ALBERT GLEIZES

For and Against the Twentieth Century

ALBERT GLEIZES
For and Against the Twentieth Century

Peter Brooke

Yale University Press • New Haven and London

Designed by Beatrix McIntyre
Set in Sabon with Gill Sans titling by Best-set Typesetter Ltd., Hong Kong
Printed in Italy

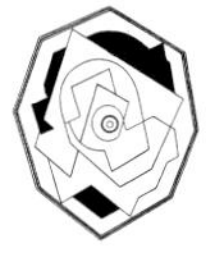

FONDATION
ALBERT GLEIZES

Library of Congress Cataloging-in-Publication Data
Brooke, Peter.
Albert Gleizes: for and against the twentieth century/Peter Brooke.
p. cm.
Includes bibliographical references and index.
ISBN 0-300-08964-3 (cloth:alk.paper)
1. Gleizes, Albert, 1881–1953. 2. painters–France–Biography. 3. Gleizes, Albert, 1881–1953–Friends and associates. 4. Cubism–France.I. Title.

ND553.G63 B76 2001
759.4–dc21
[B] 00-054076

CONTENTS

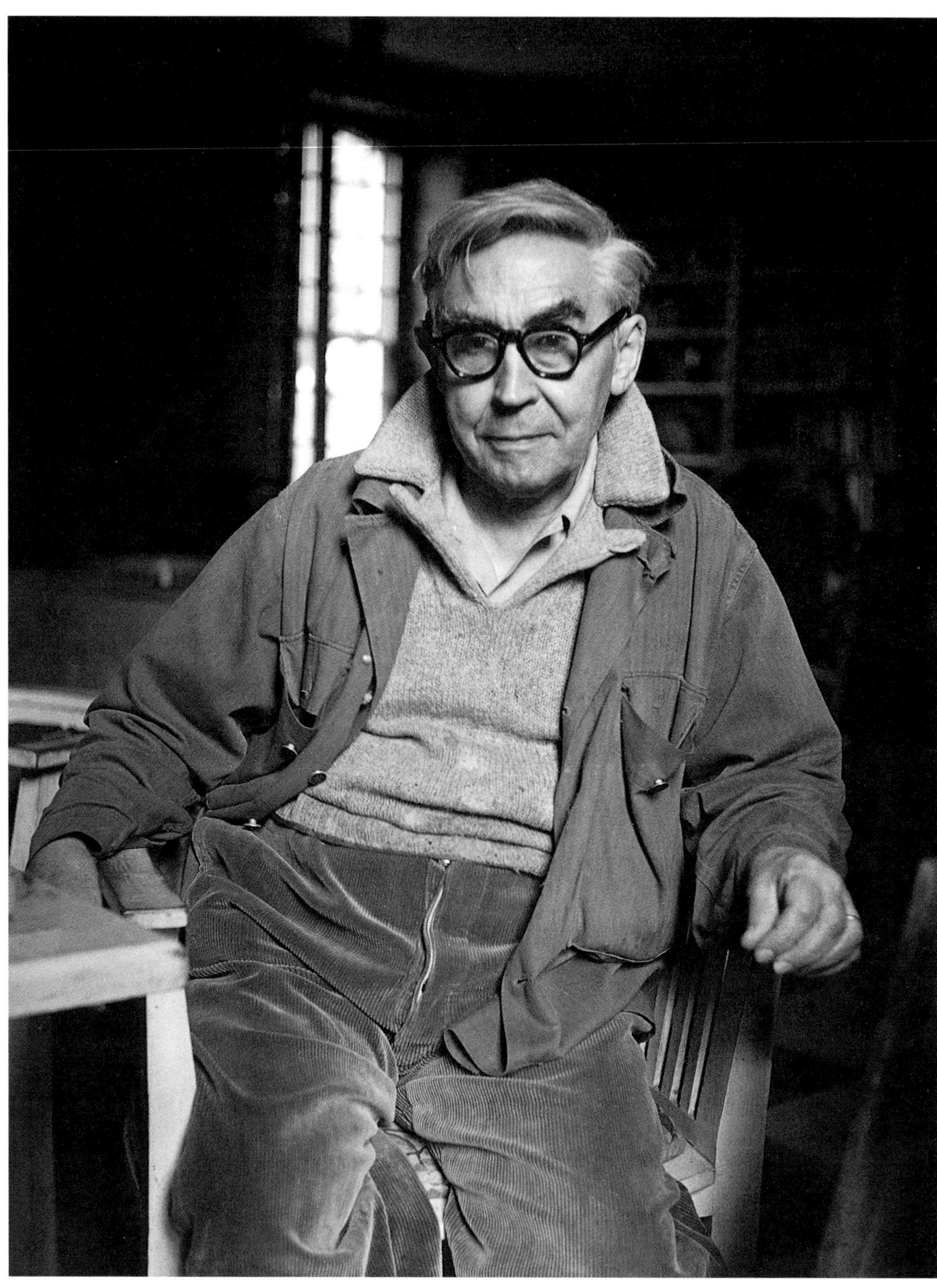

1. Albert Gleizes, *c.* 1950. Photo: Marcel Coen, Marseille. Communicated by Walter Firpo

If, I said to myself, Cubism cannot be raised to the level of a principle, of laws, in such a way as to be capable of transmission, if it does not provide a powerful framework in which individual tastes and fantasies can express themselves freely, then it will not have reached its end, whatever more or less happy successes it may produce.

Albert Gleizes

ACKNOWLEDGEMENTS

This book owes so much to so many people that it could really be regarded as a collective endeavour. In particular an important part of the job had already been done by the circle of Gleizes' friends and admirers in assembling and preserving much of the necessary material and, more importantly, in doing so much to maintain the spirit of his work.

First out of everyone I have to thank the American-French poet and painter, Walter Firpo, who introduced me to Gleizes and has for many years been a constant source of encouragement and ideas. He may be regarded as the real originator of the book. Then there is the potter, Geneviève Dalban, the teacher of Gleizes' principles and exemplar of the spirit of Moly Sabata, in the Rhone Valley, where those principles were lived not just in painting but in every aspect of daily life. Any authority I might have to speak about Gleizes comes from the time I have spent working by the side of Geneviève Dalban and of her daughter Aguilberte, herself also a very fine potter.

A large part of the book was written in one of the most beautiful parts of the Alpes de Haute Provence, at 'Aubard' where the publisher, Henri Viaud and his wife, Herviane, not only gave me hospitality but also provided me with a great deal of material and of ideas. Unfortunately, Henri Viaud died before he could see this book, to which he had contributed so much, published.

The period in which I was writing was also the period in which the Fondation Albert Gleizes was preparing their great *catalogue raisonnée*. The two presidents of the Fondation during this time, Claude Gleizes and Michel Massenet, as well as the secretary, Roberte Barrère and the treasurer, Antoine Pétri, have been most helpful and welcoming, as were Malika Noui and Anne Varichon at the different times when they were working on the catalogue. I have had very useful conversations with Henri Giriat, Henri de Montrond and Dom Angelico Surchamp. My thanks also to Pierre Georgel for giving me permission to consult the Gleizes archive in the Musée National d'Art Moderne.

I have benefitted greatly from the hospitality of André Dubois in Lyon and also from his own collection of Gleizes' work and his specialist knowledge as a historian. He should have been before me with a biography of Gleizes but was prevented by illness. The late Daniel Robbins was also working on a biography of Gleizes and was also prevented by illness from completing it. Nonetheless his catalogue for the 1964 Guggenheim retrospective and his thesis on Gleizes' early life have laid the groundwork on which anyone coming after him has to build. I was privileged to meet him on two occasions when he came to France and also to have corresponded with him.

Outside the immediate Gleizes circle I am grateful to Sophie Bowness for sharing with me her specialist knowledge on painting in the 1920s and 1930s, to Pascal Rousseau, for his knowledge of Robert Delaunay, to Bozena Nikiel for her knowledge of Jean Metzinger and to Bruce Adams for his knowledge of Anne Dangar. I was greatly helped by the staff of the documentation centre of the Musée National d'Art Moderne in Paris, in particular by Nathalie Schöller and by Nicole Bréjejère.

The idea for this book originated when I was working with Bruce Arnold on his biography of Gleizes' Irish pupil and collaborator, Mainie Jellett. I have enormously benefitted from conversations I had with him and from material he has passed on to me. I have also profited from the work that has been done on Robert Pouyaud recently in his home town of Clamecy, especially by Martine Lemaître.

My work in Paris would have been impossible without the hospitality of my friends Salah Oumohand and Michèle Bonnevin and their son, Kim. My work in the British Library in London could not have been achieved without the hospitality of many friends, but I would particularly single out Clive Boutle, Kathryn Tattersall and their son Francis. I have been engaged all this time in a work of translating Gleizes into English, and Francis Boutle Publishers have published two first instalments of these translations – *Art and Religion, Art and Science, Art and Production* and *Painting and its Laws*.

Other friends whose help, encouragement and hospitality have been invaluable for me include the Tirandaz family in Lyon, the Deleuran family in Digne, Esther Hewitt in Lisburn, the Shawcross family in Hillsborough, the de Cissey family in St Paul lez Durance, Jacques Leclerc, who has made a provisional translation of my manuscript into French, Patricia Mowbray, who secured for me a copy of Gleizes' book, *Kubismus*, written for the Bauhaus, John Minihane, who translated a large part of it for me from the German and Jean-François Delaunay, who obtained valuable information about Gleizes' pupil, Victor Poznansky, in Poland.

Finally I wish to thank my father, Arthur Brooke, whose support for what must often have seemed to be a very bizarre and impractical venture has been so consistent and unhesitating. He has made many things easy that would otherwise have been almost impossibly difficult.

INTRODUCTION

When in 1929, Albert Gleizes published a general account of Cubism, he called it *L'épopée* – 'The Epic'; and the American historian, Daniel Robbins, looking for a term to distinguish the Cubism of Gleizes and his friends in 1911–12 from that of Picasso and Braque, calls it 'Epic Cubism'.

It is this sense of an 'Epic', of an adventure story on a large scale, that I hope to convey in the following book. Of course, it is an adventure story which takes place in the realm of ideas and in their realisation in the life and painting of a single individual. But the great events which occurred during Gleizes' life – the two world wars, the rise of Communism, the rise and fall of Fascism, the universalisation of the industrial system, the changes that occurred in the domain of physics – are, in Gleizes' case, much more than just the background to a quest for personal expression. Gleizes was possessed by an overwhelming desire to understand the act of painting. What is it worth? What need does it fulfil? Why do these needs seem to change from one age to another? Why are they changing so radically in our own time? What is specific to our own time? How does painting relate to other fields of human endeavour?

Such questions carried him far, and often, it seems, beyond the bounds of painting. But Gleizes always insisted on the right, and indeed duty, of the painter to think about the largest questions, especially at a time when all the values were, necessarily and unavoidably, up for re-evaluation. It is no accident that he was friends with the most extreme of the Dada artists, Marcel Duchamp and Francis Picabia, both of whom in their different ways concluded that painting was a worthless activity. Gleizes refused this conclusion and as a result became for a while a favourite target of the Dadaists; but he had lived the same drama that they had lived and he understood their problems through and through.

At one point, in New York during the First World War, the period of a major crisis in his life and of his closest intimacy with Duchamp and Picabia, Gleizes wrote a number of poems which he grouped under the title *La Tortue emballée* – 'The Runaway Tortoise', or 'The Tortoise Overwhelmed with Love'. Beside Duchamp and Picabia, Gleizes may seem to have the slow, plodding quality of a tortoise. But what distinguishes him is the quality and steadiness of his enthusiasm, his love for the object, which was always painting. Gleizes refused brilliance and rapid movement. Fond as he was of the paradoxes of Zeno, he knew that it was the tortoise who could be expected to arrive first at the finishing post.

But his support for the steadiness of the tortoise against the speed and brilliance of Zeno's Achilles was not a sign of any sort of complacency. Although at any given moment he seems to write and paint with wonderful self confidence, the continual change and evolution of his work is proof of a driving dissatisfaction, a constant searching, not for novelty but for truth. He never settles into a repetitive formula or 'style', but, at the same time, the changes he undergoes always follow logically, one from the other. He never alters direction. Something is discovered that seems to have an absolute value. He explores its means. He finds that it is only relative. But he keeps what is positive in it. He builds, 'pierre sur pierre' – one stone on top of the other, which was one of his favourite expressions.

It is by such means that Gleizes can claim, justifiably, to have gone further with Cubism than any other painter. In the general history of modern painting, Cubism appears as the first of a series of 'isms' which succeed each other like fashions in the clothing business. In Gleizes' hands, Cubism appears as the first impulse of a process of evolution which is still far from being complete.

In this respect, Gleizes the tortoise stands as the anti-type to Picasso–Achilles. The whole history of Cubism could be written in terms of an oscillation between these two poles: on the one side fast, brilliant, playful movement – the 'shock of the new'; on the other, the search for solid principles, for firm ground, for a clear understanding of the whys and wherefores of the act of painting – an understanding that had to enter into the realm of something that could be called 'theology', since it had to address the largest question of all, the question so often derided in our own time, that of 'the meaning of life', the overall framework of thought which is necessary if painting is to be considered as something more than just a sophisticated form of entertainment.

The general state of culture at the present time reflects the victory of Picasso. Gleizes explained Picasso as being the very personification of the spirit of the age – an age in which the idea of what it is to be human which had prevailed since the Renaissance ('Humanism') has been distorted, mocked, 'deconstructed' but has not been overcome. The whole pathos and drama of Picasso's achievement lies in the fact that he remains a humanist, a classicist, through and through. The Humanism of the Renaissance, whether Christian or atheist, has long been under attack but it remains the only idea we have.

For Gleizes, the deconstruction of the humanist idea could only be of value if it represented the birth pangs of another, equally coherent, idea of what it is to be human. The external, sensual, corporeal appearance had to give way to the reassertion of an internal principle. Gleizes expressed this with the terms 'subject' and 'object'. The subject is to do with what the picture is about, what we want to say. The object is to do with what the picture is, with what we are. The first half of the twentieth century saw a widespread but unco-ordinated search for the 'object', for objective principles in all fields of human work. This was, in Gleizes' view, what was behind the development of non-figurative art – art without a subject. The second half saw the wholesale abandonment of this effort, the triumph of the 'subject', of the individual point of view.

Gleizes may be regarded as the personification of certain of the hopes of the first half of the last century, hopes which have their roots in the end of the nineteenth century when the conviction was strong that the foundations were being laid for a new religious (though not necessarily church-orientated) art. As such, he is our antithesis. He confronts us both in our modernism – the adaptation of our aesthetic tastes to suit the requirements of machine production; and in our post-modernism – the universal mockery which Nietzsche said was characteristic of the last, 'the most contemptible', men: 'they know everything that has ever been done and so there is no end to their mockery'.

My book is, obviously, partisan. I am fully persuaded that Gleizes is one of the great painters of the twentieth century and that, up until now, he has, to put it at its mildest, been underestimated. The extent to which he has been underestimated and, indeed, often abused by writers who clearly know very little about him, constitutes in itself a difficult and interesting historical problem. But the whole question of 'estimation' of course implies the existence of standards by which the estimation can be made. It has seemed to me best to present as clearly as possible the standards to which Gleizes himself was working and how they evolved before attempting, on the basis of them, to criticise or discuss the alternatives.

A brief account of my own reasons for being interested in the matter is given in the last chapter of the book.

During the time that I have been working on Gleizes, a number of studies have appeared, notably by Christopher Green, Mark Antliff, David Cottington and, most recently, the contributors to the 1998–9 Delaunay retrospective in Paris, which have done much to break down the old view that 'Salon Cubism' was only a rather paltry offshoot of the 'essential Cubism' of Picasso and Braque. A general history of Salon Cubism, however, still needs to be written, a history that could be extended to include the wonderful collective phenomenon which Christopher Green has called 'Crystal Cubism' – the highly structured work of the Cubist painters, not including Gleizes, who remained in Paris during the war, most notably Metzinger and Gris. An opening up of this early Cubism in all its intellectual fullness would, I believe, reveal it as being not only the most radical movement in painting of the past century but, still, the most rich in possibilities for the future.

Peter Brooke
Brecon
January 2000

Part One

1881–1920

1

A LITERARY PROLOGUE – THE ABBAYE DE CRÉTEIL

Albert Gleizes's first artistic ambitions were not aimed at painting but at the theatre. He tells us in his *Souvenirs* that he hated school and eventually, systematically, played truant, passing his time in the Montmartre Cemetery. He dreamed of being an actor and eventually his father agreed to let him begin an apprenticeship with a neighbour of the family in the village of Courbevoie, near Paris – a former actor who worked as a prompt in the Comédie Française. But he also insisted that the young Gleizes, very much against his will, spend each morning in his own workshop to learn a useful craft that would complement the more dubious profession he had chosen.[1]

Gleizes's father, Sylvain, was a successful industrial designer, specialising in designs for furniture fabrics. He was himself, Gleizes tells us, a talented amateur painter, as was his brother, Gleizes's uncle, Honoré, whose tastes were more advanced. Honoré liked the Impressionists and was later to defend Gleizes's first Cubist paintings against the scepticism of Sylvain. On his mother's side, Gleizes had an uncle, Léon Comerre, who was a successful portrait painter whom the young Gleizes liked very much, without in any way questioning the value of his work.

But it was poetry that was Gleizes's first love, not painting. Poetry recitation was, he tells us, the only field in which he excelled at school, though his own efforts at writing poetry were treated with scorn both by his teachers and by his fellow pupils. He entered college in 1894 and during his third year he tells us that the only tolerable moments were the four train journeys he had to perform each day between Courbevoie and the centre of Paris: 'Four quarters of an hour of liberty, of adventures, in which poetry and feeling had their place.' Playing truant in the nearby Montmartre Cemetery, 'I felt light and joyful, freed from my prison, my imagination wandering . . . In the Montmartre Cemetery, I experienced a feeling of relaxation, a love of exercise, and the only effect of the tombs was to evoke in me an ardent desire to live. What a difference to the college, which oppressed me, leaving me disgusted with any form of effort and making everything hateful to me.'[2]

Gleizes soon decided that studying with individual actors was not the way to learn and that the only proper course was to take small parts in a real theatre. He had already formed a small theatre group with schoolfriends and was acutely aware of the difference between poetry lived and the same poetry studied in the classroom. Gleizes, often reproached as an 'academic' painter and a 'theorist', started out with a detestation of the school, the academy, the university, which he never lost.

In his own later estimation, however, it was not the theatre that was the most valuable part of his youth but the apprenticeship with his father, which he had agreed to so reluctantly and which he underwent so halfheartedly. In his *Souvenirs*, he describes the methods of the workshop in some detail – the grinding of colours, the stretching of the paper, the uses of tracing paper, the importance of the 'fond', the background colour. His description of the importance of the 'fond' in his father's workshop is strikingly reminiscent of his description of the importance of the 'fond' in his own method given in *L'Homme devenu peintre*, written in 1948:

> One never paints a drawing on white paper but, so to speak, in its atmosphere. The atmosphere is the background [*fond*] which will determine the quality of the relations between the colours. This background is usually passed in the limits of a surface which occupies the centre of the sheet attached to the frame. The colourist has prepared the background colour in a pot. The apprentice applies it in the predetermined limits, showing sufficient skill to spread the colours equally, to prevent them from giving a marbled effect or going over the edges.[3]

The workshop – not the studio – was to be Gleizes's ideal condition for realising a work of art: a hierarchically organised community of apprentice, companion, master, in which everyone contributes to the finished work. In his father's case, the finished work was the industrially printed fabric, but Gleizes points out that this was much less interesting than the design as it appeared in the workshop, before it was sent to the factory: 'I often commented to my father on the disproportion that existed between the effort that was put into realising these drawings and the poverty of the effective result when the cloth came out of the factory.'[4]

Gleizes was not yet, at the age of eighteen, the enemy of industrialisation that he was later to become, but some of the main themes of his life are already present: the village, Courbevoie, subject of his earliest paintings and drawings, about to be swallowed up by the great city; the workshop, dominated by a master, his father, whose authority derives from the quality and seriousness of his work; the friendly corporate atmosphere of the workshop, based on a discipline evolved traditionally through the experience of more than one generation; the submission of this work of quality to the miserable parody produced by the machine; the concern with the art of everyday objects rather than exceptional works of genius; and the rough and tumble of theatrical life, a more magical and high-spirited artistic activity which was always to appeal to Gleizes, even when, later on in life, he sometimes seems to be the advocate of an almost monastic austerity.

At the same time, he was joined in his father's workshop by the young poet, René Arcos, with whom he was to embark on the first of his artistic projects to achieve any public attention – the Abbaye de Créteil. And, in 1902, he began his military service, a foretaste of the war and the intense concern with human and social questions which it was to provoke.

Gleizes was posted for two years in Abbéville then, for a further year, at Amiens. We will see that when Gleizes was conscripted in 1914, he was very fortunate in his superiors, who encouraged him to continue his artistic activities. He had the same good fortune during this period of military service and it was at this time that he started painting seriously. It may be noted that he still had no contact with the artistic avant garde. His uncle Honoré admired the Impressionists, but there is no evidence that Gleizes had any knowledge of

Cézanne, of the school of Pont-Aven, of the Divisionism of Seurat or Signac. He came from a family of conscientious amateurs and he found himself in front of a landscape that he found very beautiful: 'How attractive it was and persuasive for the landscape painter who came there without any formula, without the insolence of preconceived ideas [*un poncif*], but simply with a desire to serve it through understanding it, loving it, effacing oneself to give it its right of primacy.'[5] It was in the countryside round Abbéville too that he began to appreciate the beauty of small towns dominated by a church, the beauty of mediaeval architecture, probably the most important single influence of his whole career.

But despite the relative ease of his life in the army, Gleizes was filled with a lively detestation of militarism, reminiscent of his detestation of school. Gleizes, who was to be a great champion of the collective life, was always an enemy of conformism and uniformity. As later, during the war, he was engaged with his fellow soldiers in frequent and lively discussions on political and social matters. This was especially the case in his third year, at Amiens, where he became friendly with the artists Berthold Mahn, Jacques d'Otémar and Josué Gaboriaud. Mahn and d'Otémar were to be associated with the Abbaye de Créteil and later to have a reputation as Socialist artists. Gaboriaud was a pupil of Maurice Denis', and we may speculate that this was Gleizes's first encounter with the avant garde. He was later to maintain the view that, however disappointing their work may be, it was Paul Sérusier, Paul Signac and Maurice Denis, much more than the Impressionists before them or the Fauves, who had posed the basic questions on the nature of painting which the Cubists and their successors had to address.

Gleizes's last year of military service – 1905 – saw a tense moment in the long confrontation between France and Germany over Morocco. 'The garrison,' he says, 'was trembling, but not, truth to tell, as a result of any military ardour'.[6] Gleizes himself and his friends were convinced that wars were caused by militarism – a positive desire for war on the part of the military class – and that militarism was only powerful because of popular ignorance. The solution to the problem was therefore popular education, conceived on a model utterly different from that of the schools. This was the rationale behind the Association Ernest Renan into which Gleizes was to throw himself as soon as he left the army. It was launched in December 1905 in the Théâtre Pigalle, with Gleizes as secretary to the 'Literary and Artistic Section'.

His main responsibility was to organise theatrical presentations in working-class areas in Paris. He had formed a little group of experienced amateurs from among his friends from the army and from his brief theatrical career. As well as classical and modern theatre, they gave poetry readings, which included works by Arcos, Charles Vildrac, Georges Duhamel and Jules Romains, the poets, already personal friends, with whom he was to launch the Abbaye. At this time we may say that Gleizes's tastes in poetry were more advanced than his tastes in painting. Gleizes complains that the 'symbolists and moderns' were opposed by the members of the élite Ecole Normale Supérieure who made up a large part of the Association's committee, and also by the professional actors who were involved.

He himself was still working each morning for his father. He would spend the afternoon at his own painting and his evenings were given to the Association Ernest Renan. He had come to know Vildrac, Mercereau and Duhamel through Arcos. 'It's a strange thing', he comments, 'but neither Arcos nor myself, while we were painting and writing, ever dreamed of entering into any of the literary and artistic circles. It was enough for us to work passionately in our own corner.'[7] Nonetheless, Gleizes had come to know an art critic, Jean Valmy-Baysse, tenant of a friend of the family. He introduced Arcos to him. In 1904, while Gleizes was still in his regiment, Arcos wrote to him to say that Valmy-Baysse had invited him to help with a new review of modern writing to be called *La Vie*. Other contributors included 'Eshmer Valdor' (Alexandre Mercereau's pseudonym), Charles Vildrac, and Vildrac's brother-in-law, Georges Duhamel. Gleizes came to know them as soon as he left the army. He particularly liked Mercereau and Vildrac, but he had a more reserved attitude, which he develops throughout the *Souvenirs*, towards Duhamel, in whom he felt a careerist instinct that surprised him, given Duhamel's youth.

In 1906, Gleizes spent part of the summer with relatives in Gascony and Picardy. In the *Souvenirs*, he describes how he began to appreciate the diversity and, indeed, deep divisions that characterised rural France, and how much he enjoyed the farm of his cousins, winegrowers in Picardy. He spent much of his time visiting churches:

> the most exciting of which was Moissac . . . But I was hardly ready to understand that marvel of mind and body which is its doorway. How could I have been? I could appreciate these old stones, the authority of their organisation, the past they evoked. My instinct for history was awoken and engaged, but my sense of the present could not adapt to them, nor see their relevance to our own time, nor learn a great lesson on permanence and tradition, on principles and order which neither place nor time can ever change. Everything was changing from day to day at that beginning of the twentieth century, and the disorder only induced a contempt for morality. Modernism wanted everything to be decided on the instant. Why should I not have been fooled by this state of affairs since the best minds did not rise up against it, and we had not yet been warned of the collapse that was about to follow . . .[8]

The idea for the 'Abbaye de Créteil' came from Charles Vildrac. It was an attempt to address a problem that was to preoccupy Gleizes all his life. If artistic activity – poetry, painting, music – are spiritual vocations, the poet, the painter or the musician must be free to follow them independent of commercial considerations. How, then, can they earn their living? The solution proposed by Vildrac was the artistic community – a small group of artists living together, sharing their expenses, each entirely free to develop his own work, but each contributing to a common, commercially viable enterprise that would provide a regular income (Plate 2). The work chosen was fine quality printing which they were taught by Lucien Linard, a jobbing printer Gleizes had come to know at Amiens and who abandoned his own workshop to join them. Linard appears in both Gleizes's and Duhamel's accounts as the real hero of the adventure.

I have used the phrase 'spiritual vocation', but there was no religious content in the enterprise. The 'Abbaye' was based on the 'Abbaye de Théléma', imagined by Rabelais as a refuge of honest, idealistic thinkers against a hostile world. The Association Ernest Renan had been determinedly secular: 'Secular because we sincerely believed that secularism [*la laïcité*] was the first condition for establishing the rule of reason, its opposite being, naturally, an outdated heritage, source of superstition that explained all oppression and all ignorance.'[9]

The idealism of the Abbaye was in contrast with the idealism of the Association Ernest Renan. It was more individualistic, or even more selfish:

> Human problems left us indifferent, even those posed by the fact of living in a society. The tendencies I had shown in this direction only recently through the Association Ernest Renan no longer bothered me. I had again become a painter and wanted to be nothing more. The spiritual worries I had known in my adolescence had gone. I was a painter, happy to live through the seasons and the days in the company of poet friends who themselves had no higher ambitions. Irony and scepticism were enough to deal with those questions that could not fail to be posed by a little more internal life. Our belief in art was unshakeable . . .[10]

The 'poet friends' were, broadly, the group that had come together through *La Vie* – Arcos, Vildrac, Duhamel, Mercereau. They had spelt out their ambitions in an 'Appeal' launched in 1906:

> We have now arrived at the certainty that, except in unusual circumstances that have nothing to do with any real value, the writer or artist without a personal fortune must pass at least half his whole life before being freed from material worries.
>
> We know that many of our elders, despite great talent – and sometimes because of it – can only dedicate a few leisure moments left by mercenary breadwinning to the work that is dear to them.
>
> Those who want to live by their pen or their paintbrush, whatever the cost, without having to wait a long time, must stoop to prostitution and take the

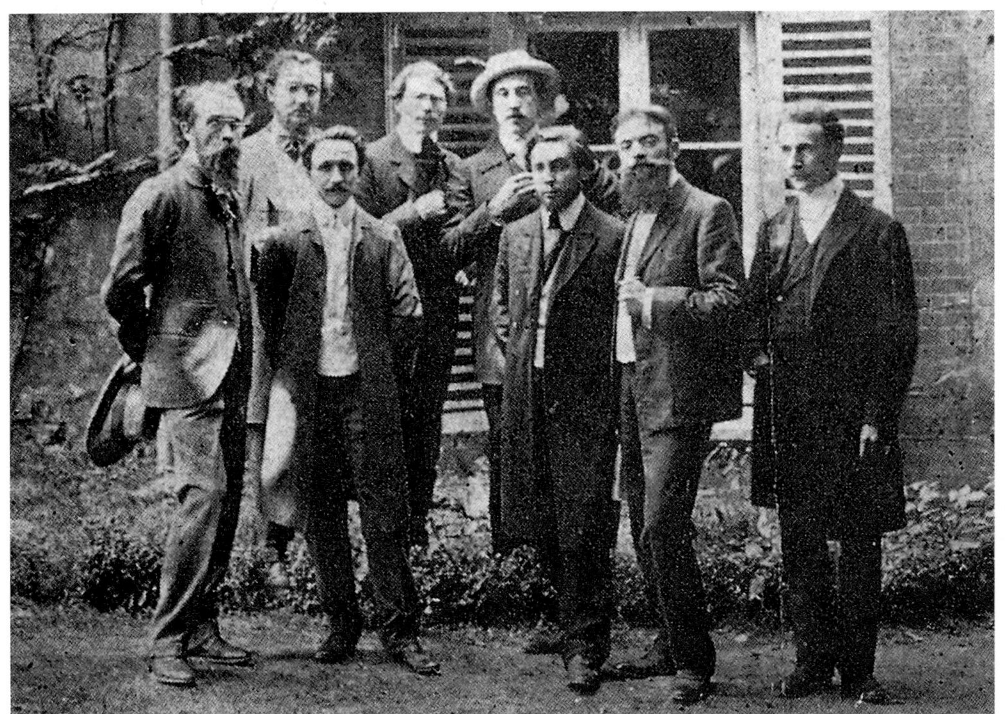

2. The members of the Abbaye de Créteil. First row, left to right: Charles Vildrac, René Arcos, Albert Gleizes, Henri-Martin Barzun, Alexandre Mercereau. Second row, left to right: Georges Duhamel, Berthold Mahn, Jacques d'Otémar

> dangerous direction of a path that descends, without the possibility of return, far below the level of their art.
>
> We do not want even to consider such an outcome; having no wealth, we have, so far, adopted the only possible solution. To live, we are either artisans or we have turned to the least literary of writing tasks.
>
> But we are not at all reconciled to such a destiny. We are young and not yet purged by a mediocre life of all tangible ideals, of all energy . . .[11]

But the solution envisaged – a communal life supported by printing – itself required capital to rent the necessary premises and to acquire basic printing equipment. The house was found, by Vildrac, in Créteil which was then, like Gleizes's Courbevoie, a small village outside Paris. There were two buildings – a house and servants' quarters – surrounded by a hectare (around two and a half acres) of land running down to the Chapître, a tributary of the Marne. It was owned by a wealthy coachbuilder who had lived there previously but had abandoned it and left it in disrepair. He had no more interest in the place and initially proposed a relatively modest rent of 1200 francs a year; but he abruptly increased it to 2000 francs a year, without repairs, when he learnt that the prospective tenants were artists.[12]

That they were able to pay (1,000 francs for the first six months) was thanks to a new friend, Henri Martin Barzun. Barzun had been drawn to the group through a brief agitation surrounding allegations of corruption in the award of a new literary prize in 1905. If Gleizes insists that the Abbaye group were indifferent to politics, he makes an exception of Barzun who, he says, constantly irritated them all by repeating that he didn't give a damn for artists, what interested him was Man. Gleizes was later to conclude that he was right, even if he only had a very limited – merely political – idea of what the term 'man' might mean.

Barzun too was a poet, the author of *La Tragédie terrestre* – 'an interminable poem in which the best and the worst rubbed shoulders lightheartedly together',[13] according to Gleizes. But he was also involved in politics and was soon to be employed in the new Ministère du Travail, created by the Clemenceau government of October 1906 under the independent Socialist, René Viviani, to address the needs of the working class. Barzun offered to help raise money for the Abbaye, but finished by providing most of it out of his own pocket on the basis of a small inheritance. Gleizes says that he also provided a source of work in the form of political pamphlets, though these do not appear in the list of books published by the Abbaye given by Christian Sénéchal in his account of the venture, published in 1930.

3. Interior of Abbaye de Créteil. Gleizes perhaps in rocking chair to left. Mercereau and Barzun at right. The painting is probably by Gleizes but does not appear in the catalogue raisonné, despite a resemblance to the *Paysage au bouquet d'arbres*

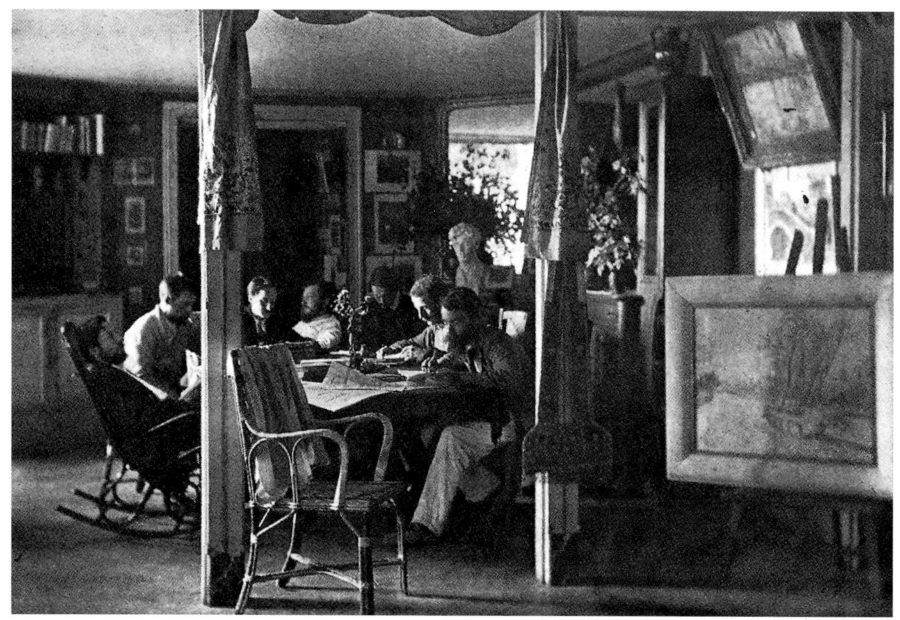

Gleizes himself was the first to move in, on Christmas day, 1906, followed shortly by Arcos, the Vildracs, and Duhamel. Duhamel was in the middle of medical studies. He had just been accepted by the Sorbonne for a year's course in histology, and it was generally agreed that he should continue, which meant that his involvement in the Abbaye was intermittent – increasingly so, Gleizes and Mercereau complain. Mercereau himself had gone to Russia in 1906 to work on the French section of a sumptuous art journal, *Le Toison d'or*, founded by Nicolas Riabouchinsky. He supported the venture in correspondence. Duhamel (bitterly attacked by Mercereau in the 1920s) complains that, given his connections, Mercereau could have given more financial help to the venture, but Gleizes says that Mercereau sent money from Russia to finance the publication of Duhamel's own *Des Légendes, des batailles*.[14]

Mercereau joined the Abbaye in the Spring of 1907, when he was sacked because *Le Toison d'or* would not sell in France. Soon, Gleizes's painter friends from his regiment, Berthold Mahn and Jacques d'Otémar, were involved, as was the musician, Albert Doyen. Of a host of others who were to be associated in one way or another with the venture, only the Mahns and Doyens, Gleizes says, were intimate friends. Barzun, he complains, although he had made the whole thing possible, only used the Abbaye as a holiday home.

Gleizes insists that, just as they were too individualistic to engage in politics, the poets of the Abbaye were too individualistic to form any definite school of poetry; but the titles of the two books already mentioned – Barzun's *Tragédie terrestre* and Duhamel's *Des Légendes, des batailles*, already suggest a common aspiration towards a large scale, epic poetry. Gleizes, putting Barzun aside, is anxious to establish that Duhamel had been won over to this poetic idea by Arcos – that Arcos' *La Tragédie des espaces* had inspired Duhamel's poem which was full of 'earthquakes, volcanic eruptions, geysers, the tumults that precede the birth of worlds'. Then 'he would quieten the elements, the first cell, the primeval egg would appear in a calmed sea and, little by little, would develop into the first man, still deprived of the word . . .'. Both he and Arcos, he admits, were very impressed, but this was before the war 'when all that *tohu-bohu* became part of the normal disorder of things . . .'.[15]

But behind this desire for a poetry that would reflect the enormity, both in space and time, of the modern scientific understanding of the universe, lay the influence of the poet, René Ghil. According to Christian Sénéchal's book on the Abbaye, Ghil was the only recognised poet who gave them his support; and the Abbaye members often attended receptions that he held at his house in Paris on Friday evenings.[16] It is surprising that Gleizes's *Souvenirs* (which are, however, in a very unfinished state) do not mention this – the more so because elsewhere he speaks very highly of Ghil, particularly in his wartime writings and in the 1920s, when he even describes him as the spiritual father of Cubism: 'the man who possesses the laws and can reveal them to those worthy of initiation . . .'.[17]

Ghil had been an associate of Mallarmé's in the 1880s. His highly influential *Traité du verbe*, advocating a music of the word based on a precise science of sonority and allusion, was published in 1885. He broke with Mallarmé in 1888. The story goes that Mallarmé declared: 'Eden exists. We must believe in Eden.' And Ghil replied, 'No, master. Eden does not exist.'[18] Which is to say that the poet was to accept the real world such as he knows it to be and not look to an imaginary sensual paradise, the world of nymphs and fauns, the world that was not just the world of Mallarmé but that of many of the painters, from Puvis de Chavannes to Matisse – 'luxe, calme et volupté.'

The title of Ghil's book of poems published in 1885 (at the time of his friendship with Mallarmé) – *Légende des âmes et du sang* – is enough to show the relationship with the poems of Barzun, Duhamel and Arcos already mentioned. It was to form part of his huge life's work, *L'OEuvre* (the final version of the *Traité du verbe* was to be published as *En Méthode à l'œuvre*). Gleizes's rather mocking description of Duhamel's *Des Légendes, des batailles* could equally be applied to *L'OEuvre* which is an account of the evolution of the whole universe culminating in an account of the evolution of human history understood as the attempt on the part of matter to enter into knowledge of itself.

Behind all these 'legends', however, the presence of Victor Hugo's monumental *La Légende des siècles* can be felt, and it may be worth mentioning in parenthesis that Gleizes's *Souvenirs* give the funeral of Victor Hugo as his earliest childhood memory.

This epic scale, which also evokes the names of Walt Whitman and of the Belgian poet, Emile Verhaeren, cannot be felt to the same degree in the poems of Charles Vildrac, which are more concerned with everyday life, albeit seen in bright colours. They are, naïvely, poems of the exuberance of youth. But there is the same emphasis on the world as it is experienced directly by the senses, the refusal of symbolism or fantasy; the same feeling that the real world contains everything that is needed for the highest spiritual ambitions of the poet – an optimism and a concern with healthy appetites and aspirations, far from the morbid obsessions with sin and mysticism that mark the generation of the *poètes maudits*. Duhamel, who collaborated with Vildrac on a *Note sur la technique poétique*, sums up their common aspirations as follows:

> We wished for a constructive reform, I repeat, not through any revolt, not by simply indulging in a disordered effort at liberation. Romains, later, with Chennevière, also published his 'art poétique' and these parallel efforts clearly show that as far as this business [he is referring to free verse – PB] was concerned neither side was blinded by the bright lights of anarchy. At the same time, our ambitions clearly went beyond a simple technical renewal. For twenty years, poetry, the poetry of the explorers, the prospectors, the symbolists, had lived on allegory; too often it had lost contact with, or indeed any feeling for, the real. Thus wandering, it risked getting lost in allusions, flying off endlessly in pursuit of the shadow which, I admit, is often more alluring than the prey. We did not for a moment dream of renouncing our masters but, more than the appearance, we hungered after the substance. All of us dreamed, more or less clearly, of a poetry capable of confronting its object directly and if, at that time, someone had asked us what this object was, we would all together, quite naturally, have replied – Man . . .[19]

However Gleizes, as we have already noted, says that all the Abbaye members, himself included, were shocked when Barzun proposed 'man', and not art, as the real object of all their efforts.

Duhamel goes on to remark that the Abbaye's ambitions for twentieth-century poetry were not realised. The followers of Apollinaire remained caught up in allegory and symbolism; the followers of Valéry fell into an aesthetically lovely despair. The writers associated with the Abbaye made their mark not in poetry but in prose.

The exception to this desire for a poetic expression of the drama of everyday life and general suspicion of symbolism, was Mercereau. Gleizes says that it was through Mercereau that he was first introduced into the fantastic world of the artistic circles of the time. Prior to going to Russia at the beginning of 1906, Mercereau organised soirées which were open to everyone. According to Gleizes, he gave the impression of being very rich while actually being very poor: 'His elegance was a masterpiece of subterfuge.' Gleizes was dazzled by his first contact with the exotic circle in which Mercereau moved but 'by the time I left this gathering I had completely recovered my assurance and was no longer impressed'.[20] He felt more at ease in the carefully selected circle round Charles and Rose Vildrac (Duhamel's sister).

Mercereau's *Contes des ténèbres*, published with a cover by Gleizes in 1912, and some of them written at the time of the Abbaye, seem to come from a different world than that of Arcos, Vildrac and Duhamel. They are fantastic allegories – the allegory allowing of no very precise meaning – often with a morbid character, as the title suggests. They belong as much to the world of Russian Symbolism as to that of French Symbolism. Nonetheless, of the Abbaye group, it is perhaps Mercereau who was to play the most important role in Gleizes's life.

He had something of the quality of the impresario – the man who helps others to express themselves. On his return from Russia in the Spring of 1907, he became particularly friendly with Gleizes. It was Gleizes and Mercereau who, against the scepticism of their friends, insisted on organising an ambitious open day at the Abbaye, with music, poetic and theatrical recitations (provided largely by Gleizes's theatrical friends), and an exhibition, organised by Mercereau, which included work by the Rumanian sculptor, Constantin Brancusi (Mercereau also introduced Filippo Marinetti, soon to be notorious as the founder and master propagandist of Italian Futurism, to the Abbaye circle).[21] The event was an impressive social and artistic success which netted a total profit of 8 francs, 75 centimes, confirming Gleizes's lifelong opinion that there was no necessary connection between artistic success and commercial success.

Later it was Mercereau who introduced Gleizes to Henri Le Fauconnier and Jean Metzinger, the two crucial encounters in his development as a Cubist painter. Mercereau also worked for Eugène Figuière, who was to publish many of the writers associated with the Abbaye as well as books illustrated by Gleizes, and most importantly, Gleizes and Metzinger's own *Du 'Cubisme'*, and Apollinaire's *Les Peintres cubistes*. After the war, Mercereau was involved with the publisher Jacques Povolozky, who was to be Gleizes's publisher in the 1920s. Gleizes in his *Souvenirs* speaks warmly of Mercereau, of his generosity, his willingness to sacrifice his own career interests to help others, and of his heroism during the war, when he refused to serve in any capacity which might involve killing the enemy but cheerfully took on the most dangerous tasks as a stretcher bearer in the ambulance corps.[22]

But of the names associated with the Abbaye, the best-known is that of Jules Romains. When Gleizes, Duhamel and Mercereau deny that there was a collective philosophy behind the Abbaye de Créteil, they are denying that it subscribed to Romains' philosophy of 'Unanimisme'. Mercereau (in his *L'Abbaye et le bolchévisme culturel*, which is largely a very embittered polemic against Duhamel and Romains) denies it with indignation; Duhamel denies it as a simple matter of fact; Gleizes seems to deny it with a touch of regret: 'We admired Romains' poems without discussing them. For if we had several points in common, we were so determinedly individualist that the desire for liberty held us together even more than the work of the Abbaye itself'.[23] We will see that Gleizes was soon to become very anti-individualist and to insist on the duties posed by the common needs of a particular age – an idea that brings him close to Romains' Unanimism. In her own *Mémoires*, Mme Gleizes – herself irresistibly an individualist despite her expressed support for her husband's ideas – refers to the Abbaye as Unanimist. Describing a reunion of the remaining members in 1951, she says that Arcos, Duhamel and Vildrac disapproved of the religious direction Gleizes had taken. Then she comments: 'It would seem, however, that faith was a fairly natural end for Unanimism. "One day we must become Humanity" is not very far from "religare" [to relate, or bring together – PB].'[24]

Romains' 'Unanimism' was, he claimed, the result of a 'vision', or a sudden, blinding intuition he had had in 1903, at the age of eighteen, that everybody and everything about him were so interrelated that they could be described as forming one huge single living being for which the poet – himself – acted as the consciousness. He was to try and express this sense of the mutual interdependence and therefore mutual responsibility – the final unity – of the world in an enormous quantity of poems, plays, novels and political writings, culminating in the twenty-seven volumes of his novel, *Les Hommes de bonne volonté*, which gives a panoramic view of French life at a wide variety of social and intellectual levels and interests from 1908 to 1933 – an invaluable aid to understanding the general atmosphere in which a large part of Gleizes's life, like Romains', was to be passed.[25]

Romains had become friendly with Arcos, Duhamel and Vildrac in 1906 (through the poet, Gustav Kahn, according to Sénéchal) but was not committed to the Abbaye project, entering the Ecole Normale Supérieure to study science just at the time that the Abbaye became viable. In 1907, however, he sent them the manuscript of his book of poems, *La Vie unanime*, and both Gleizes and Duhamel record the excitement they felt on receiving it. It was by far the most influential book published by the Abbaye, so influential that, as we have indicated, the Abbaye writers themselves began to be regarded as followers of Romains.

Apart from Romains and the Abbaye writers themselves, the Abbaye also published work by Roger Allard, who was to be one of the first literary champions of Cubism; Mécislas Golberg, the Polish anarchist whom Edward Fry presents as one of the intellectual forerunners of Cubism;[26] the poet, P. J. Jouve; the Prince de Liguori, a writer of 'cape and sword' romances who, like Golberg, was a friend of Romains'; and Robert de Montesqiou, the model for the Duc de Charlus in Proust's *A la Recherche du temps perdu*.[27] Gleizes complained that de Montesqiou's *Passiflora* cost the Abbaye more time and trouble than it was worth – among other things, the author decided at the last moment that he wanted it published on transparent paper. De Montesqiou wrote an appeal for help for the Abbaye, which was published on the front page of the *Figaro* on the day the furniture removers moved in at the beginning of 1908. Nevertheless, in a world that seems quite another to that of Gleizes, it was through de Montesqiou that Juliette Roche, the future Mme Gleizes, daughter of the powerful Third Republic minister, Jules Roche, first heard of this idealistic group of young men and their quixotic aesthetic adventure.[28]

The Abbaye only lasted a year. It was closed because of a simple inability to pay the rent. There were also tensions among the members, but these should not be exaggerated and were partly the result of the financial worries. Gleizes says that, in the early days, himself and Arcos, both bachelors, did not understand the problems and sensibilities of the Vildracs, a young family, who soon moved into the separate – servants' – building. Mercereau arrived with a Russian wife who spoke no French and seemed to have a rooted dislike for the Abbaye and its inhabitants. Duhamel and Barzun were accused of not helping enough with the serious work, especially the printing.

Nonetheless, the group continued for some years afterwards to appear as a coherent force in French literary life, mutually helping one another and gradually developing a very wide sphere of influence, to the extent that in the early 1920s they were accused by an Action Française supporter, 'Jean Maxe', of contributing to a radical weakening of the French military spirit and thus preparing the way for Bolshevism. Jean Maxe's pamphlet, *L'Abbaye et le bolchévisme culturel*, in fact gives an impressive picture of the eventual impact of what could easily be seen as, in itself, a rather unimpressive venture. Mercereau, who probably did more than anyone else to facilitate the publication of the Abbaye writers and their friends, complains that it had become just another self-serving clique. He insists, as does Gleizes, that the 'real' Abbaye were just the founders and their most intimate friends – the Mahns and the Doyens. But 'Jean Maxe''s version gives a much better idea of the Abbaye's importance. Intangible as it may have been, there was a common spirit, and this eventually touched a very wide circle which was characterised by a concern for humanity as a whole (in contrast to the individualist sentiments of the Symbolists) and which was therefore impelled into political – mainly Socialist – activity after the war. Mahn, Arcos, Vildrac, Gleizes, Duhamel and Mercereau himself all appear in the Socialist journals of the early 1920s; and the musician, Albert Doyen, pioneered the Fêtes du Peuple – festivals of popular music which impressed even his enemy, 'Jean Maxe', who exclaims rather movingly: 'Ah, si c'était ça, le communisme!'[29]

Gleizes was profoundly marked by this brief experiment in communal living. He, together with Arcos and the Vildracs, almost seems exempt from the charges and counter charges of the former associates. They were recognised as the most committed members. Gleizes was the first to arrive and the last to leave. Sénéchal says that, unable to face his family after this failure, he went to live with the painter, Henri Doucet 'in that strange house on the rue du Delta, which was made up of the remains of a hostel of the thirteenth century and the carcass of an unfinished apartment block, which also housed Drouard, Modigliani, Geo Printemps and some sons of good families who used it to hide their forbidden loves'. This was probably as close as Gleizes ever came to 'la vie de Bohème'.[30] He published an article on the Abbaye, calling it 'a communistic experiment', in America in 1918[31] and constantly evoked it as the forerunner of his own later attempts to establish artistic communities at Moly Sabata in the Rhone Valley, and at Les Méjades, near St Rémy de Provence.

I have emphasised the importance of the Abbaye in literary history and said nothing about Gleizes's painting. Gleizes is still, for the most part, a straightforward, unpretentious landscape painter using a subdued Impressionist style, who sends his work to the Société Nationale des Beaux Arts and seems almost unaware of the schools – Divisionism and Fauvism – that are battling it out in the more radical Salon d'Automne and the Salon des Indépendants. This despite the fact that, according to Sénéchal, Odilon Redon, one of the founders of the Salon des Indépendants, supported the Abbaye experiment.[32] Gleizes's work seems untouched by the ambitious literary concerns of his comrades, except insofar as he is thoroughly 'realist' – there is no fantasy in his work, and he chooses very ordinary, sometimes semi-industrial, landscapes – the suburbs of Paris in which he lived. He had not yet posed any of the fundamental problems on the nature of painting – especially on the nature of form – which were to be his life's work. Nor had he himself, surrounded as he was by writers, begun to write, at least so far as we know.

There can be no doubt of his youthful enthusiasm and passion for life in this period, from 1902, when he starts painting seriously, to January 1908, when the Abbaye was to close; but it is expressed in his enthusiasm for poetry, for the theatre, for the social ideal of the Association Ernest Renan, for the more individualist ideal of the Abbaye. His own work is cautious and steady, the most conservative and apparently immobile six years of his whole career. A detailed analysis of the paintings could indicate links with the huge, constantly developing, evolution that was to follow, but it would have been a remarkable critic indeed who could have guessed what Gleizes was capable of on the basis of what he had achieved by 1907.

2
TOWARDS CUBISM
1908–11

From 1902, when he started painting seriously, to 1905, Gleizes was in the army. In 1906, much of his time and energy was taken up with the Association Ernest Renan. Although the whole aim of the Abbaye had been to allow its members time for the free exercise of their art, a disproportionate amount of Gleizes's time seems to have been taken up with the practical work involved, especially the printing. It is therefore not until 1908 that he was able to devote all his time to painting, and it is in 1908 that his sudden rapid development as a painter begins. The change is seen in a much greater emphasis on drawing – largely ink and wash drawing – as against painting, and therefore on form as opposed to colour. At a time when the avant garde was dominated by the Divisionists, or Neo-Impressionists, led by Signac, and the Fauves, led by Matisse – both primarily concerned with bright, startling colour contrasts – Gleizes is working almost entirely in monochrome, usually black and white, though sometimes using a single, usually sombre and dramatic, colour.

There is no suggestion here of a 'reaction' against the Fauves, or of a desire to distinguish himself from them. He seems simply unaware of them, still content to record the world about him as he experiences it. His closest painter friends of the time, Mahn, d'Otémar, and Henri Doucet, would never follow him in the radical questioning of the role of painting into which he was soon to plunge; and we may imagine that Gleizes's more linear, less Impressionist drawing of 1908 could easily have developed into a Socialist Realism like that of Mahn's in the 1920s. Gleizes was still part of an essentially literary circle whose tastes in painting, with the exception of Mercereau, were conservative.

Nonetheless, Gleizes himself was prey to a deep dissatisfaction with 'the analysis and little modulations of tones' of Impressionism. He wanted something more solid and definite, and felt that it could be found in drawing, but his drawing was still derived directly from the observation of nature. He was developing a better sense of line and colour values, but this had no 'internal significance'; it provided 'a mediocre satisfaction, without any possibility of development'. 'Tonality gave way to colour and the line enfolded the drawing better, but I still felt, in spite of everything, how much this all remained tributary to the Impressionism with which I had begun.'[1]

Gleizes is referring to a series of studies of the landscape round Courbevoie, and especially of the river with its commercial life, in which we can see the emergence of a distinct 'hand', recognisably the same as that of the ink and wash drawings of the end of his life (Plates 4–6).[2] If the arabesque line is still tied to the representational subject and therefore disorganised in relation to the proportions and the two dimensions of the pictorial surface, the beginnings of an understanding of the power of line and arabesque are still present. At the

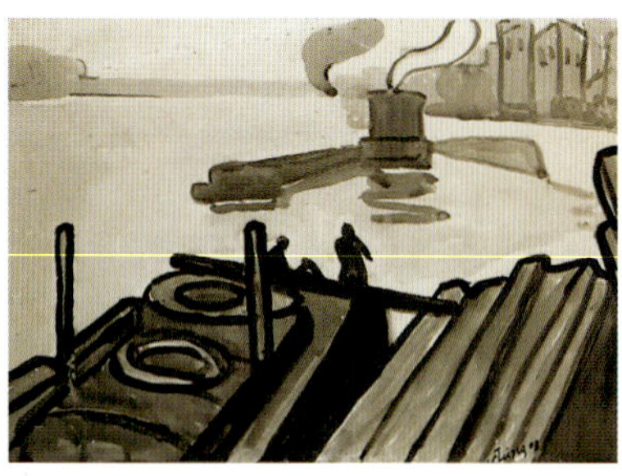

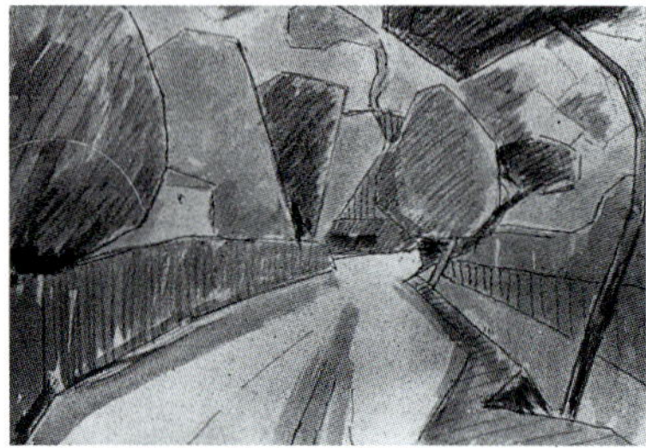

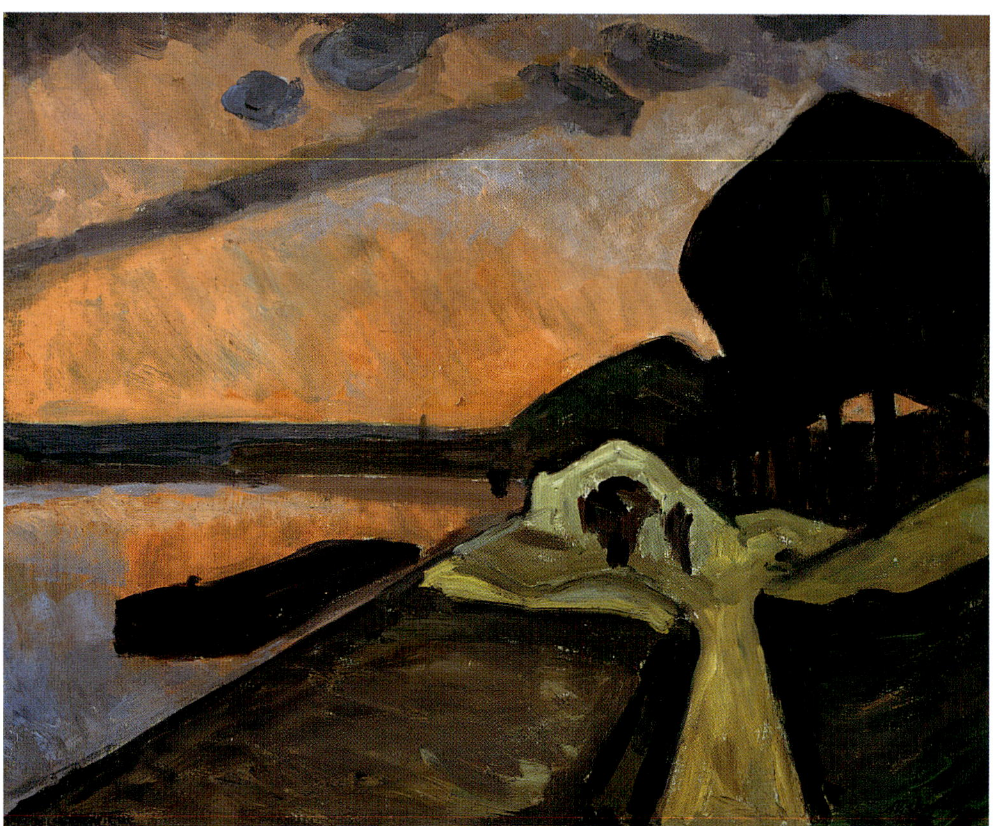

4. *Paris, les quais*, 1908. Ink wash, 30.5 × 42 cm. Fondation Albert Gleizes

5. *Environs de meudon*, 1909. Pencil, wash and watercolour, 23.5 × 31 cm. Private Collection

6. *Les Bords de la Marne*, 1909. Oil on canvas, 54 × 65 cm. Musée des Beaux Arts, Lyon

same time, some of the drawings show a much-simplified overall construction, an elementary division of the pictorial surface into a number of flat, interlocking shapes – an aspiration towards the seizure of the whole area of the painting that would be the distinguishing feature of Gleizes's Cubism.

It is all, however, still very nebulous. For Gleizes, the crucial breakthrough occurred when Mercereau introduced him to Henri Le Fauconnier in 1909. 'For my part,' Gleizes says, he felt 'the very precise sentiment that through him I could finally come to unravel my own little internal drama'. He was particularly impressed by Le Fauconnier's *Portrait du poète, Pierre Jean Jouve* (one of the poets who had been published by the Abbaye), shown in the Salon d'Automne of 1909 (Plate 7):

> This portrait was not an exact likeness of the model, but a totally different interpretation, which, far from doing away with any resemblance, heightened it by insisting on certain characteristics, and by a rigorous elimination of all useless encumbrances [*surcharge inutile*]. The colour no longer owed anything to Impressionism; it did not tickle the sensibility, it was no longer the whole of the painting, it supported the structure of the drawing by simple accords of brown-violets.[3]

For Gleizes, it marked the end of his last link with Impressionism. From now on 'lines and volumes, densities and weights, symmetrical balance of one part against another, such were our concerns and aspirations'.[4]

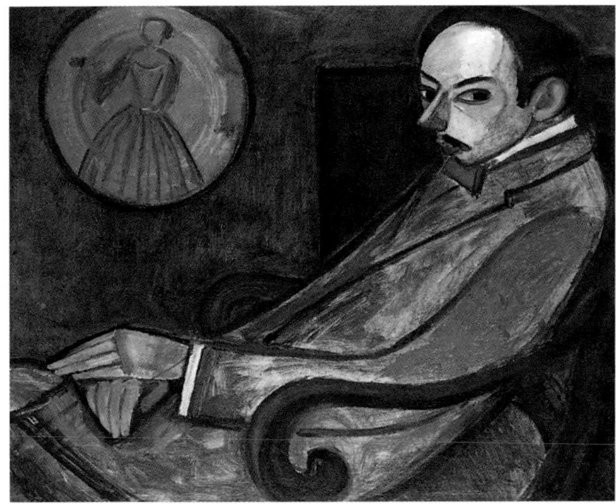

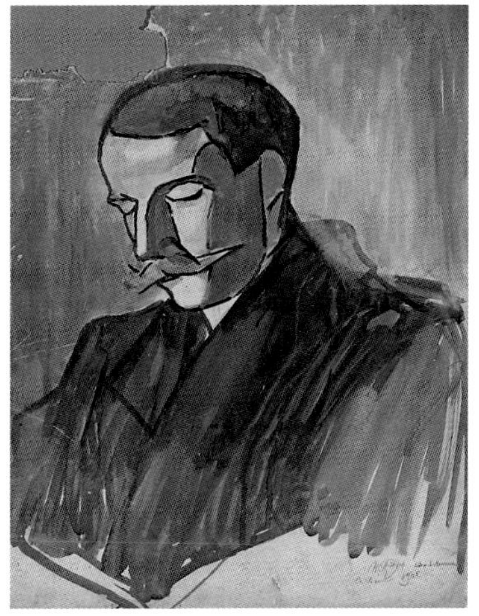

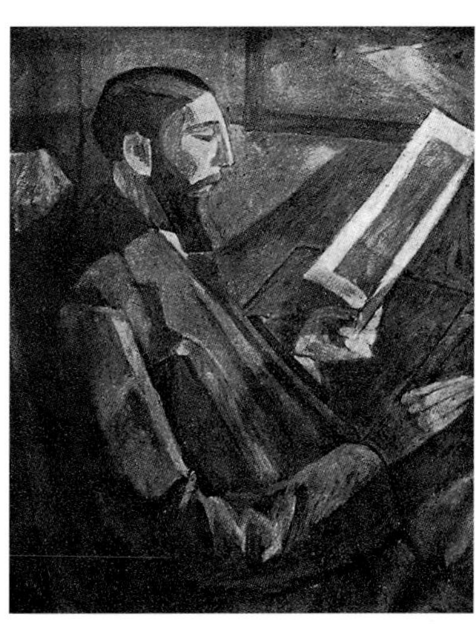

7. Henri Le Fauconnier, *Portrait du poète, Pierre Jean Jouve*, 1909. Oil on canvas, 81 × 100 cm. Musée National d'Art Moderne, Paris

8. *Portrait d'Alexandre Mercereau*, 1908. Ink and wash on card, 64.3 × 49.2 cm. Musée National d'Art Moderne, Paris

9. *Portrait de Mr Robert G*[leizes], 1910. Oil on canvas, 140 × 112 cm. Present whereabouts unknown. Photograph from Gleizes: *Tradition et cubisme*, p. 33

Unlike Gleizes, but like nearly all the other pioneer Cubists, Le Fauconnier had passed through a 'Divisionist' period, but since 1907 he had been living in near isolation in Brittany, developing an austere painting in which colour was rigorously subordinated to the requirements of structure and form. As with Gleizes, there was still no question of any radical deformation of the external appearance of the subject. The emphasis at this time was on simplification and clarity.[5]

Gleizes was later to distinguish three periods in the history of Cubism. The first was primarily concerned with volume, hence the name 'Cubism'. The whole of Cubism could be summed up as a research into form, in opposition to the formlessness that had accompanied the triumph of Impressionism. The painters' first instinct was, naturally, to seek this form in the solidity of the subject and to associate the idea of solidity with that of the third dimension. Gleizes saw this period, the shortest phase in the development of Cubism, as a return to Classicism, to the monumental painting of David and Ingres. The subsequent phases were multiple perspective and the flat surface and they will be discussed when we come to them.[6]

There is a clear similarity between Le Fauconnier's portraits of Jouve and of Paul Castiaux (co-editor with Jouve of the journal *Les Bandeaux d'or*, an outlet for the Abbaye writers which was soon to publish Gleizes's first attempts at art criticism) and Gleizes's portraits of Alexandre Mercereau, painted in 1908, or of his cousin, Robert Gleizes, painted in 1910 (Plates 8 and 9). But the problem with these pictures, as with Le Fauconnier's, is that, although the subject is given a solid, visually interesting structure, it is detached from a less visually interesting background, bounded by its own contour which, inevitably, becomes the main element in the composition. The 'lines and volumes, densities and weights, symmetrical balance of one part against another' are confined to the figure; they are not a property of the whole area of the painting.

The same problem can be seen in Gleizes's portrait of René Arcos. This was a lifesize painting which Gleizes exhibited at the 1910 Salon des Indépendants. It may be regarded as his first attempt at a monumental work. Unfortunately, the painting itself has been lost and only an oil sketch remains (Plate 10). In it, the figure is sharply defined against a rather floating background. It is a Cubist – or, at least, cubed – figure in a pre-Cubist landscape. That both Gleizes and

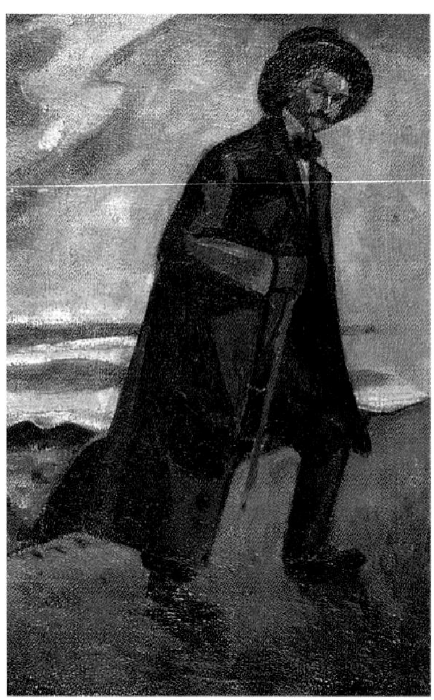

10. Sketch for *Portrait de René Arcos*, 1910. Oil on canvas, 60.3 × 38.3 cm. Fondation Albert Gleizes

Le Fauconnier were dissatisfied with this high relief given to the central subject may indicate that the strengths of Impressionism had more of a hold on them than they liked to admit. One effect of the Impressionist and Neo-Impressionist touches of colour is precisely to unify the picture plane so that each part is equally interesting. Any subject that emerges too clearly risks introducing a disruptive element – thus the nebulosity of Monet's waterlilies is a logical climax to the Impressionist experiment. Gleizes and Le Fauconnier disliked this nebulosity and wished to introduce form, but they were themselves too immersed in the Impressionist aesthetic to be satisfied with a form that was isolated from, and seemed to be imposed on, the rest of the picture surface.

Gleizes's picture, *L'Arbre*, also exhibited in the Salon des Indépendants of the Spring of 1910 is more fully 'Cubist' than the *Portrait de René Arcos* (if the latter can be judged from the sketch), in that the whole picture surface is now involved in the play of volumes. The picture, which is a radical jump forward in terms of Gleizes's own intentions, did not attract attention at the time, nor did Gleizes seem to recognise any community of intention with other painters – Le Fauconnier apart – working in a similar direction. It is doubtful if Gleizes even thought of himself as particularly 'avant garde'. The year 1910 was the first in which he passed from the Société Nationale des Beaux Arts, with its bias towards the Nabis, to the more Divisionist-Fauve dominated Salon des Indépendants.[7]

It was only at the Salon d'Automne in October 1910 that Gleizes became aware of other painters working in a similar direction – Jean Metzinger, Robert Delaunay, Fernand Léger.

Gleizes says that Mercereau had already introduced him to Metzinger and Delaunay prior to the 1910 Salon d'Automne, and that the two (Metzinger and Delaunay) had been hung together at the earlier Salon des Indépendants, but he had not particularly noticed them.[8] It was Metzinger's article, *Note sur la peinture*, in the journal *Pan* in November 1910 that first attracted his attention. Roger Allard, another writer associated with the Abbaye (Gleizes in 1910 had been working on the illustrations to a book of his poems, *Le Bocage amoureux*, published, by Eugene Figuière, in 1911[9]) had noted the emergence of a new school in his review of the 1910 Salon d'Automne, but he did not mention Gleizes. The idea of a new school was roundly ridiculed by Apollinaire in the Italian Futurist journal, *Poesia*.[10] In *L'Intransigeant*, without identifying any new school, he had sharply criticised Metzinger and, less sharply, Le Fauconnier, but did not mention Gleizes or Léger.[11] Daniel Robbins says in his thesis on Gleizes's early development that Gleizes only sent two minor works to this 1910 Salon d'Automne, but that he already had more radical work in his studio.[12]

It was after the 1910 Salon d'Automne that Gleizes, Le Fauconnier, Metzinger, Delaunay and Léger began to meet at the Closerie des Lilas, which was the meeting place of the group associated with the poet Paul Fort's journal, *Vers et prose*, for which Mercereau was working at the time. They were joined by Apollinaire, who seems to have quickly forgotten his hostility to Metzinger and Le Fauconnier, and by André Salmon. It was at the Closerie des Lilas that they plotted a virtual coup d'état against the hanging committee of the Salon des Indépendants.[13]

The Salon des Indépendants, the freer of the two great annual showcases of radical painting, was still dominated by the Neo-Impressionists led by Paul Signac, who believed that his own school, based on the scientific principles he had outlined in 1899 in his great book *D'Eugène Delacroix au néo-impressionisme*, was the way of the future. He had every reason to believe this given that painting based on small dots of primary colour in accordance with his own principles had been taken up everywhere in Europe and was still the basic technique even of the Italian Futurists, already proclaiming themselves to be the most modern of modern schools. The whole Cubist group, with the exception of Gleizes (and, as it happens, Picasso) had passed through Neo-Impressionism, but all – with the exception of Delaunay – now felt a profound dissatisfaction with it. Gleizes, Le Fauconnier and Metzinger had all three felt isolated. The realisation that there were others who felt the same discontent was exhilarating. They believed that if they could exhibit together as a coherent group, they could make a much greater impact. Gleizes complains that the arbitrary scattering of different schools of painting gave the impression of a flea market. If the schools could be grouped together, each of them could bear witness more clearly to its own essential idea.

The result of a political-style campaign which involved, among others, André Lhote, Dunoyer de Segonzac, Roger de la Fresnaye and Berthold Mahn, was an outrageously rigged election in which Metzinger, for example, was elected by 500 votes out of a total electorate of 350 voters. Le Fauconnier took the presidency. Signac and his old committee walked out in protest but in fact, according to Gleizes's account, took it in a good spirit.

The Salon, which opened in February 1911, was effectively divided in two: the Neo-Impressionists, headed by Signac and Maximilien Luce, in the centre rooms; the younger generation in the side rooms. Le Fauconnier, Léger, Delaunay, Metzinger and Gleizes had a room – Room 41 – to themselves, together with Marie Laurencin who, Gleizes says, was included at Apollinaire's insistence though she could not really be said to have been working in the same direction. Room 43 contained the work of other young painters who had also rejected divisionism and who, in their different ways, were asserting the primacy of form over colour in their work. They included André Lhote, Dunoyer de Segonzac, and Luc Albert Moreau. Room 42 contained a tribute to Henri Rousseau, 'le Douanier', who had died the previous year.

This is important. The young painters had fought for control over the hanging committee as a means of expressing as clearly as possible the ideas that motivated them. It can therefore hardly be regarded as an accident if they presented themselves grouped round Henri Rousseau as round a master. Their admiration was heartfelt and uncomplicated by any hint of a feeling of intellectual superiority. This was certainly true of Delaunay and Gleizes, both of whom, as we shall see when we come to consider Gleizes's period in New York and Barcelona, were to write comparing Rousseau favourably with Cézanne. Rousseau was a man of the people and he was monumental and direct, which corresponded well with the aims and aspirations of the so-called 'Salon Cubists'. Accused of deliberate obscurity and élitism, they all, with the possible exception of Metzinger, wanted to lay the foundations of a truly 'popular' art. There is a direct line of continuity between the young painters sitting at the feet of Henri Rousseau and the Gleizes, Delaunay and Léger who were to appear as champions of a monumental, mural painting in the 1920s and 1930s.

The painters had hoped to make an impact by being exhibited together, but they were not prepared for a riot. Gleizes describes his own astonishment as he found the crowd becoming thicker the closer he approached Room 41, culminating in a raging battle in the room itself. His description of the contro-

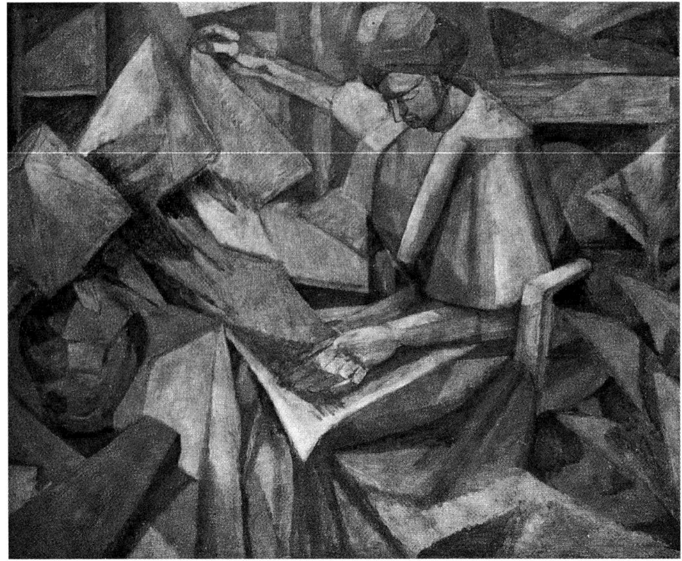

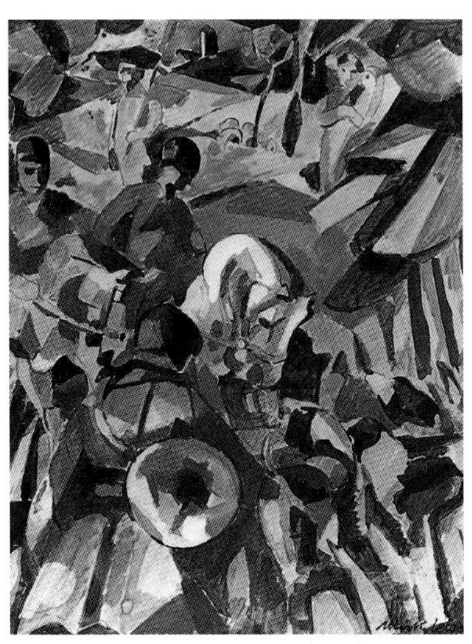

11. *La Femme au phlox*, 1910. Oil on canvas, 81 × 100 cm. Museum of Fine Arts, Houston, Texas. Gift of the Esther Whinery Goodrich Foundation

12. *La Chasse (study)*, 1911. Pencil, watercolour, gouache and ink wash, 20 × 16.1 cm. Musée National d'Art Moderne, Paris. Legacy from Dr Robert Le Masle, 1974

versy resembles descriptions of the riots at the opening of the Rite of Spring two years later. Gleizes explains the rage of the crowd by saying that the pictures looked abstract to them because they could not find the anecdotal subject. In fact, he claims, the subjects were perfectly legible and the pictures quite conservative, still for the most part observing the conventions of single-point perspective.

This was certainly the case for his own work. One of the pictures exhibited was his *La Femme au phlox* (Plate 11). Here, as in other pictures from the same period, he has addressed the problem posed in the portrait of Robert Gleizes – the matter of the fissure between subject and background – by uniting them in the same play of interdependent volumes. The distinctive pleasure of Gleizes's Cubism, and indeed of all his painting, begins to be felt – more so than in the *Arbre* of the 1910 Indépendants. The eye is free to rove over the whole surface of the painting, always finding things of interest, always impelled to move on. The pre-Cubist landscapes were simple dramatic effects which could be seen by the eye all at once. But now the spectator wants to linger, to take time to enjoy the different parts of the painting and the relations between them. Gleizes was later to write that Cubism had restored the element of 'flânerie' (rambling) in painting, the enjoyment of what lies between the main points of interest, and this 'flânerie' is the quality that is now beginning to emerge.[14]

Nonetheless, if we take Gleizes's tripartite division of Cubism – volume, multiple perspective, respect for the flat surface – then this painting is still firmly in the first stage, that of volume. Perspective unity is still respected, as is the coherence of the figure and its relation to its surroundings. Gleizes tells us in the *Souvenirs* that among those who disliked the pictures shown at the Salon des Indépendants were his old associates of the Abbaye de Créteil, the musician Albert Doyen and his wife, and Georges Duhamel. Some time later, they visited him in his studio and expressed pleasure that Gleizes was returning to conventional representational painting. The paintings they admired included those that had been shown in the Salon des Indépendants. They had simply become more used to the visual convention.[15]

The visual convention that had baffled them was the apparent disappearance of the subject in its surroundings. Although the coherence of the figure and the perspective unity are respected, they are indeed obscured by the overall movement of the painting which is its main interest and which, foreshadowing later developments, is essentially circular. But it must also be said that the Doyens and Duhamel were now seeing Gleizes's work separate from that of Delaunay, Léger and Metzinger, which had advanced further than Gleizes into the second phase of Cubism – multiple perspective.

Gleizes tells us that in the Summer of 1911, he drew very close to Metzinger who was living in Meudon, that he had lengthy discussions with him and that multiple perspective was at the centre of these discussions. Gleizes himself was reticent about what he feared was Metzinger's excessive theoretical rigour.[16] In his own work, he continued to develop the means he had begun to use in *La Femme au phlox*. The network of volumes becomes ever more complex; the eye has an ever greater variety of formations, places of interest in which to linger, like a rambler lingering over the various parts of a landscape – in fact like the figure wandering through the wonderful, multifaceted landscape of his *Paysage, Meudon* (1911), a record of his own visits to Metzinger. And I must stress that I am talking about the experience of walking through a landscape. The experience of seeing it through a train window, which interested the Italian Futurists and Léger, never had much appeal for Gleizes.

The *Paysage, Meudon* and the *Portrait de Jacques Nayral* (Plate 13), also finished in the Summer of 1911, can still be read as conventional single-point perspective paintings. In describing how he painted Nayral, Gleizes tells us what interested him: 'equivalences, echoes, penetrations, rhythmic correspondences with the surrounding elements – terrain, trees, houses'. Nayral, who, like Alexandre Mercereau, worked for the publisher Eugène Figuière and who, two years later, would marry Gleizes's sister, had asked Gleizes to do the portrait, and Gleizes had been delighted because his face seemed to correspond so well to the solid, faceted, architectural qualities he was seeking.[17]

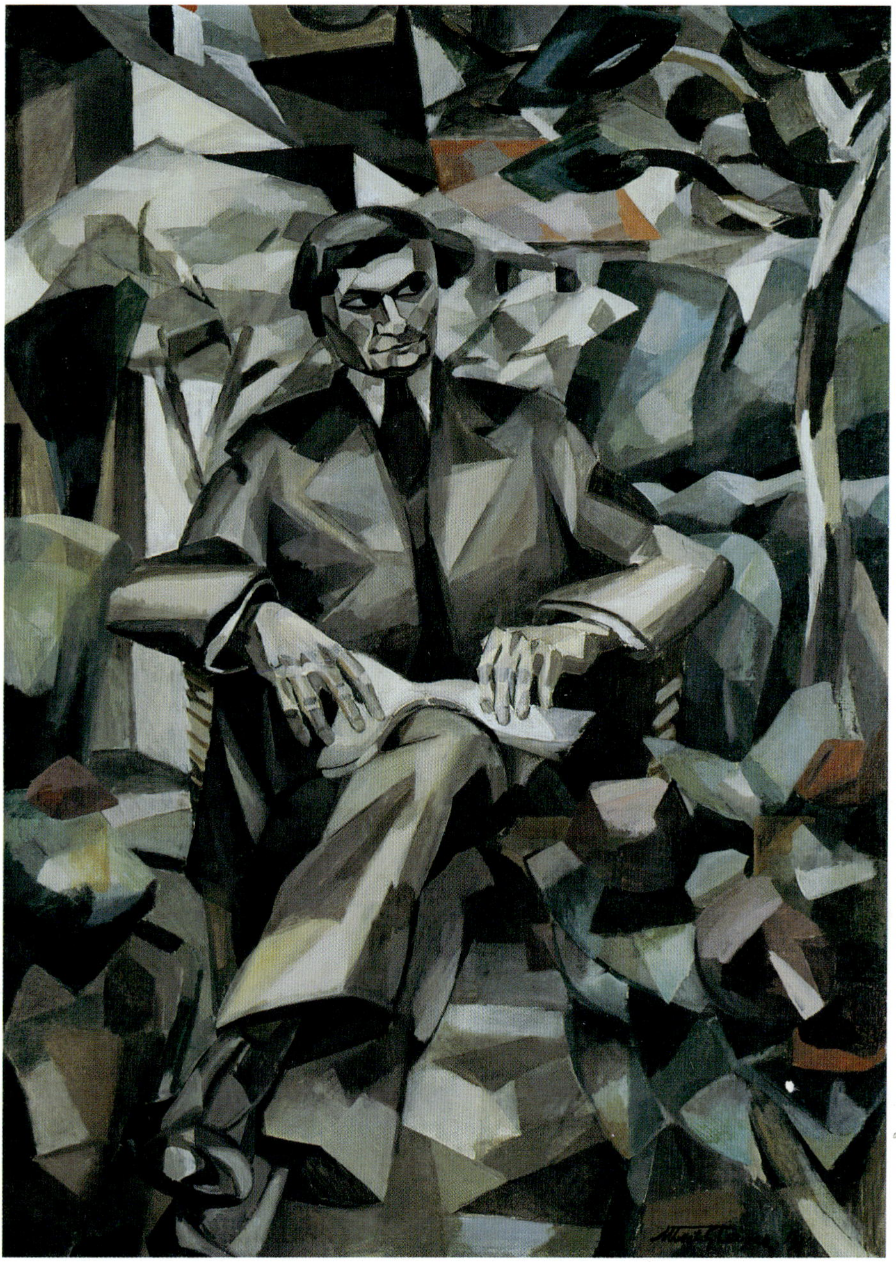

13. *Portrait de Jacques Nayral*, 1911. Oil on canvas, 180 × 130 cm. Tate Gallery, London

The emphasis on volume, and the search for a homogeneous picture surface achieved through the interpenetration of the subject and its surroundings, did not of themselves imply that the subject could, usefully, be shown from several different angles at the same time. But the interpretation of the landscape and figure in terms of simplified, interpenetrating volumes, breaks the static nature of single-point perspective. The volumes point, so to speak, in different directions so that, while the unity of the subject seen from a single perspective point is respected, the eye is still directed over the whole surface of the canvas. The multiple perspective of Metzinger was an attempt to give a fuller, more intellectual idea of the subject represented. It is not misleading to use the words 'multiple perspective' to refer to Gleizes's *Portrait de Jacques Nayral* and *Paysage, Meudon*, but it has a much more purely plastic justification in the stimulus it gives to the eye rather than to the intellect.

The visual language developed by Gleizes, still owing a great debt to Le Fauconnier, is very rich and, though it marks a logical development from the *Portrait de René Arcos*, it still represents a qualitative change: from uncertainty to

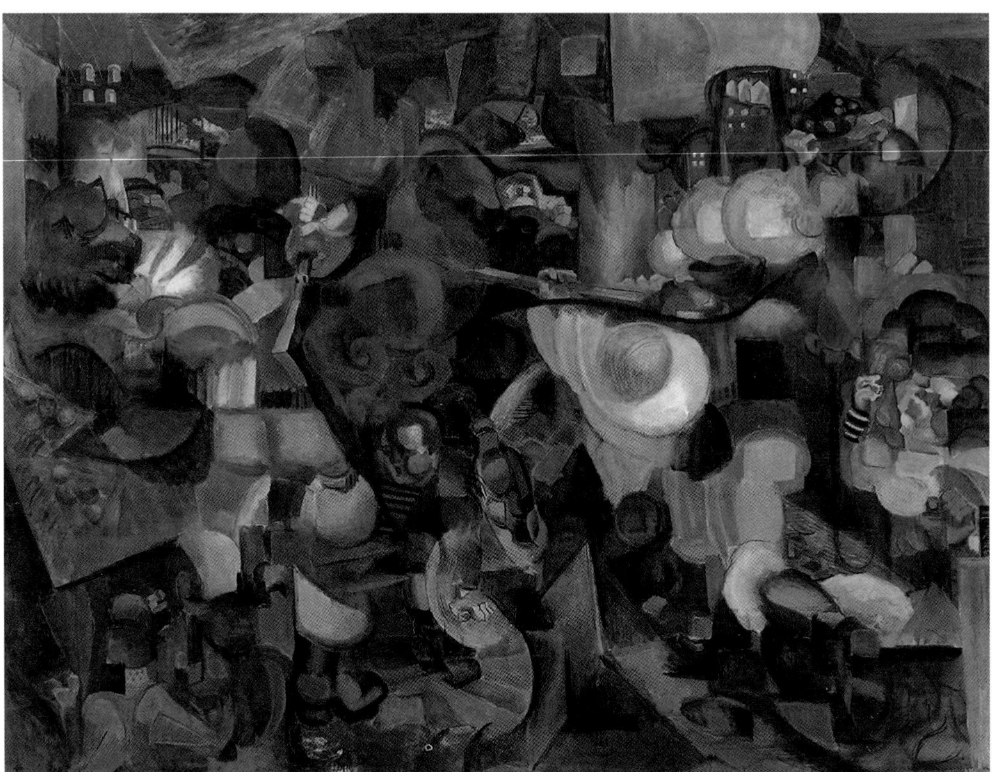

14. Henri Le Fauconnier, *Les Montagnards attaqués par des ours*, 1912. Oil on canvas, 241 × 307 cm. Rhode Island Museum of Art, Rhode Island School of Design

certainty, from hesitation to mastery. The progress made from 1907 and the period of the Abbaye de Créteil is even more remarkable. In 1907, Gleizes still has something of the character of a Sunday painter. He works within a convention that may be 'modern' in the eyes of his father who does not accept Impressionism, but which is still conservative in relation to the Fauves, the Divisionists, the Nabis. In four years – one year after his first appearance in the Salon des Indépendants – he is at the centre of a scandal and widely recognised as a leader of the avant garde, producing works which make a confident moral statement in favour of a constructive, positive painting, full of possibilities for the future.

Le Fauconnier's *L'Abondance* of 1910 is closely related to Gleizes's work of 1910/11 – especially *La Femme au phlox* and *La Cuisine*, in which the colour is very restrained. In 1911, however, Le Fauconnier began working on his monumental *Les Montagnards attaqués par des ours* (Plate 14), a complex allegorical painting which combined the elements suggested by its title with aspects taken from modern life and from *L'Abondance* itself. To combine all these heterogeneous elements in a single construction, Le Fauconnier uses a more radical development of the technique of multiple perspective. I would maintain, in disagreement with Daniel Robbins, that Gleizes was not greatly attracted by the possibility of combining heterogeneous subjects on a single canvas. Despite his association with Barzun and Romains, poets striving towards a 'synthetic' or 'simultaneist' view of human history and human life, he usually shows subjects together that would be found together in nature. But he did like large-scale subjects – the hunt; the man on a balcony with the city street behind him; the harvest threshers, with workers, picnickers and a village; the 'City and the River'.

The first of these is *La Chasse*, and it uses the same visual language as the

Portrait de Jacques Nayral and the *Paysage, Meudon*. But it is less satisfactory, perhaps because of the large scale of the subject. The hunt passes in the foreground and is watched by a shepherd and a woman and child. There is a very distinct sense of foreground and background, and the shapes of the horses and huntsmen in the foreground become an intrusive part of the composition. The picture surface is not equalised as it is in the simpler subjects of the landscape and the portrait. I would speculate that it was this problem that led Gleizes to want to go further in the direction of breaking up the coherence of the represented subject – a way that was already being pursued by Le Fauconnier and, especially, by Metzinger.

But this development, though prepared by conversations with Metzinger in the Summer of 1911, belongs to the end of 1911 and to 1912, after the 1911 Salon d'Automne, at which the scandal at the Salon des Indépendants was renewed. Here, Gleizes showed the *Portrait de Jacques Nayral* and *La Chasse*. He complains that the impact of the initial group – himself, Le Fauconnier, Metzinger, Delaunay and Léger – was a little weakened by being mixed up with painters who, he believed, had a different 'cast of mind' ['état d'esprit' – a key term in Gleizes's thinking] – André Lhote, Roger de la Fresnaye (who was responsible for the hanging), Dunoyer de Segonzac and Luc Albert Moreau. But for him, nonetheless, the Salon was of great importance because it was there for the first time that he met the Duchamp brothers – Jacques Villon, Raymond Duchamp-Villon and Marcel Duchamp – who were to play an important role in the discussions which led to the publication of Gleizes's and Metzinger's book, *Du 'Cubisme'*.

It was also soon after the opening of the Salon d'Automne that Gleizes met Picasso and visited Daniel-Henry Kahnweiler's gallery to see his work, and that of Braque, for the first time. He describes this meeting in a letter sent to the Musée National d'Art Moderne, at the very end of his life, criticising the catalogue of their 1953 exhibition *Le Cubisme, 1907–14*. The letter is largely a lively attack on the version of events given by Kahnweiler, the gallery owner who looked after the interests of Picasso and Braque and, a little later, of Léger and Gris. Gleizes says of the catalogue account (broadly based, like most of the generally available literature, on Kahnweiler's version):

> What is necessary, I'm sorry to have to speak frankly, is to take everything up again from the foundations and, to begin with, to start out from the unquestionable reality of two currents which, unaware of each other, were finally enfolded under a single heading, the movement that was called 'Cubism'. You can then avoid confusion if, right from the start, you make the distinctions that must, in all honesty, be acknowledged. The history of the 'Bateau Lavoir' belongs to those who were part of that particular grouping; personally, I only know what has been said about this history; I do not know the details, nor did my comrades of the other group – Metzinger, Delaunay, Le Fauconnier and Léger . . . But what I do know well, because I lived it and remember it perfectly, is the origin of our relations and their development to 1914, passing by the notorious Room 41 of the Indépendants of 1911, which provoked the 'involuntary scandal' out of which Cubism really emerged and spread in Paris, in France and through the world . . .
>
> The exotic expressionism, derived from Fauvism, of the *Bateau Lavoir* had as a counterpoint that 'revision of the postulates of classicism' of the French

> painters at Courbevoie [where Gleizes was based – PB] and Puteaux [where the Duchamp brothers were based – PB]. Moreover, in a recent article on Léger which appeared in *Arts* (6–12 March), Léger admits that " I was" – it is himself speaking – "too classical, with the French sense of equilibrium, to adopt the romanticism of negro art which influenced Braque and Picasso. I met them, accompanied by my friend Delaunay, at Kahnweiler's, through Max Jacob and Apollinaire. 'They are spiders' webs', Delaunay, that admirable colourist, told me, after looking at the canvasses in neutral tones, with thin lines, of those we called the 'Montmartrois'." Exactly. Léger met Picasso with Le Fauconnier, Metzinger (the only one of us who knew him) and myself in the café tobacconists at the angle of the Rue J. Goujon and the Avenue d'Autin, after the opening of the Salon d'Automne of 1911, at the request G. Apollinaire made to me on the afternoon of the opening. Some days later, we went to Kahnweiler's for the first time and saw the canvasses of Braque and Picasso which, rightly or wrongly, did not thrill us. Their spirit, being the opposite of our own, explains our reticence. The meeting to which Léger refers could only credibly have occurred after that of which I speak, which was the first. Apart from our visit to Kahnweiler's, we had never seen either Picasso or Braque. For myself, I never met Braque before 1921 or 1922, and this was a chance encounter at L. Rosenberg's [owner of the influential Galerie de l'Effort Moderne – PB] which only lasted a few minutes. As for Picasso, I met him three times in my life . . . And as far as Kahnweiler is concerned I never again put my foot in his boutique after this first visit in 1911. For Gris, it was a little different; as he exhibited at the Indépendants from 1912 onwards, we met more often, at the Closerie des Lilas, or at my house at Courbevoie, but this more often was still not very often. He was never at the Villons at Puteaux.[18]

Gleizes does not mention it, but this visit to Picasso's studio occurred at a very unfortunate time. This was precisely the moment when Picasso and Apollinaire were both implicated in the affair of the statues stolen from the Louvre by Apollinaire's friend, Géry Pieret, statues which Picasso appears to have used as models for his *Les Démoiselles d'Avignon*. Picasso had just been summoned to Paris from Céret by Apollinaire and both men were in a state of panic. Apollinaire would be arrested shortly after. Some time later it was with Gleizes's help that the charges against him were finally dropped.[19]

The question of the relations between the 'Bateau Lavoir' or 'Montmartre' Cubists (Picasso and Braque) and the 'Salon' or 'Montparnasse' Cubists (Gleizes, Metzinger, Delaunay, Le Fauconnier and Léger) is complicated. I consider the conventional opinion – that 'Salon' Cubism was a more or less original derivation from the Cubism of Picasso and Braque – to be misleading, but the literature is so enormous that a separate book would be necessary to develop the argument in detail.[20] I only wish here to indicate some conclusions which seem to me to be certain.

The painters associated with Kahnweiler did not exhibit in the great public salons. Kahnweiler assumed total control over the public presentation of their work, and his policy was to sell to a small group of discerning collectors with a taste for the esoteric.[21] Until the public scandal provoked by the Cubism of the 1911 Indépendants, there was a deliberate atmosphere of secrecy about Kahnweiler's gallery, and it was quite possible for painters working in Paris to have little or no contact with it. This was certainly the case with Gleizes and

Le Fauconnier, who were both – Gleizes especially – new arrivals on the avant garde scene. Gleizes asserts it on several occasions and nothing in the rest of his life permits us to think that he would lie on such an important matter.

On the other hand, Metzinger, who had long known the 'Bateau Lavoir' circle, notably Max Jacob and Apollinaire, was aware of Picasso and Braque and acknowledges their influence (while also confirming that Gleizes did not know them[22]). At the Salon d'Automne of 1910, he exhibited a Nude which is a more or less faithful copy of the contemporary work of Picasso and Braque and, in 1910/11, the extent and nature of this influence became a matter of controversy between himself, Apollinaire and Roger Allard who, as already noted, was an old associate of the Abbaye.

The case of Delaunay and Léger is more doubtful. Gleizes insists that Delaunay's 'spider's web' remark must have occurred after this 'first' encounter at the end of 1911. Virginia Spate, in her book, *Orphism*, suggests that it refers to the exhibition Braque held in Kahnweiler's gallery in 1908; but it fits the 1911 'hermetic Cubism' much better than Braque's 1908 work, which Delaunay would probably have liked. As a friend of Metzinger, of Henri Rousseau and of the collector, Wilhelm Uhde, Delaunay had certainly more possibilities of seeing the work of Picasso and Braque than Gleizes.[23]

But what is quite clear is that both Delaunay and Léger disclaim the influence of Picasso and Braque. We have just seen Léger disclaiming it after the Second World War. Delaunay disclaims it at the time, and very emphatically, in letters and documents that have been published under the title *Du Cubisme à l'art abstrait*. Both felt that the preoccupations of Picasso and Braque were essentially different from their own. It is only Metzinger who can be said unequivocally to have been influenced by them and even then the extent of the influence is open to question. The direction of Metzinger's painting in 1911 is completely different from that of the 'hermetic Cubism' of Picasso and Braque. Gleizes says of Metzinger's development in the Summer of 1911, when the two painters came to work very closely together: 'Metzinger, it is easy to see, wants to master chance; he insists that all the parts of his work relate logically, that the composition should be an organism as rigorous as possible and that any accidental appearances should be, if not eliminated, at least controlled . . .'[24] This is not a description that could be applied to the contemporary work of Picasso and Braque. None of the Salon Cubists show the slightest interest in the *papiers-collés* of 1912 – and both Delaunay and Gleizes in fact inveigh violently against them.[25]

That having been said, I will argue later that Braque's *papiers-collés* played an important role in the overall elaboration of Cubism as Gleizes understood it, but this argument belongs to the discussion of Gleizes's work in the 1920s. I am far from wishing to deny the importance of Picasso and Braque. It was Metzinger who had introduced Gleizes to the practice of showing the same object from different angles and Metzinger's arguments were undoubtedly influenced by the practice of Picasso and Braque. It is thus that we may say that Picasso and Braque influenced Gleizes, indirectly, through Metzinger.

A link between the two groups was provided by Apollinaire. When Apollinaire saw Metzinger's *Nu debout* at the Salon d'Automne in 1910, he saw that it was an imitation of Picasso and said so. Roger Allard, on the other hand, denied any connection between the Salon Cubists and Picasso and Braque. Metzinger explained his position, and his relation to Picasso, in the *Note sur la peinture* of November 1910, which is also full of praise for Le Fauconnier as representing the most ambitious stage yet reached by the new painting.

Apollinaire then supports the Salon Cubists at the Salon des Indépendants in 1911, and by writing a catalogue for the work of Delaunay, Gleizes, Léger, Le Fauconnier and de Segonzac at an exhibition in Brussels in June 1911.[26] He is anxious to bring the two groups together, in opposition to the policy of Kahnweiler, who wishes to maintain the distinction. At the end of 1911, as we have seen, he succeeds in introducing Gleizes and Le Fauconnier to Picasso, but the meeting is not a success. Nonetheless, Picasso and Braque have a place in Gleizes's and Metzinger's *Du 'Cubisme'*, published in 1912 (in which their chronological priority is recognised in the order of the illustrations).[27] Apollinaire himself attempts a synthesis that will allow for all the differences in his *Les Peintres cubistes*, published in 1913, though by this time he is persuaded that it is Delaunay, who refuses the term 'Cubism', who represents the way of the future.[28]

The most important question in all this is not the question of chronological priority (which can, without difficulty, be conceded to Picasso and Braque), nor even of 'influence', but the difference in intention and direction. Daniel Robbins has coined the term 'Epic Cubism' to describe the work of the Salon Cubists, all of whom were interested in large-scale subjects and none of whom, at this time at least, show any interest in the Still Life, the typical subject of Picasso and Braque.[29] All are concerned with conveying solidity and form in reaction against Impressionism and its emphasis on colour at the expense of form. Soon after Gleizes first saw Picasso's and Braque's work, he wrote an article on Metzinger in which he said that Metzinger 'perceived early on that painting was floundering about in subversive investigations touching simply the superstructure, and that the very valuable indications of Picasso and Braque did not, in spite of everything, abandon an Impressionism of form which, however, they oppose to that of colour'.[30]

The term 'Impressionism of form' expresses exactly how Gleizes would have seen the Hermetic Cubism of 1911, a painting based on the kind of spatial ambiguity which the Salon Cubists, and especially Gleizes, are most anxious to avoid. If this spatial ambiguity is seen as a necessary characteristic of 'true Cubism' – as it often is – then it is clear that Gleizes and most of his friends for most of the time are not 'true Cubists'. If a striving after solidity and a comprehensible and stable construction is a necessary characteristic of 'true Cubism', as Gleizes would argue, then it is clear that Picasso was not a 'true Cubist'. The simplest way of approaching the problem is to recognise the existence of different conceptions of the role of the work of art which, at this point in time, look superficially alike, but which are destined over the years to become ever more divergent and incompatible.

3

CUBISM 1912–14

The critical storm which had been provoked by the 1911 Salon des Indépendants continued through 1912, to the extent that, at the time of the 1912 Salon d'Automne, the Cubists, and the use of public space to present their work, was the subject of a debate in the Chambre des Députés. It was prompted by a letter sent from Mr Lampué, 'doyen' of the Municipal Council in Paris, addressed to Léon Berard, undersecretary of state responsible for the arts. It read in part:

> I hope that you will leave the place as disgusted as many people whom I know; I even hope that you will say under your breath: do I really have the right to give the use of a public monument to a band of crooks [*malfaiteurs*] who behave in the world of the arts in the way that gangsters [*apaches*] behave in ordinary life.[1]

In a letter addressed probably to the historian Bernard Dorival who was helping to organise the Cubist retrospective at the Musée National d'Art Moderne in 1953, Gleizes gives an amusing account of the background to the event. He quotes the Socialist deputy, Marcel Sembat, who spoke in the Chambre des Députés in defence of the Cubists:

> No, you have not been able to re-establish censorship under any form, neither under the broad and honest form: 'I will close the building', nor under this more indirect form: 'You will keep the building but there are certain works you will put down in the cellar!'

Gleizes continues:

> The passage about 'going down to the cellar' refers to the attitude of Frantz Jourdain, president of the Salon d'Automne, horrified by the letter of Lampué and the intervention of J. L. Breton [who had raised the matter in the Chambre des Députés – PB] and who was always our declared enemy (in his *Souvenirs*, written later about the Salon d'Automne, he does not mention the years 1911 and 1912 when we exhibited and when, without intending it, we gave rise to a violent publicity which was translated into a supplement of 50,000 francs in gold for the Society's coffers coming from visitors who had gone to see the monsters. Not even the gratitude of the stomach!)
>
> The 'scandal' we had involuntarily caused touched him particularly in a strategy for personal ends which had been upset. F. Jourdain wanted to have the cravate of a Commander of the Institute and to this end he could think

of nothing better than to invite for an 'exhibition of portraits' the Pontiffs of the [Société des] Artistes Français, who were very powerful at this time and able to do the trick for him. The room where these honoured guests had been placed, however, was situated next to that where we were to be found. Had the organisers done it deliberately? It is quite possible, since everyone at the Automne knew what was going on.

The consequences of this situation were disastrous for F. Jourdain. The crowd surged in our direction, queuing in this gallery, pressing against the picture frames and paying no attention whatsoever to the pictures. You can understand that these gentlemen were not very pleased and held it against the President, F. Jourdain, who was furious and forgot the discretion to which his role of President obliged him.

The 'Pontiffs' were not unconnected with the delivery of the letter [which had prompted the debates — PB]. On its publication, the journalists rushed to see F. Jourdain. And he, disowning the painters, whom he detested on aesthetic grounds (as he had a perfect right to do) and now detested for other reasons, since the cravate had been put off to the end of time . . . dared to pronounce the phrase . . . to which Sembat alludes, which was something like this: 'This year the Cubists are in the place of honour, but next year they will be put down into the cellar.'

We were, all of us, *members of the Society*, and, since we had committed no crime against the statutes of the Society, Frantz Jourdain, as elected President, had no right to disown us. We did not fail at the General Assembly which followed soon after to protest against this perfectly inadmissible attitude. That gave rise to a fine row, and to a proposed duel between Metzinger and the painter Chaillet, Picabia's brother-in-law, who substituted for Louis Vauxcelles, one of our worst enemies, for reasons at once of personal taste and on behalf of certain critics who felt menaced by our inopportune appearance . . .[2]

Vauxcelles, art critic in *L'Excelsior* and lifelong enemy of Cubism, was known as a particularly competent duellist. Gleizes says that he, as Metzinger's second, had managed to prevent the duel. Later he was to prevent another duel, this time between Vauxcelles himself and the Dada poet, Georges Ribemont-Dessaignes.[3]

The painters' response to the public outcry was to become ever more self-confident and assertive, working on an ever larger scale. Some of them, notably Gleizes and Metzinger, even adopted the word 'Cubism', which had originally been thrown at them as a term of abuse. Although they had not chosen this name themselves, they knew that they were part of a new collective phenomenon and, like it or not, this was the term by which they were known to the general public. Gleizes was to use it for the rest of his life to describe, not a completed 'epoch' in the history of painting, but the starting point of a long evolution which was, he believed, still far from complete at the time of his death.

Throughout this pre-war period, almost the full weight of the public controversy was carried by the 'Salon Cubists' and their associates. Even if Picasso and Braque had wanted to participate, they were prevented from doing so by the terms of their relationship with Kahnweiler;[4] and while the 'Salon Cubists' became ever more public and affirmative in their painting, the 'synthetic Cubism' of Picasso and Braque in 1912 – the period of the *papiers-collés* – shows, by contrast, a tendency towards a greater intimacy and even greater hermeticism.

•

We may speculate that this was the period when Gleizes began to develop the interest in wider human questions which was to be so much a part of his later thinking. The period, and the company he was keeping, were certainly stimulating, and a general account of the intellectual atmosphere of the time, particularly of the circle which frequented the Closerie des Lilas, would be very useful.

Some elements of such an account have already been provided in Mark Antliff's book, *Inventing Bergson*, and in David Cottington's *Cubism in the Shadow of War*. But although interesting on background, both these books are in my view too quick to attribute ideas to Gleizes simply on the grounds that they were held by people he knew. Antliff in particular develops his argument on the basis of a dispute over Bergson's philosophy which was developing in the circles of the right-wing political movement, Action Française. While we may be sure that Gleizes would have had more sympathy for the 'Bergsonian' side in this dispute than for the classical, Maurrassian, side and while he may or may not have been following it with interest there is no evidence that he attached any great importance to it; and, given his general anti-militarism and opposition to violence, which we will see when we come to discuss his attitude to the war, it seems unlikely that he would have identified with any of the tendencies in Action Francaise.

Nor does the occasional use of a Bergsonian terminology, which was very much in the air at the time, really justify the use of the term 'Bergsonian Cubist', as if Gleizes, or any of his associates were simply applying themselves to the task of translating Bergson's ideas into painting. It happens in any case, that, during the war, Gleizes wrote a large book, never published, under the title *L'Art dans l'évolution générale*, in which he tried to summarise everything he thought had been important in the pre-war period. He does not mention Bergson.

There are, however, two ways in which I think Bergson may have had an important impact on Gleizes's overall development. First, as we shall see shortly, Gleizes several times praises the Italian Futurists for having posed the problem of movement or dynamism in painting, and the debt the Futurists owed to Bergson has never been a matter of doubt. Antliff has rendered us a service in showing that related questions were being discussed in circles close to Cubism well before the Futurists arrived. Secondly, Bergson insists, particularly in the *Essai sur les données immédiates de la conscience,* that space and duration belong to different orders of reality and that the logic that applies to the one cannot apply to the other. A similar distinction between space and time, extension and duration, is, as we shall see, basic to Gleizes's thinking throughout his life. We can at least say that this is an important idea he shares with Bergson, whether or not it was actually derived from him.

Antliff's book is to some extent a critique of earlier work by David Cottington and others who had tended to present Gleizes as a classicist and traditionalist in the Maurrassian mould. Cottington's *Cubism in the Shadow of War* takes Antliff's argument on board, but, still anxious to present Gleizes as a traditionalist, uses the fact that some of Gleizes's paintings show rural scenes where he could have shown more urban scenes, to attribute to him the anti-industrialism which was to become such an important part of his later thinking. The point is certainly worth making that, even at this time, when Gleizes is developing a reputation as an outrageous modernist in company with Léger and Delaunay, his heart was not much moved by all the exciting splendours of the modern world. But the pictures can hardly be seen as manifestos against industrialisation when Gleizes himself continually insists that his commitment to the cause had been the result of a conversion undergone, with difficulty, in the 1920s.

It may be worth mentioning in this context Gleizes's fondness for painting women engaged in the quiet pursuit of a manual craft (*La Femme au phlox*, *La Cuisine*, *Les Couseuses*), which also indicates an instinctive liking for something – in this case manual crafts – which would later be developed into an ideological commitment. We might note further that Gleizes's pictorial treatment of women, usually his sisters, hardly corresponds to what Mark Antliff thinks appropriate for a painter inspired by Henri Bergson's doctrine of the *élan vital*.

Both Antliff and Cottington identify Gleizes generally with right-wing, nationalist and traditionalist, attitudes. Daniel Robbins, on the other hand, on the basis of his known liking for the poetry of Whitman, Verhaeren and Romains, and his association with Henri Martin Barzun, sees Gleizes as an enthusiast for the adventure of modern life, with left-wing and internationalist sympathies.[5] My own view is that, insofar as these speculations are viable, they mainly go to show that Gleizes's wider philosophical and political world view was still unformed. He could easily, on the basis of what little we know for certain, have developed in a number of different directions. It is the war that compels him to a serious work of intellectual reflection, which begins, in a notably impressionistic and poetic manner, in his writings in New York, but only achieves some degree of clear definition in the 1920s.

In this earlier period – as he himself frequently, in his later writings, insists – his interest is still primarily with the business of painting and with the problem of pictorial construction. This, and not any literary, political or philosophical idea that the painting might happen to express, is the centre of his interest and, since it is here that the strength and pleasure of the painting lies, it should be the centre of our interest as well.

•

The general atmosphere of public controversy provoked – involuntarily, according to Gleizes – by the Cubists had been further heightened by the exhibition held in Paris by the Italian Futurists at the beginning of 1912, claiming that their work was in advance of that of the Cubists, and supporting the claim with an impressive body of explanatory literature in the form of the Futurist Manifestos. The result was a series of intellectual skirmishes between the Futurists and the Cubists, a debate which involved, in particular, Delaunay and Apollinaire. It was a debate of very great importance with regard to Gleizes's future development because it engaged especially the idea of 'dynamism', of incorporating movement into painting.

Cubism, we may say, had been born out of a dissatisfaction with the 'retinal impression' given by Impressionism, a dissatisfaction already felt within the

Impressionist circle itself, most obviously by Cézanne, but also by the Neo-Impressionists. The glimpse of an instant in time, most obviously embodied in the work of Monet, was felt to be untrue to the fullness of our experience of the world, and it had the result of devaluing form in the painting at the expense of colour. The interest shown by the Neo-Impressionists in a precise science of colour – in particular in the writings of scientists such as Hermann Helmholtz, Ogden Rood, Eugene Chevreul and Charles Henry – indicated the desire for something more solid, more permanent than a fleeting impression. Seurat had achieved the marvel of using the pointillist technique to produce a painting that can fairly be called monumental. But there was still a feeling that the problem of form had not been tackled, and that it required more than the aggressive, purely empirical attack that had been launched by the Fauves.[6]

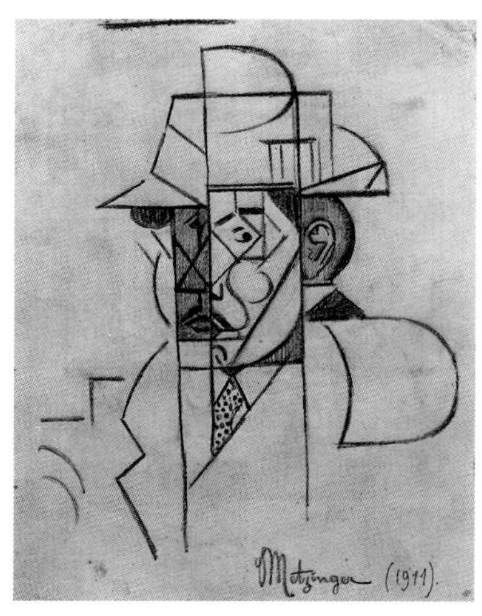

15. Jean Metzinger, Study for the *Portrait de Gleizes*, 1911. Pencil, 21.3 × 16.4cm. Musée National d'Art Moderne, Paris

Metzinger, in his *Note sur la peinture* of 1910 had put forward the idea of the 'total image', a phrase Gleizes quotes frequently in his later discussions of this period. The 'total image' was an attempt to put together the different ways in which the subject of the painting is experienced, both in the eye and in the mind. It was this ambition that would lead Metzinger himself to consider the necessity of a multidimensional space as being more real to our actual subjective experience than the abstract fiction of the three-dimensional perspective mechanism (Plate 15). In this sense a multidimensional space (Gleizes, attacking the idea some years later, was to insist that there was no need to talk about four dimensions rather than, say, fifteen) is a logical development of the idea of multiple perspective.

The 'total image' was to be achieved by a process of analysis – of identifying certain particular aspects – of the subject, followed by a process of synthesis, as the aspects that had been identified in the analysis were re-assembled. Metzinger, we have seen, was certainly influenced by the practice of Picasso and did not conceal the fact, but he was, nonetheless, attempting a much clearer expression of the idea, one whose rationality would be much more obvious. The terms 'analysis' and 'synthesis' were well understood at the time to mean two parts of a single process; it was only later that they came to be applied to two distinct phases in the careers of Picasso and Braque, and, later still, imposed as a straitjacket on the history of the whole period.[7]

The Futurist critique of the Cubist practice was that it did not take sufficient account of the destructive action of time on our formal experience of the world. The problem is of course particularly imposed by the fast movement of modern means of transport and by the moving image of the cinema, but the example given in a well-known passage from the Futurist Manifesto of 1910 is still that of a horse trotting: 'a running horse has not four legs, but twenty, and their movements are triangular.'

This proposes the very crude cinematic device of presenting movement as a series of successive stages, each one in itself static. The Futurists themselves, however, especially Boccioni, were by no means satisfied with the technique, which was only capable of showing a little fragment of movement, as arbitrary and frustrating as the frozen posture of the classical painting (it was to find its *reductio ad absurdum* in the frivolous little moving objects that were later to be produced under the name of 'kinetic art'). Boccioni aspired after:

> the creation of a new form which expresses the relativity between weight and expansion, between rotation and revolution; here, in fact, we have life itself caught in a form which life has created in its *infinite succession of events*. It seems clear to me that this succession is not to be found in the repetition of

> legs, arms and faces, as many people have idiotically believed, but is achieved through the intuitive search for *the one single form* which produces continuity in space. This is the key to making the object live in universal terms . . . We Futurists have discovered form in movement, and the movement of form . . . A body in movement, therefore, is not simply an immobile body set in motion, but a truly mobile object, which is a reality quite new and original.[8]

Still, the representation of the successive stages of a subject in motion was sufficiently identified with the Futurists to constitute an important part of the Futurist/Cubist debate. The Futurists accused the Cubists of not taking movement into account; the Cubists accused the Futurists of having a naïve idea of what movement was, an idea which was, moreover, irreconcileable with the requirements of the picture plane. However, the two sides were much closer in their concerns than either was prepared to admit. In particular there was among the Cubists (with the notable exceptions of Picasso and Braque) a real desire to tackle the problem of the subject in movement – both the movement of physical deplacement and also the movement of thought, as, most notably, in the great allegorical paintings of Le Fauconnier.

In the immediate circle of the Cubists, the presentation of the successive stages of a subject in movement had already been explored by the Czech painter, Frantisek Kupka, who had developed to a state of near abstraction a series of studies of a girl throwing a rubber ball. Although Kupka never identified with the Cubists, he was a near neighbour of the Duchamp brothers, based in Puteaux (he shared a garden with them) and he participated in their discussions, which also included Gleizes and Metzinger. Marcel Duchamp's *Nu descendant un escalier* was based on the same principle of showing the successive stages of a body in movement. We know that Gleizes, through Duchamp's brothers, persuaded him not to show this painting at the 1912 Salon des Indépendants. Duchamp later complained that this was an attempt to impose ideological conformity on the Cubist group. He was so disgusted, he tells us, that it prompted him to the extreme measure of getting a job.[9] Gleizes's reason was probably that, coming so soon after the Futurist exhibition, at a time when the Cubists were ridiculing the cinematic movement of the Futurists, it would look too much like a victory for the Italians.

The most interesting case on the Cubist side in this dispute is that of Delaunay, but I will be looking at Delaunay in more detail in a later chapter when, in the 1920s, Gleizes sees him as having embodied, better than anyone else, the real destiny of Cubism. But it is now that the problem of movement begins to appear in Gleizes's own work and, in particular, the difficulty of reconciling the movement of a moving subject with the sense of movement that can be excited in the spectator using purely pictorial means. The drama can be seen very clearly expressed in Gleizes's painting *Les Joueurs de football*, in which a very powerful pictorial construction is undermined by the idea of aggressive movement, very rare for Gleizes, conveyed in the frozen gestures of the subject, the football players (Plate 16).

Although Delaunay's hostility to the Futurists seems from his letters to have been deeply felt, it should be said that in general the quarrel was friendly. Gino Severini, who acted as the Futurists' representative in Paris, says in an essay written on Gleizes at the time of his death that the Italians had been well received by the Cubists, even if some, such as Roger de la Fresnaye, who did not have the habit of such things, were shocked by the apparent violence of the confrontations which took place. Gleizes, Severini says, had been particularly supportive: 'Gleizes was more generous [*expansif*] and supportive than anyone. . . .'[10]

All these factors contributed to the publication of Gleizes's and Metzinger's book, *Du 'Cubisme'*, in time for the first exhibition of the 'Section d'Or' in October 1912, envisaged as a new salon for the new painting.

Gleizes is best known as the co-author of *Du 'Cubisme'*, but I take the view that the book belongs more to Metzinger than to Gleizes. Although Gleizes's painting is developing with great rapidity in this period, his writing remains relatively undeveloped — certainly in comparison with what he was later to achieve. The handful of articles he wrote at this time separate from Metzinger are very different from *Du 'Cubisme'* and more modest. *Du 'Cubisme'* has something of the affirmative manifesto about it, even if it is restrained when compared with the Futurists. Gleizes's own writing, both now and later, has more a character of explanation and argument.

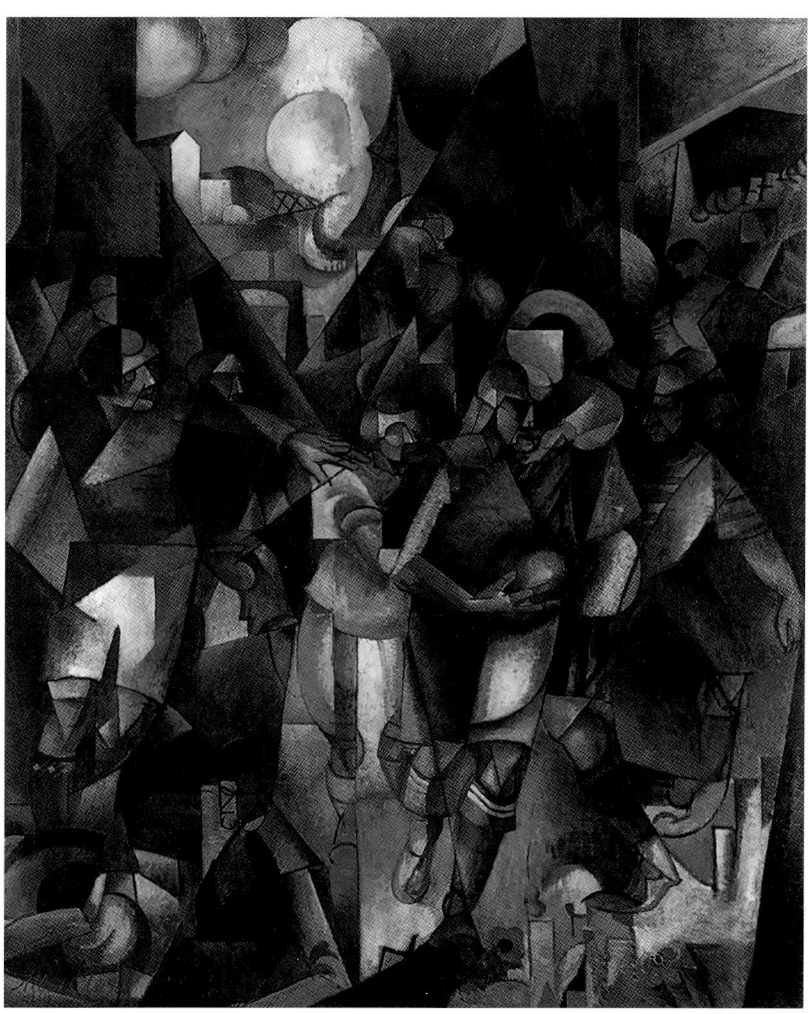

16. *Les Jouers de football*, 1912–13. Oil on canvas, 226 × 183 cm. National Gallery of Art, Washington. Ailsa Mellon Bruce Fund

The book has been dismissed as giving a dry, dogmatic, academic account of Cubism,[11] but Daniel Robbins has pointed out that it is much more a manifesto for the general freedom of the artist to interpret the subject of the painting without producing a photographic resemblance.[12] The book has little to say that could be described as distinctively Cubist. The typical Cubist device of walking round the subject and showing it from different angles (which Metzinger had invoked, talking about Picasso and Braque, in his article in *Pan*, November 1910) is only referred to in passing as a 'convention' which the public will eventually come to accept. The main thrust of the argument is that the so called 'realistic' portrayal of any subject is itself only an arbitrary convention, and a very limited one that has little to do with our real experience of the world. Since we are ourselves in constant movement, we rarely see any object from only one angle, and our act of perception is always accompanied by a multitude of thoughts and emotions. It is not a 'purely retinal' experience. As Metzinger was to comment in an afterword written when the book was republished in 1947, 'It is no longer enough to look at a model; the painter must think it.' (p.81)

> There is nothing real outside ourselves; there is nothing real except the coincidence of a sensation and an individual mental tendency. Be it far from us to throw any doubts upon the existence of the objects which impress our senses, but, rationally speaking, we can only experience certitude in respect of the images which they produce in the mind. (p.62)

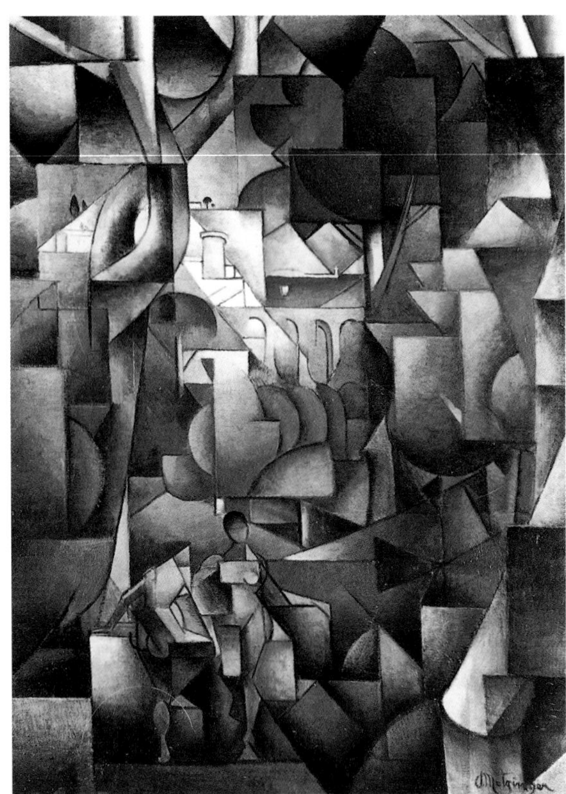

17. Jean Metzinger, *Baigneuses*, 1913. Oil on canvas, 152.4 × 108.9 cm. Philadelphia Museum of Art. The Louise and Walter Arensberg Collection

This view, that the external world can only be known as a sensation, a psychological fact, was to be axiomatic for Gleizes's later thinking, as he constantly affirms that colour, form, sound — all the means by which we experience the world — are functions of consciousness, dependent on spirit. Matter can only be known in so far as it has a spiritual existence, in our minds. Consequently, of the two orders, material and spiritual, it is the spiritual that is the more fundamental; matter is a function of spirit, not vice versa. However, although this would later lead Gleizes to argue for the necessity of a transcendent, divine spirit, in *Du 'Cubisme'* the argument is used simply to affirm the right of the painter to impose his own purely subjective and individual vision of the world on the crowd: 'A realist, he will fashion the real in the image of his mind, for there is only one truth, and that is our own, when we impress it on others . . . '.[13]

> To discern a form implies, besides the visual function and the faculty of movement, a certain development of the imagination; to the eyes of most people, the external world is amorphous . . . (p.45)
>
> The artist, having discerned a form which presents a certain degree of analogy with his own pre-existing idea, prefers it to other forms and consequently – for we like to force our preferences on others – endeavours to enclose the quality of this form in a symbol [*signe*] likely to impress others. When he succeeds, he forces the crowd to assume, in respect of his integrated plastic consciousness, the attitude that he himself assumed in respect of nature. But while the painter, eager to create, rejects the natural image directly he has made use of it, the crowd long remains the slave of the painted image and persists in seeing the world only through the symbol adopted. This is why any new form seems monstrous and why the most slavish imitations are admired. (p.46)

This presentation of the artist as the individual genius able to impose his whims and fancies on the crowd, which then becomes their slave, is consistent with the later development of Metzinger's thinking, and also with the rationale for painting given by Daniel-Henry Kahnweiler in his *Mes Galeries et mes peintres*.[14] But it does not square with the long-term development of Gleizes, for whom the artist only has the right to be respected on the basis of the objective truth of his work. If the artist is superior to the ordinary run of mortals, it is only because he is able to realise, or give concrete form to, a reality which he holds in common with everyone else. His work corresponds to the objective reality of our human nature. Gleizes would not have been able to formulate this clearly at the time of *Du 'Cubisme'* but it is doubtful if, even then, the image of the Superman imposing his arbitrary fantasies on the crowd would have greatly appealed to him. In the days of the Association Ernest Renan, he had been an enthusiastic advocate of popular education and throughout his life he saw the artist, indeed all intellectual élites (and he did believe strongly in élites) as being at the service of their fellows. We can perhaps see more of Gleizes in the passage at the end of the book which declares:

> It is in consummating ourselves within ourselves that we shall purify humanity; it is by increasing our own riches that we shall enrich others; it is by kindling the heart of the star for our own pleasure that we shall exalt the universe. (p.74)

This does at least indicate that the artist is of some use to the rest of humanity, though the idea is still Nietzschean. Nietzsche's Superman cannot prevent himself from benefiting the humanity around him through the mere overflow of his own high spirits.[15]

The passage in *Du 'Cubisme'* continues: 'To sum up, Cubism, which has been reproached for being a system, condemns all systems.' One 'system' that is specifically, though respectfully, condemned is the Neo-Impressionism of Paul Signac. In fact, *Du 'Cubisme'* could be read as a reply to Signac's *D'Eugène Delacroix au néo-impressionisme*, or, better, as a continuation of the line of thought launched by Signac. Signac claims to give a scientifically based theory of colour. Gleizes, as we have seen, had shown no interest in Neo-Impressionism, but both Metzinger and Delaunay had gone very far with it, exhibiting paintings in 1906 in which the points of colour were much bigger than those of Signac and his followers, prompting the critic, Louis Chassevent, to use the word 'Cubism', perhaps for the first time.[16]

There is much in *D'Eugène Delacroix au néo-impressionisme* that the Cubists could approve, as, for example:

> A picture organised in lines and colours will be of an organisation superior to that which the chance of a direct copy from nature can offer . . . .(p.53)

> It seems that, before his white canvas the first preoccupation of a painter must be: to decide what curves and what tones will cover it. A concern that is quite rare in an age when most pictures are like instant photographs or useless illustrations. (p.103)

But the Cubists reject Signac's central thesis that a maximum luminosity can be achieved through using only primary colours. They argue for the use of intermediary colours, such as the earth colours, and also for the luminosity of dark colours, including black. Signac had argued that, although primary colours mixed on the palette become muddy, the original brightness can be retained in the 'optical mix' of the same primary colours placed in small dots together directly on the canvas. The Cubists argue that the optical mix is likely to be as muddy as the mixture on the palette. And they call for a more discreet use of the law of contrasts (that colours are heightened by juxtaposition with their complementaries) than that recommended by Signac, or at least by some of his followers.

Robert Delaunay and Henri Le Fauconnier refused to be associated with *Du 'Cubisme'* or to allow their work to be reproduced in it, and, in Delaunay's case, this critique of Neo-Impressionist colour theory was almost certainly one of the reasons. Robbins speculates that Le Fauconnier may have refused as a protest against the inclusion of Picasso and Braque. Examples of Léger's work appear in the book. In his own theoretical writings at the time, Léger repeats *Du 'Cubisme'*'s criticism of Signac's 'optical mix', but he argues that the violent use of the law of contrasts is the basis of all the new painting, as it is of the commercial art of the advertising poster. What is distinctive about the new painting, in his opinion, is that now it is extended from colour to be applied to form.[17]

Du 'Cubisme' has been interpreted as advocating a 'system' based on non-Euclidean geometry.[18] Metzinger was profoundly interested in non-Euclidean geometry and in his 1947 afterword to *Du 'Cubisme'*, he suggests that, in considering the subjective space of the painting, which does not correspond to a three-dimensional world nor, he believes, to its own two dimensions, it may not be misleading to talk about a four-dimensional space (p.81). The 'fourth dimension' as such is not mentioned in the book, but non-Euclidean geometry is. Gleizes and Metzinger say that the space of the painting should not be confused with pure visual, or Euclidian space, and hence that classical geometry is not a useful science for the painter. Classical geometry presupposes that a form put in movement does not change its shape; but in painting, every form modifies every other form: 'Every inflection of form is accompanied by a modification of colour, and every modification of colour gives birth to a form'. (p.61)

This is not the colourless, abstract, essentially static world of classical geometry; but, they say, if there is a geometry that corresponds, it would have to be non-Euclidean geometry, as in 'certain theorems of Rieman's'. (p.49)[19]

Gleizes later insists that this passage is a declaration that painting has nothing to do with any geometrical system: 'We spoke of the sterility to which the dangerous incursions into the squaring of the circle, or the absolute mathematics of a Henri Poincaré would lead in art; we foresaw before their birth the dogmas and hermeticisms, destructions under the guise of new constructions'[20] but many readers, probably including Metzinger himself, drew the opposite conclusion. In 1913, Mikhail Matyushin, a friend of Kasimir Malevich's, published an article in Moscow which consisted of parts of *Du 'Cubisme'* interspersed with extracts from P. D. Ouspensky's argument for a mystical fourth dimension, *Tertium Organum*.[21] *Après le Cubisme*, published by Amédée Ozenfant and Charles Edouard Jeanneret (better-known as the architect, Le Corbusier) attacks the Cubists for their interest in a non-Euclidean geometry they could not possibly understand. They give *Du 'Cubisme'* as their reference.[22]

Perhaps the main interest of *Du 'Cubisme'* lies in the fact that, after claiming great liberties with regard to what we might call the 'photographic' image (though the term does not appear in the book), of the subject, the painters go on to discuss painting in purely 'abstract' terms – the balance between straight line and curve, warm and cold colour, light and darkness – though the same could also be said of Signac's *D'Eugène Delacroix au néo-impressionisme* and indeed of much of the contemporary writing of Maurice Denis. In the passage Gleizes quotes most often, *Du 'Cubisme'* envisages the possibility of a fully non-representational art, while saying that the time is not yet ripe:

> Let the picture imitate nothing; let it nakedly present its motive, and we should indeed be ungrateful were we to deplore the absence of all those things – flowers, or landscapes or faces – of which it could never have been anything other than a mere reflection. Nevertheless, let us admit that the reminiscence of natural forms cannot be absolutely banished; as yet, at all events. An art cannot be raised to the level of a pure effusion at the first step. (pp.48–9)

Possibly the thought had been suggested by Kupka's work – or even by Delaunay, who was busy with his great, and nearly abstract, *Fenêtres* series. We may also note that the invitation to the Section d'Or exhibition was signed by the painter Henry Valensi, best known as the leader of the 'Musicalist'

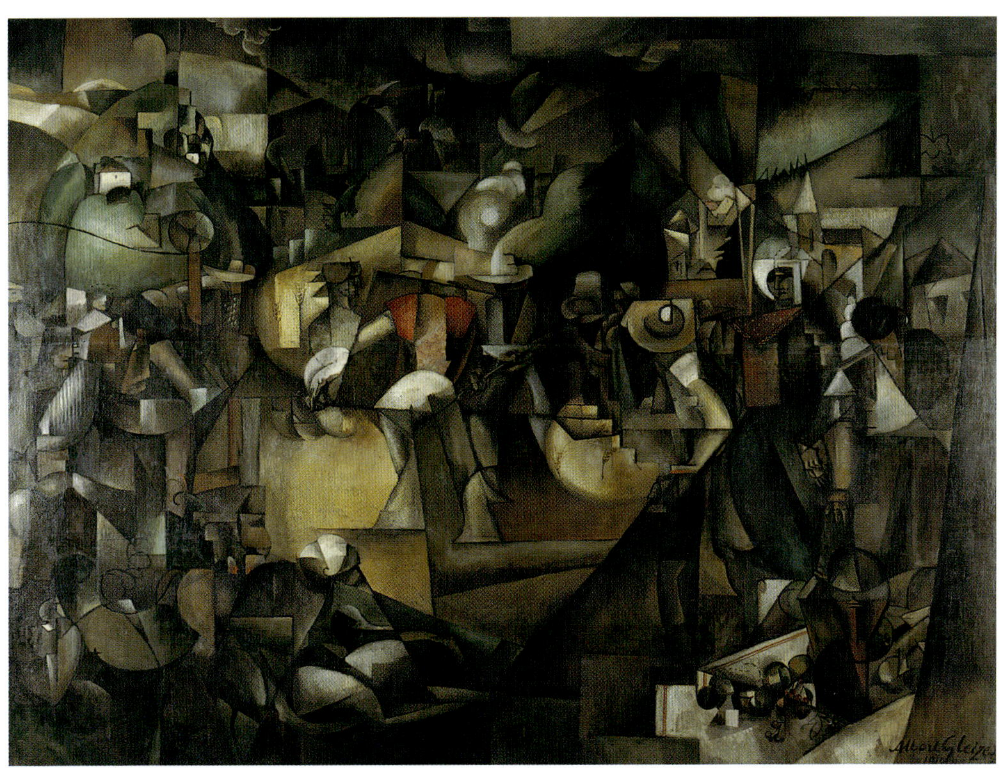

18. *Le Dépiquage des moissons*, 1912. Oil on canvas, 269 × 353 cm. Private Collection

school of abstract painting in the 1930s. Valensi is like a shadow figure in Gleizes's life. Gleizes rarely if ever refers to him but he is often present where Gleizes is, engaged in the same projects. He was in New York during the war, he was active in the Unions Intellectuelles in the 1920s, in Abstraction-Création and the Salon d'Art Mural in the 1930s and in the Salon des Réalités Nouvelles in the 1940s. In the review, *Montjoie!*, shortly after it published Gleizes's essay *La Tradition et le cubisme* which we shall be looking at shortly, Valensi published what must be one of the first arguments – certainly in France – for a fully non-representational art.[23] At any rate for Gleizes this passage from *Du 'Cubisme'* was an exact statement of the stage the artists had reached on a course which logically and inevitably led to non-representation. Metzinger, on the other hand, never became a non-representational painter and insisted, as firmly as Kahnweiler was to do, that, however valid non-representational painting might or might not be, Cubism was essentially to do with variations on a representational subject.[24]

•

While writing *Du 'Cubisme'*, Gleizes was working on what can certainly be described as his masterpiece of the pre-war era – *Le Dépiquage des moissons* (Plate 18). It is only with the greatest reluctance that I include a photograph of this wonderful painting. Photographs can never convey the real experience of looking at a painting, but they can convey some idea of what that experience might be.[25] *Le Dépiquage des moissons*, however, escapes all attempts to convey

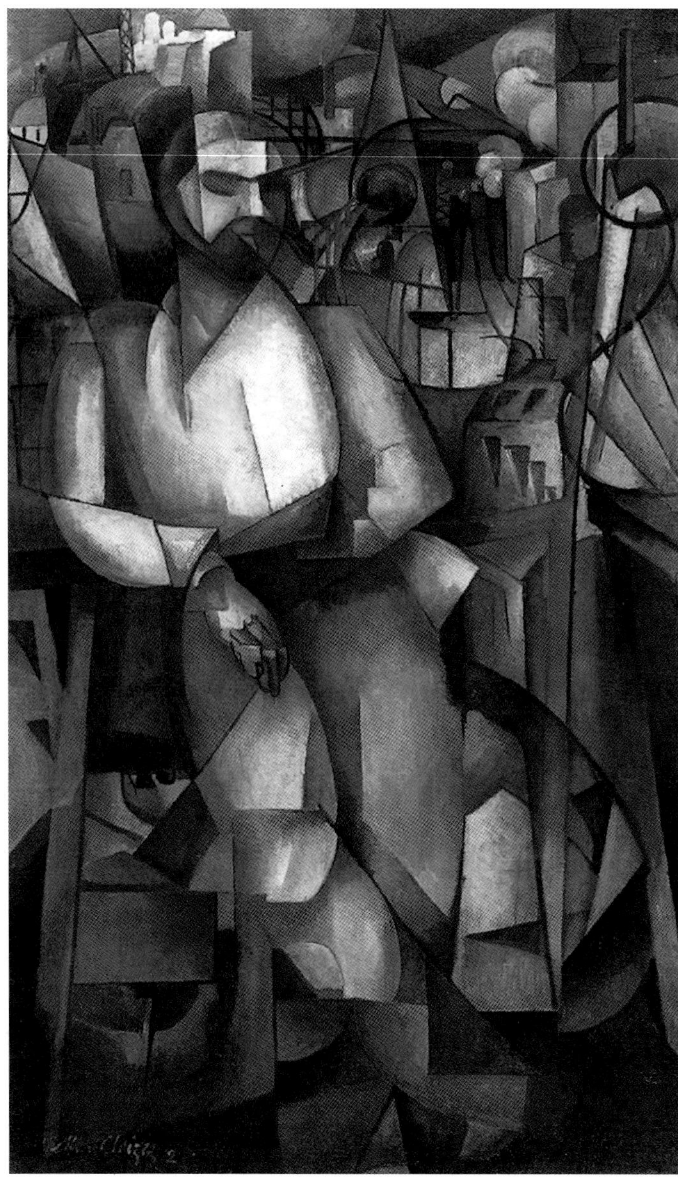

19. *L'Homme au balcon*, 1912. Oil on canvas, 196 × 115 cm. Philadelphia Museum of Art. The Louise and Walter Arensberg Collection

even such an idea. It is a large painting, 269 × 353 cm, and, much more than Delaunay's large-scale *Ville de Paris*, it requires this scale if it is to be appreciated at all. It could be seen as a manifesto painting for *Du 'Cubisme'*, which argued for a balance not based on an exact equivalence, between straight lines and curves, light and dark, restful areas and busy areas – all of which can be seen in *Le Dépiquage des moissons*. In particular, the large restful areas play an important role that is not typical of the work of the other Cubists and that is lost in the smaller-scale reproduction. *Du 'Cubisme'* insists that dark colours can be luminous: *Le Dépiquage des moissons* is both very dark and very luminous. Gleizes was soon, quite deliberately, to put his ability to use darkness aside; it is only towards the end of his life that he is once again tempted by the shadows. *Du 'Cubisme'* calls for a balance, but not an exact equivalence, between areas in volume, in three dimensions (the idea conveyed by the word 'cube'), and areas that are flat. This again can be seen in a masterly fashion in *Le Dépiquage des moissons*. Again, Gleizes was soon to reject the use of volume altogether. Though we will justify this decision, we cannot help feeling some regret when we see what he was able to do with volume in this pre-war period.

Le Dépiquage des moissons also uses multiple perspective more radically than the *Portrait de Jacques Nayral*, the *Paysage, Meudon* or *La Chasse* in which, although the eye is pointed in different directions in the play of volumes, the perspectival unity of the subjects – the person, the tree, the house – is respected. Now the individual subject is shown from different angles, but in a way that could still be described as conservative in comparison with the contemporary work of Picasso and Braque. The fact is that Gleizes is only interested in this multiple perspective as a means of opening the subject up into a play of lines and colours that will embrace the whole surface of the painting. He is not interested in creating variations on the appearance of the subject – he may even be said to regard the deformation of the appearance of the subject as, in itself, regrettable. In general, he still respects the subject's unity – as in *L'Homme au balcon* (Plate 19), also of 1912, in which, to the critic Edward Fry's disgust, the man's head is visibly on his shoulders, his body is on his legs, he is visibly propped against the balcony and is quite distinct from the street behind him.[26]

Nicholas Berdyaev was to criticise the Cubists and the Futurists for destroying the integrity of the person, and reducing the world to a playground for impersonal, supra-human forces.[27] Gleizes would perhaps have been more sensitive to such criticism than some of his fellows. For Gleizes, multiple perspective is justified primarily as a plastic device to help in the whole construction of the painting. His concern here is simply an extension of the

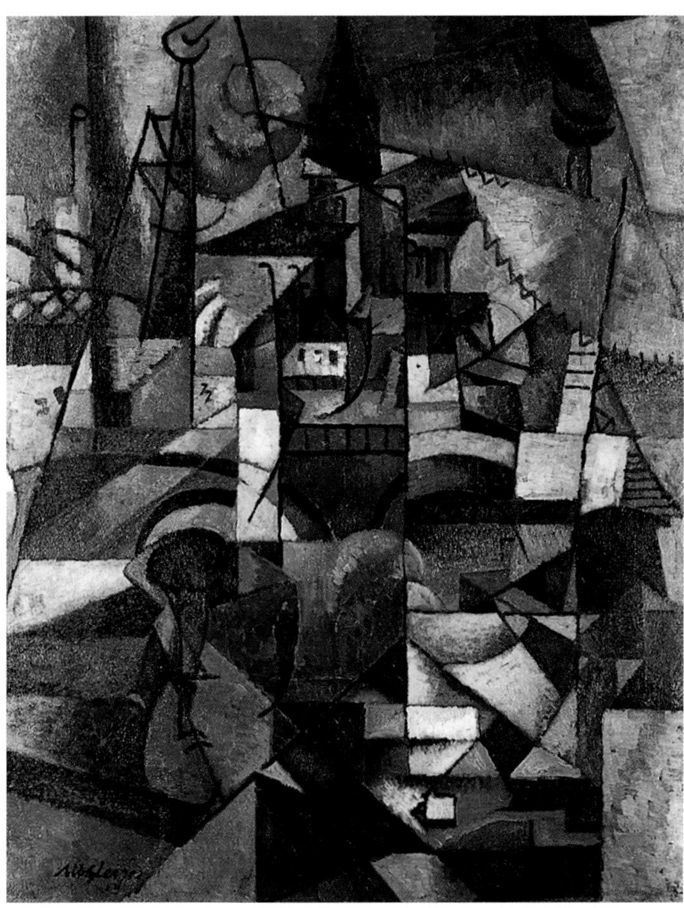

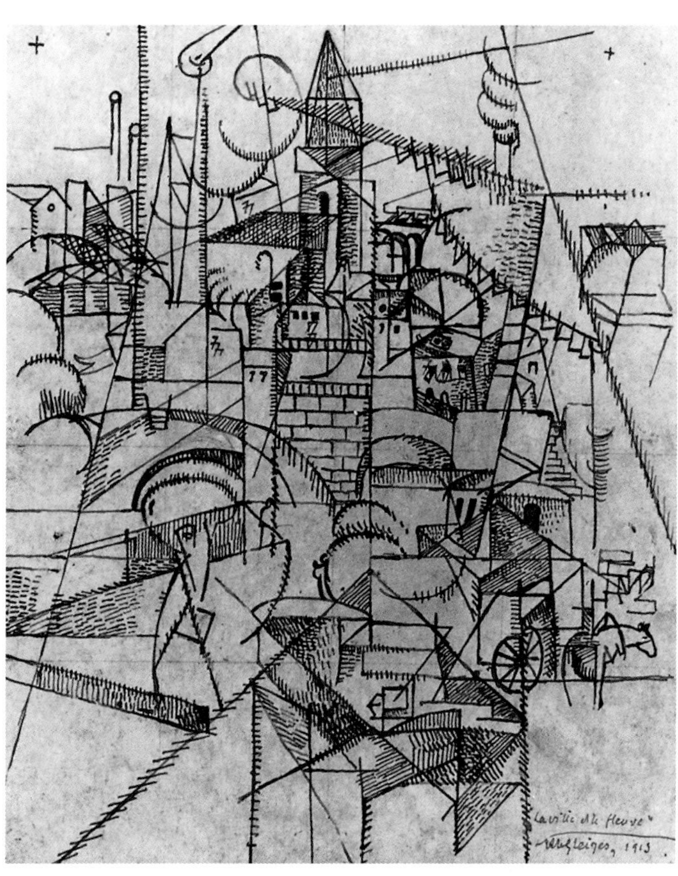

20. *La Ville et la fleuve*, 1913. Oil on canvas, 80.6 × 64.6 cm. Collection of Ursula and R. Stanley Johnson, USA

21. *La Ville et la fleuve*, 1913. Ink with pencil on paper, 19.7 × 15.9 cm. Solomon R. Guggenheim Museum, New York

concern which led him in 1911 to unite subject and background in the same play of interlocking volumes.

The question of the overall construction of the painting is addressed in *Du 'Cubisme'*, which talks of two possible conflicting principles: a principle of convergence to a common point, and a principle of divergence, which, it is said, is the practice of Chinese painting (pp. 49–50). The principle of convergence may be related to single-point perspective and that of divergence to multiple perspective. Ultimately, it is through a circular or spiralling movement that the two can be reconciled, but Gleizes is not yet ready to say this. In his act, however, in *Le Dépiquage des moissons*, he has realised it in a masterly fashion. The eye is directed from one thing to the other in a continual movement that may be slowed down, but is never stopped (as it is by the face in the *Portrait de Jacques Nayral*) and which, ultimately, since it never goes beyond the limits of the painting, is obliged always to return upon itself like a circle or a spiral (or, to use an image that comes from much later on in Gleizes's thinking, like a rubber band that can be pressed into many fantastic shapes without losing its essentially circular nature).

Signac's *D'Eugène Delacroix au néo-impressionnisme* quotes Delacroix as saying: 'There are lines that are monsters: two parallels', and, in Gleizes's painting of 1911–12, one senses a conscious desire to avoid parallel lines. In fact, in 1911, Gleizes could still be said to be sufficiently 'Impressionist' to want to avoid lines of any sort, in accordance with Delacroix's famous dictum: 'There are no straight lines in nature'.[28] Gleizes is aiming for a unity of the whole picture plane but the tendency of the straight line is to divide it. Increasingly through 1912, Gleizes makes use of this 'divisive' property of the line, clearly defining one area from another, as a positive element in the construction of the painting – a positive constructive element which has the effect of distancing it further from the appearance of things in nature. In 1913, these divisions become yet more affirmative and more regular, with a particular emphasis on parallel vertical lines.

The effect of the parallel vertical lines is to emphasise the monumentality and stability of the painting. We have seen Gleizes wanting to direct the eye about the canvas – 'flânerie' (rambling) as he would later call it, 'plastic dynamism', as it is called in *Du 'Cubisme'*. But Gleizes also aspired after monumentality or solidity, which in turn implies stasis. The reconciliation of these two apparently contradictory aims would later be formalised as 'translation' and 'rotation', but the broad principle of counterposing static verticals and dynamic diagonals and curves is already beginning to emerge — most strongly perhaps in his large painting, *La Ville et la fleuve* (Plates 20 and 21), which could be described, in terms of its scale (220 × 187 cm) and ambition, as the 1913 equivalent of *Le Dépiquage des moissons*. The painting itself is lost, but a drawing, an oil sketch[29] and photograph exist and the photograph may give a better idea of the original than any photograph of *Le Dépiquage des moissons* precisely because of the greater regularity provided by the vertical parallel lines. Gleizes would later argue that the reassertion of the verticality of the picture plane had been the great achievement of Cézanne and, if it is not so explicit in Gleizes's own previous paintings, it is still powerfully present. It is this that lagely accounts for the well-known phrase in Apollinaire's *Les Peintres cubistes*: 'Majesty, that is what characterises the work of Albert Gleizes.'[30]

Gleizes's friend and pupil, Walter Firpo has pointed out that Gleizes's life was always a struggle 'with and against'[31] and we will soon see how Gleizes, who has brought this monumental verticality to some degree of perfection in *La Ville et la fleuve*, is to become increasingly committed to a struggle against the fixity and immobility that it implies.

4
IN THE SHADOW OF WAR

Gleizes met his future wife, Juliette Roche in 1913. She has left us an account of her first impression of him:

> The big studio of Albert Gleizes opened on to a garden with well-tended lawns under chestnut trees in flower. In a great disorder, canvasses, gouaches, drawings, tracing paper, pots of glue, papers, journals, boxes of colours, books.
>
> Very brown, with a very meridional appearance, extremely lively, agile, adroit in all his movements, Albert Gleizes made one think of a *pelotari* [player of the Basque game, pelota – PB]. But his strongly modelled face, sharply delineated, was rather that of a monk in meditation. What was most striking in him was his regard, very black, very luminous, very changeable, but always equally attentive and possessed of an extraordinary intensity. He conveyed an agreeable impression of solidity, of precision, of openness . . .
>
> He did not at all have a Bohemian air about him. He wore a Bordeaux cravate . . .[1]

The studio in question was still Gleizes's studio in Courbevoie, in his father's house, which had now become an important meeting place for the avant garde artists – at least for those who were based in the semi-rural villages north and west of Paris, the 'artistes de Passy' – Gleizes at Courbevoie, Metzinger at Meudon, the Duchamp-Villon brothers at Puteaux (the 'artistes de Passy' formed themselves into an Association in 1912). We know that Gleizes's father disapproved strongly of the direction his son's painting had taken.[2] Under the circumstances, we can only admire the forbearance he seems to have shown.

Juliette Roche came to Courbevoie looking for someone to explain Cubism to her. She had been perplexed by Ricciotto Canudo, editor of *Montjoie!*, and by Delaunay but, she says, Gleizes cleared the whole matter up in a few minutes. Juliette Roche is a quite remarkable person in her own right, and a worthy subject for a book, though perhaps a novel would be more appropriate than a historical account. Indeed, since early childhood, she had been close to Robert de Montesqiou and Elaine de Greffulhe, models for the Duc de Charlus and the Duchesse de Guermantes in Proust's *A la recherche du temps perdu*. She was the daughter of Jules Roche, an important figure in the history of the Third Republic who, at different times, was Minister of Commerce, of Posts and Telegraphs, and of Colonies, long-time president of the Commission for National Defence, involved in the establishment of the Office of Labour (where Barzun worked) and owner and editor of the journal *La République française*. Since 1871, he had been the deputy for Serrières, in the Ardèche, which was later to be an important centre for Gleizes. Juliette Roche tells us that her father was a champion of European unity and of understanding between France and Germany. He was chatting to the Kaiser on his yacht at the Kiel Regatta at the moment when news of the assassination at Sarajevo was received (he said that the Kaiser had been in exceptionally good spirits that day but turned livid on receiving the news and shouted: 'They want war. But they won't have it.').[3]

Juliette Roche herself was an only child, very intelligent and much loved by her father. She spoke both English and German fluently and was herself a painter, moving in the circle of the 'Nabis'. She was friends with Redon, Bonnard, Vuillard, Sérusier, Denis, Vallotton, with the musicians round Ravel and the writers who were soon to found the *Nouvelle Revue française*. There are stories in the Gleizes's circle of her attending anarchist meetings and police reports of inflammatory speeches by her being passed on to her father. She describes her artistic circle in terms that emphasise its remoteness from Gleizes – though Gleizes greatly admired Redon and Bonnard as painters, and Sérusier and Maurice Denis as theorists.[4] In contrast to Gleizes's collectivist ideals they constituted a circle of highly refined individuals. A cathedral decorated by Redon, Denis, Vallotton and their friends would, she suggests, 'have produced something like the Théâtre des Champs Elysées'. It was a magical world. She speaks with rapture of productions at the Théâtre des Arts, with sets designed by Bonnard, but she quotes a friend as remarking: 'After them, we need the barbarians'.[5]

In 1913 and 1914, the subject in Gleizes's painting reaches a level of disintegration that can be compared to that of the paintings of Picasso and Braque in 1911 – thus leading Edward Fry to suggest that it was only in 1913 that Gleizes begins to understand them.[6] But Gleizes's paintings of this period are characterised by a much more definite construction than the earlier work of Picasso and Braque. The lines of division increasingly tend to traverse almost the whole area of the canvas, and they now (especially in 1914) tend to define areas of elementary, uniform, usually bright, colour. An example is the *Portrait d'Igor Stravinsky* of 1914 (Plate 22). The earlier *Portrait de l'editeur Figuière* has already very much distorted the face but, in my opinion, this is not sufficiently compensated by a greater strength in the construction (Plate 23). The figure is surrounded by a space that could be characterised as dead, without interest, and the colour is reduced to neutral greys and browns – two characteristics that recall Picasso and Braque. By contrast, the colour in the *Portrait d'Igor Stravinsky* is strongly affirmed and there is no dead space – the whole pictorial surface is brought into play. One senses here a desire for clarity – that each element in the painting should assert itself as something quite distinct with a clearly comprehensible role to play in the whole work. Here too, although there is still a sense of depth, the different divisions of the painting appear as planes parallel to the picture surface. This is not always the case. The landscapes in particular still use perspective techniques.

In an essay published in February 1913 in *Montjoie!*, Gleizes outlines his own practice of the time:

> It is sufficient for me to say, quickly, that painters today only consider the object in relation to the totality of things and, with regard to itself, in relation to the totality of its aspects. As they are not unaware of the fact that a form which is more pronounced dominates those which are less pro-

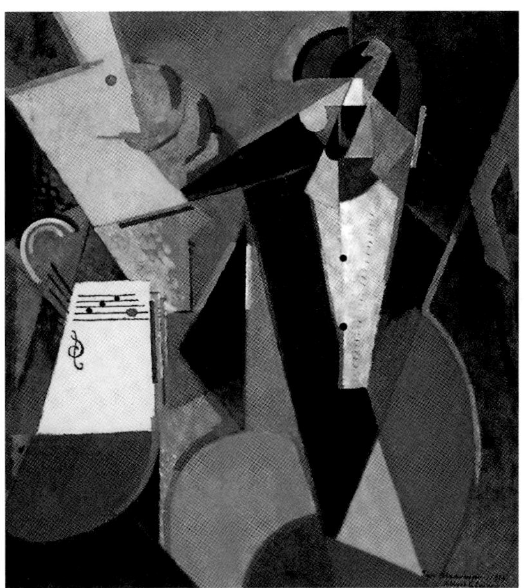

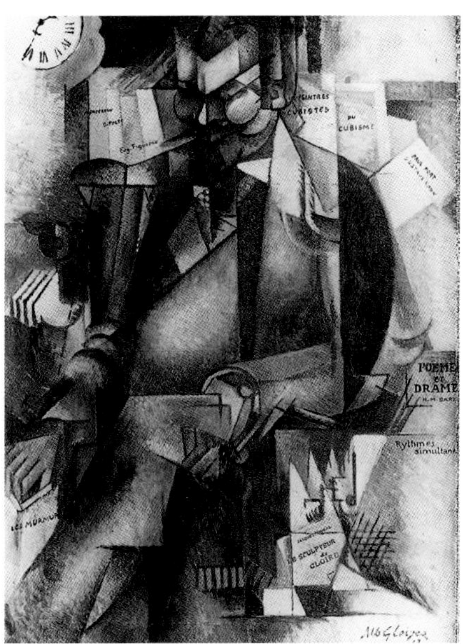

22. *Portrait d'Igor Stravinsky*, 1914. Oil on canvas, 131 × 115.5 cm. Present whereabouts unknown

23. *Portrait de l'editeur Figuière*, 1913. Oil on canvas, 143.5 × 101.5 cm. Musée des Beaux Arts, Lyon

> nounced, the plastic dynamism will be born from the rhythmic relations of objects to objects, as with the different aspects of one and the same object, juxtaposed – not superposed, as some would like to believe – with all the sensibility and taste of the painter for whom those are the only rules.[7]

One could hardly ask for a more succinct statement. 'Sensibility and taste' are the only rules. The confusing appearance of the painting is due to the fact that the painters feel free to use all aspects of the subject not just one, as in conventional painting (Gleizes has not yet drawn the crucial distinction between 'subject' and 'object' so that what will later be called the 'subject' is referred to here as the 'object'); and they want to refer it to the 'totality of things' which, in practical terms, means the total surface of the painting not, as the Futurists might think, the totality of things that exist in the street, or in the mind of the painter while he is working. The term 'plastic dynamism' appears in *Du 'Cubisme'* as well, when Gleizes and Metzinger say that it has been 'negligently confused with the agitation of the street' (p.68). This is a clear reference to the Futurists. It is nonetheless the Futurists who have established the word 'dynamism' at the centre of the artists' debates (and later, free from immediate polemical needs, Gleizes would acknowledge the fact[8]). But the key thought here is that the 'rhythmic relations' must be 'juxtaposed', not 'superposed'. This marks an important difference from Picasso and Braque who, both in the 'Hermetic Cubism' of 1911, and in the 'Synthetic Cubism' of 1912, superpose the elements of their painting in a way that is highly ambiguous in 1911, but which achieves much greater clarity in Braque's *papiers-collés* of 1912. We will see that Gleizes later changed his mind about juxtaposition not superposition but at the moment he sees 'superposition' as inseparable from the visual ambiguity, or 'impressionism of form' he is anxious to avoid.

Gleizes aspires to clarity. But what is it that is to be clear? Obviously not the appearance of the subject, which is becoming ever more obscure. It is the 'object' – the plastic properties of the painting itself. But what does clarity mean if it does not mean something that is clearly comprehensible? And who understands the plastic properties of the painting itself? Kahnweiler, in his seminal *Das Weg zum Kubismus*, describes the Cubism of this period quite correctly as a tension between the representational image and purely plastic qualities. But he writes as if the purely plastic qualities are known. The representational image is known but at this time the purely plastic qualities are not. As Gleizes says (and he is still making a principle of it) the painter only has his taste and sensibility to guide him. This taste and sensibility dictate that, in addition to being clear, the painting must also be complex: 'the plastic continuity must be broken into a hundred surprises of light and shade', to quote *Du 'Cubisme'*. If it was just a question of plastic clarity based on juxtaposition not superposition we would have something resembling Mondrian's 'Neo-plasticism'. Finding out what clarity and complexity might mean in purely plastic terms – translating into a conscious and intelligible principle what is still a matter of taste and sensibility – will be the great work of the rest of Gleizes's life.

•

This essay, *La Tradition et le cubisme*, lies at the centre of Mark Antliff's argument in *Inventing Bergson* that Gleizes's painting was an attempt to express an *élan vital* of a specifically Celtic nature – that Gleizes was involved with, and indeed deeply committed to, a rather unsuccessful Celtic nationalist movement founded, again in reaction against the classicism of Charles Maurras, by a certain Robert Pelletier. Again, the strength of the argument lies in the fact that some of Gleizes's friends, most notably the group round the publisher, Eugène Figuière, seem to have been involved – Figuière himself, Alexandre Mercereau and Jacques Nayral.

Gleizes was certainly sympathetic, as he says in *La Tradition et le cubisme*: 'Today, when we have a better understanding of our old Celtic origins, we must honour those who have preserved and passed on . . . the inheritance of our fathers' (p.22). But this is far from showing the degree of commitment that Antliff claims. The word 'Celt' appears many times in Antliff's summary of *La Tradition et le cubisme* but this is the only appearance it makes in the actual text. Gleizes's main intention is to situate Cubism within a specifically French tradition going back to a French Renaissance which occurred in the thirteenth century and which corresponds to what we would call 'Gothic'. The essay is an argument against Italian influence and, as such, takes its place in the general context of the dispute with the Futurists. Antliff, perhaps following a lead given in a little book on *Montjoie!* by Anna Campro,[9] treats that journal itself as an organ of the Celtic revival, but I found very few references in it to support this case. Its main bias seemed to me to Latin, which is hardly surprising given that its editor, Ricciotto Canudo, was Italian (though the Italian Latin-orientated Severini, perhaps with this in mind, was later to complain that it was too eclectic, it allowed too many conflicting opinions).[10]

In *L'Art dans l'évolution générale*, written very shortly afterwards, Gleizes gives quite a clear picture of his notions about France and about its racial composition. It was, he says, nothing more than 'the bastard child of ancient Rome' but, thanks to its geographical position, it became the meeting point of the Mediterranean and Nordic cultures: 'The perfectly playful superficiality of the first came up against the dark, brooding thoughts of the second . . . Nature has reconciled everything in France. The two forces met and from the shock a whole forest [*buisson*] of sparks shone forth.' (pp.128–9). All he has to say about the Celts is that the Gauls, the first possessors of the the soil, had welcomed the Franks who got rid of the Romans. This hardly squares with Antliff's thesis, especially when he presents Gleizes as anti-German. That is quite plainly not the case. Neither before, during or after the war can Gleizes ever be presented as anti-German; we will soon be seeing the energy with which he opposed French anti-German propaganda during the war. The 'Gothic' art which Gleizes admired at this time (though he would later question it, settling for Romanesque) may have had a 'Celtic' character, but it also has a distinctly Frankish and Germanic character, which Gleizes never attempted to repudiate.[11]

The important point in all this is that it is not the race *per se* that interests Gleizes. It is totally misleading to see Gleizes's painting, even at this time, as the simple expression of a racist or nationalist ideology of any sort. What interests him is a tradition of pictorial construction, sobriety and popular realism, which he identifies as specifically French, in opposition to a tradition of aristocratic elegance, which he sees as specifically Italian. Antliff (p.118) correctly observes a difference in this respect from Metzinger, whose preferences in art history were indeed for the elegant, Italianate and aristocratic eighteenth century.

Having said that Gleizes's principle 'racial' bias is anti-Italian it will be useful to remember Severini's comment, quoted in the last chapter, that Gleizes had been particularly supportive of the Italian Futurists. Gleizes himself, in his *Souvenirs (*'Retour à la France, 1919–26', p.7), evokes the enthusiasm of Severini's support for the Futurist cause (an enthusiasm Severini seems to have lost by the time he wrote his autobiography), and continues: 'This attitude, which I did not share, nonetheless rendered him extremely sympathetic to me, as indeed were all his friends, among them, in the first place, Boccioni.'

In the Spring of 1914, Juliette Roche introduced Gleizes to Jean Cocteau whom she had known since childhood. Cocteau was Jules Roche's godson. She had not intended to introduce the two men and was surprised by the result. Cocteau – known at the time as *le prince frivole* – was opposed to the new developments in painting and she claims that it was Gleizes who converted him, with consequences that Gleizes himself would later regret. This is how she describes their meeting:

> I had been imprudent enough to start a portrait of Cocteau. During the Easter holidays in my studio I did the portrait, or rather tried to do it. His continual agitation and too amusing comments prevented me from working . . . An unexpected ring at the doorbell alarmed me. It was Albert Gleizes, whom I hadn't been expecting. It was a catastrophe . . . For a year Cocteau had been pleasantly making fun of 'my' Cubists, and also of those of Roger de la Fresnaye, and we politely replied that he was ripe for the academy. Terrible things were about to happen. I pronounced the two names as badly as possible in a strangled voice in the feeble hope that they would not understand them, and, so as not to be present at the probable outcome, I disappeared backstage to make some tea. When I reappeared with my teapot, they were sitting close to each other with a delighted air, exchanging cards, telephone numbers and arranging a further meeting. Eight days later, Cocteau

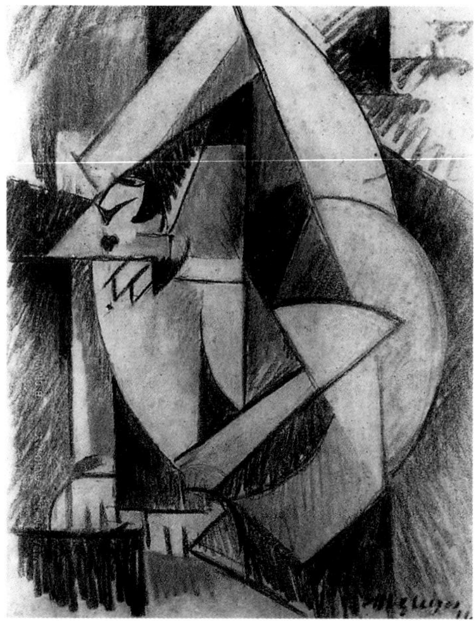

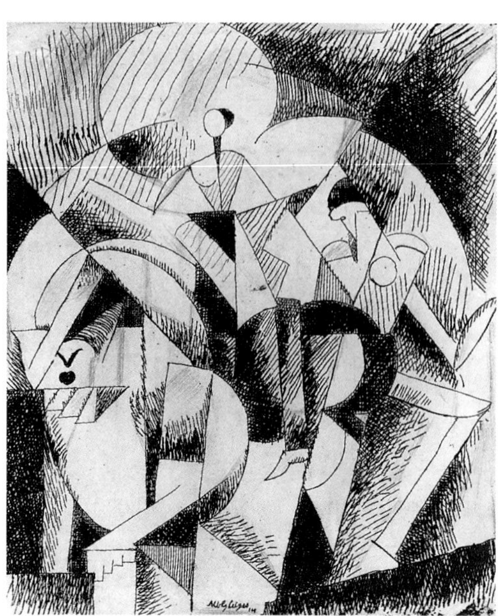

24. *Tête de clown*, 1914. Charcoal on paper, 62 × 48 cm. Private Collection

25. *Sur une Ecuyère de cirque*, 1914. Etching, 23.9 × 18.9 cm. Private Collection

> could no longer talk about anything other than Jacques Villon, Duchamp-Villon, Albert Gleizes. Misia Godebska reproached me severely: 'Why did you put Jean in touch with the Cubists? He is a man of the right, he isn't a man of the left . . . He will be lost in that crowd.'[12]

Gleizes was to be strongly opposed to Cocteau's influence in the 1920s but in the *Souvenirs*, talking about the war years, he speaks of him fondly and especially of a project Cocteau devised for a production of *A Midsummer Night's Dream*, presented as a circus performance, with sets and costumes by Gleizes and Lhote and music by Georges Auric, Erik Satie and Edgar Varèse.[13] About this time, the circus – clowns, bareback riders – appears as a theme in Gleizes's paintings, the closest he ever came to the *commedia dell'arte* figures who were to feature so much in the work of Picasso, Gris, Metzinger and Severini (Plates 24 and 25). However, these pictures do not imply any interest in the circus in its own right. Mme Gleizes remembers his going to the circus twice, in Paris in 1914 and in New York in 1916.[14] But, together with the portraits he did at the same time of Cocteau and of Juliette Roche (and indeed the portrait or, more so, the sketches for the portrait of Stravinsky) they represent a new departure in his work. It is as if Gleizes – praised by Apollinaire in *Les Peintres cubistes* for his 'majesty' – had decided he needed to lighten his touch. Perhaps the influence of Cocteau had something to do with it, or perhaps Cocteau had responded to a need that he already felt. The portraits of Cocteau and of Juliette Roche show a sense of humour which Gleizes often revealed to his friends but is rarely seen in his work. But the continued concern for pictorial construction is never far from his mind, and certain of the circus themes, most notably the *Ecuyère* – the bareback rider – will recur over the next ten years, becoming the pretext for a great dramatic struggle between the apparently conflicting claims of the lightness of touch (which Gleizes will never want to abandon), the fast movement suggested by the subject, and the pictorial construction which, in the first instance at least, implies a certain monumentality and stability.

Cocteau made his proposal (never realised, though Gleizes did his costume designs[15]) soon after the war had broken out. Gleizes had immediately been conscripted and sent to the garrison town at Toul in the north-east of France. But here we can see the extraordinary good fortune that seemed to pursue him through his life. When he gave his name to the young sergeant who was charged with receiving new recruits, he was asked if he was any relation to the Cubist painter. When he replied that he was the Cubist painter, he was asked to stand aside. The sergeant in question was Raymond Vaufrey, later a distinguished palaeontologist, who was an enthusiastic admirer of the new painting. Gleizes soon found himself assigned to the congenial task of providing entertainment for the troops.[16]

While it may not appear obvious that a 'Cubist painter' would be well qualified for this job, it happens that Gleizes personally was very well suited through his early interest in theatre, his involvement in the Association Ernest Renan, and his sympathy for those who, like himself, had had little formal education. As in the Association Ernest Renan, he was responsible for literary and artistic activities, and he was lucky in having a 'star' in the person of a well-known actor of the time, Maxime Levy. The harpist, Carlos Salzedo, was responsible for musical activities. Gleizes soon found himself in sympathetic company, which included Théo Morineau, a dentist, one of the earliest friends of his youth at Courbevoie, and possibly the model for several paintings including *L'Homme au balcon*.[17] There were also the painters, George Valmier (who had not yet developed into the non-representational artist he was soon to become) and Paul Colin (who was to acquire a considerable reputation as a poster designer in the 1920s). They were soon joined by the composer, Florent Schmitt.

Gleizes describes his activities as literary and artistic impresario for the garrison. He worked with a team drawn largely from the kitchen staff and he offered a judicious mixture of 'monologues that were stupid or in questionable taste' with 'classical and romantic poems, and I even several times risked myself reciting Paul Fort, Laforgue, Rimbaud . . . '. He says that Laforgue, Rimbaud and Tristan Corbière went down well, but that Valmier told him about 'the effect produced by the mysterious poet', Mallarmé: 'Laforgue and Rimbaud, that's OK, you can understand it even if you don't understand it. But Mallarmé, that's the pits [*Mallarmé, c'est la chiotte*].'[18]

The period of Gleizes's involvement in the war, then, was not an obstacle to his development as a painter. He found it difficult to work on a large scale and therefore produced only one major canvas – the *Portrait d'un médecin militaire* (Plate 27). But he made many drawings and gouaches – notably a wonderful series of sketches of the landscape round Toul, in which he develops a technique of punctuating his drawing or watercolour with clearly defined areas of black (Plate 26). It is a device which will recur throughout all the different phases of his career. Some of the work he did at this time, notably the portraits of Florent Schmitt, were turned into major oil paintings once he went to New York.

He tells us that he kept his drawings and gouaches in drawers until one day he found that the private who was responsible for looking after his room, a young miner, had taken them all out and made a little exhibition of them, using toothpicks to attach them to the wall. Gleizes, here as elsewhere, insists that the ordinary soldiers or people without intellectual pretensions had less difficulty with his painting than the more educated or cultured ones. An example of this is his description of the reaction to the *Portrait d'un médecin militaire*. This is a portrait of Dr Lambert, Professor of Physiology at the Faculty of Nancy, who was responsible for the infirmary and did much to help the cultural activities of Gleizes and his friends. Lambert was less than enthusiastic about his portrait by Gleizes. He preferred that of Valmier:

> The portrait that he [Valmier] made of the Doctor was excellent, a very good likeness that remained in the classical idiom. But for myself, I wanted to remain faithful to Cubism and not to play games with my own convictions. So the portrait I envisaged was a little surprising for the good doctor's habits of mind. He did not conceal his way of thinking, but he let me do what I wanted. I made of him, from memory, a large number of drawings in pencil, in pen and ink, in ink wash. I made a series of watercolours and gouaches. When he saw them, the model was pretty shaken. When my studies seemed to be ready, I did the oil painting. I painted the portrait in Marshall Ney's room. I nailed a canvas I had ordered from Nancy to the wall and got down to work. When it was finished, it received the approval of my friends, the unsophisticated ones, who were all able to recognise Dr Lambert perfectly well. The others were divided. As for the interested party, he refused, definitely but amicably, to take possession of it. To please me, he only accepted the final little gouache which I had used for the execution of the canvas.[19]

26. *Paysage*, 1916. Gouache, 103 × 81.2 cm. Columbus Museum of Art, Ohio

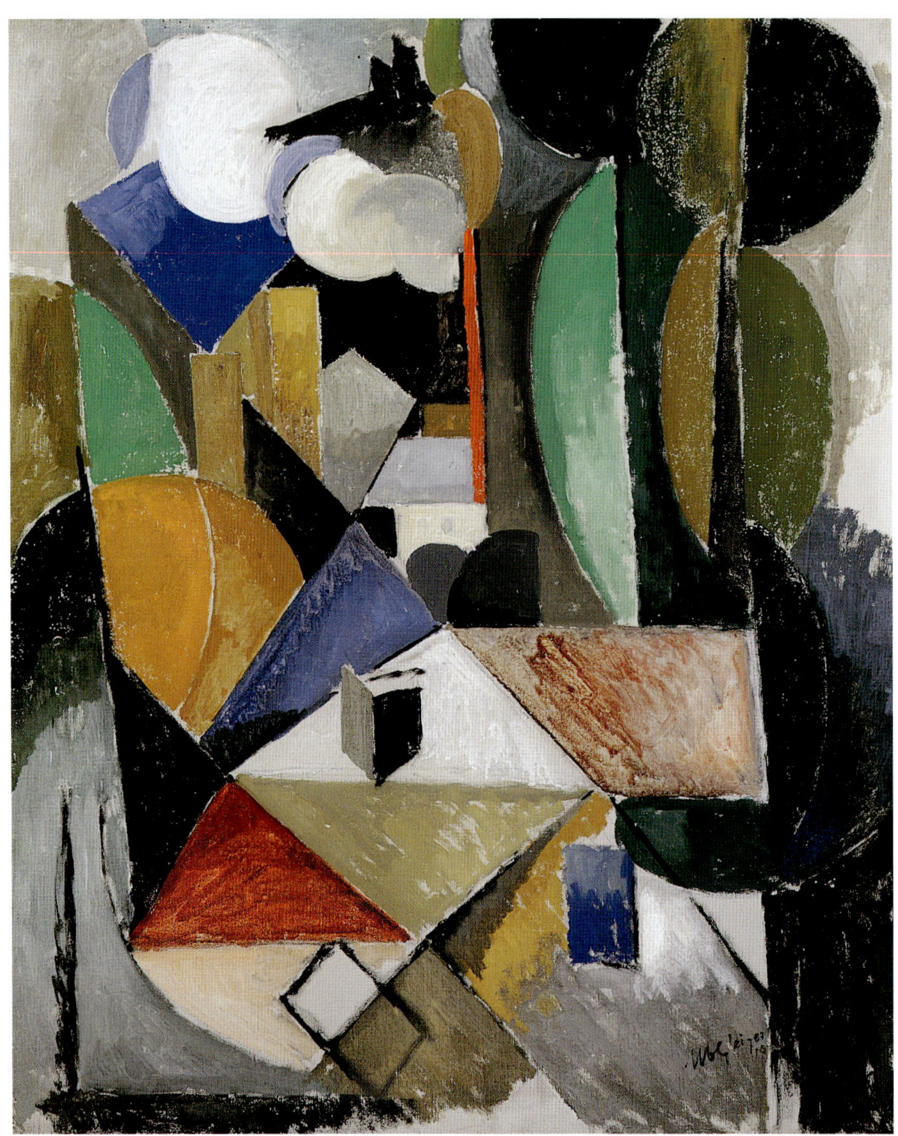

The *Portrait d'un médecin militaire* is very impressive. Although Gleizes tells this story lightheartedly, it is a serious, almost tragic painting, in which the subject (the poor Dr Lambert) has almost disappeared – reduced to a presence rather than a likeness – in a construction in which vertical parallel lines, and therefore a static, monumental character, prevail. Together with the second *Portrait of Florent Schmitt* (the *Chant de guerre*), it could be described as the furthest point reached by this Cubism striving towards the laws of the 'object' – the properties of the picture space itself – but still taking the 'subject' – the thing represented – as its starting point.

Gleizes himself says that these paintings represent the rupture with the 'Cubism of analysis' that had followed the first period – that of volume; and that he was now embarking more courageously on 'a

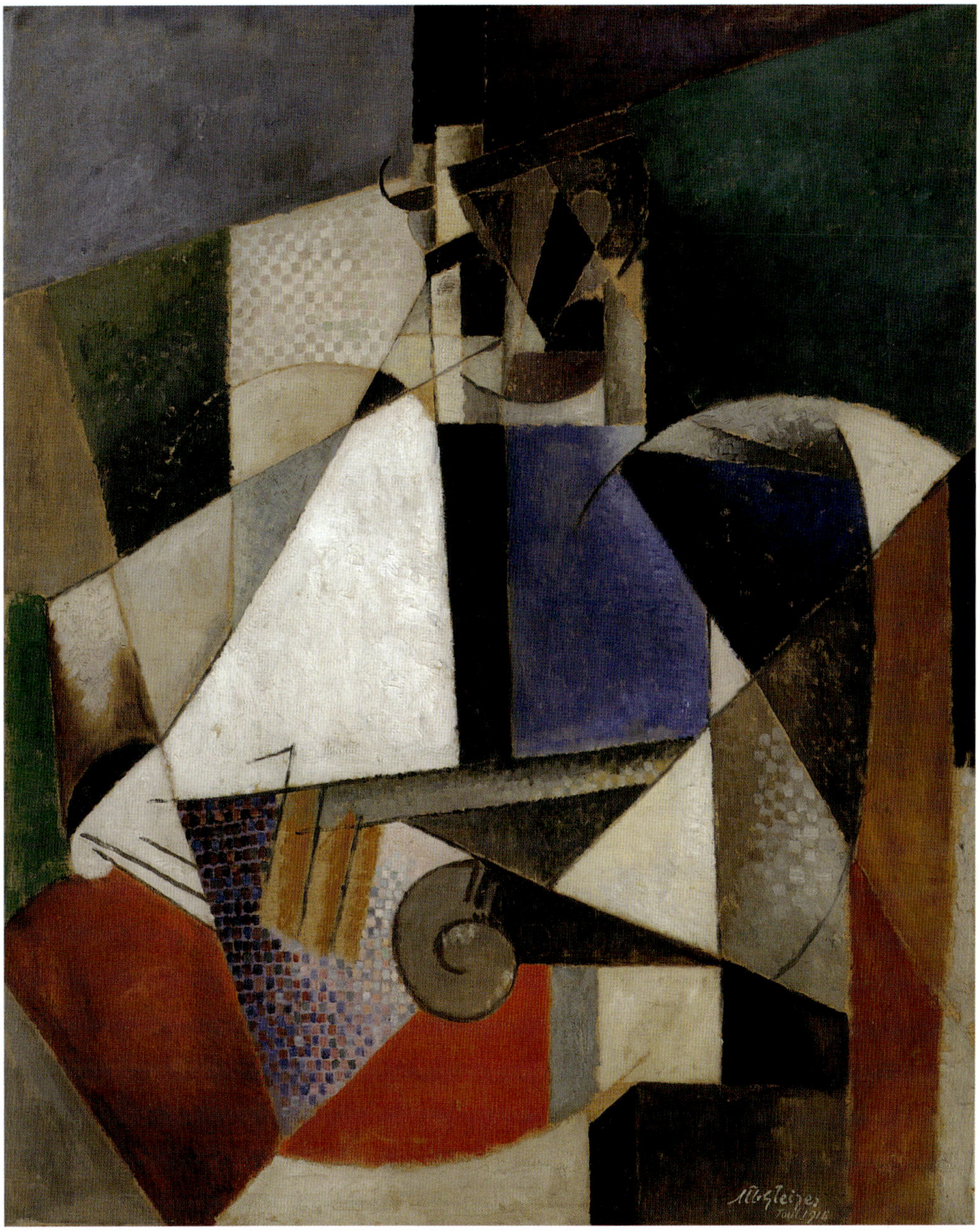

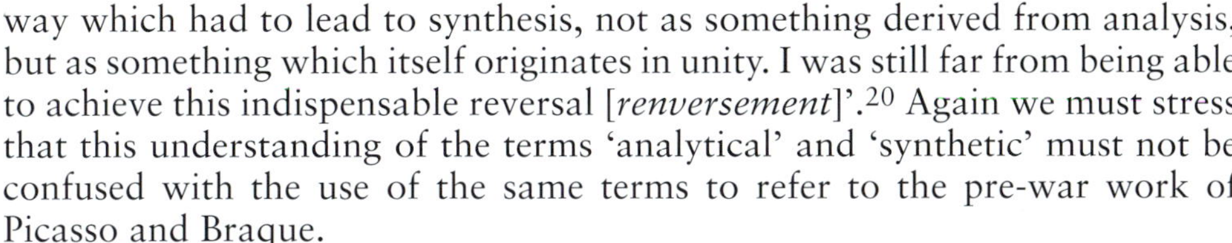

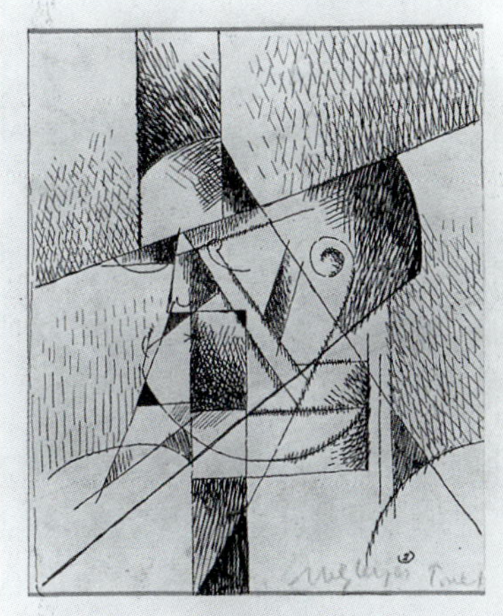

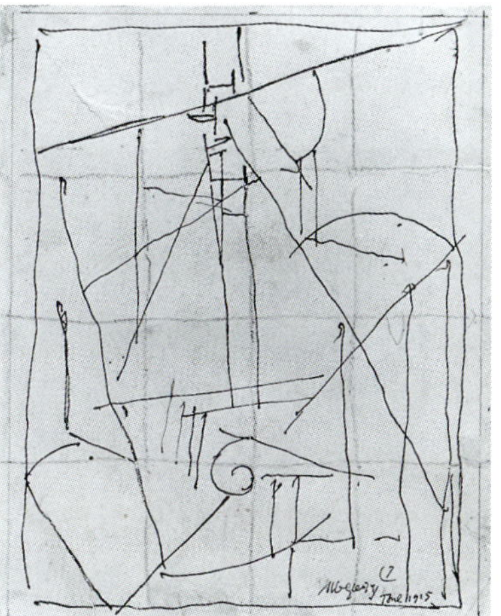

27. *Portrait d'un médecin militaire,* 1915. Oil on canvas, 120 × 95 cm. Solomon R. Guggenheim Museum, New York

28. *Portrait d'un médecin militaire, study no. 2,* 1915. Ink on paper, 19.4 × 15.3 cm. Solomon R. Guggenheim Museum, New York

29. *Portrait d'un médecin militaire, study no. 7,* 1915. Ink with crayon on paper, 24.4 × 19.8 cm. Solomon R. Guggenheim Museum, New York

way which had to lead to synthesis, not as something derived from analysis, but as something which itself originates in unity. I was still far from being able to achieve this indispensable reversal [*renversement*]'.[20] Again we must stress that this understanding of the terms 'analytical' and 'synthetic' must not be confused with the use of the same terms to refer to the pre-war work of Picasso and Braque.

The composer Florent Schmitt had been brought to Toul by Lambert in order to help with these artistic activities, and the ambitious *Chant de guerre* was his response, a difficult score given its first performance by the orchestra Carlos Salzedo put together with mainly amateur players. Gleizes was present at rehearsals and was fascinated both by the work itself and by the sight of

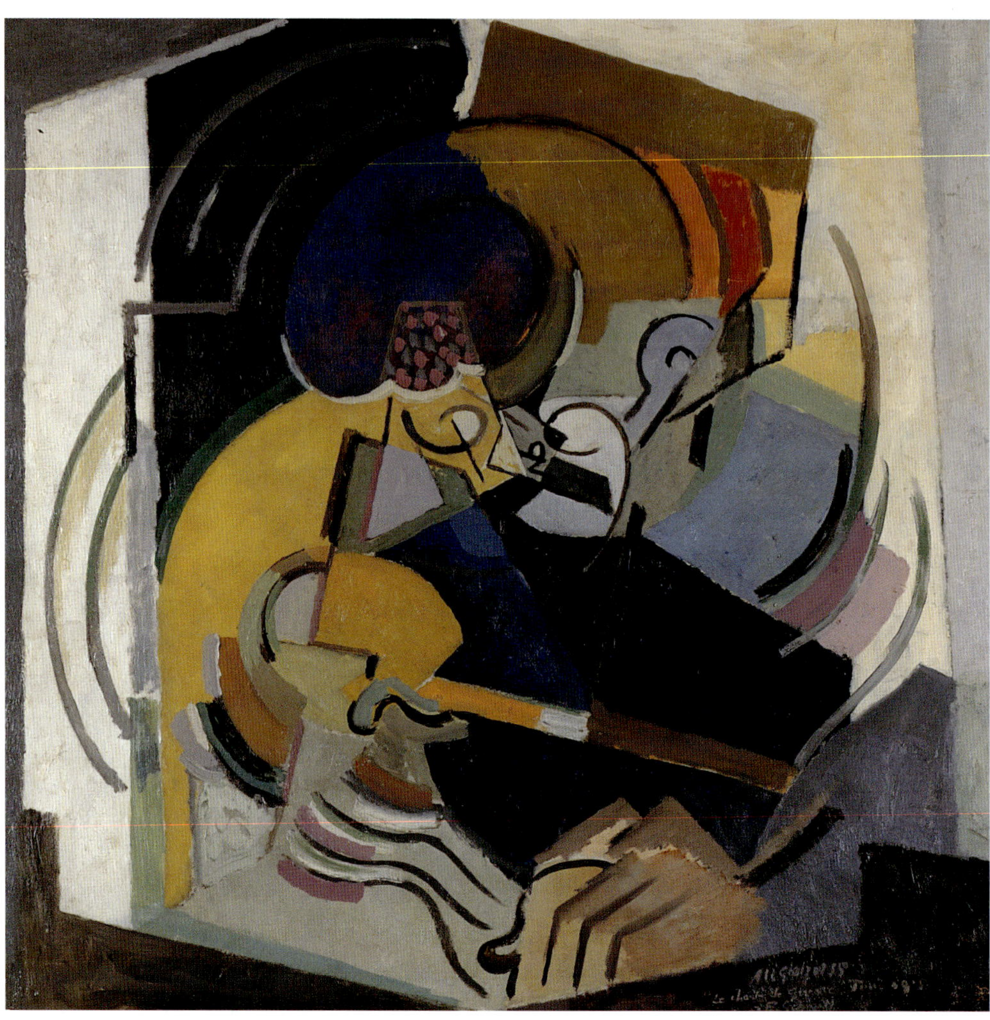

30. *Portrait de Florent Schmitt – Chant de guerre*, 1915. Oil on canvas, 101 × 101 cm. Musée National d'Art Moderne, Paris

Florent Schmitt conducting it. He says that the lines made by the movements of the conductor's hands were the starting point for his *Portrait de Florent Schmitt – Chant de guerre* (Plate 30). Where Dr Lambert is static and monumental, Schmitt (here, much more than in the almost-representational first portrait) is all movement and, in a prophetic letter sent by Gleizes to Schmitt in April 1915, Gleizes, describing his reactions to the *Chant de guerre*, seems to foresee the spiralling movement of his own mature painting:

> I have in vision the image that is made in the water by a stone which one has just thrown into it. A circle and, all around, vibrations which are translated into concentric waves that widen to arrive at a supreme development, finally dying in the whole that has, once again, become calm. I followed clearly the pattern of this drawing interlaced with arabesques in which all the fantasy of your art was woven together in capricious dissonances. I saw circles spread out and stretch into ovals, these ovals turn, serpentlike, multiply in infinite folds, brutally, suddenly brought back to the pure form which they fled, playfully . . . Perhaps that is not what you wanted to convey, this game, this round of circles developing, interpenetrating, escaping, breaking up, going in waves,

> incidentally assuming the characteristics of straight lines. It is doubtless not this explanation I have given that can translate the secret aims of your mind. But even if I am very far off the mark, my dear Florent, I don't mind. Once it has left you, your work is no longer yours, and it is I that listen to it.[21]

Altogether, it may appear that Gleizes had fallen on his feet; that the garrison, with its mixture of working class and intellectual, was almost the perfect social environment for him; and that he had been assigned duties which were congenial and for which he was exceptionally well qualified. But his attitude to the army and to the war remained one of absolute outrage. Very early on, he had the news of the deaths of his two brothers-in-law, Captain Alphand (killed almost as the war began on 15 August) and Jacques Nayral. Nayral – close associate of the editor Eugène Figuière, probably responsible for the decision to publish *Du 'Cubisme'*, and subject of Gleizes's great portrait of 1911 – had been much less fortunate than Gleizes and had spent three months in complete spiritual isolation before he was killed. In the garrison at Toul, Gleizes sketched a second *Portrait de Jacques Nayral* which he turned into a full-scale painting in 1917 (Plate 31). A sombre construction of browns and blacks in which the lively, intelligent face of the 1911 portrait is reduced to anonymity dominated by a number, it is the closest Gleizes ever comes in his painting to a howl of anguish.

Gleizes was not an absolute pacifist, but he regarded war as a specialist vocation in which possibilities of human worth and heroism depended on the relation between man and weapon. A war using long-range weapons of mass destruction in which whole populations were mobilised regardless of their skills and aptitudes revolted him. At least, that is how he interprets his feelings in the *Souvenirs*. He says that he frequently saw the soldiers leaving, terrified, for the front and returning, shattered. He was disgusted by the morale boosting lies of the propaganda machine – the attempt to portray the war as a battle of good and evil, with all the evil ascribed to the German side, and the attempt to underestimate French losses and exaggerate the losses of the enemy.

31. *A Jacques Nayral*, 1917. Oil on board, 76 × 60 cm. Columbus Museum of Art, Ohio

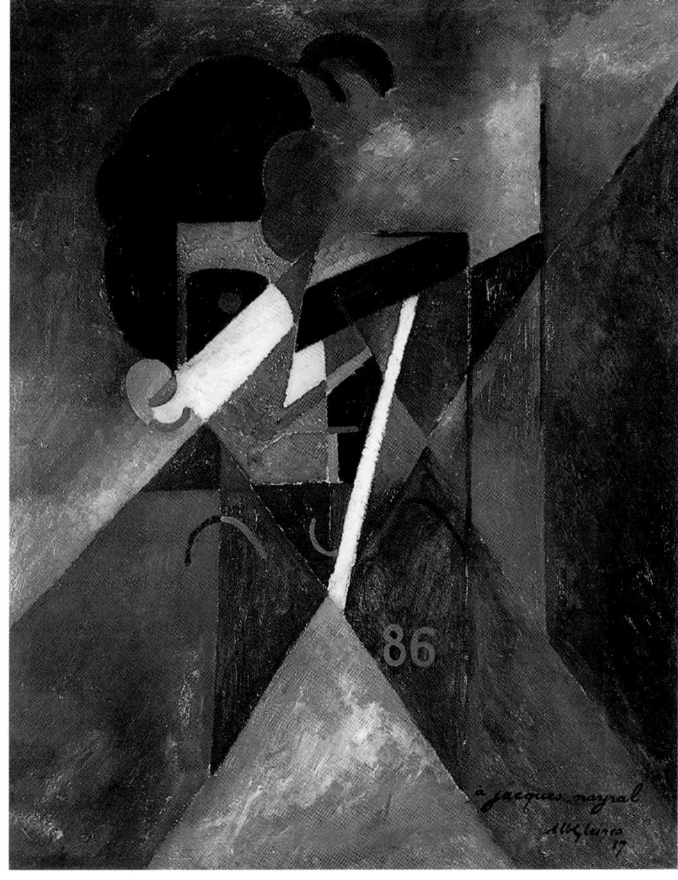

Cocteau in Paris had launched a new journal called *Le Mot*. Gleizes regretted its conformist chauvinism, but concedes that without it the magazine could not have been published in Paris at the time. 'Conformist as he was,' he says, 'Cocteau wasn't taken in'. Cocteau invited him to contribute to the paper and Gleizes sent an article in which he attempted, within the limits that were allowed by the censorship, to give some idea of the reality of the situation: 'I thought that the best way of overcoming the difficulty was to fix the attention on a main proposition that looked conformist, and to place ideas that were more or less seditious in the field of propositions that seemed to be secondary. The attentive reader would himself know how to redress the balance.' He also sent a brush drawing, the *Retour de Bois le Prêtre* (Plate 32), a Cubist treatment of a group of wounded soldiers returning from the front:

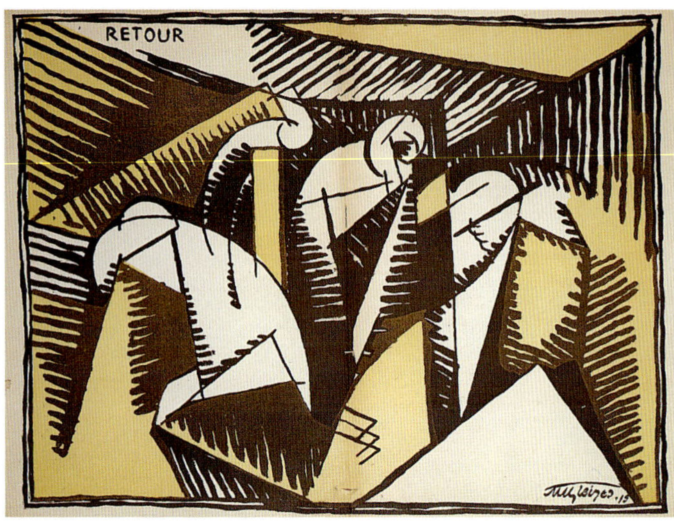

32. *Retour de Bois le Prêtre*, 1915. Wood engraving, 39 × 50 cm. Printed in *Le Mot*, no. 20, 1 July 1915

'The wounded clung to their comrades like frightened children clinging to their mother's hand . . . The group went beyond any misery one could possibly imagine . . .'.

Cocteau gave the drawing a double-page spread and it excited an avalanche of indignant letters, nearly all signed by groups: 'the sub-officers of the third platoon of the xxxxth regiment of cavalry etc'.[22]

We have seen that at the time of his national service, Gleizes blamed war on 'militarism'. Now he was inclining more towards economic explanations, largely influenced by an anti-war literature which included Norman Angell's *La Grande Illusion* and *Faites un Roi ou faites la paix* by Marcel Sembat, the Socialist deputy who had defended the Cubists in the 1912 debate in the Chambre des Deputés. Gleizes's growing conviction that modern war was inseparably linked to industrial overproduction was to be greatly reinforced by his experience in New York as he watched America being drawn into the conflict.[23]

It was his opposition to the war that brought him particularly close at this time to Juliette Roche, whom he married in September 1915. He had sent her a postcard shortly after being enlisted, just to indicate that he was still alive,[24] and he was surprised to receive in return a long, impassioned attack on the war. As the daughter of a prominent member of the government, Gleizes had assumed that she would take the patriotic side. She in turn, disgusted by the war-enthusiasm of such as Apollinaire, was impressed by what she saw as Gleizes's level-headedness.

She had, she tells us, already set in motion a procedure for extracting him. As soon as war was declared, she had gone to see Aristide Briand, an old family friend, to protest against his continued involvement in government. He replied, predictably, that he was there to try to limit the damage. She replied that he could start by taking some of the best minds in France out of the war. She presented him with a list which included Gleizes and the composer Edgar Varèse, both of whom were demobilised in the following year.[25] Gleizes says that she also tried to release Alexandre Mercereau but failed because of a strong prejudice against him, due to his widespread international connections – precisely a reason why the war was especially painful for him.

Gleizes never apologises for taking advantage of such privileged treatment. As far as he was concerned, the war was not his business. He had a long, difficult and important work to do and it was absurd that he should be taken away from it and his life put at risk for something that was of no concern to him. A large part of his attitude may be summed up in a story he tells about Florent Schmitt. Schmitt was reprimanded by a young sub-lieutenant for failing to salute him. He replied: 'Do you really think I can be bothered to look at what stripes people are wearing? I have other things to do.'[26]

Gleizes's attitude to the war, unrestrained by the censorship, is developed in what is probably the earliest unpublished manuscript we have from him. It is the text of a talk he gave in November 1915, in New York and is worth pausing over in the hopes of removing any last lingering impression that Gleizes was a right-wing nationalist, a 'soldier patriot', as Kenneth Silver calls him.[27] He begins by saying that, once the initial surge of German militarism had been halted at the Battle of the Marne in September 1914, everything possible should have been done to secure peace. The war was being prolonged by the hopes of both sides for an outright victory (Gleizes sees the war simply in terms of a French-German confrontation, taking little account of what was happening in the East). The French were as much to blame in this respect as the Germans, because both sides were engaged in an unforgiveable project of cultivating a state of mutual hatred between their two peoples. He says that shortly before the war, he had had a young German art critic staying with him and both had shared their dismay at the propaganda which was already being put out by their two respective sides.

He insists that he is speaking because many people still engaged in the war and unable, unlike himself, to speak freely had asked him to speak for them, to say what they really felt and not what they were said to feel by the propagandists of their own side. He admits that he himself had been swept up in the hysteria at the beginning and had joined almost joyfully, though he insists, not for the last time, that he had had no great interest in political matters prior to the war. His disillusionment, however, had begun during the train journey to his garrison, surrounded by young, drunken recruits, full of fantasies about what they would be able to do once they entered German territory. It was reinforced as he saw how shamelessly the vulnerable situation of the recruits was exploited by those, both miltary and civilian, who were responsible for their provisions. As the hellish nature of the war became more clearly defined, it was principally the propaganda, the efforts by those who were well entrenched behind the lines to cultivate hatred of the enemy, which aroused his disgust:

> I have to admit to my shame that I have never been able to understand what the protests that follow torpedo actions mean, nor those that are heard after the raids conducted by airships or by aeroplanes against open cities . . . All of a sudden one expresses amazement that war is war, that evil is evil, that hate is hate, that the work of death is the work of death . . . At the same time one insists above all on respect for non-combatants when, in a system of general conscription, there is no respect whatsoever for the individual conscience which refuses to kill. One forgets all too easily that the soldiers, whatever the country they come from, are there (I attach no importance to the unquestionably factitious delirium of the beginning) because they could not do otherwise. What can be said for certain is that it is not among them that the most bloodthirsty are to be found.
>
> Coldly, one accepts the massacre of millions of boys in capes and military hats in a deluge of flame and steel poured out on them by an artillery well laid out at several kilometres distance. That is war as it should be. But one is enraged by the death of a handful of children, of women, of old men killed by chance in open towns which, however, are not free of arsenals, arms manufactures, garrisons, which provide a military justification for aerial bombardment.
>
> If we want to give any substance to such a sentimental view of the matter, all right. Let us follow it right through and reflect that there is hardly any more respect shown for a mother or a wife, who is mortally wounded when her child or her husband is torn away from her and sent to die like a dog, his stomach ripped open in some corner by shrapnel, or stuck by a bayonet;

> that those who return, crippled, riddled with tuberculosis, blind, mad, will surely be a poison to the lives of those who are close to them and whose hearts have not been closed up by a convenient, brutalising, fanaticism . . .[28]

Far from accusing Gleizes of a militant and aggressive nationalism, it would be more reasonable to accuse him of being a traitor to his country. Mme Gleizes presents him as being engaged in a small campaign to argue against American intervention in the war. He was, in other words, profiting from the privileged position which had freed him from the army in order to undermine what was widely seen as his country's best hope of victory. Gleizes, however, believed that it was such hopes of outright victory that were prolonging the war. The sooner the two sides were compelled by the hopelessness of their situation to come to terms the better. In the event, he was, as we shall see, horrified by the overwhelming victory won by 'his own' side and by its predictable consequences, including the rise of Hitler, which he always saw as being as much the responsibility of the French and British as it was of the Germans.

Gleizes was demobilised in August 1915 and married Juliette Roche on 8 September. His witnesses were Henri Martin Barzun and Alexandre Mercereau. Hers were Jean Cocteau and Edouard de Prémoréal.[29] It was a strange marriage between two people who, one might have thought, were temperamentally unsuited to each other. There was little in common between the down-to-earth, morally earnest son of a prosperous artisan, Albert Gleizes, and the witty, sophisticated, high-society woman, Juliette Roche, more than able to hold her own in the world described in the novels of Marcel Proust.

In fact it has something of the appearance of a marriage of convenience. It got Gleizes out of the war and greatly helped him to achieve the independence from commercial constraints which enabled him to pursue his often very unfashionable research. Mme Gleizes continued to paint but never showed much interest in applying her husband's principles. She never shared his religious commitment. She is often described by those who knew her as a 'snob'[30] – not a word that could ever be applied to Gleizes himself. Yet in her *Mémoires* and other writings she shows herself well able, if in a rather detached and ironical tone of voice, to explain and defend his arguments. On certain matters, mainly political and pacifist, it was she who took the lead. The couple had frequent, sometimes blazing, rows, but everything either of them did was discussed and executed together. They were never separate for any length of time (they even painted their very different pictures side by side in the same studio). There is not the faintest hint on either side of any sort of infidelity. It is a relationship, puzzling to their friends, which can in the end only be explained on the assumption that, against all probability, they loved each other very much.

They left for New York on 11 September, Gleizes being allowed to leave France through a correspondent's card from Jules Roche's paper, *La République française* (Mme Gleizes had a correspondent's card from *Le Gaulois*). Robbins points out that Jules Roche misspelt his name – 'Gleyzes' – and that this may give some idea of the hurry in which the move was made.[31]

5

NEW YORK AND BARCELONA

The transition from the garrison at Toul (followed by a brief spell in the Military School in Paris) to New York was abrupt and disquieting. It had a disorientating effect on Gleizes's work. There was, however, at least one element of continuity. They were met on the quay by Carlos Salzedo, Gleizes's musician friend from Toul, who introduced them to New York. They also soon made contact with Marcel Duchamp (Duchamp's brothers had been conscripted and Raymond Duchamp-Villon, for whom Gleizes had a very high regard, was to be killed in the war).

Gleizes was initially quite dazzled by New York. He expressed his feelings in a poem, 'Dieu Nouveau', later published in *La Vie des lettres et des arts*, which describes the experience of coming into New York harbour:

> With a bad-tempered abruptness
> The rain stops and the mist disappears
> And the enchantment surges up before the prow,
> A gigantesque flowering of towers
> Arises in a contagious emulation . . .

> The vertical lines are taken with vertigo and bend as they rise. Whole planes fall backwards and stop suddenly, supported by other planes that fall forwards . . .
>
> The rows of the windows are not parallel to the surfaces they gut. These stubborn souls cast off the disciplines of architecture to follow their disordered fantasies . . .
>
> All the fleeting lines turn like the spokes of a wheel moving on its axis. They are impossible to grasp, and the very moment one thinks one has uncovered their intentions, they turn brutally on themselves and swoop down upon the eye, which has no time to avoid the attack . . .[1]

The poem is a good description of Gleizes's paintings of New York. These paintings mark something of an abandonment of principle for Gleizes and it is perhaps not surprising that they are admired by critics who otherwise dislike his work in general.[2] In *La Tradition et le cubisme*, Gleizes had proposed the principle of 'juxtaposition not superposition' as necessary to the clarity of the painting, in opposition to the visual ambiguities of Picasso and Braque in 1911. But now he indulges in superposition – and visual ambiguity – with a vengeance.

The resemblance to Picasso and Braque in 1911 is heightened by the fact that, almost for the first time, he uses lettering as a prominent part of the pictorial construction. The earlier *Portrait de l'editeur Figuière* shows Figuière surrounded by the titles of his books, but they are discreet. They are given as information, so to speak; the lettering does not play an important constructive role. Now disembodied phrases – 'Chal Post', 'Kelly Springfield' – feature prominently.[3] Both Gleizes and Mme Gleizes have poems dating from this period which consist entirely, or almost entirely, of advertising slogans. Gleizes is spiritually closer than he ever was before or ever will be again to Delaunay's friend, the poet Blaise Cendrars, for whom the impact of America and of New York also played a very important role – with this difference, that in the case of Gleizes it was to be temporary, in the case of Cendrars, it was permanent.

The visual ambiguity, the superposition of transparent planes, the lettering, are all suggested by the actual experience of confrontation with New York – with its skyscrapers, dizzying speed, publicity, shop windows. Gleizes was to become the most resolute opponent of the purposeless agitation of the great city but at this time he seems to have found the perfect language in which it could be celebrated. By this we can see that another principle has been thrown to the winds. He could easily be accused, in the words in which *Du 'Cubisme'* condemns the Futurists, of confusing plastic dynamism with the agitation of the streets. But, given that this is the aim he has now set himself, I believe that he does it with remarkable success. He has a strong claim to be regarded as the first European avant-garde painter to respond to the rhythm and vitality of New York, the first – before any of the musicians, and thirty years before Mondrian's *Broadway Boogie Woogie* – to celebrate jazz. It is only in a very intellectual manner that the work of his colleagues in New York – Duchamp, Picabia and Duchamp's brother in law, Jean Crotti – could be described as responses to the New World. Gleizes also had an impact on the way in which the New York artists themselves experienced their city. There is an obvious comparison to be made between the ways in which the Brooklyn Bridge was seen by Gleizes and by Joseph Stella – a painter for whom Gleizes had a high regard.[4]

His thinking of the time is shown in a letter, almost certainly addressed to Barzun, written probably in 1916. It is an attack on any attempt to reduce painting to a systematic formula, but an attack that is still grounded in the subject – in the enormity of what the painter must represent if he is to be faithful to the experience of living in the modern world. Gleizes is of course frequently criticised as a dogmatic painter who believed in systems, and many of his articles in the 1920s seem to argue the opposite of the case he makes here; but in Gleizes there is always a dialectic between what we might call the 'finite', which is susceptible to a geometrical system and the 'infinite', which is not. Later, the 'infinite', which he associates here with the infinite range of sensations given by the outside world, will become an internal characteristic of human nature, of the spirit. He will never lose sight of it:

> We are in the age of synthesis. An hour in the life of a man today raises more levels, insights, actions, than a year of that of any other century. That is what I try to say in my art. The rapid sketch of an Impressionist crystallised the fragility of a sensation; it was immobilised in his picture. The painting of today must crystallise a thousand sensations in an aesthetic order. And I see that for that there is no need to reveal other laws, other theorems with definitive forms. A beauty achieved through a mathematical order can only have a relative life; the universal kaleidoscope cannot be fitted into the framework of a system; it

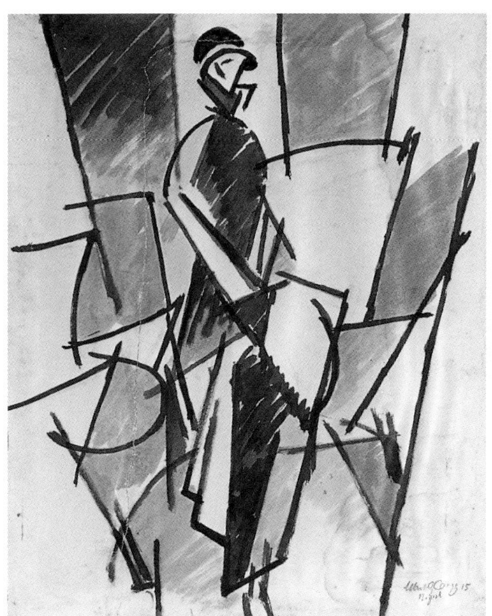

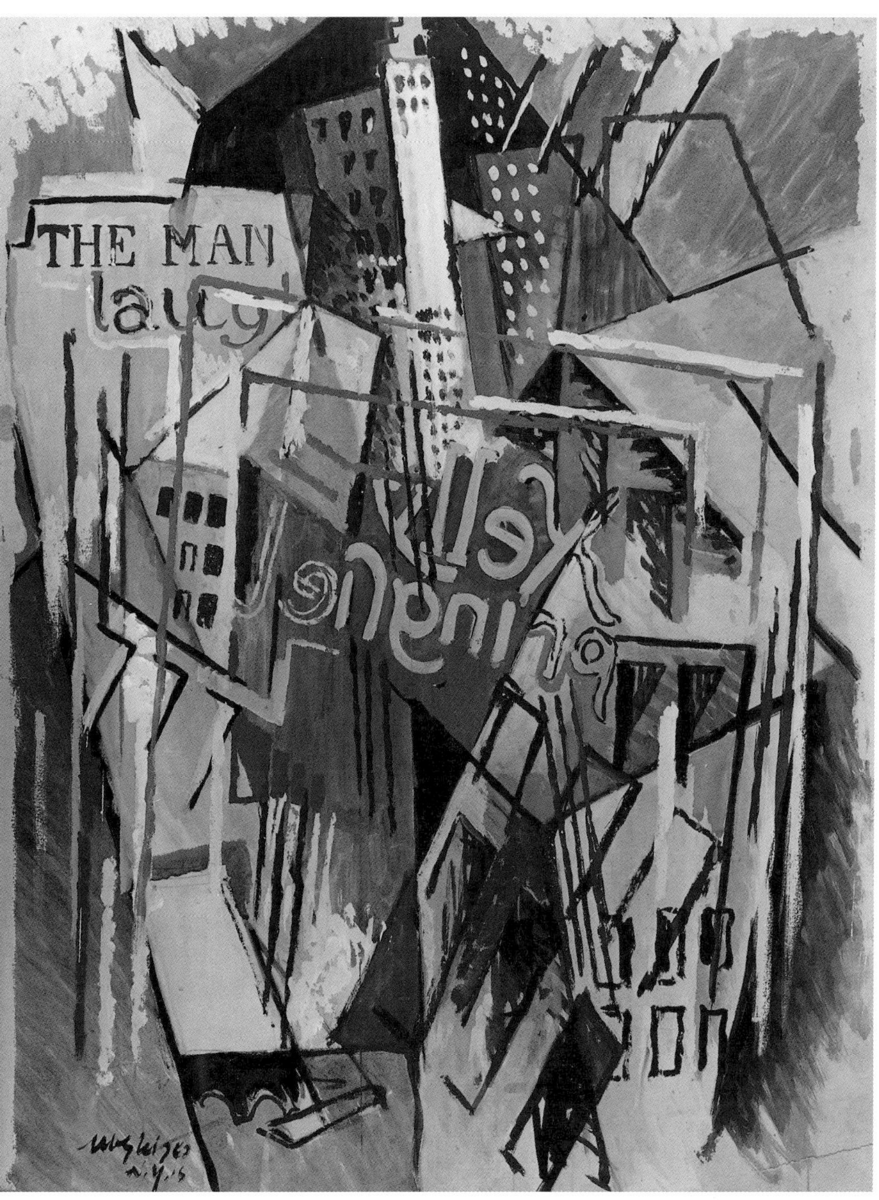

surprises through the unforeseen and is re-newed by it. We should regard 'the system' with suspicion. It limits our possibilities. How, for example, can we give the equivalent of the enormous 'Broadway' – that fantastic river with a thousand currents going against each other, interweaving, rising up over its banks – if, in our painter's expression, we apply little principles just about good enough to describe a very simple object, an inkstand, a box etc. With one blow, the truth blinds us [*crève les yeux*] and rises up to scatter the system's charm . . .[5]

33. *Portrait de Mme Gleizes* [probably, in fact, a portrait of Bessie Brener], 1915. Sepia ink brush and wash on paper, 48 × 38.2 cm. Musée National d'Art Moderne, Paris

34. *Kelly Springfield*, 1915. Gouache and oil on board, 102 × 76.5 cm. Solomon R. Guggenheim Museum, New York

We may note in passing the similarity between this description of 'the enormous Broadway' and the description he gives Florent Schmitt of the effect the *Chant de guerre* had on him – the concentric circles produced by a stone thrown in the water. Mme Gleizes describes how, in an Italian restaurant in New York in 1915, Gleizes defended the culture of the Celts by drawing 'convincing spirals' on a paper napkin.[6]

Gleizes was already known in New York. He had featured in the 1913 Armory Show and in 1914, a number of his paintings had been taken when the collector John Quinn had sent Walter Pach to Paris on the outbreak of the war to buy works by artists who had been called up. The result was two exhibitions held in 1915. Gleizes had sold well and was now owed quite a lot of money. He found, however, that the purchasers were in no hurry to pay, and he was strongly advised not to press for payment, since, if word got about that he needed money, the result would be socially disastrous.

Any impact Gleizes might have made on New York, however, was as nothing compared to the impact made by Marcel Duchamp. We have seen that Gleizes, through Jacques Villon and Raymond Duchamp-Villon, had persuaded Duchamp not to show his *Nu descendant un escalier* at the Paris Salon des Indépendants in 1912. But the picture had an enormous *succès de scandale* at the 1913 Armory Show in New York.

Gleizes explains why:

> The title was a promise; the work a mystery. Between the promise and the mystery lay the reality, the fruit, the kernel, the pleasure that the sight of a nude descending a staircase could not fail to provoke. In fact, Marcel Duchamp had wanted within a given space to schematise the series of displacements of a body in movement. The idea of a 'nude descending a staircase' was his starting point. But in developing it, in stripping away all accidental characteristics, he had ended up almost completely suppressing the figurative, anecdotal element with which he had begun . . .

Nonetheless, he had used his starting point, quite innocently, as the title of the painting. Normally, even in the more radical circles, the title of a painting had something to do with the content. But in this case, no-one could see the connection:

> Discussion seemed impossible. A nude descending a staircase was announced but it could not be seen. To these Protestant minds, for whom introspection [*refoulement*] was the rule, what a pretext this provided for an examination of their conscience. In this case, examination of a painting. It became an enormous success. Poor Marcel had never foreseen anything like it.[7]

The result was that Duchamp began to conceive of the disjunction between title and subject as a psychological, emotional event more interesting than that provided by an actual work of art. Hence the appearance of the 'ready-made', often with an incongruous title attached – the snow-shovel called 'In advance of the broken arm', the urinal entitled 'Fountain'. The circle of New York admirers of Cubism – John Quinn, Conrad Arensberg, Walter Pach, Alfred Stieglitz – were enchanted by this phenomenon. Gleizes detested it, and his detestation appears in a number of texts – poems, stories and essays – written at the time, in which Duchamp and the 'officine intellectuel' (intellectual drugstore – almost certainly Stieglitz's Photo-Secession gallery) are satirised mercilessly. Duchamp and the ready-mades are also largely the target of Mme Gleizes's satire – *Le Minéralisation de Dudley Craving McAdam*.[8]

In the calmer mood of the *Souvenirs*, however, Gleizes says that he had quite failed to understand the phenomenon, which was only an extreme version of what he himself was doing, and of what all the painters had been doing since the idea that 'art is nature seen through a temperament' had become generally accepted. He thought he was witnessing something strange, exotic; but increasingly he saw the same spirit invading all spheres of human activity – a spirit in which the individual who is sceptical of everything, who has lost all sense of personal responsibility, who has no solid principle within himself, nonetheless wishes to express himself.

The means of this self-expression is to take a subject from outside himself and to deform it, provide variations on it, in accordance with his own temperament. Duchamp had simply recognised that this could be done directly, with a minimum of effort, by lifting the subject bodily out of its normal context and placing it in the new context of the art gallery, in the new atmosphere provided by an incongruous title. There was no difference in principle between a coffee-grinder placed in a gallery and a painting of a coffee-grinder placed in a gallery. In this approach, which eliminates all the unnecessary effort of the painter's craft, Duchamp was simply following the tendency of the age:

> the suppression of all effort in the name of a mechanical progress advancing with giant steps, the anguish and emptiness which are the price of a life without purpose, the substitution everywhere, from top to bottom of the scale, of symbols for the authentic reality, the reality one makes oneself, whose growth one follows with one's head, one's heart, one's hands . . .[9]

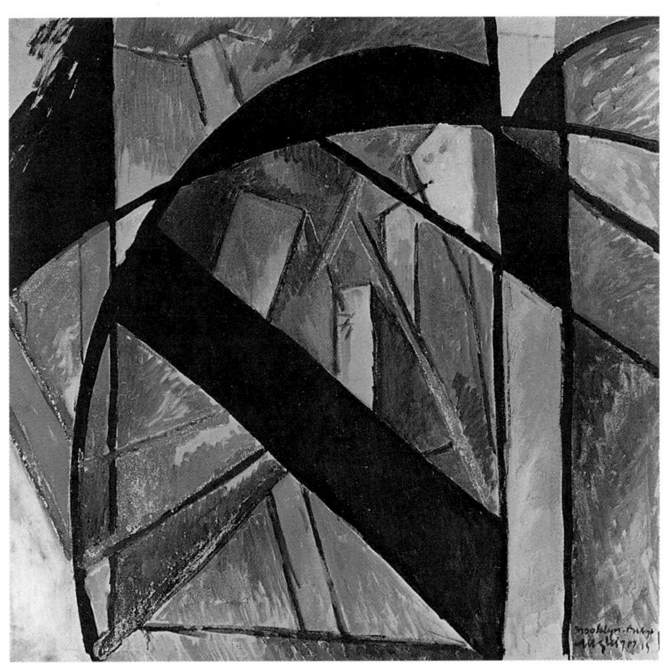

35. *Brooklyn Bridge*, 1915. Oil and gouache on canvas, 102 × 102 cm. Solomon R. Guggenheim Museum, New York

Mme Gleizes tells us that Gleizes's enthusiasm for New York was shortlived, that he quickly realised that behind the fascinating spectacle of 'the enormous Broadway' there lay a great mass of human misery. She describes how, one day, they got lost 'in an endless street "uptown", in the Bronx or in Harlem':

> Around us was a desolation of reinforced concrete and old twisted metal, a succession of massive blocks, all exactly the same, one after the other, pierced by sash windows behind which only sinister things could take place, striped with the metal bars of fire escapes . . .
>
> It was a space that was morally empty, deprived of all organic life and destined soon to disappear, to be replaced by another, just as utilitarian and dehumanised . . .
>
> Albert Gleizes walked along, his eyebrows contracted, with a very dark manner, without saying a word, which was not like him. Suddenly, he exploded: 'See where it leads when we live only for the transport of packages. Over the whole earth, millions and millions of beings who have no thought but to send packages to each other.' . . .
>
> He had lost all restraint and continued on the theme. He could not admit this devitalisation, this mechanisation, this loss of everything that gave value or charm to life. When a society had lost its head to the extent of no longer preserving the sense of its essential needs, and no longer thought of anything but transporting packages, by hand, by air, by sea, one could only conclude that it was very sick and one could expect nothing from it but convulsions. The war was one. A war so mad, so monstrously stupid, little by little polluting the whole planet, could only have occurred in a world that was completely brutalised. We could never forgive this war. But not to forgive was not enough. We must learn how to say No. In all our thoughts and in all our

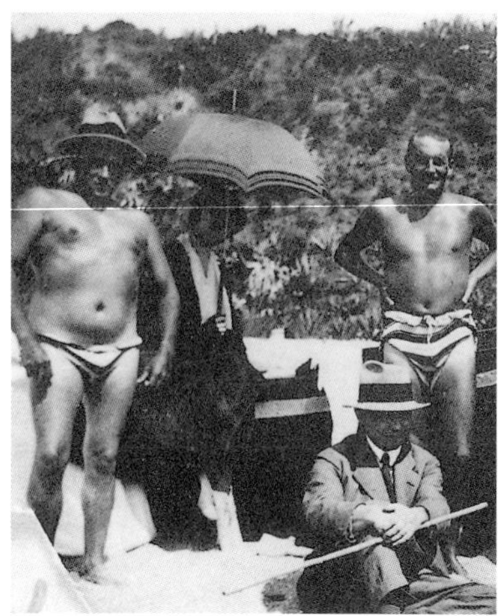

36. On the beach at Tossa del Mar, 1916. To left, Francis Picabia and Juliette Roche Gleizes (with parasol). Seated, Albert Gleizes. Note the difference in vestimentary style

> acts to separate ourselves from everything that could, even very remotely, contribute to giving birth to war or making it possible. That was the only programme of life that could be admitted for those who survived the war, if there were any survivors.[10]

Gleizes tells us how he watched America change as it was brought into the war. It could not avoid entering it because the economic rewards were too great. Henry Ford had been passionately opposed to the conflict, but he made a fortune out of it all the same. Gleizes took Ford as a type of the modern man, unable to see the cleavage between his own entirely personal decency and the immense horror he was creating in the world through his daily work. War was a necessary consequence of industrial capitalism because only the enormous needs created by war corresponded to the scale of industrial production – only war could keep it fully occupied. But modern war required a modern, centralised nation able to act, inhumanly, as one man. This was what was implied in the idea of total mobilisation. In America, the economic principle had developed in a cruder, less restrained fashion than in Europe because there was less of an inhibiting traditional culture. But at the time of Gleizes's arrival, America was still too decentralised and individualistic to act as a proper nation. He saw it become a nation as it whipped itself into a war fever on the basis of lies to which he, as a Frenchman, was expected, but refused, to contribute. He congratulated himself on his good fortune in having been able to observe America, and hence industrial capitalism at its least restrained, in an exceptionally revealing moment.

Among his writings at this time, is a piece dated December 1915, thus not long after his arrival, which confirms what he says in the *Souvenirs*, that his disillusionment with New York had set in at an early stage.[11] It is called *Le Miracle du 5th Avenue* and it presents a schematic history of the western world from the Middle Ages in the form of a conflict between two 'spirits' – the spirit that built the cathedrals and the spirit that was to build the skyscrapers. For a long time the former has disappeared from the world, leaving only the dead stones to testify to its previous existence. When even the dead stones have disappeared and the new, brutal, commercial spirit has triumphed completely, the old spirit will redescend upon the world, and a new Age will begin.[12]

In a fanciful, fictitious form, this is the first example we have of the vision which will inform all Gleizes's historical writing. Indeed, it is during this period that Gleizes's career as a writer begins. The point is worth stressing. Gleizes is often portrayed as primarily a theorist, all too anxious to rush into print. But until the age of thirty-five he had actually published very little – a handful of articles and a small book written in collaboration with another painter. We have now reached the first period in which we have a substantial collection of his own writings (earlier unpublished material may have been lost but I have seen no record of it). Even now, it is not until the 1920s, when Gleizes is in his forties, that he begins to publish on a large scale. For Gleizes, in general, writing is inseparable from action. It is a means of clarifying actions already realised with a view to preparing for actions to come.

Nevertheless, these wartime writings are much more literary than his later writing. They can be divided into three general categories:

1. prose poems gathered under the general heading *Le Cavalier du dimanche;*
2. poems in free verse, gathered together as *La Tortue emballée;*

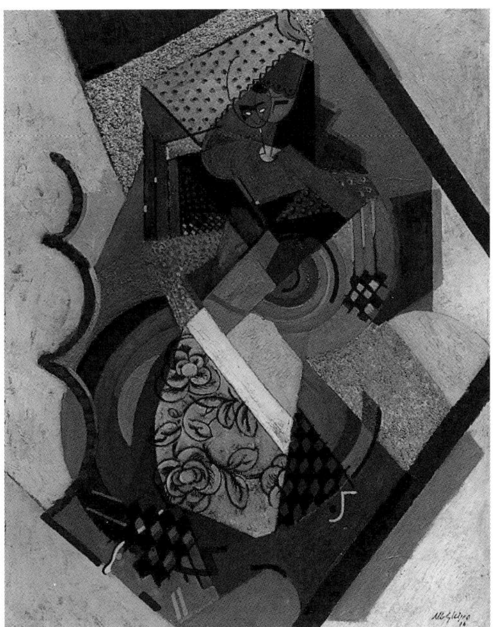

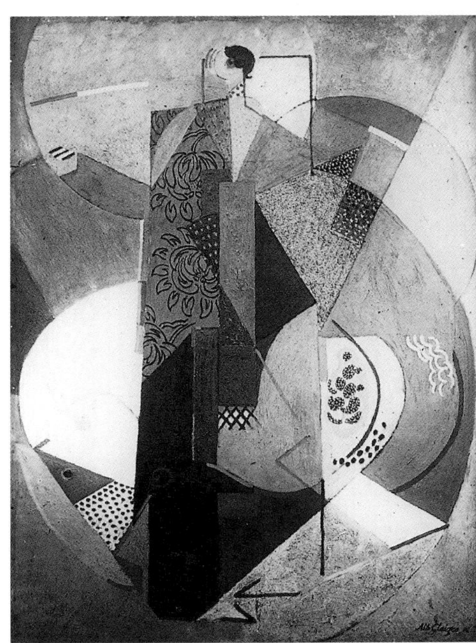

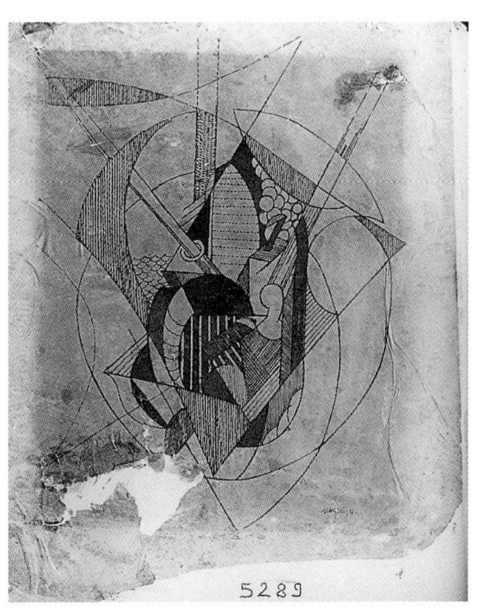

37. *Danseuse Espagnole*, 1916. Oil with sand on board, 101 × 76.4 cm. Solomon R. Guggenheim Museum, New York

38. *Sur une Ecuyère de haute école*, 1916. Oil with sand on board, 101.8 × 76.2 cm. Solomon R. Guggenheim Museum, New York

39. [Sur le bateau à voiles de Picabia], 1918 (*sic*. More likely 1916). Ink on paper, 32.5 × 22.5 cm. Musée des Beaux Arts, Lyon. Photograph taken before restoration

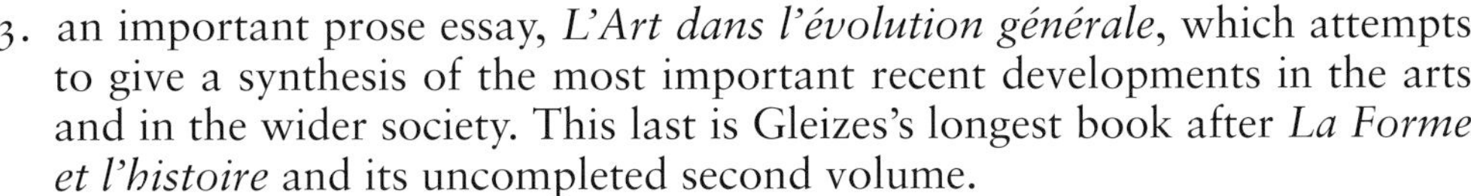

3. an important prose essay, *L'Art dans l'évolution générale*, which attempts to give a synthesis of the most important recent developments in the arts and in the wider society. This last is Gleizes's longest book after *La Forme et l'histoire* and its uncompleted second volume.

It is possible that Gleizes turned to writing during the long sea voyages he made at this time. In May 1916, the Gleizes travelled to Spain and, on their return to New York in December, they took a long detour which included Cuba. Soon after, they travelled again to the Bermudas where Gleizes painted some curious landscapes in which he seems to be looking back to the style of his earliest Cubist work. *L'Art dans l'évolution générale* is dated – at the end of the book – January 1917 and *Le Cavalier du dimanche* contains a number of rather tedious accounts of his travels. Although Gleizes was to give lectures in Germany, Poland and England in the 1930s, this is the only case I know after the Cubist period of his travelling for pleasure – though it was not wholly for pleasure, since he was in Barcelona for a one-man show in the Dalmau Gallery, which had already shown itself to be supportive of the Cubist painters.

While in Spain, they were particularly close to Francis Picabia and his wife, Gabrielle Buffet-Picabia, who had joined them in June. Picabia was a rather suspect person in the pre-war Parisian avant-garde. Coming from a very wealthy family, he had achieved considerable success with an insipid but commercial Impressionist style. He had then transformed himself into the most radical of the moderns and in this circle had rapidly made himself indispensable. It is probable that he helped to pay for the publication of *Du 'Cubisme'* and certain that he supported Apollinaire's *Méditations esthétiques (Les Peintres cubistes)*. There had been a sort of competition between him and Delaunay for the affections of Apollinaire and according to Sonia Delaunay it was because of the inclusion of Picabia that Delaunay had refused to appear in the illustrations to *Du 'Cubisme'*.[13]

Picabia had been in New York prior to the war, the only one of the Cubist group who was actually present at the 1913 Armory Show, and he had served as a useful contact between the French painters and their American buyers. He could make a strong claim to be regarded as the first of those directly associated with Cubism to pass into non-representational painting.

The Picabias and the Gleizes passed the Summer together in the resort of Tossa del Mar where, according to the account given by Mme Gleizes to Picabia's biographer, Maria Lluïsa Borràs, they spent much of their time in the local casinos. The period sees a number of paintings based on the theme of Spanish dancers, continuing the interest in performance (of the body moving in a precise, rhythmic manner) which we have seen in the circus paintings (Plates 37, 38 and 39). Another theme which appears at this time is *Le Bateau de Picabia*.

According to Borràs, Gleizes's journeys on his return to New York were done at Picabia's suggestion. In the summer in New York the two couples met up again and shared a house with the composer Edgard Varèse. According to Varèse's wife, Louise, 'it was a very hot summer. Varèse and Picabia walked about the flat entirely naked and it was in this state that they received their female guests . . .'. It was a time when Picabia was taking a great deal of cocaine and alcohol, which would eventually necessitate his taking a cure.[14]

It all seems very unlike Gleizes. Some of the pieces in *Le Cavalier du dimanche* have a fantastic, satirical element which may suggest a determined effort to fit in to the social circle in whch he found himself. But *L'Art dans l'évolution générale* is quite consistent with Albert Gleizes as we know him in the rest of his life. As the title suggests, it is concerned with the relations between the artist and the wider society. Like many of the prose pieces in *Le Cavalier du dimanche*, it is an impassioned attack on the 'cénacles', the little élitist groups for whom art is a matter of self-indulgent expression, who cultivate eccentricity, sensuality, the disordering of their senses through drugs and alcohol, with a view to better expressing their own individual peculiarities. We have seen that in *Du 'Cubisme'* the artist was seen as a Superman, able to conceive of forms in a world that to most eyes is purely amorphous. The artist loves his form – because it is his own – and forces the crowd to adapt to it. But in itself the form is arbitrary. The moment that the crowd begins to understand it – the moment it becomes a collective possession – the artist moves on.

I have suggested that this view belongs more to Metzinger than to Gleizes who, even in 1912, was unlikely to be attracted by it. *L'Art dans l'evolution générale* could be described as an attempt to find an alternative. Its very length and breadth (it touches on an enormous range of subjects) testifies to the difficulty of finding an alternative. Broadly speaking, Gleizes argues for the existence of an instinct, or a spirit, that goes beyond the individual to express the common needs of the collectivity at any given time. Although the spirit corresponds to a collective need, it is only an exceptional individual who is capable of realising or expressing it. It is certainly not an individual who is obsessed with his own psychological peculiarities. Gleizes here draws the important distinction between the individual and the person – a distinction that is also crucial to the philosophy Nicholas Berdyaev was developing at about the same time. It is in the depth and solidity of the person that the artist can speak to the collectivity. But one of the greatest obstacles to realising what is solid and permanent within oneself is education, such as it is understood at the present day – the accumulation of information, of a series of purely external acquisitions; the person seen essentially as an empty vessel that needs to be filled up with material from outside itself. This education

creates a conformist attitude of mind which for Gleizes is the opposite to the constructive, collectivist mentality he wishes to develop.

In this context, there is a most interesting comparison between Henri Rousseau and Paul Cézanne in which he argues that Rousseau was the more successful of the two painters. Cézanne's life was a long, heroic struggle against his own education; but Rousseau was able to go straight to the point:

> His craft is simple and unworried; he talks to us as well as he can; he knows exactly what he wants to say when he begins his painting, and when he has finished he has attained his end fully and in a relaxed fashion. . . . Cézanne all his life advanced towards a meeting with himself; Rousseau did not have to take a single step. He had always been there . . . (pp.38–9)

There is a very similar comparison between Rousseau and Cézanne in the papers of Robert Delaunay which are reproduced in *Du Cubisme à l'art abstrait*, where it is ascribed to 1911.[15]

Gleizes discusses the new spirit that he saw developing about him in all the arts – in poetry (with René Ghil, Emil Verhaeren and Gustav Kahn), in music (in the work of Stravinsky) and in the theatre (with Cocteau's project for *A Midsummer Night's Dream* – a theatre that would address all the senses at once, like a circus. We may note in parenthesis the parochial nature of Gleizes's comments on other artists. Both here and in his subsequent writings, he rarely mentions anyone he has not known personally). In all these fields, there is an interest in 'primitive' forms. This is not sufficient in itself, but it is a step in the right direction. Cubism itself is described as a reaction to the new architecture of the metal bridges and the Eiffel Tower – an emphasis on scaffolding and construction rather than on decoration. But Gleizes is already sceptical about the contemporary enthusiasm for machines. He is not opposed to them, but he does not believe that, in themselves, they have any value for the spirit.

These wartime writings, which have never been published, are a rich source for understanding the ferment of ideas out of which Gleizes's mature thought was to develop. Keeping to Gleizes's terminology and talking about the transition from the subject to the object, they represent the last moment in which the subject is dominant. Mme Gleizes says that Gleizes was very quickly dissatisfied with *L'Art dans l'evolution générale*. Nonetheless, it contains much that the mature Gleizes would be able to approve – he later, probably in the early thirties, began to prepare it for publication, and the changes he made in the text would make an interesting study in themselves. In particular, the book points clearly to the next important development in his thought – his conversion to belief in God, which he saw as a necessary corollary of his belief in something of solid, permanent value in our common human nature – a real value which he was particularly anxious to reassert in the face of its negation in the war, in New York, and in the attitudes of the 'intellectual drugstore' which revolved round Marcel Duchamp.

The years 1916 and 1917 see the emergence of a new technique in Gleizes's painting that corresponds to the ideals expressed in *L'Art dans l'évolution générale* and in the letter I have already quoted to Barzun. Far removed from the proto-Dada jokiness of Picabia, it is a return to the 'majestic' Albert Gleizes. The elements – circus, Brooklyn Bridge, skyscrapers, Picabia's boat, dancers – which had first been painted sketchily, dynamically, are now crystallised, so to speak, organised in a tight structure of lines of construction which cover the

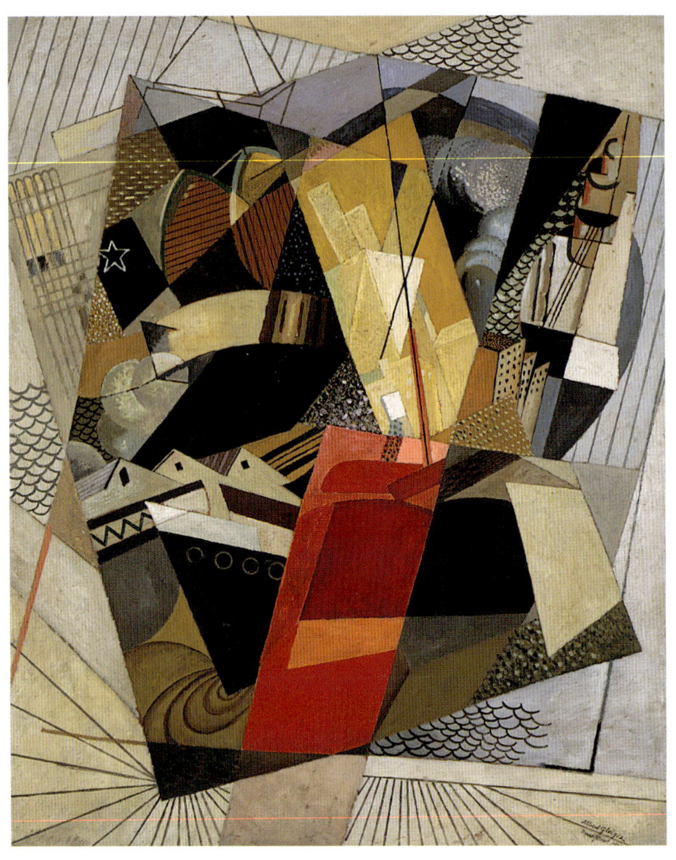

40. *Dans le Port*, 1917. Oil and sand on board, 153.3 × 120.6 cm. Thyssen-Bornemisza Museum, Madrid

whole area of the canvas. They are much more ordered than even the *Portrait d'un médecin militaire*, but they also cover a much broader subject matter. In contrast to the first paintings done in response to New York in 1915, they reaffirm the principle of 'juxtaposition not superposition'. The whole has the effect of reinforcing the flatness of the canvas, its two-dimensional nature, and we begin to see signs of the organisation on the basis of planes derived from the proportions of the overall picture surface which will be Gleizes's starting point for the whole development that continues from 1920 until his death. It is no accident that in *Kubismus*, published in 1928, he chooses one of the *Bateau de Picabia* paintings of 1916 to illustrate the third stage in the common history of Cubism – affirmation of the flat surface – as it appears in his own work.

In the letter to Barzun, we see Gleizes full of confidence, full of excitement at his own achievement, even treating his own earlier work with a note of contempt:

> The little researches in which my desire to expand myself [*mon désir de rayonnement*] was wasted, I have transformed them into something more universal, more synthetic. I have become conscious of the planet. The limited horizon which I thought was the only horizon is finally opened up and stands revealed. I look with a little scorn on the Albert Gleizes of yesterday, and a little pity, for the credulity which, finally, only ended up in a narrow sectarianism.'

It is difficult to believe he is talking about paintings like *Le Dépiquage des moissons* or *Les Joueurs de football*.

So, Gleizes believes that he now possesses the means of synthesis, the ability to give form to a 'planetary' vision. And these resemble the means which will characterise his mature work – the interplay of two-dimensional planes presented brutally as rectangles (something he carefully avoids prior to the New York period) and the circle and circular curve, also presented straight, in a manner that is reminiscent of Robert Delaunay, whom he met during the visit to Spain in 1916 (the Delaunays passed most of the wartime period in Portugal). Indeed discs, clearly derived from Delaunay, appear in some of the paintings of this time, notably the 1917 *Brooklyn Bridge* (Plate 41). Borrowings as flagrant as this are rare in Gleizes's work. It is almost as if, in attempting the synthesis of everything that excites him in the surrounding world, he is also trying to synthesise everything that excites him in the work of his colleagues.

And yet, suddenly, Gleizes stops; there are hardly any paintings done by him in 1918. It is difficult to say why. The circumstances seem more favourable than in the earlier period. I know of no major journeys undertaken by the Gleizes' at this time. Mme Gleizes says that they were living in Pelham, which was then a quiet rural suburb of New York. The mystery is all the greater when we learn, as we shall shortly, that on his return to Paris Gleizes thought of destroying his wartime paintings, and that he agreed with a severe critique made of them by Metzinger. It all points to a major crisis of confidence, perhaps (though this is a pure speculation on my part) something that could be called a nervous breakdown. It is in this context that we may begin to understand the most important event that we know of in 1918 – Gleizes's conversion to belief in God, 'consequence of feelings and of reason pushed as far as it can go'.[16]

Mme Gleizes describes what happened. She was tranquilly painting a picture of circus acrobats when Gleizes burst in in a state of great distress and declared: 'A terrible thing has happened to me. I have found God [*je retrouve Dieu*]. God exists. We cannot do without Him . . .'. According to the story as she told it to Walter Firpo, she replied: 'Well, Albert, don't worry. Take a cup of tea and you will soon feel better.'[17]

Gleizes had developed a means of celebrating the noise and agitation of the great city, of jazz, of the circus; but he himself had no real interest in these things and, instinctively or consciously, associated them with the horrors of the war. He was closely associated with Duchamp and Picabia who, in their different ways, were expressing their sense of the pointlessness of artistic activity. He had spent what was probably for him an intolerable summer with Picabia who was destroying himself with drugs. His own work seems to suggest all the means which he would later develop with such astonishing success but, seen in the light of his later achievements, it appears relatively arbitrary, disorganised and melodramatic – indeed even histrionic. We may imagine that Gleizes who always, to some extent, lived in the future, judged what he had done severely in the light of what he felt instinctively might be possible but which he was still unable to do.

The realisation that was coming upon him was that the quality he was aiming for – and which, to a large extent, despite everything, he had managed to achieve – had nothing to do with the appearances of the world, 'the enormous Broadway'. There was a distinction to be drawn between a 'universal' consciousness and a 'planetary' consciousness. The 'planetary' was of the nature of appearances, of the senses. The universal was a property of consciousness itself. The former – the appearance of phenomena – was an obstacle to the latter – the 'universal'. But only in the light of faith in God – a consciousness that transcends the individual consciousness – did this notion of the 'universal' have any meaning.

The 'revelation' had been prepared for some time. Gleizes says in the *Souvenirs* that he had the 'sense of the divine' in 1917. It is already almost manifest in *L'Art dans l'evolution générale*, most of which was written in 1916. It implied no conversion to any church; Gleizes was to continue for a long time to argue that the churches had lost all spiritual value. In the very short term he was to turn rather to the Russian Revolution. His conversion to God was an extension of his belief in human nature and in the need for a great, popular, collective culture.

In *L'Art dans l'evolution générale*, Gleizes distinguishes two 'forces' – reminiscent of the two 'spirits' of *Le Miracle du 5th Avenue*. One goes from the collective to the particular, the other from the particular to the collective. Both, he argues, are necessary and

41. *Sur le Brooklyn Bridge*, 1917. Oil on canvas, 162 × 129.5 cm. Solomon R. Guggenheim Museum, New York

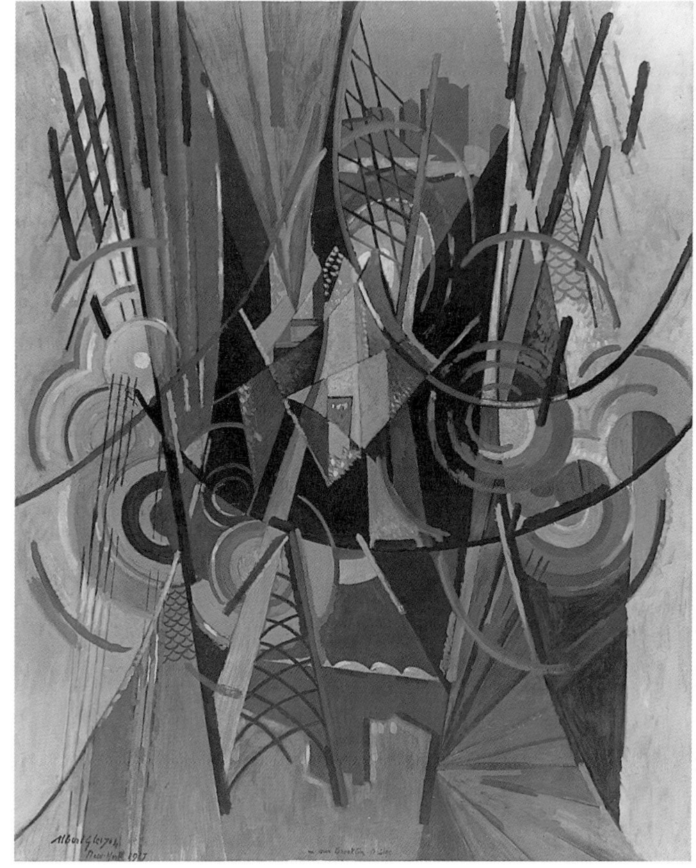

interdependent. Some ages of history are dominated by the one, others by the other. We are passing from an age in which the individual and the spirit of analysis have been paramount (the age of capitalism, of the division of labour, of the skyscrapers) to an age in which the collective will be paramount (a return to the spirit of the cathedrals). This is not yet obvious. The individualist spirit is still predominant, it has launched the war to defend itself, but it is in full decomposition. The other is on its way, and Cubism is its herald. What Gleizes feels within himself as a Cubist painter is much stronger than a subjective preference, a matter of taste and sensibility, something that could be picked up one day and discarded the next. It is the presence of a great truth which is objective even though it has been forgotten, which corresponds to a deep-seated human need which everyone should be able to feel, as everyone had once been able to feel the power, dignity and truth of the cathedrals.

The two antagonistic but complementary forces are personified as if they were gods acting out their conflict within us. What is new in his conversion, is that Gleizes is no longer satisfied with God as a symbol for something else. The 'subject', product of our own imagination, is to become the 'object' – with its own real, independent existence. In love with the mystery of human nature and of the universe, and feeling deeply that it obliges us to aim higher than our immediate whims, fancies and sense impressions, Gleizes is now convinced that this desire for transcendence must be directed towards an actual objective reality. God must exist. If He doesn't, then our highest aspirations are merely arbitrary and we cannot escape the subjectivism of *Du 'Cubisme'* and, ultimately, the logic of Duchamp's individualist despair. Already he senses that, in painting, he is approaching an objective reality, essentially common to all men, which exists independently of his own ideas and wishes. Already he knows that this reality is embodied in the cathedrals, and that they could only have been built by faith. Now he realises that they could not have been built by faith in God as a symbol of mankind (as He is portrayed in *L'Art dans l'evolution générale*) but only by faith in God as really existent, a point of excellence to which all mankind aspires.

The consequence of his conversion for his painting was soon to be the abandonment of the turbulent agitation of the New York period in exchange for a new seriousness and sober discipline. Belief in God was belief in the importance of his own work, the willing acceptance of an enormous responsibility. But this was not experienced as a desire to escape from the real world, from its political and social problems, or even its variety and turbulence. If such a belief transcends everything, it also incorporates everything. It is a development, not a denial, of the Unanimism of the Abbaye de Créteil.

6

PARIS AFTER THE WAR – I

It is only in 1922, when he writes *La Peinture et ses lois* that the consequences of Gleizes's conversion are fully realised. The period from 1919 to 1922 may be called a period of transition, but one in which, unlike the previous New York period, the end is in sight. Gleizes says that his paintings of 1919 were no different in principle from those of 1914, but that he had a quite different

> consciousness and of a different order . . . Cubism was changing in its meaning and its end. If, I said to myself, Cubism cannot be raised to the level of a principle, of laws, in such a way as to be capable of transmission, if it does not provide a powerful framework in which individual tastes and fantasies can express themselves freely, then it will not have reached its end, whatever more or less happy successes it may produce.[1]

This is the theme of *Du Cubisme et les moyens de le comprendre*, published in Paris in 1920: 'The time for theorems is past: now is the time for axioms'. But the qualitative difference between *Du Cubisme et les moyens de le comprendre* of 1920 and *La Peinture et ses lois* of 1922 is that the former expresses an aspiration, the latter realises it. In *L'Art dans l'evolution générale*, Gleizes had expressed a desire for construction equivalent to the construction of the metal bridges and the Eiffel Tower; but this is really a preference for the appearance of construction – it is still an external aesthetic effect. By *Du Cubisme et les moyens de le comprendre*, he knows that this appearance would be mere theatre if it is not based on a real spiritual principle, in accord at once with the nature of the painted surface and of that of the human being who looks at it. In *La Peinture et ses lois*, he gives the first clear indication of what this principle (which was to be developed over the rest of his life) might be.

Mme Gleizes says that Gleizes's friends had some difficulty persuading him not to destroy his New York output.[2] Gleizes says that, on his return to Paris in April 1919, his work was subjected to withering criticism from Metzinger, which hurt him deeply at the time, but which he had to agree was essentially right. On the other hand, he was praised by André Lhote. During the war, Lhote, together with Metzinger, Juan Gris, Gino Severini and Diego Rivera (and Picasso, but Picasso was keeping his distance from the other painters) had developed the Cubist language in Paris into what Gleizes called the third phase of Cubism: the respect for the flat surface (Plate 42).[3]

The first and second phases – volume and multiple perspective – were still based on the classical perspective mechanism, giving the appearance of a fictitious third dimension. This third phase did not abandon the idea of depth and the third dimension, but it no longer attempted to realise it by means of per-

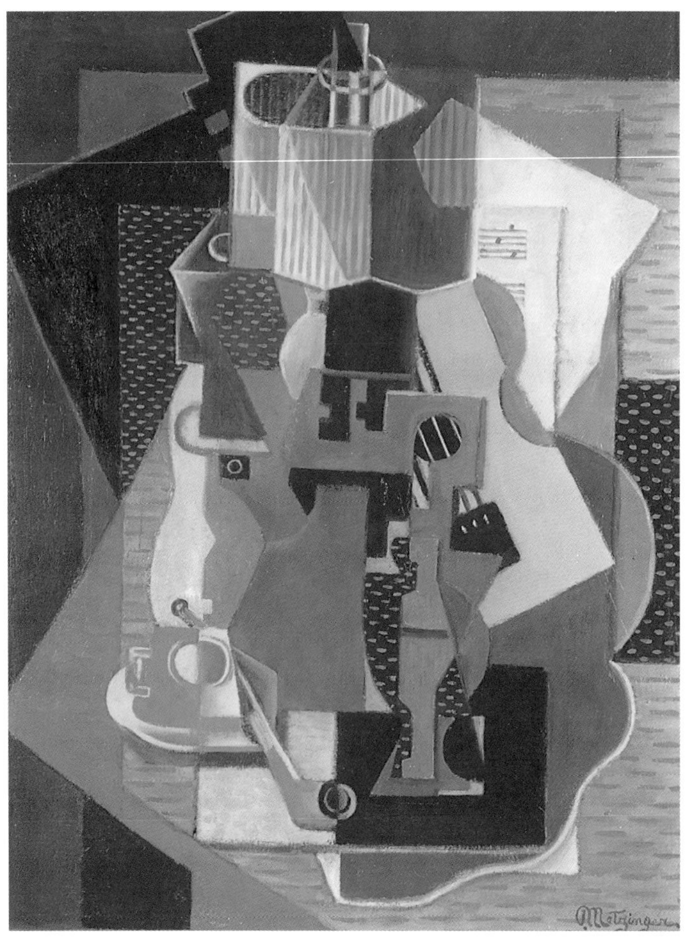

42. Jean Metzinger, *Nature morte? la lampe*, 1916 (sic. more probably 1918). Oil on canvas, 81 × 61 cm. Museum of Modern Art, New York

spective. All the different planes used in the construction of the painting were, so to speak, parallel to its surface, so that the real – two-dimensional – nature of the canvas was respected. Gleizes frequently acknowledges Metzinger and Gris as the great pioneers of this development.[4] Lhote, Severini and Rivera had also, however, played a role; but by the time Gleizes arrived in Paris, they were in retreat and rather publicly so, since Lhote and Rivera were being praised by the old lifelong enemy of Cubism, Louis Vauxcelles. This retreat, and its impact at the time, is the starting point for Christopher Green's discussion of the fate of Cubism in the 1920s, *Cubism and its Enemies*.[5]

It is doubtful, then, if Gleizes would have appreciated Lhote's admiration, though the two painters were friends. Lhote was attempting in the pages of the *Nouvelle Revue française* to define what was specifically 'French' in French painting, to distinguish it from what was specifically 'Italian'. This is also, of course, the theme of Gleizes's 1913 essay *La Tradition et le cubisme*. Lhote argues that the Italians aspire to paint the gods directly, as they are; the French start off from the human, and it is from the human that they arrive at the divine. Thus the Italians are much more easily attracted by the abstract – the ideal, the intellectual, the mathematical. That becomes their starting point and they then give it a human form. The French are more empirical; a love for the appearances of the real world is their starting point: the ideal, the intellectual and the mathematical comes afterwards. Gleizes, on the strength of his wartime work, and especially the paintings done during his visit to Spain in 1916, is praised as a typically French painter, but Gleizes was soon to disappoint Lhote and to show, if we continue to use Lhote's terminology, that he was the most 'Italian' of them all.[6]

The Italian Lhote had specifically in mind was Gino Severini, formerly one of the most extreme Futurists, Marinetti's agent in Paris. In about 1915, Severini had begun to change radically and was now insisting on a return to 'Classicism' and to the principles of the Renaissance, especially the early Renaissance, when the religious principle was still predominant, before the corrupting influence of sensuality set in. It was not the external appearance of the Renaissance painting that interested Severini so much as the internal principle which, he argued, was based on mathematics. His *Du Cubisme au classicisme*, published in 1921, argued that painting had to be based on a good working knowledge of geometry – not the fantastic, non-Euclidean, four-dimensional geometry which had attracted Metzinger and, after him, Duchamp; but normal Euclidean geometry, which is perfectly adequate for what painting is – a three-dimensional projection on a flat surface. The pleasure of painting derives from the ability of the eye and of the mind to grasp and appreciate the geometrically rational relationships of lines and colours (his mathematical understanding of colour is especially interesting).

Du Cubisme au classicisme was published with a preface by Dr René

Allendy, a specialist in the symbolism of numbers and in what we might call the 'pre-scientific' sciences, such as alchemy and astrology. He was soon to be instrumental in introducing the thought of Sigmund Freud into France. Allendy's *Le Symbolisme des nombres*, also published in 1921, is an argument for the numerical basis of the universe – he uses the term 'arithmosophie' to describe his subject. Allendy was also a close friend of Gleizes's. Severini frequently refers to the mathematician Charles Henry, director of the 'Laboratory of the Physiology of Sensations' at the Sorbonne. Henry had developed a complex mathematical understanding of the difference between what is pleasing and what is displeasing in the relations of forms and colours. He had already had a considerable influence on Signac and on the development of Neo-Impressionist colour theory and he too was soon to become a close friend of Gleizes's. We may note in passing that similar ideas on the relation between mathematics and painting can be found in the *ABC de la Peinture* of the 'Nabi', Paul Sérusier, also published in 1921; and that Sérusier had been greatly influenced by the mathematical art of the German Benedictine monastery of Beuron, to which Severini refers.[7]

Whole passages of *Du Cubisme au classicisme* arguing that a common, intelligible, mathematically (and therefore objectively) based theory of painting is necessary could have been written by Gleizes; yet it would be difficult to imagine anything further removed from Gleizes's aspirations than Severini's return to the Italian Renaissance. *La Peinture et ses lois* can be read as a reply to Severini, and thus as a continuation of a long and very rich debate that goes back at least to Signac's *D'Eugène Delacroix au néo-impressionisme*, published in 1899.

Two other important developments which had occurred in Paris during Gleizes's absence were the emergence of the 'Purists', Amédée Ozenfant and Charles Edouard Jeanneret (soon to be better known as the architect, Le Corbusier) – and of Léonce Rosenberg's Galerie de l'Effort Moderne, as the centre and showcase of the new painting. Kahnweiler had been in Switzerland when the war broke out. As a German citizen, he was unable to return to Paris and his property – including the paintings – was confiscated. A group of painters, including Picasso, had approached Rosenberg, a specialist in antiquarian art who collected modern paintings for his own pleasure. Rosenberg agreed to support the new painting and, throughout the war, signed contracts with a number of painters, which, for most of them, including Juan Gris, was almost their only source of income. Like Kahnweiler's contracts, these gave Rosenberg full control over the painters' work.[8]

Rosenberg's approach was very different from that of Kahnweiler. He believed in the new painting with an almost religious fervour. Gleizes says of him: 'Léonce Rosenberg felt that a world was about to be born and, without ceasing to be a merchant, he gave it his faith, even to the detriment of his commercial interest. This is such an exceptional fact that it must be affirmed, loudly and clearly.'[9]

Where Kahnweiler chose a select group of painters and sold to a small, specialist élite, Rosenberg bought everything and believed that the 'effort moderne' he was promoting would eventually change the world – architecture, industrial design, advertising posters, indeed, more fundamentally, the whole state of mind of the age, as much as the fine arts. Like Gleizes, he had the collective art of the mediaeval cathedrals as an ideal in his mind. He ran a very disciplined house; the artists who signed contracts with him were

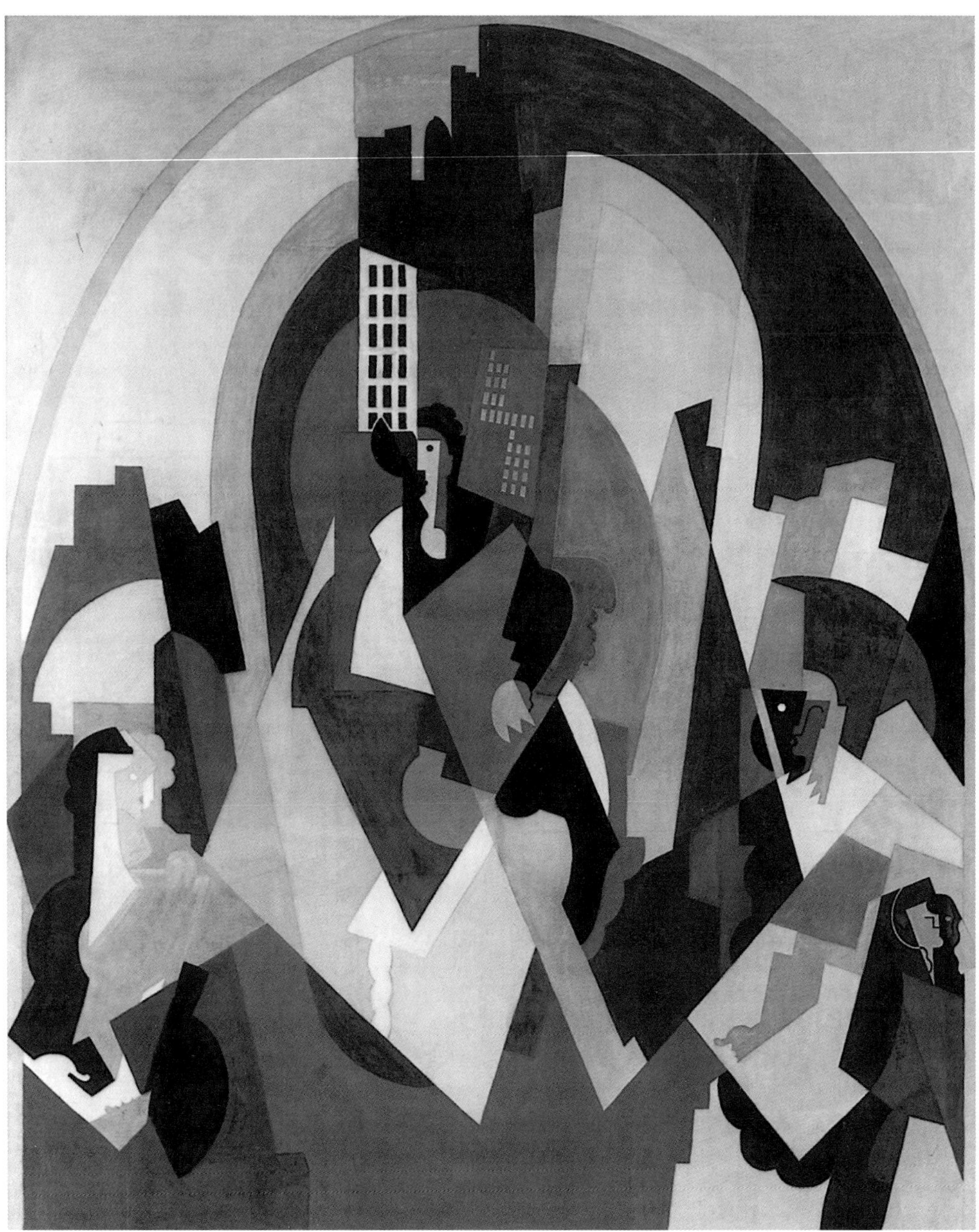

43. *Peinture pour une gare*, 1920 (?). Oil on canvas, 357 × 276 cm. Musée de Grenoble

expected to abide by his collective ideals and even to conform to what might be called a 'house style'. The collective ideal was later to be developed in his *Bulletin de l'Effort Moderne* and in the sometimes quite bullying letters he sent to his artists.

Despite all this, Gleizes suggests that he lacked confidence in his own judgment and was easily influenced. Gleizes himself did not sign a contract with Rosenberg and says that, initially, Rosenberg was reluctant to buy his work. He thinks that he may have been influenced in this by the opinions expressed by Metzinger, but it should be noted that Gleizes had returned to Paris with a rooted dislike of all art dealers, epecially art dealers with pretentions to telling artists what they should be doing. And, as we shall see in the next chapter, he tried to organise an artists' union to control the activities of the dealers. Under the circumstances this could only have been interpreted as an attack on Rosenberg. Nonetheless he found Rosenberg fascinating: 'What a strange figure Léonce Rosenberg was, continually torn between his commercial interest and the most disinterested idealism. Never in one man have I seen the struggle between matter and spirit revealed so clearly.' He says that he had many long conversations with him. Certainly he was a frequent contributor to the *Bulletin de l'Effort Moderne*.[10] Perhaps the most typical expression of the aesthetic favoured by Rosenberg at this time was to be found in the work of Ozenfant and Jeanneret – the 'Purists'. Their pamphlet, *Après le Cubisme* of 1918 was the manifesto of a clean, greatly simplified and ordered Cubism, a mechanical style suitable for mass production, aiming to reproduce the 'pure' aesthetic of utilitarian architecture and factory-produced objects of everyday use. This is 'modernism' as we know it today and it may be noted that Mondrian was in Paris at the time and supported by Rosenberg, who published (in a very cheap and unattractive edition) his essay – *Le Néo-Plasticisme*.

Much in all this was calculated to appeal to Gleizes, especially the emphasis laid on architecture as the mistress of the plastic arts, the denial of any absolute distinction between arts and crafts and, here as in Severini, the insistence on an objective, mathematical basis for the arts. The similarity is so close that Reyner Banham, high-priest of modernism, treats *Du Cubisme et les moyens de le comprendre* as a typical modernist text.[11] But it is hardly surprising that he much prefers *Après le Cubisme*. Gleizes was never, even at this time, a real 'modernist', in Banham's sense of the word. He gives his opinion of the Purists in his essay *Vers une Époque de bâtisseurs* of 1920, contemporary with *Du Cubisme et les moyens de le comprendre*:

> As we live in a heavily industrialised age, we are surrounded by machines, by factories and by rudimentary constructions with a limited purpose. This is all they need to declare that these machines, these factories and these constructions are the perfect types of Beauty. They have forgotten only one little thing that needs to be said: this is, that a work of art is, strictly speaking, useless in the material meaning of the word. But all these industrial realisations are strictly useful. Their appearance is logical like numbers, but with the precision and coldness of numbers. A work of art must combine these numbers with other, less precise elements which destroy the possibility of measure. These elements cannot be controlled because they are of the nature of love . . .[12]

'Other, less precise elements, which destroy the possibility of measure . . .'. The phrase should be retained, because it marks a major difference between Gleizes on the one hand, and both Severini and the Purists on the other. The painting is a game played between what is finite and measurable and what is infinite and immeasurable – that idea is already present in *Du 'Cubisme'*. The theory of Severini and the Purists is confined to the finite

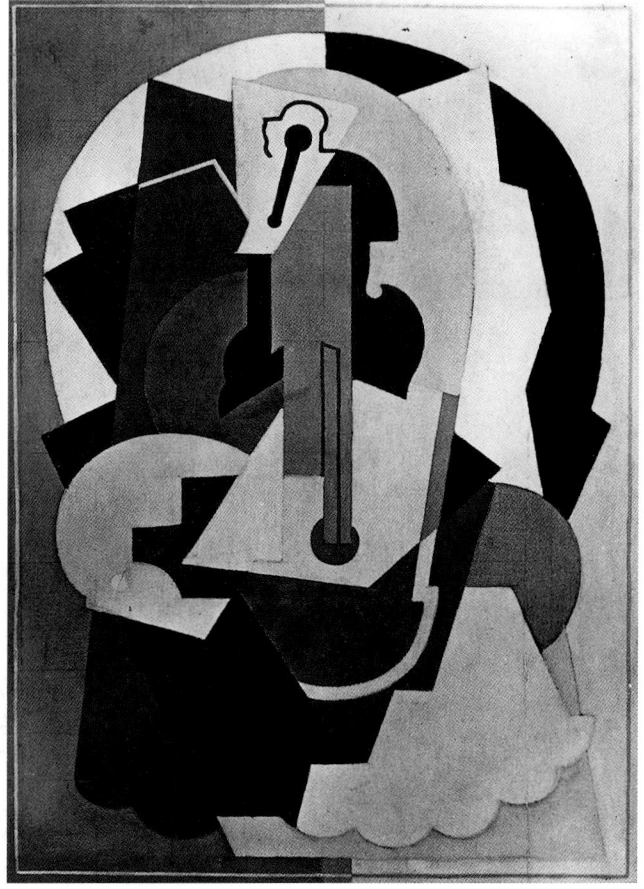

44. *Ecuyère*, 1920. This photograph probably shows an earlier state of pl. 60

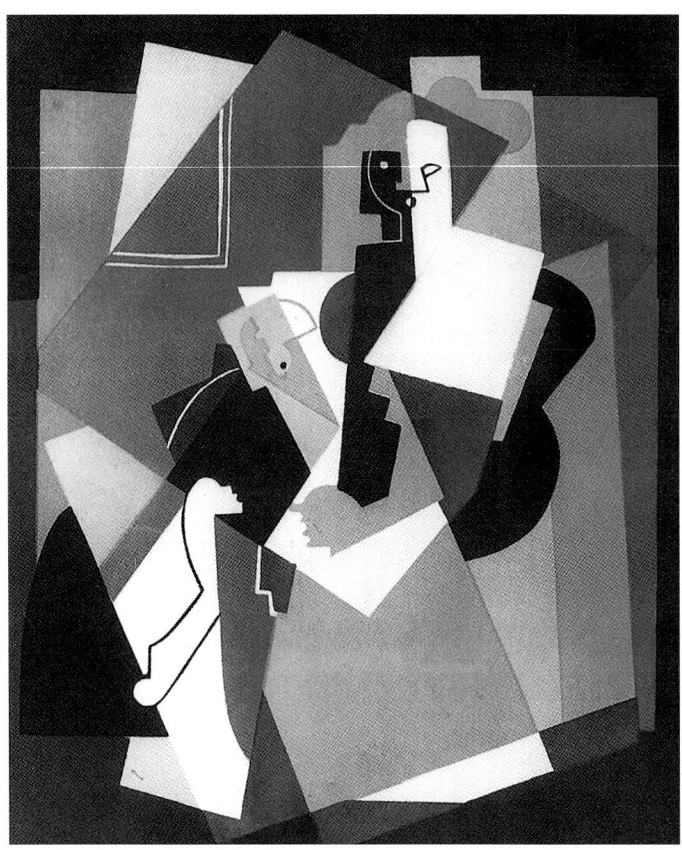

45. [Sans titre], 1920. Oil on canvas (?). Dimensions and present whereabouts unknown

and measurable. But the infinite and immeasurable is still nebulous in Gleizes's mind. It still belongs to the realm of taste and sensibility.

Gleizes's own painting changes abruptly on his return to Paris and in a way that accords with the general mood surrounding the Galerie de l'Effort Moderne. The definite collective gain of the war years in Paris was, in Gleizes's eyes, the abandonment of perspective: the acceptance of the real, two-dimensional, nature of the canvas. This enables a rational construction based on the nature of the surface with which the painter is working, not a mere appearance of a construction taken from the outside world. Instead of a presentation of the idea of construction, we have an actual constructive act; and because the painting is no longer a window which the eye must pierce horizontally to see an imaginary third dimension, it is now free to assert its real vertical nature. The eye – and with it the mind or spirit – moves up and down; the act of seeing engages the soul in a vertical movement; the soul, so to speak, stands up. This is a clarification of something already achieved in pre-war Cubism – the clarification lies in the fact that the contradictory in and out movements of multiple perspective have been done away with.

Secondly, and also in line with the general direction of the Effort Moderne, Gleizes is using mainly bright and well-defined colours (though they include black). He does not confine himself to primary colours (black, white, red, yellow and blue) as recommended by Mondrian, but the ochres and intermediary and dark colours recommended in *Du 'Cubisme'* have gone. *Du Cubisme et les moyens de le comprendre* insists that painting is an art of light and cannot compromise with darkness. At the same time, all the subtle modulations of colour which are very typical of his wartime painting disappear abruptly. *Du Cubisme et les moyens de le comprendre* also suggests that modern painting – simple, rational, flat, unmodulated – lends itself easily to being copied and that this could have radical effects: 'The multiplication of a painting strikes at the very heart of bourgeois thinking and its economic ideas.' Such painting 'can no longer lend itself to speculation. No longer can we twist its neck the moment it appears and put it in a necropolis. No longer is it a corpse as soon as it is born.' (pp.54–5)

Thirdly, though this could be seen as an inevitable complement of the simplification of the colour, the principle of 'juxtaposition not superposition' is back with a vengeance. Everything is clearly demarcated (though not with thick black lines as in Mondrian's work). The picture is held together by large, simple lines of construction, which do not differ in principle from those of the pre-war Le *Dépiquage des moissons* or *La Ville et la fleuve*, except that they are presented as demarcations of areas of colour rather than explicitly as lines. The imagery, since these pictures are still drawn from a 'subject', is still in the shadow of New York: architectural, monumental, an attempt to humanise modern architecture by combining forms suggestive of skyscrapers with forms suggestive of the human body – both rigorously adapted to the objective needs

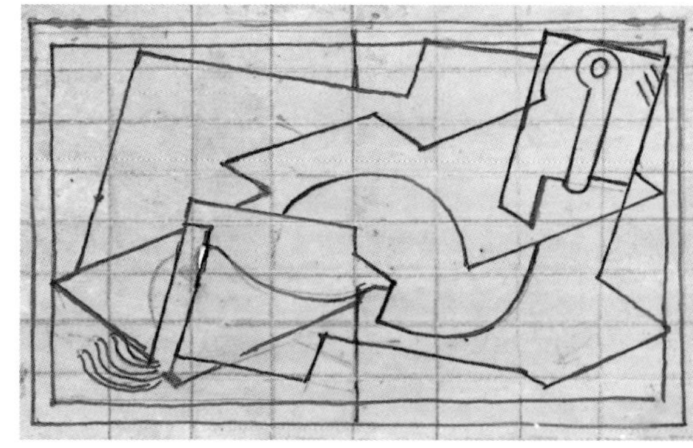

of the painting. There is no illusionistic element left. One almost feels that Gleizes is trying to make life difficult for himself, and later, talking about this period, he refers to 'the voluntary abandonment of all aesthetic tricks'[13] – the third dimension (including the third dimension suggested by transparency or superposition), modulations of colour, chiaroscuro effects and intellectual games (the literary, or artistic references beloved of those who write about painting). To use the subject/object terminology again, Gleizes has made a negative decision to exclude everything that belongs to the subject, except the most rudimentary of figurative indications; but the means he has at his disposal to realise the object are still very limited.

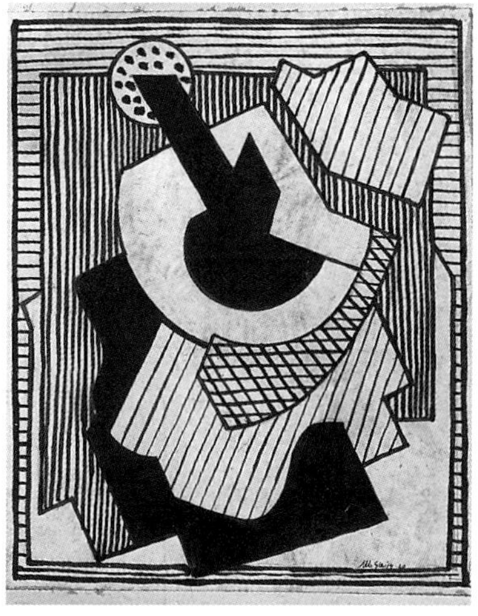

46. *Composition*, 1920 (?). Pen and ink on tracing paper squared up in blue pencil, 9.6 × 15 cm. Musée National d'Art Moderne, Paris
47. *Composition*, 1920. Ink on card, 29 × 24.5 cm. Private Collection

These means were soon to be enlarged by a device that was to be crucial to the development of Gleizes's thought, a device that, with hindsight, may appear to be almost absurdly elementary and obvious. When Gleizes denounced 'superposition' in 1913, he was thinking of the superposition of transparent planes in the hermetic Cubism of Picasso and Braque in 1911. This transparency contributes to a disagreeable flickering effect, as we do not know if the planes are in front of each other or behind each other or at what angle they are placed, whether they are turning inwards or falling outwards – exactly the disorientating effect Gleizes was soon to experience when he went to New York, as he describes it in his poem *Dieu nouveau*. New York compels Gleizes himself to engage in the superposition of transparent planes, though by this time he is sufficiently experienced in the art of construction over the whole surface of the canvas to be able to keep the spatial ambiguity under control.

In 1912, Picasso and Braque both moved on to the *papiers-collés* of which – and in very similar terms – both Gleizes and Delaunay expressed their strong disapproval.[14] In one important respect, however, the *papier-collé* contributed to resolving the problem of spatial ambiguity. The strip of newspaper or of wallpaper or whatever, placed on the canvas, automatically creates an opaque plane; the power of this is felt much more strongly in Braque's *papiers-collés* than in those of Picasso. Critics often say they have difficulty distinguishing the 1911 hermetic Cubism of Picasso from that of Braque, but already the key to the distinction lies in Braque's better sense of construction. Braque is closer to the object; Picasso is closer to the subject. The difference is unmistakable once we move to 1912 and the *papiers-collés*. Picasso uses the *papier-collé* (pioneered by Braque) as a means of engaging in a wide variety of ways of interpreting the subject. Braque sees it as a means of construction. It is at this time that a tension begins to develop between the two friends, leading to their final separation.

I have already remarked that the 'Salon Cubists' showed little interest in the *papier-collé* as such. Juan Gris used it, but in a very painterly way. Where he does use it, he could equally well have used paint. However, during the war, both Gris and Metzinger (both, unlike Gleizes and Delaunay, admirers of Picasso and Braque) advanced towards a much simpler, more rational painting, whose simplicity and rationality is based on the superposition of opaque planes, often in the form of the St Andrew's Cross – a plane tilted to the right and another to the left – which was to be the basis of Gleizes's 'translation/rotation', the key to the 'laws' of *La Peinture et ses lois*.

From 1920 onwards, Gleizes uses the superposition of opaque planes and this enables him, so to speak, to interweave the different shapes he uses into a

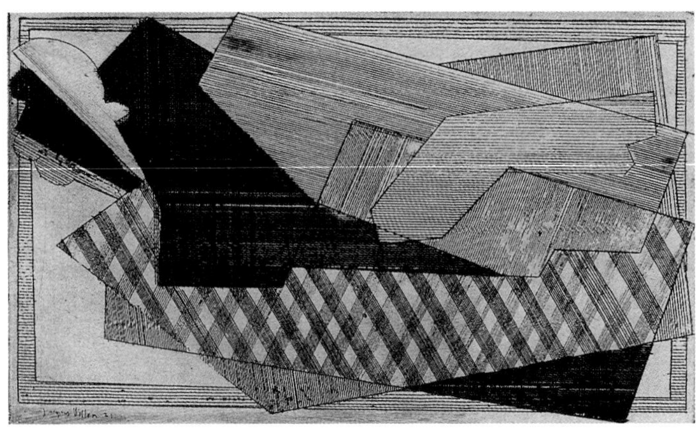

48. Jacques Villon, *Le Cheval*, 1921. Etching, 7.8 × 12.8 cm. Musée du Dessin et de l'Estampe, Gravelines

coherent unity; and this in turn enables him, for almost the first time, to realise fully non-figurative paintings. I say 'almost' the first time because a *Composition* of 1915, probably derived from the *Portrait de Florent Schmitt, Chant de guerre*, is generally regarded as Gleizes's first non-figurative painting; and letters of Metzinger's addressed to Gleizes in New York, which attack the possibility of non-figurative painting, suggest that this possibility (already indicated in *Du 'Cubisme'* in 1912) was very much on Gleizes's mind at the time.[15] Nonetheless, in reflecting on the development of 1920, we can see that such nearly non-figurative paintings as the *Portrait d'un médecin militaire*, the *Chant de guerre*, the *Cruche Lorraine*, all of 1914, are still highly dependent on their subject: it is the presence of the unified subject that enables us to feel them as an organic unity. It is only in 1920 that Gleizes begins to have the means to realise a form that will correspond fully to the nature of the canvas and that will work as a natural, visually interesting organism in its own right, without reference to anything outside itself. The 'object' is almost manifest.

During this important period of 1920/21, Gleizes was closely associated with Jacques Villon, eldest of the Duchamp brothers. On his return to Paris, Gleizes moved into a Paris apartment which belonged to Mme Gleizes, but Villon also gave him the use of his brother Raymond Duchamp Villon's studio in Puteaux. Jacques Villon's work at the time shows close parallels with that of Gleizes. He says that, while serving in the army, he had become interested in maps, and especially in the use of contour lines to convey the idea of depth on a flat surface. The map maker could be said to imagine the mountain as a series of planes superposed on top of each other.[16] The device of superposed planes is typical of Villon's work at this time when he too seems to have reached a point of complete abstraction. 'Abstraction' is the right word because, normally, he 'abstracts' from a figurative basis – often an analysis of a subject in movement after the manner of his brother Marcel's *Nu descendant un escalier*, though in a visually much more satisfying manner.

The parallel between Gleizes and Villon is reinforced when we realise that, until *La Peinture et ses lois*, Gleizes is still preoccupied with the problem of depth. He has abandoned perspective, but he still sees the third dimension, achieved by means other than those of perspective (perhaps like the map-maker's contour lines), as a necessary characteristic of painting, related to the need to address the 'infinite' capacity of the soul. This idea of depth still lingers even in *La Peinture et ses lois*, but by this time Gleizes knows that it is by entering the realm of time and rhythm that the 'finite' painting can speak to the 'infinite' soul.[17]

7

PARIS AFTER THE WAR – 2

The period between 1919 and 1922 was also a very active period for Gleizes outside the immediate development of his painting. It sees him attempting to establish an artists' union as a means by which artists could defend their spiritual freedom against the depredations of the merchants. The scheme is given at the end of *L'Art dans l'évolution générale*. The period also sees him becoming involved with the Socialist and pacifist journal *Clarté*; and with Raymond Lefebvre and Paul Vaillant-Couturier, soon to be founders of the Parti Communiste Française.

In this, Gleizes shows himself still faithful to the impetus given by the Abbaye de Créteil. If the members of the Abbaye in 1907 were, with the exception of Henri Martin Barzun, disinterested in political activity, they still shared a moral earnestness and a concern for the social relevance of their work that contrasts with the mood of the 'cénacles' or coteries which Gleizes abuses so freely throughout *L'Art dans l'évolution générale* – the believers in 'art for art's sake', or in sensuality as a stimulus to artistic endeavour. And, together with Gleizes, we recognise in *Clarté* the names of René Arcos, Charles Vildrac, Georges Duhamel and Berthold Mahn. Indeed, Duhamel and Jules Romains were among the first directors of the international movement, *Clarté*. At about the same time, Albert Doyen, the musician of the Abbaye, founded the Fêtes du Peuple, with a view to re-establishing a popular basis for the arts. Gleizes was involved in helping to launch the Fêtes du Peuple in Lyon.[1]

Gleizes believed in 'élites' – that those who devoted their lives to pursuing a particular discipline were the best judges of that discipline and should be respected as such, even if they appeared to be going against the public taste. But the élite, in Gleizes's eyes, still exists for the sake of the people as a whole; they have a social function, which is to raise the general level of the quality of life, spiritual and material.

The attempt to form an artists' union was, according to the *Souvenirs*, Gleizes's first project on his return to Paris. The aim was to secure the control by artists of the art market. It was, in Gleizes's view, the lack of solidarity among artists that had enabled the merchant to gain control over the sale of their works. The subjective preferences of the merchants – non-specialists – had become the criteria of excellence, and the merchants used the critics – also non-specialists – as publicity agents. This was a theme that was to remain dear to Gleizes all his life and indeed its origins go back to the days of the Abbaye de Créteil.

The union would decide a minimum price for the artist's work based on its dimensions, and it would control the merchant's profit margin. 'It follows from this that the merchant would once again become uniquely a merchant, not an inspired prophet' (*L'Art dans l'évolution générale*, p.275). The union would ensure that the artist received a percentage on subsequent sales of his work. He hoped that it would eventually gain control over the sale of past works of art and be able to ensure the distribution of works of art of value to small towns. 'The corpses must not be allowed to swallow up the living' – the state should buy old works of art to clear the way for new ones. The union would initially be funded by subscribers, but eventually also by a percentage on the sales of paintings. This would enable it to help artists in the case of illness, accidents etc. The artist was in a similar position to the worker, except that society recognised the need for the latter's work, but the need for the spiritual element represented by the artist was not recognised:

> A new age of cathedrals is opening for anyone who knows how to understand the tremblings, the advance signs that announce the birth of a god. The human race has suffered too much from the materialism in which it has fallen; it must find peace in love, it must believe in something other than what falls directly before the evidence of the senses, something other than the worn-out consolations of the Church, where the divine has become the prey of merchants. (p.278)

It is hardly necessary to say that Gleizes was unsuccessful in establishing his artists' union. He says he attempted to launch it at a series of meetings in the Closerie des Lilas, where he read his *L'Art dans l'évolution générale* text. The better-known artists who had established their links with the galleries stayed away. Léger expressed interest in private conversation but did not turn up to the meetings. A committee was formed but Gleizes himself soon lost interest because of the *beaux-arts* conservatism of his colleagues, and he turned to more radical circles.[2]

Among those who supported the artists' union project were Alexandre Mercereau and the writer, Carlos Larronde, curator at the Musée Balzac. According to Mme Gleizes, it was through Larronde that they met the Polish painter, Mela Muter. She was engaged to the novelist, musician and Socialist orator, Raymond Lefebvre, and it was through him that the Gleizes' entered the *Clarté* circle. Mme Gleizes also says that an old friend of hers, the American Professor Ida Treat, was married to Paul Vaillant-Couturier, a prominent member of the *Clarté* group. Ida Treat was a palaeontologist and had thus come to know the young priest, Pierre Teilhard de Chardin. A small group was formed which included the Gleizes, Vaillant-Couturier and Teilhard de Chardin, a combination of names which is, to say the least, intriguing. Mme Gleizes comments that she and Gleizes were worried about 'compromising' Teilhard by drawing him into their political circle, but they soon realised that he was perfectly capable of compromising himself without any help from them.[3]

The *Clarté* group had been formed in 1919 by Henri Barbusse as a movement for international reconciliation. The Gleizes' had already wanted to meet Barbusse on the strength of his highly influential anti-war novel, *Le Feu*, published at the end of December 1916. In 1917, Barbusse had formed the Association Républicain des Anciens Combattants, with Lefebvre and Vaillant-Couturier. *Clarté* itself had an international directorate which included, in addition to Romains and Duhamel, Thomas Hardy, Upton Sinclair, H. G. Wells and Stefan Zweig. Initially it was simply pacifist, opposed to the Western intervention against Bolshevik Russia, but during 1920, largely under the influence of Gleizes's friends Lefebvre and Vaillant-Couturier, it became itself increasingly Bolshevik in character.[4]

Although *Clarté*, both as a movement and as a magazine, was clearly intellectual in its orientation, it was involved in organising large-scale meetings and demonstrations, which Gleizes said he greatly enjoyed. He was especially impressed by Vaillant-Couturier, soon to be a leading figure in the Parti Communiste Française. Gleizes said of him 'I immediately had the feeling of being in the presence of a rare personality, and of having found what I was searching for'. Vaillant-Couturier came from a Catholic background and Mme Gleizes says that he had been intensely religious prior to the war; she insists that she always saw an essentially religious fervour in him.[5] Lefebvre came from a Protestant background and was, according to Gleizes, more introverted: 'Paul drew you along after him; Raymond made you think'.[6] Lefebvre was drowned in suspicious circumstances while returning from the founding Congress of the Third International in 1920.

The year of Gleizes's closest involvement in politics, 1920, was an exceptionally important one for the development of French Socialism. The war had seen a dramatic shift in France towards large-scale industrial production and by January 1920, the main federation of unions, the CGT, had over 2,000,000 members (compared to 600,000 in 1914). It was still dominated by the revolutionary syndicalist tradition which believed in direct action by workers and was suspicious of political parties. We may imagine that Gleizes would have been sympathetic to this syndicalist tradition, derived from Proudhon rather than from Marx. In May 1920, however, the CGT was pressed into calling for a General Strike in support of the railwaymen's union, which was firmly suppressed by the government. After three weeks, it was called off. Many of the strike leaders were imprisoned and 22,000 railwaymen lost their jobs. It was a terrible blow to the CGT which, by Spring 1921, was reduced to 650,000 members according to its own figures. Edward Mortimer states that it took fifteen years before trade unionism again became a force to be reckoned with in France.

The end of the war had also seen a large increase in the membership of the Socialist party, the SFIO (Section Française de l'Internationale Ouvrière) founded in 1905 by the Marxist, Jules Guesde, and the former radical, Jean Jaurès. The SFIO had, like all European Socialist movements, been badly split between those who supported the war effort and those who opposed it. In 1920, its political life was dominated by quarrels between those who wished to affiliate to the Third International, run by Moscow, and those who supported the renewal of the old Socialist Second International. The increase in membership was not translated into an increase in parliamentary seats, largely owing to the introduction of the 'list' system of voting, which favoured the anti-Socialist 'Bloc Nationale'. The 'Chambre Bleu Horizon' of 1920 was, according to Mortimer, the most right-wing parliament France had known since the 1870s.

The SFIO split at the Congress of Tours in December 1920, when the supporters of the Third International won a majority and went on to form what was to become (in October 1921) the Parti Communiste Française. Despite his friendship with the Communists, it is reasonable to attribute Gleizes's withdrawal from political circles in 1921–2 at least in part to the harsh and apparently arbitrary discipline imposed by the Third International in these years.[7] However, the series of articles he published in *Clarté* in 1920 already show a wide divergence from the main direction which his friends were taking. According to Mme Gleizes, the articles aroused strong objections among the *Clarté* circle (though the only reaction I have seen published in *Clarté* itself was a highly favourable one from a group of supporters in Lyon, probably connected with Doyen's Fêtes du Peuple, and perhaps including César Geoffray, the musician, who was to be closely associated with Gleizes in the 1930s). Gleizes summarises his argument in the *Souvenirs*, showing why the *Clarté* readership might have objected to it: 'I tried to present the general direction of the social transformations taking place as a return to the traditional religious spirit. In the Russian Revolution of October 1917, I wanted to see the seeds of a reappearance of this spirit, still burdened with irritating hangovers from the past, but already active.' He says that Lefebvre and Vaillant-Couturier both supported him.[8]

His argument was broadly that as the war had revealed the inherent rottenness of the old economic order, a new economic order such as that demanded by the radical Socialists was indeed necessary. But the Socialists still had an old mentality; they had a spiritual outlook that belonged to the bourgeoisie, essentially that of the French Revolution. A spiritual revolution, as radical as the economic revolution, was necessary. In the intellectual sphere – in painting, in poetry and in science – it was already taking place in a very piecemeal fashion, but insofar as the Socialists had noticed it they had opposed it, despite the acceptance of the radical painters in Russia itself.

Vers une époque de bâtisseurs was published in five parts, but the sequence was interrupted first at the time of the General Strike, then at the time of the Congress of Tours. A sixth, concluding, part was promised but did not appear. There was nothing by Gleizes in the heavily Bolshevik *Clarté* of 1921, but that he was still approved of is suggested by two articles in December 1921 by André Gybal. The first, called 'Les tendances de l'art moderne', is a defence of modern art based on a rather watered down version of Gleizes's views on the need for construction and rhythm. Architecture is praised because it is its nature 'to represent eternity', though, for Gybal, doubtless more of a 'materialist' than Gleizes, this is to do with its solidity. The second article is an enthusiastic account of the modernist tendencies at the Salon d'Automne, which Gleizes was busily denouncing in the pages of *La Vie des lettres et des arts*. The article finishes with a long interview with Gleizes, which repeats the main ideas of *Vers une époque de bâtisseurs*, especially condemning the return to classicism that was becoming the fashion, led by Severini, in Rosenberg's circle. Referring in particular to the imitation of Ingres, Gleizes comments: 'Seriously, those who try to do this do not have either his reasons nor his humility, faced with the external forms of the Renaissance.' Gybal finishes by praising 'an extraordinary still-life' by Gleizes at the Salon d'Automne. 'It is, I think, serenity itself . . .'.[9]

As late as 1923, an article by Gleizes – *L'Art moderne et la société nouvelle* – was published by the *Monitor of the Socialist Academy* in Moscow. Gleizes's eccentricity with regard to the Socialists in this period should not, perhaps, be exaggerated. As we have seen, *Clarté* started with very wide terms of reference – the desire for radical change which would render a war such as the 1914–18 war impossible. Gleizes's desire for a spiritual/religious renewal was not necessarily alien to it, especially given his continued anti-clericalism. The Bolshevik leader who features most prominently in the pages of *Clarté* was Lunacharsky, Lenin's Commissar for Education. Lunacharsky had been prominent among the so-called 'God-builders' – a Bolshevik grouping which was atheist but which nonetheless developed a metaphysical system, of which Lenin disapproved. In 1908, Lunacharsky had defended Bolshevism on the grounds that it was based on faith as against the materialist Mensheviks. He saw Marxism as a 'religion', albeit a religion without God.[10] Barbusse did not join the Communist Party until 1923, but even then, when he became one of the most loyal Communists, he was accused of mystical tendencies. In 1927, he wrote a 'biography' of Jesus – *Les Judas de Jésus* (in which the disciples kill Jesus when He refuses to declare Himself the Son of God). Alexandre Mercereau, replying to the attack on the Abbaye de Créteil by the Action Française supporter, 'Jean Maxe', talks of:

> that Communism of which Christ was the instinctive and inspired prophet; the Communist Christians the millenarian example; Karl Marx at present the best-known theorist; Tolstoy the most powerful pioneer; Lenin the most mystical practician [*réalisateur*]; Trotsky the most realistic organiser; the crooked dealings of the powerful and their war the richest and most nourishing of fertilisers, the most undeniable ferment.[11]

Even after it had fallen completely under the control of the Third International, the French Communist tradition allowed a considerable degree of latitude to sympathetic writers and intellectuals, beginning with the strange relationship that was established with the Surrealists. *Clarté* itself, to Barbusse's disgust, fell into the hands of the Surrealists in 1925 (in 1927, after Trotsky's final defeat in the Russia at the hands of Stalin and Bukharin, it became the shortlived Trotskyist *La Lutte des classes*).

Gleizes's mediaevalism – his evocation of the cathedrals and of the 'revolution' which he believes occurred in France in the ninth century – may seem to strike an odd note in a French context, given the strong association between the romantic mediaevalism of Châteaubriand, de Maistre and Montalembert with a still-powerful Roman Catholic Church. But read in an English context it immediately suggests William Morris, one of the founders of the Social Democratic Federation, the first British Marxist grouping. And we will again be reminded of Morris when Gleizes turns against industrial production in all its manifestations. Gleizes's refusal of any party affiliation recalls Romain Rolland, the main target of Jean Maxe's attack on the Abbaye de Créteil, and a close associate of Barbusse's in 1919. Rolland quarrelled with Barbusse in 1921–2 over the latter's increasing commitment to Bolshevism. He was himself strongly attracted by Indian mysticism,[12] and this left-wing mysticism is very much the atmosphere that pervades the journal with which Gleizes was to be most associated in the period – *La Vie des lettres et des arts*.

•

In the course of his *Clarté* articles, Gleizes is obliged to admit that if the Socialists have not appreciated the spiritual revolution, those involved in the spiritual revolution have not appreciated the importance of the material revolution; that Cubism had been taken up by the 'right', that 'the decrepit and constipated spirit of the boulevards needed a certain rejuvenation and has now turned to the condemned painters'.[13] A leading agent of this marriage of the avant-garde and the 'grande bourgeoisie snob' was Gleizes's old friend, Jean Cocteau. Throughout 1916, Cocteau had become especially friendly with Picasso and had introduced him to the aristocratic circle of the Comte and Comtesse de Beaumont. In 1917 he wrote an article for the journal *L'Excel-*

sior in which he argued for an alliance between 'right-wing' money and 'left-wing' art. The year 1917 also saw the production, on Cocteau's initiative, of the ballet *Parade*, with music by Satie and sets and costumes by Picasso. Picasso had replaced Gleizes as Cocteau's main Cubist mentor.[14]

Mme Gleizes says that she had greatly liked Cocteau prior to the war but that after the war he took himself far too seriously as the arbiter of Paris fashions – without attending to really serious things such as the need to implement Wilson's Fourteen Point Plan. Gleizes, she tells us, detested his lifestyle – the life of the Paris bars and night clubs. Gleizes 'had an insurmountable horror for drugs and alcohol', and wrote to Cocteau to formally end the contacts between them, against Mme Gleizes's protests.[15]

According to Pierre Alibert's account, based on his conversations with Mme Gleizes, this was a very serious incident for the Gleizes'.[16] Juliette felt at home in the Paris café life, and still enjoyed the brilliance and wit of Cocteau's circle. Gleizes, however, insisted that if she did not break off the contact as well, he would leave her. Subsequent accounts by people who knew the Gleizes' well in the 1940s sometimes represent Gleizes as a rather henpecked husband, over-submissive to Mme Gleizes's whims. But it should be remembered that Juliette Roche made an enormous sacrifice when she accepted and agreed to co-operate with her husband's idealism which was to take them ever further away from the intellectual and cultural coteries of Paris in which she had been brought up. Intellectually she accepted and defended Gleizes's arguments but it is doubtful if she ever felt entirely at ease with them.

Gleizes, too, sacrificed much in breaking off his friendship with Cocteau at a time when friendship with him was a key to financial and social success. That Gleizes, as Cocteau's first Cubist friend, rejected the possibilities that were open to him, says much for the seriousness of his attack on fashionable 'snob' art. There is a rather sad little letter from Cocteau to the Gleizes', dated August 1920, in which he says: 'They tell me you no longer like me. But I never believe what people say and, myself, I like you and embrace you.'[17]

•

Mme Gleizes was equally unhappy about the confrontation which took place in 1920 between Gleizes and the Dadaists, led by Francis Picabia and the poet, Georges Ribemont-Dessaignes. Gleizes had two articles in Picabia's magazine, *391* – the first in June 1917 and the second, *Voyage circulaire*, affirming 'LA LOI UNITE DIEU', in December 1919. In the pages of *391*, his calls for a constructive art, equivalent to the cathedrals, and for a return to the religious spirit seem even odder than *Vers une époque de bâtisseurs* in the pages of *Clarté*. In fact, even before the second article had appeared, Ribemont-Dessaignes had already attacked him in the pages of *391*, in November 1919, ridiculing his seriousness and his commitment to the well-being of the working class. The attack was renewed in February 1920, after Gleizes had voted to exclude the Dadaists from a proposed revival of the pre-war Section d'Or group.

For Gleizes, the revival of the Section d'Or was another attempt to instil a sense of collective purpose among the artists. The artists' union was to deal with purely practical interests, disregarding the question of tendencies and movements. The Section d'Or had been the name under which the Salon Cubists and their immediate circle (without Le Fauconnier and Delaunay) had exhibited in 1912. This immediate circle had included Picabia, who had also featured in the illustrations of *Du 'Cubisme'*, and Gleizes, always anxious to establish the credentials of the Cubists as a team, continued to list Picabia among the group. It seems that Gleizes had agreed that Picabia and his friends could give readings at the proposed Section d'Or exhibition but that this decision was challenged at a meeting in the Closerie des Lilas on 25 February, when it had become clear that the provocative methods of the Dadaists would attract all the attention of the public, at the expense of other, more serious contributions. Gleizes changed sides and voted with Braque, Léger and Laurens against them. Hans Richter in his account says that Gleizes changed his mind after seeing a small work by Max Ernst, probably his *Hypertrophic Trophy* which was submitted for the exhibition and refused. Mme Gleizes gives Marcoussis, Archipenko and Survage as among those who voted against the Dadaists (Picabia, Breton, Soupault, Dermée and Tzara).[18]

The Dada attack on Gleizes included an extraordinarily cruel 'interview' given by Metzinger to Tristan Tzara and published in *391*.[19] Mme Gleizes also came under fire, to her great annoyance. She had only recently been mentioned in an article by Picabia as being, in contrast to her husband, at 'the Dada hour' in company with Alfred Stieglitz, Gabriel Buffet, Marcel Duchamp, Tristan Tzara, Hans Arp, Jean Crotti and Manuel De Zayas (Gleizes appears in the same article, outside the Dada hour, in the company of Marie Laurencin and Metzinger).[20] She says that she had done everything in her power to prevent the confrontation, and especially to prevent Gleizes from launching into a powerful polemic against the Dadaists, *L'Affaire Dada*, in the pages of the journal, *Action*.

L'Affaire Dada is a comprehensive demolition of the Dadaists – not on the grounds that they are frivolous, which was part of their programme, but on the grounds that they are safe. They do not challenge the existing order of things in any substantial way. They represent simply the existing trend towards individualism pushed to its logical conclusion: 'The presentation of the Dada work is always full of taste, the paintings reveal charming colours, all very fashionable, the books and magazines are always delightfully made up and rather recall the catalogues of perfume manufacturers.' They boast of their individuality, but they do not have the internal resilience or self confidence to live and work alone. 'They cannot live alone. They seek the crowd, in which they believe. They are flat on their bellies before it, or else they engage in all sorts of clowning in order to coax catcalls or invective from it.' They had enough taste and intelligence to come close to the worthwhile trends 'but their total lack of a constructive faculty has kept them in a distrustful relationship to those trends. Their works have always been the blurred image of a face whose architectural determinant they did not discern.' They persuade others who lack any constructive ability that it doesn't matter – anything will do. They talk about instinct, but the instinct of animals is a simultaneous translation of command into execution, not a mere, useless disordering of the senses. Nonetheless, although they claim to deny everything *a priori*, 'we must, in spite of that denial, which strikes me as rather premature, recognise that they are full of conviction when it comes to those ornaments with which babies are made and which they so love to toy with'.[21]

Dada, in Gleizes's view, was the artistic equivalent of modern-day capitalism, and this is why it had so quickly become acceptable. We may note in passing that Gleizes had a rather different attitude to Surrealism. He disliked it very much but did not engage in polemics with it. In the 1930s, he specified his differences in an essay, *Cubisme et surréalisme, deux tentatives pour redécouvrir l'homme*. The very title shows that he recognised a seriousness of purpose in Surrealism, just as he recognised a seriousness in the despair he attributes to Duchamp.

Gleizes was invited to write *L'Affaire Dada* for the journal *Action* by its editor, Florent Fels. Fels was also editor of *L'Art vivant* which, as Green shows, had a commitment to the social role of painting – its involvement in 'real life' – that complemented that of Gleizes, except that it argued for a realism which the people could understand and accept. It stood, in fact, for the kind of 'social art' that Gleizes was attacking in the pages of *Clarté*. Mme Gleizes says that Gleizes's relations with Fels were good, but we may speculate that Fels, thoroughly committed to his expressionist realism, was not unhappy to see dissensions develop in the old avant garde.[22]

•

If Gleizes sits oddly in the pages of *391* or *Clarté*, he found a much more congenial home in *La Vie des lettres et des arts*, which was to publish many of his most important articles written between 1920 and 1925, including *La Peinture et ses lois*. *La Vie des lettres et des arts* was connected with the publisher and gallery owner, Jacques Povolozky, who was to be Gleizes's – and Mme Gleizes's – publisher until the early thirties. Povolozky specialised in Russian literature, but it is interesting to note (in an advertisement placed in *La Revue de l'epoque*, March 1922) that his list includes Kautsky's *Terrorism and Communism*, part of his series of highly perceptive and prophetic Marxist attacks on the Russian Revolution, together with works by A. Axelrod, another Socialist leader who opposed the Revolution, V. N. Lvov, a minister in the provisional government who left Russia after the Bolsheviks took power, and A. Denikin, one of the leaders of the White military campaign.

A series on the poetry of different nations entitled *Les grandes Anthologies* was edited by Alexandre Mercereau, and Povolozky published Mercereau's 'fairy tale', *La Conque miraculeuse*, with illustrations by Gleizes. These were woodcuts, and the work of turning them into woodcuts was done by A. P. Gallien, who features prominently in the pages of *La Vie des lettres et des arts*. Povolozky also published a book by Barzun – *La Fondation de l'Europe, 1916–1920*, an ambitious attempt to summarise the whole experience of the war, calling for a united Europe on the basis of a radical new social order.

Gleizes held a one-man show in Povolozky's gallery in 1921 and Jacques Villon, with whom Gleizes was very closely connected at this time, exhibited there in 1922. We may speculate that the connection was formed through Mercereau, who had also been Gleizes's connection to Eugène Figuière, publisher of *Du 'Cubisme'*, of Apollinaire's *Les Peintres cubistes*, and indeed of the whole circle connected with the Abbaye de Créteil. In his very embittered epilogue to *L'Abbaye et le bolchévisme*, Mercereau complains that the Abbaye group, which had now become just another self-serving clique, had exploited Figuière ruthlessly.[23]

La Vie des lettres et des arts does not especially reflect the influence of the Abbaye, but it includes among its contributors – in addition to Mercereau – Carlos Larronde who, we have seen, played a role in introducing Gleizes to the

Clarté circle. It was edited by the poet Nicolas Beauduin, who had been connected with the Cubists since before the war.[24] The painters who wrote for it include – in addition to Gleizes – André Lhote, Picabia, Kupka, Mondrian, and Ozenfant. In January 1921 – at a time when it carried a cover designed by Gleizes – an address by Ribemont-Dessaignes given at a Picabia exhibition held in Povolozky's gallery declares that 'Bouguereau was certainly a much more perfected painter than Matisse, Cézanne or Albert Gleizes's (a statement with which, taking the word 'perfected' in a very mechanical sense, we may well agree). Jean Cassou, soon to become a leading intellectual in the Communist movement and later curator of the Musée d'Art Moderne de la Ville de Paris, is a frequent contributor. In particular, he inveighs against the emphasis of Gleizes and Lhote on the need to develop an objective theory of art, arguing that art must be essentially anarchic. This may be the first time that Gleizes and Lhote are bracketed together as the 'theorists' of Cubism.

As a magazine of poetry, *La Vie des lettres et des arts* had a very definite character, largely determined by Beauduin and by his friend, the Polish mystical poet, O. V. de L. Milosz.[25] Both wrote on an epic scale, seeing poetry as the link between man and the universe – poetry as the means of developing a genuinely universal vision, not just little day-to-day insights. There are frequent references to René Ghil, who was still living (he died in 1925),[26] and who is praised by Gleizes in *Vers une Époque de bâtisseurs* as 'the man who possesses the laws and can reveal them to those worthy of initiation . . .'.[27] Ghil had been present in Gleizes's mind at least since the time of the Abbaye de Créteil and, to prepare for developments that are about to come, it may be worth pausing here to consider him in some more detail. He had made his mark at the end of the nineteenth century with the publication of his *Traité du verbe* in 1885. We have already seen that at this time he was associated with Mallarmé but that he separated from him in protest against his attachment to the ideal of the earthy paradise – to 'Eden'.

The *Traité du verbe* went through several editions with radical changes until the final version of 1906, under the title *En Méthode à l'œuvre*. The changes took him progressively away from Symbolism towards what he regarded as a rigorous science of poetry. *L'Œuvre* was the title of his life's work, a vast epic which aimed to cover the history of the universe, broadly following the evolutionary theory of Darwin but with the emphasis on the development of thought in matter:

> While the science of Origins spins about our heads like the whirlwind of stars which the eternal stream eternally becomes, see how – not knowing that our sensations can only provide materials for the Idea that tries, through its waves of Intelligence in the greater than unity-science, to reproduce in itself the Universe and its rhythms – nearly all the poets are but the degenerate leftovers of the rhapsodies of pleasure and sadness, and philosophers who cannot do without Eden.[28]

Ghil is not easy to translate but we can already see a relation with Gleizes in the rejection of sensuality and the insistence that, through our senses, an Idea, which is objective and greater than the individual consciousness, is attempting to reflect the universe by means of rhythm. Ghil had an enormous admiration for the great religious poems of India and, through the discoveries of modern science, he believed that such an epic vision was again becoming possible: 'our modern knowledge which, I believe, has but rediscovered the meaning of the sacred by which, under a monstrous symbolism, the Initiates, in occult fashion, carried the burden of the people.' (p.203)

Ghil was greatly taken with the work of the nineteenth-century German physicist Hermann von Hemholtz on harmonics in music – that each note carries with it a series of barely audible harmonics which determine its character. Since words too, like musical notes, are vibratory, Ghil argued that they too had their harmonics:

> A poetic work, for me, is only of value if it prolongs in suggestion the laws that order and unite the total-being of the world, evolving according to the same rhythms – "there is a universal meaning in every letter [*caractère*]", as Goethe says'. (p.227)[29]

Everything is in vibratory movement: 'So, matter does not exist. And, in the perpetual diversity of its way of producing itself, which is movement, from eternity to eternity, without limits – it comes into existence.' And this imposes the necessity for 'a work of art which will itself be movement – movements of thought'. Following Helmholtz, 'the instrument of the human voice is, with varying notes, a reed – completed with a resonator, with varying possibilities of response' (p.228). To have some idea of the importance of this emphasis on movement and vibration, and the full weight of the word 'resonator', we will have to know something of Gleizes's relations with Charles Henry, who – in conjunction with Seurat and Signac – was elaborating his own scientific theory of the visual arts, also much influenced by Helmholtz, at the same time as Ghil was writing *En Méthode à l'œuvre*. Ghil also evokes a universal circular movement that in itself is perfect and cannot evolve without departing from its own perfection. It evolves through developing into an ellipse. Here again, we can only evoke these notions whose full relevance to Gleizes will be indicated later, again especially after passing through Charles Henry.

So Ghil called for a poetry which overthrew the classical norms but which was still to be rigorous and 'scientific' in its principles, drawing on the scientists' realisation of the importance of waves, vibrations and movement, as opposed to the inertia of matter in classical mechanics. This poetry, for all its modern, scientific nature, was a return to an earlier conception of poetry, oral, rhythmic, epic, which Ghil believed (as did Gleizes) was also based on a science, known to an inner circle of initiates. The voice of this poetry was not the voice of an individual but the voice of the universe itself, seeking to know itself through thought, through human consciousness. The distinction between matter and spirit was a false distinction. 'Spirit' is matter conscious of itself. Consciousness without matter is nothing; matter without consciousness is nothing. Again, as we shall see, we are close to Charles Henry, who claimed to have identified, in addition to what he calls 'gravitic resonators' and 'electromagnetic resonators', a level of 'biological resonators', which he identified with life and consciousness. Gleizes's language at this time evokes such concepts. It is not until later that he will be able to express clearly what he has drawn from them.

One other name associated with *La Vie des lettres et des arts* should be mentioned. This was Edouard Dujardin, like René Ghil an important figure in the late nineteenth century, who has since been largely forgotten. In 1885, he founded the *Revue Wagnérienne* in conjunction with Wagner's son-in-law,

Houston Stewart Chamberlain, best-known as a theorist of racism. Dujardin claims to have been the first theorist of free verse, a claim disputed in the 1920s by Gustav Kahn who worked with and succeeded him in the 1880s as editor of *La Revue indépendante* (not to be confused with the shortlived journal which was later to publish one of Gleizes's first articles, on Metzinger, in 1911). Gleizes often expresses his admiration for Kahn, and was soon to remark that free verse had been at the origin of Cubism.[30]

The 'Wagnerian' element in this epic vision of art and poetry, with its correspondences between the arts, established according to common rhythms, is evident (and is drawn out in an article on Ghil published in *La Vie des lettres et des arts* in July 1920). In the 1920s, Dujardin was editor of *Les Cahiers idéalistes* which published Gleizes's *Individualisme* and *Originalité collective*, both in 1921. Mme Gleizes had a particular fondness for him and, in the 1930s, the Gleizes' published his play, *Le Retour éternel*, at Moly Sabata. I mention him here to stress the late nineteenth-century origins of Gleizes's thought – in Renan, in Ghil's rejection of Symbolism, in the enthusiasm for a 'total art' which may be associated with Wagner (though I have never seen Gleizes refer to Wagner as such and it is unlikely that he would have favoured Wagner's luscious sensuality), in Verhaeren's poetry of modern life. The 'Epic Cubism' of 1911–12 is part of this same current and, though Gleizes's pictures of the 1920s look very different ('serenity itself' as Gybal said in *Clarté*), Gleizes never abandoned it. He is part of a continual movement (perhaps the only part still going forward by the 1930s) whose origins can indeed be traced back to René Ghil.[31]

Part Two

1920–34

8

PAINTING AND ITS LAWS

The year 1921 finished with what was perhaps the most important external event of this whole turbulent period – the arrival on his doorstep in Paris, one rainy night, of two quite unknown Irish art students, Evie Hone and Mainie Jellett. They were to be Gleizes's first pupils and it was in teaching them that he was forced to clarify his thought sufficiently to be able to write *La Peinture et ses lois*.

So far, we have seen Gleizes, who always insisted on the 'collective' nature of artistic activity, working and disputing with painters and writers who, rightly or wrongly, considered themselves to be equals. Increasingly from now on we will see him as a 'master' surrounded by pupils. This aspect of Gleizes life is lightly ridiculed in Metzinger's anecdotal memoirs:

> The canvas on its wooden stretcher before the first stroke of the brush; the frame which was to isolate it and to justify the more or less thick and diversified coloured coating it would receive, these were the elements that would enable Gleizes to fulfil himself. They are, moreover, the only real things the painter meets while exercising his art. It was enough for him [Gleizes] to practise on the rectangle he had before him several very simple operations in elementary geometry to enable a rhythm, a poetic means of expression, to appear. Such a method obliged its inventor to seize the idea of the picture, something he could not have done without such help [*une telle méthode obligeait son inventeur à saisir l'idée d'un tableau ce qu'il n'aurait pu sans secours*]. In fact, he enjoyed, or suffered from, a spiritual abundance that left him with no choice in the matter. Of course it could only work for him alone. I didn't like to tell him. Already his religious generosity was leading him towards proselytism. He dreamed of forming pupils . . .
>
> I had measured the difference that separated art prior to 1900 from the art which I felt was being born. I knew that all instruction was at an end. The age of personal expression had finally begun. The value of an artist was no longer to be judged by the finish of his execution, or by the analogies his work suggested with such-and-such an archetype. It would be judged – exclusively – by what distinguished this artist from all the others. The age of the master and pupil was finally over; I could see about me only a handful of creators and whole colonies of monkeys. But I could not ask Gleizes to see it that way. Happily, nothing of his social or mystical opinions remained when he was engaged in the work of painting. The work of reconciling an oval and a lozenge, a yellow and a blue, prevailed and saved him.[1]

I have quoted this passage in full because it expresses so well one of the common assumptions of much thinking about modern painting. By contrast, we have already seen Gleizes declare that: 'If . . . Cubism cannot be raised to the level of a principle, of laws, in such a way as to be capable of transmission . . . then it will not have reached its end'.

Nonetheless, Gleizes was very reluctant to take pupils at this time. He describes his first encounter with the Irish women in a *Hommage à Mainie Jellett* written after her death in 1944. They asked to become his pupils: 'What you do corresponds exactly to what we are looking for.' He knew nothing about them and had no intention of taking pupils: 'I already have all the problems in the world trying to sort myself out personally, how do you want me to help you?' They said that they were currently studying with Lhote and Gleizes tried to evade the responsibility by saying that Lhote was his friend and he did not want to rob him of his pupils. They replied that they had a right to choose their own master. Eventually, he gave way before their persistence. Mme Gleizes adds that the Allendys, René and Yvonne, were visiting at the time and were present during the conversation. When Hone and Jellett had left, they said that, since Gleizes was now taking pupils, he could take Yvonne's sister, Colette, as well. Victor Poznansky, who had known Mme Gleizes since 1912, heard about it some days later and asked to join the group. Colette Dumouchel-Nel was later to marry René Allendy after her sister's death, and she became director of the influential Galerie Colette Allendy in Paris.[2] Victor Poznansky, son of a wealthy Polish banker, sank much of his own private fortune in 1925 into organising the exhibition 'L'Art d'Aujourd'hui', the first serious attempt to present an international survey of non-representational art in Paris.

Mainie Jellett and Evie Hone came from similar wealthy Anglo-Irish Protestant families, based in Dublin. Jellett's father was a prominent barrister, involved in Unionist politics; Hone's father was a businessman and a Director of the Bank of Ireland. The two women met and became lifelong friends at the studio of Walter Sickert in London. They went to Paris together in 1921 to study with Lhote, and together they turned to Gleizes.

It is not clear what attracted them to Gleizes. Bruce Arnold, in his excellent biography of Mainie Jellett, quotes her as saying that she wanted to go further in the direction of 'extreme Cubism' and he speculates that she was attracted by the radicalism of Rosenberg's circle, which Lhote had abandoned. He also quotes Anne Dangar, a later pupil of Gleizes's, as saying that they had seen Gleizes's paintings prior to meeting him, and that 'they had a construction which reminded them of the Irish books of the seventh century in the University of Dublin.' They may have seen the exhibition Gleizes held in the Galerie Povolozky in Spring 1921.[3]

At any rate, it was a remarkable and courageous choice, since the general mood in Paris, including that of the circle around Rosenberg, was hostile to non-representational painting. Lhote in particular emphasised the importance of the subject, and they continued to work with Lhote for some time after starting to work with Gleizes. Whatever the initial reason, it was to be the beginning of a lifelong commitment on the part of the two Irish artists. Mainie Jellett was to describe it as the 'third' – and definitive – 'revolution' (after Sickert and Lhote) in her life. It was also very important for Gleizes. Referring to *La Peinture et ses lois* in the *Hommage à Mainie Jellett*, Gleizes says: 'I owe it to Mainie Jellett and to Evie Hone'.

La Peinture et ses lois begins with an apocalyptic vision of the present state of the world:

> We are living in an extraordinarily interesting time. It seems that we are dragged along by a current of unheard of power which flings against a rock men and their works as if for the purpose of wiping them out and destroying their memory forever. We see the wrecks pile up of shattered groups of human beings and nothing can persuade us that it won't be the same for us tomorrow. A madness seizes those who feel themselves irresistibly drawn into the maelstrom. Their actions, instead of stopping or protecting them, seem to move with the current and to push them further into its headlong flow. Those who are aware of the phenomenon speak of the danger that civilisation is in, but remain unable to understand what is causing it. Humanity, caught in a panic, acts as it usually does in such circumstances. It splits into ever smaller groups, each of which accuses the other of having provoked the catastrophe, gets caught up in it, and is finally swept away. Unknown forces have begun to move. Men's own wishes have little enough importance in the march of events; something very basic breaks the resistances and initiatives of individuals; the final overthrow is but a matter of time.[4]

There exist several rough drafts of *La Peinture et ses lois* all beginning with this same passage or something like it. It is his response to the war; to the Treaty of Versailles and its treatment of the defeated enemy which shocked him profoundly; and also, perhaps, to disillusionment with the Communist movement, since by June 1922 the Parti Communiste Française, formally constituted in October 1921, had already revealed its spirit of absolute devotion to the rough and apparently arbitrary discipline imposed by the Third International.

But Gleizes's anxiety is more than just political – enormous as the issues raised by the war and the Revolution were. In the early twenties, he wrote reviews of the Paris salons in *La Vie des lettres et des arts*, in which he argues that the chaotic state of modern painting reveals that mankind is undergoing a spiritual crisis. It is, in a sense, the coherence of the human soul that is at stake.

We have already seen Gleizes pointing to 'the cathedrals' as representing the collective, integrated spiritual effort he wants to see in the 'age of builders', to borrow the title of his *Clarté* articles. He is looking back to the Middle Ages. Even in *La Tradition et le cubisme* of 1913, he took 'the cathedrals' as his starting point. In this case, the 'tradition' he evoked was a French popular realist tradition that he traced from the cathedrals, through Fouquet, 'our most glorious ancestor', Chardin and Courbet to the Cubists. It was a polemic against the influence of the Italian Renaissance but it enthusiastically invoked an earlier French Renaissance in the thirteenth century, corresponding to the transition from Romanesque to Gothic. But in the New York writings, particularly *Le Miracle du 5th Avenue* and *L'Art dans l'evolution générale*, we see that the whole period between 'the cathedrals' and the present day is characterised by the triumph of a 'spirit' opposed to the spirit of the cathedrals. Gleizes is no longer seeking continuity with a tradition that passes through the last six or seven centuries. He is seeking to renew with a tradition which is dead. He is beginning to develop his quarrel with the Renaissance.

But it is still vague and impressionistic. *La Peinture et ses lois* is much more concrete. In it, Gleizes argues that the central idea giving coherence to Western civilisation and to the constitution of the individual soul was Christianity; that Christianity was a 'science' – a whole philosophy which situated man in relation to God, the individual consciousness in relation to the universal consciousness; that there must have been a time in which Christianity manifested clearly the truth that was in it; that it is obvious that by the Renaissance, by the sixteenth century, Christianity was hopelessly corrupt and had been in a state of disintegration for some time; therefore, if we seek a period when Christianity was rising rather than declining, we must go back earlier, to the period that is characterised in the English language as the 'Dark Ages', the period prior to the twelfth century.

I believe that this is the first time Gleizes draws the distinction, which would be crucial to the rest of his life, between Romanesque and Gothic (though he does not use the terms). He is no longer content simply to counterpose the Middle Ages and the Renaissance. He now sees clearly that the Renaissance has been prepared in the Middle Ages and that 'the cathedrals' do not make a uniform spiritual witness. Between the church or cathedral prior to the thirteenth century and after the thirteenth century – between Romanesque and Gothic – there is a considerable difference; this difference is seen clearly in painting. The conventional history of painting (enthusiastically repeated in Severini's *Du Cubisme au classicisme*) begins with Cimabue in the thirteenth century. Prior to Cimabue, everything is 'primitive' – charming perhaps, but in the way that children's drawings are charming. Cimabue of course is still primitive and 'stiff', but something more sophisticated is beginning to appear; and it becomes clearer still with Giotto at the end of the century and the beginning of the fourteenth century. What is this sophisticated thing? It is the ability to imitate the external appearances of nature – the ability to convey an illusion of three dimensions on a two-dimensional plane.

In his 1932 lecture *Art et religion*, Gleizes says that at about this time he began to realise that Cubism was retracing the history of art backwards. The Romanesque painters, and indeed Cimabue himself, had mastered the art of painting on a flat surface. Giotto and his immediate successors had introduced an illusory aspect, but the illusion was not total. Their first concern was to tell a story and each incident in the story occurred in its own 'space', each space determined by its own perspective point or even, since the illusory aspect was still of secondary interest, several perspective points. This was a phase of 'multiple perspective'. With Uccello, the whole painting was organised round a single perspective point.

This was accompanied by the development of a very sophisticated science – the science of optics. One only has to read the treatises of Alberti or Leonardo to realise the complexity of the theory that underlay Renaissance painting. From the point of view of Severini, this science was definitive. Severini sees the science of painting as a matter of representing the subject as we see it and not as we know it (the reverse of the formula for explaining Cubism that was developed by Metzinger and Apollinaire). This could only be done through a precise knowledge of the mathematical principles of perspective. In a passage that is heavily marked in Gleizes's copy of *Du Cubisme au classicisme*, Severini says:

> Effectively, before and during the twelfth century, the geometrical laws which the Greeks had developed to a very high level were almost entirely

forgotten. Only the Byzantines still possessed some of them but clearly only as a 'formula' . . . Before him [Giotto], art was merely decorative and the forms only had two dimensions . . . (p.39)

For Severini, then, the perfection of the scientific knowledge of painting was realised with Leonardo and Dürer. After them, painting degenerated into sensuality and individualistic self expression in which the objective – mathematical, rigorous, intellectual, spiritual – principle was lost.

Later, Severini, rejecting the arguments advanced by Peter Lenz, a monk of the German Benedictine monastery of Beuron, says that it is impossible to go back to the Primitives, the Egyptians or the Orientals because 'Painting, in the true sense of the word, came after them, and we cannot ignore this fact.' The Greeks were the first painters. They invented the perspective mechanism 'precisely with a view to realising a synthesis of plan and elevation, to express space in such a way that mind and senses would both be satisfied. The Egyptians, Hindus, Chaldaeans etc are decorators. The Byzantines who inherited the means of the Orient are decorators too and only the genius of Giotto was later able to bring the plastic art back to the West once it had fallen into oblivion after the Greeks.' (p.75)

This is effectively the view of history that has prevailed in western Europe since at least the seventeenth century. A certain level of knowledge and enlightenment had been achieved by the Greeks and was consequently manifest in the largely Greek-influenced culture of Rome. Then Humanity (since in this view of things Humanity has its highest development in Western Europe) falls into darkness until the Renaissance, or the period immediately preceding the Renaissance.

It is a view that is, to say the least, unfavourable to Christianity which must, reasonably, be seen as a catastrophe, since its triumph more or less coincides with the fall of the Roman Empire and the end of the free development of Greek classical culture. Yet this historical perspective is broadly accepted by the Western Christian churches themselves. Neither Roman Catholicism nor Protestantism have any profound historical memory of the 'Dark Ages' (say, between the sixth and twelfth centuries). Both have a lively memory up to the great debates on the Trinity and the work of Augustine in the fourth and fifth centuries, but the Roman Empire is still alive at this time. Both see the succeeding period as a blank period in which nothing of great importance happens until the thirteenth century and Thomas Aquinas, in the case of the Roman Catholic Church; and the sixteenth century and Luther in the case of the Protestants.

What is surprising, and indeed revolutionary, in Gleizes's thought is that he sees this 'empty' period between the sixth and the twelfth centuries as the period in which the truth of Christianity asserts itself. The destruction of the Roman Empire was not a catastrophe to which Christianity contributed, as Gibbon might argue, nor an accident that happened to accompany the rise of Christianity, as a Christian apologist might argue. It was a positive achievement on the part of Christianity. 'A monumental fact such as Christianity cannot be born of a mere error; it would not have been able to hasten the fall of the Roman Empire if it hadn't been based on unquestionably true foundations' (p.4).

Gleizes regards Byzantium, which preserved the Roman Empire, with some suspicion. For Gleizes, Christianity found its natural home among the barbarians and it was complemented, not contradicted, by the rise of Islam:

> the violent influence of the new, living, eastern abstract vision introduced by the Muslims marks the beginning of western[5] Christian art. The remnants of the Greek-Latin ideas are wiped out by new Christian ideas of construction. The Arab art is not opposed to the spiritual state of Christianity which is developing as a Catholic faith with the help of the barbarians. The arithmetical art of the Arabs harmonises with the first impulse of Christianity which, likewise, is based on numbers. The new Merovingian and Carolingian development gives a new life to representational art by treating purely plastic principles as being of equal importance with the natural forms and images taken from the world about them. When I talk about representation, I am thinking of something rather more than simply the appearances of things. It is precisely as a result of our failure to disentangle the real meaning of the painter's work in its dualism – spiritual and material – that we have established the one-sided myth of what we insist on calling ignorance. The word primitivism hides, under an elegant title, contempt for a form that is considered childish by those who think they have brought it to its fullest possible development. On the basis of this calculation they are keen to believe that the laws governing the painter's work have been fixed for all time. (p.6)

In the 'Dark Ages', then, painting is dominated by its purely plastic principles, which are based on numbers and proportions. The illusory representation is secondary. It is sufficient that we know what is being symbolised. In the case of Muslim art, it is eliminated altogether. Because we cannot separate the idea of art from the idea of an illusory representation, all we can see in early Christian painting is an inadequate illusory representation. The whole contemplative, or 'rhythmic' aspect of the painting, which is purely plastic and based on numbers, and on a science as rich and complex as that of the Renaissance, escapes us. This is because we are entirely materialistic, which is to say that we are only interested in the external appearance of phenomena in the universe; we have no understanding of the inner, rhythmic principle of life and intelligence, including our own intelligence. This rhythmic principle begins to be lost between the twelfth and the thirteenth centuries:

> The painting of the Middle Ages was seen as something that raised the soul. The head of the man who looked at it was raised and the mind followed, or submitted to, the unfolding of the rhythm without the intervention of any little optical tricks. But the painting which is prompted by the desire to establish resemblances, in which the imitative element intervenes, cast the verticality which dominated the eleventh century down, and created an artificial, illusory ambiance out of a geometrical projection that robbed it of its true nature. Three centuries were necessary before the work of the painter evolved from the law of rhythm to the law of perspective. Instead of the painting with a centre, moving round this centre, the Renaissance saw a collection of external images gather together on the line of the horizon. The man who looks at an eleventh century wall-painting is drawn into its spiralling movement. The rhythm seems to start from him, to belong to him, to expand around him in concentric waves. It is the stone which falls into the quiet water and brings about the waves which each produce the other. The stone is the action which is conveyed to the water – lifeless matter which awaits the command. (p.18)

The change that takes place between the twelfth and thirteenth centuries can be seen most easily in two fields – art and philosophy. In art it sees the gradual emergence and triumph, between Cimabue and Uccello, of the imitative principle (based on external appearances) over the purely plastic principle (based on 'rhythm'). In philosophy, the period is marked by the great debate between 'Realism' and 'Nominalism'. Realism argues that the categories of thought – Beauty, Justice, Equilibrium, Harmony etc. – are real, pre-existent and eternal; things are beautiful, just, balanced, harmonious to the extent that they participate in the real nature of Beauty, Justice, Equilibrium, and Harmony, which can be understood as ideas in the Mind of God. Nominalism, on the other hand, argues that they are only 'names' and have no existence outside the beautiful, just, balanced or harmonious object that presents itself before the senses (Gleizes would later call it the 'subject'). For the Realists, only the Universal is 'real'; for the Nominalists, only the particular is real. The debate took the form of a confrontation between Plato (who, mediated largely through Boethius, dominated the thinking of the 'Dark Ages', at least from the Carolingian period), and Aristotle, largely introduced via Islam in the twelfth century. Once Aquinas had succeeded in 'baptising' Aristotle, the way was open for the triumph of Nominalism which, in Gleizes's eyes, was a reversal of the Christian principle.

The advance of Nominalism coincides with the advance of the perspective principle in painting, and with the development of the Church into a political institution seeking temporal power. The change is completed by the sixteenth century, and the world is ready for the development of modern physics, which is entirely based on the observation of the external appearances of nature. Gleizes was later to comment that Auguste Comte's division of the intellectual history of Europe into three successive phases – Theology, Philosophy and Science – had always struck him as a self-evident truth.

With this difference, of course, that he saw it as a regression rather than a progress.

But the key word in all this – the characteristic that distinguishes the religious, Christian culture prior to the twelfth century from the materialist, Humanist culture that followed it, is the word 'rhythm'. Although the word appears in Gleizes's earlier writing, it is, in the use he now makes of it, a substantially new development in his thought.

We have seen Gleizes frequently puzzling over the possibility of movement in painting. Both *Du 'Cubisme'* and *La Tradition et le cubisme*, in reaction to the Futurists, talk about 'plastic dynamism'. The letter to Florent Schmitt in 1914 gives the image of the concentric circles made by a stone thrown into the water that we have just seen again in *La Peinture et ses lois*; the letter to Barzun of 1916 invokes the endless pulsating movement of 'the enormous Broadway'. In one of the pieces in *Le Cavalier de dimanche* ('Bals Mornes III – Génie', dated New York 1917, and clearly written in a state of great depression) he says: 'There are always the same images around my new self, the same immobile images that now I hate, the same images which, however, I played with, only a very few centuries ago.'

This is a protest against the immobile Renaissance image. If, as I have suggested, the New York paintings represent an abandonment of principle on Gleizes's part, it is under the pressure of the desire, still dictated by the 'subject', to capture the energy and movement of the city. In *Art et Religion*, Gleizes gives 'our artists' despair as we compared our fixed and frozen images with the bustling images that succeeded each other on the cinema screen' as one of the motives that led to the period of multiple perspective.

But immediately prior to *La Peinture et ses lois*, Gleizes seems to have reconciled himself to the essential immobility of painting. *La Peinture et ses lois* poses the question: 'How can a flat surface be brought to life?', and answers: 'By endowing its space with rhythm.' The same question is posed in the essay *Choses simples*, published in October 1921, but the answer is very different:

> By using the principles of perspective considered in relation to the surface – not imposed on it with a view to projecting an external representation of the world. The present day problem turns on this solution. The plastic revolution which has been developing for over ten years has no tendency other than to realise a clarification of the truths of perspective – the mechanism of the eye.[6]

'Life' is identified, not with movement, but with the organic unity of the painting that is true to is own nature as a two-dimensional space but which, without losing this reality, can realise depth, through the superposition of planes. This is an application of the principle of perspective that respects the real nature of the plane, unlike illusory painting, which imposes a reality which is essentially alien to it.

A similar idea is given in *La Mission créatrice de l'homme dans le domaine plastique* of December 1921, where he invokes: 'The rational application of the perspective law, which no longer sustains a crude illusion based on imitation, but evokes a possibility of spatial depth on the canvas, in harmony with our system of vision'.[7] And in *Des 'ismes' – vers une Renaissance plastique*, published in April 1922, thus on the very verge of *La Peinture et ses lois*, he asserts bluntly that the idea of movement had to be abandoned. He criticises the Futurists' longing for 'dynamism' and then proclaims in bold capitals that: 'THE CHARACTERISTIC OF OUR PRESENT AGE IS A SURE DEVELOPMENT TOWARDS REST AND SILENCE. The mistake of Cubism and Futurism was that they did not see it. The arts are tending towards reflection [*recueillement*] and meditation, which demand immobility and silence.' He relates this to the whole development of technology in the age whose tenden-

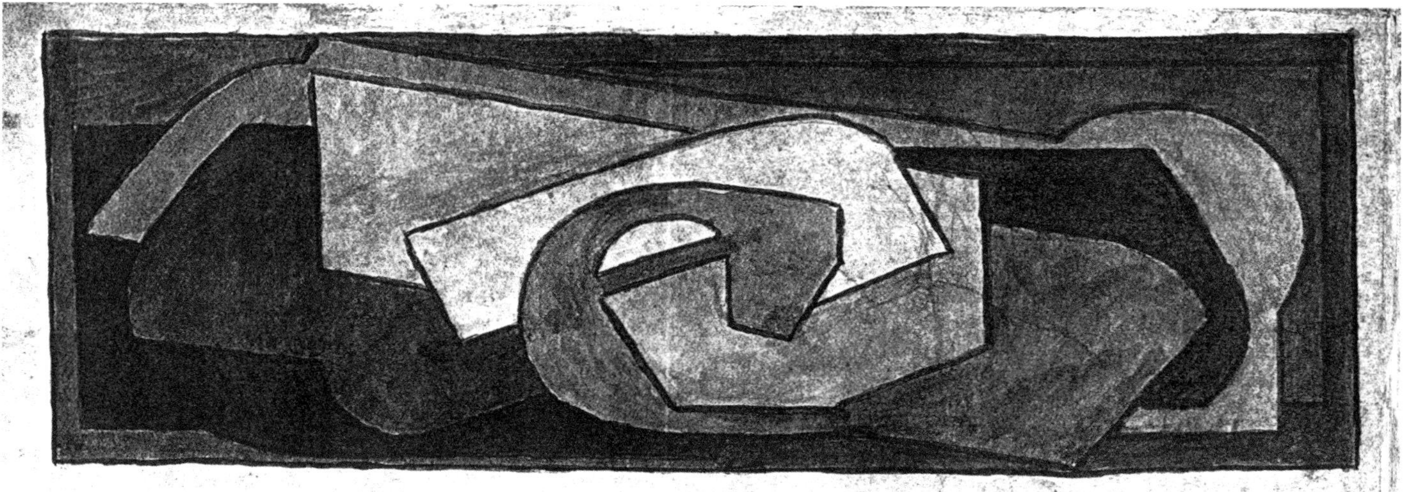

49. Mainie Jellet, *Drawing in Long Rectangle*, c. 1922. Sepia ink on card, 7.6 × 23 cm. Private Collection

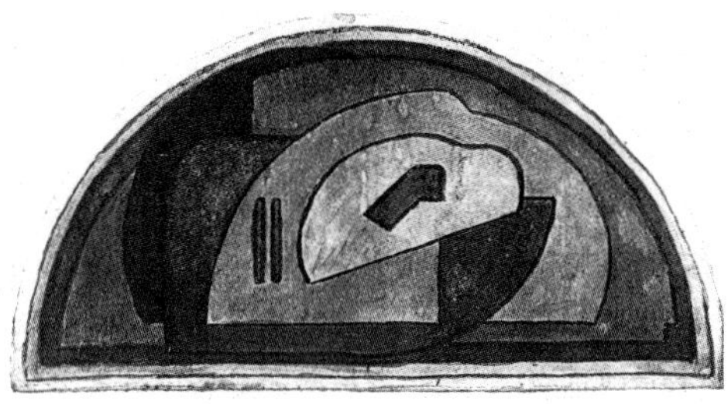

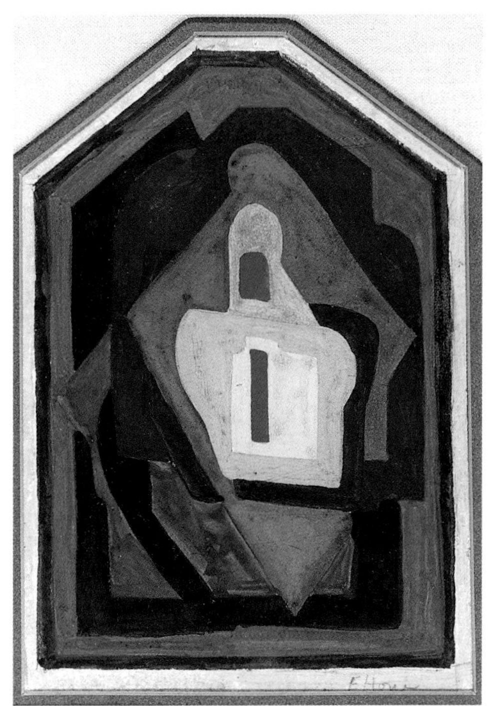

50. Mainie Jellet, *Drawing in a half circle*, *c.* 1922. Sepia ink on card, 10.5 × 20.5 cm. Private Collection

51. Evie Hone, *Abstract Composition*, *c.* 1922. Gouache, 18.5 × 12.7 cm. Private Collection

cy is to reduce human movement, human muscular activity:

> Man has seen his agitation reduced in favour of his immobility . . . The means of communication, post, telegraph, telephones, have brought human muscular movement to a halt and demand silence . . . the possession of the world takes place by virtue of the laws of an economy of human muscular movement, while the mental – individual and collective – develops in silence, enriching itself by perceiving the laws of the universe more exactly.[8]

We are far from the letter to Barzun and 'the enormous Broadway', but there is a remarkable similarity, especially in this use of the word 'economy', to the contemporary thought of Kasimir Malevich in Russia. In his *God has not been Deposed*, also published in 1922, Malevich argues that the development of technology is an attempt to do away with the body altogether, to become entirely spiritual and to emulate the condition of God on the seventh day, when He rested from His labours.[9]

Consequently, when Mainie Jellett and Evie Hone began to work with him, Gleizes was arguing for an essentially immobile painting, identifying immobility with meditation and using the superposition of opaque planes instead of conventional perspective as a means of invoking depth. Mainie Jellett has left us a rich documentation in the form of sketches, gouaches and drawings on tracing paper, through which the course of her work with Gleizes – and, consequently, of Gleizes's thinking – can be followed through the 1920s. The earliest of these, doubtless going back to the beginning of 1922, are simple arrangements of sometimes slightly bizarre planar shapes placed one on top of the other, sometimes with the 'depth' between one plane and the other emphasised by a false shadow. There is a conscious attempt to interweave the forms. But there is no method in it. It is still an empirical, hit or miss affair (Plates 49 and 50).[10]

Gleizes himself refers in the *Souvenirs* to his own lack of method at this time:

> Around 1920, my practice was ahead of my intellectual opinions. I sorted myself out sufficiently to make things presentable. But with regard to theory, that is to say, to the lucidity of my acts, I had not got very far. I've already said what forced me to become conscious of this activity – those young painters who came asking me to teach them. I had necessarily to

> explain myself to myself before being able to explain it to others; from the practice I had to disengage the theory. It was a particularly hard pregnancy, passionately exciting, but exhausting. At the end of it, I knew clearly what I was doing – I was able to follow the process of my plastic act. Consequently, this action became capable of being taught, passed on in its principle.[11]

Hone and Jellett worked with Gleizes from December 1921 to March 1922, when they left Paris, but Hone returned in June. She wrote back to Mainie to say: 'I went out to Gleizes yesterday, getting there at one. I never arrived back till after 7 o'clock. He was most excited over his book. He began writing it just after we left and he says he can't sleep at all at night it is so enthralling.' Gleizes set them (Evie Hone and Colette Dumouchel-Nel, the future Colette Allendy) exercises, then 'he retired behind a barrier of pictures and wrote his marvellous book and forgot all about us . . .'.

She continues that Gleizes's teaching was much the same as it had been,

> except that if people ask 'what are the laws that the Cubists work on' that one could answer Rhythm and Spacing – space taking the place of the perspective that you see in pictures by Raphael etc – and obtained by placing one object over another – he said this idea of space was rather like Einstein's theory, do you know it? – I don't – he said the picture of the future the next generation would tend to more and more to be circular and revolve inside itself not like as in Giotto or in those things we have done which go in planes but like this [drawing of a spiral].

Gleizes referred to Leonardo's *Treatise on Painting* (which is frequently quoted by Severini) 'but he said L. was full of contradictions and so complicated that it would give you a *dégoût* for painting for ever to have to follow all those rules whereas the work he is arriving at is all based on Rhythm and repetition and is simple in itself . . .'[12]

Space and rhythm are the two basic categories given in *La Peinture et ses lois*. The science of Christianity prior to the thirteenth century is based on the knowledge of rhythm, which can be seen in the art. The science of the Renaissance, developing from the thirteenth century onwards, is focussed on space, hence the concern with perspective: its logical culmination is the aeroplane (foreseen, appropriately enough, by Leonardo). Space is to do with what is external to man: rhythm and movement are to do with life and spirituality, and hence with the 'contemplation' he had invoked in *Des 'ismes' vers une Renaissance plastique*.

The secret to understanding how rhythm and mobility can be part of a painting lies in a phrase in *Du Cubisme et les moyens de le comprendre*: 'A painting is a manifestation that is silent and immobile. The movement that it provokes can only exist in the mind of the spectator' (pp.30–1); and the particular importance that Gleizes attached to the 'mind of the spectator' may have been reinforced at this time by his relations with the scientific community, which had suddenly become very close. This had come about partly through Gleizes's political connections, and partly because he and Mme Gleizes had started visiting Cavalaire, then a sleepy fishing village on the Mediterranean coast. Among his political friends was the physicist Paul Langevin, and among the Summer residents at Cavalaire was Jules Drach,

Henri Poincaré's successor in the Chair of Celestial Mechanics at the Sorbonne.[13] Evie Hone says in her letter that Gleizes's 'idea of space was rather like Einstein's theory, do you know it? – I don't', and it happens that Gleizes, who had never previously shown much interest in science, had fallen in with the physicists at precisely the moment when Einstein's theory of relativity was beginning to attract attention. Paul Langevin in particular was active in introducing Einstein's thought in France.

Einstein's theory of relativity posed questions as to the 'absolute' nature of time and space, as we experience them. Without going into what he actually taught (Gleizes was later to argue that his 'space-time continuum' was actually a desperate attempt to restore the absolute nature of time and space as we experience them[14]), he was generally believed to have taught that our ideas of time and space are only relative, depending on the point of view of the observer. In December 1922, the French mathematician Charles Henry, whom we have already mentioned in our discussion of René Ghil, published an account of the theory of relativity in which he suggested that Einstein had not taken sufficient account of the point of view of the observer. He was, Henry argued, treating the phenomena he describes as if they could be known independently of the operation of the senses.[15]

Earlier in the same year, Henry published a series of articles under the general title *La Lumière, la couleur et la forme* in Ozenfant and Jeanneret's journal, *L'Esprit nouveau*. Henry's interest in aesthetic questions derived from his conviction that since the world could only be known through 'representations' in the mind, any attempt to express reality mathematically must take account of the human sensibility. Physics must become 'psychophysics' and must be prepared to consider the aesthetic sense – whether phenomena are pleasing or displeasing. Henry uses the terms 'rhythmic' and 'non-rhythmic', in relation to pleasing and displeasing, giving them a very precise meaning that is of great interest to the long-term development of Gleizes's thought.[16] Gleizes had known Henry since 1920 or 1921, and according to Mme Gleizes, Henry was impressed by *La Peinture et ses lois*: 'he offered to collaborate with Albert Gleizes with a view to clarifying what seemed to both of them to be the most important points'. They had many discussions, but the project was halted by Henry's death in 1926. Gleizes published an article in homage to Charles Henry in the journal *Les Cahiers de l'étoile* in 1930.

There is much that could be said on the relation between Henry's thought and that of Gleizes but the main point I want to make here is that, in the debate around Einstein, the idea is being expressed among the scientists that the object of our consciousness cannot be anything other than consciousness itself; that the external world, including the fundamental categories of time and space, only exist for us as a function of consciousness: 'there is nothing real except the coincidence of a sensation and an individual mental tendency . . . rationally speaking, we can only experience certitude in respect of the images which they produce in the mind', to quote *Du 'Cubisme'* (p.62); 'Everything we know is based on sensation', to quote Charles Henry's *Sensation et energie* (pp.160–1). Consequently, space and time too must be understood as categories of consciousness.

Neither Henry nor Gleizes were depressed by such thoughts, as if the world and its myriad wonders were to suddenly become a mirage. Nor did the idea imply that the world and its myriad wonders were entirely arbitrary and subjec-

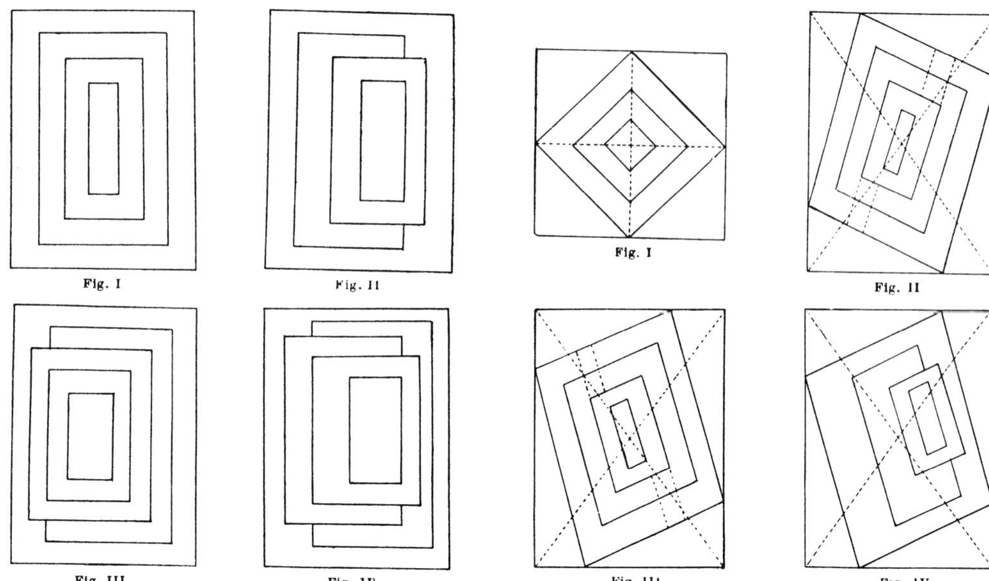

52. *Movements of translation of the plane to one side*, 1922–3. Illustration from *La Peinture et ses lois*

53. *Simultaneous movements of translation and rotation of the plane*, 1922–3. Illustration from *La Peinture et ses lois*

tive, which is what is suggested in the argument of *Du 'Cubisme'*. If Henry's arguments were accepted, consciousness itself was structured according to an objective, mathematical order. Gleizes saw in this emphasis on the objective nature of consciousness a sign that the scientists were rejecting Nominalist conceptions (by which the 'external' phenomenon is more fundamentally real than the idea) just at the time that the painters were overcoming their enslavement to the sense-based illusion of external space, as expressed in the theory of perspective. He says in *La Peinture et ses lois*: 'The ideas of time and space are those which have proved the most inspiring for the men of the present century. Painting has to reflect this passion if it is to discover new reasons for its existence.' (p.28)

Gleizes was very far from arguing that painting should be based on the discoveries of the scientists. He had been strongly opposed to the idea that painting had anything to do with non-Euclidean geometry, and he was certainly not now applying Einstein's theory of relativity, or even Henry's more directly relevant colour circle and 'aesthetic protractor'. It was the parallels between the directions taken by independent researchers honestly following their own particular discipline that interested and encouraged him.

Time and space are the basic categories in which we experience the world. Both are functions of consciousness. The sensation of space derives from the comparisons our mind makes between different magnitudes, shapes and colours – themselves all sensations. The sensation of time derives from the mental functions of memory and anticipation. It implies direction. Both these mental functions could be exercised by the painting. Consequently the painting, tissue of space and time, could stand in the same relation to the world, as the microcosm to the macrocosm (and in early drafts of *La Peinture et ses lois*, he calls this new painting a new 'naturalism').

Gleizes calls the distinctive operations by which the painter works with space and time respectively by terms that are derived directly from the language of physics (and which occur frequently in Einstein's theory) – 'transla-

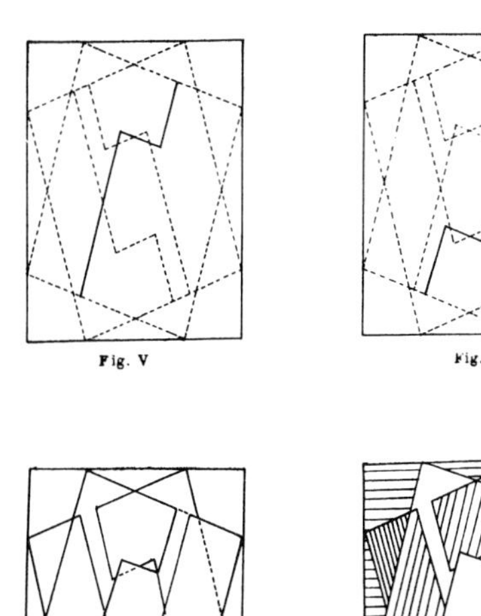

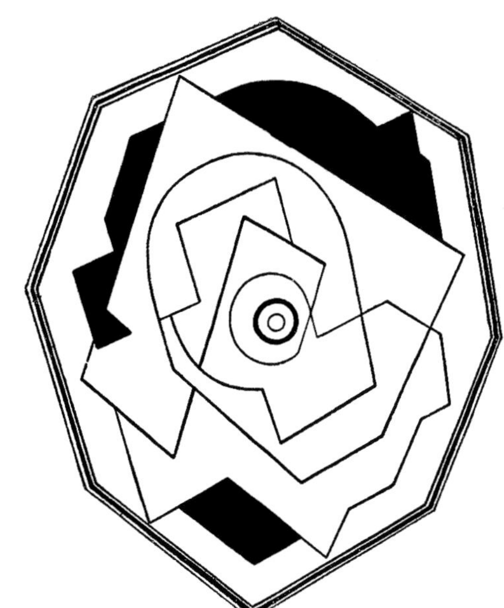

54. *Simultaneous movements of translation and rotation of the plane resulting in the creation of a spatial and rythmic plastic organism*, 1922–3. Illustration from *La Peinture et ses lois*

55. Illustration from *La Peinture et ses lois*, 1922–3

tion' and 'rotation'. In physics, translation is the movement of a body in relation to another body; rotation is the movement of a body in relation to itself. The Earth going around the Sun is moving in translation; the Earth turning on its axis is moving in rotation. This was not the first time these terms had been used by the artists. They appear with much the same meaning in Severini's essay *La Peinture d'avant garde*, published in 1917 and claiming to reflect ideas that were generally accepted among the painters Severini knew (Metzinger, Gris, Rivera et al).[17] Nonetheless, the terms were to become so central to Gleizes's thinking from the 1920s onwards that they may fairly be regarded as his personal property.

Gleizes illustrated the two 'movements' of translation and rotation with diagrams showing a simple repetition of the basic shape of the canvas or panel – in this case, the rectangle (Plates 52–55). Gleizes is anxious to show his two principles at work with the minimum of intervention on the part of the artist. In the translation, the eye makes a comparison between the different magnitudes of the shape of the rectangle repeated inside the initial form. It thus has the idea of space. In the rotation, the rectangles are tilted – to the right, to the left, and to right and left at the same time. This disequilibrium establishes a sense of direction. The angle between the vertical plane and the tilted plane creates the anticipation that the movement will continue in the same direction. The mind imagines and follows (in time) the displacements that have already taken place and that could take place in the future.

Gleizes shows how the two 'movements', the one suggestive of space, the other suggestive of time, could be woven together into one coherent, unified form – always with a minimum of intervention on the part of his own subjective tastes. Throughout the explanation there is a sense in which he is trying to say as little as possible, to remain at the highest possible level of generalisation, to leave the greatest possible liberty to the individual artist. But he nonetheless insists that if the painting is to live its own life, independently of forms borrowed from the natural world, then it must address the two most irreducible functions of perception, of the consciousness of the person looking at it – the sense of space and the sense of time.

Both of these are numerical; the sense of space, based on comparisons made between closed forms, is geometrical; the sense of time, based on a series of numbers in movement, is arithmetical. In practical terms this means that the artist's starting point must be the numerical proportions given by the surface he is working with – a simple relation of height and breadth in the case of a rectangle, though Gleizes illustrates *La Peinture et ses lois* with a most beautiful octagonal construction, and an interest in eccentrically shaped pictures can be seen in the earliest of Mainie Jellett's exercises. Everything in the painting must stand in some relation to that initial given proportion. 'Rhythm' is a matter of the recurrence with variations of one and the same phenomenon. Gleizes argues that in the painting it is, first and foremost, the recurrence with variations of the initial proportions given by the picture surface.

This emphasis on the limits of the picture surface as the element that gives birth to everything else is quite unique to Gleizes. Both Mondrian and Malevich in their different ways aspire to give a sense of spatial infinity that must transcend the limits of the painting, but for Gleizes, the sense of infinity could not be given by entering into infinitely large magnitudes (the line that, going beyond the picture area, could continue into infinity). The infinity with which the painter has to work is for Gleizes a function of the consciousness of the person looking at the painting and it can best be engaged by an unceasing movement of lines and colours. And this can only be realised within and on the basis of clearly defined limits. The moment the movement goes out of the frame, it stops, as it does in the case of any living organism once it is cut open, once its limits are not respected. The means by which spatial limits can be reconciled with infinite movement in time is the spiral which Gleizes invoked in his conversation with Evie Hone, but a spiral, or a circle that must be born from the static geometry of the initial proportions of the picture surface.

Kandinsky's *Point, Line to Plane*, begins with the point, not the plane, and indeed the plane, when he realises it, is not the whole surface of the picture but just another element (it could be a large point, or a thick line) to be placed on the picture surface. Of the picture surface itself and its proportions he has virtually nothing to say.

Gleizes sums up his argument with the formula: 'To paint is to give life to a flat surface; to give life to a flat surface is to endow its space with rhythm' ('Peindre, c'est animer une surface plane; animer une surface plane, c'est en rhythmer l'espace' – p.41). He was later to be very critical of *La Peinture et ses lois* and we will see why. But the book, vastly richer than any summary could suggest, is still the seedbed of all Gleizes subsequent development. If some of its formulations were to be abandoned, others were to lie dormant and only reveal their full meaning much later. He says that, in 1920, his theory lagged behind his practice; he was now, in 1922, to enter a period in which his practice became a slow, steady effort to realise the fullness of his theory.

9

BACK TO THE BEGINNING

La Peinture et ses lois was published in *La Vie des lettres et des arts* in 1923 and in Rosenberg's *Bulletin de l'Effort moderne* in 1924–5. A very short extract from the technical part – 'la mécanique nouvelle' – appeared in German in Herwarth Walden's paper *Der Stürm* in 1925. Jacques Povolozky, who published *Du Cubisme et les moyens de le comprendre* and later, *Tradition et cubisme* and *La Forme et l'histoire*, declined to publish *La Peinture et ses lois* as a book, and Gleizes had it published privately. Although it is of immense importance for Gleizes himself and for his immediate circle, it had little impact on the wider artistic world. It is doubtful if more than a handful of people understood it. His later pupil, Anne Dangar, reading it in Australia in 1929, already convinced that it contained the answers she was looking for, admits that she found it difficult.[1] Jacques Villon was attracted by it, but was already moving in a different direction.[2] The central idea of an analogy between Cubism and early mediaeval art would appear much less far-fetched in the 1930s than in the 1920s, but the Romanesque fashion of the 1930s was still unfavourable to the sort of precise thought and discipline envisaged by Gleizes. Eventually, as we shall see, the later development of the line of thought begun in *La Peinture et ses lois* was to have a marked influence on the development of Gleizes's old friend, Robert Delaunay.

For the moment, however, the book had the effect of confirming Gleizes's growing isolation from the Paris art world. Already in 1920 he had denounced the shift of the Cubist painters to 'the right', as they were taken up by the *beau monde*, influenced largely by the master of fashion, Cocteau. Christopher Green has commented on the luxurious aspect the Cubism of the 1920s was adopting, as the austere still-lifes of the pre-war period were garnished with bunches of grapes and exotic fruits; the open window showing a comfortable landscape began to appear; and *Commedia dell'arte* figures abound.[3] Writing about the Salon des Tuileries in June 1924, Louis Vauxcelles, the lifelong enemy of Cubism, rejoiced that 'Montparnasse Cubism is hardly the rage; and Cubism has also lost its charms for Picasso. Almost all that is left is the ferocious Albert Gleizes, whose stubbornness is unshakeable. Even Marcoussis, following the example shown by Juan Gris and Metzinger, is flirting with nature.'[4]

Green suggests that Gleizes was the only one of the Cubist pioneers who was to remain faithful to the end;[5] but it is probable that in the early twenties even the champions of Cubism would have been unhappy about the direction he was taking. In his articles on the 1920s Salons Gleizes remarks on how the superficial aspects of Cubism had become acceptable, but these were precisely the aspects he himself was trying to eliminate. To a painter such as Lhote,

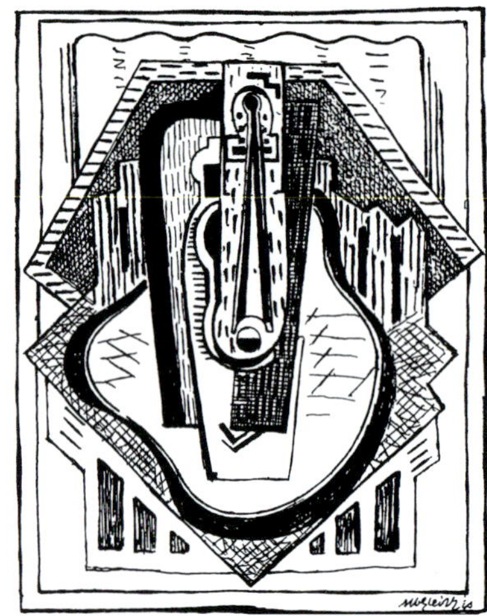

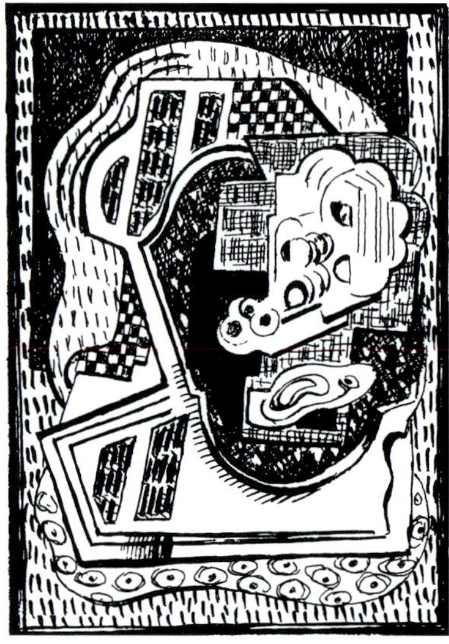

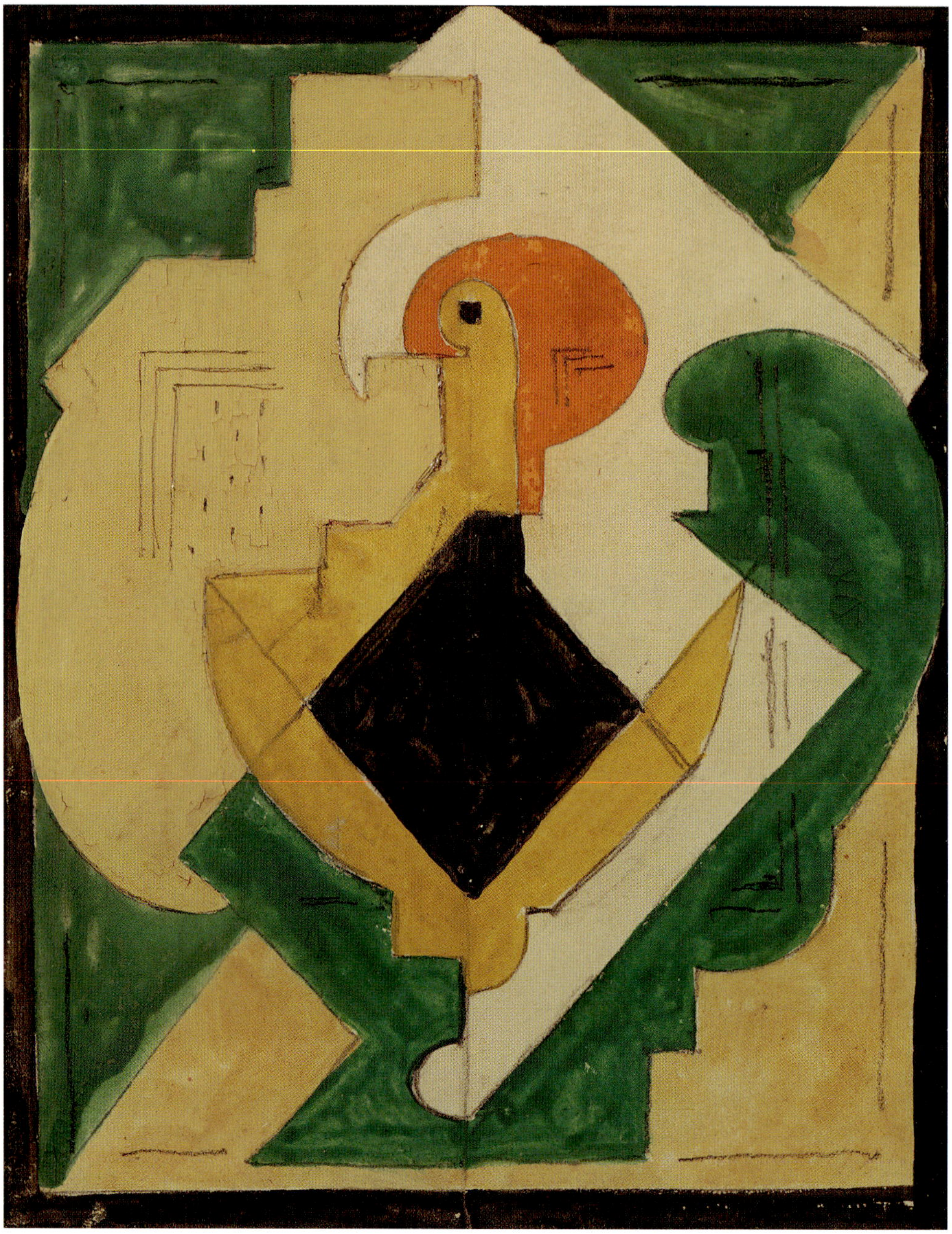

56. *Example of a drawing of a picture-object realised on the basis of the mechanism relating to the plane (free execution for a familiar painting)*, 1922–3. Illustration from *La Peinture et ses lois*

57. *Another example of a picture-object – free execution, familiar painting*, 1922–3. Illustration from *La Peinture et ses lois*

58. *Le Coq*, 1922. Gouache on paper, 17.5 × 13.5 cm. Present whereabouts unknown

who had praised Gleizes's wartime work as being a more human kind of painting than that of Severini or Juan Gris, it must have seemed that Gleizes was deliberately negating his own virtues.

The 'new mechanism' outlined in *La Peinture et ses lois* was still at a very primitive stage of development. Gleizes was confident that it was right in principle, but it was still far from revealing all its possibilities. In a letter written to Lhote in 1943, he says of this period:

> With a candour and audacity that now make me smile I dared to show, to exhibit, those poor efforts which, for all their sincerity, could not arouse

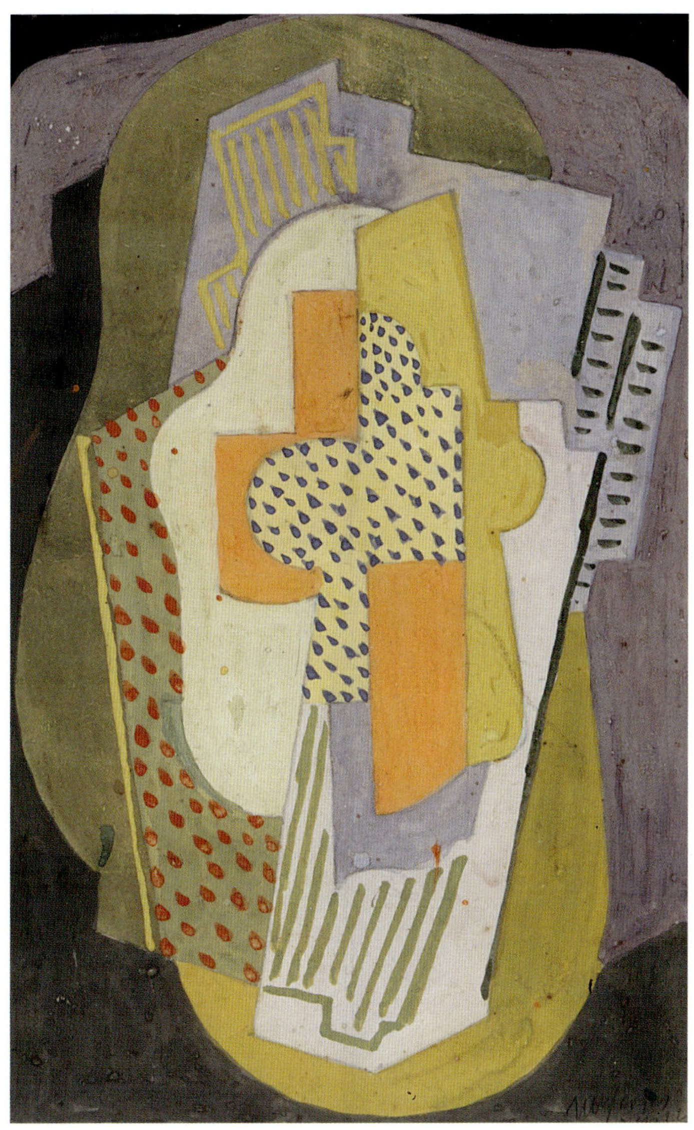

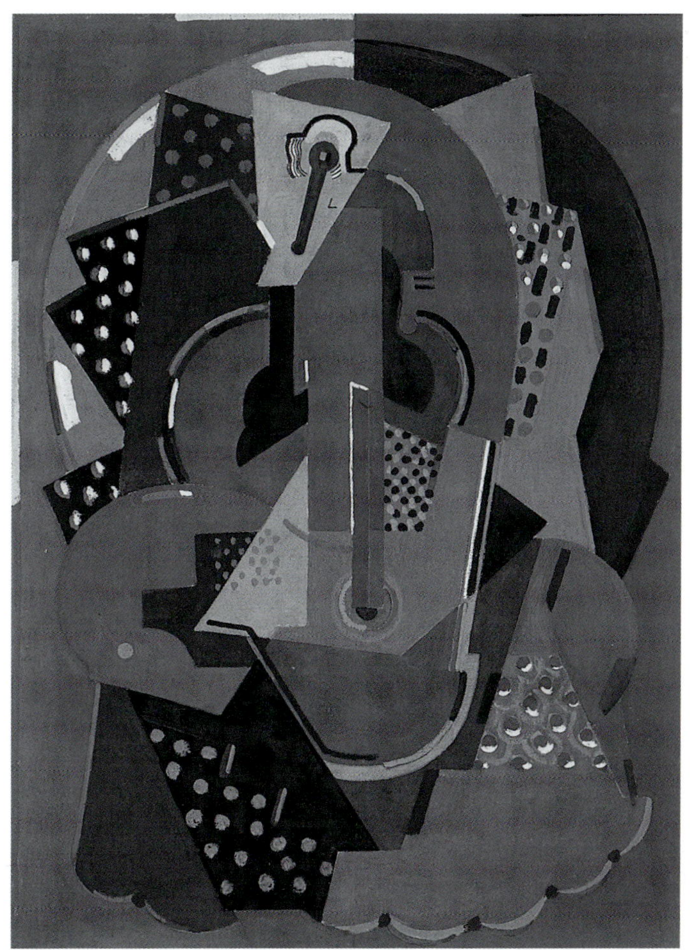

59. *Composition*, 1922. Gouache on paper, 27 × 17.5 cm. Fondation Albert Gleizes

60. *Ecuyère*, 1920–3. Oil on canvas, 130 × 93 cm. Musée National d'Art Moderne, Paris

> any sympathy for me, or any intellectual interest in the surrounding world. I was certainly made to feel it. Only faith kept me going.[6]

And at the time, in the essay *L'Art moderne at la société nouvelle* (in which he was still hoping that the conditions of the newly emergent Soviet Union would be favourable to the development of the new art), he said:

> At present the struggle is taking place on the slippery slopes of Reason and Argument. The most recent paintings and sculptures are in an intermediate stage between the new order in the process of formation but still broken down into its constituent parts, and aspirations which have no sense of direction or co-ordination at all. The best of them, those which come closest to the laws which are in the process of being discovered, are still too intellectual to really appeal to people who can only respond to paintings by means of their feelings, their tenderness.

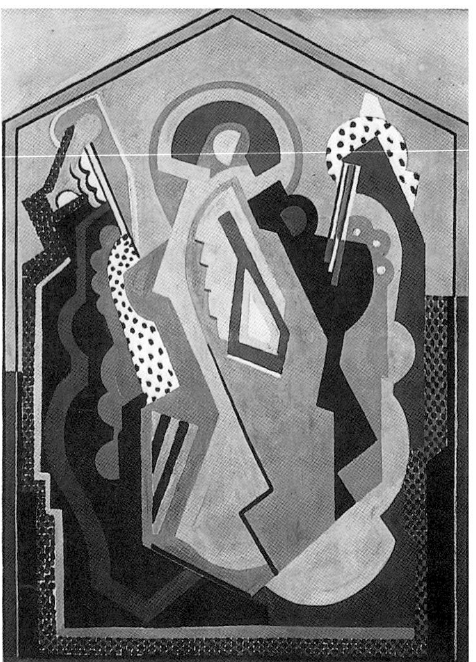

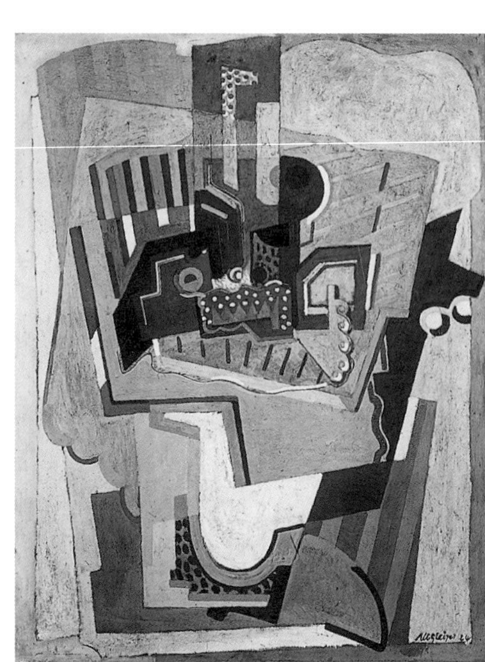

61. *Composition à trois éléments*, 1923. Oil on canvas, 193 × 144 cm. Private Collection

62. *Nature morte imaginaire (verdâtre)*, 1924. Oil on canvas, 101 × 75 cm. Wadsworth Atheneum, Hartford. The Ella Gallup and Mary Catlin Sumner Collection

> But this need not worry us. It is the fate of all work which rejects dead principles of organisation to achieve a new order whose life is only beginning. Basic principles take up all the artist's attention and therefore take on an importance in the external appearance of the work going far beyond the essential but internal role which they must play in what will finally be achieved. . . .[7]

Indeed, if *La Peinture et ses lois* marks an extraordinary step forward in Gleizes's thought, the work associated with it, that of 1923–4, does not immediately appear as a great improvement on the work of 1920–1 (Plates 56–62). In practice, all Gleizes has is the superposition of a number of plane forms, creating a – still three-dimensional – impression of space, together with the notion that by their inclinations to left and right, an element of 'time' or 'rhythm' can be introduced. The illustrations accompanying *La Peinture et ses lois* (plates 56 and 57), with the exception of the lovely *Octagonal Composition* (plate 55), are unconvincing. By the standards which Gleizes would later apply, following from the argument of the book, their organisation is arbitrary; they only bear an approximate relationship to the scheme of the 'new mechanism'. Two of them are called 'peintures familières' – familar paintings. In the *Souvenirs*, he describes the thinking behind the familiar paintings. As well as the austere organisation of planes, 'I made more approachable compositions, of the sort I called familiar paintings, in which the planes were loosened up with the lines, and in which picturesque elements broke the rigour of the law.'[8]

This indicated Gleizes's continuing desire for a more accessible, popular painting, one that would 'appeal to people who can only respond to paintings by means of their feelings, their tenderness'. At the same time, Gleizes made no fetish of abstraction and many of the paintings of this period contain representational elements – usually the human figure or landscape, sometimes using subjects that appear in his earlier work. There are also some 'imaginary still-lifes', perhaps conceived in a spirit of mockery against the association between Cubism and the still-life, which Gleizes had always resisted. What was important for Gleizes was that the starting point and end of the work was not the subject but the organisation of the painting. In this, he comes close to Juan Gris, who, however, adopted by Kahnweiler, was being tempted by the harlequins. For Gleizes, champion of the 'big' subject – 'the enormous Broadway' – the modesty of his subjects in this period marks a significant change. It is not any lessening of his ambition. On the contrary, where the painting of a subject copies a small part of the universe, the 'painting-object' was to stand in the same relation to the whole universe as the microcosm to the macrocosm.

•

An ambivalent attitude towards his 'laws' may be reflected in Evie Hone's letter to Mainie Jellett of June 1922, when he was in the full feverish enthusiasm of writing *La Peinture et ses lois*. She says:

> I really don't think one can keep the exact measurements 1 – 1/2 – 1/4 etc all through in working out the design. I do to start with, and for the very long lines, but not afterwards when I put in the curves, and I know he does not at all himself – as he took a design I brought and worked it out and showed it to me afterwards and he had not done it a bit.[9]

In other words, what the 'new mechanism' of *La Peinture et ses lois* really offered was not 'laws', but a number of underlying principles from which the laws could be developed. Gleizes in 1922–3 had no particular notions as to how to incorporate colour into his method, and only the crudest notions as to how to achieve the interlocking of his planar shapes. The 'laws' still do not exist. They will develop steadily through the 1920s in a very moving dialogue with his pupils, Mainie Jellett, Evie Hone and Robert Pouyaud.

Indeed it is probably easier to follow the evolution of the idea through the numerous sketches and preparatory drawings and paintings that Mainie Jellett has left us than through the work of Gleizes himself. 'We went back to the beginning with him', she remarked.[10] There was little in her own formation as a pupil of Walter Sickert and André Lhote that could help her with the problems Gleizes was posing, whereas Gleizes had been working with similar problems, in a more or less empirical fashion, for the previous fifteen years. He was able to 'cope sufficiently well to produce a presentable result (*je me débrouillais suffisament pour me tirer d'affaire*)'.[11] A considerable knowledge lies behind the simple, harmonious, unified forms of the 'compositions' of 1920, which owe little or nothing to any representational subject. But they are static, in accordance with the immobilism he was preaching immediately before *La Peinture et ses lois*. In terms of Gleizes's later terminology (developed around 1927), they are not 'forms' but 'figures'. How could the same coherence and unity be achieved once their repose is broken, once their essential verticality is 'turned' in an oblique direction?

Gleizes is enough of an old empirical Cubist to be able to make something

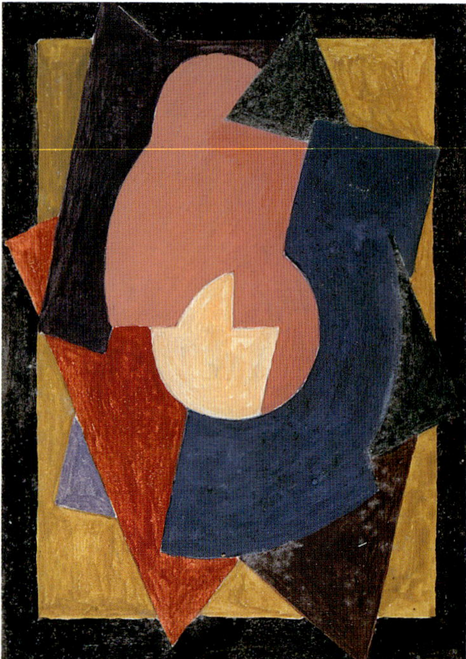

63. Mainie Jellet, *Abstract Composition*, 1922. Oil on canvas, 89 × 45.5 cm. Private Collection

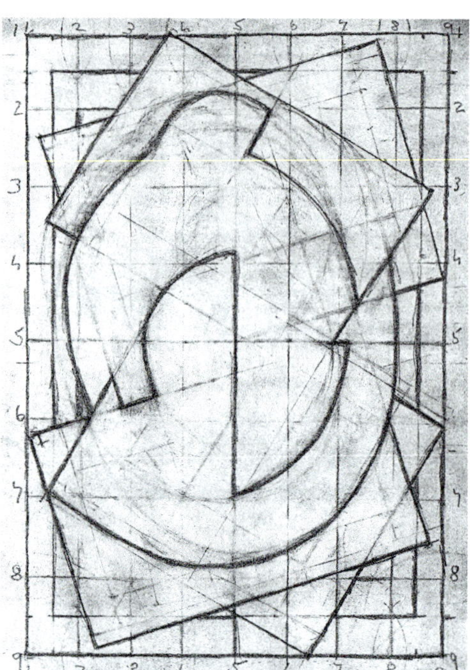

64. Mainie Jellet, *Construction derived almost automatically from a simple exercise of translation-rotation*, *c.* 1922. Pencil on paper, 23 × 16.3 cm. Private Collection

more or less presentable, whether it is yet fully incorporated into the theory or not. But in Mainie Jellett's work of the 1922–4 period we feel that a new, strange, unknown world is being explored (Plates 63–73). Initially, apparently arbitrary shapes are placed one on top of the other and often it seems that they stand in no relation to each other and are about to fall off the canvas. Sometimes an awkward 'space' is established between one shape and the shape beneath it by means of a 'shadow', in accordance with Gleizes's notion, still to be found in *La Peinture et ses lois*, of a new perspective (the perspective of Villon's map-maker). The same effect is found in some of Gleizes's paintings through the use of different thicknesses of line. The 'peinture familière', in *La Peinture et ses lois*, (Plate 56) is an example. But steadily Jellett learns to relate the different shapes to each other in such a way that they lose their individual autonomy and contribute to a more organic whole, the larger shapes embracing the smaller: 'he said each line must be belonging to another, *un père et mère et des enfants*, rather a good description, I think', as Hone wrote to Jellett in 1922.[12]

The constructions were worked out on squared paper, and there are many exercises which attempt to derive them 'automatically', after the manner of the 'spatial and rhythmic plastic system obtained by the combination of simultaneous movements of the rotation and translation of the plane and of movements of translation of the plane from side to side' of *La Peinture et ses lois* (Plates 54, 65 and 66), from the basic scheme of interlocking rectangles – the scheme that in principle gives a rational underpinning, unifying the whole work. But she seems to want to conceal this underpinning as far as possible, as if already trying to minimise the 'external appearance' of the principles in favour of 'the internal role which they must play in what will finally be achieved'. The result is a preference for irregular, rather

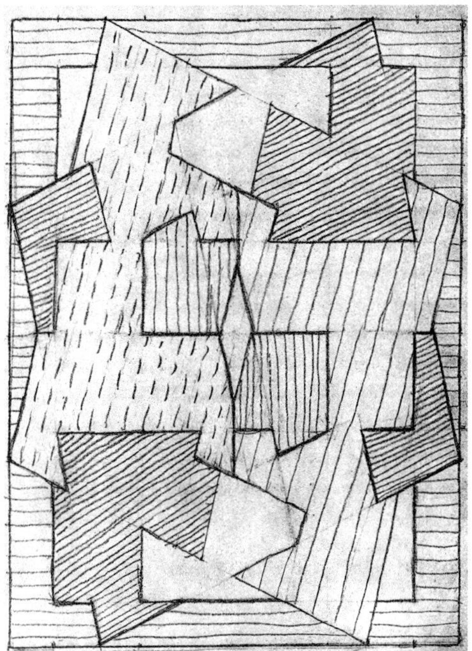

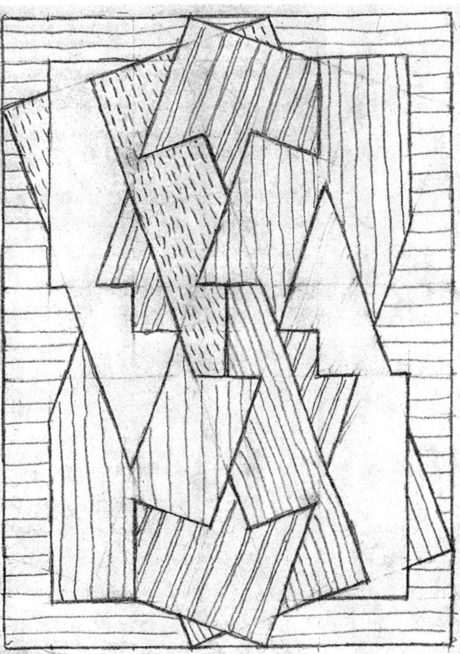

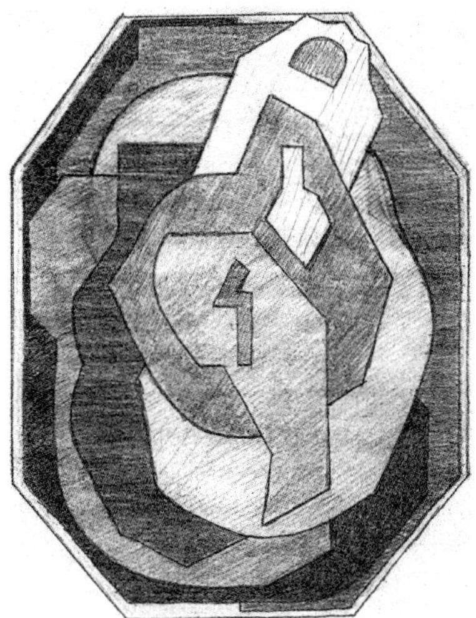

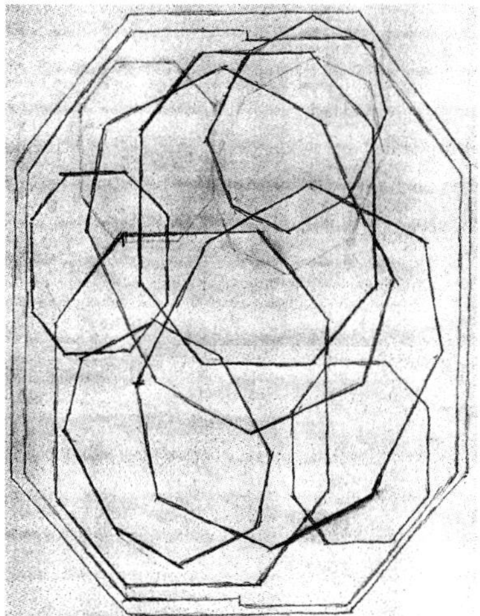

bizarre shapes which may recall the 'First Principle' of *La Peinture et ses lois* that: 'All imaginable figures determined by the point and line are capable of being used without destroying the nature of the picture surface.' (p.37) Later, Gleizes would be more particular as to what figures would be compatible with the picture surface.

It is in the very nature of these series of shapes superposed one on the other that they will become smaller and smaller coming to a centre, and this is implicit in Gleizes's remark to Evie Hone that the painting of the future would increasingly take the form of a spiral. The nature of this centre and its relation to the rest of the painting were soon to be very important in Gleizes's thought, but for the moment it is just another element in the painting. It is not mentioned as part of the argument of *La Peinture et ses lois*. Indeed, sometimes Jellett seems to want to avoid it. It has its dangers. At this stage, in which the movement of the painting is at such a crude level of development, the tendency is for the eye to be brought into the centre and fixed by it. The elimination of the centre keeps the eye moving round the periphery (and we may remember the comment in *Du 'Cubisme'* on the two ways of organising the painting: concentration towards the centre, as in the perspective system, and dispersal, which is attributed to Chinese painting).

In 1923–4, Gleizes began to argue for the introduction of several different centres, or 'elements', in the one painting. Jellett's own work has already become much more coherent. There is much less of a feeling of a number of disparate shapes put together; the eye is more easily led to pass from one thing to another. The first paintings with several elements give the impression of a river in which different currents are active. The 'elements' are dispersed arbitrarily. At the same time, the different plane shapes are more extravagantly decorated with variously sized dots and dashes, after the man-

65. Mainie Jellet, *Preparatory drawing derived from simple exercise in translation and rotation*, c. 1922. Pencil on paper, 19 × 12.5 cm. Private Collection

66. Mainie Jellet, *Construction derived almost automatically from a simple exercise of translation-rotation*, c. 1922. Pencil on paper, 23 × 16.3 cm. Private Collection

67. Mainie Jellet, *Preparatory Octagonal Drawing*, c. 1922. Pencil on paper, 17 × 13 cm. Private Collection

68. Mainie Jellett, *Octagonal Drawing*, c. 1922. Pencil on paper, 17 × 13 cm. Private Collection

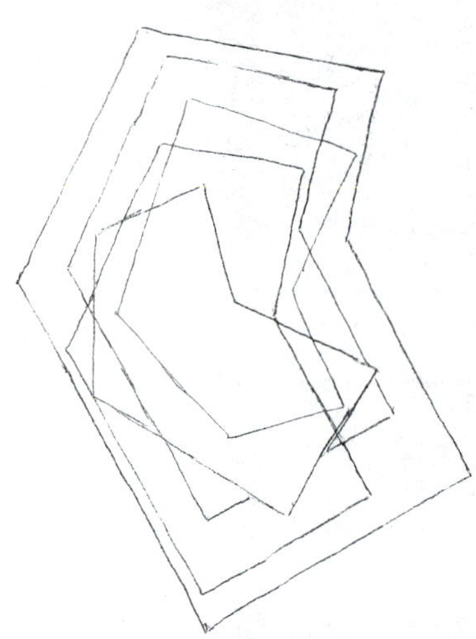

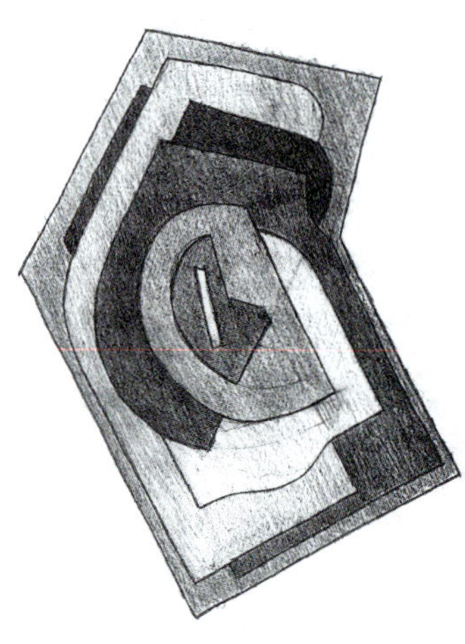

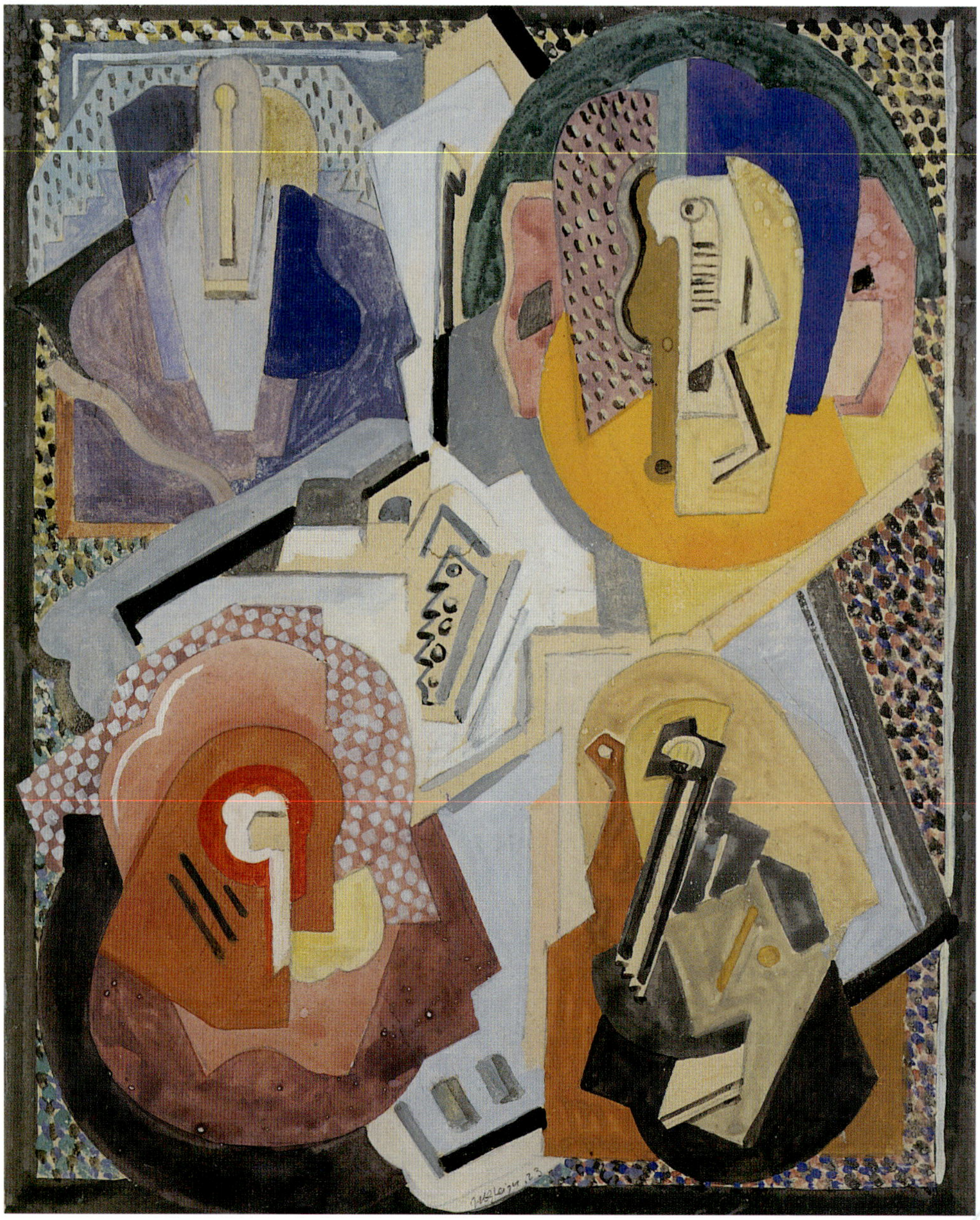

69. Mainie Jellett, *Preparatory drawing in an irregular shape*, c. 1922. Pencil on paper, 23 × 16.5 cm. Private Collection

70. Mainie Jellett, *Drawing in an irregular shape*, c. 1922. Pencil on paper, 23 × 16.5 cm. Private Collection

71. *The Tetramorph*, 1923. Gouache on paper, 26 × 21 cm. Private Collection

ner of Gleizes's *peintures familières*, perhaps indicating a rather desperate desire to 'animate the flat surface' with still insufficient means. In a letter to Robert Pouyaud written in 1934, at a moment when he was bringing all these researches to a fulfilment, Gleizes says:

> When I indicated the possibility of paintings with several elements, we first started without order, you remember? We had to go back on ourselves and end up being modest once again, dividing the canvas into equal parts. Now [he is referring to 1934 – PB], after having mixed everything up, we must put everything in order, separate things out, give each value its autonomy, and learn how to bring it all together.[13]

That is a good summary of the developments of 1924–6. Far from bringing order, *La Peinture et ses lois* initially introduced an element of disorder – the aspiration after 'rhythm', the *schemae* which were better understood in principle than in practice. Evie Hone comments on the difficulty of doing curves in 1922, but curves abound in the 1922–3 work. From 1924 onwards, curves, with the easy impression of movement they automatically convey, are used more sparingly; the rectangular *schema* becomes more – not less, as we might have expected – obvious in the final appearance of the work. In 1922, Evie Hone was grumbling about the difficulty of keeping the same proportions throughout. It is not so obvious, however, that the shapes are proportionately related to each other in the work of 1922–3; this becomes much clearer in the later period, as does the constancy of the angles of the inclined planes. Furthermore, the colour is more restrained and is beginning to be incorporated into the theory.

This is an important point. The whole of Gleizes's development from now until his death in 1953 is a movement towards greater discipline. The 'laws' were not just a necessary training, a period the painter must pass before claiming his freedom. They are inseparable from the painter's freedom. Freedom in painting, as in any other craft, comes with mastery of the laws. In the 1930s and 1940s, Gleizes was much freer than he was in the 1920s. He was also much more disciplined. The territory covered by the theory, which is only sketched in *La Peinture et ses lois*, was much greater: 'We had to go back on ourselves and end up being modest once again'.

Interesting and moving as the arbitrarily disposed elements of 1923–4 – the

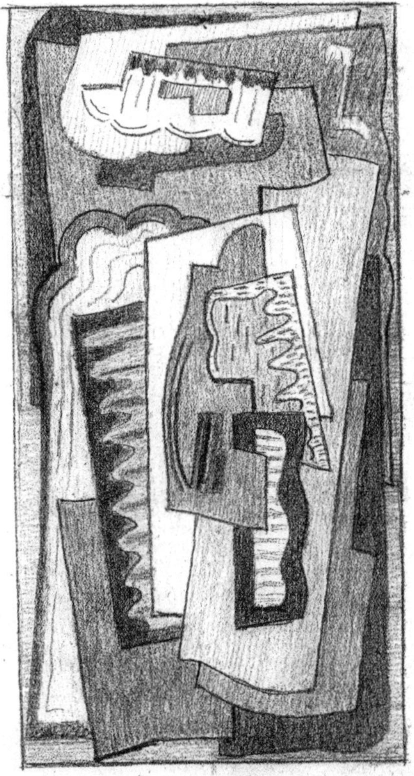

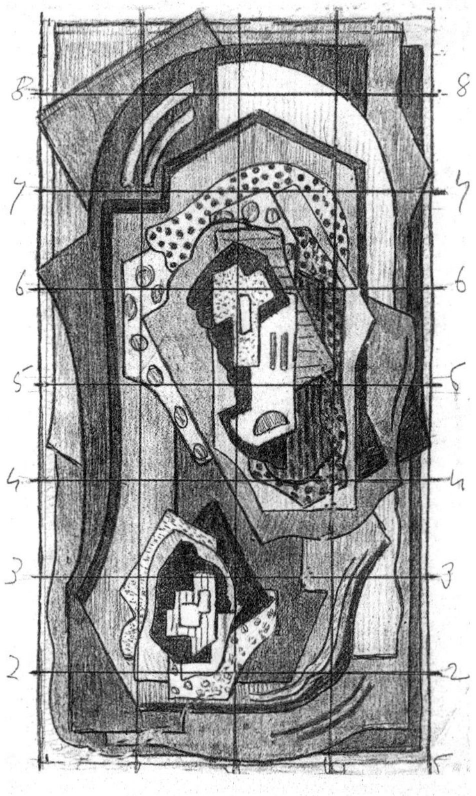

72. Mainie Jellett, *Drawing with two elements*, *c.* 1923. Pencil on paper, 23 × 11.7 cm. Private Collection

73. Mainie Jellett, *Drawing with two elements*, *c.* 1923. Pencil on paper, 26.5 × 13.7 cm. Private Collection

river giving rise to different currents – may be, they seem to indicate a misunderstanding of the central idea of 'rhythm' in *La Peinture et ses lois*. If 'rhythm' is understood as 'the result of the continuity of a certain phenomenon that repeats itself in analogous conditions at intervals which may be variable or invariable according to a progression established on the basis of a mathematical relationship . . .', what can the 'certain phenomenon' be other than the overall dimensions of the painting itself?

> To endow a flat space with rhythm is to determine the movement of the organs in accordance with the extreme possibilities of the whole surface itself. Consequently, it is to bring it into harmony with the measures of the surface through the arithmetical relation of its dimensions and of the width of its angles (pp.38–9).

The overall proportions of the painting itself establish a numerical relationship of height and width together with the principle of verticality and horizontality, which is 'turned', with a corresponding adjustment of the angles, in the movement of rotation. Consequently, the initial proportion, and its verticality and horizontality, are immensely important. Everything else derives from them, and the eye must grasp them if it is to follow all the subsequent developments. Gleizes had in fact been asserting the frame of the painting in a more or less emphatic manner ever since the Cubist period. It is a constant feature in his work. But in a painting in which several elements are arbitrarily disposed, the 'frame' of each individual element cannot be affirmed and, consequently, cannot act as starting point for the rhythm. Hence the need to give each of the separate elements its own clearly defined space.

A similar problem is posed in relation to colour. If the whole painting can be logically derived from the 'extreme possibilities of the whole surface itself', is there an equally logical principle by which colours can be derived one from the other? The question of the evolution of Gleizes's understanding of colour will be discussed in more detail later on but for the moment colour was still an arbitrary, empirical factor. If Gleizes's use of colour does harmonise to some extent with the later elaboration of the theory it is simply because he is already a highly experienced painter: 'I had necessarily to explain things to myself before I could explain them to others; from the practice I had to disentangle the theory.'[14] Jellet's colours, rather less compatible with the later theory, are still very striking, but in a way that often tends to separate rather than unite her shapes. The tendency of the line of argument launched by *La*

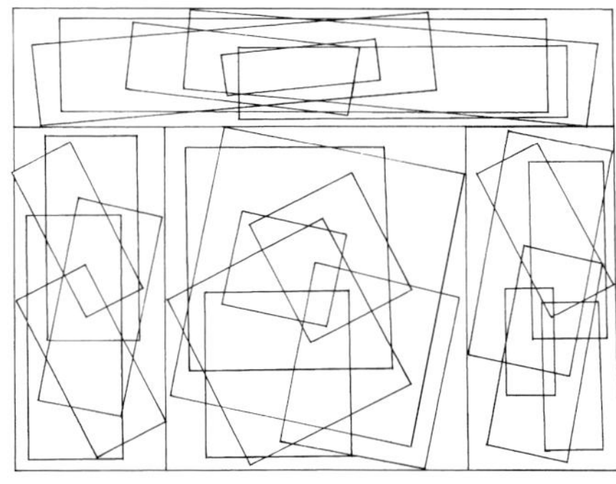

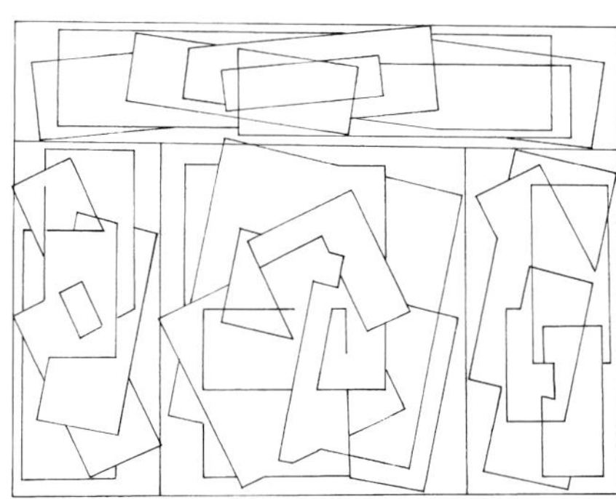

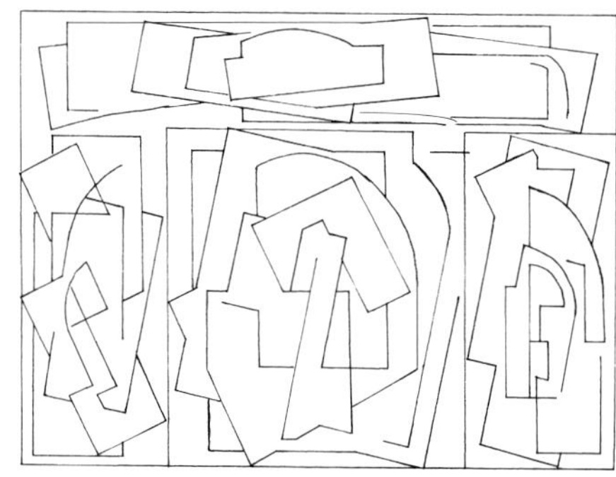

Peinture et ses lois will be to search for a means by which one colour will guide the eye to another in a movement starting from the initial 'extreme possibilities of the painting itself', and going towards the centre, then returning to the frame. This will become Gleizes's preoccupation in the late 1920s and early 1930s. But the first approach towards a coherent notion of the use of colour, in 1926–7, concentrates more on an overall harmonious effect than on a movement from one colour to the next. A single colour, with slight variations, is allowed to dominate the whole surface and other colours – most notably, in very small quantities, the complementary (either stated as such, or appearing as a result of using a neutral grey) appear simply in relation to it, modified by the 'atmosphere' it creates.

I am tempted to suggest that in the first instance Gleizes and his pupils struggled against the 'laws' of 1922 and the impression of rigour that they would, necessarily, convey. Although Gleizes is constantly arguing in this period for rigour and the application of collective, objective standards, he is himself a product of an age that favoured the arbitrary and the individual. The resistance he encountered in the world about him had first to be overcome in himself.

Gleizes's paintings with several elements are very beautiful, and the device permits the necessary reconciliation of order and complexity. The eye which, in a painting with one element, risks being immobilised by the centre (a problem Gleizes would later address and overcome) is able to ramble from one element to another in an effect not unlike that of the several different scenes, each with its own perspective point, placed side by side in the work of the early Renaissance painters – a practice Gleizes defends in *La Peinture et ses lois* against the criticisms of Leonardo.[15]

The 'manifesto' painting for this more ordered approach is the large *Quatre éléments* or *Centre noir* in the Musée des Beaux Arts in Lyon; and in the Mainie Jellett archive in Belfast there is a remarkable series of sketches showing successively how closely it, or a more abstract composition very closely related to it, is based on an initial, rigorously organised, scheme of rectangles, each, for each of the elements, maintaining constant proportions and angles of inclination (Plate 74). The sketches also indicate the extent to which Gleizes was engaged in a collective work with his pupils. Was this, one of his most important paintings, derived from a composition originally worked out by Mainie Jellett? Was she copying him? The question is irrelevant. They were simply both working on the same problems. According to Anne Dangar, writing in 1931, Mainie 'says she has helped him paint more than half his pictures'.[16]

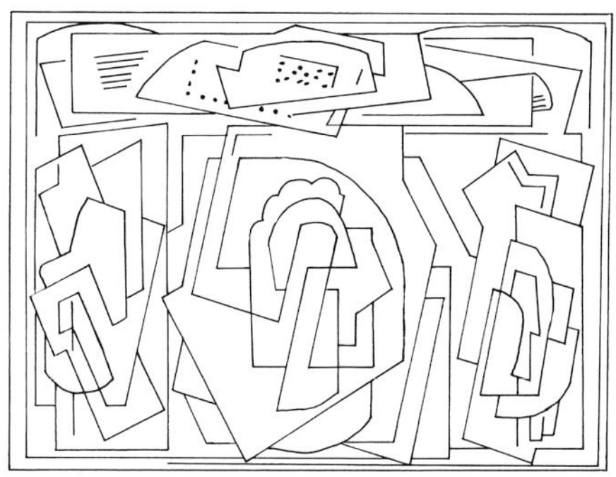

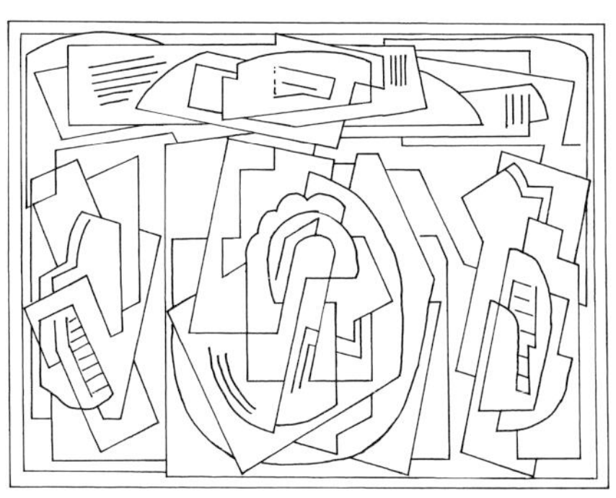

74. Schematic presentation of five drawings by Mainie Jellett, showing the evolution of a design related to Gleizes's *Quatre éléments, or Centre noir*, of 1925. The original drawings, in pencil on tracing paper, are in the Ulster Museum, Belfast

•

Gleizes says that he sent the *Quatre éléments*, a very large painting, to the Salon des Tuileries in 1926, and that 'By them [the critics] I was, that year like all the other years, following the attitude they had adopted towards me, copiously denigrated and insulted'. He claims that Louis Vauxcelles declared in *L'Excelsior* that Gleizes had not exhibited that year.[17]

It is easy to see how this period of hard, uncompromising research would have been displeasing both to the critics and, more especially, to the commercial galleries. For Gleizes, this was the turning point of Cubism; either Cubism would show the ability to develop new principles strong enough to replace the principles of the Renaissance, or it would fall back on itself as just another fashion, giving way to the next fashion without having resolved the problems it had posed.[18] In Gleizes's view, most of his comrades fell back, and the reason for this was largely financial, the understandable desire to make a living after all the hard work and sacrifice of the early years.[19] But Cubism was not like Impressionism – an idea that was just a little ahead of its time but still fully in accord with a bourgeois and materialist world view, however shocking it might have appeared at the start. Cubism was a much more profoundly radical challenge to the assumptions of the era, and could not accomodate itself to the age without betraying itself.

That Gleizes was able to continue his researches regardless of the opinions of critics and the market was largely due to the financial independence he enjoyed as a result of his marriage with Juliette Roche. She already owned their apartment in Paris, and together they had bought the property in Cavalaire, where a house and studio were built for them by the painter Emmanuel Gondouin. Jules Roche died in 1923, leaving Juliette, his only child, his house in Serrières in the Rhone Valley, where Gleizes was to spend an increasing part of his time. He also left a portfolio of shares which, according to Mme Gleizes, soon became a burden on Gleizes's conscience, though she claims that their value was greatly exaggerated by envious fellow artists.[20]

But if Gleizes, from his position of relative financial security, was showing 'candour and audacity' in exhibiting 'those poor efforts', as he later said to Lhote, we can only the more admire the courage and fidelity of his pupils. Mainie Jellett exhibited in Dublin in 1923, and if Gleizes's work was misunderstood in Paris, it is easy to imagine what sort of reception she could expect from critics in the newly independent Republic of Ireland. Yet not only did they persist with Gleizes, but they were joined in 1924 by another pupil who was to prove equally, if not more, faithful and helpful to Glezes' own development – Robert Pouyaud.

Pouyaud wrote to Gleizes in August 1924, a letter that already expresses the mixture of self-effacement, self-importance and earnestness that was to characterise him all his life and make his correspondence with Gleizes so very interesting and moving:

> Forgive me the audacity which pushes me to write to you.
> I think my letter will be well received.
> I am a painter of the young generation – that following the war – artist – ardent searcher after the purest form of art. I have seen the error of my artistic education and devote all my efforts to freeing myself –
> I felt attracted by Cubism before I understood it.

> It has become the new orientation of my artistic instinct.
> I have read your books.
> I have seen your paintings.
> I have worked.
> Many things have become clear to me but many are still obscure.
> I have arrived at a point where I can no longer advance.
> I need something solid to underpin my ideas.
> This thing that I cannot grasp discourages me.
> In one of your books, you say that the laws of painting can be learnt by everyone.
> So I allow myself to turn to you, Monsieur, to ask for your advice.
> Are there books that can teach me these laws?
> The gift – my idea of the infinite – only asks for the true materials by which it can express itself. . . .[21]

The book Pouyaud refers to is almost certainly *Du Cubisme et les moyens de le comprendre* in which, as in his articles of the time, Gleizes announces the existence of his laws rather prematurely. Pouyaud had first seen Gleizes's work in 1920; he was doing his military service and had taken a day's leave to go round the galleries. As with Jellett, Hone and Anne Dangar, this first encounter with the work, not with the man, was of the nature of a revelation which was to be decisive for the rest of his life. His family background was modest; his father was a manufacturer of picture frames and canvas stretchers. Gleizes tells us that, in order to gain his living without compromising his art, Pouyaud himself worked at painting window-display mannequins with a spray gun. His hours of work made contact with Gleizes – and painting in other than artificial light – difficult.[22]

It is worth noting that Pouyaud, like Hone and Jellett and, later, like Anne Dangar, approached Gleizes not knowing whether or not Gleizes took pupils. Gleizes never sought pupils and certainly never advertised for them. Accused of being an 'academic Cubist', he never, unlike Lhote, Ozenfant, Léger or, later, Metzinger, taught in an academy. He didn't have many pupils, and his relations with what pupils he had were friendly, informal and collaborative. His ideal was the master–apprentice relationship, not the teacher–pupil relationship. Jellett and Hone paid for their lessons,[23] but I have seen no reference to Pouyaud, who was much poorer than they were, or Anne Dangar ever paying anything.

Gleizes replied to Pouyaud, sending him a copy of *La Peinture et ses lois* – 'a little pamphlet, an article which appeared in *La Vie des lettres* over a year ago, which has not yet been put in the bookshops.'[24] In the first instance, according to Anne Dangar, Gleizes handed him over to Mainie Jellett and 'the proud Robert Pouyaud' hesitated for several days before he would submit to the indignity of being taught by a woman. He very quickly developed a lively respect for Jellett which developed into a lifelong friendship.[25]

In June 1925, Pouyaud married, which prevented him from accepting an invitation to visit Gleizes in Serrières. But in July, Gleizes arranged for him to meet another of his pupils – Yanaga Victor Poznansky – to help him with the congenial task of organising an important exhibition – 'L'Art d'Aujourd'hui'.[26]

•

I have stressed Gleizes's isolation from the general direction of artistic life in Paris, but many of the characteristics that differentiate him from his French

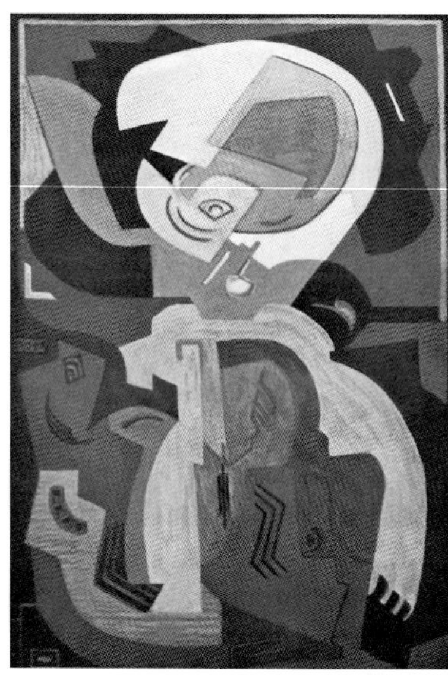

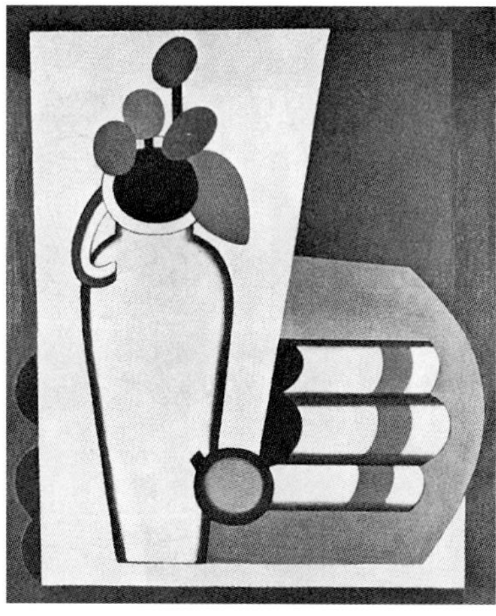

75. Y. Poznansky, *Composition with Two Elements*, 1925. Illustration from Gleizes, *Kubismus*

76. Marcelle Cahn, *Still Life*, 1925. Illustration from *Gleizes, Kubismus*

contemporaries were shared with painters elsewhere, most notably in Russia, Germany and Holland. Gleizes, as a contributor to *Clarté*, had a political sympathy for Russia, and also for Germany which he believed had been treated outrageously in the post-war settlement. In 1921, he organised an exhibition with *Der Stürm* in which, he says, he introduced the 'captivating work of the Polish painter living in Paris, Louis Marcoussis'[27] to the German public. *Der Stürm* also published a German edition of *Du Cubisme et les moyens de le comprendre*.[28] *L'Art moderne et la société nouvelle* was published in Moscow in 1923. In it, and in the other articles of the same period collected in *Tradition et cubisme*, Gleizes constantly refers to the work of finding solid principles for the new painting as a collective, or at least as a common, work, international in its scope. The artists, he argues, were obliged by the pressures of the age to work separately, each in his own little corner, often unaware of what his neighbour was doing. Yet they were all faced with the same essential problems and they all shared a common, radically new state of mind. The end result of their endeavours had to be, not a wide variety of subjective opinions, but a single common truth, like the common truths to which the scientists aspired; and it was highly desirable that painters should write, and that they should not allow critics, who had no practical experience and knew nothing about the problems involved, to speak for them.

It is easy to see how Gleizes would have found much to interest him in the schools that were developing in the Soviet Union, the Bauhaus in Germany, and the Dutch De Stijl. They too were talking about collective work based on objective principles, eliminating the figurative element as something alien to the real nature of painting, yet it is difficult to get a clear idea of Gleizes's attitude to his contemporaries from his writing. He very rarely mentions any painter by name other than those of his own immediate Cubist circle. The evolution of his own work suggests that he would not have favoured the teaching of the Suprematists, the Constructivists, De Stijl or even the Bauhaus, despite the connections he had with it which will be looked at shortly. His whole concern had long been with the evolution of a coherent, unified, organic form corresponding to the specific nature of the space that is being covered with paint. He was opposed to the idea of imposing something – whether a copy of something in the external world or an idea in the mind of the painter – onto that space. Much of the contemporary non-figurative work he would have seen as arrangements within a given space of elements that did not belong to it. Whether these elements were nudes, guitars, or squares and circles made little substantial difference.

Nonetheless, it was Gleizes's pupil Poznansky who organised the first major attempt in Paris to show what was happening in painting on an international scale. And although Gleizes worried that Poznansky would (as he did) lose a great deal of money on the project he was nonetheless excited by it – as his related essay *Cubisme et culture générale*[29] and a number of unpublished texts on the 'Exposition de 85 artistes de 24 nations' show.

The exhibition opened in December 1925. Christopher Green comments that 'Poznansky's exhibition was designed to fix in the minds of those who visited it the idea that current art at its most up-to-date and international was moving irresistably towards abstract and non-objective art. By displaying the Cubists as precursors, the challenge to Cubism's avant garde status could hardly have been made clearer'.[30] Though the exhibition did feature a number of Surrealists, notably Arp, Ernst, Masson and Miro.

Among the French painters, those who were most representative of the international tendency towards an impersonal, collective and non-representational art were Gleizes and Léger, both of whom appeared surrounded by pupils – Hone, Jellett, Poznansky himself and Pouyaud in the case of Gleizes; Marcelle Cahn, Otto Carlsund, Francizka Clausen and Florence Henry in the case of Léger. Léger had started to give afternoon classes in Ozenfant's 'Academie Moderne' in 1924.[31] Green quotes the critic Maurice Raynal in the pages of *L'Intransigeant*, fulminating against the claim of the exhibition to represent a 'young' art. The younger generation, he complained, were merely pupils of Léger, Ozenfant, Gleizes and Delaunay, reducing Cubism to a copiable formula.[32]

We can imagine how the older generation of critics who had defended Cubism on the basis of freedom of subjective expression could dislike the new emphasis on objective principle; but it must have been strikingly obvious that the work of the young painters, whether grouped round Gleizes or round Léger, was very different from pre-war Cubism, and much more in tune with developments outside France than the other French-based painters represented – Picasso, Gris, Marcoussis, Lipchitz, Laurens, Villon, or even Ozenfant and the Delaunays. By 1925, Villon was much more representational than he had been in 1922. Ozenfant had always made a principle of maintaining the representational element. The case of Delaunay will be discussed shortly. Braque, to Gleizes's disgust, did not reply to his invitation to participate. Gleizes also regretted, without explaining it, the absence of Metzinger.

Léger wrote to Gleizes at the time of the exhibition to say that he himself and Gleizes were now the only French painters who were going forward:

> The exhibition of L'Art d'Aujourd'hui has made things clear. I can see only your influence and my own dominating the present situation. The 'curve' Picasso, Braque, Gris, is flattening out and has stopped moving. It is on the way down. The world, mural, collective movement is predominant, that is incontestable. So in a few days I will send you the photos of my pupils. Around three of each.[33]

These photographs were for *Kubismus*, a book Gleizes was writing for the Bauhaus in Germany.

Although *Kubismus* was not published until 1928, Gleizes was already working on it by September 1925, in the period in which Poznansky was organising L'Art d'Aujourd'hui. It was published in the same series as Klee's *Pedagogical Notebook*, Kandinsky's *Point, Line to Plane* and Malévich's *The Non-Objective World*. It is divided into two parts – a historical account of the development of Cubism, and a theoretical 'attempt at generalisation', which is heavily cut in the German version. These are followed by a set of illustrations (Plates 75–78), divided into two parts: the older generation (in alphabetical order – Braque, Delaunay, Gleizes, Gris, Herbin, Le Fauconnier, Léger, Marcoussis, Metzinger, Picasso, Villon and, slightly out of alphabetical order, Valmier). The younger consists largely of Léger's and Gleizes's pupils.

Each of the illustrations is accompanied by a commentary – invaluable as a glimpse into Gleizes's thoughts about his contemporaries. The commentary is the best statement we have of Gleizes's argument for the three stages of Cubism – volume, multiple perspective and respect for the flat surface – so much simpler and more comprehensive than the model of 'analytical and synthetic' Cubism developed only a little time later by the art critic, Carl Einstein.[34] Each

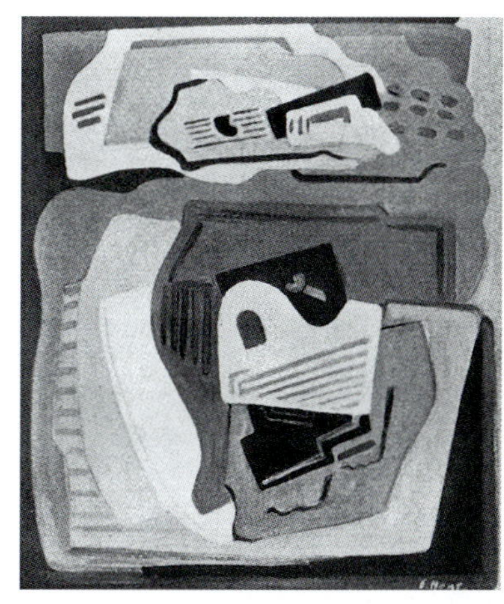

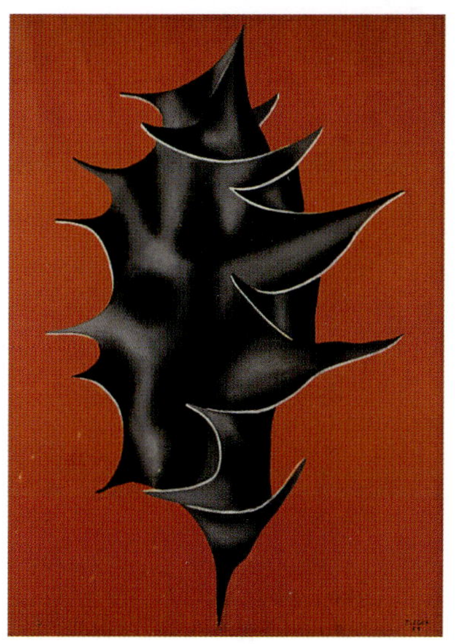

77. Evie Hone, *Composition with Two Elements*, 1925. Illustration from Gleizes, *Kubismus*

78. Fernand Léger, *La Feuille de houx sur fond rouge*, 1928. Oil on canvas, 92 × 65 cm. Private Collection

of the offerings of Gleizes's generation is described, convincingly, as adhering to one or more of these phases. Gleizes is especially enthusiastic about the wartime work of Metzinger and Gris. Of a Gris *Nature morte* (1921) he says:

> An outstanding example in which the new plastic order opposed to the descriptive principles of the Renaissance is now brought clearly to light. Gris, following the logic of the struggle against the Renaissance dogma, has gone beyond the second phase of Cubism. Here he shows, with a rare clarity, all the dynamic possibilities contained in the surface and expressed in movements of translation and rotation. And, not just for the eye, but also for the spirit, he conveys the idea of the circular form which is governed by time.[35]

He contrasts Metzinger and Gris favourably with Picasso:

> Picasso is certainly a man of unusual instinct, but he is considerably less rigorous with regard both to his conscience and to his intelligence than either Gris or Metzinger. It is this that gives him his charm, which has proved to be irresistible, the particular attraction he holds for a public who are infatuated with whatever is conventional and who are willing to forgive him his excursions into the uncouth world of the craftsman so long as he remains, first and foremost, an artist. Picasso was brought up in a spirit of love and reverence for the old masters and for the museums, and the proof of this can be seen in all his work. Hence the dichotomy there is between a descriptive painting – the product, up to a certain point, of his initial training – and work which is entirely inventive, entirely creative – the product of his own temperament. But there is nothing in his individual style which can be relied upon. Gris and Metzinger have contributed more in the way of discoveries. Their influence, their success, has been less than that of Picasso, but their radiant power – even in their weaker moments – is greater. The future, free of the errors of the present time, will be the proof. It is from those two painters that the young painters will find that they have most to learn.

Alas, Metzinger was soon to disappoint him. In the 1920s Metzinger could almost be said to have abandoned serious painting and certainly to have abandoned the researches he had taken so very far during the war.

Of Léger and his pupils he says that they, like all the others, had reached the third stage of Cubism – the respect for the flat surface – and touched on the first necessary characteristic of that surface: translation, the organisation of the spatial relations. 'But its capacity to enter into rotation is not taken into account' (in Léger's *Femme à la toilette*, 1925). The theme recurs in his comments on all Léger's pupils: 'The surface is confined to the movement of translation' (Marcelle Cahn: *Nature morte*, 1925); 'Depth has reasserted itself through the emphasis on modelling and this has the effect of weakening the realisation of the rhythm' (Otto Carlsund: *Peinture murale*, 1925); 'movements of translation are accomplished through the surface' (Franciska Clausen: *Composition*, 1925).

Taken in conjunction with his remarks on his own pupils it amounts to a slap on the wrist, an indication that, though Léger had done something, he had not done very much. Worse, Gleizes was criticising the master in front of his pupils, some of whom, since they were an international set, could certainly read German.

In fact, Léger was already turning in a direction almost the opposite of that recommended by Gleizes. Gleizes complains that Léger has not yet understood the principle of 'rotation' (the introduction of a circular movement through the inclination of planes still clearly derived from the overall picture surface). But Léger was even beginning to abandon those elements of translation he already possessed, which is again a matter of derivation from the overall picture surface. Free-floating 'organic' forms, unrelated to the overall surface, appear in his work. He is interested in the advertisers' technique (later to be exploited by the American pop artists Lichtenstein, Oldenburg and Warhol) of presenting an object, in itself banal, enlarged to monumental dimensions.

We may imagine that Gleizes has Léger in mind when he says, commenting on a *Composition à deux éléments* (1925) (plate 77) by Evie Hone:

> A field full of flowers is only a plurality of individual flowers, each of them, equally, embodying the same principles of construction; a tree is not a magnified leaf. So, monumental painting is not just one element magnified beyond all measure, but a multiplication of elements which are able to relate one to the other in a way that is natural. Here we can see the movement of the surface both in translation and rotation.

A painting such as *La Feuille de houx sur fond rouge* (1928) (plate 78) could almost be seen as Léger's reply – a reply that goes far towards vindicating Gleizes's argument. On a more positive note, the publication of *Kubismus* marks the beginning of a closer and more fruitful relationship between Gleizes and Delaunay, whom Gleizes praises for having been the first to see the 'end' (*dénouement*) towards which Cubism was heading. But this will be the subject of a later chapter.

Gleizes was the only French painter who contributed to the Bauhaus series, and his status as French representative of the more advanced modernist schools can also be seen in the invitation he received in 1926 from the German group Die Abstrakten to organise the French side of a new international journal – *Ars* – to be published in four languages – German, French, Italian and English. The German representative and overall editor was the painter and sculptor, William Wauer and the Italian representative was Marinetti. Russia was to be represented by Kandinsky, a choice that may reflect the closing down of the Russian modernist schools, since Kandinsky was now permanently resident in Germany. Wauer asked Gleizes to find him an English representative, and Gleizes approached Mainie Jellett, who said that she could not do it herself because, living in Dublin, she could not keep in touch with what was happening in London. She suggested Wyndham Lewis, who was in full retreat from his Vorticist days, or the critics Roger Fry and Frank Rutter. Gleizes read Fry and Rutter and dismissed them with contempt – 'Fry surtout est fantastique'. In a manifesto he wrote for his French section (which Wauer approved), Gleizes expressed his determination to avoid the critics: 'How little the opinions of critics count in history, how childish they appear when they are not completely forgotten; and how the words of the painters remain exciting and always true.' He did, however, conceive of the idea of inviting intelligent amateurs, those prepared to put their hands in their pockets to buy paintings, to express their views, as the best way for painters to have some idea of the impact their work might have. To this end, at Poznansky's suggestion, he approached the Vicomte de Noailles, a patron of the Dutch De Stijl artist Theo Van Doesburg, who had bought several paintings including some by

Mondrian, albeit at derisory prices, from L'Art d'Aujourd'hui.[36]

In the event, *Ars* never appeared, and it was not until Abstraction-Création in 1931, with which Gleizes was also closely associated, that the non-representational artists were able to organise themselves in a coherent international structure.

In all these activities, Gleizes has the appearance of a 'Modernist', a painter whose art is spiritually in tune with the development of modern technology. Gleizes did not share the passionate enthusiasm of Le Corbusier or Ozenfant for the machine aesthetic; he often expressed reservations about 'modernolatrie', and he was deeply unhappy about the economic shape of the society about him and about the relation between the economy and war. Still, it was the uses of technology not the technology itself that worried him, and in this respect, the year 1926 marks a turning point. An intense reflection on the 'anxiety' of the age in relation to his own anxiety as a painter and the means he had found to resolve it, led him to see the development of the city and mechanised production, together with the destruction of the life of the countryside and of the skills of the craftsman, as major evils to be confronted. It is from 1926 onwards that the second term of my title – 'Against the Twentieth Century' – begins to have meaning.

10

THE END OF AN ILLUSION

Towards the end of *La Peinture et ses lois*, Gleizes gives a variant of the typical modernist argument that says spectacular developments in technology have so changed our perception of the world that a corresponding change must take place in the nature of painting. He has already argued for an art of 'rhythm', an art of time, as against the exploration of 'space' which was the principle concern of the Renaissance. Now he says that a sense of the rhythmic, repetitive, periodic nature of life has been imposed by the regular throbbing of the machine. Metal is to the engineer what the surface of his canvas is to the painter: an inert vehicle waiting to be 'animated' rhythmically by means of 'la mécanique nouvelle'. At the same time, new means of transport have had the effect of changing our ideas of the relation between space and time. In thirty years the Atlantic Ocean had shrunk from a distance of fifteen days to a distance of five. Space and volume were becoming ever less burdensome. We may remember that in *Choses simples*, Gleizes, like Malevich, argues that technology, relieving us of so many burdensome activities, would lead to a new age of motionless contemplation.

A similar account of the relation between technology and the painter's idea of form can be found in one of the essays that Gleizes wrote for the L'Art d'Aujourd'hui exhibition. He develops an elaborate analogy between the problems faced by the painter and those faced by the mechanics who had had to devise a chassis for the horseless carriage. The appearance of the horse and carriage had seemed complete and perfect: the notion of a carriage moving without a horse appeared aesthetically repellent. But after thirty years, the automobile had been justified: 'Though still unsure of itself, the external form was sufficiently sturdy to protect the internal thought and its faith. The internal thought had first conceived, then searched for the means to live; slowly, by perfecting its means, it had to harmonise its organic system and its outward appearance.'[1] If the motorcar, 'an invention that was nonetheless positive', had encountered such opposition on aesthetic grounds, it was hardly any wonder that the painters, whose utility was rather less obvious, had run into difficulties. But, as he says in *La Peinture et ses lois*: 'The painter and sculptor can no longer misinterpret their role, in spite of the opinion of the old woman who continues to visit her friends in a buggy drawn by a bay in the middle of the confusion of streets full of automobiles whose diabolical creation she curses.' (p.53)

Although Gleizes is always careful to dissociate himself from the extreme enthusiasm for machines shown by his colleagues Ozenfant and Jeanneret in the pages of *L'Esprit nouveau*; and although he several times declares that he finds the humblest natural phenomenon more wonderful than the most sophisticated machine; nonetheless, there was little in what he had written so far to indicate that he was about to become the fierce opponent of all forms of mechanisation and of the city.

Mme Gleizes, however, gives the impression that this had been a long-standing theme of his conversation, dating back to his rapidly developed disillusionment with New York: 'It was in New York during the 1914 war, in an endless avenue "Up Town", in the Bronx or in Harlem, that Moly Sabata was born . . .'[2] She says that she herself was sceptical about Gleizes's anti-industrialism until one day when she was perched on a stepladder in the library at Serrières and a book fell on her head. She climbed down to look at it. It turned out to be *Entre deux Mondes* by the Italian historian and political philosopher, Guiglielmo Ferrero, best known for a major study on the *Grandeur et décadence de Rome*. Ferrero had, she says, been 'one of my father's best friends', and she had known him and his wife, Gina Lombroso, since childhood. *Entre deux Mondes* was an account of the Ferreros' experience of America that seemed to coincide with that of the Gleizes'. Like them, they saw America as a tendency in European culture developed without restraint, and as the future to which Europe was inevitably bound. And like the Gleizes' – or at least like Albert Gleizes – they found the thought repellent. The Ferreros were solidly rooted in the Italian classical tradition; Gleizes was, and had been for some time, on the side of the barbarians. Mme Gleizes claims that she found the coincidence of their views on the evils of industrialism convincing. She describes this incident under the heading – '1925'.

Gleizes himself tells us in the *Souvenirs* that he was much preoccupied with these questions in 1925 and that he was working on a book which intended to distinguish the good and the bad aspects of machine production. He was already convinced of the dangers of overproduction which he invoked in the 'Essai de généralisation' he had written as part of *Kubismus*:

> These machines, wonderful instruments if they could be disciplined by a moral standard, will soon accumulate dangers in the game of chance into which our general system coming apart has fallen. The natural tendency of these machines to annul space to the benefit of time will become dangerous because of the fever of possession which the new way of looking at things inflates constantly, because it will use the machine perversely, to exaggerate the product-volume. Space will seem too small; individualisation, whether personal or gathered together in arbitrary, temporary groups, will be insufficient to contain the expanding action of the machine; conflicts between individuals, groups, nations, leagues of nations, will break out, tenacious, wearying, without any possible resolution.
>
> The too slow consumption of a too great product will create a monstrous state of affairs. Open conflicts to crush competition and establish monopolies will, in the course of our everyday experience, reveal what the best industrial product and its best application is – the application that seems to be the very reason for the machine left to the fantasies of the individual, the inevitable end of the terrible use of those characteristics of intense, rapid production and accelerated distribution; the product which finds a consumption-disaggregation worthy of it, a demand that is thus appropriate to its needs. Scientifically, this product is the product that corresponds to a state of war. Engines and munitions of all kinds can in fact be made as abundantly and as fast as possible; consumption will always be able to follow, no matter how fast it goes . . .[3]

The book Gleizes was working on was to be called *La Machine-modernolatrie*. He says that it was in writing his last chapter, in January 1926, that he realised his mistake. He had wanted to distinguish good machines from bad but now he could see that 'the two types of machine were the same . . . there were only bad machines, enemies of man, killers of men, whose evil would soon spread like a leprosy across the world . . .'.

'For an artist who had a certain sensitivity and no dogmatic preconceptions, the aesthetics of the machine had a charm which had lasted for years; this infernal beauty which hid the evil nature of the machine had lulled me to sleep.' But now,

> the role of the machine was clear to me. There was nothing in its aesthetic appearance which could not be found elsewhere in the humblest of plants, in an animal, in the human body. By contrast, its destructive force belonged to it alone. Incapable of building anything at all, of competing with what the hands of men, helped by the tool – which is anything but mechanical – had produced in every domain, the machine is power pushed to the point of abolition. It destroys the physical, the moral, the spiritual, stimulating the idea of possession to a state of frenzy where it no longer has any sense of its limits . . .
>
> I am persuaded that if man has not been able to breathe a soul into this machine, it is because he has already lost his own. When he has found it again – and this will happen sooner or later, though through what suffering! – he won't turn towards the machine any more but towards himself, possessed again at all his levels. To a world that the machine has ground into dust will succeed a world to be rebuilt in the spirit.[4]

Gleizes implies that he had virtually written *La Machine-modernolatrie*, but I have only seen notes for it. These, however, do convey some idea of the distinction he initially wanted to draw between the proper and improper uses of the machine:

> The good = speed.
> The bad – those which give too much weight reality to space.
> First: transports, locomotion. Steamboat, Auto, Aeroplanes, Telegraph, Phone, Wireless, Gramophone etc. etc. Show how the Reality of Space is relative and free Time from the measure in which we have sought to [confine] it. . . .

Here again, we have the idea that the machine complements the religious-rhythmic nature of the new painting because it renders space, identified with the senses, less cumbersome and time, identified with the intelligence, more flexible:

> So the machine in its true nature, annulling space in favour of time, has allowed the senses to realise relations that are more certain and, independently of any practical application, to take a step towards intelligence-time . . .
>
> Unfortunately, Man uses the machine to crowd space, giving it a more solid reality – overproduction compromises the social equilibrium. A bad notion of plastic reality searches outlets which themselves are only similar productions – renders space rigid. The burdening of the senses is not a plastic realisation – arterio-sclerosis is not more plastic than the suppleness of healthy

> veins. Terrible error that turns the social body to a corpse. The little Universe thinks that it can forget the laws of the great which condition it. . . .

The good machines, then, are those that augment the speed of communications; the bad those that clutter up space through the overproduction of material goods. It is easy to see that this distinction could not be maintained for long. Speed and abundance of communications are precisely a requirement of overproduction. Something of the internal struggle Gleizes may have had in renouncing the automobile, the railway train, the aeroplane, may be seen in a footnote to *Vie et mort de l'occident chrétien*, the book in which his change of attitude was expressed in the most uncompromising terms:

> The railways, for example . . . seem a definite gain, one of the finest examples of progress, a means of emancipation and of human communication: an opinion that is without serious foundation and which collapses with a little critical effort . . . Few people, even among the cultured classes, have thought about the fact that society taken as a whole serves the railways much more than the railways serve society. First, has anyone asked where the enormous personnel they require comes from? A personnel, from engineers to track-layers, that has been taken away from real human work, taken from the land and from the crafts. And then, does anyone think there are enough people wanting to travel to cover the costs of running them? If they were to transport only people, with only those products that are useful to them, they would soon be ruined and suppressed. Thus the railways have become an essential cause of overproduction; thanks to overproduction they have been able to live – but to live poorly, because, in spite of the immense transportation of merchandise at prohibitive prices, the State still has to give them guarantees and financial help, money that comes from the taxpayer. So, people are all at the service of the railways . . . (p.39)

But Gleizes's criticism of the machine is much more than an economic argument, important as the economic argument is; and his remarks on space and time are more than just an eccentric way of expressing himself. In order better to understand this crucial turning point in the development of his thought, we will have to look a little more closely at his religious belief and also at his relations with the mathematician, Charles Henry.

We have seen that in *La Peinture et ses lois*, Gleizes argues that the monuments of the early Middle Ages were the product of a 'science' – a body of knowledge possessed by an élite who directed the society. This science was no less objective or sophisticated than our own, but it was differently orientated. Where we regard the evidence of the senses as primary, and consciousness as little more than its reflection, the early medieval science regarded consciousness as primary and the evidence of the senses as doubtful. Certitude was to be found in 'intelligence', not in the fleeting appearances of the world. The art of this period was an art of rhythm and number, the means by which the static nature of the figurative image could be accomodated to the mobile nature of consciousness. In the art of the Renaissance, by contrast, the figurative image is rendered immobile so that the senses may have time to appreciate its luscious qualities: similarly in science, as it has developed since the Renaissance, the fleeting appearances of the world are immobilised so that they can be taken apart and studied at length. Consciousness adapts itself to the slower pace of the senses.

The confused aspiration after movement and dynamism of the Cubists and, more so, the Futurists, were a sign that man, wearied after five or six centuries of submission to the senses, wants to return to the mobility of consciousness. The increasing need felt among the scientists to incorporate time into their calculations as a 'fourth dimension'; the tendency for matter to appear ever more nebulous, less solid the more it was studied; these too seemed to point in the same direction. And, as we have just seen, Gleizes initially saw the development of the machine as part of the same tendency, favouring time over space.

In the early 1920s, Gleizes was deeply interested in early Christian literature. After the death of Jules Roche, he had free access to the library at Serrières, which included a substantial theological collection from the library of Jules Roche's uncle, who had been Bishop of the town of Gap, in the south-east of France. Gleizes himself often refers to the fifth-century Christian philosopher, Augustine of Hippo, and later defends what he understands as the spirit of Augustine against that of Thomas Aquinas and of the thirteenth century.[5] In June 1925, Pouyaud wrote to Gleizes to say that he would study Augustine's *Confessions*, obviously in reply to a suggestion from Gleizes.[6] Anne Dangar was set to reading Augustine and later, in 'Talks' which she sent to her friends in Australia, she recommends what the *Confessions* have to say on memory and on time.[7]

The reflections on memory, time and consciousness occur at the end of the *Confessions* (Bks x–xiii), together with a critique of scientific curiosity, which he likens to the curiosity that brings people to see freak shows. It is a manifesto for a different orientation of consciousness – away from the senses and the external world, towards itself and thence towards God, whose image it is. In his treatise *On Music*, written soon after his conversion to Christianity, he argues that it is through 'numbers' (translated in the authoritative French Etudes Augustiniennes version as 'rythme') that the soul can use the sensible to turn to the intelligible, whose source is God, in Whom the diversity of the world is assembled and brought to a state of unity. In the *Confessions*, time is understood not as something external imposed on the consciousness, but as a function of consciousness. The senses cannot grasp the past or the future, and yet the 'present' has no existence for the senses independent of past and future.

> The present cannot possibly have duration . . . (p.266)
>
> We measure time as it passes . . . but while we are measuring it, where is it coming from, what is it passing through, and where is it going? It can only be coming from the future, passing through the present and going into the past. In other words, it is coming out of what does not yet exist, passing through what has no duration, and moving into what no longer exists. (p.269)
>
> It seems to me, then, that time is merely an extension, though of what it is an extension, I do not know. I begin to wonder whether it is an extension of the mind itself. (p.274)

Augustine is writing as a Christian Neo-Platonist, and his reflections on time – particularly his argument against the view that time can be identified with the movement of any material body such as the Sun or the stars – is very close to the argument of Plotinus (*Enneads*, 3.7), who concludes that 'Time, however, is not to be conceived as outside of Soul' (p.278) – in this case, the 'World Soul', the third emanation out of the original divine and eternal Unity. It is this World Soul that 'animates' and gives form to the visible world. The second emanation, proceeding directly from the One, is the 'Intellectual Principle', distinct from its Source, but living in perpetual adoration of It. In the *Confessions*, Book xii, commenting on *Genesis*, Augustine gives a definition of the 'Heaven of Heavens', which he regards as a conscious, spiritual being, which resembles Plotinus' definition of the Intellectual Principle. Plotinus, Augustine and Boethius may be described as three of the architects of the Christian 'science' that, in Gleizes's view, underlies the Christian achievement of the early European Middle Ages.

The Neo-Platonist scheme of a series of emanations descending from the Eternal One to the lowest levels of temporal reality and thence returning again is the theme of *Le Symbolisme des nombres*, published in 1921 by Dr René Allendy, at a time when he was particularly friendly with the Gleizes'. There is no doubt that Gleizes's thinking is very close to that of the Neo-Platonists, and that he read Allendy's book with a sympathetic interest, but his language is still very different. Gleizes is scrupulous not to write anything whose truth he has not felt within himself, mainly through his work as a painter. He is suspicious of preconceived ideas and ready-made symbolic formulae. We will see this more clearly when we come to the vexed question of his relations with the esoteric philosopher, René Guénon.

For the moment we must retain the fact that, through Augustine, Gleizes saw the Christian cycle as beginning with a reflection on time and on the nature of the material world which seemed to resemble the reflections of the scientific milieu – Langevin, Drach and Henry – with which he was involved. He already has the idea that the essential meaning of the word 'religion' is *religare* – to bind or bring together – to return the disparate world to an essential unity – and it is thus that he understands the task of the painter: a task that is complemented by the need to restore a human sense of community in opposition to the atomisation and individualisation that characterise industrial society, an individualisation that was all too powerful among the artists. When Gleizes evokes 'intelligence', he does not mean the powers of the individual 'intellect',[8] but rather an objective awareness of the reality of things that may be said to correspond to Plotinus' 'Intellectual Principle' – inseparable from the love of God, or of essential Unity, incessantly searching for the means to bring things together, religiously, for synthesis as opposed to the analysis to which the individual intellect is prone, tied as it is to the activity of the senses.

However, if the achievements of early Christianity are the work of an élite with a highly developed 'theocentric' science, where was this élite to be found? Gleizes never seems to be tempted by the thesis of a secret knowledge passed on through a Rosicrucian-style brotherhood, though the idea was to appeal to many of his French associates, notably Pouyaud. Gleizes himself believed that what he was beginning to grasp was the mainstream teaching of the early Christian Church, beginning with the Fathers. It was then clear that this élite who possessed the necessary knowledge must be found, from the fourth century onwards, in the monastic movement, the foundation stone on which Christian Europe was built. But the most obvious characteristic of the monastic movement was its flight into the desert – its rejection of the city and of its highly sophisticated literary and sensual culture. The monastic movement turned towards the country, towards agriculture and towards manual work. Without underestimating the importance of the thought of the Fathers, its 'science' was practical rather than verbal: the movement was, at least initially, suspicious of words, and this is why its science, its knowledge, is as invisible to our own over-intellectual age as is the knowledge of a peasant who farms using traditional methods. Like the monastic movement, we must reject intellectualism to turn to intelligence, and the best way to achieve this – recommended by St Benedict – is through manual work.[9] But if Gleizes admired the early monastic movement and the Fathers of the Church, how did he stand in relation to the contemporary Church?

In his immediate circle, Poznansky was a Third Order Dominican, and Hone and Jellett were both serious, practising Anglicans – Anglo-Catholics in the Church of Ireland, which has a distinctly Protestant character. In December 1925, Evie Hone entered an Anglican convent – the Convent of the Epiphany in Truro in Cornwall. Her religious interest had been long established. Winifred Nicholson remembers 'an idea for a picture that she chalked of St Francis' at Byam Shaw's Art School in London, where they were both studying before the First World War: 'It was pristine like early Christian art, and showed all the fervour of her promise.'[10] She had considered entering the Truro community in 1919, shortly before going to Paris to study under Lhote. Among Gleizes's books there is her copy of *Le Tourment de Dieu* by Dom Willibrod Verkade, a painter and friend of Sérusier and of the Nabis, who belonged to the Benedictine monastery of Beuron in Germany. We have already mentioned the role of the School of Beuron, with its flat, hieratic, mathematically based painting, in the theoretical literature published by Sérusier, Denis and Severini in the early 1920s.[11]

Hone stayed in the convent through 1926, becoming a novice in June, but she left in 1927 without taking her final vows. Both Gleizes and Mainie Jellett disapproved of her initiative,[12] but there was a logic to it which Gleizes must have felt and which may have contributed to his, or, rather, Pouyaud's decision to launch Moly Sabata as a 'lay convent' in 1927.

Gleizes expressed his opinion on the difference between the early monastic movement and the present day monasteries in a text which seems to form part of *La Machine-modernolatrie*:

> The monasteries were ready to receive the disappointments of men, turning from the illusions that the spectacle of the old civilisation had maintained. Based on the soil, they must have surprised those who fell upon them all of a sudden, who had forgotten the truth of the soil and of the law that cannot be deformed. Already organised when everything was falling hopelessly apart, they had to offer a refuge to all who were in flight and so to restore the human tendency to come together in a community. The discipline of the monasteries, rigorous and realistic, assured safety from the social system that was disappearing. Nowadays, the word 'monastery' is used to refer to degenerate orders where for the most part a flock of neurotics and weaklings swarm, but that is no reason to confuse this end, as lamentable as it is, with their origins. The monasteries of the present day have nothing to do with the monasteries that saved the species when Roman Statism collapsed into rottenness. . . .

We can see that the old leaven of Gleizes's anticlericalism is still at work. In relation to Evie Hone's entering her monastery, he wrote to Mainie Jellett that the monasteries were nothing more than 'empty shells, deserted by the spirit'.[13] It was an opinion he would soon have to modify as he came to regard the religious orders with increasing respect. But he never believed them to be fully worthy of the role they would have to fulfill if, once again, the West was to be 'saved' from the collapse of its own civilisation.

•

The year 1926 – the year which Evie Hone passed in the convent at Truro, and the year of Gleizes's definitive disenchantment with the machine – was also, according to Mme Gleizes, the year of his closest involvement with the mathematician, Charles Henry, who may, as I have already suggested, have had a considerable influence on the thinking of *La Peinture et ses lois*, and particularly on Gleizes's use of the word 'rhythm' as a possible and desirable characteristic of painting.

Henry's influence may also be seen in a development in Gleizes's terminology which takes place around 1925 in his essays *L'Inquiétude: crise plastique* and *Cubisme: essai de généralisation* (a title which echoes one of Henry's most important studies, the *Essai de généralisation de la théorie du rayonnement*, also published in 1925). Put very crudely, it is the language of wireless telegraphy. The phenomena of the world are conceived of in terms of an exchange of vibrations, transmitted or received. We may note that it was also in 1925 that Prince Louis de Broglie, a radio expert and enthusiast for chamber music (and, incidentally, for medieval history) put forward his thesis that the operation of the atom could best be understood in terms of 'waves', vibrations, like the vibrations of sound, rather than solid particles or billiard balls moving round a centre.[14] Gleizes regularly sent copies of his books as they appeared to de Broglie, who politely acknowledged receipt of them, but I am not aware of any closer relationship between them.

Henry, an admirer of the German physicist, Hermann von Helmholtz and of his work on sound waves and music (which we have already mentioned in the discussion on René Ghil), had long thought of the world as vibratory rather than solid, but in his case, this was not a hypothesis about an imagined external reality. As we have seen, he argued that 'physics' had to become 'psycho-physics'. It is as vibration – sound and colour – that we receive the world. It is only as vibration that we can know it. Anything else he characterised as 'metaphysics', which, as a good empiricist and one-time laboratory assistant to the theorist of experimental science, Claude Bernard, he regarded as a term of reprobation.[15]

Henry's general theory recognised three levels of radiation – the generally admitted electro-magnetic radiation, but also the 'gravitational' (*gravitique*), corresponding to mass and weight, and the 'biological', corresponding to consciousness. Henry believed that he had proved the existence of his 'biological resonators' (which 'have nothing in common with those ideas of spirit, too imprecise to be useful, which arrive from time to time to clutter up the bibliography'[16]). He could see no reason why the biological resonator, corresponding to consciousness, should not be able to function independently of the electro-magnetic and gravitational resonators:

> The stationary equilibria established between the biological resonators on the one hand and the gravitational or electrical resonators on the other,

> imply a stationary equilibrium between resonators of a different quality. This equilibrium, condition of life as it appears to us, is broken in death as it appears to us . . . The rupture of this equilibrium, by freeing the biological resonator from its stationary mechanical liaisons, frees it from relativity [he argues that the laws of relativity are confined to the electro-magnetic level – PB] and do not imply the cessation either of a consciousness or of an elementary personality.[17]

Both Gleizes and Mme Gleizes in separate articles on Henry quote him three months before his own death as saying: 'Death is only a physico-chemical phenomenon of no importance; it is only after my death that I will seriously begin to enjoy myself.'[18]

In *Vie et mort de l'occident chrétien*, Gleizes observes of contemporary scientists:

> Everything is vibration, they say, thinking they are only adding another observation, a new fact; the Universe is a curve, is finite; time and extension dispute with each other, what is relative and what is absolute . . . all of this is tending to break away from the narrowness of intellectual argument, and aspires to the level of intelligence, bearing witness to an agonised longing for unity; vaguely we can see an irrational, active, imperturbable, unapproachable cause behind facts that are only passive, agitated, endlessly fleeting . . . (pp.51–2).

The appearances of the world are essentially vibrations that assume forms. It is in our consciousness and nowhere else that these forms are assumed; they only exist because our senses are capable of transforming them, because they correspond to our nature. We can say nothing about their existence outside our own nature. Henry wrote a great deal about the way in which the human sensibility receives forms and colours – the effect of the vibration on the resonator, and also the effect of the resonator on the vibration – the difference between the world as experienced by a healthy organism and the world as experienced by one that is sick or tired. Although his historical conclusions did not coincide with those of Gleizes (Gleizes claimed that he was coming round in their conversations before his death[19]), he had long argued that the human sensibility has changed over the course of history. At different epochs, man has experienced the world differently. For Gleizes – the moral thinker which Henry, the scientist, tries not to be – these differences coincide with the youth, adulthood and decrepitude of a people which has its birth in an idea, essentially a religious idea – in our case, Christianity. For both Henry and Gleizes, the state of health of the sensibility of the age, the quality of the resonator, can be seen in the monuments it has left.

The words that now begin to appear in Gleizes's thought, and that present great difficulties for a translator, are words like 'résistances', referring to the limits that the human sensibility as a receiver imposes on the signals it receives; 'le ralenti des sens', the slower rate of the senses, referring to the time it takes for the senses to absorb the stimuli they receive – and this was the subject of numerous experiments of Henry's; 'résonateur' itself; 'vibration' itself, as when the different arts from dance to architecture are discussed in terms of the number of vibrations they are able to bring together; and a particular use of the word 'biologie', where another writer might have used the word 'spirit', to refer to a self-regulating process that, when it is functioning properly, will automatically defend itself against excess.

The particular relevance of all this to machine production, to the city, to agriculture and the manual crafts, and to the work of the artist, is that if the human frame is conceived of as a resonator, receiver of vibrations and creator of forms, then the relation between vibration and receiver becomes of enormous importance. The work of the artist, in whatever field, is precisely to manage the vibrations to which his work gives rise in such a way as to contribute to the health of the human beings about him, not to harm it. And this is true not just of works of art but of all realisations in space and time. But it is precisely this vibratory quality, this interaction between the object and the sensibility, that machine production and commercial interest cannot admit. At best it is an optional extra, at worst an encumbrance. For Gleizes, in his article, *L'Inquiétude: crise plastique*, this was the source of the 'anxiety' of the age: 'Anxiety is always a plastic crisis, because plasticity is the very tendency of the being in space.'[20]

We do not like the things with which we surround ourselves. We are ill at ease with them, whether they are utilitarian or decorative. This is the source of our anxiety. The problem is a problem of form, of our own act of forming things, of our 'plastic' act. It is therefore a matter that must engage the interest and the sense of responsibility of those engaged in the arts – of the whole continuum of the arts, since essentially it is the same problem throughout; but it is especially the problem of painters, sculptors and architects because these are the arts in which form is presented most completely. Form is glimpsed through the successive changes of music and dance, but it is seen simultaneously and permanently in painting, sculpture and architecture, the 'plastic arts'.

From now on the word 'plastic' becomes particularly important in Gleizes's thought, and it too is difficult to translate because of the negative connotations that the word has acquired.[21] Gleizes wrote several books and essays (including *Cubisme: essai de généralisation*) under the general title *Vers une Conscience plastique*. The 'plastic conscience' (since it is a moral consciousness that is referred to and not just consciousness in and of itself) is a consciousness of our responsibility towards the plastic nature of the world about us, susceptible of receiving form:

> Every act is a formal function [*fonction formelle*]. The human organism, whether individual or collective, never manifests anything other than its power to form [*former*]. To form is temporarily to stop the principle of energy that flows eternally, to transform arithmetic into geometry;[22] it is all the mystery of creation, and we find it everywhere and always.
>
> Biological creation, whether in the natural or in the human order, is achieved when certain quantities – which, being quantities, are measurable – of space are drawn together by periods of quality that cannot of themselves be measured but which, nonetheless, are rendered perceptible.[23]

In *L'Inquiétude: crise plastique* and *Cubisme: essai de généralisation*, the different art forms are discussed in terms of the quantity of vibrations they are able to associate, passing from dance – 'the first formal [*plastique*] emanation', in which the form disappears as quickly as it appears, to architecture: 'the whole world is regulated by the speed of the [human] being, the senses enjoy their plenitude, a complete agreement is achieved between the, usually antagonistic, numbers and measure, movement and rest. The theoretical dance has become a fact . . .'[24] Once all the different arts are understood as associations of different orders of vibrations, they can be understood as a continuum. The differences between them can be understood as a matter of the speed and quantity of the vibrations they are able to associate, dance being the slowest, most tentative effort towards form, and architecture being the fastest and fullest.

The whole world, then, can be conceived of in terms of an exchange of vibrations, given a more or less fleeting form, whose ultimate source is, in Gleizes's view, not of the nature of time and space. This being the case, the nature of these vibrations – the nature of form – is not a matter of indifference: 'Do you begin to understand the importance of the formal realisation which our species, at different stages of its growth, has surrounded with a mystery as great as the intensity of its longing – its joy when it sees the association being born; its regret as it feels that it is coming apart?'[25] The forms, colours and sounds that we as resonators receive are as important for our well-being, for the quality of our being, as the food we eat. At the very least, they must correspond to our own human order of magnitude; but we have wanted to project ourselves far beyond our own means, into the infinitely great (the universe observed externally) and the infinitely small (the atom observed externally).

The natural world, the raw material with which we work, is wonderfully adapted to our human nature:

> These materials that lie at the disposal of the human consciousness, are already so moving and so living when we think that the fundamental principle has elaborated them in their stable consistency adapted to the speed of our senses, following the same law that we have to follow, obliging an enormous number of vibrations to hold together in the shortest possible time.[26]

Our anxiety – the sense of insecurity that pervades modern society – derives from the fact that we have abused the relationship between ourselves and the natural world, and between ourselves, the natural world and our own formal realisations, which are grossly out of scale, conceived for abstract, intellectual, commercial reasons, without reference to human nature, consequently inhuman. The two essays in which Gleizes begins to work out a language that corresponds to the view of the world as an exchange of vibrations were written before he developed his radical opposition to the machine, but it is clear that that is where the tendency of his thought must lead. The formal question has become a question of the form that can correspond to human nature in the fullest sense of the word; this in turn requires the recovery of that human nature from the Tower of Babel which it has built about itself; and this requires a re-establishment of contact with the elements of the natural world about us, which already possess the perfect adaptation to our own human nature that we seek.

The first essay in which Gleizes argues for the return to the soil is *La Terre et les métiers manuels*, published in *Les Cahiers de l'étoile* in 1928 and later included in *Vie et mort de l'occident chrétien* when this was published in book form in 1930. Thus, between 1926 – when, he tells us, he abandoned *La Machine-modernolatrie* – and 1928, he is uncharacteristically silent, at least on this subject, which must have been very much on his mind. The Gleizes possessed a motorcar, which may have inspired his 1925 reflections on the shape of the car in relation to painting. However towards the end of 1926 he was involved in an accident. He was thrown out of the car and had to spend two weeks in a hospital in Toulon with two fractured legs.[27] It is tempting to think that this accident might have contributed to his disillusionment with the machine, but it must be admitted that the Gleizes' still had a car in the 1930s.[28]

It was about this time that either he or Juliette decided to buy a substantial rural property – Les Méjades and Archaimbaud – near St Rémy in Provence. Mme Gleizes says that it was his idea; that her father's portfolio of shares had become intolerable to him and that he insisted on investing it in the land. She says that he learned about the region round St Rémy while he was in hospital. He, on the other hand, says that it was her idea; that he was perfectly happy to play Cassandra and lament (or look forwards to) the imminent collapse of civilisation, but that she insisted that something practical had to be done.[29] Some time later, Anne Dangar complained in a letter to her Australian friend, Grace Crowley, that: 'You know she [Mme Gleizes] made Mr Gleizes put all his [sic – PB] money in a property; well, by mismanagement the property costs more than it brings in and he has never had a new pair of socks since his father-in-law died in 1920 [sic – PB].'[30]

However, it was not until later that Les Méjades became an asset rather than a liability in Gleizes's life. Much more important in the immediate circumstances was the establishment of Moly Sabata in 1927.

The initiative for Moly Sabata came from Pouyaud, writing to Gleizes in the Summer of 1927 to ask if he could help him to escape from the town to begin the work of rebuilding himself in the country in accordance with Gleizes's ideas – ideas which, it will be remembered, Gleizes had not yet published. Gleizes was worried about Pouyaud's health, which had been adversely affected by the job he had painting with a spray gun, but he was reluctant to launch such a thoroughly town-bred couple into what could be a dangerous and difficult way of life.[31] Pouyaud, however, insisted, wanting to settle near Serrières, where he could keep in contact with Gleizes. At the end of the year, after exploring several other possibilities, the Gleizes' rented 'Moly Sabata', a large house in Sablons, the village facing Serrières on the other side of the Rhone Valley. From now on, the story of Moly Sabata and of its inhabitants (especially Anne Dangar, the Australian potter who maintained it, often in very great difficulties, for twenty years until her death in 1951) will accompany Gleizes like an alter ego – the practical application of his ideas, the proof or otherwise that they were viable. Although it will involve jumping a little ahead of Gleizes's own development, this seems to be a good moment in which to give a brief account of its early history.

11

MOLY SABATA

Sablons and Serrières are two villages facing each other across the Rhone Valley, about half way between Lyon and Valence. Sablons is in the department of the Isère, Serrières in the Ardèche, but this reflects a more ancient division between the Vivarais, part of the Kingdom of France (Serrières), and the Dauphiné, once part of the Germanic Holy Roman Empire (Sablons). The two are joined by a bridge and the Roche family house, where Gleizes was now spending much of his time, was just beside this bridge, in Serrières, on what is now called the Quai Jules Roche. Jules Roche had been the deputy for Serrières since 1871 and the villagers had known the eccentricities of his daughter since childhood. According to Anne Dangar, they felt that she was much improved.[1]

Moly Sabata is a long, low, rambling house running alongside the river at the extreme southern end of Sablons (Plate 79). It was owned, appropriately enough, by a community of nuns, and had a garden with spreading chestnut trees and three outhouses. The main building consisted of two wings, separated by a large central room. As it stands now (it has been repaired by the Fondation Albert Gleizes after a fire in the 1980s) this room is tall but previously the ceiling was lowered by an attic floor. With paintings by Gleizes, Metzinger (*L'Oiseau bleu*) and Delaunay (*Formes circulaires, soleils N° 1* – one of the first of his series of 'Soleils'), and a soft light reflected from the Rhone playing on the walls and ceiling, this room was, by all accounts, extraordinarily beautiful.

The director of the Museum at Annonay, further south in the Rhone Valley, researched the origins of the name 'Moly Sabata'. According to Anne Dangar, 'He was vibrating with excitement when he heard it was probably a Moorish name meaning "Repos du Seigneur" [The Lord's Rest]. But later evidence shows plainly it is very ancient French for "Sabots Mouillés"' – 'wet clogs', referring to the tendency for the Rhone to flood its banks.[2] When I mentioned the name to a friend who is a mediaeval scholar, she suggested that it could be derived from a Latin phrase meaning 'the Women's Sabbath' – the place where women went to enjoy themselves in their own company. This seems to me the most probable explanation, the more so because the house is situated near a spring where the women would have met as they went to fetch water.

Gleizes outlined his hopes for Moly Sabata in a talk given in April 1932 in Dassau, at the Bauhaus, and in Poland. He began by evoking the memory of the Abbaye de Créteil, and it is perhaps worth noting that 1928–9, the period when Moly Sabata was being established, was also the period when Christian Sénéchal was researching his book on the Abbaye, published in 1930. Gleizes quoted the Abbaye manifesto which I have discussed in my first chapter. The problem had not gone away. The artist, standing for the values of the spirit, was an anachronism, a luxury in our resolutely materialist society which had no time for anything that did not pay: 'The whole of the nineteenth century is a long martyrology of artists, poets, writers . . .'. Nowadays, artists and intellectuals were multiplying 'in a proportion as great as tinned foods and automobiles': a recent survey had counted 40,000 artist painters,[3] but only a handful of these could live from their art. Musicians had been able to find work playing in cinema orchestras, but the advance of progress had been able to synchronise the cinematic image with recorded sound and the musicians were being thrown out of work. Poets and writers had traditionally been able to find office jobs but even they were threatened by the advance of the typewriter. At any rate, it was almost impossible for artists in any field to find the time that was necessary for learning their craft. Only a handful of spectacular and flexible talents could expect to succeed in the conditions of the market.[4]

The result was that the artist was becoming something of a monstrosity. This was how the world saw him and, increasingly, it was how he saw himself. We will remember that this whole problem had been one of Gleizes's major preoccupations on his return to Paris after the war, when he had proposed the formation of an artists' union.

In the first instance, then, Moly Sabata was an attempt to reassert the idea of the Abbaye de Créteil – a refuge where artists could concentrate on their work, sheltered from commercial pressures. The group that formed the Abbaye had intended to earn their living through the practice of a craft compatible with their artistic aspirations – in their case, fine printing. And they had tried, in the most rudimentary and incompetent fashion, to cultivate a vegetable garden. Moly Sabata's garden could be more or less self sufficient in food and its inhabitants could provide for their other needs through the practice of a craft.

There was now a further dimension to Gleizes's thought, though he still sees the seeds of it in the Abbaye de Créteil. The Abbaye had organised open days, and a great Summer Festival, with theatre, music, poetry readings, paintings. Gleizes saw the whole of the spiritual life of the nation converging on the towns. The country had been left desolate. Everything – cinema, radio, newspaper – was calculated to demoralise the peasant, to persuade him that real life occurred in the city. The problem of the depopulation of the countryside was

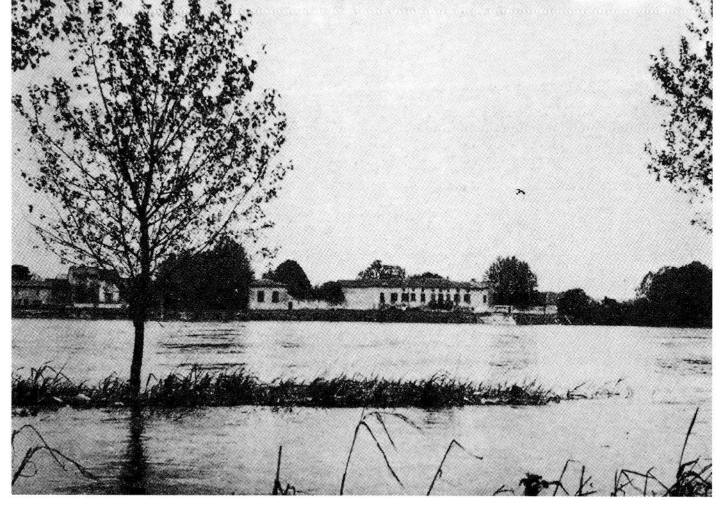

79. Moly Sabata seen from across the Rhone

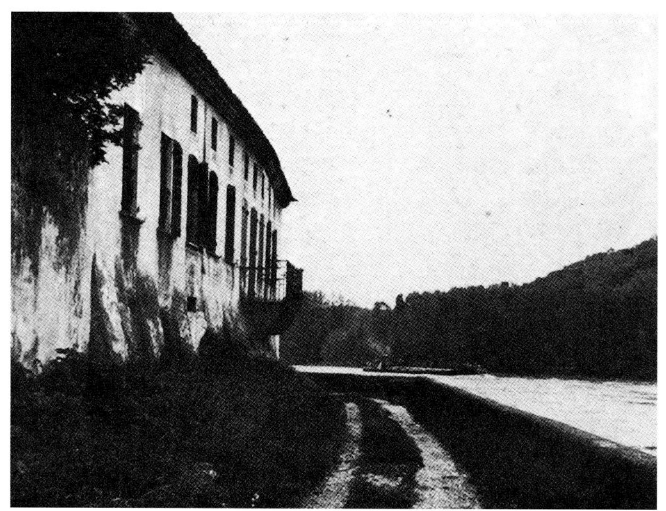

80. Moly Sabata beside the Rhone

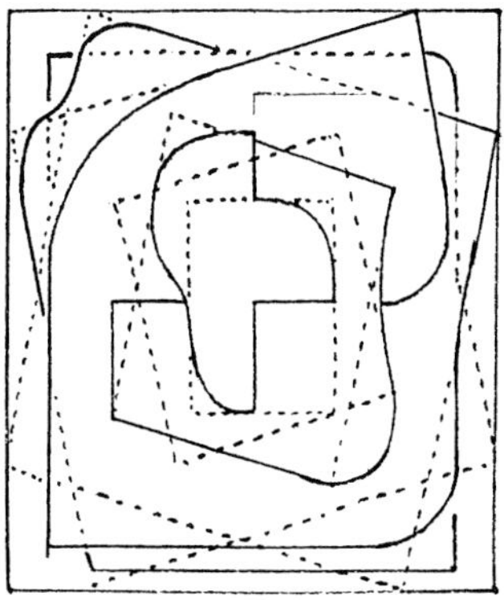
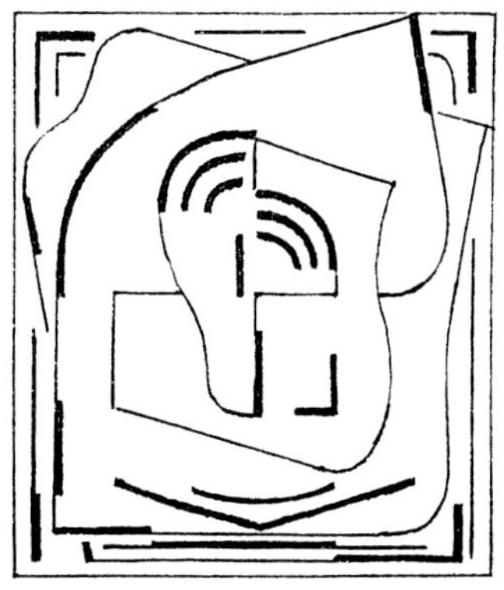
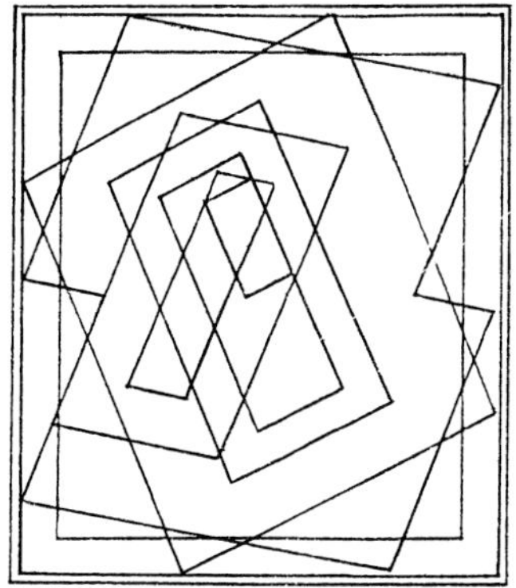
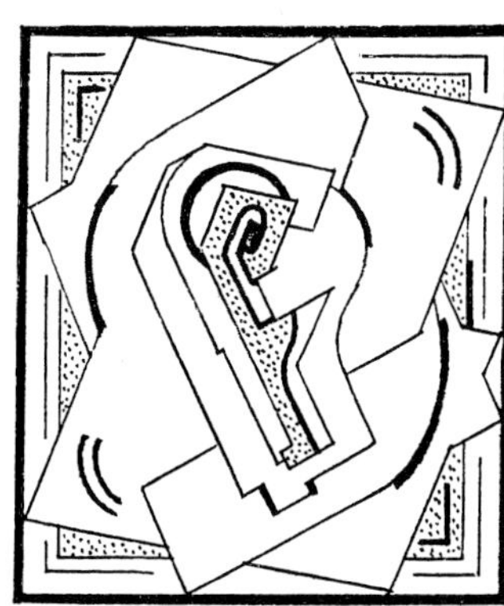

being posed in the political discussions of the time. The solution usually proposed was to create outposts of an essentially urban culture – school, cinema, 'dancings' – in the village. For Gleizes, this was ridiculous. These could only be a means of propaganda for the town. Sooner or later, the young peasant would tire of the imitation and want the real thing.

What was required was a radical decentralisation of our cultural life. The 40,000 artist-painters seemed a grossly inflated number when they were all herded together in the town, all competing for the same handful of successful galleries. But it was by no means an excessive number if they could be dispersed about the country. Gleizes's idea – and it was an idea of genius – was that in this way the artist could recover the social usefulness he so obviously lacked. He could bring back to the villages the spirit that had long been lost to, and corrupted by, the towns.

The Pouyauds moved into Moly Sabata at the end of 1927. In January 1928 they were joined by a Romanian poet, Georges Dobo. In February, the Rhone burst its banks and Moly Sabata and the area around it were flooded and isolated for several days. The Pouyauds' initiation into their new life was a hard one.[5]

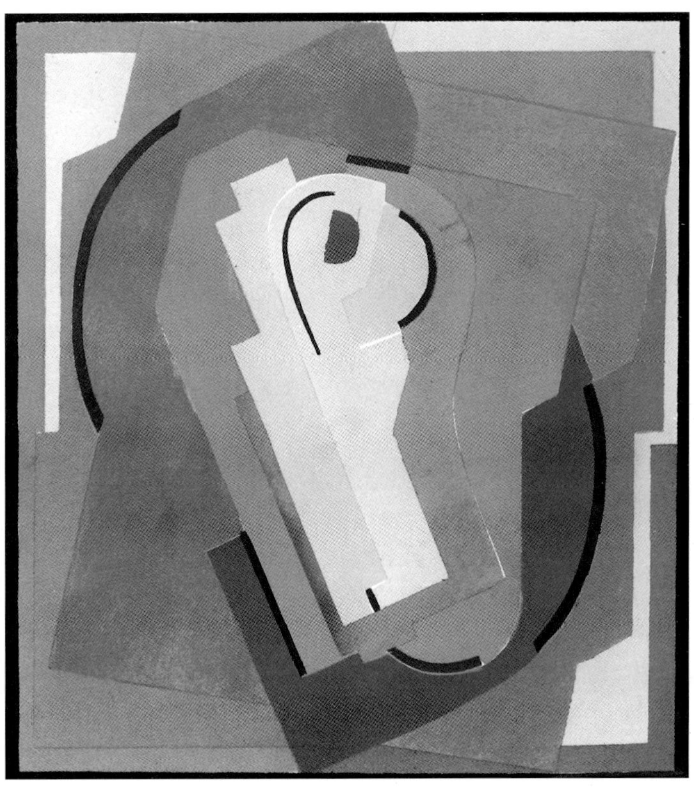

81. Drawings by Robert Pouyaud, probably *c.* 1930, showing how a pictorial construction can be derived from simple exercises in translation-rotation

82. Robert Pouyaud, Pochoir prepared for C.Geoffray and R. Pouyaud's *Suite de sons et de couleurs*, *c.* 1931, 20 × 17 cm. Private Collection

By June 1928, they had a small vegetable garden, rabbits and beehives.[6] Gleizes, in addition to providing the house, also wanted to help the project by providing work and he commissioned Pouyaud to make a series of pochoirs based on Gleizes's own paintings. The pochoir was traditionally the means by which playing cards were reproduced. It is a method of painting in *série* rather than of printing as such. Each colour is painted through its own stencil, normally cut out of a zinc plate. The method allows great precision and liveliness, but it is very time-consuming. Trial runs by Pouyaud annotated by Gleizes have survived (as have the zincs themselves) and they show how demanding he was and how much importance he attached to the precise relations of the colours. Pouyaud's pochoirs – both those based on Gleizes's paintings and on his own – are masterly.

In *Du Cubisme et les moyens de le comprendre* (1920), Gleizes had argued that the new painting, simple in form and colour, lent itself to reproduction in series, which would bring down the price, undermine the mystique of the unique piece, bring the artist closer to the craftsman, and contribute to breaking the power of the commercial galleries. But even then, although he had not yet publicly developed his opposition to machine production, Gleizes is arguing for the painstaking pochoir method. According to a review of an exhibition Gleizes held in New York in 1923: 'Albert Gleizes's later work is purely flat. He has confessed that his desire is to repeat his canvasses exactly by means of stencilling and later by filling in the colours with the same mechanical precision. In this way there need be no dispute among buyers over the possession of the same picture.'[7] This was of course the period in which Gleizes was closest to Jacques Villon who, realising after the failure of an exhibition held in Jacques Povolozky's gallery in 1922 that he would never be able to live from his painting, had devoted himself to making high quality prints, including a very impressive series based on paintings by his more successful contemporaries.

Dobo's involvement with Moly Sabata was shortlived,[8] but in October 1929, the Pouyauds were joined by François Manevy and his wife. Gleizes had met Manevy in 1920, when he had been invited to Lyon for the inauguration of the Lyon section of the Fêtes du Peuple, the movement launched by his old friend from the Abbaye de Créteil, Albert Doyen. The Lyon section was organised by Manevy. It was about this time that *Clarté* published a letter from a group of artists in Lyon supporting Gleizes's article, *Vers une Epoque de bâtisseurs*, and we may speculate that Manevy was among them.[9] Later Manevy opened what he claimed was the first art gallery specialising in modern work in Nice. He wrote to Gleizes on the basis of their earlier encounter, inviting him to exhibit.[10] He had also become friendly with a young painter, Walter Firpo. Firpo was working as a bank clerk at the time and tells of an occasion when one of the clients protested to the manager against his employing a man responsible for such ferocious, barbaric painting.

Manevy put Firpo in contact with Gleizes who agreed to hold an exhibition with him in Manevy's gallery in 1929. It was an extraordinary decision since Firpo was an unknown painter and Gleizes had never seen his work. He explains it in the Introduction to an exhibition of Firpo's held in 1947:

> The letters which Firpo addressed me on that occasion had struck me forcibly. This American handled French with a mastery that was astonishing and his enthusiasm overflowed in words; I was enchanted by his understanding of painting. Our friendship, founded on the spirit, was immediate. . . .[11]

In fact it was an inspired decision. Firpo, without ever renouncing his own very distinctive approach to painting, was to become a lifelong champion of Gleizes, one of the few who fought – in lectures, articles and a wonderful, wide-ranging correspondence – to keep his name alive in the difficult years after his death.

The following year, 1930, after the gallery had closed, Firpo organised an exhibition in Nice of himself, Gleizes, Jellett, Hone, Pouyaud and Ben Nicholson. We may assume that Nicholson had been involved through Evie Hone. She had been a friend of Winifred Nicholson's since before the war and since 1925 was involved with the '7 + 5 Group' in London, which Nicholson chaired. Winifred Nicholson says that between the wars she and Ben often visited Evie Hone in Paris: 'Ben and Evie talked of squares and rectangles, and of this dawn of art which was discovering the possibilities of the potencies of shapes and their relationships in space, when nothing but shape alone was under consideration.'[12] We may note that at this time, unlike Hone, Nicholson had not yet become a convinced non-representational painter.

When Manevy's gallery failed, Gleizes invited him to go to Moly Sabata, and initially Pouyaud was delighted with the decision: 'We already think they are just the "monks" that were needed here'.[13] It was, however, fairly clear that the Manevys were not deeply committed to the venture: 'neither of them seemed to be possessed by "the agricultural mystique"', as Mme Gleizes was to put it.[14] It was merely a means of coping with a temporary difficulty.

About the time that the Manevys moved in, in October 1929, Pouyaud was also working with an Australian painter, Grace Crowley – 'very nice, we are already good friends and we work together'.[15] Mme Gleizes says that in September she and Gleizes returned from a conference in Barcelona to find Evie Hone, Mainie Jellett, a young German architect who specialised in the Romanesque and two Australian girls who had worked with Gleizes in the previous Summer – Grace Crowley and Dorrit Black.[16] Crowley and Black had initially been told they should make contact with Gleizes by their friend, Anne Dangar.

Anne Dangar had an already well-established reputation in Australia as an associate of Julian Ashton, founder of the Sydney Art School, who could be said to have introduced the techniques of the pre-Impressionist Barbizon School to Australia. The Sydney Art School as such had been founded in 1907, though Ashton had been giving private classes (nicknamed the 'Academie Julian') for many years previous. Dangar, according to her own account,[17] served an apprenticeship of nine years with him and then became his closest associate, helping him to run the school, for another nine years ('I bet if any pupils do come in his [Gleizes's] absence they'll get Gleizes's methods better than Miss Jellett or Pouyaud could give them because Julian Ashton taught me to teach, to give my all, and never think another was less worthy to receive than myself'[18]).

In the mid-1920s, she went to London to visit some of Ashton's old associates but on the way she passed through Paris and was overwhelmed by the difference between what was happening there and what she had been up to in Australia. She was to tell her pupil Geneviève de Cissey that 'At your age I did not yet know Cézanne. It was in 1923, I think, that I first saw a reproduction of one of his pictures.'[19] This was after she had already been painting with Ashton for at least fifteen years. She decided that she had to stay in France to study the new painting and in 1925 and in 1926, she sent letters to Australia describing her discoveries, which were published in the Sydney Art Students Club magazine, *Undergrowth*. She and Crowley took lessons with Lhote and Crowley wrote to Ashton to say that 'to my amazement, his teaching was only the confirmation of the WANT I had been feeling so long without knowing exactly what the want was'.[20]

Nonetheless, it appears from a letter Dangar wrote to Gleizes in 1941 that 'After three years in Europe, we simple Australians ("innocents abroad") were terribly depressed and disillusioned'.[21] The art which had seemed to proclaim a new, lofty, moral idea was dominated by commercial interest. It was in this mood of disillusionment with Europe, shortly before she had to return to Australia, that she fell upon the paintings of Albert Gleizes:

> I had seen the pictures of Mr Gleizes in the Salon des Tuileries in June 1928. After having looked at hundreds of canvasses in this exhibition, I reached

> the depths of the wooden building and found myself in a little room with three large astounding pictures. In front of these canvasses, I was filled with a perfect satisfaction, with an internal joy that the Hindus call 'intellectual beatitude' and describe as a 'savorous taste'. It was the same peace for the heart that I feel in front of a mediaeval cathedral or the wall-paintings of the same period.
>
> Although I had to return to Australia, I could not forget the experience of this hour passed with Gleizes's pictures. I didn't have the compositions of these pictures clearly in my mind, but more even than the colours, the long lines that had evoked a divine music within me were constantly in my thoughts. Fourteen months after my return to Australia, I came back to France, directly to Moly Sabata, and I have stayed here because I found in my master's work what I was looking for.[22]

Mme Gleizes says that Dangar had tried to contact Gleizes prior to returning to Australia but failed. She told her friend Grace Crowley about her discovery, and Crowley seems to have made contact in 1929, taking lessons with Gleizes in Paris during the Summer. Back in Australia, Anne Dangar could not resume her old life. Her relations with Ashton, who had become a fierce opponent of the new painting, had become very difficult. She set up classes of her own and was immediately successful, but she had to teach a representational painting in which she no longer believed. The mood of depression which she had felt in France deepened as she was torn between the intuition of a religious dimension she had had before Gleizes's painting (almost certainly three paintings on religious themes he had prepared, working closely with Mainie Jellett, for the church at Serrières) and the heavy naturalism and materialism of the art world about her. As she wrote to Grace Crowley:

> I suddenly got a deep desire to draw nearer to God. Sydney . . . the commercial outlook on Art . . . etc. shocked me after Lhote and the Primitives and Chartres and Italy and my three pure vision years and my whole thought was a prayer to be rescued from that dreadful throng I found myself amongst. *La Peinture et ses lois*, although so hard to understand, was to me the one confirmation of my belief in Art being God's creative spirit, therefore my hopes clung to the name of Albert Gleizes. You were sent to Gleizes and you sent for me to come – I was already there in mind. . . .[23]

In Serrières, Grace Crowley had worked with Pouyaud and seen Moly Sabata. When the Gleizes' arrived to join them she told them about Anne Dangar and suggested that Moly Sabata would be ideal for her. They sent a telegram inviting her to come and were surprised to receive a reply almost immediately: 'Will leave February if position certain'.[24]

Anne Dangar arrived in March 1930 and was met at the station at St Rambert by Pouyaud and Manevy. The beautiful house, the beautiful setting and the extraordinary character of Pouyaud (nicknamed 'St François' in her correspondence with Grace Crowley) immediately impressed her. But in fact a very fraught situation had developed between Pouyaud and Manevy; and in the exchange of telegrams, nobody seems to have explained to her exactly what Moly Sabata was intended to be.

•

Pouyaud wrote to Mainie Jellett in June 1930, three months after Anne Dangar's arrival, to say that he had definitely decided to leave Moly Sabata. Part of the reason was that his parents had left Paris and gone to live in the village of Asnières sur Bois, near Vézélay. His father was old and ill and needed help to continue working and supporting himself, but Pouyaud was also disappointed in the direction Moly Sabata had taken.[25] Without going into the details of his problems with the Manevys we may note that underlying them was a difference in principle between Pouyaud and Gleizes that was soon to cause much difficulty for Anne Dangar as well. Pouyaud took the 'monastic' aspect of Moly Sabata seriously, believing that it could only work if those living there had a common 'state of mind' – essentially a common faith in Gleizes's teaching, though 1930 is precisely the moment when Pouyaud discovers a second 'master' in the person of René Guénon. In June 1930, the same month in which he wrote to Mainie Jellett to tell her of his decision to leave Moly, he wrote to Gleizes to tell him in great and very excited detail about his thoughts on reading Guénon's *Le Roi du monde*, and Anne Dangar, seeking God in the teachings of Albert Gleizes, seems to have received a heady mixture of Gleizes and Guénon in her early days with Pouyaud.[26]

Pouyaud, then, wanted a community disciplined around a common faith. When he had argued this case with Gleizes, Gleizes had said that he would take anybody at Moly Sabata.[27] For Gleizes, Moly Sabata was an attempt to address a social problem concerning, for a start, the 40,000 artists of Paris. Obviously he would hope that those who came to Moly would accept his own philosophy, but the principle thing was to start a process of decentralisation, to get them out of the town. The result of this view, which was shared by Mme Gleizes, was that for much of her life, Anne Dangar had to put up with a succession of intellectuals of different kinds with whom she had very little in common and whose lack of commitment to the hard everyday work of maintaining the house and garden was a constant source of irritation to her.

In the dispute with the Manevys, Anne Dangar sided with Pouyaud but Gleizes seemed, incomprehensibly, to side with the Manevys. From Pouyaud's account, it appears that Gleizes lost patience with Pouyaud when Pouyaud told him that he intended to leave. Pouyaud's decision was also related to the needs of his family and therefore was not totally a matter of his feelings about Manevy. Why should Gleizes try to sort Manevy out if Pouyaud was leaving in any case? At this time, Gleizes had little reason to have confidence in Anne Dangar who, in the earliest days, felt this lack of belief sorely ('He thinks he's struck a dud'[28]). For a while he seems to have thought of abandoning the whole venture and simply subletting the house to the Manevys and to Anne Dangar if that was what they wanted.

In the middle of all this, in the Summer of 1930, Serge Charchoune arrived. Charchoune had been in Barcelona at the same time as Gleizes, in 1916–17, and had been regarded as one of the most important of the painters associated with the Dalmau Gallery. He had broken off what appeared to be a promising career to go to Russia in 1917 to join the Revolution but in the event he failed to reach Russia and was soon to be disillusioned by the Revolution. On coming back to France, he was associated with the Dadaists and, later, with the group that gathered round Delaunay. He too had no particular commitment to Gleizes's ideas. He told the historian, André Dubois: 'I had to choose between life under the bridges and Moly Sabata. I had nothing to eat. I heard about Gleizes's phalanstery on the grapevine, but I wasn't interested in Gleizes's ideas . . .'.[29] Nonetheless, as André Dubois has remarked, Charchoune's often delightful, lyrical non-representational painting is perhaps closer to the spirit of Gleizes than he was prepared to admit. Walter Firpo arrived at the same time and, for all his enthusiasm for Gleizes's ideas, his explosive temperament may have had more in common with the wild man Charchoune than with the slow, patient, perhaps rather plodding Pouyaud. Neither Charchoune nor Firpo stayed very long.

In the event, the Manevys left, rather suddenly, in September. This did not alter the decision of the Pouyauds who left in November. Pouyaud seems to have felt that he could no longer trust Gleizes sufficiently to be dependent on him, though their friendship and correspondence continued. He also told Anne Dangar that he believed Moly Sabata was an idea which was too far ahead of its time.[30] The Gleizes were worried that Anne Dangar was now alone in this large house, but she might have preferred to have been left that way.

Anne Dangar had arrived as a painter, wanting to learn from Albert Gleizes. That was her sole motive for coming to France. She was forty years old, with twenty years experience of painting and teaching behind her and was well-known and liked in Sydney. She knew of Gleizes's ideas through *La Peinture et ses lois* but she knew nothing of his belief in decentralisation, in the return to the soil or return to the crafts. Mme Gleizes describes the shock with which Anne Dangar learned what Moly Sabata was about :

> The countryside, which was nothing but a white and pink mass of fruit-trees in flower, the nobility of the Rhone, the contours of the hills on the right bank, the old house so contemplative, the dinner rich with local tastes, everything enchanted Miss Dangar – but when Pouyaud showed her the square of garden she had to cultivate and the cabin where the rakes, the spades, the picks were stocked, she underwent one of the worst shocks of her life. To have broken with her entire past, and to have travelled 20,000 km to find nothing but agricultural implements was a tragedy – With her accent that was so distinctive and that scorn for genders she would never lose and which we all learned to appreciate so much, she declared: 'But I am a [feminine] painter, I'm not a [masculine] gardener.'[31]

Anne Dangar was soon to have reason to complain at Mme Gleizes's aristocratic amusement and aesthetic appreciation of the poverty in which she was often obliged to live. Pouyaud had written to Gleizes in 1929 to say that the work of maintaining Moly and of making pochoirs was such that, although he had learned a great deal and developed spiritually, he had been unable to do any painting.[32] Anne Dangar's career as a painter more or less stops at the moment of her arrival at Moly Sabata. She seems to have thought that Gleizes was offering her work and she arrived with very few financial means to find that, almost immediately, she had to buy elementary furnishings for the house. Pouyaud taught her to make pochoirs and Gleizes paid her in advance for a commission of 400. In the event, she never completed this commission, which ceased to be urgent because, in the conditions of the economic crisis in France, Povolozky was unable to sell them. Anne Dangar eventually repaid Gleizes in 1934.[33] In the early days, two of her Australian pupils

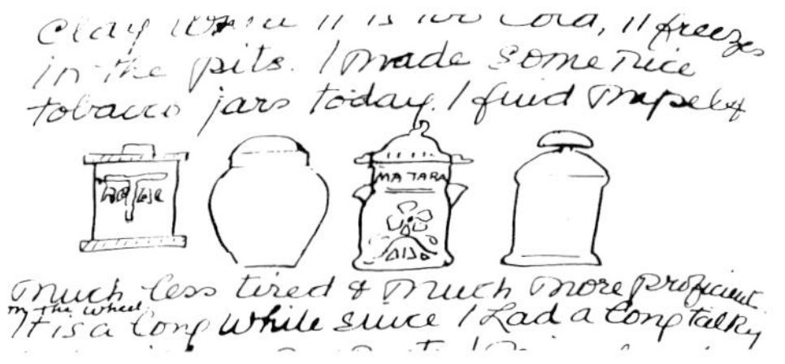

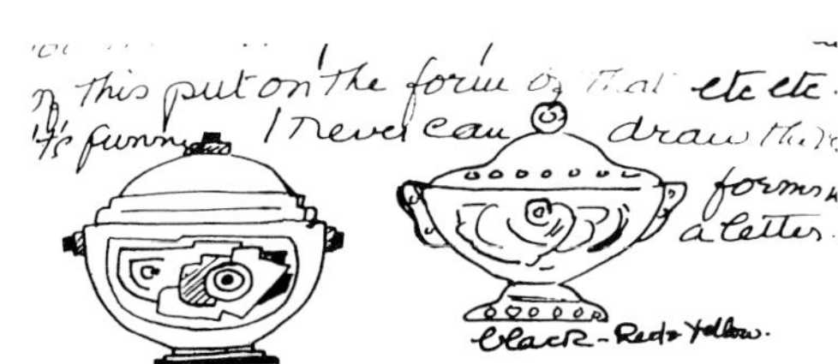

83. Anne Dangar, Drawing from a letter to Grace Crowley, 15 November 1932. Mitchell Library, Sydney

84. Anne Dangar, Drawing from a letter to Grace Crowley, 11 July 1933. Mitchell Library, Sydney

joined her at Moly Sabata and paid for lessons, but otherwise it was only help from Grace Crowley – which she was ashamed to have to accept – that saw her through her first two years in France.

While she was living in Paris she had spent some months studying pottery – 'rather on the artistic side', as Gleizes remarked, disapprovingly[34] – with a potter called Bernier, at Viroflay. Pouyaud suggested that she should go and work with one of the local potters. Small potteries using traditional techniques could still be found in the French countryside in the 1930s, albeit in a dilapidated and anachronistic state. The potters in the Rhone Valley area round Sablons used the 'glazed earth' technique. They found the clay in local claypits, washed it themselves, turned, decorated, glazed it with a lead-sulphate glaze, and fired it in a wood-fired kiln. In England, such techniques were being revived by potters such as Bernard Leach as part of the Arts and Crafts revival; but there was no character of 'revival', or any sort of ideology in the work of these French potters. They were simply providing for the needs of the people around them.

The first reference I have seen to her work as a potter in Anne Dangar's correspondence is in a letter to Grace Crowley, dated September 1930. She says she had made a whole coffee set 'as well as many other things these last four days'. We may assume that she started in the Summer. She worked at St Désirat, south of Serrières, travelling there on foot, under the direction of a potter named Pignot. On Pignot's death in 1934, she wrote:

> I am so thankful to have worked with Pignot, for I fear he is the last of his tribe of grand old workmen of a bye-gone age. Certainly, he was the best potter I have known and I owe him all I know regarding real pottery. 'La poterie n'est pas fait par un coup d'oeil, ni un coup de main, c'est construite, c'est le mouvement de la forme qui fait la poterie bien' ['Pottery is not made by a trick of the eye or a trick of the hand, it is constructed, it is the movement of the form understood that makes good pottery']. Imagine that from an ignorant old dirty workman! I could look at his rows of 'pots' and see the same movement in each one of the 500, and the result was the same pleasure to look upon as the parade of magnificently built beasts at the Easter Show. Thank God I was led to old Pignot. He always got drunk when I needed him most, he caused me every species of despair known, but he made me understand pottery, and much about the true meaning of Cubism, for what is Cubism but 'the movement of form understood'?[35]

By 1931, Anne Dangar was also giving painting lessons to children from Sablons and Serrières, a work that was to become increasingly important for her and that fulfilled Gleizes's desire that the artists, returned to the village,

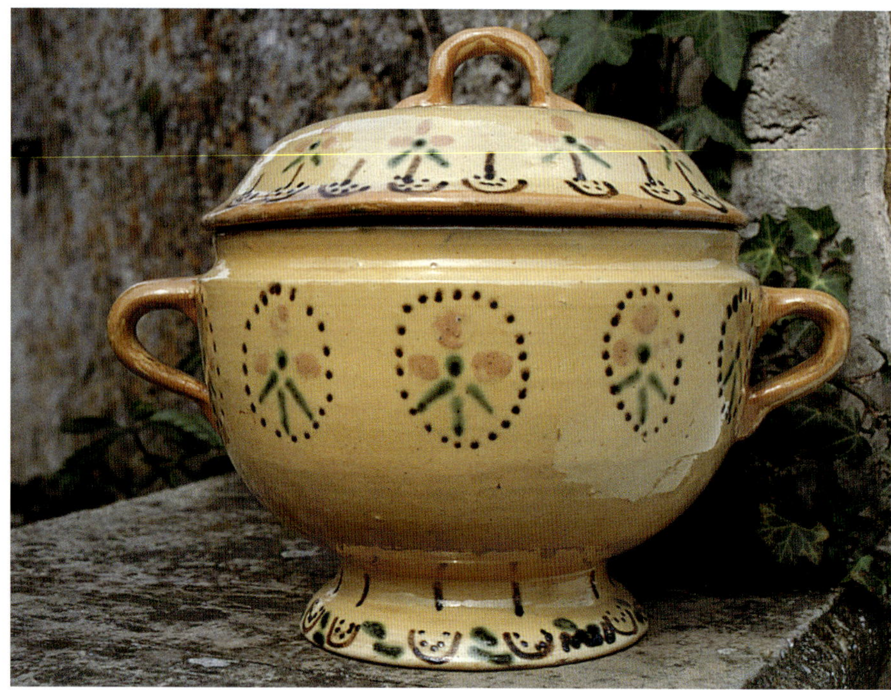

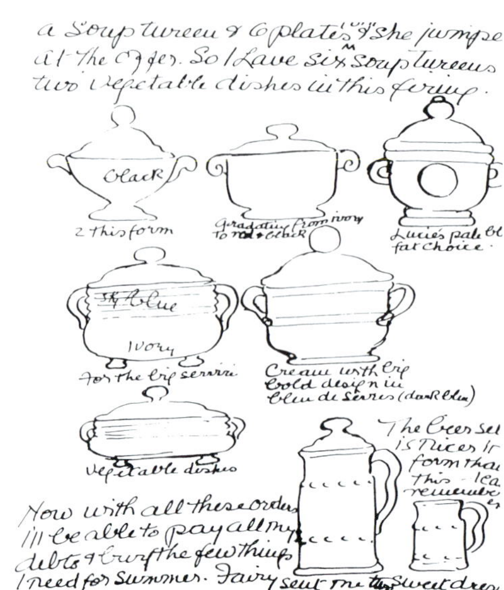

85. Anne Dangar, Large Soup Tureen, *c.* 1931–2. Glazed earthenware with slip decoration, h. 25 × w. 30.5 × dia. 23 cm. Sablons, Moly Sabata. Gift of Mido Geoffray

86. Anne Dangar, Drawing from a letter to Grace Crowley, 17 May 1935. Mitchell Library, Sydney

should contribute to the life of the community. But although these lessons were greatly appreciated, there could be no question of asking for payment for them. And it would be some time before she could think of earning money from her pottery. In the Summer of 1931, she earned the paltry sum of 120 francs for a large amount of routine work done for the Nicholas', who owned the St Désirat pottery:

> I am staring at the future in terror, for there is NOTHING and this 120 francs I got just now I must hand over at once to pay my month's bread bill and the coal I have been owing over a month. I am so old and I work with all my strength from 6 in the morning till 10 at night and never paint and only read in the train, but I earn 10fr a week and spend 50 in living and train fares. The Gleizes' urge me to do pottery but they give me no definite commissions for it nor make any arrangement with Nicholas . . . .[36]

It was not until March, 1932 that her career as a potter – more or less earning her keep with very great difficulty – began, with the first firing of her own work. The Gleizes, and a friend, were with her when the kiln was opened: 'I couldn't walk, broke into a run, and we all four ran up the hill like a pack of kids. Who couldn't love the French, who are always kids?'[37] When they saw the result, the Gleizes' were delighted. '"Now we've got something to brag about and WON'T WE JUST!!" cried Madame.' The talk Gleizes gave in Poland the following month, in April 1932, could be described as a case of 'bragging'. He boasted that Anne Dangar had revived the traditional pottery of the region, singlehandedly.

Anne Dangar's early pottery is indeed delightful, a remarkable achievement for the little time she had had to work on it (Plate 86). But it would still be some years before her real greatness as a potter would become evident.

In his 1932 talk, Gleizes, still remembering the Abbaye de Créteil, said that he could think of no better way of interesting local people in the imaginative work of Moly Sabata than music, which he had long argued was more sensual, therefore lower but also more easily accessible than painting. He was very taken with the idea of restoring the Festivals of the agricultural year:

> These festivals seemed to me to be a splendid means of keeping the activity of youth constantly alive, and even that of adults and of the old. For the preparations and the rehearsals required long weeks even if the festival itself would only last a few hours, and during these weeks, the work of the imagination, of invention and fantasy, could maintain and develop an active, captivating life for the spirit.[38]

But for this, musicians were necessary, and it was only in the previous year that the musician had been found. César Geoffray had started out as a child musician working in a circus. He had been involved with Manevy in the Lyon Fêtes du Peuple and, like Manevy, had met Gleizes in 1920, when he had read and been impressed by *Du Cubisme et les moyens de le comprendre* and by the articles in *Clarté*. Soon after, in 1921, Florent Schmitt, Gleizes's old army colleague, came to teach at the music school in Lyon where Geoffray was studying. Geoffray regarded Schmitt and Gleizes as the two great masters of his life.[39]

Geoffray's was the classic case described by Gleizes of the musician put out of work by the introduction of sound movies. He had been the conductor of a small Music Hall orchestra in Lyon; his wife, Mido, played the piano. Then the Music Hall was converted into a talking cinema and, as Gleizes put it: 'In accordance with the generally accepted idea that all progress liberates man from manual tasks and turns him into a thinker, the orchestral players saw their chains mercifully broken and were free to go off and think where they pleased.' He says that, by a remarkable stroke of good fortune, Geoffray had another offer of work, but that by this time he was enthusiastic about living and working at Moly. Anne Dangar mentions the Geoffrays as having spent a month there in 1930, probably with Manevy. In the same year he worked with Pouyaud on a *Suite de sons et de couleurs*, a book with pieces of music written by himself interspersed with pochoirs by Pouyaud (Plate 82).

The Geoffrays seem to have come back again in January 1931 only to leave again shortly for Paris. They finally moved in in May. With César, his wife, Mido, and their young daughter, Gilka, they had a maid, Lucie Deveyle, a peasant woman who had joined them after finding life working in a factory intolerable. Lucie was soon to join Anne Dangar's classes and to become increasingly interested in weaving. She left the Geoffrays in 1934, moved in with Anne Dangar and, as a weaver, became one of the most faithful and distinguished of Gleizes's pupils.

César Geoffray is best known as the founder of the popular choral movement, 'A Coeur Joie', which originated in the Choir of the French Scout movement, also founded by Geoffray, in 1940. The A Coeur Joie movement still exists throughout France. Through Geoffray, its origins go back to the Fêtes du Peuple. But his period at Moly was something of an interlude in his career. He himself says that he had spent most of the 1920s doing uninteresting and tiring commercial work and that he saw his life at Moly as a period of recovery. He liked the idea that 'Moly Sabata' might mean 'the Lord's rest' (himself being 'the Lord'). Apart from the annual festival of Moly Sabata, he contributed little to the development of the house or to relations with the village, and spent an increasing amount of his time in Lyon, where he gave music lessons. The result was a considerable tension between the Geoffrays and Anne Dangar, who felt that he was just using the house as a hotel. In fact, though neither she nor Geoffray himself were aware of it at the time, he was preparing himself for his later career, a work of promoting a decentralised, popular, non-commercial musical activity of very high quality, largely inspired by his conversations with Gleizes.[40]

The tension between Geoffray and Anne Dangar can be seen as reflecting the same two, not necessarily contradictory, tendencies in Gleizes's own thought that we have seen in the tension beteen Manevy and Pouyaud – the 'monastic' tendency, emphasising discipline and longing to re-establish the consciousness of a transcendental reality; and a more outward going, theatrical tendency – the Gleizes who had wanted to be an actor, who had organised plays and poetry readings for the Association Ernest Renan and for the garrison at Toul, the Gleizes who had wanted to collaborate with Cocteau (it happens that, in the late 1920s, when Moly was founded, Gleizes was working with Léonide Massine on costumes for a ballet, *Jane d'Aimé*, to be performed in America. The contact between Gleizes and Massine had been made by Delaunay, but the project bored him – 'c'est de l'eau de rose', he wrote to Mainie Jellett[41]).

In Poland and at the Bauhaus Gleizes gave a glowing account of the Geoffrays' activities, saying that 'their arrival in the region made more impact than that of the painters and of the poet . . .'[42] and that already he had worked with the local priest and with the schoolteacher, thus reconciling the great antagonism that ran through French rural life. The Gleizes' returned from Poland in the Spring of 1932 to see the first 'Spring Festival' of Moly, with ninety children directed by Geoffray singing music by Rameau, Couperin and Lully and dressed by Anne Dangar and Lucie Deveyle in those 'gauzes spangled with often very agreeable colours which stall-holders used to protect their wares against the flies'.[43]

By this time, Moly Sabata had survived for five years, easily outliving the Abbaye de Créteil, and it was beginning to make a significant impact on the life of the region – at the very least to render country life more interesting, though, in the event, it could do practically nothing against the increasing industrialisation of the Rhone Valley and the conversion of independent peasants into wage earners. From the point of view of what may be called Gleizes's political ambitions, it was to be a spectacular failure, but both César Geoffray and Anne Dangar in their different spheres testified to the possibility that, without becoming in any way 'commercial' or being 'vulgarised', the arts could serve as a spiritual refreshment to ordinary people. Geoffray taught children and untrained adults from all social backgrounds to sing the music of Lully and Couperin; Anne Dangar taught peasant children Gleizes's 'laws of painting', and sold her pottery at normal prices at the local market. Moly Sabata was the proof that Gleizes's thought, difficult and abstruse as it may sometimes seem, was indeed capable of assuming a popular dimension.

12

THE MYSTERY OF THE BREAD AND WINE

The period in which Moly Sabata was established was a period of intense activity on Gleizes's part, as a painter, as a writer and as a lecturer – the period in which the intuitions of the early 1920s begin to assume a definite form in preparation for the 'dénouement' of 1934.

I have mentioned that Gleizes lectured on Moly Sabata to a conference in Poland in 1932, and that he attended a conference in Barcelona in 1929. These were both held under the auspices of the 'Unions Intellectuelles Européennes', founded in 1921 by Prince Charles de Rohan with a view to encouraging understanding and dialogue among the intellectual élites of the different European countries after the disaster of the First World War. It was not an internationalist or pan–European venture; in the 1930s, Rohan was to become an apologist for German National Socialism. But nor was it right-wing or nationalist. The intention was to represent the widest possible range of opinions. Gleizes served on the French Committee of the Unions Intellectuelles together with, on the one hand, the Archbishop of Paris, and on the other, the 'rougissime' ('Ultra–red' – Mme Gleizes's phrase) Paul Langevin, soon to be a leading member of the 'Vigilance and Anti–Fascist Action Committee'. The Unions Intellectuelles Committee also included the poet Paul Valéry, the scientist Emile Borel, Henri Lichtenberger (specialist in German literature and, especially, Goethe) and the mathematician–politician, Paul Painlevé. Mme Gleizes mentions Oswald Spengler, Nicholas Berdyaev, Guiglielmo Ferrero, Gina Lombroso, Rabindranath Tagore, Herman Keyserling and Aldous Huxley as among the participants.[1]

For Gleizes, this was congenial company; all those mentioned were concerned with the great theme of the relation between science, philosophy and religion. It is interesting to see how easily Gleizes, whose formal education had been unsuccessful and as short as he could possibly manage, moved in these circles. Rohan's central idea was the creation of a European intellectual élite, and the necessity for an 'élite' had also long been a preoccupation with Gleizes – it is already evident in the articles in *Clarté*. But for Gleizes, this élite had to be primarily a moral élite, acquiring its status through renunciation, as the early Christians had done. Such an élite could not emerge naturally out of the existing system of education and nor could it be purely intellectual. A sense of the reality of things could only be acquired through the practice of a craft and in this respect Gleizes felt that he had the edge on his more academically orientated colleagues.

Gleizes first spoke to the Unions Intellectuelles in March 1927, when he gave a paper on *Peinture et perspective descriptive*, which marks a significant step forward in his understanding of the mediaeval sense of form. It is the first time that he evokes the contrast between the 'rhythmic' lines of the garments in twelfth-century sculpture, and the more representational, immobilised sculpture of the thirteenth century. The essay is also interesting for its discussion of Cézanne, whose greatness was recognised by everyone because he was made up of contradictions: the new plastic/formal spirit struggling with the old fidelity to the external appearances of nature. It was, Gleizes suggested, because the problems are posed but not resolved in Cézanne that everyone can find something to their fancy. The lecture was given to the French Unions Intellectuelles under the auspices of the Carnegie Foundation, but the Unions Intellectuelles also organised all–European conferences. Gleizes was present and spoke at the Barcelona congress of 1929,[2] in the context of the Spanish Universal Exhibition shortly before the overthrow of the monarchy, and at Cracow in 1930.

Most important was a lecture tour in Germany and Poland in April/May 1932, when, in addition to his paper *Art et production*, which he thought was to be given under the auspices of the Intellectual Unions (to his dismay, he found that the meeting had actually been organised by the Polish Foreign Office), he also spoke on *Art et science* in Lodz and in Stuttgart, at the invitation of an old friend, the engraver, Gottfried Graf; on *Art et religion* in Dresden; and on Moly Sabata in the Bauhaus, at a meeting chaired by Kandinsky, as well as in Warsaw. *Art et religion* had first been given in Paris in March 1931 to the Fédération Française des Associations Chrétiennes d'Etudiants, at a meeting chaired by Jean Baruzi, Secretary of the French Intellectual Union. The three papers *Art et religion, Art et science,* and *Art et production* have been published together and constitute perhaps the best general introduction to Gleizes's thinking.[3] They follow from the publication, in 1930 and 1932 respectively, of two of his most important books: *Vie et mort de l'occident chrétien* and *La Forme et l'histoire*.

•

Mme Gleizes says of *Vie et mort*: 'No book was ever worse received at its birth than these 220 pages which attacked everything.'[4] It is easy to see how the book could have upset Gleizes's immediate circle. Painting is hardly mentioned at all, except when Gleizes insists that the craftsman has the right and duty to address the general problems of mankind. It is the first book in which he expresses his general opposition to machine production and the city – though the most forthright essay on the subject – *La Terre et les métiers manuels* – had already been published in *Les Cahiers de l'étoile* in 1928.[5] But perhaps the most 'offensive' part of the book is the last of the three essays – *Le Mystère du pain et du vin*, in which he defends the Catholic doctrine of the Eucharist. To defend 'religion' in general terms, or even a now-forgotten esoteric Christian 'science', was one thing; but to defend the central mystery of the Catholic Church was quite another – though Gleizes's defence was as likely to offend Catholics as it did Gleizes's own rather anticlerical circle (when *Vie et mort* was published in an English translation shortly after the war, the argument on the Eucharist was criticised in *The Tablet*[6]).

Vie et mort de l'occident chrétien and *La Forme et l'histoire* both take up the cyclical view of history that is expressed in *La Peinture et ses lois* and develop it much further. *La Peinture et ses lois* studied the question in the history of painting and, despite the apocalyptical opening, was broadly optimistic in tone. Painting was renewing itself and therefore society as a whole could renew itself. But now Gleizes puts much more emphasis on the death of the old order. An old man, whose body is weak and painful, becomes obsessed with his bodily functions and can think about nothing other than how to overcome them, how to go beyond them. For Gleizes, that is the essence of the machine. It is an 'orthopaedic material' for a man who is sick, who is ready to die, but who does not wish to die:

> The West was sleepy with exhaustion, experiencing those discomforts of old age that make the organs, the articulations, the flow of blood so to speak conscious of themselves and close the mind, making it heavy, robbing it of the physical freedom of youth, filling it with their own miseries, irritating it with their too great sensibilities. So, under this pressure, the West has dreamed intellectually of an unheard of age when solid, material heroes would prance about in a world that was infinitely great, suddenly become infinitely small, where organs, articulations, veins and arteries would assume fabulous proportions and, inflating human knowledge, would boost the power of man and make him happy. (pp.xv–xvi)

Our distrust of our own human resources, our reliance on the machine, the concentration of all our energies round a single centre – the great town – the depopulation of the countryside, our conviction that reality is external to ourselves, that we are only observers – these are all signs of extreme old age, and a crabbed, bitter, undignified old age at that. But wherever one cycle ends, another cycle must begin. We are repeating the old age of the Roman Empire and at that time the renewal was brought about by Christianity. Christianity was radically opposed to the towns: the monastic movement was a flight of the best elements of the society into the desert. The Bible is full of the destruction of cities – Babel, Sodom, Jerusalem itself, Babylon, Rome (under the image of Babylon in Rev. 18):

> Would we not smile if we heard some madman say to the urban developer with his collection of wonderful plans for rapidly building an ideal, hygienic, silent town in conformity with our modern aspirations: "Verily I say unto you, there shall not be left here one stone upon another that shall not be thrown down."' (p.63. Quotation from Matt 24:2)

Christianity promoted a radical decentralisation and move away from the towns, to such an extent that by the eighth century there were no major European towns left, apart from Rome itself, which had long been stagnant. Gleizes regards the role of the barbarians in this process as essentially positive:

> Devitalised populations, impotent authority, collapse at all levels of activity, the Roman mortar was insufficient to hold its internal edifice together; through the cracks an external pressure was beginning to pierce, to widen the gaps, to throw down what appeared to be so high, periodical return to the soil . . .[7]

The knowledge of agriculture had greatly declined in Italy as wheat became an article of international commerce, and North Africa became the granary of the empire. But wherever the Christian monks went among the barbarians, they promoted agriculture, and especially the cultivation of wheat for bread, and the grape for wine, the sacramental elements.[8] So the sacramental bread and wine is not in any way separated from everyday bread and wine. The bread and wine necessary to our spiritual life is not separated from the bread and wine necessary to our corporeal life. And the process of the transubstantiation of the bread and wine into the Body and Blood of Christ is only a continuation, a culmination, of the many transubstantiations they have already undergone in the process of becoming bread and wine – a process that Gleizes describes in passages of captivating beauty.

The return to agriculture, then, was pioneered by the monks, who were themselves an intellectual élite prepared (unlike the self–indulgent Roman intellectual élite) to undergo the most rigorous discipline. This agricultural work was in itself an education in the physical reality of things. To produce good bread and to produce good wine, an immense knowledge of the quality of different soils, the quality of different seeds, the action of the seasons, the process of fermentation is needed, a knowledge that can only be acquired over generations of slow, patient, loving, disciplined work. It is an idea of knowledge that is radically different from our present idea of knowledge – the accumulation of observations about a world that is assumed to be external to ourselves. The illusion that we are mere observers of events for which we have no essential responsibility is not possible in a Christian agricultural society. There it is known that the world is created in us through the work of our own senses and that the manner in which our senses work is very largely determined by our own intellectual attitude, our 'state of mind'.

Augustine, in a number of his writings, but most notably in *The Teacher*, argues (following Plato) that all knowledge is a recognition of knowledge that already exists within us. This idea of 'innate' knowledge is basic to early Christian thinking. It is only at the end of the seventeenth century that the opposite idea, that our mind can only work on the basis of information about the external world conveyed to it by the essentially passive senses, becomes predominant, though its victory was prepared in the great scholastic debates from the eleventh century to the fourteenth. In *La Forme et l'histoire*, Gleizes argues that the two notions, of innate idea and external impression, can be reconciled once we understand the implications of the 'vibratory' nature of the world:

> Our ears are made, not to receive a sound that has no existence in itself, but to make it concrete, though this is unknown to most of those who are used to thinking that sound has its own reality . . . whatever we do, we will never be able to study sound, but only our ear . . .
>
> Hearing can only recognise what it knows, so that that order of vibrations that resonate upon it and that it translates into sonority has no reality of its own as sound other than that of a relationship. So, the conflict between innate ideas and ideas that only derive from sensations could thus be resolved without either of the adversaries losing face. If nothing exists outside our senses, could it not be precisely because our senses are like radio receivers organised in such a way that they take in certain magnitudes of external vibrations? They transform them into quality, and these qualities have a different character according to the nature of the senses in question. Numerically, our senses are tuned to all the vibratory magnitudes. They

> receive, according to their individual capacity, their resistance, such and such a numerical order and they make it conscious. Innate ideas, then, would be no more than these rhythmic capacities that are pre–existent to the sensation . . .
>
> Our senses are established on the basis of a fixed magnitude, the variable external world falls upon them, is measured against them, and from the resulting relationship a third state is born which we call, variously, sound, light, line, plane, volume, whose nuances and modes of action can be varied to infinity. (pp.218–20)

For Gleizes, the continual work of perception is a work of creation, endlessly astonishing and delightful, the transformation of numbers (quantity – the vibrations we receive) into quality (the spiritual resonance that these perceptions wake in us). The transformation of numbers into quality could be described as the whole theme of Augustine's *On Music*. What damns our civilisation is its complete lack of this sense of quality, its utterly passive and intellectual treatment of its sensations, beginning with the most elementary and life–giving – the eating of bread and the drinking of wine:

> The bread in the past did not look like anything much; it was excellent to the taste, and perfectly adapted to that lifegiving journey it was to realise through the flesh of the person who eats it; but for a purchaser who can read and write, who votes, and who freely agrees to undergo his military service, 'it looks bad', it isn't worthy to be sold.

Hence the need for 'those discoveries of talent and seduction which the citizen and the independent woman are unable to resist'. (*Vie et mort*, pp.161–2)

Gleizes elaborates at length on the degeneration of both bread and wine as they submit to the needs of international commerce:

> Under the cudgels of science, the soil became feverish, its pulse grew quicker, its temperature rose; the seeds reacted, they caught the fever, they hastened to grow, were abnormally prolific. Man had no understanding of the underground struggle that could be seen in the plant. He thought himself the master of agriculture, able to do what he liked, he swapped the different natures according to his fancy and changed the patterns of cultivation of different regions. He misunderstood the result of this scientific violation of the sources of life and, because it seemed good for his bank balance, he decided that a great progress had been achieved. Strange destiny of man! You only have to pass a certain order of things to an imperceptible degree and your life is in danger; and if you go too far beyond the order of things, it will cease altogether. There is no great white stone marking the danger, no boundary line between the rule of evil and the rule of good. St Augustine meditated long and hard upon this mystery. If man cannot understand the problem at a level that goes beyond sensory perception, he is lost because he will lose the awareness of his own levels of resistance. Animal manures were good for the soil, she knew how to assimilate and to be revived by them. Sometimes she could even profit from some mineral additions, natural and close to the fabric of her own varying nature, such as marl, or lime; but still it was necessary to treat them prudently and to go back to the

> manures and to that intelligent cadence of crop rotation which, by alternating periods of rest and different crops, repaired her, and enabled her to recover from the fatigue of her work . . . . (pp.154–6)

The result of the new methods was a dull, standardised wheat, with little nutritive content, when it was not positively harmful through adulteration: 'So, of the bread recommended by Jesus as the essential substance of life, what is left? A word, a verbal memory we continue to apply to something whose real, vital cause has become secondary, but whose commercial cause is in charge, exclusively . . .' (p.165)

Gleizes was writing this at almost exactly the same time (1928–30) that the provençal writer, Jean Giono, was publishing his trilogy of novels, *Colline*, *Un de Baumugnes* and *Regain*, which also calls for a return to the life of the countryside, the renewal of the villages, and lays great stress on the importance of bread. I have seen no evidence that Gleizes was in contact with Giono at this time, but he was soon to be involved with the rapidly developing 'Naturist'[9] movement, particularly with the journal, *Régénération*, and there were a number of other currents going in the same general direction – Guiglielmo Ferrero's *Entre le Passé et l'avenir*, published in 1926; René Guénon's *La Crise du monde moderne*, published in 1927; Gina Lombroso's *Le Rançon du machinisme*, published in 1931 and, also published in 1931, Louis Hoyack's *Où va le Machinisme?*. Gleizes's relations with Guénon will be looked at in a separate chapter. We have already seen that Gina Lombroso and her husband, Guiglielmo Ferrero were old family friends of the Roches. They were also involved with the Unions Intellectuelles, and Mme Gleizes says that they were frequent visitors with the Gleizes'. Hoyack was to play an important role in the key development Gleizes was to undergo in 1934.

Hoyack and Guénon both place the return to the earth and to handicrafts in the context of a religious scheme strongly influenced by oriental thought – Sufism in the case of Hoyack, Hinduism in the case of Guénon.[10] We may note in this context that in 1925 and 1927, Gleizes published articles in a journal called *Vers l'Unité*, 'revue internationale de synthèse spirituelle', a paper associated with his old friend Dr René Allendy.[11] The 1925 article – *Cubisme et culture générale* – is published in an issue which also contains Guénon's *La Métaphysique orientale*. The journal also includes an advertisement for a paper called *Les Cahiers anonymes*, 'sous la direction de R. de Maratray'. De Maratray was a Buddhist and 'Naturist' who was to write both for *Les Cahiers de l'étoile* and *Régénération*, and who was to visit the Gleizes' and Moly Sabata in the early 1930s. Although Gleizes's concerns were now out of keeping with those of his old acquaintances, both artistic and political, they were shared by a new circle that was gradually gathering around him.

This may be an opportune moment to point to a change in Gleizes's political connections. *Vers l'Unité* was combined with another paper, *France–Europe*, described as the 'Organe de la Droite Nouvelle', which gave opposition to Bolshevism as the cornerstone of its political outlook. The association is strange given the already well–established link with Allendy, a lifelong supporter of the Communist Party.[12] Gleizes himself was not involved with the 'New Right' or with any other political organisation at this time. His attitude towards the existing division between Right and Left may be summed up in an extract from *L'Inquiétude: crise plastique* of 1925:

> The species is a huge animal collapsed on the ground, wanting to get up on its feet. But, ignorant of its own constitution, it becomes desperate and, through impatience, becomes ever more tangled up in the network of its own members which, no longer able to recognise one another, wound each other horribly, every time the common desire brings them together in the same effort; the right legs and the left legs hit each other obstinately, instead of co–ordinating their action, and the huge inert mass of the body, caught in this double madness, is exhausted and sinks down ever deeper in despair. (ms version, p.1)

Within both Right and Left, Gleizes then recognised a desire for radical change, a feeling that something was gravely wrong and had to be changed. But, in his view, neither were prepared to go to the heart of the problem which lay in the relations between man and his environment, man and his work, man and his own formal realisations. The quarrel between them was absurd, especially since both wanted to perpetuate the supposed advantages of the machine and its production at a speed that went far beyond the rate that human resistances could absorb.

In *La Forme et l'histoire*, Gleizes evenhandedly criticises both the Communists and, more particularly, Action Française, the most powerful, both intellectually and politically, of the French Right-wing movements. He was in little danger of sympathising with the Action Française leader, Charles Maurras, soaked as the latter was in the classical culture Gleizes disliked. Maurras was a passionate Nationalist, who looked back to the great days of Louis XIV and the strong French monarchy. For Gleizes, looking back much further to the early days of Christianity, the nation was already too large a unit. Its emergence was a sign of the break–up of the original Christian universality.[13] He refers to 'the national fatherland, too big in space to be accessible to the senses, too small for the intelligence, inhabited by the Universal'.[14]

Nonetheless, the fact that Gleizes could publish side by side with the anti–Bolshevik New Right marks a change from the days of *Clarté* and *Vers une Epoque de bâtisseurs*. Gleizes says that it was when he explained his new radical opposition to the machine (thus, in early 1926) that Paul Vaillant–Couturier (who that year became editor of the Communist Party journal, *L'Humanité*) stopped visiting him.[15] It is also about this time that Gleizes begins to express admiration for a number of writers usually associated with the Right, including the theorists of Racism, le Compte de Gobineau and Houston Stewart Chamberlain, and the theorists of the early nineteenth-century counter–revolution, Joseph de Maistre and Louis de Bonald. His admiration for Gobineau and Chamberlain must be seen in the light of his regionalism, his attachment to very small local units; it carries no implication of an idea of racial superiority. In evoking the names of Gobineau and Chamberlain, he says: 'I love the varieties of expression of the human family too much not to deplore this dissolution of particular characteristics that destroys all character'.[16] He mentions Chamberlain again in *La Forme et l'histoire*, referring to his *Birth of the Nineteenth Century* 'where the most extraordinarily true insights swarm together with the most arbitrary opinions . . .' (p.335)

But to return to the views on the machine and 'machinisme' that were being expressed in Gleizes's immediate circle. Gleizes refers to Ferrero and to Gina

Lombroso's *Le Rançon du machinisme* in *Art et production*. He says that Ferrero had performed the great service of launching the terms 'quantity' and 'quality' into the general debate. The whole of current political and economic thinking turned on quantity. The problem of quality, which Gleizes understands as the life–giving quality of the product rather than just the effectiveness of the machine, was never raised. He may have in mind Ferrero's *Entre le Passé et l'avenir*, published in 1926, which criticised 'our quantitative civilisation' and ridiculed the idea that machines were saving labour:

> This immense activity of iron moved by steel would be impossible if we too did not work with greater intensity, if an ever more considerable number of men did not learn to produce and consume in ever larger quantities . . . The rapidity of means of communication is the thermometer that measures the fever of modern activity. The more rapidly we move in space, the more we have to work . . .'

And this feverish activity was unfavourable to 'any serious, disciplined religion' which required 'a reflection, a continuity of thought, a self–control that become ever more difficult in the fever that has attacked the world (pp.30–2).

Like Gleizes, Ferrero looks to social units smaller than the nation. Between the twelfth century and the French Revolution, Italy had been made up of ten regions, each 'a world that was complete, original, alive, developing according to its own law' (pp.37–8); and, like Gleizes too, he saw the Russian Revolution as little more than an extension of the French Revolution: 'The workers' and peasants' state they thought they had established in Moscow is governed by the bourgeois intellectuals and civil servants, just like the French Revolution or the German Republic' (pp.47–8). All the revolutions since the French had done no more than to complete its work of toppling the monarchies.

Le Rançon du machinisme, by Ferrero's wife, Gina Lombroso, is a history of the development of the machine, most interesting for her argument that, intellectually, the machine had always been possible. Mankind did not suddenly become immeasurably cleverer in the eighteenth century. She argues that if the principles on which the machine is based were not much discussed prior to the eighteenth century, it was because our minds were engaged on other things. Insofar as the problem was posed, the tendency of legislation and of the action of guilds and corporations had been rather to discourage technical innovation, rightly recognising its socially destructive effects. The early philosophers and moralists were all agreed that the emphasis on material goods, on utilitarian interests, on commerce were to be despised. The emphasis of the craftsman was on quality rather than on quantity:

> We find in old objects, even the most everyday and familiar, which come to light after many centuries – keys, pots, cradles, tombs, lamps, cups, boxes, children's toys – such a research after perfection and elegance, so much care, so much love, that we are amazed, and we smile, we, their distant descendants, used as we are to separate the useful from the beautiful, to decorate only what is meant to be seen, to concentrate our efforts only on what sells. (p.47)

Like Ferrero, Lombroso regrets the loss of the religious dimension of life but, also like Ferrero, one feels that she herself does not believe in it. She regards it as unreal, a magnificent dream:

> Christianity brought to its highest degree of development the faculty of 'conceiving', of imagining what is not, of rejoicing and suffering over unreal joys and evils, future, imaginary joys and evils. This orientation had developed the imagination in all the forms of art, of morality, of aesthetics. (p.51)

People slept in unlit stables and measured their water sparingly in the little towns of Assissi, Siena, Pisa, but they had magnificent wall–paintings in their churches:

> What did all that mean? That the ideal of wealth, of health, of trade with their neighbours awoke no echo in that period by comparison with beauty, with local patriotism, with morality.
>
> It meant that to be sure of Paradise and have in the town square a church more beautiful than that of the neighbouring village brought more pleasure than the selfish desire of having a fabulous wardrobe or living a long time.
>
> It meant again that the citizen tasted the beauty of the place where he lived, of its bell–towers, the angels sculpted on his church, more than he suffered from being deprived of water and light.
>
> That these monuments, which raised the prestige of his village (to which he was more attached than to himself), these sacrifices, guarantees of eternal joy, represented for the citizen of that time a good that was vague and indefinite, but much superior to real goods. That he could hardly enjoy the roads, the gutters, the aqueducts, the commodities of life that we esteem to be essential. (pp.54–5)

For Gleizes, of course, this 'good', the good of the Kingdom of Heaven, was far from being unreal, and this capacity to 'conceive', to 'imagine', was the normal exercise of young and healthy human senses in touch with the Intelligence, source of their creative activity. For Gleizes, the mystery of the Eucharist was based on the most solid, tangible realities – the realities of bread and of wine and their transubstantiation into flesh and blood, a transubstantiation that occurs every time we eat bread or drink wine, the wine that 'by another series of transformations, even more mysterious, penetrates as far as the network of arteries, of veins and minuscule vessels where it finally becomes the blood with which Jesus, in the supper of the last night, identified it'. (*Vie et mort*, p.168)

The transubstantiation of bread and wine into body and blood is an everyday fact; what the Eucharist says is that we are all of one body and blood. It asserts the fact that in our inmost being we are of God and we return to God; and that is the source of the unity of humanity, not any arbitrary political division, national or international.

The principle of the Mass, Gleizes argues, can be found in our modern scientific applications – and we remember that Gleizes used to argue that new developments in technology were bringing us back to ancient truths. The wireless, for example, seemed to be miraculous:

> but no-one has remarked that the wireless is no more extraordinary than what occurs when every one of us is simply listening to the person with whom he is talking, at a distance of 50 metres. But we have always pre-

> ferred the acrobat to the man who, staying within normal limits, is distinguished from his fellows by the perfection of his acts. The wireless is only a piece of acrobacy performed on the basis of the normal process of hearing; it alters the space and time – at least in appearance – of the transmitter and receiver. But it violently, brutally draws attention to a phenomenon to which, normally, we pay no attention, we are so used to it; which is that ONE transmission can resound, in variable intensities, at the same time, in an infinite number of receivers that are tuned to its cadence. And that is how, without our wanting it, or even being aware of the fact, the mechanical application brings us back to the Mass.
>
> The Mass, in fact, is, for the spirit, the consecration of the Unity of Cause, whose nature is not in the slightest altered by the multiplication of tangible effects at an infinite variety of magnitudes; that is to say, that these effects which really embody the Cause in its entirety, no matter how numerous they may be, do not diminish it and do not change its quality. That is the truth on which Christianity was built; and the ceremony of the Mass had no aim other than to spread it, to let it be heard, let it be understood, or at least to let it be felt. (pp.202–3)

Gleizes cites a seventeenth-century collection of writings of the Church Fathers on the Eucharist to show that the word spoken by a single mouth and received by a multitude of ears, 'where, individually, each seized it in its entirety without its being in any way diminished' (pp.206–7), was often given as an analogy for the Mass.

The quality of the 'message', the Word which was in the beginning and by which all things were – and are being – made, is eternal and unalterable; but the quality of the reception changes, and changes radically. If our minds are in tune with the source of our being, then we have life – the life that Jesus came to give. Our senses are healthy and we are capable of creation in harmony with the natural order that is about us. But if the receiver is old, busted and cantankerous, then we have the world as we know it today.

We can see here a theological conclusion drawn from the 'vibratory' nature of the world, a conclusion which, if there was space to develop the argument, could be shown to relate closely to the thinking of Plotinus, Augustine and Boethius. One of the arguments of *Vie et mort de l'occident chrétien* – an argument that was to cause problems for its English translator[17] – is that the scientist of today is destined to become the theologian of tomorrow. Another of the scientific theses in which Gleizes saw a theological implication was that 'the universe is a curve, is finite' (p.51–2). And this brings us to one of the central arguments of *La Forme et l'histoire*.

•

La Forme et l'histoire was Gleizes's most ambitious book – 460 pages, and he envisaged it as the first of three parts (the second part was largely written during the Second World War, but never published). He began writing it in 1928, and finished it in April 1930, submitting it to Povolozky, who agreed to publish it in June. In the event, owing to a series of difficulties, it was not published until 1932, to Gleizes's great annoyance. Gleizes was already com-

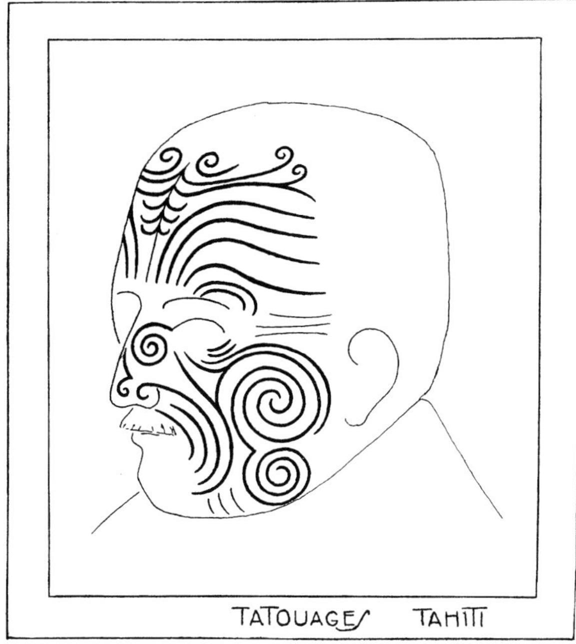

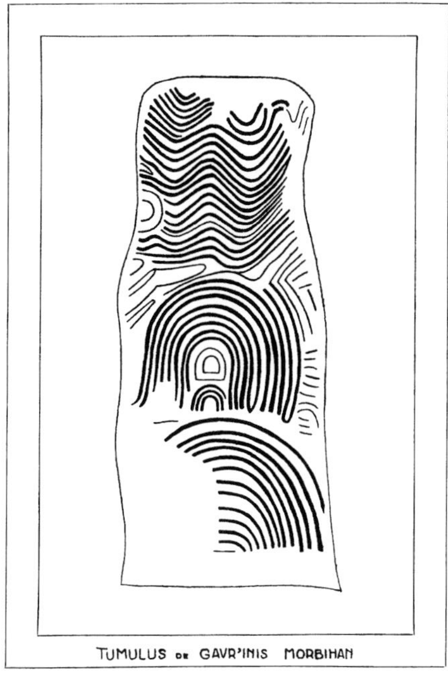

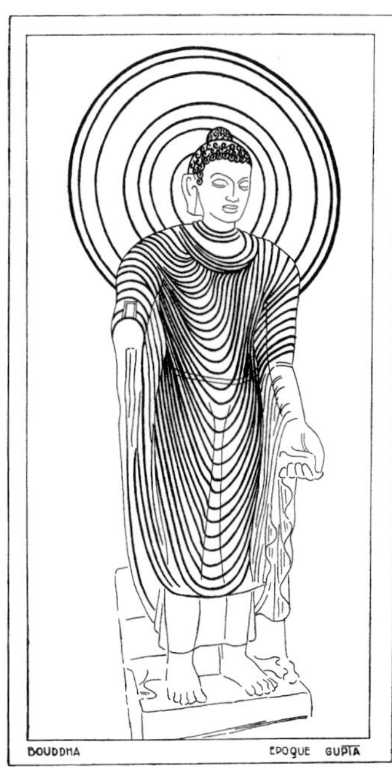

87. Robert Pouyaud, *Tatouages. Tahiti*, *c.* 1930–2. Illustration from Gleizes, *Vers une Conscience plastique: la forme et l'histoire*, p. 67

88. Robert Pouyaud, *Tumulus de Gavr'inis*, *c.* 1930–2. Illustration from Gleizes, *Vers une Conscience plastique: la forme et l'histoire*, p. 81

89. Robert Pouyaud, *Bouddha – Epoque Gupta*, *c.* 1930–2. Illustration from Gleizes, *Vers une Conscience plastique: la forme et l'histoire*, p. 95

plaining about the slowness of publication in October 1930. Part of the problem was that Povolozky wanted it to be beautiful: 'We see things differently – for you, the book is only the printed content of your thought that you want brought to light as quickly as possible – for me it is a technical realisation of important, highly interesting ideas in the form of a book that must, before anything else, give satisfaction by that very form.'[18]

It is indeed a beautiful book – the only book Gleizes published that has a presentation worthy of the power and beauty of the thought. From 1927 onwards, with the exception of *La Forme et l'histoire* and the English translation of *Vie et mort*, Gleizes published all his books himself, under the imprint Editions Moly Sabata, and it must be admitted that, despite his insistence on craftsmanship and perfection, they are all clearly published as quickly and as cheaply as possible. In order to support the region in which he lived, he used the local printer at Serrières, and Mme Gleizes points to the difficulties this caused – the large number of misprints in *Vie et mort*, for example.[19]

La Forme et l'histoire was illustrated by Pouyaud, and these drawings, showing the difference between the 'rhythmic' and non-rhythmic art of religious and non-religious ages, are perhaps the best illustrations we have of Gleizes's central historical thesis (Plates 87–9). I have no intention of attempting a summary. Much of it covers the same ground as *Vie et mort*, but in much greater historical detail, answering many objections (the intolerance, violence, serfdom of the religious epoch of the Christian West, for example) and also discussing much of the literature available on the main subject – the development of the sense of form between the fourth and twelfth centuries. This straightforward discussion of a very wide range of references is unusual for Gleizes who is normally coy about his sources.

I will finish here by opening the discussion of a key development in his thought which relates to what has just been said about the single cause simultaneous to an infinite number of effects. This is the distinction that Gleizes draws between what he now calls 'form' and what he calls 'figure'. I will concentrate for the moment on the purely 'theological' argument.

In the nineteenth century, the 'Non–Euclidean' geometers who were so interesting to Metzinger and Duchamp, developed a geometry based on the assumption that parallel lines always, eventually, meet. In the twentieth century, physicists found that certain phenomena could only be explained mathematically by applying their methods – by assuming, in effect, that the Universe is spherical. In *Vie et mort*, Gleizes evokes the drama of the physicist who finds that conventional notions of space and time which imagine them as an infinite plane, or an infinite straight line, do not work. Suddenly, 'in an intuition of genius, he realises that the mystery of these partial figures does not lie in themselves; they tend towards it indefinitely; their ultimate reality is the sphere, and at that moment they touch the mystery, they have come close to it, going as far as sensation can go.' (pp.xxi–xxii)

For a moment, then, the scientist has a glimpse of the form, the sphere, the real nature of the universe. He has passed from the realm of physics to the realm of theology – of the creative, formative work of God. But alas! he is still only a physicist. He is absolutely confined to the realm of sensation. He continues his researches and finds that the spherical model does not, after all, go very far towards helping him to account for the innumerable sensations he encounters. These sensations are of the realm of the relative. It is only more or less approximately that they approach the sphere, which is of the realm of the absolute. They tend towards it, but since that tendency is never realised, the physicist cannot take account of it.

The mathematician is more fortunate. He is not tied to the nature of the external world, to the nature of the sensations. He can take account of the absolute in his calculations and for this reason, Gleizes argues that he is closer than the physicist to the artisan, the man who continues the work of creation, its tendency towards the absolute, with the work of his hands.

We have seen that Gleizes argued, with Charles Henry, that all physical facts are 'representations' in the mind – they result from the interaction between a vibration and a pre–existent configuration of the mind. Henry argued that pure, unapplied mathematics also conforms to the configuration of the mind, so the mathematical formula and the external appearance are of the same – 'psycho–physical' – nature; hence 'the deeply held intuition of the geometer that every new analytical function will, sooner or later, find its application in physics'.[20]

Thus the ideal sphere is not without its significance. Put crudely, it is not without significance that we want to believe in it, or in its equivalent on the flat surface of the painting – the circle. They are in conformity with our own nature. Henry, in his 'Laboratory of Physical Sensations' at the Sorbonne, performed a large number of experiments on the stimuli that people found restful, lifegiving, or irritating and inhibiting. Our experience of the world, he argued, after the arguments of quantum theory, is discontinuous but, nonetheless, we aspire after continuity, and the appearance of continuity is achieved through 'rhythm', whose regular repetition evokes the continuity of the circle 'to which the ideal mechanism of the living being can be assimilated'.[21]

Thus, Henry's 'aesthetic protractor' (*rapporteur esthétique*), conceived to distinguish those angles, proportions and relations of lines that are pleasing and 'rhythmic' from those that are irritating and non–rhythmic, is based on a formula devised by the German mathematician, Johann Gauss, to express the characteristics common to all the polygons that can be inscribed in a circle. The polygon is the discontinuous sensation, the circle the continuous ideal. In *La Forme et l'histoire*, Gleizes argues that it is the Ptolemaic universe, in which man is at the centre of a series of concentric spheres, that corresponds to our real nature, and it is this universe that we would construct for ourselves if we used our senses creatively instead of as mere devices for recording whatever seems to lie outside us.[22]

If we see reality as lying outside ourselves – a series of causes and effects going back in time to some First Cause such as the Big Bang – then this longing for the circle is of little importance. It may even be seen as a temptation to be resisted in the name of honesty, of loyalty to the Truth. If, however, we see the phenomena of space and time as eternally derived from a single source lying outside space and time, and much closer in its unknowable nature to what we think of as consciousness than to what we think of as matter, then the ideal form becomes of much greater importance, is much closer to the cause, than the observation; and this is a large part of the teaching of Pythagoras, Plato, Plotinus, Augustine and Boethius (not to mention the neo–Platonist philosophers of Islam and of Judaism).

There is a close analogy to be drawn between the physicist multiplying observations about the external world and the painter copying the appearances of the external world. Both have subjected their Intelligence to the accidental appearances that flit before it. In the nineteenth century, the Intelligence began to revolt. The result in physics was the emergence of non–Euclidean geometry, precursor of quantum theory and of relativity. In painting, it was the turbulent struggles of Cézanne and Van Gogh, precursors of Cubism. But relativity theory and Cubism are only compromises. The problem is not resolved. All that has happened is that the accidental fleeting appearances have been deformed under the pressure of a force which has not yet been understood. The problem can only be resolved by a radical reorientation of our minds – the equivalent in reverse of the transition that occurred between the eleventh and fourteenth centuries between 'Realism' and 'Nominalism', between the primacy of Intelligence and the primacy of the senses.[23]

The accidental appearance studied by the landscape painter or the physicist is only a 'figure'; it is immobilised. The life and movement have been knocked out of it in order the better to see it. But this is based on a radical misconception of the nature of the eye. The eye does not just exist to observe this, that or the other thing. Much more than the ear, it is of its nature to be able to enter into movement, to follow lines, shapes, colours, one after the other:

> To see the mobile is, obviously, an act of the mind but one that implies a perfect consciousness of the means. These means belong to sight, which is the most complete and most noble instrument for realising movement . . . The eyes have this advantage over the ear that they move more rapidly, they are much more sensitive than the ear to frequency, less sensitive to duration; the number of vibrations per second that they need for their normal functioning is enormous.[24]

To immobilise the eye in representational painting was already to rob it of a great deal of its vitality; but the representational painter had enough skill and control over his means to give some stimulation to the eye's capacity for movement despite his obligation to copy and thus to freeze external appearances. The photograph and the cinema immobilise the eye completely. They render it completely passive and destroy what is left of the sense of form. The figure is static; the form is in movement, continuous, contemplative, ultimately tending towards the circle, the sphere, common to all human beings in all human cultures as is their common Source in a single, unique, eternal Cause: 'the infinite is without form, not because it is lacking but because it is the principle from which the intelligible forms derive'.[25]

As Pignot, the old drunken potter at St Désirat, told Anne Dangar: 'Pottery is not made by a trick of the eye or a trick of the hand, it is constructed, it is the movement of the form understood that makes good pottery.' What this means in practical terms for the painter will be the subject of the next two chapters.

13

ROBERT DELAUNAY

In *Kubismus*, Gleizes evokes the case of 'Robert Delaunay, finally, too abundant, too little master of himself, but having, intuitively, the exact idea of what the destiny of Cubism was to be . . .'.[1]

In his essay on Delaunay, written for Abstraction-Création (the society that had been founded in 1931 to group all the non-representational painters of the time together in a coherent movement), Gleizes says that it was only twelve or thirteen years later that 'through my experience, [I] joined up with the spirit of his works of 1913 . . .'.[2] This, then, was in 1925–6, after *La Peinture et ses lois*. The thinking of this book, all to do with manipulations of the plane surface based on essentially rectilinear shapes, was influenced by the wartime work of Metzinger and Gris. It is only later that he begins to understand the radicalism of what Delaunay had been doing.

In fact it is clear that Delaunay's achievement had been at work in Gleizes's mind from a much earlier period. The two characteristics of Delaunay's pre-war work that distinguish him most obviously from his colleagues of the time are his use of bright colours and his use of circular forms. Both are characteristic of Gleizes's wartime work, starting with the *Clowns* of 1914. Indeed, we may say that the circle is one of the elements that is severely curtailed and disciplined when he returns to Paris in 1919. The new order, explained in *La Peinture et ses lois*, emphasises shapes that are compatible with the flat surface of the canvas, which is, typically, a rectangle. Gleizes, of course, uses the term 'rotation' and envisages the eye turning in a rotary or spiralling movement. The problem is already posed: how to move from the static rectangle to a movement that is essentially circular – a problem that is not unconnected with the old geometrical conundrum of 'squaring the circle' (that is, calculating the area enclosed by a circle by treating it as if it were a square). But the circle presented baldly seems to be of another nature from the plane surface, and Gleizes treats it with suspicion.

As for colour, Gleizes says nothing about it in *La Peinture et ses lois* – a strange neglect in a book on the laws of painting. His ideas in *Du Cubisme et les moyens de le comprendre* are elementary; he recommends bright, simple colours because painting is an art of light and cannot compromise with the shadows. In a letter to Evie Hone, written in 1922, he says 'Your colour is logical and you have understood the advantages of knowing how it works – all the variety it allows, which is to say, all the liberty of the painter, beyond the system in which those artists close themselves up in exercises of quantity, who use only two or three colours and never break away from them.' He recommends that she should soften her tones and try to maintain a uniform level of tonality throughout.[3] Despite the reference to the 'logic' of colours, this amounts to little more than advice in good taste. Later, in November 1926, he tells Pouyaud: 'Let the forms follow each other better and the colour will come of its own accord.'[4]

So for a time, all his theoretical work is concentrated on form, and colour is treated as a matter of instinct. But in March 1927, Pouyaud asked him for something more definite:

> I have been thinking ceaselessly about the laws of the plane which demand a mechanism for colour through which we can understand the painting in its verticality.
>
> I am looking for the means to paint the different parts of the plane in such a way that they hold, each beside the other, not one in front of the other.
>
> I lack knowledge.
>
> Can you tell me where I might find the documentation which I lack on the laws of harmony and on the relations of colours between each other?
>
> For the moment, I can explain the mechanism of the plane relative to the form in a logical fashion, but I cannot explain the mechanism of colour relative to the plane.
>
> I feel that there is something there to be found – a problem both terrible and captivating . . .
>
> Tell me, please, where I can find a good document that will explain the matter of colour and enable me to work in a more solid fashion.[5]

When Anne Dangar arrived in Moly Sabata in 1930, Pouyaud had a well-worked-out theory of colour, based on *La Couleur: ses manifestations, son rôle dans les arts, ses harmonies*, published in 1916 by F. Forichon, director of the Regional Arts School at Clermont Ferrand.[6] We know that Mainie Jellet also used Forichon's book[7] and Gleizes defends Forichon when, later, Pouyaud begins to have doubts about him.[8] It seems reasonable to infer that Gleizes produced Forichon's book in reply to Pouyaud's letter – and this is confirmed by the more disciplined use of colour which we see in the work of all these painters – Gleizes, Jellett, Pouyaud and, once she had returned from her convent, Evie Hone – about this time.

Forichon's book is a continuation, but also a critique, of Eugène Chevreul's *De la Loi du contraste simultané des couleurs* (1839) and *Des Couleurs et de leurs applications aux arts industriels à l'aide des cercles chromatiques* (1864). Forichon begins by evoking the Neo-Impressionists, led by Seurat and Signac, who had been much influenced by Chevreul. Modern painters had made good use of their discoveries but 'unfortunately, many painters abused them by applying, without discernment, violent colours whose incoherent juxtaposition only produced an ungracious mess.' (p.1)

The problem was that the science of colour harmony was so little developed in the West. The science of sound harmony was well-established, so that bad harmonies could instantly be detected by the ear, but our eyes are very ill-informed. Forichon assumes that artistic painting is a matter of copying the external appearances of nature, so the painter can modulate the harsh effects of bright colours by using dull combinations of tones in the shadows: but the decorator, working with bright colours on a plane surface, had no such advantages. He needed a theory of colours as solid as the theory of musical scales. But, although a very valuable work had been done on colour by the scientists (a literature still not well enough known by the painters) no-one had yet found a means to reproduce and identify any given colour value quickly and precisely – the range of the colour scale was simply too great. Every workshop had its own colour charts, but these were arbitrary and could not provide a basis for a general discussion. The most ambitious attempt at methodically cataloguing colour had been Chevreul's, but even the enormous number of tints that he gives in a prohibitively expensive book, is not complete and, Forichon argues, he had imposed a scheme on his colours that was false. A method for quickly identifying the complementary of any colour was necessary, and Chevreul's colour circle, in which each colour is supposedly faced with its complementary, was misleading.

Forichon proposed a system by which any desired tint could be obtained from the primary colours, with white and black, not through mixing them as paints, but through an optical mix achieved by the use of spinning discs, a device that had already been used by the American theorist, Ogden Rood. Two or more colours could be placed on the disc in such a way that, when it was spun, they would combine in the eye to give the desired result. The complementary of any given colour could be found in that colour or combination of colours which, when spun with it, gave a neutral grey. Neutral grey was to the pigment colours what white light was to the coloured rays of the spectrum. Where all the rays of the spectrum combined to give white light, all the pigment colours combined to give neutral grey. The whole range of colours was contained in the relation between the colour and its complementary, which added up to grey.

By the use of this method, Forichon demonstrated that Chevreul's complementaries were inaccurate. They did not add up to grey. For example, Chevreul assumed that the complementary of a vivid red, midway between violet and orange, would be a vivid green, midway between yellow and blue. In fact, according to Forichon, it is a blue-green.

The importance of this question of complementaries was that, in Forichon's scheme, the complementary colours provided the key to colour harmony. This had long been felt, but the direct juxtaposition of colour complementaries had been found to be too violent, partly because they were, in Forichon's view, inaccurate. Nonetheless, his conclusion is that if a painting is to be harmonious it must embrace the whole possible range of colours, which is what happens when a colour is juxtaposed with its complementary: 'If an assembly of colours is to be harmonious, all the colours that feature in the whole must be able to produce, when mixed together, neutral grey' (p.134).

Following the German physicist, Hermann von Helmholtz (who had also, we have seen, greatly influenced Ghil and Henry) and the English Thomas Young, Forichon argued that different 'fibrils' in the eye corresponded to different colours and that there was a constant coming and going between them:

> Everyone knows that one cannot concentrate for too long a time on one single point without being tired. So this organ is in perpetual movement, directing sight from one object to another . . . after having first looked at a yellow tone, for example, it will be pleasant for the eye to pass afterwards to a blue violet, since all the nervous fibrils that are sensitive to yellow will then enjoy a complete rest. Any nuance other than blue-violet would have the effect of stimulating a certain number of the nerves that have already been working under the action of the yellow rays, so the rest could only be partial. (pp.135–6)

He likens this, rather prettily, to a man walking from a station carrying a heavy suitcase, who is constantly obliged to change the suitcase from one hand to the other.

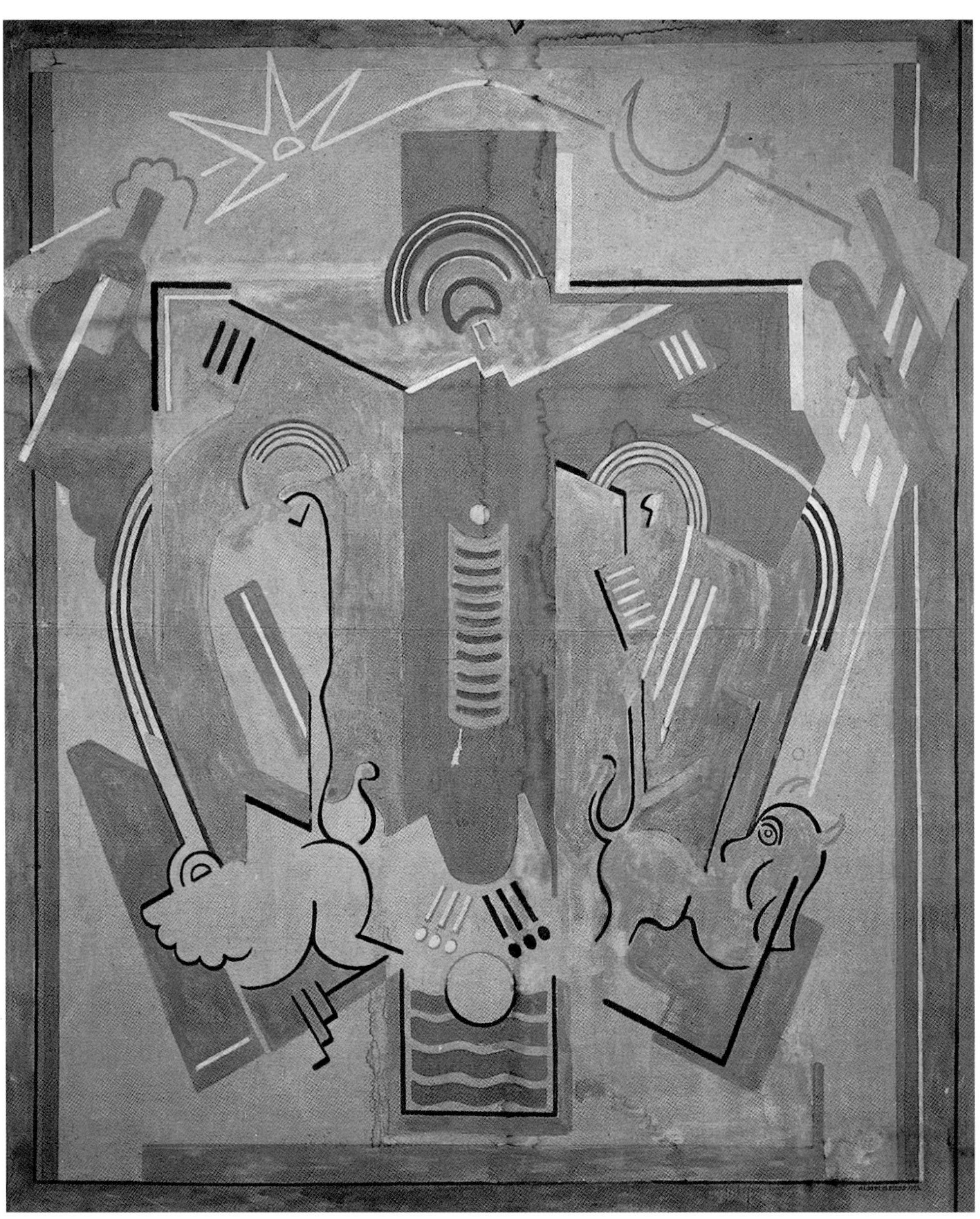

90. *Crucifixion*, 1927. Size on canvas, 214 × 175 cm. Musée National d'Art Moderne, Paris

However, a simple juxtaposition of a bright colour with its bright complementary can itself be very tiring – the movement from one to the other is too fast – and one way of attenuating this is simply to use a neutral grey: 'The grey or black are then strongly tinted with the complementaries, thus with the simultaneous contrast, and the effect is often very successful.' (p.118)

Forichon evokes the possibility of using more than one set of complementaries, but he insists that this should be done with great caution and that 'there must . . . be a dominant colour which imposes on the work in a lasting manner and characterises the tonality of the rest.' (p.119)

Forichon's book includes an advertisement for the equipment – metal discs etc – necessary to find the complementaries and other colours using this method. Pouyaud had this equipment and doubtless used it to realise the exact tones necessary for his pochoirs. Anne Dangar was confronted with it on her arrival at Moly Sabata: 'They have only one book on colour and its terribly scientific. I have to study it with a big brass revolving dial which of course I'm scared of'.[9] But by June, she was reconciled to it:

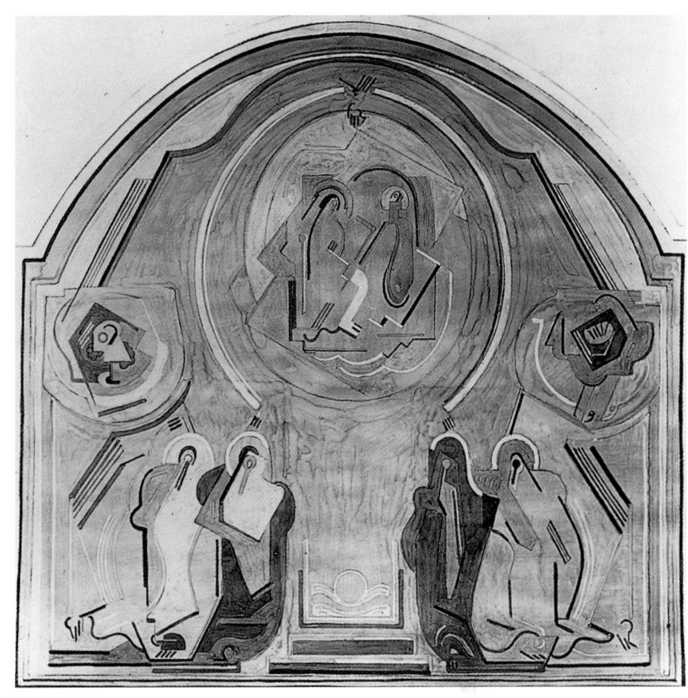

91. *Couronnement de la Vierge*, 1927. Gouache or watercolour (?) Dimensions and present whereabouts unknown

> Our great effort is to create light by colour in our painting, not by black and white (how often Lhote advised this, but he didn't show how to do it!) . . . As it is impossible with pigment to get white by colour, we can only achieve a perfect grey *sans* colour when revolved (the disc I told you of before is how you rig your perfect greys). Now, say you start a background in red ochre and black and white mixed. Placing the black and white thereon, you get your blue-green complementary. That is the complementary because the eye calls for light, and light is only created when the missing colours are added to a colour already there. Red ochre contains yellow, red and violet. But it has neither blue nor green in its composition. It calls for them, and a perfect neutral like black and white recalls them to the eye. Now proceeding, you will use colours which go towards your blue-green, but always mix a little background colour with all, except when you get right near the centre, then you work towards greater movement. When colours are very close to one another, the movement is slow, but put blue and yellow/orange together in pure and separate colours and you have the maximum of movement – the whole circle. So with all the complementaries.[10]

I have quoted this at length because it seems to me to be a good summary of the practice of Gleizes and his colleagues in 1927–9, just prior to Anne Dangar's arrival, and it more or less accords with Forichon's formula: a single overwhelmingly predominant colour, offset by its complementary in very small quantities if used pure, in rather larger quantities when introduced as a neutral grey. There is also a greater sensitivity towards regulating the intensity of the colours so that they hold together on the same plane. Pouyaud had said he wanted 'the means to paint the different parts of the plane in such a way that they hold, each beside the other, not one in front of the other' and the problem is addressed by Forichon, who explains how his discs can help to resolve it.

The most ambitious work of the period is the series of three paintings devised in 1927 for murals for the church at Serrières – the *Crucifixion* (Plate 90), *Descente de croix*, and *Couronnement de la Vierge* (Plate 91) – Gleizes's first use of explicitly religious themes, and almost certainly the paintings which so overwhelmed Anne Dangar just before her return to Australia. Although Pouyaud was to make pochoirs of them, he does not seem to have been closely involved in working them out, probably because at this time he was deeply immersed in the work of putting Moly Sabata in order; but the final work, especially the *Couronnement de la Vierge*, seems to owe as much to Jellett as it does to Gleizes. The project had been refused at the last moment. This was

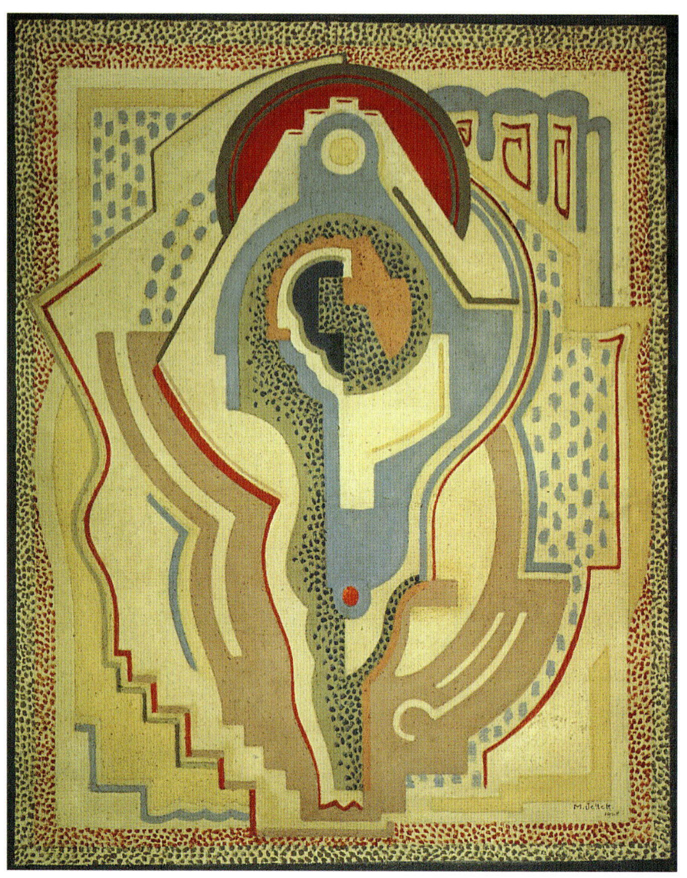

92. Mainie Jellett, *Abstract Crucifixion*, 1928. Oil on canvas, 107 × 87 cm. Private Collection

to be the typical fate of Gleizes's mural projects – forcibly stopped after all the preparatory work had been completed. It was a fate he had already encountered with a project for a classroom – three panels round a blackboard – for the Ecole de Pharmacie, Paris, in 1925.[11]

These paintings also mark a progress away from the impression often given in the work following *La Peinture et ses lois* of a number of shapes placed one on top of the other. They are more fluid and linear, and the 'translation/rotation' schema of vertical and inclined planes, is less obvious. It is perhaps not without significance that this tendency away from the explicit statement of the translation/rotation is less marked in Gleizes's *Crucifixion* and *Couronnement de la Vierge* than it is in Mainie Jellett's *Abstract Crucifixion* (Plate 92) and *Homage to Fra Angelico* (Plate 93).

Gleizes remains faithful to this scheme all his life – much more than Jellett – and it constitutes one of the strengths of his painting. Nonetheless, he does not discuss 'translation/rotation' in his major essay of 1927 – *Peinture et perspective descriptive* – nor indeed in the whole 460 pages of *La Forme et l'histoire* – even though, in both, the theme is the existence of solid principles of painting that will put the eye in movement. 'Rhythmic' art is illustrated throughout *La Forme et l'histoire* through a play of curved lines, not of planes. The point is not that Gleizes has abandoned the 'new mechanism' of *La Peinture et ses lois* but that his mind was concentrating on a further development, the next stage of the problem to be resolved.

•

The link between this period and the pre-war painting of Robert Delaunay is not yet obvious. Delaunay's tempestuous character seems far removed from the cool calculations of Forichon's colour theory and the manipulation of his colour discs – though Delaunay had a lively interest in Chevreul and in Ogden Rood.[12] But something of Delaunay can be seen in Anne Dangar's statement that 'Our great effort is to create light by Colour in painting, not by black and white (how often Lhote advised this, but he didn't show how to do it!)'.

Light is the uncoloured source of all colour just as, in Plotinus' teaching, the One is the immobile source of all movement, the eternal source of all time, and the formless source of all form. It is not in the external world that colour comes into existence, but in the eye. The whole created universe is revealed to us through colours and the whole range of colours is pre-existent in the eye. The eye's need for the complementary – the fact that each colour calls on its complementary – is a need for totality, a need to embrace the whole, and that whole is of its nature circular. It is no accident that, since Newton, the circle has been considered the most appropriate way to present colours. Starting from any given colour and running through the whole range of colours, we will arrive back at our starting point: red-orange-yellow-green-blue-indigo-violet-red.

Charles Henry attached great importance to our tendency to react to any given sensation by evoking its complementary: 'Complementary reactions ensure, by definition, a functional stability; rhythmic stimuli also have the same effect, because they tend to diminish the energy of the sensation; they all help towards auto-regulation, the most essential mechanism of life.'[13] It should be noted that, for Henry as for Gleizes, a healthy organism did not need strong stimuli. The weaker the sensation, the more the senses themselves are required to act. A need for violent sensations is a sign of weakness.

We have seen that the eye cannot concentrate on a single colour for a long time without evoking its complementary. Which is to say that the eye itself is in constant motion; change and movement are natural to it. Gleizes has already approached the problem with regard to form, and has argued that a simple movement of displacement in space – the movement of translation – cannot satisfy the eye's demand for movement, because it is not a whole movement. A whole movement is one that turns back on itself – the movement of rotation: the circle. Henry said that the circular form is 'the elementary, normal and persistent form of the living mechanism'.[14] Now we begin to see the same phenomenon in colour – the need for a totality that is circular in its nature. And it is here that we rejoin Robert Delaunay.

Between 1909 and 1914, Delaunay passed through one of the most moving dramas in the history of modern painting. In his Abstraction-Création essay, Gleizes emphasises Delaunay's isolation from his colleagues. They were searching for form in opposition to Impressionism. Impressionism had emphasised colour at the expense of form; the Cubists were therefore suspicious of colour. They looked for form initially in its most classical expression – volume, the three dimensions that properly belong to sculpture. They were then disconcerted by the changes form undergoes in time – a problem that was forced on their attention by the more rapid displacements in space introduced with the railway, the aeroplane and the cinema. In fact, Gleizes now believed that what they had been studying was not 'form' at all but 'figures'. A geometrical figure is a schematic representation of a phenomenon that has been rendered immobile for the purposes of study. The painting of a portrait, a still-life, a landscape, is equally a schematic representation of a phenomenon that has been rendered immobile. It is partial. A painter of great skill can make it look as if it is living but the life is false and can only give rise to a longing for the real life it can never achieve.

93. Mainie Jellett, *Homage to Fra Angelico*, 1927. Pencil drawing, dimensions and present whereabouts unknown

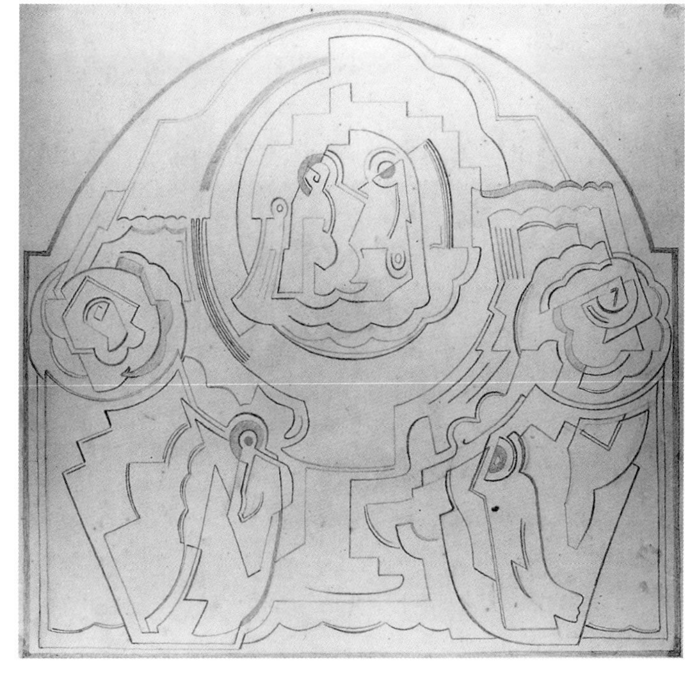

The word 'form' implies totality. Like colour, it is a capacity of the eye. The eye is in constant movement. Nothing immobile can satisfy its need for movement. But nor can it be satisfied by a movement that is only partial. A whole movement can only be a movement that turns back on itself – a circular movement. 'Form is movement, despite appearances,' Gleizes says in *Peinture et perspective descriptive* in 1927.

> If it was otherwise, there would never be any growth. Only we no longer know, exactly, what movement is,

> because we confuse it with agitation, which is only a parody. Movement is not external, it is an internal unfolding; the painted work is something that has been slowed down so that the eye can move with the form, can appreciate it sensually – without confusing sensuality and concupiscence. . . . ('Peinture et perspective descriptive', in *Puissances du cubisme*, p.87)

It was this identification of form, movement and colour which distinguished Delaunay from his colleagues and put him ahead of them. Colour is a problem for classical drawing, a nature added to it that does not naturally belong to it. This is why the early Cubists, identifying form and classical drawing, suppressed colour; and why the Impressionists, also identifying form and classical drawing, suppressed form. 'Colour', Gleizes says in *Robert Delaunay*:

> is a nature that is mobile in itself; it is an accident of light which tends to run back to light by the most direct ways, those of simultaneous or successive contrasts; how could it not throw the immobility of classical space into confusion, colour, that is time itself . . .
>
> The formal rhythm, inseparable from colour, realised the plastic fact through its own action alone; no need to look elsewhere – in retrospective images, in more or less literary motifs, in geometrical formulae whose exactitude is guaranteed. The coloured rhythm was of the nature of life. . . .

It is surprising to see how close Delaunay's writings of the pre-war period, and especially of 1913, when he produced his *Formes Circulaires*, are to this line of argument developed by Gleizes in the 1920s and early 1930s. Gleizes insists on Delaunay's 'intuitive' nature: 'Delaunay played with moons and suns like an amazed child' as he says in *Kubismus*,[15] but although Delaunay never wrote a book, he continued all his life to reflect and write notes on his work. The far from complete collection of his writings, *Du Cubisme à l'art abstrait*, is one of the most precious documents of twentieth-century painting. He also had his friends, the poets, Cendrars and Apollinaire to try to articulate what he was doing.

In fact, by 1912, Delaunay had every reason to believe that he held the future in his hands. When Apollinaire published his *Les Peintres cubistes*, he did not discuss Delaunay: he envisaged a second volume which was to deal with 'Orphism' – essentially Delaunay's painting – which he saw as the true successor to Cubism.[16] Gleizes's essay on Delaunay says of this term 'Orphism', which Apollinaire first used at the opening of the Section d'Or exhibition in Paris in 1912: 'The word was wonderfully well chosen, we must admit. Above all well chosen for the time. 1912 would not have accepted a more universal title, being unable to understand that between "orphic" and "religious", there was only a difference in name.'

While enjoying the admiration of Apollinaire and Cendrars, Delaunay was also the virtual founder of an interesting school of American painting – the 'Synchromatists'; and he was the Parisian who excited most interest among the painters of the Blaue Reiter in Munich – Franz Marc, August Macke, Wassiliy Kandinsky, Paul Klee. His letters to them are almost the letters of a master to his pupils. But behind the brilliance of his position there is a considerable anguish – the anguish of a man who knows that he has touched something of great importance but who does not have the language to understand or explain why it is important. His best-known writing of the time is the wonderful manifesto on Light, translated into German by Paul Klee and published in *Der Stürm*.[17] The text is well known, but I quote it at length to show the remarkable similarity there is to Gleizes's later thinking:

> Without visual sensibility no light no movement
> Light in nature creates the movement of colours.
> Movement is given by the relations between unequal measures, contrasts between the colours that constitute reality . . .
>
> Human vision is gifted with reality because it comes to us directly from the contemplation of the Universe.
> The eye is our highest sense, that which communicates most directly to our brain, our consciousness . . .
> Auditive perception is not sufficient for our knowledge of the Universe. It has no depth.
> Its movement is successive, it is a sort of mechanism, its law is the time of mechanical clocks which, like it, have no relation to our perception of visual movement in the Universe . . .
>
> Art in Nature is rhythmic and has horror of any constraint.
> If Art is tied to the Object [the thing represented – PB] it becomes descriptive, divisionist, literary . . .
> It is conventional, it doesn't reach formal purity, it is an infirmity, the negation of life, of the sublimity of the art of painting –
> Art, like nature, is rhythmic, that is to say, Eternal.

The last sentence indicates that Gleizes was not far off the mark in saying that this painting had religious implications and that these were felt by both Delaunay and Apollinaire despite both men's lack of any explicit religious belief. Apollinaire, in one of his essays written under Delaunay's influence, even evokes the Trinity:

> This simultaneity is life itself, and the succession of elements in a work, whatever it might be, leads inevitably towards the end, which is to say, death, while the creator can only know eternity. The artist has for a long time aspired after death by putting together the sterile elements of art; it is time that he arrived at harmony, fecundity, trinity, simultaneity.[18]

Successive movement goes towards death, which is identified in Delaunay's essay with the machine. Why? Because it is only a partial movement. It is the equivalent of what Gleizes was to call 'agitation'. The movement that does not go towards death but towards life, the movement that is endlessly renewed, is a circular movement. Mixed in with the thinking of Apollinaire and Delaunay at this time is a polemic against what they saw as the mechanical 'dynamism' of the Italian Futurists, based on their enthusiasm for the machine. Delaunay, with his Eiffel Tower, his Big Wheel, his *Hommage à Blériot*, the French aviator, was by no means hostile to the machine, but he felt that its movement was something different from the movement required in painting. As Gleizes would later define the difference, the mechanical movement is something essentially inert put into movement by a force coming from outside itself. The painting which shows its subject in an inert state, the photograph, the diagram and figure – even the cinema, which is a succession of 'stills' run together – all reinforce this idea of movement. But the living thing has its own principle of growth and movement inside itself. Its movement is not an effect that follows a cause, even a divine, transcendent cause. In life, Gleizes increasingly argues, cause and effect are simultaneous.

In addition to his polemic against the Futurists, Delaunay was also anxious to distinguish himself from the Cubists. He is particularly savage – and unreservedly xenophobic – with regard to Picasso:

> Moreover the importers of these bluffs were foreigners, not recognised in their country nor really at bottom in Paris; what are commonly described as profiteers. It is thus that certain of them tried to pass off as French art (made in Paris) various obfuscations, pastiches of the ancient sculpture of the Africans, others introduced bits of newpapers, nails, broken glass . . . These incoherent divisions had for leaders, Picasso, Boccioni . . .[19]

He rejected the name 'Cubist' and, as we have seen, refused to be included among the illustrations in Gleizes's and Metzinger's *Du 'Cubisme'* (to their regret). The approach of *Du 'Cubisme'* would certainly have appeared to him to be far too cerebral, and he would not have liked the criticism – respectful though it is – of Neo-Impressionist colour theory. But among the Cubists, he draws an interesting distinction between those who are attached to the 'Object' – 'Derain, Picasso, Braque, Metzinger etc.' and those attached to the 'Image' – 'Gleizes, Le Fauconnier, Herbin, Henri Rousseau, Seurat, P. Gauguin, Signac, H. Matisse etc . . .'. The fact that he separates Gleizes and Metzinger and attaches Metzinger to Picasso and Braque is itself interesting. The 'object' here is of course what Gleizes would call the 'subject' – the chair, the mandolin, the city, the nude or whatever. These are painters who want to interpret such things intellectually, a work that has nothing to do with the work of painting. Gleizes, on the other hand, finds himself in the splendid company of Seurat and Rousseau, Delaunay's favourite painters. The 'image' is much closer to painting than the 'object'. What is wrong with it? It is static: 'Without the sensibility (the eye), no movement'.[20]

In a letter to Auguste Macke, Delaunay said:

> Above everything else, I always see the Sun. As I want the identification of myself and others, it is here and there the halo, haloes, the movement of colours. And I believe that that is rhythm. To see is a movement. Vision is the true creative rhythm: to discern the quality of the rhythm, that is movement, and the essential quality of painting is representation, the movement of vision which functions through objectivising itself towards reality.[21]

But Delaunay had immense difficulty conveying this idea to those about him. One of his correspondents, perhaps Kandinsky, wrote to complain: 'Then the movement of colours, what is it? A physical word. Everything is movement. The line of a pencil is nothing other than movement. One explains nothing about art with words like that.'[22] Delaunay replied:

> I find, and I am very distressed after reading your letter, that you have understood nothing of my worker's comments which shed some light on my personal means in their craft, in relation to their works. I am not talking about

> a movement that is mechanical, but harmonious, since there is simultaneity, that is to say, depth. 'We see as far as the stars.' There is movement. My visual sensibility conveys to my consciousness depth; in the universe of simultaneity, none of the senses is equal to that of sight.[23]

In another letter, certainly addressed to Kandinsky, he says: 'So I am no longer surprised that people do not see. These are realities that are unintelligible for them at the moment . . .', and he continues: 'I am often also driven to ask myself if there is any need for these things . . .'.[24]

•

Delaunay's development as a painter was badly hit by the war, which he spent in Spain and Portugal. Sonia Delaunay had had a comfortable income from property held in Russia, but this was abruptly cut off with the outbreak of the Russian Revolution. From 1917 onwards, the Delaunays were dependent on Sonia's flair for adapting Robert's ideas to commercial ends. The coloured circles continue in his wartime work, but the figurative side becomes more dominant. He is in full retreat from his discoveries of 1913–14, a retreat that continues after his return to Paris, where he and Sonia initially moved in the fashionable Dada circles Gleizes disliked so much. In *Kubismus*, Gleizes, after praising Delaunay as having gone furthest towards realising the destiny of Cubism, continues: 'In saying that, I will probably surprise plenty of people who think of Robert Delaunay as he is today, once again taken over by the descriptive image.' This was published in its French version in the journal *Le Rouge et le noir* as late as 1929.

Gleizes corresponded with Delaunay throughout the 1920s and Delaunay helped Poznansky and Pouyaud with L'Art d'Aujourd'hui in 1925. But it was in 1929, after the publication of Gleizes's article in *Le Rouge et le noir*, that their friendship began to flourish again. Delaunay wrote to Gleizes to say how much he appreciated the article. Gleizes wrote back to explain why he was no longer living in Paris:

> I no longer believe that this society can last, rotten to the marrow as it is with mercantilism, and I believe that we must, as far as we can, turn decisively to what will succeed it . . . What you say about my history of Cubism pleases me . . . What shows how bad the rot has become is that I am sure that many of the painters agree with me but that, for certain reasons to do with the age, they keep from approving me so as not to displease their masters, merchants, critics etc. . . . They no longer dare – and this is true for all the painters who write – say a word about Gleizes, because, it seems, I have become the *bête noir* of commerce. . . .[25]

In complaining that the painters dare not agree with him openly, Gleizes is probably referring in particular to his account of Picasso. The letter was written shortly after an exchange in *L'Intransigeant* with the art critic, Guillaume Janneau who, Gleizes felt, had treated him disgracefully in his book *L'Art cubiste* – possibly the first major book on Cubism written by someone who had not actually played a role in its history.[26] The falsification of the history of the pre-war period was a theme dear to Delaunay's heart. In an undated letter to

Gleizes, probably from 1931, he refers to 'a combination that dates back to the cut-up Cubism of Kahnweiler's boutique . . . our clan has been too individual . . . and the crooks have taken advantage of it'[27] and, advising Gleizes on his proposed book for Abstraction-Création, he urges him to give 'the reasons for my antagonism with the traitors, the sowers of confusion like Picasso – and his commercial combination that has been going on since the start'.[28] Gleizes did indeed write a very interesting critique of Picasso, though perhaps it is a little more balanced than Delaunay would have liked.[29]

In 1930, Delaunay was involved in a project for establishing an artists' community in the countryside, at Nesles-la-Vallée, near Paris. Both he and Gleizes saw this as complementary to what Gleizes was doing at Moly Sabata, and Gleizes wrote enthusiastically that 'we must bring the state of mind of these dispersed elements to fruition, they must know each other and unite, exchange men and works, but keeping their own freedom, their independence, and that will be the real symbol of the age in this total decentralisation.'[30]

But most significant – given that the Nesles-la-Vallée project did not, in the event, go very far – was the change that takes place in Delaunay's work at precisely this moment. It is very simply registered in the titles of Guy Habasque's catalogue of Delaunay's work, included in *Du Cubisme à l'art abstrait*. A seemingly endless list of *Portraits, Coureurs, Tours Eiffel* suddenly gives way in 1930 to *Formes Circulaires, Rythme – Joie de Vivre, Rythme – Relief*, etc. In *Robert Delaunay*, Gleizes refers to 'the very legitimate worries and hesitations of a man who had gone ahead too soon and who felt alone. He has admitted it to me since I joined up with him again and since I told him unreservedly what I had discovered in him.' In 1930, Gleizes wrote to Delaunay commenting on one of his numerous portraits of Mme Jacques Heim:

> Independently of the pleasant impression I had of the portrait of Mme Heim, very attractive both in the successive stages of its realisation and in the final success, I repeat what I said in the house. Take the discs up again. Without a subject other than their mobile life, their living life, for life isn't in the image but the movement of the spirit. And you will really have developed what you felt in 1913–14. . . .[31]

It is impossible to resist the conclusion that Gleizes helped to give Delaunay the confidence he needed to return to a wholly non-representational painting in the 1930s; and this is confirmed in the entry on Gleizes in the *Dictionary of Abstract Painting* by Michel Seuphor, the Belgian writer and critic, who knew both painters well.[32] Throughout the 1930s, Gleizes and Delaunay regard each other as colleagues, as members of the same school and when in 1934 Gleizes feels that he has fully understood the idea towards which they had been working, he notifies Delaunay, just as he notifies Pouyaud, Jellett and Anne Dangar. In 1937, they collaborated on a number of great mural panels for the Paris Exhibition, and in 1939, Gleizes joined Delaunay in giving a series of lessons for younger painters in the latter's studio in Paris. In his essay, *Spiritualité, rythme, forme*, written in 1943, shortly after Delaunay's death, Gleizes represents himself and Robert Delaunay as the only members of the original Cubist team who had seen the adventure through to the end.

14

1934

In various notes on his own development as a painter, Delaunay distinguishes two periods which he calls 'destructive' and 'constructive', corresponding more or less to what Gleizes and the other Cubists would call 'analytical' and 'synthetic' – not to be confused, we have seen, with the terms 'analytical and synthetic Cubism' generally used to characterise the work of Picasso and Braque. Delaunay's 'destructive' Cubism refers simply to the 'destruction' of the representational 'object'. It begins with Cézanne: 'Cézanne's watercolours announce Cubism. The coloured or rather luminous planes destroy the object . . . but the object remains in its broken state.'[1] In Delaunay's own work, the 'constructive' period begins with his *Fénêtres* of 1912, and begins to be fully realised in the circular forms of 1913:

> The dynamism of the colour contrasts where the linear element has entirely disappeared, it is the form itself, product of contrasts in simultaneous vibrations of colours, which is the subject – the total mobile form – neither descriptive nor analytical as in the earliest Cubism. It is form in movement, static and dynamic. The elements that make it up are colours; some vibrate slowly, in opposition to others which are fast, or very fast. Their height, on the surface, in relation to their width, relative to each other – their spaces, intervals, intensity, number, interference – so many basic elements which have their numerical relations, their dominant, in the evolution and direction of form. . . .[2]

This is Delaunay writing in the period when he was closest to Gleizes and the similarity to Gleizes's thinking is obvious. But the identification of form and colour is perhaps the major point that, from the start, distinguished Delaunay from the Cubist group. Delaunay was the first to recognise that when Cézanne broke the representational subject the effect was to liberate the power of the colour. Cézanne has been widely represented as standing for construction in opposition to the Impressionists who stood for colour. For Delaunay, however, Cézanne was the greatest of colourists – his formal innovations enabled him to move towards the fulness of colour. Colour is a force that cannot be contained within the representational scheme. The effect of the triumph of perspective is a progressive diminution of the power of colour,[3] but nor can colour reveal its strength when it is split up into the myriad little dots of the Impressionists and Neo-Impressionists. It is too divided to be properly seized by the eye. It is inseparable from form, but a form other than representational form.

Even in 1927, when he is thinking about the problem of colour and about Delaunay, Gleizes, in *Peinture et perspective descriptive*, only discusses Cézanne in terms of a drama of form, independent of colour – the struggle of the power of the circle (the circle of a bowl or of a plate) and the weak oval that it becomes under the deformation imposed by the perspective system.

Delaunay from the earliest days has wanted the fullness of colour – the fullest possible saturation of colour, the full colour circle: and he saw it in Cézanne. And he knows from Cézanne that it can only be achieved through clearly demarcated areas of colour, areas that have been given by the destruction of the figurative image, reducing it, not to little points, but to larger divisions that can be siezed by the eye. And Delaunay has been able to carry these larger divisions over into his circular forms.

So far, we have discussed the circle very much in the abstract, as if the mere fact of drawing circles was itself revolutionary. If the introduction of non-representational circles was of itself the revolutionary act, then we would have to recognise Frantisek Kupka, who, we have seen, had known Gleizes prior to the First World War, as the real precursor of this development in Gleizes's thought. But the power of Delaunay's *Formes Circulaires*, as opposed to Kupka's *Disques de Newton*, lies in the colour, and the power of the colour is released because the circle is broken into clearly marked divisions which can be seized and appreciated by the eye. If we simply draw a circle, the eye takes it in all at once. It may follow the line round, but the operation is performed so quickly that there is no sensation of movement, or only the sensation of a movement that is unpleasantly fast. If the eye is to 'taste' the circular movement, it has, in a sense, to be slowed down; And this is done by the division of the circle into what Gleizes was now beginning to call 'cadences'.

•

The period when Delaunay, in alliance with Gleizes, returns to a purely non-representational painting, is also the period when the relation between Gleizes's own work and Delaunay's becomes more apparent, largely through this question of cadences. Gleizes, we have seen, has had Delaunay on the mind since, perhaps, 1925–6, and he is also much preoccupied with problems of colour, but Gleizes's colour in this period of searching for a precise discipline, using Forichon, bears very little resemblance, at least superficially, to Delaunay's. Delaunay aimed for his 'plenitude' by presenting an abundance of very bright colours 'simultaneously' – and he was saved from catastrophe by his innate colour sense. Gleizes too had been able to present daring colour combinations (never so powerful as Delaunay at his best) by means of an innate good taste – the good taste in colour that, in *L'Homme devenu peintre*, he attributes to children, before they are corrupted by their art teachers.

Now, however, under pressure from his pupils, he has to try to understand what he is doing, and in searching for the same totality that Delaunay seeks, he takes up Forichon's idea of the necessity of presenting the whole colour spectrum, which can be done with one predominant colour, giving the 'atmosphere' of the painting, placed in relation to its complementary. This, however, is still a static presentation of colour. It enables a harmonious composition, satisfying the eye in its state of repose, without stimulating it into movement. What movement there is in 1927–30 is given much more by the drawing than by the colour.

At the same time, Gleizes has a problem with his 'mechanism' of translation/rotation, independent of colour – a problem that has been touched on before. This is that if by the superposition of planes, the eye is drawn into a centre, that centre risks becoming a point of immobility, as wearisome – if not more so – as the vanishing point of the perspective mechanism. The danger is that the attention is immobilised on the centre and the subtle game of planes in translation and rotation recedes into the background. Initially, Gleizes called on his pupils to 'animate' the planes with various patterns to make them more interesting, but this rather patchwork effect could only be a temporary measure. A more substantial solution begins to appear from around 1926 onwards. This is that the eye, drawn into the centre by the game of the planes, could be drawn out again by a game of 'accents'. Again, we must stress that Gleizes has been doing this for a long time; it can be seen in his wartime work. We may say that he has to theorise it in order to explain why his paintings are more successful than those of his pupils. In Gleizes's work, the practice normally comes before the theory – but the elaboration of the theory enables him to carry it further.

In the last chapter, I quoted Anne Dangar telling Grace Crowley that the painting starts slowly, with minimal colour changes, and becomes much faster in the centre. A 'slow' colour change may be from blue to blue-green; the fastest possible colour change would be from blue to yellow-orange, its complementary. So, following this scheme, there is much greater variety of colour at the centre than at the outside. We are soon going to encounter the Dutch philosopher, Gleizes's friend, Louis Hoyack. Hoyack has an interesting and analogous view of traditional oriental music. It starts slowly and majestically. It ends very fast. In this it reproduces the development of societies. Their youth is characterised by dignified and graceful movement, their old age by very fast speed and agitation. Very fast speed is the prelude to death, to immobility.[4]

Of course, the centre of the painting risks being its death – its immobility. To avoid this, the eye is guided back to the frame of the painting by the accents, small touches of colour which, in the slower atmosphere of the initial colours pick up the faster colours of the centre. Thus an in-out movement is established, like breath, which, also like breath, can be kept up indefinitely. We are beginning to replace harmonious arrangement with an idea of movement that is specific to colour.

The theory of colour Pouyaud used in teaching Anne Dangar was a combination of Forichon with Gleizes's scheme of translation/rotation. It proposed a distinction between movements of colour in translation and movements of colour in rotation. The movement of colour in translation was the movement of one and the same colour through all its different tones from dark to light. The movement of colour in rotation was the movement of one colour to another round the colour circle. The sense of direction is easily established in translation. It can immediately be appreciated by an eye following a series of degradations of a colour towards white or towards black. But in order that a colour should move towards another colour, a connection must exist between them. They must both be of the same tone. They must both occupy the same band of a colour circle in which the different tones from black to white, from night to day, are recorded.

For Pouyaud, the movement of colour in translation corresponded to the movement of form in translation, that is to say, to vertical figures; the movement of colour in rotation corresponded to the movement of form in rotation, that is to say, to inclined figures. Anne Dangar found this very difficult, especially since many figures combine traits of verticality and inclination. Gleizes said that it was a good general rule, but not one to be obeyed slavishly.[5]

By 1930–1, Gleizes was intensely involved in the problem of the movement of

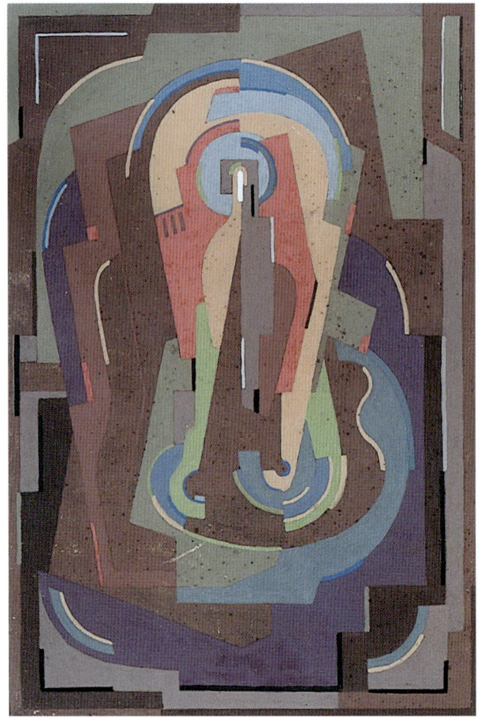

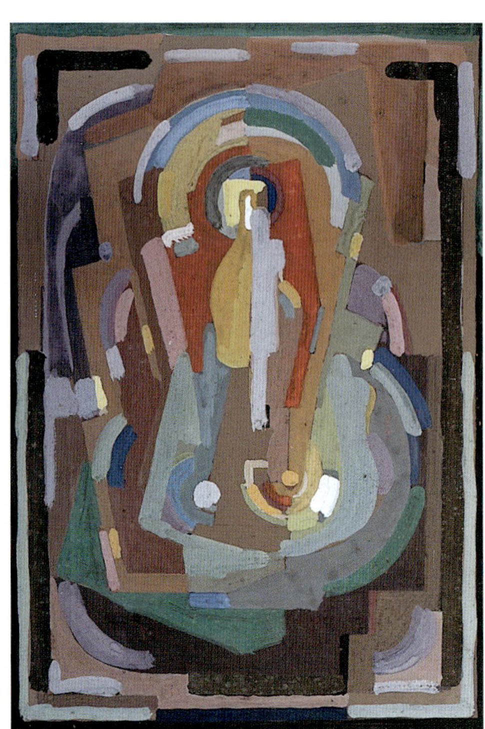

94. Robert Pouyaud, *Composition*, 1926 (1931?). Gouache, *c.* 30.2 × 20 cm. Private Collection

95. [Re-working of a gouache by Robert Pouyaud], 1926 (1931?). Gouache, *c.* 30.5 × 20.3 cm. Private Collection

colour. Indeed, he almost seems to be re-living the conflict between form and colour, the drama between the Cubists and the Neo-Impressionists, except that this time he is on the side of the Neo-Impressionists. He is now almost uniquely interested in 'cadences' of colour – to such an extent that the form – or, rather, the figure, the construction – risks disappearing altogether, buried under the weight of a mass of cadences turning round a centre, cadences that could be said to have evolved out of the earlier coloured accents. In *L'Homme devenu peintre*, he invokes the authority of Odilon Redon:

> Someone who knew Odilon Redon very closely told me that he[6] once heard him reply to a young painter who asked his advice: 'Open your box of pastels. Choose the one that pleases you most, and crush it on your paper. Surround it with what suits it, and in that way organise your picture.' That is painting expressed in its object. Beginning with the feeling of sight, and finishing with the formed work; between these two limits, the movement of cadence and counterpoint. The order is perfect. It only remains for us to acquire through experience the secret of the rules through which we can correct the vagaries of our feeling, though still constantly taking it into account; that is what is meant by mastery. (p.37)

This is very close to Gleizes's own practice in this period of intense research on colour. In a letter written early in 1931,[7] Anne Dangar describes Gleizes working on a drawing by her own Australian pupil, Estelle Creed:

> He covered a long narrow panel with cobalt, then put her drawing down[8] and made the centre orange-red [the complementary – PB], and then he worked out from that centre on one side with orange, yellow, yellow-green, green, and on

the other red, crimson, violet-blue. But so gradually! and in such tiny morsels of the bright colours near the centre! Then the border lines, he just used black and white and they looked quite near enough the complementary . . .

The foundation colour is laid down; its complementary is put in the centre, and the two are linked by the cadences – little touches of colours moving in the two different directions suggested by the centre (in this case orange towards yellow or orange towards red, since orange is made up of yellow and red) round the colour circle. In a letter of February 1931, Dangar illustrates the meaning of the word 'cadence' with a number of concentric circles made up of dotted lines: 'The dictionary definition, as applied to music is quite in keeping with Gleizes's use of the word. The measures following one another really make your composition, but those measures lost through the power in which they have conducted you to the thought behind is what he calls 'rhythm'.'[9]

'Measure, cadence, rhythm' – this is the terminology in which Gleizes is now thinking. The 'measure' is the individual area of colour, sufficiently definite (unlike the Impressionist dot) to be measured by the eye. But it establishes a direction. The eye does not concentrate on it; it is directed to the next, then to the next. That direction gives the 'cadence'. As the individual measure is lost in the cadence, so the different cadences are lost in the overall, unified, ultimately circular movement, which is what Gleizes calls the 'rhythm'.

It is here that Gleizes is closest to Delaunay. The development belongs mainly to 1931. Pouyaud had already left Moly Sabata, but he was still sending his work to Gleizes for comment and correction. In January 1931, Gleizes wrote to congratulate him on a gouache he had sent (Plate 94) but to say that it needed to be more supple: 'The painting that is fully realised will be that which will impose the form on the figures. One will experience only the form, the cycle, and it will only be later that one can analyse and grasp the fragments . . . '.[10]

Helped by Jellett, Gleizes reworked Pouyaud's gouache (Plate 95), and the difference between the two versions is remarkable. Essentially, Pouyaud's con-

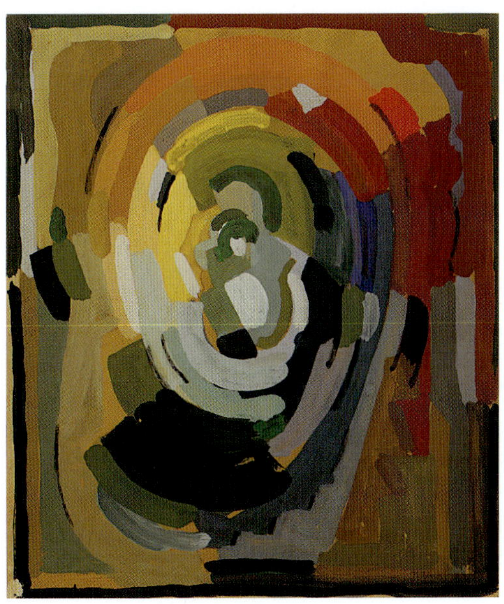

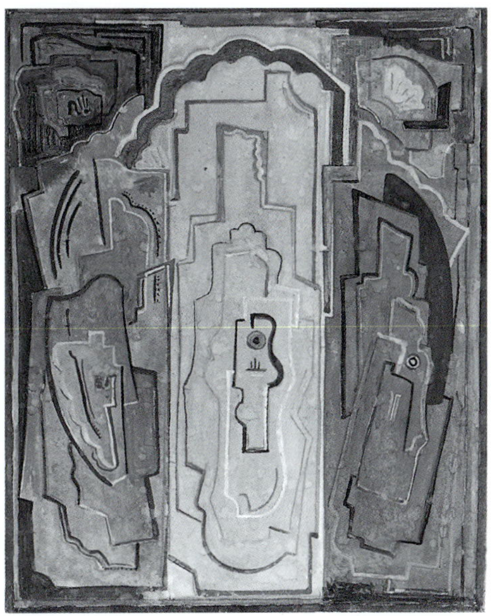

96. *Study for Cadences*, 1931. Gouache on cardboard, 30 × 24.1 cm. Fondation Albert Gleizes

97. Mainie Jellett, *Five Elements*, 1929 (?). Watercolour, 27.5 × 22 cm. Private Collection. The three principal elements are, from left to right, in red, yellow and blue. The central motifs are in neutral grey

struction (impressive enough in its way) has been used as a base for the elaboration of the cadences. The eye is never allowed to rest for any length of time on any part of the painting, and the main stimulus which compels the eye into a coherent, directed movement is not the structure, the drawing, but now almost uniquely the – often very small – divisions, or 'measures' of the colour.[11]

Although this work is a considerable advance on the work of the 1920s, Gleizes in 1932–3 is still restless and dissatisfied. It was an exciting period for his pupils because the concentration on colour posed a host of problems which he discussed with them. He was much more interested in this studio work than in exhibiting. Anne Dangar wrote to Grace Crowley (nicknamed 'Smudge') in March 1932 to say that he had been offered a one-man-show, but had replied:

> 'I don't know enough. I am not ready' . . . We tell him the thing he has done is the beginning of perhaps four hundred years of thought and technique in art. He says 'I'd rather show with you – I don't want this work to appear as an individual's idea but as a school of artisans. I want to work on your pictures and I want you to help me with mine and no names appear at all as it was in the Middle Ages.' (He is a dear, Smudge).[12]

Mainie Jellett complained about his refusal to exhibit and his insistence on the importance of his books: 'It is inevitable that if they [younger artists] read the books and have no way of seeing what kind of art the books are defending, that they will be driven more and more to copy Picasso and artists of his type whose work they see, for want of a better example.'[13]

Gleizes was of course involved with Abstraction-Création, set up, largely on the initiative of Auguste Herbin, in 1931. He was on the organising committee, but his involvement was only half-hearted. Herbin wrote complaining in February 1933 that 'your removal from the scene leaves you ignorant of the works and decisions of the committee of which you are a member'.[14] Gleizes had told Delaunay back in 1927 that he now regarded visits to Paris as an unpleasant duty and he believed in principle that work in his own locality was much more important than jostling for position in the metropolis.[15] In any case, though he supported Abstraction-Création and encouraged his pupils to participate in it, its central organising principle of 'abstraction' had little interest for him. He disliked the term 'abstraction', just as he disliked the term 'non-objective'. For Gleizes, a painting that copied the external appearances of nature was a subjective (therefore non-objective) abstraction: 'nature seen through a temperament' – nature subjectively abstracted from its own reality and placed on the canvas. A painting which was faithful to the nature of painting – the flat surface and the laws that regulate colour and drawing – was concrete and objective. And so long as it was faithful to its own objective nature, there was no reason why it should not embody figurative elements, if these were subordinate to the rhythm of the painting and not dominant over it.[16]

Gleizes's discontent and reluctance to exhibit do not indicate any lack of self-confidence. The talks he gave in Germany and Poland in 1932 are full of certainty, as is the essay on Delaunay, written in 1933. He gives the impression that the destiny, the end (*dénouement*) of Cubism has now been realised – that Delaunay's circular forms provide all the means that are needed for a complete renewal of painting, independent of classical representation. The problem is now to understand and master those means.

However, in undated notes, almost certainly written in the early 1930s,[17]

Gleizes indicates some dissatisfaction with Delaunay's means:

> On reverie, on imagination – in the first Cubist pictures (multiplicity of perspective points) there was the return of a spirit of rambling, of giving nuances to the different paths taken; it was the opposite to the modernist tendency that scorns whatever lies between two points = ultra-rapid voyages of which aeroplanes represent the means that most suppress whatever is intermediate; Man becomes ever more stupid and uniform and we're not even aware of it.
>
> Delaunay, exclusively painting the true principle, suppresses the movement, which makes the sinusoide faithful to the curve through its distancing and its approach. He only paints the final curve-principle. The curve must be followed faithfully in the figures that mark its different stages = nature of the form and natures of the figures. . . .

In 1934, explaining his own latest development to Delaunay, he defends the earlier slowness of himself and his colleagues prior to the war:

> Realism is not below, in the senses, but, making use of them, and making use of the memory, it is above. That is the secret of the religious periods. It will be our secret. You felt it a long time before the rest of us. You had a stroke of genius in 1914. But the analysis that we were engaged in, methodically, was not sterile, I beg you to believe; it allowed the regulation of the lower, terrestrial parts of the work. You saw the end, the culmination. But the feet and the heart have to be brought along as well . . .[18]

Gleizes described 1934 as 'the year that I consider as the most decisive in my life'.[19] He gives a detailed account of what happened in the *Souvenirs* and, at the time, in a letter to Anne Dangar in September. The 'revelation' came in two parts – the first in March, the second in Autumn. What happened in March is described, rather pleasantly, by Anne Dangar:

> Mr Gleizes has been passing through a very strange experience in his work. He says that the first work of March 1934 will stand out in his memory as the most important work of his career. He thinks he has discovered the secret of the 'Moyen Age' art. I looked at his work for an hour or so. He has encircled and bound every picture with a grey line of even dimension and perfectly neutral tint – a firm, relentless, inflexible line. The effect is very fine. The pictures possess an austerity and unity such as I have never seen, except in primitive art . . .
>
> Mr Gleizes explained his revelation. Hoyack – a professor of philosophy from Holland – came and spent a week with him. He is a heavy, university brained creature who can understand nothing until it has been put on the dissecting table and cut up in morsels. He said he couldn't understand *La Forme et l'histoire* at all. He demanded explanations of the words used – 'space', 'time' etc etc. Mr Gleizes made him define these words because he [Hoyack] said Mr Gleizes was wrong in saying God was not in either space or time because God was unchangeable and space and time is changeable. Hoyack said space was unchangeable. Then when demanded to define it, he

said it was the distance from one object to another. Mr Gleizes said: 'Well – take the flower in your hand for instance and its distance from me – a dimension. Now, how long will that flower endure if you keep it in your hand?' 'Two days, perhaps,' Hoyack replied. 'Yes. In two days, the space will have changed because the flower will be dead.' etc etc etc

But Mr Gleizes went to his studio. He looked at his pictures. The lovely dimensions of colours – the rhythm, movement, time. But – the unchangeable? He realised he had missed the very thing he had been searching since 1926. He sent me word he was going to burn all his work since 1926. Knowing the French temperament, I only missed two hours sleep and had wild dreams one night. He didn't burn 'em. He reflected long and I think prayerfully, for he spoke of his gethsemane, on the nature of God. In two days he had this revelation. . . .[20]

Louis Hoyack was a disciple of the Sufi teacher, Inayat Khan. His book *Où va le Machinisme?*, published in 1931, develops an argument on the nature of the machine that is very close to Gleizes, and he contributed, with Gleizes, to the Naturist journal, *Régénération*. His *Spiritualisme historique: étude critique sur l'idée du progrès* of 1932–3 and *Les Aubes de l'humanité* develop a cyclical view of history,[21] but his cycles do not correspond with those of Gleizes. Essentially, he sees the cycles of history as being launched by the divine revelations of the 'Messengers of God' – the founders of the great religions. The appearance of Muhammad in the seventh century means therefore that the Christian cycle had come to an end. He could not agree with Gleizes as to the spiritual greatness of the period from the fourth to the twelfth centuries. At the same time, he admired the Renaissance, seeing it as a fruit of the revelation of Muhammad.[22]

Gleizes describes his conversations with Hoyack at length in the *Souvenirs*.[23] They turn on the distinction between 'absolute' and 'relative'. The confusion in Hoyack's understanding of time and space is due to his defining Time as a duration and Space as an extension; he could see only the relative to which he ascribed the value of an absolute. To understand this, it may be helpful to remember Gleizes's interest in the mediaeval debate between 'Realism' and 'Nominalism'. The advance of Nominalism in the philosophical debates from the eleventh to the fourteenth centuries was the equivalent of the advance in the external aspects of nature in painting. The Realists maintained that the characteristics of the world were reflections in space and time of absolute, unchanging realities. The Nominalists maintained that these spatial, temporal, changing realities were complete in themselves. They were created by God, but they did not otherwise participate in any absolute nature.

Gleizes had long believed, in principle, that the Absolute was the source of unity in the world, the origin and end of all the disparate phenomena of the Universe – eternity source of time; immobility source of movement; light, colourless source of colour. This was the essence of his idea of religion – that everything is related. His Christianity was Neoplatonist: the temporal was a reflection of the eternal not, as it is in a Nominalist theology, a completely different order of reality. He nonetheless drew a clear distinction between Absolute and Relative. He accuses Hoyack of 'pantheism', of confusing the Relative and the Absolute. Hoyack – if we are to believe Anne Dangar's second-hand account – says that God is in space, that space is unchangeable; and then he defines space as extension – the distance between two points. In Gleizes's view, if we are to understand what God has to do with space or with extension, we must recognise 'space' – the abstract meaning of the word, so to speak – as a reality other than that of any given extension, or even the sum total of all possible extensions: as lying in the Absolute, which is unattainable to us but which is the necessary ground of everything that is relative. However, in the course of these conversations, Gleizes begins to realise that if Hoyack confused the Absolute and the Relative in his thinking, Gleizes himself had confused them in his act:

> It was in one of these moments of relaxation [from his exhausting conversations with Hoyack – PB] that I saw clearly, spontaneously, the *quidproquo* in which I had been struggling for years and which was the reason for my dissatisfaction with regard to the technical means I was using. My compositions remained fragmentary and, in spite of certain intuitions that had led me to adopt a coloured curvature round the central theme, I felt clearly that the unity had not been achieved.
>
> Why? It was in vain that I divided tones, modulated and multiplied nuances, the result was not what I wanted. I couldn't understand the reason. Suddenly, while I was reflecting before my canvasses on their easels, still under the influence of the formal clarifications we had just been making with regard to certain key words, a ray of light crossed my mind; it struck the canvasses scattered before my eyes by a ricochet.
>
> I understood now, at least partially.
>
> Translation and Rotation were certainly the principles on which I had based myself to 'realise my painting-objects'. But I had only touched on ROTATION; I didn't see it, therefore I didn't unleash it . . . What came to me clearly now was that, even though I had aimed at rotation, which would have truly realised a mobile form that would have drawn the eye into its movement, I had up till now only indicated the opposing phases [of this movement – PB], and I was still static.
>
> Despite the modulations I was using, following the suggestion of the colours of the rainbow, it [the rotation – PB] did not follow categorically. Something definitive was missing which I now glimpsed; it is movement itself, in which the modulated interlinking of the colours would find their end.
>
> This movement is the rhythm of the picture, expressed by the linear arabesque that describes its form. It is this form that must unite all the organic fragments which give only a promise of unity.
>
> I had finally understood. 'How', I said to myself, 'did I dare ask Hoyack to give me precise definitions of the words he used. I pride myself on not acting towards words like an intellectual without hands, always to render objective whatever I have in my head, and here I have the proof that for years I have been as incapable as him or any other intellectual of making concrete what I had as an idea. I spoke of rotation without being capable of doing it, and it is only now that I see it.'
>
> So, I armed myself with a brush in one hand, and a cloth soaked in turpentine to be able to correct and rapidly wipe out anything I might repent. I made

a mixture of white and black, which gave me a grey of a certain intensity corresponding to the general tonality of the canvas I had in front of me. And, with this tone alone, I superposed an arabesque on the coloured composition, the simplest I could, which summed up in a line the intentions that were contained in the different directed currents of the canvas. I stepped back. This time I had realised the rotation I had been speaking about so long . . .

The composition which until then had been inert, waiting, was thrown into action and the colours called and replied to each other.

Unity was established. The explanation was easy. The drawing was affirmed by these combinations of grey curved lines. These grey lines – I insist, a grey obtained by a mixture of black and white and consequently not at all coloured – were like luminous resonators on which the colours sang in softened complementaries. As the order of my colours more or less modulated had, once they had parted from the central colour harmony, respected the order of the chromatic circle, one can understand that the grey resonator woke the eye to the contrast. On a red, the grey drawing took on green, and everywhere that the grey line passed, the same phenomenon took place. In my coloured combinations, a red, or several reds, would be found at one side of the canvas – a green, or several greens on the other. Between them, from top to bottom, the intermediary chromatic successions were divided. So that on the coloured reds the resonator sang green and on the coloured greens the resonator sang red.

And everywhere the contrast opposed a subtle nuance to the colour, changing intensities and creating a real symphony. Hence, unity found again on a basis of plurality and in movement.[24]

In the 1920s, Gleizes had aimed for 'rotation' by presenting two stages of a rotating figure – the first vertical, the second inclined – and hoping that the eye would imagine the inclination continuing in a circular movement. In 1930–1, he added the cadences, small measures of colour placed beside each other in a given order, which could be followed by the eye round the colour circle (the order of the spectrum; of the rainbow). But here again, the eye was being invited to jump, so to speak, from one essentially static measure to the other. Effectively what was happening was that a 'figure' – static in its own nature (the basic 1920s construction) – was being bent into a movement by the addition of the cadences. It is the same process that Gleizes describes in the painting of Van Gogh.[25] Gleizes already had the idea of the distinction between

98. (below) *Pour Méditation* (this is the title given to the version which appears in the Pensées de Pascal), 1934. Without grey circles

99. (below) *Pour Méditation*, 1934. With grey circles. Oil on canvas, 65 × 135 cm. Present whereabouts unknown

100. (top right) *Rythmes*, 1934. Without grey circles

101. (top right) *Rythmes*, 1934. With grey circles. Oil on canvas, 108 × 78 cm. Present whereabouts unknown

102. (far right) *Spirale brun et vert*, 1934 (1932–3). Without grey circles

103. (far right) *Spirale brun et vert*, 1934 (1932–3). With grey circles. Oil on canvas 168 × 78 cm Present whereabouts unknown

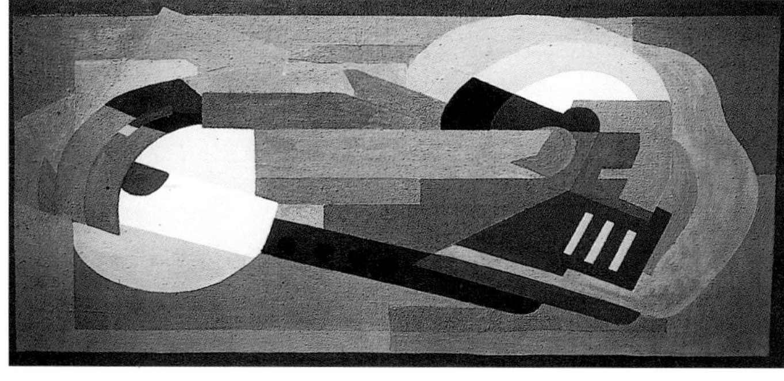

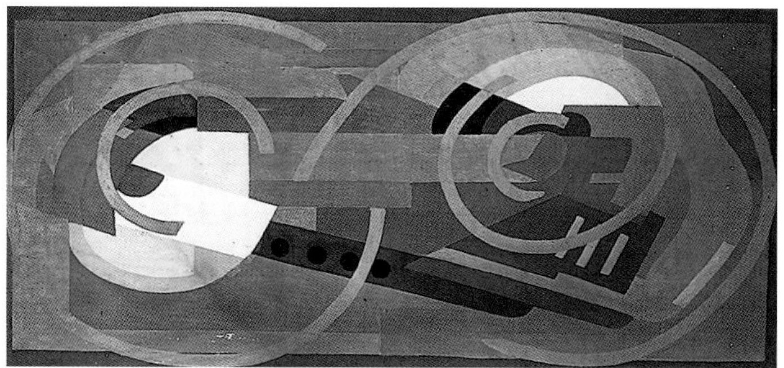

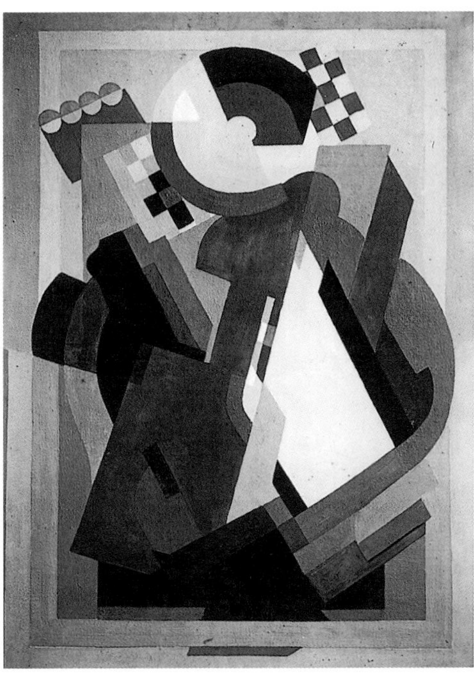

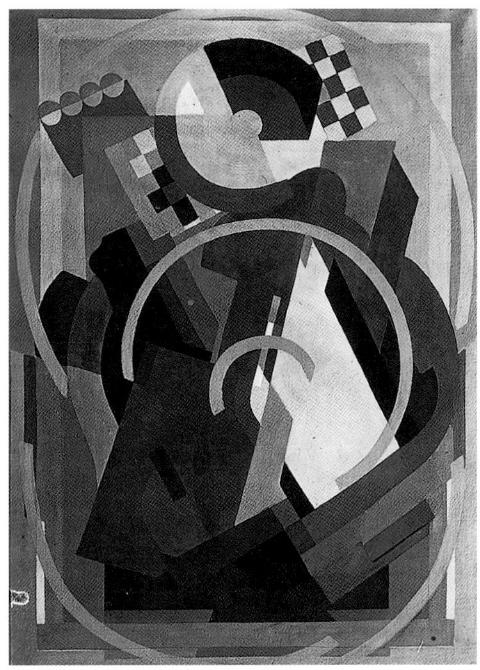

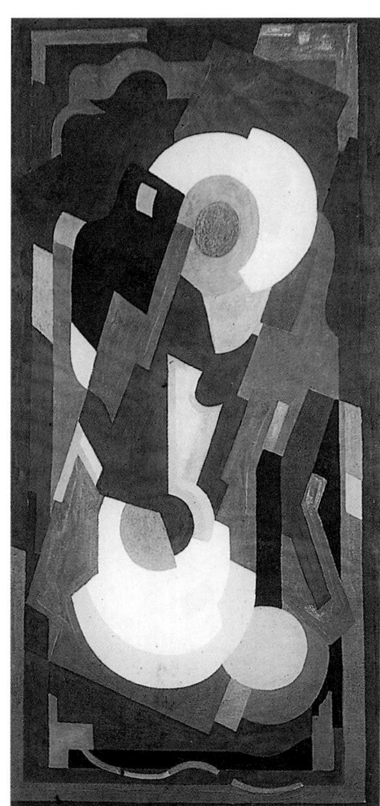

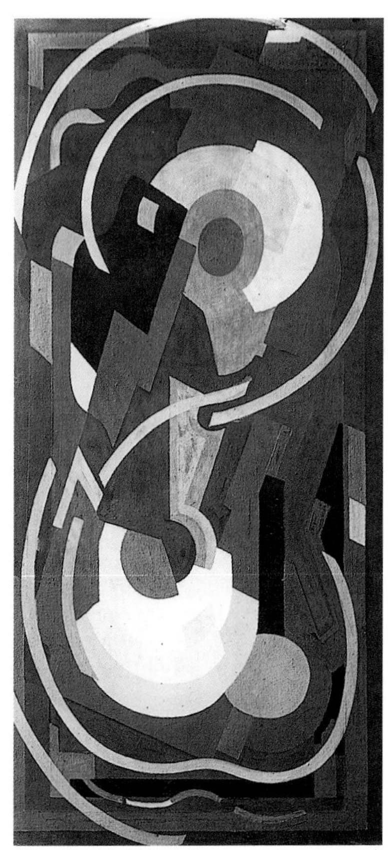

mobile form and immobile figure, but he was still confusing the two in his painting, trying to bully the figure into becoming a form. The addition of the grey lines gave the form as simply and explicitly as possible, conferring unity and simplicity on the diversity and complexity of the figures and cadences.

Gleizes subjected all the canvasses of 1932–3 that he could to this treatment, with the result that it would have been difficult to imagine what they were like without it if we did not possess a good black-and-white photographic archive of the paintings in both states. The immediate effect in relation to his earlier work is that the pictures are much easier on the eye, simply because the eye has less work to do to penetrate the painting. However, the canvasses to which Gleizes applied his grey lines had not originally been intended for them. He had taken a great risk with some of his best paintings (the ones he told Anne Dangar he wanted to burn) – including the monumental *Sept éléments*, which he had been working on since 1924 (Plate 104). Here in particular – in a construction developed before the colour researches of the late 1920s and early 1930s, we can see that he could not use a simple uniform grey and had to modulate it according to the differing tones of colour it encounters.

Anne Dangar, despite her praise for their 'austerity and unity' was not wholly enthusiastic:

> But, although I see and feel the architecture of the Romanesque period, there is something lacking. Jacopo Bellini gives all that Gleizes gives but also that golden light of pure love and a Oneness between the symbol (the Virgin Mother – the sheltering body of the Church) and the spirit – also the humility of the painter offering his all in worship . . . Ah, we are far from the spirit of *le moyen age*, we *pauvres analystes* of 1934.[26]

Mainie Jellett was more directly critical. Gleizes later wrote to her to say that:

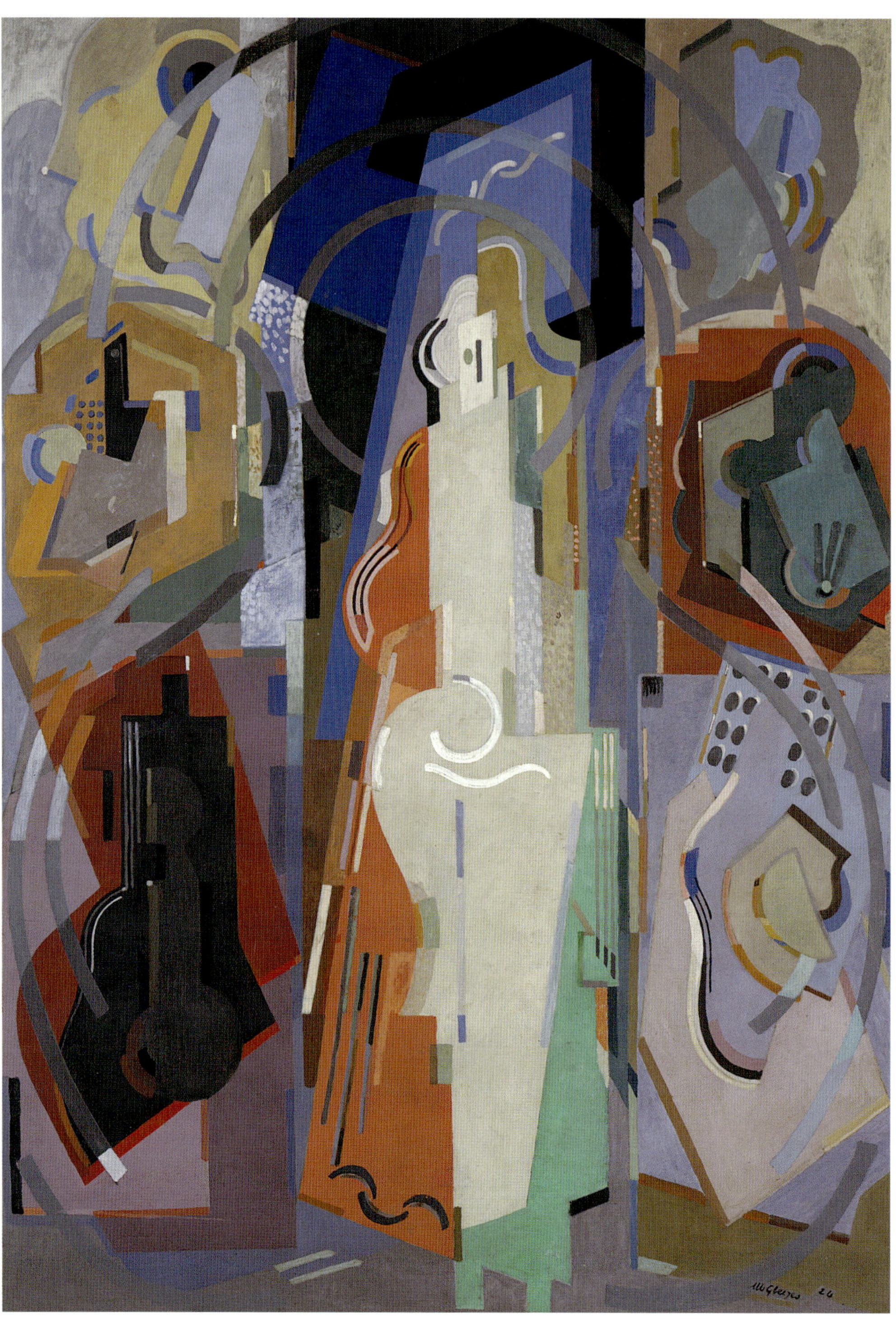

104. *Sept éléments*, 1924–34. Oil on canvas, 261 × 181 cm. Musée National d'Art Moderne, Paris

'Your comments were judicious, and I realised that my grey circles were too much outside the composition.'[27]

Gleizes descibes how he resolved the problem in a letter written to Anne Dangar:

In the canvasses which were waiting for me, which I felt to be very incomplete, which did not satisfy me, I tried the impossible – to bring them to their end, the integration of the curves, the game of light.

You know the result. But perhaps you do not know that despite my apparent joy, I still wasn't content. In fact these canvasses, when I conceived them, didn't embody this end because I couldn't definitely envisage it. They behaved well and didn't protest too much when I imposed it on them; they did what they could and I am grateful to them. But – but – it was insufficient, and my criticisms quickly replaced my pleasure. The final circles were too much outside the translation and rotation; or rather these last were revealed, by the very rigour of the newly arrived circles, as imperfect, confused, disordered, badly arranged.

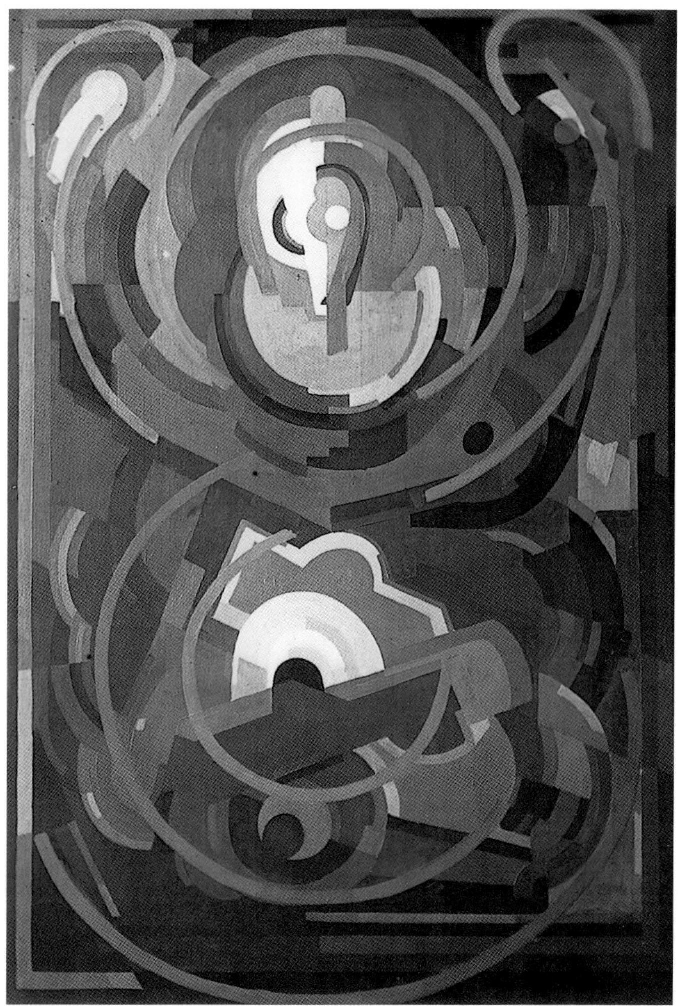

105. *Symphonie de violets*, 1934 (1930–1). Oil on canvas, 196 × 131 cm. Present whereabouts unknown

So that the decisive circles should be logical and really an end, an apotheosis, the translation and the rotation had to prepare their arrival methodically, clearly, finally in order. The three stages of the construction of the monument had to appear successively in the whole of the work. Successively, you understand? That is to say that the first with the foundations should be in its place, the second also, and the third, with the roof, should be a natural conclusion. In other words, that the static space accessible to the senses – translation – should be the base; that time – cadence, rotation – should put it into movement; and that, to finish, this cadence should become rhythm, form, light. So: figures, dominated by straight lines; then, periodical displacements of straight lines and curves; finally, unity, the circles.

1) Organisation of combinations of colours, following all the games of the fancy.
2) These combinations are arranged in the order of the coloured cadences, transformed in the order of the chromatic circle.
3) These chromatic cadences are integrated following their natural tendency into grey – intensity of a mixture of black and white, the equivalent in painting of the intensity of light.

When these stages are found in their regular succession, their natural order, there is truly unity. The circular light arrives as a necessity and not something just thrown into the bargain, as in the canvasses you have seen, which are above all interesting for their intention and intuition, but badly organised. Now the light is something expected, satisfying, conclusive.[28]

The letter is illustrated with three small drawings showing 'space-translation', 'time-rotation', and 'the end – simultaneously space and time'. This is the scheme that now replaces the 'space/rhythm' or 'translation/rotation' of *La Peinture et*

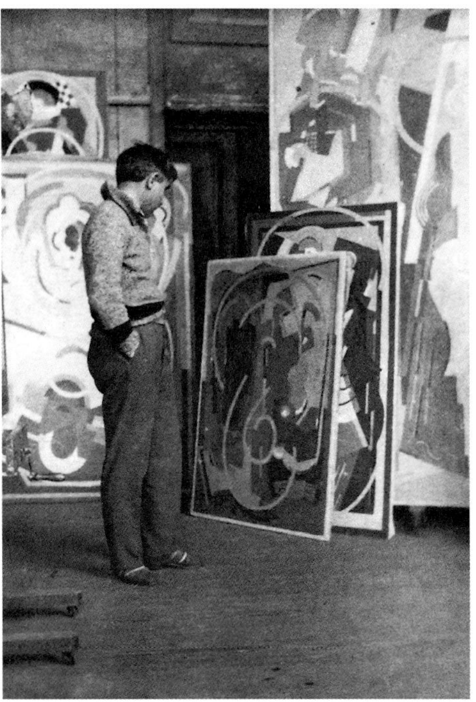

106. Gleizes in his studio. The paintings are all from 1934

ses lois. The earlier scheme had not been abandoned, but it now occupies entirely the lowest level of the edifice – the figure, essentially static, but beginning, through the inclination of the planes, to hint at the possibility of rotation. The second level is the element introduced by Delaunay. The colours are given by the initial translation-figure, but they are displaced round an essentially circular 'rainbow', and ordered, so that they pass from one to another following a definite direction round the colour circle – red, orange, yellow, green, blue, for example. The existence of several different rows of cadences means that this can be done without monotonous repetition. The different areas of colour are divided according to lines given in the initial figure, made up, as it is, of straight lines. Integrated into the circles of differentiated colour is the third level, the simple grey circle that unifies, softens and enlivens all the rest.

In these three stages of the painter's work – translation, rotation, rhythm, analogous to the three necessary conditions of reality – space, time, eternity – Gleizes believed that he had found the key to the painting of all the great religious epochs of human history. It was the return to 'traditional painting' – the end of the domination of consciousness by the senses (an imitative, 'humanist' art and science) and the beginning of the reign of the spirit (a creative, theocentric art and science). Gleizes's evolution does not stop in 1934, but he now understands the means by which the rhythmic, religious painting that he wants can be realised. From now on, it is a matter of learning how to master them.

15

FROM FIGURE TO LIGHT

One immediate consequence of the 'revelation' of 1934 was the return of a recognisable representational imagery. Gleizes never totally abandoned such imagery for very long and this has led some commentators, including Daniel Robbins and Bernard Dorival, to deny that he was ever really an 'abstract' or 'non-objective' painter (Gleizes, we have seen, objected strongly to both terms).[1] He wrote to Pouyaud in 1926 to explain his position. As regards:

> the evocation of representational images . . . it doesn't worry me. All the more so since there is a world of difference between the representational image that the painter has set out to realise and an image evoked in the memory that appears as accidental to the act of painting. I don't fear the consequences of such an evocation if, in your work of construction, you finish up with an image that suggests the idea of a form that is known – it may even be a proof of the rightness of your work. In this way, you join up with a language that is known, but without taking it as a starting point. You see the difference? There is at the present time a tendency among young painters to only accept canvasses without a subject. Without a subject, that is to say, without an anecdote, this is fine, but I think they are in error as to their terms because they talk about abstract art and concrete art, concrete art being that in which the memories appear, while abstract art is that in which there are only geometrical forms. For me, the question is at once more simple and less simplistic. Your imagination brings you a formal system, an order of images. Through your construction, you allow it to be born. Whether it is born without evoking any memory, or whether it is born provoking an analogy, doesn't matter. What is important is that you have the means to bring this system to birth, independent of any element of fantasy. These means are abstract and must result in something concrete. A table is as concrete as a horse; but the tablemaker starts from principles that can also be found in the structure of the horse. The painter who starts from the horse to make an image of it, to reproduce it, has no principle. I would go so far as to say that he starts from the concrete (the horse) to arrive at the abstract (the image of the horse); while the tablemaker starts from the abstract (the principle of equilibrium, of movement, the relations of each part to the other) to arrive at the concrete. Oh, words! . . .[2]

Gleizes takes up much the same line of argument in the letters to Anne Dangar and to Mainie Jellett in which he explains what he had learnt in 1934, and we find it again, developed at length towards the end of his life, in *L'Homme devenu peintre* (p.132 et seq.). Nonetheless, in the early 1930s, the period of his involvement with Abstraction-Création and also of his researches into colour, his work is almost entirely non-representational and he comes close to making a principle of it. In *La Forme et l'histoire* (submitted to Povolozky in 1930) he develops an argument that the earliest distinctively Christian art in the West (as opposed to an essentially Roman art using Christian imagery) must have been entirely non-representational. If examples have not been found it is because at that time the artists, unworried by the fugitive nature of all worldly things, and anxious not to impose human constructions on the creation of God, used perishable materials.[3] In the earliest Christian art we know, the representational element is creeping back in, but is still subordinate to the rhythmic principle which it will eventually displace. This is why we, who only have eyes for this representational element, see this work as 'primitive' and even as 'stiff' and 'rigid'. The implication is that, in accomplishing a 'revolution' equivalent to the revolution that separates late classical and early Christian painting, Cubism must become entirely non-representational, and this is the argument he develops in an important letter addressed to his German friend, the engraver, Gottfried Graf, in September 1932: 'The image as figure [*l'image figurée*] has been exhausted in our biological cycle . . .'.[4]

The argument is not incompatible with that of the letter to Pouyaud of 1926, or those addressed to Jellett and Dangar in 1934; it is the image as starting point that he condemns. Similarly, Gleizes strictly forbade Hone and Jellett to use any representational images in their first work with him in 1922, at a time when he himself was quite happily evoking landscapes and human figures in his own painting. Gleizes has to stress different sides of his argument depending on whether he is talking to Graf, who is still defending the image as a starting point, or to Pouyaud, Dangar and Jellett, who have accepted the discipline of translation/rotation as starting point. But there is more to it than that. After telling Graf that 'the image as figure has been exhausted in our biological cycle', Gleizes continues: 'Space must, once again, give way to time.' The 'non-representational' is specifically related to time.

The apparent weakness of the representational image in early mediaeval painting is due to the fact that the Christian painter knows that all things are constantly altered by time, and that time (known to us through our capacity for memory and for anticipation) is as 'real' if not more so than space (known to us through the senses). He therefore does not trust the immediate sensorial impression, and does not wish to give it the illusion of permanence. The transformation of something that is impermanent (an immediate sense impression) into an illusory permanence is the basis of classical art and also of the neo-classical art of the Renaissance (and also, in its most degenerate form, of modern photography). The Christian painter, on the contrary, uses the principles of rhythm to awaken the eye to an activity, an organised movement, which in turn awakens the mind to an activity other than that of a mere observer, a recorder of sense impressions – the activity of contemplation.

We have also seen Gleizes about the same time, in his book on Delaunay, identify time and colour – 'colour, that is time itself'.[5] I suggested that in the early thirties Gleizes, concentrating on a research into colour, was re-living the conflict between the Cubists and the Neo-Impressionists, but that now he was on the side of the Neo-Impressionists. The structural elements of Cubism (the schema of translation/rotation) had become almost, if not entirely, invisible, swept away by the essentially circular 'cadence' of the colour. Gleizes's circular cadences may be distinguished from Delaunay's (despite the immense debt to Delaunay that he never hesitated to acknowledge) by their greater complexity. He uses much smaller elements, or 'measures' and, consequently, many more of them, and he organises them much more methodically. This methodically organised movement distinguishes him from the Neo-Impressionists whose very rational, very well-informed use of colour is still trapped within and subordinate to a representational *schema* that is essentially alien to it and prevents the colour from manifesting its propensity to movement. This is why Gleizes, re-working the Neo-Impressionist experiment, but with over thirty years' collective experience behind him, now renounces the representational element (even subordinated to Cubist principles) altogether.

It was this period of principled non-figuration, coinciding almost providentially with the period of Abstraction-Création, that enabled the first stage of the development of 1934 – the addition of the grey arabesques, giving the paintings the simplicity and form that they had hitherto lacked, or which had been insufficiently manifest. This addition of simple grey circles and spirals would have been almost impossible had the paintings been representational, which is to say, if there had been a (representational) figure sufficiently manifest to interfere with the statement of the 'form'.

Gleizes had drawn the distinction between the 'figure' (essentially static) and the 'form' (essentially mobile) at the end of the 1920s, and it was a basic idea of *La Forme et l'histoire*. In the early 1920s, prior to *La Peinture et ses lois*, he only knew the figure, which he presented as if it was a form, sceptical as to the possibility of movement in painting, even though this had been at the centre of his researches during the war. Throughout the 1920s, using the principles of translation and rotation, he attempts to put the essentially static figure into movement, an effort that comes to the end of its tether in the *Triptyque* for the church at Serrières. It is then that he draws the distinction between figure and form, but in *La Forme et l'histoire*, this is discussed almost entirely in terms of line, not of colour, and the tendency is to condemn the static figure in favour of the mobile form. In fact, as we have seen, his practical researches into form were to concentrate on colour. Initially they are hampered by what remains of the old formal (now understood as figurative) construction. Gleizes more or less abandons it and concentrates his attention on the need to establish an ordered succession of colours which is then able to receive the grey arabesques as a simple statement of form, now understood as an overall, essentially circular, direction whose movement has been slowed down (so that the eye can appreciate and enjoy it) by the coloured cadences.

This period, however, is very short. It lasts from March to August 1934 and is marked by a radical re-working of the entirely non-representational paintings of 1931–4. It was far from being in itself a dead-end, and it was to provide many suggestions that Gleizes was able to take up again, especially during the 1940s, when he once again became almost entirely non-representational. We have nonetheless seen that he was discontent with the relation between the original coloured-cadence painting and the grey lines that had been imposed on it, but had not been born out of it. Their success, insofar as they are successful, was accidental. They did not offer a real programme for methodical work.

Now, in Autumn 1934, each of the three stages was clearly separated, but each nonetheless prepared the way for the other. The figure is much more strongly asserted and it is in this context that the representational image returns. It returns severely subject to the principles of translation/rotation as understood in the 1920s. But where, in the 1920s, this, together with 'combinations of

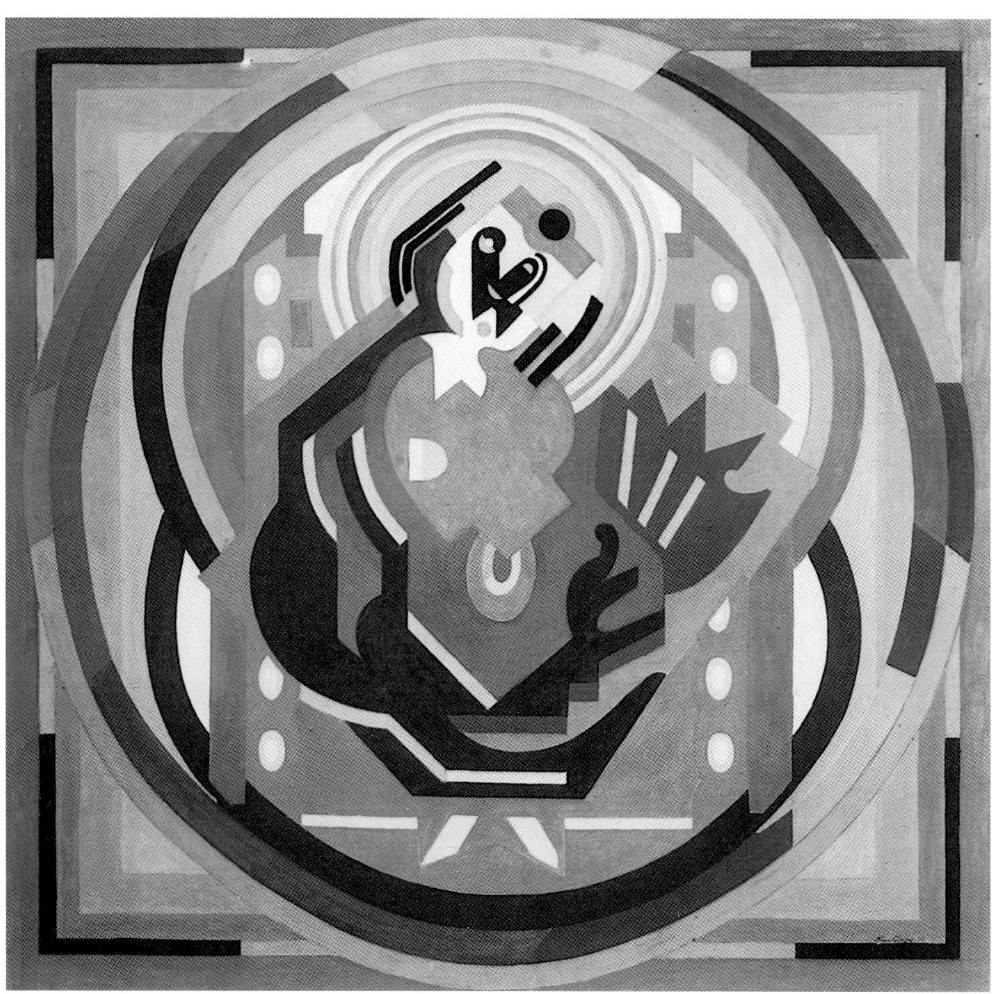

107. *Terre et ciel* 1935. Oil on canvas, 135 × 135. Present whereabouts unknown

colours, following all the games of the fancy' would have constituted the whole of the painting, it is now a preparation for something else. This something else is the equivalent of the whole period of the early 1930s, the coloured cadences, but once again, where in the early 1930s they would have constituted the whole painting, they are now organised into a strict halo or rainbow, a straightforward circular movement in which the colours and the divisions between the cadences are given by the colours and the lines that have been used for the first stage. In turn, the circle given by the rainbow prepares the way for the unifying grey circle, in which all the complications of the painting are resolved into the simplest possible overall form.

Out of this, Gleizes was to develop an argument as to the nature of man, the sensibility that creates and receives the painting, which he published in his book *Homocentrisme*. This will be looked at in the next chapter, but the point I want to stress here is the centrality now given to the static figurative and representational element. By the end of 1934, Gleizes seems to have been withdrawing from Abstraction-Création; he was irritated by its internal divisions, and his colleagues were irritated by his prolonged absence from Paris.[6] In any case, from now until the period of the war, it would have been impossible for Gleizes to accept the society's strict refusal of any representational element. The formula that Gleizes

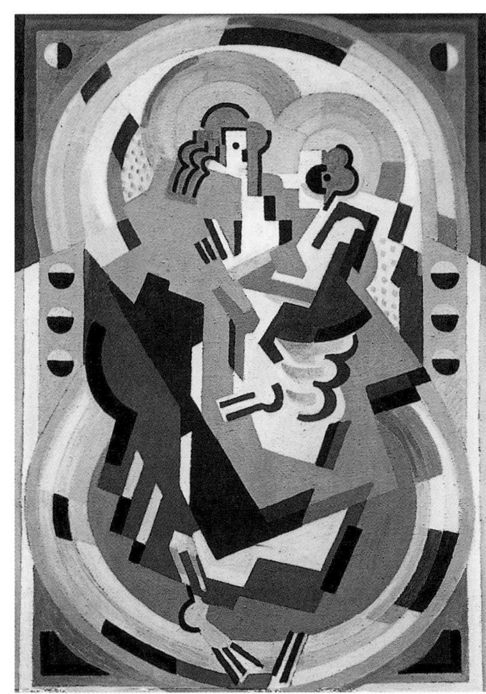

has now found and which will be the basis of all his work until 1938, is one that lends itself to representational imagery. The figure is at the centre and the rest is built upon it. At this time he seems to have felt that a purely geometrical figure would not make a sufficiently interesting centre.

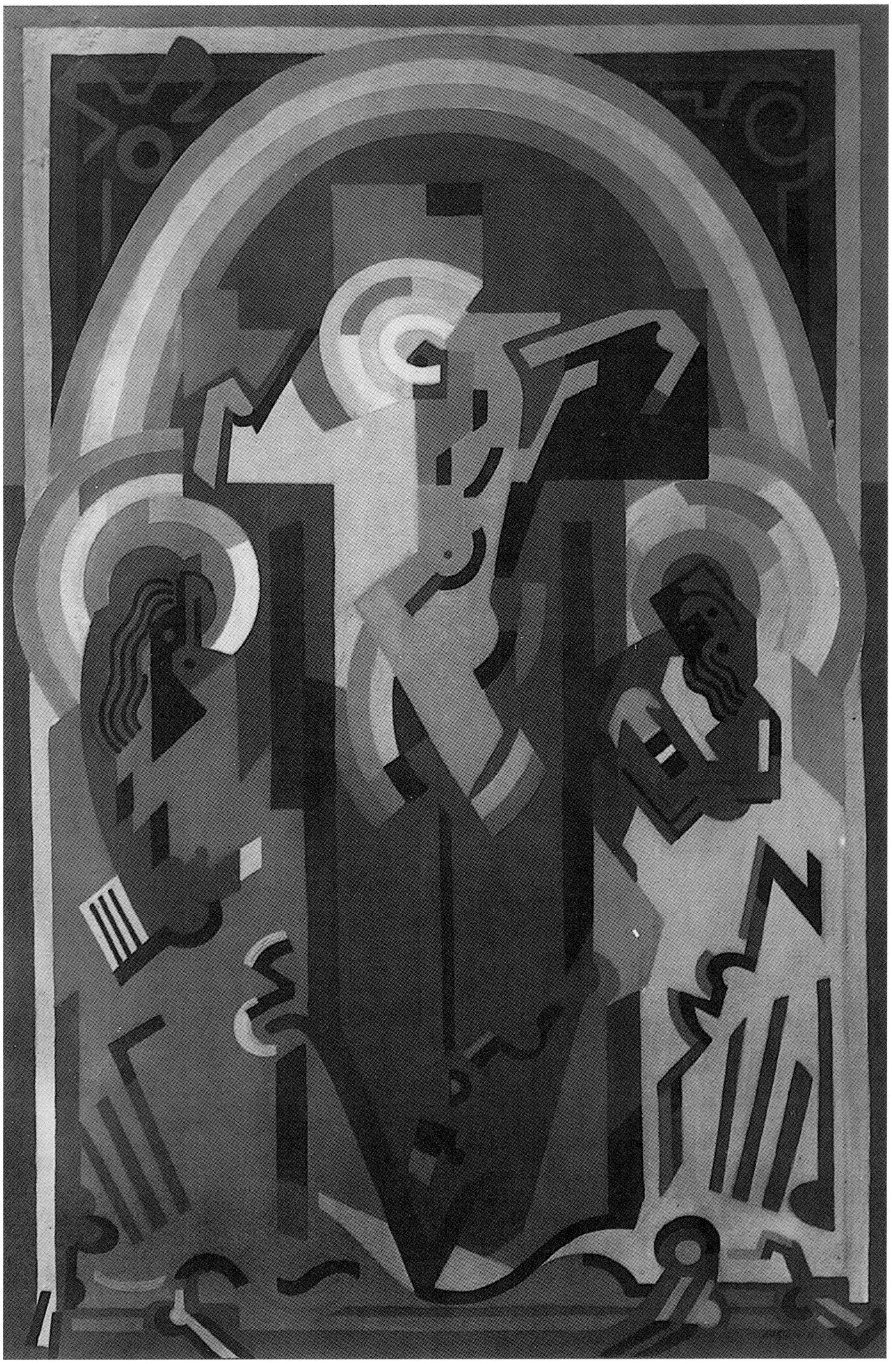

Almost immediately, in Autumn 1934, Gleizes takes to re-working the stock of representational images that he had developed in the 1920s in accordance with his new principles. In theory he could have re-worked his existing stock of non-representational images, but in practice he didn't. The *Trois thèmes* of 1934 takes up the representational central element of the *Centre noir* or *Quatre éléments* in the Musée de Lyon, and adds a representational dimension to its non-representational side elements. The *Femme et enfant*, *Femme au gant* and the *Ecolier*, all 1920s images, are re-worked throughout the 1930s. The historian André Dubois has shown that one of the most important 'new' images, the *Terre et ciel* of 1935 (Plate 107), is derived from an earlier *Figure avec un éventail*. Several long paintings under the title *Figure en gloire* or *Christ en gloire* may owe something to the (originally non-representational) central element of the *Sept éléments*; and the *Crucifixion* of 1935 (Plate 109) is developed from the Crucifixion prepared for the church at Serrières (plate

108. *Figure suggérée dans une peinture*, 1935. Oil on canvas, 139.4 × 84.5 cm. Present whereabouts unknown.

109. *Crucifixion*, 1935. Oil on canvas (?). Dimensions and present whereabouts unknown

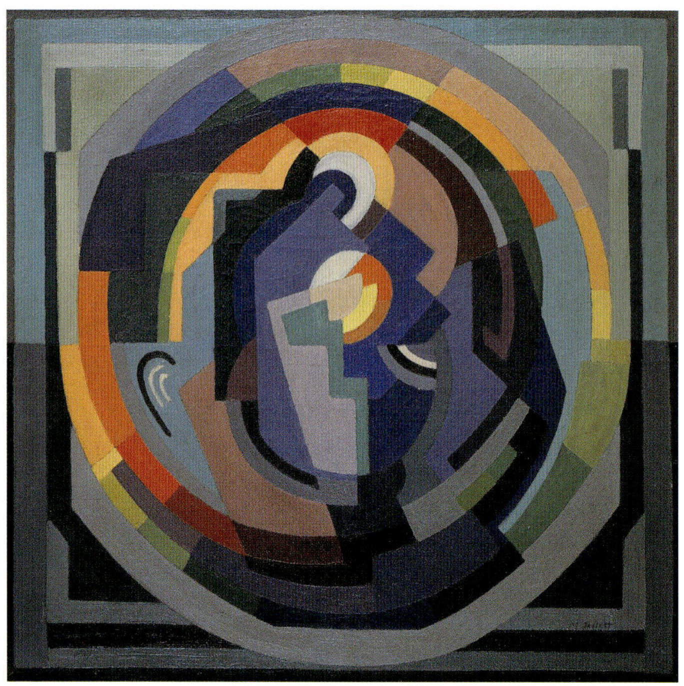

110. Mainie Jellett, *Mother and Child*, 1937. Oil on canvas, 76 × 76 cm. Private Collection

90). Gleizes, who constantly urges a principle of 'renunciation', never really lets go of anything that he feels may be useful to him. He always evolves out of what has gone before, he never eliminates it entirely.

What did Gleizes's pupils and associates think of this development? In fact, this period represents something of a rupture with his pupils of the 1920s. Evie Hone was beginning to establish herself as one of the leading stained-glass-window makers in Ireland. It was an extraordinary craft to choose, given her severe physical disability, the consequence of a polio contracted in childhood. We can see a parallel with Anne Dangar – both painters by formation, both learning very difficult crafts at the same time, and both moved by a remarkable spirit of selfless devotion. But whereas Anne Dangar was devoted to Gleizes's teaching, through which she had come to define herself as a Christian, Evie Hone had long been devoted to the Church (she was to enter the Roman Catholic Church in 1939. Until then, herself, Mainie and, largely through their influence, Anne Dangar, were all High Church Anglican). As a servant of the Church rather than specifically of the teachings of Albert Gleizes, Evie Hone was prepared to do the entirely representational stained-glass work that the Church required – though her first efforts were non-representational and her representational work is always simplified and harmonious. Gleizes, to the extent to which he was able to follow it at such distance, liked it. It was only, however, in spirit rather than in method that it could be described as a continuation of her work with Gleizes.

Mainie Jellett had been closely involved with Gleizes's work of the 1930s, the period of the 'cadences', and she had realised some ambitious paintings in this manner. We remember that it was she who had started the 'correction' of Pouyaud's gouache in 1931. Bruce Arnold's *Mainie Jellett* gives a reproduction of a painting which is almost a text-book illustration of the three stages: representational figure developed according to the principles of the 1920s, giving rise to a circular movement of colours in an organised cadence, the whole unified by a simple grey circle. He attributes it, rather surprisingly, to 1937 (Plate 110). The mid-thirties is nonetheless a period in which Mainie Jellett too begins to distance herself from Gleizes, though at first this appears as a rather unfortunate, in my view, development of Gleizes's current argument. Gleizes has argued that figure, cadence and form should be separated out, and that there is now no problem about the figure being representational, thus facilitating a use of religious iconography. In Mainie Jellett's work of the 1930s, there is a tendency for the representational figure to become more three dimensional and for the 'cadences' to become more marginal and decorative. The tendency towards illusionistic space was reinforced by her enthusiasm for a major exhibition of Chinese painting shown in London in 1935–6. This Chinese art suggested the possibility of an essentially representational art organised rhythmically. With this painting, she became successful and well-liked and was able to conduct a courageous struggle on behalf of modern art in a still generally suspicious Ireland; but her last work is disappointing when we compare it with the austere work of the 1920s. While still closer to Gleizes in her method, I would suggest that she moved further away from him in spirit than did Evie.

Since leaving Moly Sabata, Robert Pouyaud had been building a new life for himself in the village of Asnières sur Bois, not far from the great Romanesque basilica of Vézélay, which was to provide a rich source of reflections for him for the rest of his life. In order to make a living for himself he had, since 1933, taken up sculpture – an entirely representational sculpture for churches and memorials after the manner of Pierre Vigoureux, a monumental sculptor who also lived in the same area and who had been his first teacher, prior to Gleizes. He wrote to Gleizes about his first commission (a *Ste Thérèse de l'enfant Jésus* for the church at Clamecy, the town nearest to him):

> This proposal had seemed to me to be unacceptable, given my ideas – you know my dogmatic intransigeance. After ripe reflection, I thought that, on the contrary, this affair could bring me some marvellous outlets with regard to the Clamecian mind which I had already tried to approach but without result. You know the classic line: 'You do this sort of painting . . . because you're incapable of doing anything else.' How to reply – the *Ste Thérèse* will be my reply . . . I will always have, placed in the cathedral, the proof that my painting is a matter of will and not the result of any inability . . .[7]

Gleizes surprisingly approved of Pouyaud's sculpture and used almost the same argument about proof of ability in discussions with Camille Mauclair, a critic known as a fierce opponent of modern art who had, nonetheless become friends with Gleizes, largely through their common interest in the return to the soil.[8] Gleizes told Pouyaud of the new development of his thought in August 1934 and in his reply Pouyaud said: 'I have produced practically nothing, but I meditate. Little by little, I am building up documents drawn from different sources – I begin to see my way through the world of symbols used by the races at the different periods of history.'[9] In fact, Pouyaud was going more and more deeply into the philosophy of his other master, René Guénon. Through the 1930s, he explains what painting he does in the light of its symbolism rather than according to the principles now being proclaimed by Gleizes. When Gleizes explained his thinking in more detail in a letter of February 1935, Pouyaud replied with a reflection on the spiral, on space and time which, though interesting, does not connect with the point Gleizes was making.[10] He was developing a line of argument which, although it had started with Gleizes, was now very much his own. Never-

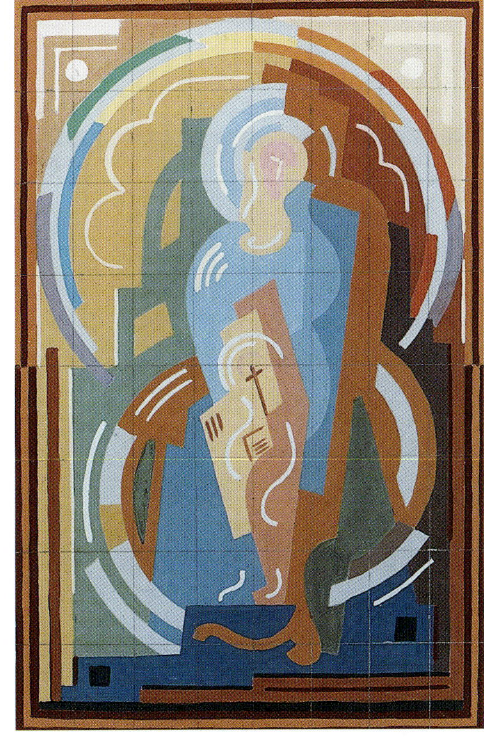

111. Robert Pouyaud, [Figurative Composition], nd. Gouache, 27 × 17 cm. Private Collection

theless, his paintings include many quite straightforward 'traditional' paintings on the 1930s model (Plate 111) and his little pamphlet *Du 'Cubisme' à la peinture traditionnelle*, published in a first version in 1942, remains faithful to the principles of translation and rotation and was greatly appreciated by Gleizes.

Robert Delaunay, of course, cannot be regarded as of the school of Gleizes, but the two painters viewed each other as comrades in arms throughout the 1930s and followed each other's development closely. From Gleizes's point of view, Delaunay relied too much on his coloured circles, corresponding to the faculty of time, or memory, and did not give enough attention to the figure, which was needed if the senses were to be fully engaged. This is what Gleizes emphasises in a letter sent to Delaunay in February 1935:

> The spatial image obviously cannot be the renaissance image, which ends up in photography and the cinema – it will be an image which enters into time, in the development of the chromatic circle which, I repeat, is only a preparation for the intensity of light, consequently of grey. That is why this new image has been won through the analytical researches of the Cubists [with which, Gleizes insists, Delaunay had had little patience – PB]. It prepares what you were the first to find: the stage above in which mobile time is no more than a regular succession of coloured durations. The modulations of these durations are dependant on the nature of the image underneath them; mobile time is, in a way, a fugue based on space, accessible to the senses, apparently static . . .[11]

Although Delaunay did not do much to develop this figurative, spatial base, he does experiment with neutral grey, introduced among his bright, primary colours, which does something to relieve their intensity without, however, as Gleizes would have wished, appearing as a fulfilment of them.

It was of course Anne Dangar who was closest to Gleizes in this period but, like Evie Hone with her stained glass and Pouyaud with his sculpture, her time was taken up with a demanding craft that kept her away from painting. Gleizes left some of his gouaches with her to study and in January 1935 she wrote to him to say:

> I fear I did not realise the completeness of the movement of translation in the first (the pink), but the further I went on in the work the more I saw how the translation was accompanied in dimensions by the rotation and how beautifully each opened the way for the other and lead on to the pure form – the circle.

She developed a moving comparison with the work of a clockmaker she had known, who had lovingly presented all the pieces of an old clock to the pupils at the Sydney Art School.

> After working upon your pictures I looked at the Cimabue composition I had analysed three weeks ago. It is not at all the same thing. It is a mere chart, not a living organism. I feel a contempt for my slight designs for twenty-franc plates. They are mere fancy, with a touch of sentiment.[12]

In July 1933, she had written to Grace Crowley to say that it was impossible for her to create pottery other than that which would be commercially viable and that, consequently, she could not devote as much time as she would have liked to developing what she had learned from Gleizes.[13] In March 1935, her inability to follow Gleizes in her painting broke his patience:

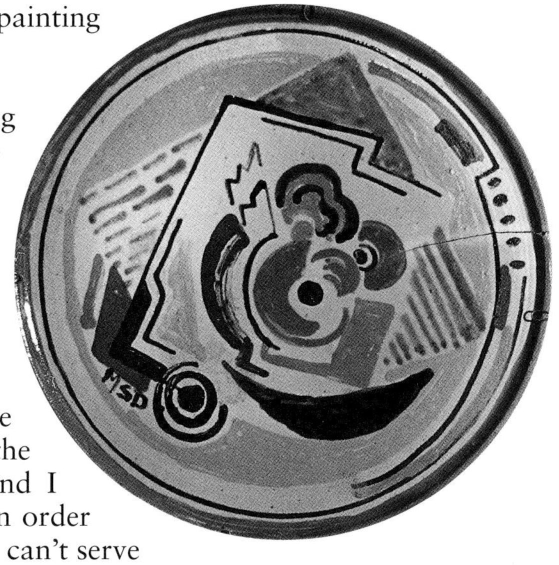

> I've just had a real trouncing from him, he was terribly impatient and severe because I showed him some drawings I had done for a mural decoration. He said they were analytical and academic and the contrary to his teaching, whereas I thought them quite Cubist in accord. But I see he divined the truth, it was the subject which interested me and I merely used Cubism to put it in order although I didn't mean to. 'You can't serve God and Mammon'. I felt tingling with the lashes I received on my cringing back but all the same invigorated and spurred on to show my grand master that I'm no jib, it was only the fault of having worked with blinkers on so long I was led to follow the old track I knew, instead of taking the sharp turn to the right.[14]

112. Anne Dangar, *Plate with Cubist still-life*. Glazed earthenware with slip decoration, dia. 39 cm. Fondation Albert Gleizes

In fact, Anne Dangar's life was soon to improve, partly because of the sympathetic interest of an enterprising gallery owner, Marcel Michaud, in Lyon, who gave her an outlet for more experimental work, and partly because of the interest Gleizes began to feel in the possibility of translating his pictorial constructions into the medium of pottery (Plate 112). Her friend, Grace Crowley, constantly feeling guilty that she had been responsible for putting Anne Dangar in an impossible position, often urged her to return to Australia. In June 1935, Anne Dangar replied to one of these letters to say that she had promised to help Gleizes with the great exhibition envisaged for Paris for 1937 (though it was still by no means obvious that either Gleizes or Moly Sabata would have a role to play in the 1937 exhibition). She told him, she said:

> I'd do my utmost to show work which would merit being known as the offspring of his teaching . . . No, I can't leave Mr Gleizes and this wonderful world of miracles happening all around me – miracles I would have been too stupid and blind to see if it hadn't been for the light of Albert Gleizes. Oh Smudge, really its much more exciting than pretty clothes and pink nails – and as for reflection and study, I don't believe money brings that, I never reflected or studied really until I had to walk 10 kilometres a day to work – that's when I can think clearly.[15]

•

Gleizes showed two paintings at the 1934 Salon d'Automne whose titles were a virtual manifesto in themselves: *De la Réalité des sens à la réalité de l'esprit* and *Les trois Degrés de la réalité plastique*. The dealer and gallery owner, Léonce Rosenberg wrote, full of enthusiasm:

> What a joy, after having passed through kilometres of horrible canvasses to arrive in front of your two pictures at the Salon d'Automne . . .
> Can I speak frankly?
> If you had always made pictures of this class the great collections would have long since been open to you.
> You have attained fulness, in purity, knowledge and precision.
> There is a perfect equilibrium between the internal life and the external life, in a few words, you have just succeeded in going beyond intentions, towards accomplishment.
> Everything at the Salon d'Automne could be suppressed except your two canvasses.
> While Braque, Picasso, Léger, Metzinger decline, drowning in a cubisto-surrealism, you, on the contrary, are becoming radiant in your own line. Your old colleagues become baroque but you, you remain classical . . . .[16]

He asked Gleizes if he could show the canvases in his gallery and Gleizes gave his permission.

Rosenberg had corresponded with Gleizes throughout the 1920s and several times invited him to contribute to his *Bulletin de l'Effort moderne*, but he had only showed an active interest in his work since 1930, when he commissioned him to decorate his daughter Jacqueline's room in an apartment he was renting in Paris (in January 1929 he had written to say that commissions for the apartment had been given to Léger, Herbin, Metzinger, de Chirico, Viollier, Valmier, Ozenfant, Rendon, Beaudin, Savinio and Picabia, but not, regrettably, to Gleizes because of his distance from Paris[17]). Gleizes produced maquettes at the beginning of 1931, Rosenberg proposed to pay by instalments, and the work was finished by September – one of the very few of Gleizes's mural projects to be actually realised. From then on, Rosenberg's correspondence largely consists of a series of apologies for being unable to pay the instalments owing to the seemingly endless financial crisis and its effects on the art market. In 1934, these letters take the form of a list of all the galleries that were going bankrupt, news that Gleizes, with his well-known detestation of the whole gallery world, greeted with some satisfaction.[18]

Gleizes of course believed that with his initiative at Moly Sabata he had indicated the solution to the crisis, at least as far as artists were concerned: a radical decentralisation and return to the soil. The artist could ensure his own survival by what he could grow himself, and anything he might need in addition could be had by selling his work to the local community. He would thus be freed from the vagaries of the international art market and would become part of a real human community, aware of and responsive to its needs. Gleizes argued this case in an article published in the journal *Beaux-arts* at the end of 1934.[19] At that time, the permanent residents at Moly included, in addition to Anne Dangar and the Geoffrays, a weaver, Jacques Plasse, with his family. The Plasses had arrived at the beginning of 1933, but were soon to leave.[20] The letter I have just quoted from Anne Dangar in May 1935, affirming her determination to stay in Moly, was partly a reaction to their departure, which had been very disappointing for Gleizes. Otherwise, Anne Dangar's letters are a long litany of complaints at the poor quality of the people who arrived at Moly and at their inability to assume the responsibilities of a difficult if, ultimately, personally rewarding, way of life.

At the same time, it seems that the estates the Gleizes' had bought near Saint Rémy had run into difficulties. Mme Gleizes tells us that in 1935, most of the local landowners had been obliged to lay-off their workers. The Gleizes's two estates, at Les Méjades and Archaimbaud, supported a community of around forty-five people – ten men with their families. Gleizes, she says, summoned the men to tell them that he could no longer pay them but that they could cultivate the land for themselves, paying him 12% of their produce. He would pay taxes, water and insurance, and he asked them also to be willing to welcome unemployed intellectuals who wished to learn farming.[21] There was talk in the journal *Régénération* of establishing a colony near St Rémy along 'naturist' lines.[22] Mme Gleizes tells us of four such intellectuals, four 'students' who, however, did not get on with the farmers whom they found to be very 'materialist'. One of the students was to become a shepherd in the community formed by the novelist Jean Giono at Fourcalquier in the Alpes de Haut Provence.[23]

One of the many victims of the financial crisis was Gleizes's publisher, Jacques Povolozky, who was also trying to sell Gleizes's pochoirs (the work of Pouyaud and of Anne Dangar) and books. We have seen that Povolozky had irritated Gleizes with the time he had taken to produce *La Forme et l'histoire*, and Gleizes had irritated Povolozky by criticising him for it publicly. Povolozky went bankrupt in 1935 and the stocks of Gleizes's books, including *La Forme et l'histoire*, reverted to Gleizes. In August, Povolozky wrote to say that he had had to transport nearly 2,000 copies to the Gleizes's apartment in Bld Lannes, Paris, but that since the concierge had refused to allow them to use the lift, he had had to employ two men for a day and a half, and despite this there were still fifty-six packets left (it is a very large book).[24]

Rosenberg took over from Povolozky as Gleizes's principle dealer and from now on his letters are full of the efforts he was making on Gleizes's behalf. These were to begin very soon with an exhibition intended as the first major retrospective of the history of Cubism – Les Créateurs du Cubisme, organised by *Beaux-arts* in conjunction with the more prestigious and conservative *Gazette des beaux-arts*.[25] The exhibition opened in March 1935. Rosenberg was on the organising committee and at the end of February and the beginning of March he sent Gleizes reports almost daily on its progress.

In the event, of course, the exhibition was to consecrate the by now generally accepted view that Cubism had been the work of four great painters – Picasso, Braque, Léger and Gris – and that the rest were followers, more or less interesting 'minor cubists'.

It was dominated by one large square room in which Picasso, Braque, Léger and Gris each had a wall, featuring more paintings than any of the other exhibitors. Delaunay wrote to Gleizes, furious:

> What use are all those books you've written . . . Léger who . . . wanted to claim the principle of formal colour for himself but who does not understand that life and technique both exclude chiaroscuro in its *trompe l'oeil* manifestation. He could see nothing in my paintings but circles but from the dealers' point of view he looks good in the square room . . . Should we send?[26]

Rosenberg explained the predominance of Picasso, Braque and Léger by saying that they had turned up in person to insist that their work be well-presented and that Wildenstein, director of the *Gazette des beaux-arts*, in whose gallery the show was being held, was afraid that they might withdraw if he did not give in to them.[27] This, however, hardly explains the favour given to Juan Gris, who had been dead since 1927. Gleizes would certainly have felt that the division of the exhibition corresponded to the dealers responsible for the painters concerned. Picasso, Braque, Léger and Gris had all passed through the hands of D-H. Kahnweiler, who still controlled the legacy of Gris. Picasso, Braque and Léger were all with Léonce Rosenberg's brother, Paul, a tough businessman and one of the few dealers in modern art, as Léonce points out, to survive the financial crisis (Léonce also dealt in antiquarian art, which had a more stable market. But he claimed that, even so, he only survived by imposing immense sacrifices on himself and on his family).[28] The second room, in which Gleizes found himself in the company of Valmier, Metzinger and Herbin, consisted of the painters attached to Léonce Rosenberg himself, though Gleizes had objected to the inclusion of Valmier as a 'creator' of Cubism when Valmier's first Cubist work had appeared after the war (Valmier, we remember, had been with Gleizes in the garrison at Toul in 1915 and at that time his work had been entirely conventional).[29]

The last room showed Delaunay, Le Fauconnier, Lhote, De La Fresnaye and Marcoussis, for all of whom except Delaunay (but only with regard to his pre-war work) Rosenberg had nothing but contempt. Indeed at the beginning of the project it seemed as though Delaunay was going to be excluded altogether and Gleizes had insisted on his inclusion. Rosenberg, who disliked Delaunay's current work, felt less strongly on the matter. For Rosenberg, the stars of the show were Gleizes, Léger, Gris, Metzinger and Valmier:

> The new Picassos are deplorable, laboured and exotic . . . All the artists, even those who used to be Picasso's most ardent defenders, were horrified. Braque, together with little things that are charming, poetic and full of good taste, has shown some smoky, dark, almost sepulchral canvasses. Very late Empire . . . They are, all the same, great painters, but one wonders, looking at their contribution, if they are still current, in other words, if they have not been and if they are still.[30]

Part of the problem was of course that Rosenberg, like Gleizes, still believed in Cubism as a living and evolving force in art – Cubism understood in the most basic terms as a desire to affirm structure in painting and to subject the representational, figurative element to its requirements. Even as a Cubist, Picasso had been more interested in variations on the representational element than in an overall, purely plastic structure, and this interest took a large variety of forms. Les Créateurs du Cubisme brought the work up to date, but Picasso's work of the 1930s was not at all Cubist.

We have seen Rosenberg congratulating Gleizes on his 'classicism', a term Gleizes would not have appreciated, and this reflected a difference between the two of them. Rosenberg loved what was static and monumental, hence his enthusiasm for Léger and Herbin, and we may imagine that he preferred Gleizes's work from the end of 1934 to the earlier period, dominated by the cadences, because the static, figurative element – the 'translation' – is so much more clearly affirmed. Gleizes, on the other hand, now seeing the need for the three stages – the static, the mobile and the unifying rhythm – but recognising the mobile as the most radical of the three, could only see everything, apart from his own work and that of Delaunay, as a falling away from the heroic period of collective Cubism, from 1910 to 1920. Nonetheless, he wrote a very favourable review of the exhibition, stressing the points he wished to emphasise – that Cubism had been a collective effort, that all the individual talents had been necessary to it, and that it was still alive, not in its original form, but in constant evolution. Picasso and Braque had been important in developing the analytical side, but in an intuitive fashion. They had no clear understanding of what they were doing or why they were doing it. Delaunay, equally intuitively, had seen the possibility of synthesis, of overall form, but Metzinger and Gris had had the necessary clear-sighted deductive understanding of their own act and 'that is why they were the first to establish the solid foundations on which it would be possible to build a lasting edifice'. As for himself, Gleizes claimed that his own distinctive contribution had been to raise the discussion from the level of purely aesthetic preferences to the level of the general culture and of a new understanding of the nature of man.[31]

This is broadly the view that is developed in his 1925–8 essay for the Bauhaus, *Kubismus*, which was already a polemic against what Gleizes saw as the deformation of the history of Cubism under the pressure of commercial interest. The unpleasant exhange of letters between Gleizes and Guillaume Janneau in *L'Intransigeant* over Janneau's book, *L'Art cubiste* has already been mentioned. Gleizes wrote at the time to Mainie Jellett to say that the book had been written for commercial reasons, to raise the value of the Zoubaloff collection (an important collection of modern, largely Cubist, work with which, as it happens, Rosenberg was closely involved at the end of 1935).[32] In 1934, Gleizes was involved in another, though private, exchange of letters with the very influential critic René Huyghe, who threatened to sue him if he said in public what he had said in private, that Huyghe's journal, *L'Amour de l'art*, and in particular a series he was publishing on the history of modern painting, was dictated by commercial interests.[33]

Gleizes would certainly have seen the confirmation of his view that the presentation of contemporary art was being distorted by commercial interests in a letter Léonce Rosenberg sent him in August 1935. Léonce said that his brother Paul had offered him a position in America that was extremely attractive especially since he had just visited America and greatly liked it. There was only one condition; that Léonce should not concern himself with any contemporary painting and that all the work he held by living artists should be put in the cellar.[34] As we have seen, his first interest in art had been as an antiquarian. His current idea was to combine modern and antiquarian art to show what the great monumental ages of history had in common. He had told Gleizes in his response to the 1934 Salon d'Automne: 'In the new programme I have outlined for myself, your works can find their place. I see them very well on each side of a beautiful Egyptian sculpture. I am going to attempt the last experience of my life: the modern in every age. The sun is still modern, despite its formidable age: the pyramids too.'[35]

Léonce refused Paul's offer, though it obviously tempted him. What it amounted to was an attempt on Paul's part to suppress the second room of the Créateurs du Cubisme exhibition and the only dealer who was still prepared to defend the so-called 'minor Cubists' and a view of the history and values of Cubism other than that which favoured the interests of himself and Kahnweiler. The 'Essential Cubism' of Picasso, Braque, Léger and Gris was to have the monopoly of what was still, at the time, a small and very fragile market.

Part Three

1934–53

16

THE UNIVERSAL EXHIBITION

Gleizes's article on *Les Créateurs du cubisme* was published in *Sud Magazine*, which had now become, with the 'naturist' paper *Régénération*, the main outlet for his writings. This marks a change since the 1920s, for while *Sud Magazine* was based in Marseilles, the journals in which he published at that time – *La Vie des lettres et des arts*, *Vers L'Unité*, *Les Cahiers de l'étoile* were of course based in Paris. The earlier journals were also following a programme, attempting to work out a view of the world in which the most recent developments in science and culture were given a religious or mystical interpretation, more in line with the various 'esoteric' philosophies than with any orthodox Christian doctrine. In these journals, Gleizes appears as one of a number of people with similar concerns, working on a coherent project. It may be, however, that this is an optical illusion, and that what we are witnessing is the last remnant of the impulse given to French cultural history by the Symbolist movement.

Régénération has been characterised by Romy Golan in her book *Modernity and Nostalgia* (p.105) as a Fascist paper on the strength of articles which express sympathetic interest in Nazi agrarian policy, and in the Nazis' avowed aim of encouraging city dwellers to turn to farming. These articles, however, constitute only a small part of a journal which was essentially pacifist in its political orientation. It expressed more admiration for Gandhi than it did for Hitler and its interest in Nazi agrarian policy was accompanied by a perhaps even more naive sympathetic interest in the Soviet *kolkhoz* system.[1]

For a period, Gleizes seems almost to be running *Régénération*. It features a large number of his own articles as well as articles by his associates, including Hoyack, and the poet and Sanskrit scholar René Daumal. The paper was later to change its name to *Harmonie* and Gleizes's involvement declined as its founder, Jacques Demarquette, became increasingly committed to living and working in Morocco.

In general, then, even as he is feeling more sure of himself and of the means he has discovered, Gleizes is becoming more isolated. His thinking is in a line that he can trace back, in painting, to Delacroix, but the rising tendencies within painting, even those that are closest to him, are not in that line. The concerns of Surrealism are radically different. The 'abstract' painting with which he is most closely associated, sees itself as marking a radical break with the past, a leap into an unknown and unprecedented future. Gleizes's insistence on a slow and continuous research that spans several generations is alien to it, as is his conviction that the whole movement of this history, this research, is towards not some form of individual self-expression, but an expression of, or response to, human nature in its fullness, which is, necessarily, religious.

The three stages of space, time, eternity; translation, rotation, rhythm; measure, cadence, form, are only valid and necessary because they correspond to the threefold nature of Man – the body, or the senses; the soul, mind or intellect; and the spirit, or intelligence. This understanding of human nature as three-fold, not two-fold (body and soul, matter and spirit) or single (matter or spirit) is, from now on, at the centre of all Gleizes's thinking. He has, essentially, found the basis of what he believes to be the craft of painting as a religious art. It corresponds, as we have seen, to the teaching of the early Church and it has been maintained within the Orthodox 'hesychast' tradition, but what is remarkable about Gleizes is that, even if he has come across a version of it in Augustine's writings, it only becomes real for him when it imposes itself as a practical necessity in the act of painting. The translation/rotation of *La Peinture et ses lois* is dualist. In 1934, he recognises that the translation and rotation, corresponding to the fixed senses and the mobile intellect, could only function when the longed-for 'rhythm' or 'form' was recognised as being something qualitatively different, for the moment expressed as the grey arabesque or the grey circle, though later it would be stated less overtly.

The implications of this development for his understanding of human nature were worked out in his book, *Homocentrisme*, written in 1935 and published privately in 1937, though a very substantial extract was published the same year under the title *Le Problème de la lumière* in the Marseilles based journal *Les Cahiers du Sud*. In it he defines his own philosophy – 'homocentrism' – in opposition to 'humanism', arguing that humanism reduced man to the simple level of a sensory mechanism. The humanist perceives the world with his senses and then uses his mind to reflect on what he has perceived. He thus reverses the human hierarchy. The mind and what remains of the spirit are subordinate to the senses; the internal is subordinate to the external:

> The senses on the one hand, observation on the other; and there you have the whole of humanism summed up. It separates man from the world about him. Man is reduced to his senses. The surrounding world exists outside him. The only way to know the world is to observe it with the senses . . . Sensation can be measured, can be weighed. Which amounts to saying that it is fixed, immobile, unchangeable so long as it lasts. A reason which cannot see the weakness of such a belief, which lets itself be carried away by such sophisms, which surrenders its right to lead and allows itself to be led seems to me right from the start to be suspect. (p.43)

In the humanist system, the role of the reason is to reflect on the observations brought to it by the senses. It is therefore passive, subject to them. But nothing is less certain or reliable than the senses. Their apparent fixity, solidity, measurability is swept away by the action of time. The sensations they convey are 'fugitive, partial, prejudiced, troubled, incapable of serving anything other than practical applications and usages' (p.44).

For the homocentrist, on the other hand:

> the 'spirit' had no need of the senses to know and 'the intelligence' only needed them in a very relative manner. By contrast, the senses were indispensable for the realisation of man at once in his body and in relation to the world to which he belongs. We see at once that, in opposition to the

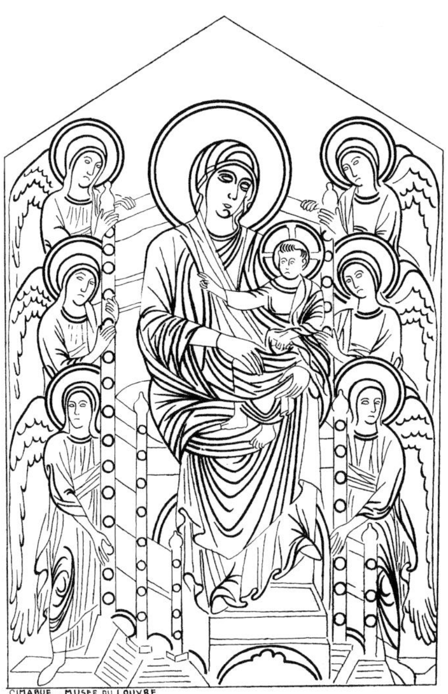

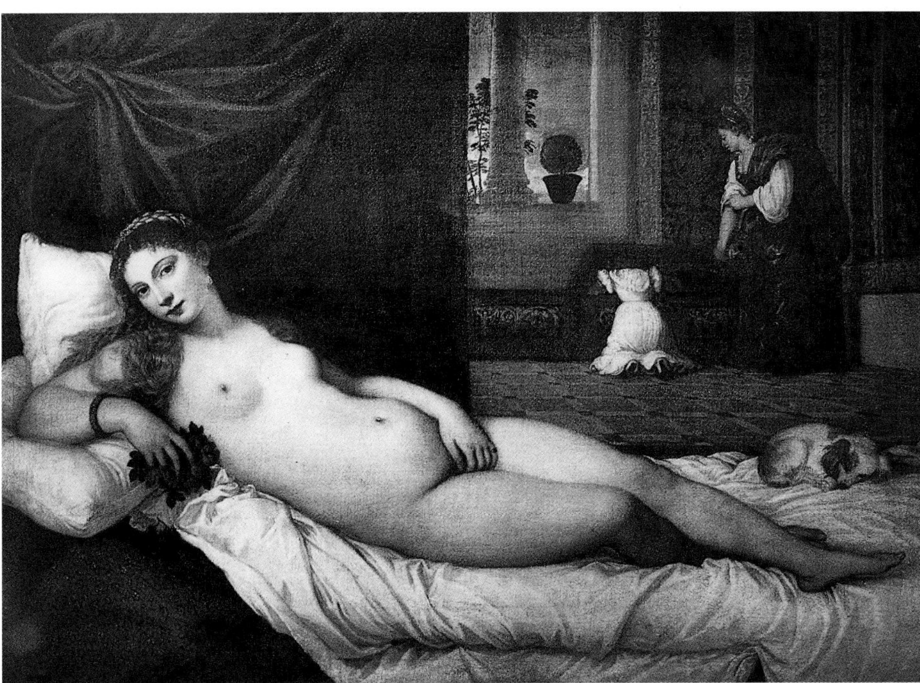

humanist attitude, which separates man from the surrounding world, the homocentrist unites man and the world intimately, in an indissoluble alliance. Remove the man and you remove the world. Remove the world and you suppress man (p.45).

113. Robert Pouyaud, [Drawing of Cimabue's Virgin with Angels]. Illustration from Gleizes, *Vers une conscience plastique: La forme et l'histoire*

114. Titian, *Venus of Urbino*, *c.* 1538. Uffizi, Florence. Illustrated in Gleizes, *Homocentrisme*, facing p. 26. A handwritten comment by Gleizes on his photograph reads 'Renaissance! The progress of the human spirit'

Gleizes argues that Europe had been 'homocentrist' for a thousand years, the Christian millennium from the third to the thirteenth century. He is reaffirming the argument of *La Peinture et ses lois*, of *La Forme et l'histoire* and of *Art et religion*, but this time he uses for his example a major exhibition of Italian art which was held in Paris late in 1935, and contrasts Cimabue's *Virgin with Angels* and Titians's *Venus* (Plates 113 and 114). The Cimabue is a work of the intelligence in which external observation has had very little part to play. The Titian is a work in which the intelligence or, rather, reason, merely served to adjust an image that was copied from an external sensation. Where a modern intellectual, still thoroughly formed in the humanist mould, would see a progress in the accuracy of the observation of nature, Gleizes saw a collapse in the internal life of the painter.

But why, if the old mechanical way of looking at things is able to achieve the spectacular results of modern technology, should we not be content with the humanist observer? The answer is that his observation only corresponds to a small part of our nature and, consequently, as his realisations become ever more enormous and menacing, our fuller human nature becomes ever more oppressed and frustrated. This order is inscribed within us and it really does yearn for and strive to advance towards the Absolute, towards Light and Eternal Life. Where it is free, all of our acts are invested with poetry – the rhythmic, numerical, ordered poetry that is the subject of Augustine's essay on music. Where it is not free, there is no possibility of poetry, and human nature, for all its technical ingenuity, becomes small and frivolous, like the crowds Gleizes watched as they passed through the rooms of the Italian Exhibition in Paris:

> The faces showed clearly enough their inability even to dream that each of these canvasses affirmed a moment that had been lived, passionately; that each century, even the ages in decline, proclaimed, through its masters, its uncompromising faith in itself. [But when] the past overwhelms desire, when desire envisages nothing more than a vain physical agitation of winning races and beating records, it means that the living action, that which strives towards the reality of the spirit and leaves monuments behind, is no longer thinkable. From one stage to the next, from one renunciation to another, the West has come to produce these amorphous crowds, brutalised with illusory worries, incapable of imagining that man could be anything other than just his bodily appearance. (p.22)

Central to Gleizes's argument is the conviction that the human being can only be formed, only become what he or she really is, through the practice of a manual craft. If the worker performing a mindless routine in a factory has little possibility of self-formation, the same is true for the 'pure intellectual', who only knows words and ideas and does not enter into the living relation with an object – 'in running after diplomas, he has turned away from real experience, that which involves the whole man-in-his-act' (p.10). But among the pure intellectuals, the philosophers and scientists, Gleizes indicates that there were some exceptions who had done valuable work: 'One of the greatest, in my view, is unquestionably René Guénon. Artists looking for the way of salvation have a definite interest in entering, through his writings, into a relationship with him.' There are others but 'there are few who are so clear-sighted or so perfectly objective; there are few, moreover, who have his immense erudition. In this respect I only know Ananda K. Coomaraswamy.' Coomaraswamy has a complete knowledge of oriental and western mediaeval philosophy: 'By knowledge, of course, I mean a deep and truthful understanding' (p.12).

Gleizes tells us, in his *Spiritualité, rythme, forme,* that Coomaraswamy had contacted him on the strength of *La Forme et l'histoire*. He had probably come to hear of Gleizes through Guénon and his *Études traditionelles*; but he was also associated with the English art historian, E. B. Havell and the second chapter of *La Forme et l'histoire* is devoted to a discussion of Havell's *Ideals of Indian Art*, which Gleizes may have known through Mainie Jellett. Havell was an ally of Coomarasamy's in the effort to understand Indian art according to its own values and not according to Western judgments (he quotes an official handbook to the Indian section of the Victoria and Albert Museum as saying: 'Painting and sculpture are unknown as fine arts in India'[2]). Gleizes praises Havell for recognising that Indian art is based on an idea of form that is completely different from our own but analogous to that which can be found in the European Middle Ages, and that it cannot be understood or appreciated except in its own religious context. He presents Havell as the model of what an art historian should be and contrasts him favourably with the French specialist in mediaeval art, Emile Mâle, subject of the third chapter of *La Forme et l'histoire*.

Gleizes and Guénon had met each other at least once prior to the latter's departure for Cairo in 1930; they moved in similar circles. We have already remarked that Gleizes's *Cubisme et la culture générale* appeared in 1925 in the same issue of *Vers L'Unité* as Guénon's *La Métaphysique orientale*, and Guénon's books were reviewed in the journals which published Gleizes throughout the 1920s. They had a common acquaintance in the Polish poet, Oskar Milosz.[3] Robert Pouyaud, however, claims that it was he who awoke Gleizes's serious interest in Guénon and Alibert is probably right to suggest that it was Pouyaud who prompted Gleizes to enter into contact with Guénon in 1931.[4] We have already seen how Anne Dangar, arriving in France in 1930 in search of religious truth found Pouyaud in the full flush of his first enthusiasm on discovering Guénon's *Le Roi du monde*. Anne Dangar herself was briefly carried away by it; in a very untypical letter, she wrote to Grace Crowley in September 1930 to inform her that the centre of the world was a subterranean city in Tibet whose priests were in direct contact with God, knew all the secrets of the modern sciences and constituted the real government of the world and the real source of the only true religion ('You may think we're a nest of silly, spooky spiritualists, but its TRUE'). She said that it was extraordinary how many of Gleizes's ideas could be found in a book which he had not yet read.[5] Later, Anne Dangar was to become very hostile to the influence of Guénon.

What Gleizes, Guénon and Coomaraswamy had particularly in common was the view, powerfully expressed in Guénon's *La Crise du monde moderne* and *Orient et occident* (books which Gleizes singled out as particularly important), that modern Western society – secular, mechanical, commercially minded, cruel in war, incapable of poetry – is in terminal decline; and their common desire to form an 'élite' of people conscious of the problem and capable of envisaging what might replace it, taking societies such as that of mediaeval Europe, in which there was a well-established religious authority, as a model. The three clearly regarded each other as members of a common school of thought. Coomaraswamy and Guénon both promoted Gleizes in their own circle – Coomarasamy through the influential *American Art Bulletin* and Guénon in his own *Etudes traditionelles*.[6] Gleizes in turn encouraged his circle to read Coomaraswamy and Guénon. Their reaction was varied. Rosenberg wrote in January 1936 to say that he did not know *Etudes traditionelles* but he used to read its predecessor *La Voile d'Isis*: 'I stopped because there was, as you say, the best and the worst . . . more of the worst than the best. Most of the works of theosophy are like that. One looks forward to seeing Isis unveiled and . . . one is lost in endless nebulosity . . .'[7] (It should be said that Guénon was strongly opposed to the Theosophists). Delaunay, Hone and Jellett showed no interest, but a new generation which began to gather round Gleizes towards the end of the 1930s was to be more receptive, and Gleizes's continuing admiration for Guénon, despite the differences, was to pose problems for him when, during and after the Second World War, he entered into closer relations with the Roman Catholic Church.

In *Spiritualité, rythme, forme*, Gleizes says:

> I readily acknowledge that what I painted at that time was very poor, my means being very limited – with hardly any chance of attracting the atten-

> tion of a world in quest of aesthetic titillation, a world every day more convinced that works of art could only be produced through the spirit of individualism. And what I was saying and writing could hardly be understood even by the best-informed of intellectuals since their opinions were all built upon all-exclusive formulae derived from rationalist premisses that were beyond discussion. I was not, then, unaware of the enormity of what I had undertaken. But what I had already glimpsed at the other end of a thousand difficulties was enough for a faith to be born in me which enabled me to go after it unhesitatingly. (p.318)

This seems to refer to the period between the publication of *La Forme et l'histoire* and the clarification of his idea in 1934, but he several times refers in similar terms to the whole of his work of the 1920s. We have already seen how diffident he was about exhibiting, but from 1934 this mood changes. He is now sure that he has something worth presenting and he is anxious to exhibit where he can. His style of life, however, his dislike of Paris, his even more visceral dislike of the art market and of anything resembling publicity, made this difficult. He was fortunate that Rosenberg took an active interest in him, though he was less than impressed by what he had been given in the Créateurs du Cubisme exhibition. Gleizes was also fortunate in exciting the interest of the American collector, Solomon R. Guggenheim, and of his secretary Hilla Rebay, herself an important collector.

Mme Gleizes tells the story of Gleizes's encounter with Guggenheim.[8] Gleizes was told that Guggenheim intended to visit him and to buy his paintings, but that he had to propose a price that was higher than the normal, otherwise Guggenheim would think him stupid and refuse to have anything to do with him. He had already sacked a doctor for failing to overcharge him:

> Albert Gleizes protested, agonised. He wasn't a crook and he had a horror of swindling. Jean de Mare and myself explained to him that, after all, money was only an utterly subjective point of view and one shouldn't attach such importance to it. And since the Copper King absolutely insisted on being swindled. . . .

Gleizes eventually gave in, and then insisted that Guggenheim should also visit Robert Delaunay, who was a great and unjustly neglected painter. Given a certain rivalry which set in later between Juliette Roche Gleizes and Sonia Delaunay, we might be suspicious of this picture of Gleizes patronising Delaunay, but it seems to be confirmed by the reserved attitude towards Delaunay shown in the letters of Hilla Rebay, acting as Guggenheim's agent: 'I like Delaunay well enough but his canvasses are decorative art and that isn't enough to win and, what can one do, he's so nice – We're working for something else, they will never understand it in Paris – where sacrifice for this idea of education through intuition is entirely unknown.'[9]

Guggenheim also bought paintings (including the *Portrait d'un médécin militaire* of 1915) from an important exhibition Gleizes held in the René Gimpel Galerie in New York in December 1936 to January 1937. This seems to have been Rosenberg's doing. Rosenberg wrote in October 1936 to say that he had recently visited René Gimpel and met 'this splendid Sidès' (Fredo Sidès, who was to be behind the Salon des Réalités Nouvelles, the most important French showcase for non-representational painting immediately after the Second World War):

> To stimulate the enthusiasm of these two very sympathetic opportunists who, only eight months ago, were still denying that Cubism had any interest or future, I let them know about the change that has taken place in the official world on the spiritual level and assured them that if they act with vigour in New York, they would be surprised by the results they could obtain.[10]

The 'change that has taken place in the official world on the spiritual level' refers to the interest the State seemed to be showing in the possibility of a Cubist contribution to the Universal Exhibition being planned for 1937. We have seen Anne Dangar in 1935 promising Gleizes that she would stay in France to help him with the Exhibition, and Rosenberg wrote to him in February 1936 to say that he would be able to participate if he made an application to the Fine Arts Director, Georges Huisman. He had himself warmly recommended Gleizes and, a week later, he said that the Exhibition administrators were enthusiastic that the Cubists should participate and interested in Gleizes, but wanted 'some material proofs of his aptitudes'.[11] Mme Gleizes tells us that Gleizes was scandalised by the idea that he should have to write a begging letter to justify himself before a crowd of bureaucrats.[12] He says in a letter written to Delaunay about the same time:

> I'm very touched by the effort being made in my favour by the person who is very big [in English in the original – PB] in the court . . . and I will do what he recommends.
>
> But I'm very sceptical. The administration is not at all ready to understand what we have to offer. Despite its good intentions and its courtesy. Later, when its no longer afraid of creating 'a scene', when it is no longer afraid of compromising itself, then, yes. But, now!
>
> I see in this morning's *Figaro* some names of painters who have been chosen to decorate the building which is to replace the Trocadero. And I remain not defeated but on the defensive. I think an important wall will be given to Utrillo, to Vlaminck, to Derain. With those who have been put forward, that will be in the order of things. What makes it ludicrous, however, is that, apart from one or two names, most of those who are going for commissions for 'mural decorations' are the very ones who the most rejected, and with such impressive dignity, the very idea of mural painting. We are easel painters, godammit. That is chic and superior. Cubism is to do with decoration, with the wall, with the art of the wall-painter. Horror! Haven't they thrown this reproach at us for years.
>
> But now that decoration is required we find all these indignant people and champions of easel painting lining up.
>
> It is in the order of things. . . .[13]

Gleizes, as he says, did what he was recommended to do, urged on by Mme Gleizes and Anne Dangar, but after a very polite letter from Mr Huisman,

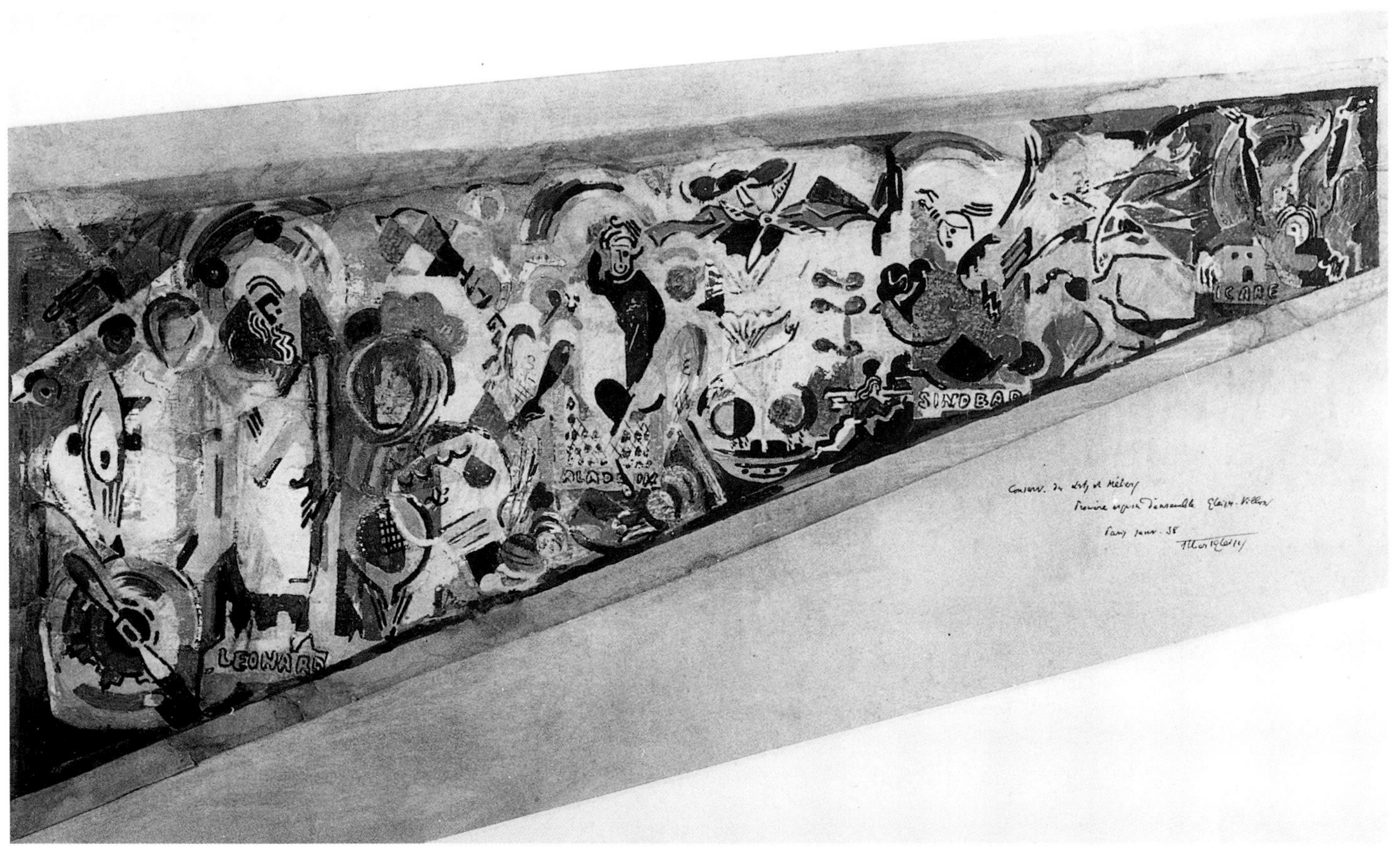

115. With Jacques Villon, *Quatre Figures légendaires du ciel* (project for the decoration of the Institut des Arts et Métiers), 1938. Gouache on paper, 24.5 × 60.5 cm. Fondation Albert Gleizes

there seemed to be no result. Rosenberg said in September that Valmier, Herbin, Metzinger and Léger all had commissions. But it was not until February 1937 that he wrote saying that he was on the committee of the important exhibition of modern painting to be held at the Petit Palais, and inviting Gleizes to participate. He congratulated Gleizes on his success in New York (presumably the Gimpel show): 'What contrast with what is still going on here, where the battle against Cubism and everything that is abstract is still ferocious'.[14] Inclusion in the Petit Palais exhibition was by election and some Cubists had only got in by a single vote after lively debate, but de Segonzac, Dufy, Rouault and Utrillo each had a room to themselves. Among the Cubists, only Picasso and Braque had whole rooms to themselves. Léger had half a room, and the others, including Gleizes, were all together in two large rooms. Csaky, Herbin and Valmier had not got in.[15]

The exhibition opened in June and, together with some of his own paintings, Gleizes's contribution included four plates and a ceramic tile-panel done after his paintings by Anne Dangar. Describing the exhibition to Grace Crowley she said that 'his pictures were not at all up to his usual standard as he had all his recent work in America'.[16]

In addition to his involvement with the Petit Palais exhibition, Gleizes realised two enormous mural paintings, one for the Pavillon de l'Air and the other, done in collaboration with Léopold Survage and Fernand Léger – two artists whose work he normally disapproved of – for the Union des Artistes

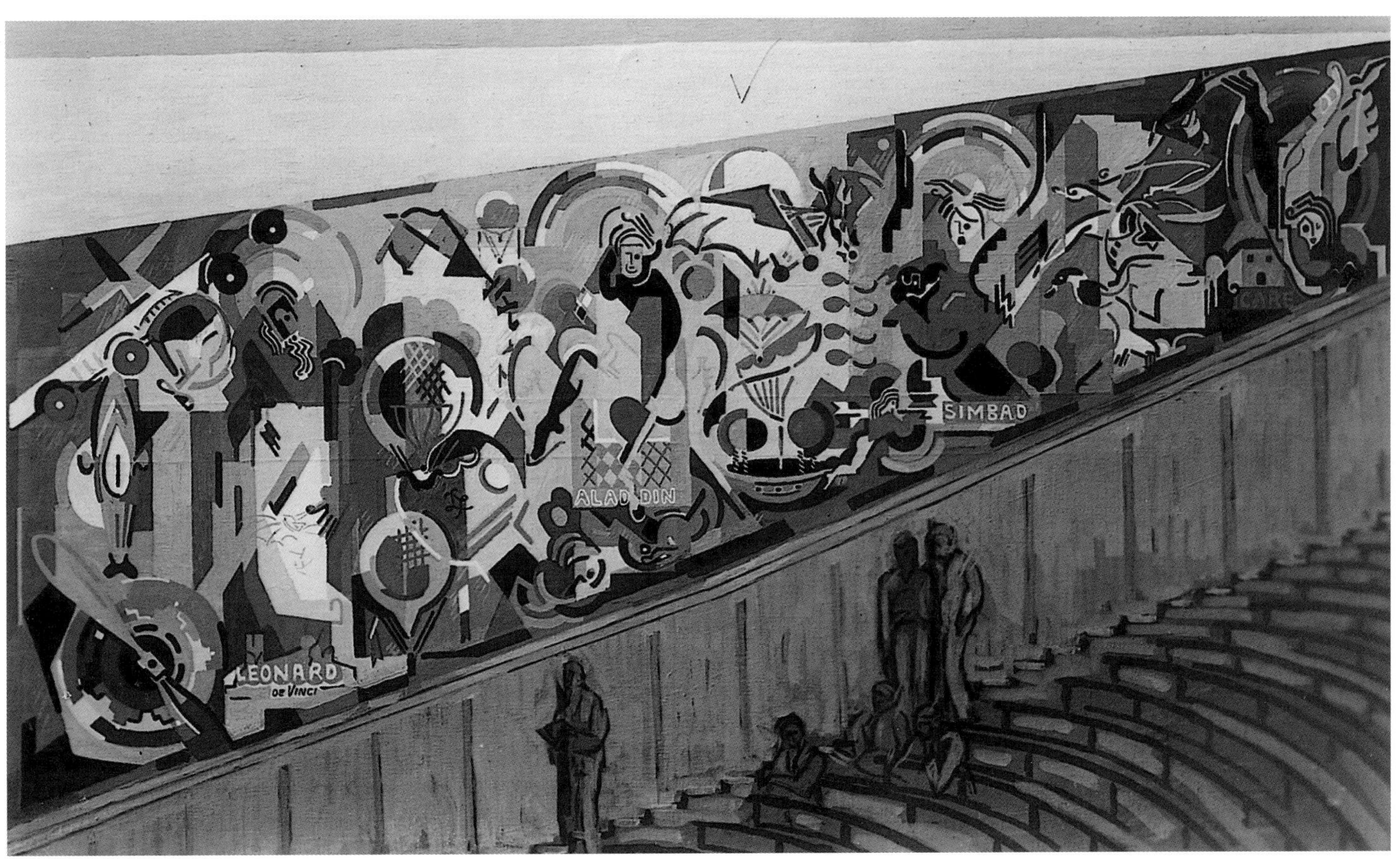

116. With Jacques Villon, *Quatre Figures légendaires du ciel* (project for the decoration of the Institut des Arts et Métiers), 1938. Oil on canvas, 89.5 × 147 cm. Fondation Albert Gleizes. Probably a version painted by Villon in order to clarify the figurative elements in the painting, in an effort to secure approval for the project

Modernes. It is possible that this second project had been planned long in advance, and that it explains Anne Dangar's promise in 1935 to help Gleizes with the 1937 exhibition. In 1934, Gleizes was informed by the general secretary of the Union des Artistes Modernes, the architect G. H. Pingusson, that he had been unanimously elected as a member of the group:

> I add that you are the first painter to join the Union des Artistes Modernes and that, in this respect, we hope you will be willing to collaborate effectively with us for the defence of our ideas . . . The great manifestation of 1937, which should theoretically bring together the efforts of all classes of creators in French art, should give an important place to the Union des Artistes Modernes. We are doing our best at the present moment to secure it.[17]

Gleizes had given a talk in June, under the auspices of Abstraction-Création, looking forward to the day 'when the painters would be judged by architects'.

The Pavillon de l'Air (Aviation Pavilion) commission had been secured by Delaunay – after much effort, Mme Gleizes remarks. Delaunay also had responsibility for the Railways Pavilion. These were projects on a large scale and to realise them, Delaunay put together a team of about sixty unemployed painters, gathered together in a 'huge garage' with buckets of paint two metres in diameter and, Mme Gleizes tells us, perhaps exaggerating a little, rolls of canvas meas-

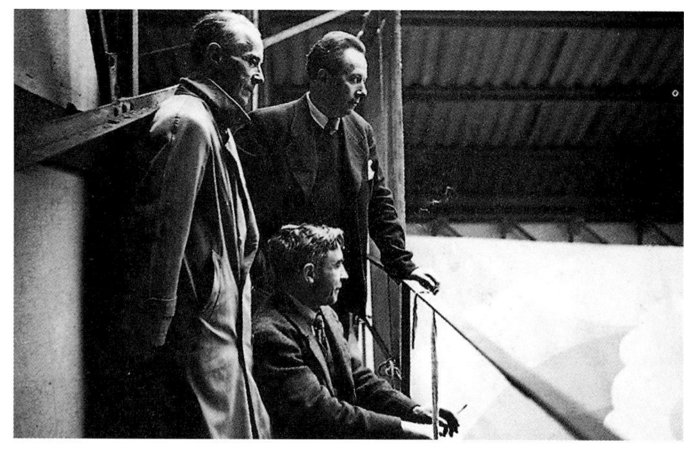

117. Jacques Villon, Robert Delaunay and Albert Gleizes (crouched) in 1937

ured in kilometres (Plates 117 and 118).[18] It was Delaunay in his element. In 1935, he had written to Gleizes on the need for intense research into the materials suitable for such large-scale work (Gleizes replied that it was very interesting, but that the really important thing was the three levels of plastic reality and Delaunay's need to incorporate the lower, earthly, figure and the higher, heavenly, simple form – the grey circle – with his intermediate colour circles).[19]

As Gleizes says in his remarks on the champions of easel painting lining up for commissions, he and Delaunay had long been advocates of mural painting – a painting conceived for a definite place, structured architecturally. When Cubism was described as a merely decorative art that had found its proper home in the 'Art Deco' of the 1920s, Gleizes accepted the description as a compliment. His Bauhaus essay – *Kubismus* – appropriately enough for the Bauhaus – argues that Cubism marks the desire of the artist to once again become a house painter.

Gleizes was involved with a Salon de l'Art Mural, which held its first exhibition in 1935, shortly after Les Créateurs du Cubisme. The Salon had been established on the initiative of the Spanish writer Eugenio d'Ors, together with a young French painter, St Maur, whose catalogue entry declared: 'We wish to be gathered under the leadership of the architects. We want to work by the hour, by the square metre. We wish to be workers in art and nothing more.'[20] Indeed, the Salon was in part designed to promote the idea of mural art as a solution to the problems of unemployed artists such as those Delaunay was to bring together for his two pavilions. It was in a paper given to the Salon de l'Art Mural that Gleizes posed a question that is central to *Homocentrisme*, particularly that part of it published in the *Cahiers du Sud* as *Le Problème de la lumière*: 'Has anyone seen light?' And he developed an argument that Michelangelo's work on the Sistine Chapel was not mural painting but easel painting blown out of proportion. It did not correspond to the nature of the wall ('the result could have been worse', commented one of the critics[21]).

Moly Sabata itself also had a role in the Universal Exhibition as part of the pavilion devoted to the region Forez-Vivarais (archaic names for an area which covered the departments of the Loire and Ardèche, including Serrières, but not, strictly speaking, Sablons). Mme Gleizes claims that it was she who applied, furious that the administration had not thought of it themselves.[22] Although the exhibition included work by Mme Gleizes herself and by Lucie Deveyle, the emphasis was on the work of the children. As a result of it, Moly Sabata was awarded a diploma of honour for technical instruction, as well as a gold medal for craftsmanship.[23]

Gleizes too won a diploma of honour and suddenly found himself in the unusual position of being in official favour. He was invited to organise a group exhibition in the Petit Palais in 1938, with full freedom to choose his own collaborators, an experiment that was repeated at the Salon d'Automne at the end of the year.[24] And the painter, Othon Friesz, old associate of Signac and the Neo-Impressionists, invited him, together with Robert and Sonia Delaunay, Lhote and Villon, to prepare ten large panels (two each) for the Sculpture Hall at the Salon des Tuileries. At the same time, Mme Gleizes was invited, on the strength of the success of Moly Sabata, to organise an exhibition of craftwork under the auspices of Arthur Sambon, President of the International Chamber of Art Experts. Sambon, essentially an antiquarian, had been interested in Gleizes and active in promoting his work since the Créateurs du Cubisme exhibition in 1935 and again it seems to have been Rosenberg, with his own interest in the links between the archaic and the modern, who was responsible for making the connection.[25]

But the first of the honours conferred upon Gleizes was to follow a more familiar course. At the end of 1937, André Lhote passed on to Gleizes and to Jacques Villon a proposal that they should collaborate on a major painting of sixty square metres for a lecture room in the Conservatoire des Arts et Métiers. Lhote had been invited to paint the other wall. Gleizes's and Villons' wall was to represent mankind's striving towards the sky, and Lhote's was to represent the more earthbound crafts. The idea that Gleizes and Villon should work together on a single painting may seem extraordinary, but there was a precedent for it in the work Gleizes had done with Survage and Léger for the Union des Artistes Modernes. Gleizes and Villon had, as we know, been very close in the early 1920s, but they had since drifted apart, Villon insisting on a figurative idea as the starting point of his work. Villon's greatness moreover is revealed in his etchings; a fine, intimate work which does not at all suggest an aptitude for mural painting on a large scale. Mme Gleizes suggests that both had been successful in 1937 and the state wished to award both with a wall, but that this was the only wall that was available. There is a letter of Lhote's to Huisman complaining that Gleizes and Villon 'have not yet had any official confirmation of the proposition which I passed on to them to study this project' and it talks of the 'panel which is to replace that of Gromaire' – the painter, Marcel Gromaire, best-known for powerful schematic representations of the miseries of modern life. A letter from Lhote to Gleizes, saying that the project had been approved by Huisman and by Anatole de Monzie of the Conservatory, is dated November 1937.[26]

In the event, however, the project for the conservatory was refused after all the preliminary work had been done. Lhote withdrew his own painting in protest.[27] Gleizes was to realise his part of the work, the 'legendary' part – Leonardo (Plate 119), Aladdin, Sinbad, Icarus (Plate 120) – in four magnificent paintings of 1939–40. After Gleizes's death, it was at the suggestion of André Malraux that the state commissioned the Gobelins Manufactory to weave a tapestry based on the joint venture.[28]

Soon after this setback, it seemed as if the Gleizes' were about to face another blow, even more severe – the loss of Moly Sabata. Moly Sabata was rented from an order of nuns, the Trinitaires de Saint-Félicien, who were keeping it with a long-term project of opening a school in Sablons. Once the project was formally abandoned, they were able to sell to the Gleizes', but the Gleizes' were deeply in debt. The money that Gleizes made from sales throughout 1937 was going to pay off a huge debt to their bank and various bills that had been run up in Paris (friends of the Gleizes' say that their financial troubles were mainly due to the extravagance of Mme Gleizes, a woman from a very

118. Gleizes, in white smock, working on his painting for the Aviation Pavilion at the 1937 Exposition Universelle

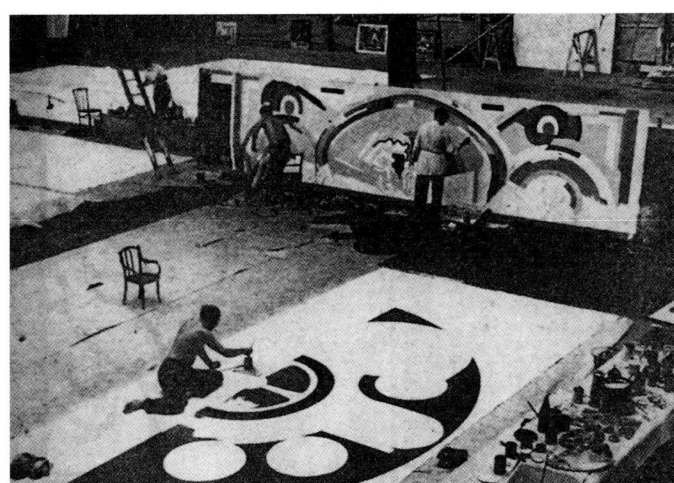

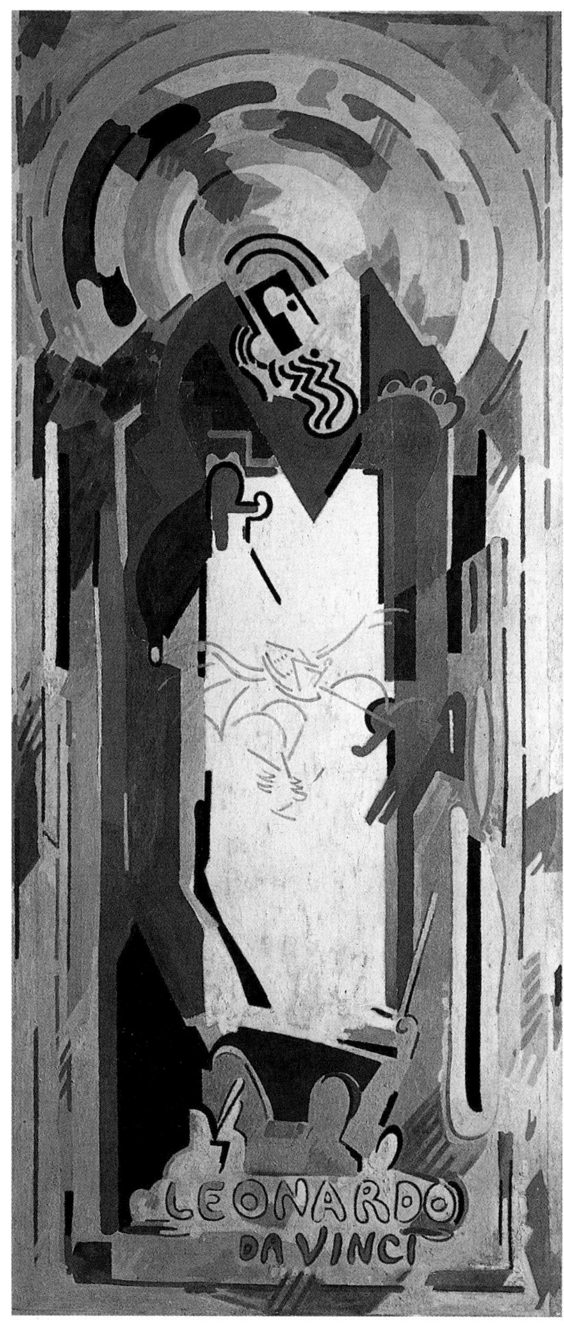

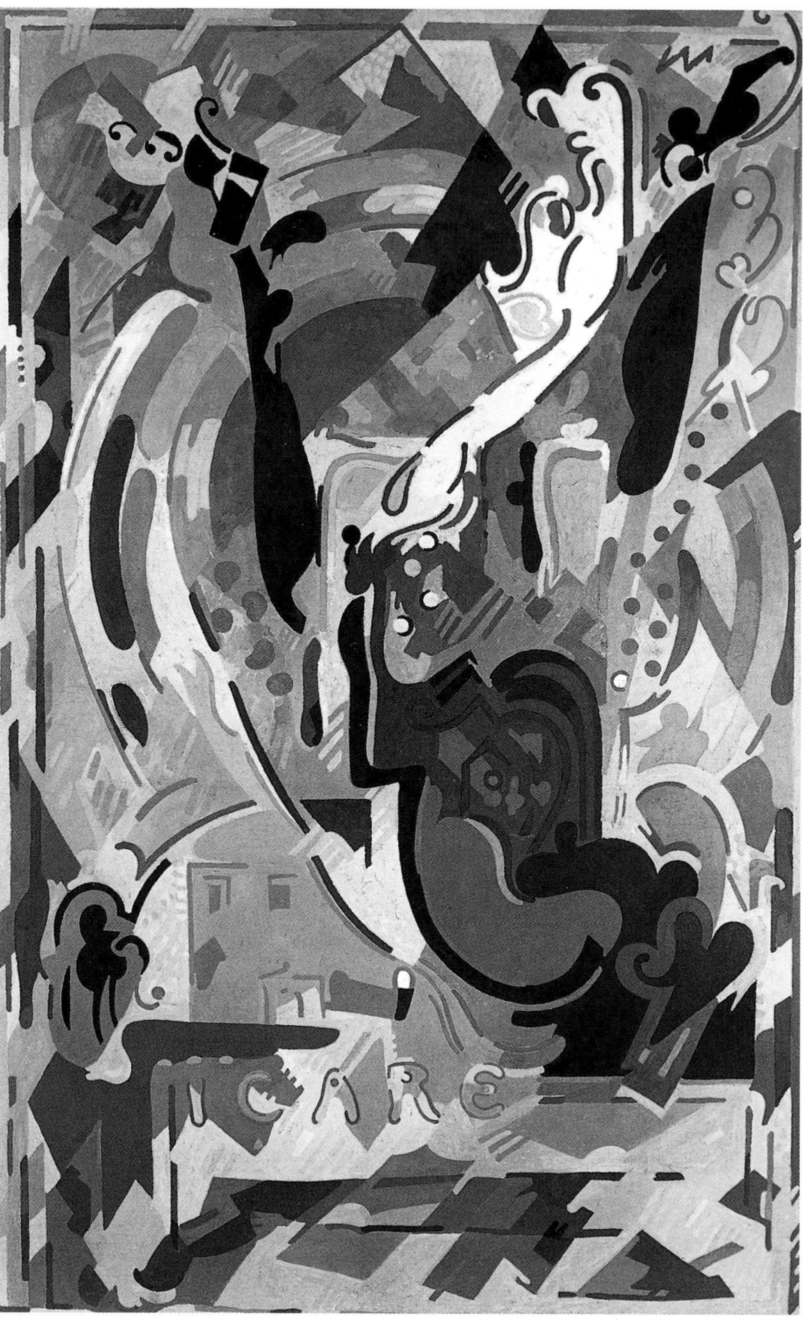

119. *Figures légendaires du ciel – Léonardo da Vinci*, 1940. Oil on canvas, 300 × 127 cm. Marion Koogler McNay Art Institute, San Antonio, Texas

120. *Figures légendaires du ciel – Icare*, 1940.Oil on canvas, 309 × 189 cm. Marion Koogler McNay Art Institute, San Antonio, Texas

rich family, used to having whatever she wanted). By 1938, they were still without financial means and faced with a large tax demand because they had failed to pay taxes on Les Méjades. A prize of 6,000 francs – the Prix Davilliers – was not enough to get them out of their difficulties.[29]

In these circumstances, Mme Gleizes saw an advertisement in the *Figaro* for a philanthropic agency offering to lend money for the purchase of properties. She signed 6,500 francs away as a guarantee to the group, who immediately disappeared with it (they were later arrested but, so far as I can see, the money

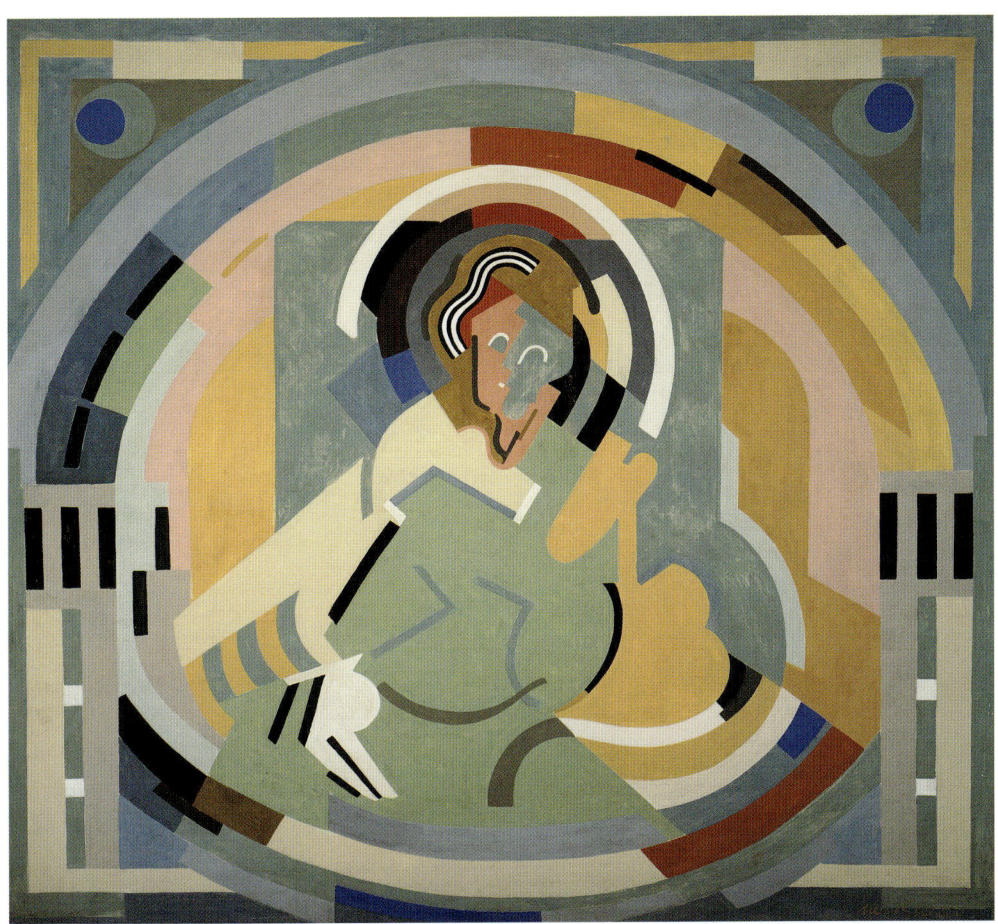

121. *Grande composition – dominante verte*, 1938. Oil on canvas, 536 × 536 cm. Musée d'Art Moderne de la Ville de Paris

was not recovered). To Anne Dangar's annoyance this money included 4,000 francs that had been awarded as a prize to the Moly Sabata children's exhibition – money she felt she herself and the children could have put to good use.[30] This was in March 1938. In the event, the Gleizes were able to stop the sale of Moly until June, when the exhibition at the Petit Palais opened and Gleizes sold enough – mainly to Guggenheim – to be able to resolve the problem.

The pictures sold to Guggenheim included the monumental *Dépiquage des moissons* which Gleizes had very much wanted to see in a French museum. A letter of Hilla Rebay's in August encloses a draft for 210,000 francs.[31] The story is worth telling because it modifies the picture that is often drawn of Albert Gleizes living off his wife's fortune. Most of Juliette Roche's inheritance had gone into land and the most important part of this land – Les Méjades – was badly managed and losing more money than it was yielding. In this particular case, it was very much Gleizes's own work that enabled the purchase of Moly Sabata.

However, despite the disappointment over the Conservatoire des Arts et Métiers and the anxiety over Moly Sabata, 1938 continued the tide of apparent success that had begun the previous year. The panels for the Salon des Tuileries were realised by the same team Delaunay had assembled for the Aviation and Railway pavilions. Gleizes's panels were six metres in height, treatments of his *Terre et ciel* and *Grande composition – dominante verte* (Plate 121), both typical constructions of this period from 1934 to 1938. The Petit Palais exhibition and the Salon d'Automne exhibition (*L'aspect actuel du Cubisme chez quelques aînés et quelques jeunes*) were designed to show that Cubism was alive and well ten, fifteen even twenty years after the critics had written it off. Anyone with eyes, Gleizes believed, could see that Cubism had proved itself in the 1937 Exhibition and its aftermath as the school of twentieth-century painting best able to assume the monumental dimensions of the wall. It was the true decorative art of the twentieth century and, for Gleizes, that was no word of reproach. But this small success, like the small successes of the Cubists of 1913–14, was about to be blown away by the outbreak of a European war.

17
UNDER THE OCCUPATION

Gleizes was struck down with a severe attack of 'flu at the beginning of 1939 which confined him to his bed in Paris. He was in Paris, he says 'above all to satisfy my taste for spreading the Gospel'.[1] The events of 1937 and 1938 and especially, perhaps, the emergence of a team of both younger and older painters sympathetic to Cubism put together by Delaunay, seemed full of possibilities. Following on from the collective exhibition Gleizes had organised for the Salon d'Automne in 1938, Delaunay opened his studio for regular discussions every Thursday evening which provided both himself and Gleizes with an opportunity to affirm the importance and continuity of their researches since the early Cubist period.[2] Mainie Jellett attended one of these sessions, but was critical of their lack of method:

> I was interested by the evening at the Delaunays' studio, only felt it was not very well organised and that the students' work should have been corrected, also I don't feel the students will learn very much that way, they would need to be made to work there in the studio and given principles. I think Delaunay is an 'instinctive' painter, as you have always said, and I don't imagine has much to give to students except what they can learn from looking at his pictures. I feel his theory of colour is very primary. It seems to consist of contrast only, it is not sufficiently organic. He is naturally a fine colourist and his taste will bring him a certain distance, but I don't feel he has advanced much since those early pictures he showed us, in fact I think they are more interesting than what he does now. Though he seems afraid of your idea of form being mechanical, I think his ideas of colour contrast are very mechanical or his application of them is mechanical.

She regretted that Gleizes intended to leave Paris 'as I feel you could give those students something solid to build upon. It was not much good me showing them those few primary principles, as they must learn to work them out and go into the matter deeply if it is to do any good. . . .'[3]

Gleizes, in the *Souvenirs*, acknowledges that the discussions were a little undisciplined but nonetheless certain definite postulates were given and painting was presented as a real activity and not just as a material suitable for the production of sentimental commentary. Nonetheless, he wanted to be able to talk in a less specialised way, to put the problem in the larger context of the arguments he had advanced in *Homocentrisme* – that the radical change that painting had undergone presupposed a radical change in our understanding of the nature of Man. Without such an understanding, painting remained a matter of aesthetic taste, an activity of marginal importance, its 'principles' had no objective base, it had no sense of direction, no sense of a future.

Gleizes's desire to raise the discussion to a more general plane was reinforced by his horror at the imminence of war. Mme Gleizes describes him at the time of the crisis over the Sudetenland in anguish, unable to paint, gathering and colouring roots and vinestocks and making 'little malevolent creations which I didn't dare to look upon. One of them especially, a sort of sea monster, a bit like a horse, garnished with orange spikes and laughing with a horrible laugh of a black and white keyboard. The spirit of evil in person. . . '.[4] It is worth bearing this in mind, it seems so untypical of Gleizes and stands in such a contrast to the serenity and confidence of his wartime work.

Shortly after the French declaration of war, Gleizes, in Serrières, began to write a second volume of *La Forme et l'histoire*, subtitled, *Mort et résurrection de l'occident chrétien*. The subtitle indicates that it was not just a sequel to *La Forme et l'histoire*, but also to *Vie et mort de l'occident chrétien*, and in what was written (four chapters more or less complete, and extracts from six further chapters), the emphasis is more on the history, especially political history, than on the form. The book is very distinctly a response to immediate events:

> Oh yes, I know the enormous responsibility of my family [France – PB] in the drama which is now unfolding before us. Since 1914, not a day has passed, perhaps not even an hour has passed, when I haven't thought about those events that have followed one another implacably heading in the same direction, despite the appearances of peace, since the 2nd August, 1914; when I haven't seen the character they bear that marks the end of a civilisation and the catastrophe in which they will finish when all the resistances are finally worn down altogether. But also when I haven't been struck by the contrast between these failures and those elements which, timid, weak, loaded down with the remains of modernist prejudices, nonetheless strangely recall doctrines that belong to the distant past, doctrines that are rejected, thought to have disappeared for ever and which are only remembered through the existence of monuments that cannot be destroyed and of chronicles covered in dust. (ch.1, p.30)

The theme of *Vie et mort de l'occident chrétien* was, we remember, that our civilisation is old, that we have no internal force within us – the force that was capable of building the monuments of the past or even giving a rich, human quality to the humbler crafts – and that, obsessed by our sensory functions because these are seizing up, we seek to reinforce them by the use of a huge, elaborate 'orthopaedic material' – industrial production. Imagining that highly perfected crutches are superior to living limbs, we see this development as a 'progress' and we see the whole of human history as a continuous, rising straight line, with ourselves as the highest point it has yet achieved. For Gleizes, by contrast, the movement of history, like the movement in the painting, is circular. Each individual phenomenon can only be understood in relation to what came before and what came after: it is part of a cadence with its own direction. And our civilisation, like all the empires and civilisations of the past, is destined to fall. The absence of a principle of life within it, which is the meaning of our dependence on the machine, indicates that the fall is imminent.

The Second World War appeared as proof that he was right. Since at least 1925, Gleizes had argued that there was an intrinsic connection between machine production and war. The essential characteristic of modern industry was overproduction. It required very high levels of consumption. This in turn required a constant search for new markets, hence Imperialism, and hence colonial wars. But even with captive markets in foreign lands, moments arrived when the market was saturated. Factories closed and unemployment increased. The unemployed had lost all possible means of living independently of the factory system. War was a perfect answer to the problem, because it provided a market that, destroying as quickly as it produced, could never be saturated.

Gleizes saw the new war as largely a continuation of the previous war. He had been lecturing in Germany about the time that Hitler took power and he had been appalled by the poverty and demoralisation he found in what had been, prior to the First World War, a great nation. There was nothing surprising in the fact that a movement to pull it out of its misery should assume a violent and dictatorial form, and France, which had been largely responsible for the problem and which had what he saw as a different, more hypocritical form of totalitarian dictatorship under the guise of democracy, was not in a position to assume an air of moral superiority: 'The military industrial dictatorship which we represent has no business turning up its nose at the anti-liberal dictatorship which is represented by Hitler.'[5]

In addition to Gleizes's general sympathy for Germany – his feeling that Germany had been treated unjustly after the First World War – there were aspects of the National Socialist programme which aroused his sympathy, especially the theme of a return to agriculture and craftsmanship which we have mentioned in relation to *Régénération*. His impressions seem to have been formed through his correspondence with the German Expressionist engraver, Gottfried Graf. Gleizes had known Graf since before the First World War and there is an important correspondence in the 1920s. Graf was a friend of the abstract painter, Willi Baumeister, who lost his professorship when the Nazis took power and was soon forced to leave the country. Nonetheless, Graf told Gleizes that the atmosphere of demoralisation in Germany was now lifted: 'in my whole life I have never seen a more magnificent [*grandiose*] spectacle; it isn't a spectacle, it is the miracle of the integral union of a great nation'. 'Nowhere has any act of cruelty been committed, despite what has been said to defame Germany throughout the world', though there had been a 'virile severity'. Given the general hostility to Germany in the world, Graf was deeply moved by Gleizes's support: 'Patriots that we are, each of us, we feel the need for an understanding between neighbouring peoples in the name of human culture . . .', and he even thought there was some possibility of interesting the new rulers in Gleizes's ideas: 'I am sure that the opinion of a famous Frenchman will be accepted with the greatest sympathy by the government of the Reich. . . '.[6]

Gleizes speaks favourably of the Nazi 'revolution' in the first version of his essay on Robert Delaunay and we may imagine, though I have seen no hard evidence one way or the other, that this was one reason why it was not published, given the general concern within Abstraction-Création for the fate of the German non-representational painters. Delaunay himself does not seem to have raised any objections. The introduction to the second draft of *Robert Delaunay*, prepared in 1937, however, suggests that Gleizes's enthusiasm had cooled:

> Since 1933, what have those countries that are at present considered as having realised profound social changes contributed in the aesthetic field?

What was shown by Russia in its pavilion in the International Exhibition in Paris in 1937 is instructive. Never has so-called bourgeois art shown itself to be in such a state of collapse as the official Russian art. As for Italy and Germany, they have revealed through their aesthetic manifestations what the transformations they claim to have brought about at the social level are really worth. Which is to say that, despite their proclamations, these countries have at the most been reformist, reconciling opposites, always sacrificing Man to entities whose failure is manifest in their death, trying to give new life to them, showing, in a word, that they haven't touched the essential. And that is a good illustration of what I've just been saying: a social mass can only operate certain reforms to prolong its own existence up to the day when it gives way altogether, when its resistances are exhausted. Only individuals can renew themselves, make a revolution, totally change their way of thinking and be reborn to life in the way in which a grain that has fallen from the plant that produced it, which rots in its compost, can give life a new body and a new life to the seed that it contains . . .' (p.46)

The conclusion – that the desired revolution can only be realised at an individual level – may be described as Gleizes's bottom line; he was constantly obliged to fall back on it. But in himself he wanted, and continually hoped for, a revolution that would compass the whole society. The second volume of *La Forme et l'histoire* was his most ambitious attempt to indicate what such a social revolution might be, an attempt to apply the argument of *Homocentrisme* to the organisation of society, on the grounds that what is true for the microcosm had to be true for the macrocosm. The project of putting such a social ideal forward seemed particularly worthwhile once it appeared, after the Franco-German armistice of June 1940, that Germany had won the war and that, consequently, a radical change of some sort was about to take place.

•

The war had caught Anne Dangar in Fez, Morocco, where she had been invited by the wife of the French Resident General, General Noguès to help in an attempt to revive the local pottery industry. She was in Morocco from May to December 1939 and this may be described as one of the happiest and most satisfying periods of her life since her arrival at Moly Sabata. There was a much more lively sympathy established between her and the Muslim potters of Fez than there had been between her and the Communist potters of Roussillon, but there were disagreements with Mme Noguès. Anne Dangar's idea was to restore an ancient craft, to oppose the use of French chemical colours, to encourage freer, less imitative designs, while still maintaining traditional principles, ideally to go beyond the traditional appearance to understand the theory that had given rise to it. Mme Noguès' idea was to encourage work that would appeal to a French cosmoplitan taste. Nonetheless, Dangar claimed that her approach was as commercally viable as Mme Noguès'.[7] Inevitably, she established a children's drawing class:

On Friday afternoon, some very clean (so clean one feels they have not only been scrubbed and half boiled but oiled with sweet scented oils and powdered

> also) boys of 12 to 14 come to me for drawing. They are very attentive and interested and talented. I would love to have a photograph of my little class, these white-robed, shaven-headed boys with such refined, intelligent faces![8]

Certainly she felt that she had as much to learn as she had to teach. She even tried to learn Arabic and she wrote to her French pupil, Louis Raibaud, that, according to her teacher:

> Mohamet said that to read the Coran is to remain in the space of its parchment pages; it is better to put it into the memory; in this way it is put into time, but 'the celestial word' is neither in space nor in time – it is the light within you alone that enables you to hear 'the celestial word' – its Homocentrism, isn't it?[9]

Despite her disagreements with Mme Noguès she had been well received and so successful and popular with the potters that she was invited to stay for another six months. The atmosphere, however, changed sharply once war was declared. The engagement to prolong her stay was broken: 'For me it was unbelievable that one could break the agreement that had so clearly been entered into, without even telling me and without any excuses. On the contrary, I was sent my ticket for the boat with a letter as if the agreement had never been made. . . '. The master potters of Fez had sent a letter asking that she be allowed to stay, but it had no effect. At Moly Sabata, she continued to receive friendly letters from them which, she felt, made a cruel contrast with the attitudes of many of the French.[10]

Anne Dangar belonged to the generation of the ANZACs – the Australians and New Zealanders who had volunteered with enthusiasm for service in the First World War. Many of her schoolfriends had been killed at Gallipoli and she remembered their idealism and loyalty to the Crown with pride. She was deeply shocked by the mixed attitude to the war and to the English ally that she found in France, especially after the armistice, when some of the parents of children in her class insulted her, and when she was, initially, refused permission to leave the department (the Isère, which meant that she did not have the right to cross the bridge to Serrières, which was in the Ardèche) and denied the status of 'artisan', without which she had no right to sell her work. For the first year after the armistice she was living off money she had earned in Morocco and put aside in the hopes of being able to build her own kiln in the grounds of Moly Sabata. It was all the more painful for her when she found that this hostility to the war, and to the English, accused of fomenting and perpetuating it, was shared by the Gleizes.[11]

The Gleizes' were still in Serrières when Anne Dangar returned from Morocco, and Gleizes gave her some lessons in the winter of 1939–40, which she passed on to Louis Raibaud and which show signs of an important change in his approach to painting, which will be discussed in the next chapter. The Gleizes' left Serrières in January 1940. Serrières and Sablons were occupied by the Germans (after a short battle with French Moroccan troops) in June, shortly before the armistice, and Anne Dangar, describing the scene in a letter to the Gleizes', assumes that they will shortly be back. Gleizes's house was occupied by the Germans. She was told that there had been a hundred of them in it but later corrected this to ten – 'the other ninety must have been visitors'. Describing the condition of the house, she commented that, compared to the ravages performed by the people who came to live in Moly Sabata, the bathroom had been left in tolerably good shape. In fact, Gleizes was to settle at Les Méjades for the rest of his life and, apart from a few brief visits, never returned to Serrières (Plates 122 and 123).[12]

The Gleizes had been in Cavalaire when the war broke out and they had visited Saint Rémy on their way back to Serrières. They found it in very bad condition. The system of tenant farming that they had instituted in 1935 had broken down completely. The land was barely being worked because the farmers found that they were better off working as salaried labourers in nearby estates. Under the circumstances, the Gleizes' decided that they would have take charge of the estate themselves, especially given the likelihood of food shortages in the conditions of the war. They sold half their property, the domain of Archaimbaud, and to work Les Méjades they took on a small team of Spanish Republican exiles. The Spaniards – four men with their families – were all Communists, and Spanish Communist exiles had been one of the categories of people most at risk in France even before the government was installed at Vichy. Whatever political differences they may have had with Gleizes, however, a close mutual friendship and respect developed between them, especially between Gleizes and Pelayo, the man who was to become informally the head of the group. Gleizes had long talked about a return to an agricultural way of life, but this was his first real experience of it. Within a short period of time he had taken to it so completely that it was impossible

122. Albert and Juliette Gleizes at Les Méjades

123. Les Méjades. A pottery panel by Anne Dangar – *From the Reality of the Senses to the Reality of the Spirit* – can be seen on the bottom right

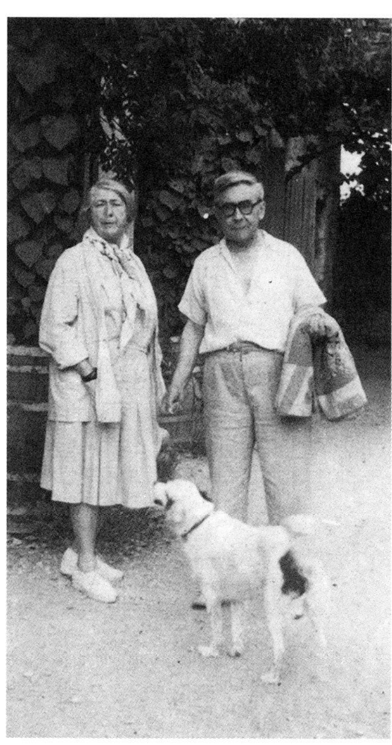

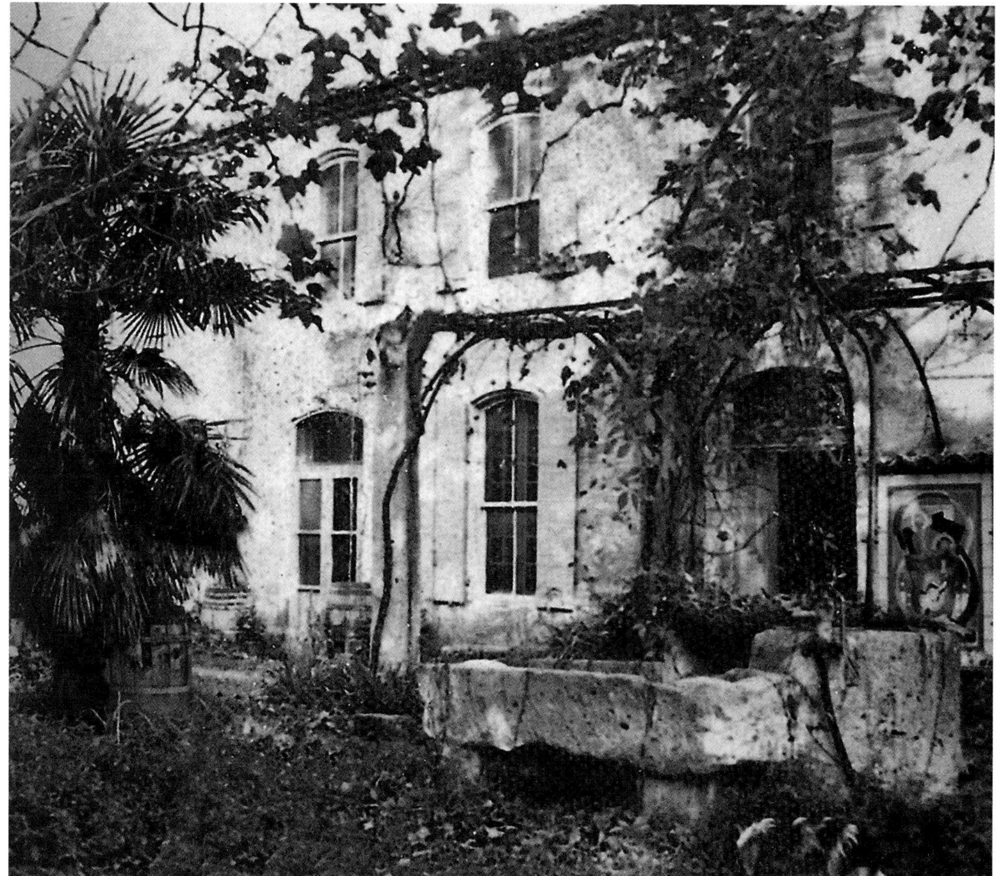

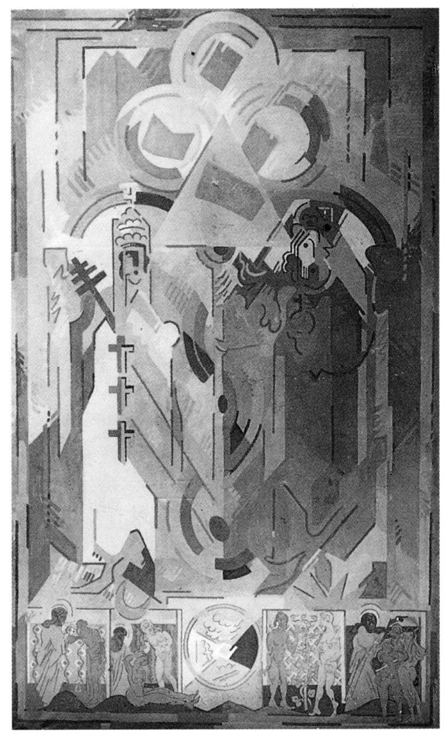

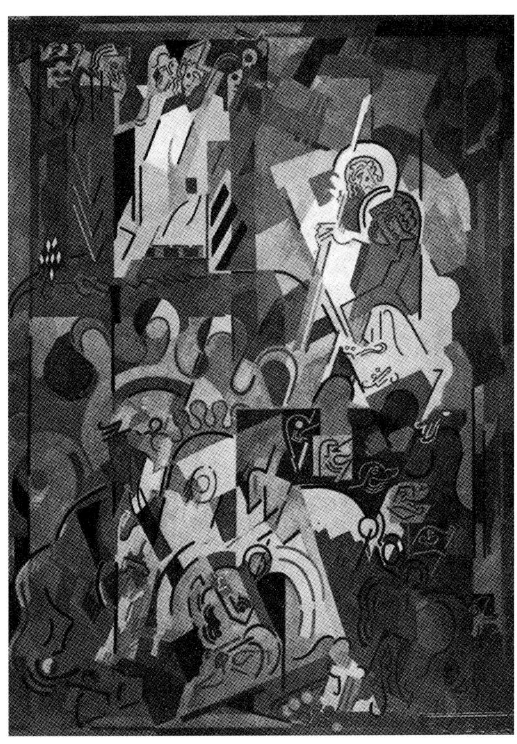

124. *Le Pape et l'Empereur – Autorité spirituelle et pouvoir temporel*, 1939–40. Photograph taken before restoration. Oil on canvas, 336 × 203 cm. Musée des Beaux Arts, Lyon

125. *Chute de Babylone*, *c.* 1939–40. Oil on canvas, 360 × 265 cm. Present whereabouts unknown. Photograph from *Albert Gleizes – 50 ans de Peinture*, Lyon, 1947

for him, perhaps to the despair of Juliette, to imagine anything else.[13]

Nonetheless, when Anne Dangar visited Les Méjades in November 1940, she found them both tired: 'They talk all the time (especially Madame) about their age – that their life is finished – that they're old etc. It is very bad for Mr Gleizes . . . Mr Gleizes's work up until now has been a preparation – it is from now on that he can give the world his noble teaching – free from all the difficulties created by the work of his research.' She goes on to say that he was working on his painting – not yet finished – *Le Pape et l'Empereur* (Plate 124).[14]

•

Le Pape et l'Empereur is also called *Autorité spirituelle et pouvoir temporel*, and André Dubois insists that this should be regarded as the true title, that *Le Pape et l'Empereur* is just a nickname.[15] 'Pope' and 'Emperor' are particular applications of a general principle and it is with the general principle that the painting is concerned. Both Guénon and Coomaraswamy wrote books entitled *Spiritual Authority and Temporal Power* and Pouyaud says that Guénon's was the book that had aroused Gleizes's interest in him ten years previously. Together with the monumental *Chute de Babylone* (Plate 125) of the same time it could be described as his 'manifesto' for the period of the war, the equivalent in painting of the unfinished second volume of *La Forme et l'histoire*.

From 1935 to 1938, Gleizes had remained faithful to the formula of 1934 – the figure, in principle static, derived from the proportions of the plane surface and giving birth in turn to the circle, divided into cadences of colour arranged according to the order of the colour circle, the whole unified in the simple circular form given in a neutral grey. Gleizes's writings of the time, gathered

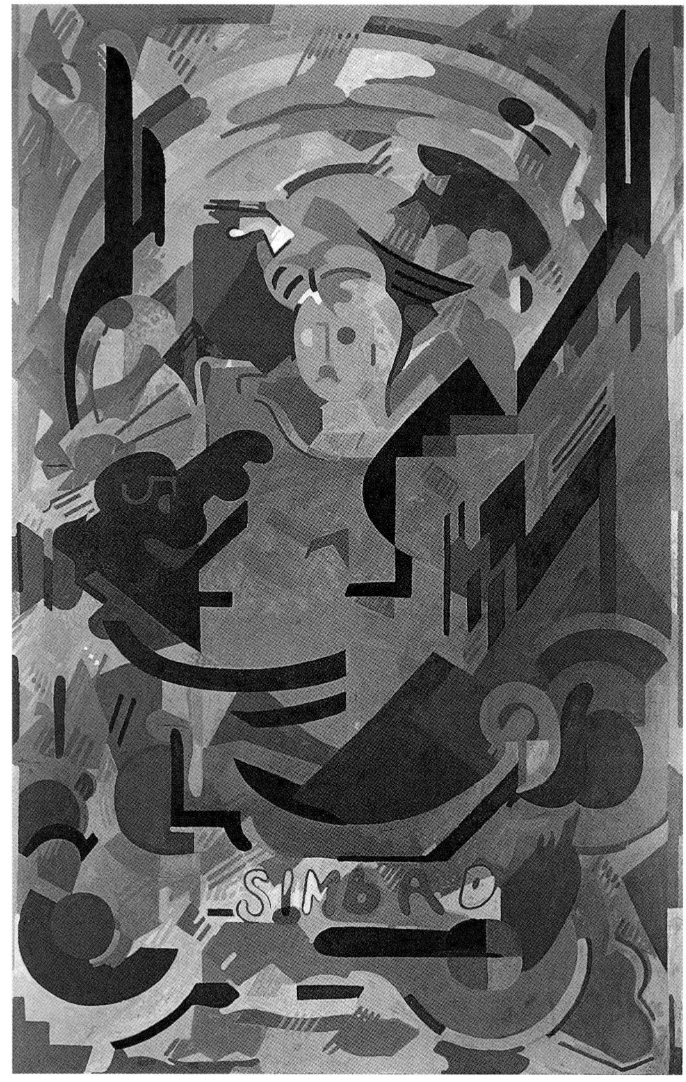

126. *Figures légendaires du ciel – Simbad*, 1938. Oil on canvas, 308 × 189 cm. Marion Koogler McNay Art Institute, San Antonio, Texas

together in the collection *Puissances du Cubisme*, really give the impression that from now on all painting must conform to this 'traditional' model. Increasingly, however, the 'model' was to become a principle, capable of a wide variety of applications.

Both the *Figures légendaires du ciel* (Plate 126) and *Autorité spirituelle et pouvoir temporel* are marked by a greater compexity of the figure. In his argument of 1934, Gleizes had stressed that the figure, made up essentially of straight lines, is static and that the two aspects, the vertical and the oblique, which he had previously characterised as 'translation' and 'rotation', of the nature of space and of the nature of time, were both equally 'static'. They were both now grouped under the heading 'translation' – of the nature of space.

There is an ambiguity here, because there can be no doubt that the oblique does prepare the eye for an entry into movement, that it invites the curve and the change in colour which are of the nature of rotation. The problem is a delicate one. The flaw in the paintings of the 1920s, culminating in the *Triptyque* for the church at Serrières, is that a closed figure, static in its nature, is being distorted into an appearance of movement by the use of curves. The curve in its mobile nature is not sufficiently distinguished from the figure in its static nature, a problem that remains characteristic of the work of Mainie Jellett. The distinction is understood and clearly made in 1934. If the curve is to enter fully into its mobile nature, it has to be detached from the figure and to be revealed as part of a full circle. The movement has to be a total, completed movement. Gleizes then applies this discovery dogmatically ('dogma' meaning 'teaching') for four years; but once the separation of the principles is fully understood and mastered, then it becomes possible to combine them in ways that are more subtle and complex than in the paintings of 1935–8, without falling back into the deformed statism of the 1920s.

I should perhaps stress that I do not really accuse the paintings of the 1920s of 'deformed statism'. This was simply a tendency of the way Gleizes thought about them. He had sufficient innate good taste to be able to avoid it. Nonetheless his inadequate understanding of his own act was a limitation on his practice. The dogma, when it is true, gives us the freedom to go further.

In the paintings of 1935–8, the fullness lies in the cadences of the circle, the 'halo' or 'glory' which surrounds the figure. There is a very subtle and complex interaction between the figure and the cadences to which it gives rise, but the two are clearly distinguished. The halo is still present and still important for *Figures légendaires du ciel* of 1938, but it is beginning to recede in importance, while a host of cadences and curves begin to appear suggested by and interwoven with the static straight lines of the figure. The circle which is presented as distinct from the figure is giving way to the spiral which moves within and about the figure.

Autorité spirituelle et pouvoir temporel represents another departure from

Gleizes's normal practice which seems to indicate another and perhaps more surprising line of development. It is divided horizontally in three parts, and the bottom part is wholly representational. It shows the creation of Adam, the creation of Eve, the temptation and the expulsion from Eden. Although the flatness of the picture plane is respected, there is nothing in it of Gleizes's distinctive principles of construction, of translation and rotation. It tells a story, simply and naively. The organisation of forms and colours is pretty, but no more than pretty. It is entirely static in its nature, without even trying to affirm stasis as a principle through an affirmation of the rectangle. There are many sketches from this period in a similar style which suggest that Gleizes was seriously interested in the possibilities of a purely representational portrayal of religious subjects.[16]

Above this bottom level, there are the figures of the 'Pope' and the 'Emperor', and it is here that Gleizes's distinctive principles are felt. The 'figures' are of a radically different nature from the figures of the bottom level. They are suggested in a play of lines each one of which has a dynamic function asserting either stasis (vertical and horizontal lines, changes in tonality) or movement (oblique lines, curves, arabesques, delicate accents, changes of colour). Each of the heads has its 'halo', but these halos, circular curves divided into cadences, are only one of the means by which the rotation is suggested and not at all the most important. While in 1934, the 'halo' was required to incorporate all the colours used in the painting and to cover the whole spectrum of colours organised following the order of the chromatic circle, these halos are barely coloured at all. The main explicit statement of circular curves in cadence is a series of curves in the middle of the picture, placed between the Pope and the Emperor, the effect of which is not to enclose the area of the painting but, on the contrary, to open it up to the third and highest level with its three very rapid circles, each embodying one of the primary colours, and its simple triangle, the whole dominated by the neutral grey which Gleizes saw as the pictorial equivalent of light.

The symbolism of these three levels is obvious, corresponding to the three levels of human reality which we already know: (1) the senses – space; (2) the soul, intellect, memory, reason – time; (3) the spirit, unity, Trinity – eternity. In this case, the 'senses' are shown by a painting that appeals uniquely to the senses, a purely anecdotal painting that conveys information without exciting the temporal activity – activity in time – of the soul. It is appropriate that the story is the expulsion from Eden. Guénon in *Le Roi du monde* (p.53) characterises the expulsion from Eden as the loss of the ability to see how things stand in relation to eternity, to perceive uniquely what can be perceived by the senses. The 'Pope' and the 'Emperor', or the spiritual authority and the temporal power, by contrast, restore to the soul the activity that is proper to it, the one raising the material to the temporal, the other the temporal to the eternal, the highest level, in which the principle is given in its simplicity.

The *Figures légendaires du ciel*, *Autorité spirituelle, Chute de Babylone*, *Consécration* and the great religious triptych (Plates 128–30) in the Musée de Lyon all indicate Gleizes's interest in allegory, in an anecdote which attracts the senses, the presentation of a literary idea or subject which is then converted into a pictorial act. But this is also a period of great non-representational painting, starting with the *Pour l'Esprit: les rouges* and *Pour l'Esprit: les verts* of 1939 (Plate 127), Gleizes's first major non-representational paintings since 1934. *Les Rouges*, in particular, could be described as a non-representational equivalent of

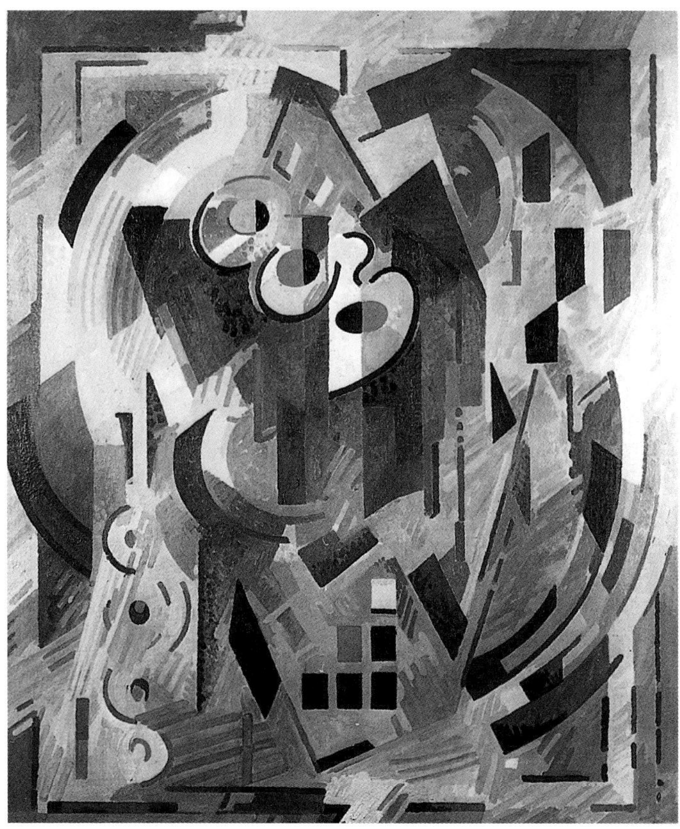

127. *Pour l'Esprit: les verts*, 1939. Oil on canvas, 183 × 148 cm. Present whereabouts unknown

the middle portion of *Autorité spirituelle*, with its series of circular curves rising (this time obliquely) from the bottom up in the centre of the canvas. In both paintings, especially in *Les verts*, the chromatic circle is, as it were, broken and dispersed about the canvas. It is present but no longer embodies all the colours used for the figure. The distinction between static figure and mobile circle has become a matter of inflexions, vertical inflexions for the stasis, inclined and curved for the mobile.

It is almost entirely by means of inflexions and directions rather than geometrical figures that the great lines of the composition are now suggested. We remember that the figure had all but been swept away in the early 1930s, when Gleizes concentrated all his attention on the 'cadences' of colour. The figure returned, and with it the monumental, constructive aspect of the painting, in 1934. Now the figure – in the sense of a closed geometrical shape – has all but disappeared again, but the monumental, constructive aspect remains, achieved by a multitude of relations which the eye establishes without the mind even being aware of the fact – a straight line that disappears and is picked up further on as an accent and then again as a change in colour; a series of colours that take the eye in a particular direction through changes of tone or through slight changes in colour, a blue edging into green, a red to orange. Nothing now is fixed or closed or capable of being measured; it is, to use Gleizes's terminology, a thoroughgoing advance from geometry to arithmetic, from figures to numbers.

And yet in his lessons given to Anne Dangar in the winter of 1939–40, he is still insisting on apparently very elementary exercises in translation – relations of rectangles parallel to the overall frame, equivalent to the first set of illustrations in *La Peinture et ses lois*.[17] Anne Dangar wrote to her friend Gaston Grimaud in Annonay to say: 'There are so many things to be done even with these first exercises. Carpets, woodwork, architecture etc above all require the straight line. Don't imagine that it is a little thing to begin with. It is the division of the plane surface and very important.'[18] It was indeed to be the basis of nearly all Lucie Deveyle's work as a weaver. Here it should be said that at the easiest and most elementary level, it enables the eye to see the plane as a rich, indeed inexhaustable, source of possible directions. 'Every line, every form and every colour comes from somewhere and goes somewhere' as Anne Dangar put it, summing up the whole of Gleizes's teaching.[19] Simple and naive as these exercises may appear to be, they are of a single fabric with the astonishing virtuosity which Gleizes had achieved by the early 1940s.

18
FIRST COMMUNION

The writer and poet, Henri Giriat, worked at Les Méjades as a farmhand from 1940 (after the armistice) until the end of the war. He says that, initially at least, life there was hard. Les Méjades had been a vineyard but Gleizes had torn the vines up to convert it to a varied agricultural production more suitable for a self-sufficient community. 'During this period, life was very difficult in the Midi. At Les Méjades, the basic nourishment consisted of barley, maze, pulses, potatoes, a daily quarter-litre of wine and green vegetables and fruit in the Summer. But no milk, no butter, and rarely any oil. The hen-coop, the rabbit-hutch, the pig-sty were not big enough for the needs of the farm. The workers were hungry.' The Spanish workers did not come from an agricultural background any more than Giriat or Gleizes himself. Everyone had to learn from scratch. It was not until 1942–3 that Les Méjades began to yield something of the riches of which it was capable.[1]

It was in this difficult period of 1940–1 that Gleizes entered into a more formal relationship with the Roman Catholic Church. This is sometimes represented as Gleizes's 'conversion' to Catholicism, but Gleizes had regarded himself as a Catholic since the 1920s. The problem was that his Catholicism – his reasons for being a Christian – had nothing to do with the contemporary nature of the Roman Catholic Church. Gleizes, as we know, regarded his Christianity as corresponding to the Christianity of the period prior to the twelfth century. It was not a matter of doctrine but of 'state of mind'. Christianity had brought about the state of mind which Gleizes called 'rhythmic' and which was the obverse of the static, classical state of mind of the Roman Empire. But the classical state of mind had begun to rise again from the thirteenth century onwards. The difference was evident in the works of art those periods had left behind. It was the rhythmic state of mind that interested Gleizes and the modern Christian churches did not possess it and had no conception of it.

Nonetheless, he had, in *Vie et Mort de l'Occident Chrétien*, written a defence of the Eucharist. Even if he did not believe that the priests understood it, he believed that he had some understanding of it and consequently that he appreciated how necessary it was. There was something illogical about not taking communion, as there was about not participating in the life of the Church while engaging in theological discussion and working, in his paintings and in his writings, for its conversion and regeneration.

We may imagine that in his instincts, Gleizes was still an anticlerical. Anne Dangar tells of a conversation she had with Mme Lhote, who had known Gleizes prior to the First World War. She had been very surprised to learn that he had become a Christian because at that time he had been just as intense and serious as ever but intensely and seriously anticlerical.[2] Talking after the

Second World War to the Benedictine monk Angelico Surchamp about his decision to take communion, Gleizes remarked: 'You don't refuse to eat bread just because all your life you've been cheated by the bakers.'[3]

Thomas Greenwood, an English Roman Catholic who had come to know Gleizes through the Unions Intellectuelles (he was secretary to the English Union) tells us that he discussed these issues with Gleizes in the early 1930s and that he persuaded Gleizes of the inconsistency of his position. He says Gleizes used to go with him when he went to mass. Shortly before reaching the church, however, they would part company and Gleizes would return home. One day, however, Greenwood said to him as they were about to part, that everything Gleizes said about the communion was splendid but that it was impossible to take him seriously unless he took it himself. Gleizes acknowledged that he was right and, thereafter, Greenwood says, he frequently went to church and frequently took communion.[4]

Mme Gleizes, however, recounting what happened in 1941 says that though he prayed frequently, he rarely went to church because he found it so ugly, and she gives the impression that he never took communion.[5] This is confirmed in Giriat's account. One thing is certain. Whether or not Gleizes had previously taken it, it was at the end of 1941 that he formally took his First Communion.

Gleizes had been baptized, but it was in discussion with a Belgian Carmelite priest who came to Les Méjades in 1940, Père Jérôme, that he realised that more than that was needed before he could have the right to share in the Eucharist. According to Mme Gleizes, they had indeed been married in church, but the priest who officiated, Abbé Mugnier, well-known as one who took an accomodating attitude towards the needs of high society, had not enquired too closely into their credentials. Gleizes told the more demanding Père Jérôme that, at the time when he should have been confirmed, his mother was going through a period of enthusiasm for the esoteric doctrines of 'Papus', pseudonym of Gérard Encausse, founder, or he would claim renewer, of the Rosicrucian and Martinist Orders.[6] Most of what was occult or esoteric in France, including Guénon, had, at one time or another, passed through some sort of relationship with 'Papus'.

Being confirmed and taking his First Communion involved learning his catechism (though Giriat says that Gleizes began studying the catechism prior to his meeting Père Jérôme – 'What a lot of pious superficialities. But, never mind, behind all that there's still the sacrament').[7] Anne Dangar visited Les Méjades at the beginning of 1942 and was impressed by the change she found in him:

> Mr Gleizes was very nice. Never have I known him so simple, so human. I think he's changed a lot. His daily contact with the workers, the earth, the worries of the real life of men and of animals, have helped him to understand the difficulties of existence. Then his conversion and the moral effect of taking his first communion and being confirmed have had a very great effect on him. . . .[8]

Anne Dangar herself was by now strongly attached to the Oxford movement in England, an attachment encouraged by Mainie Jellett and Evie Hone, who sent her books by Pusey and Newman and kept her informed of developments. Prior to the war she had tried to attend Holy Communion once a month at the Anglican church in Lyon. I have seen no sign of any interest on her part in the Eglise Reformée although her friend Mme Steinbach of the Château de Peyraud, facing Moly on the other side of the river, came from an old French

Protestant family.[9] The Oxford movement was of course the wing of the Anglican church closest to Roman Catholicism, and Evie Hone, after much soul-searching, had entered the Roman Catholic Church in 1939. Anne Dangar's isolation in wartime France as an Australian citizen – an Australian of Irish and possibly French descent who counted herself as 'English' – led her to reaffirm her English and Anglican identity, and therefore to come up against the anti-English feeling and new commitment to Roman Catholicism of Gleizes.[10]

Mme Gleizes says that after his First Communion, Gleizes went to church and communed frequently. But this 'conversion' did not imply any very obvious change in his view of the world. In *Spiritualité, rythme, forme*, written at the end of 1943, he said:

> For us, Frenchmen and occidentals, it is Christianity that is the religious reality and sole traditional spirituality. Since tradition is older than Christianity, as the beginning of the world is older than Christianity, all that was said before it prefigured it. Christianity radiated spirituality up to the day on which we stopped building the cathedrals, up to the day when the ARCHITECTONIKE, who possessed knowledge of the sacred, gave way to the ARCHITEKTON, who knew only how to construct secular buildings. From that moment onwards, the Occident passed under the domination of the sensible; a period of preoccupation with space began, with its illusions, its seductions, its splendours that dazzled without ever satisfying, with its reality that was mortal, of the nature of death, and which, as the illusions vanished, no longer sought to conceal itself, to pretend to be other than what it is. (*Puissances du cubisme*, p.324)

The idea that Christianity is part of an older tradition, though expressed delicately (in the way it is expressed, it is uncontentious, since it could simply refer to Judaism) nonetheless evokes Guénon's idea of a great world tradition of which Christianity is simply a part. Guénon himself, in Cairo, became a Muslim, but he argued that the only two valid expressions of the tradition in Western Europe (for 'Frenchmen and occidentals') were Roman Catholicism (not any form of Protestantism) and Freemasonry. For other peoples other religions constitute the 'religious reality and sole traditional spirituality'. But perhaps more obviously dangerous from an ordinary Catholic point of view is the idea that at a particular point in history, and a long time ago at that, Christianity ceased to radiate spirituality.[11]

Such ideas soon began to create difficulties between Gleizes and Père Jérôme. Initially, they were close friends. Jérôme, a Belgian, visiting chaplain to the nearby convent of St Paul de Mausole, with a particular interest in sacred art, anxious to introduce modern art to the church, gave classes and lectures in St Rémy and Gleizes encouraged his circle to attend them. There was talk of organising meetings for 'a small group of young artists interested in spiritual questions'.[12] But the atmosphere began to change in 1943. Henri Giriat says that the problems began when Jérôme passed Gleizes a book of essays by Jacques Maritain on Being and Mind. Maritain was perhaps the most influential Roman Catholic philosopher of the period who, for the previous thirty years, had been working to establish the relevance of Thomas Aquinas' writings to present-day problems. Many of those converts to Catholicism who, like Gleizes, were associated with 'modernist' tendencies, had been influenced by Maritain. But Gleizes had definite ideas about Thomas Aquinas. He saw him as the intellectual personification of a period, the thirteenth century, in which the primacy of spirit is giving way to the primacy of the senses.[13] Aquinas in these circumstances was certainly fighting the battles of the faith, but he was obliged to use the weapons of the new state of mind, the sense-, and observation-, based philosophy of Aristotle. Gleizes himself frequently quotes him, but this is because his *Summa Theologiae* is a summary of existing knowledge, including a great deal of knowledge from the previous period – the period that interests Gleizes – that had not been written down.

> In the thirteenth century, the period of the *Summae* (which attempt to settle accounts with the earlier period) St Thomas, writing on the problem of religious art in his *Summa Theologiae*, recalls the old order and reveals nothing of the thinking behind the art of his own time, which is more and more freeing itself from the traditional, Christian, popular and, as such, metaphysical technique . . . (*Spiritualité, rythme, forme*, p.334)

But, in his own thinking, Thomas is a man of his time and as such he lies at the beginning of the evolution that is now coming to an end. To go back to him is to go back to Humanism in its embryonic form. Gleizes was therefore not sympathetic to the project of Maritain.

Thereafter, Giriat tells us:

> The Père Jérôme attempted his own critique of Gleizes's writings in which he thought he could see signs of Nietzsche's notion of Eternal Recurrence.
> He accused Gleizes of underestimating human liberty in favour of the determinism of the theory of cycles: 'You are guilty of naturalism, Mr Gleizes.'
> Gleizes defended himself, good humouredly at first, but firmly: 'Father, you're not going to accuse the farmer of a lack of initiative because his work is subject to the rhythm of the seasons. He is precisely the representative of Mind that knows how to correct the determinisms of nature. Its the same for someone who is conscious of the rhythms of history.'
> The Père Jérôme argued the opposite case and the polemics began to develop, until the day when the Père Jérôme exploded in the great room of Les Méjades: 'Monsieur Gleizes, your thought is not Christian.'
> Gleizes understood him as asking him to give up the struggle he had been waging for decades. Sooner tear out his own entrails!
> 'Monsieur Gleizes, you must give up your favourite ideas.'
> 'But, father, you don't understand. These ideas aren't mine. They don't belong to me. They were given to me, and I'm just serving a cause that goes beyond me.'
> Thus was the knot of misunderstanding tied with the best intentions of both men. Each retired to his tent. Gleizes said 'A malevolent monk'. Mme Gleizes: 'Torquemada in person.'
> The Père Jérôme went for his daily walk along the great ally of the pines in Saint Paul de Mausole, and pondered on his annoyance. 'I will tell him: "Monsieur Gleizes, you want to measure everything. You, too, you will be measured, you will be measured . . . in your coffin." '[14]

There are some letters of Père Jérôme to Gleizes which give us other glimpses of this quarrel and which show that a part was played by Gleizes's continued loyalty to Guénon:

> I deeply regret, dear Mr Gleizes, that our relations have come to a stop. Certainly, I have been wanting with regard to you, in more than one way, and I humbly ask your forgiveness. On the other hand, you can't be surprised that I react when I hear you say, for example, that 'the whole of theology needs to be taken up again', or certain ideas on the subject of the Person and of the reality of Christ which the Church does not and never will allow [. . .]
>
> Since I saw you the last time, I have had the occasion to read several works by René Guénon, among others his *Introduction générale à l'étude des doctrines Hindoues*. I found some very fine things in them, together with others that are irreconcilable with the teachings of the Church [. . .]
>
> I fear that our old discussions will just start all over again, and what's the use. We will stick, each of us, to our guns. . . .[15]

The last correspondence between them was, it should be said, friendly. But these themes – Gleizes's distrust of Thomism, his insistence on a cyclical view of history, his sympathy for Guénon, and a tendency to lay the emphasis on the universal reality of Christ rather than on the historical individual – were to continue to pose problems between Gleizes and the Church in the period after the war.

The year of Gleizes's First Communion and the great period of the reorganisation of Les Méjades, 1941, was a comparatively fallow year in his career as a painter, though it was probably then that most of the work was done on preparing the great *Triptyque* at Lyon (Plates 127–9): 'I think that it is there, in the Triptyque, that I have gone furthest,' Gleizes told Angelico Surchamp after the war: 'Five tones used without any mixture, flatly, without variations in tone, together with black. That is all. I rediscovered an austere palette, that of the Romanesque painters: yellow ochre, red ochre, ultramarine, chrome green and violet grey: the earths.'[16]

It was in 1942 and 1943, however, that Gleizes realised what are, in my opinion, his greatest paintings, the paintings that could almost be seen as the 'end' to which he had been working all his life: the *Support de contemplation* of 1942 and the *Peinture à sept éléments* of 1943 (Plate 132), the *Composition: Dominantes roses et vertes* of 1942 and the undated *Composition abstraite* (at least that is the title given in catalogues though Gleizes himself objected to the term 'abstract' (Plate 134). A postcard-size gouache based on the same composition dated 1944 and intended as a gift for Anne Dangar, is called *Contemplation pour Anne Dangar*). The first two of these paintings are particularly impressive in their massive verticality, recalling how, back in the 1920s, Gleizes had declared that the great achievement of Cézanne, or at least the great aspiration embodied in Cézanne, had been to reassert the verticality of the wall that had been punctured by perspective. The person standing in front of the painting is once again able to stand upright, to be upright internally. The *Sept éléments* of 1943 is of course related to the *Sept éléments* of 1924 and of 1934 (essentially the 1924 painting re-worked with the grey circular curves), both of which have this same powerful verticality. The 1943 painting observes the same division of the plane – the great central element flanked on each side with three subordinate elements, the same construction as Gleizes had seen in the megalithic carvings of Gavr´inis in Britanny (Plate 131) and in Cimabue's *Virgin with Angels* (Plate 113), proof, in his view that 'tradition' is a matter of recovering

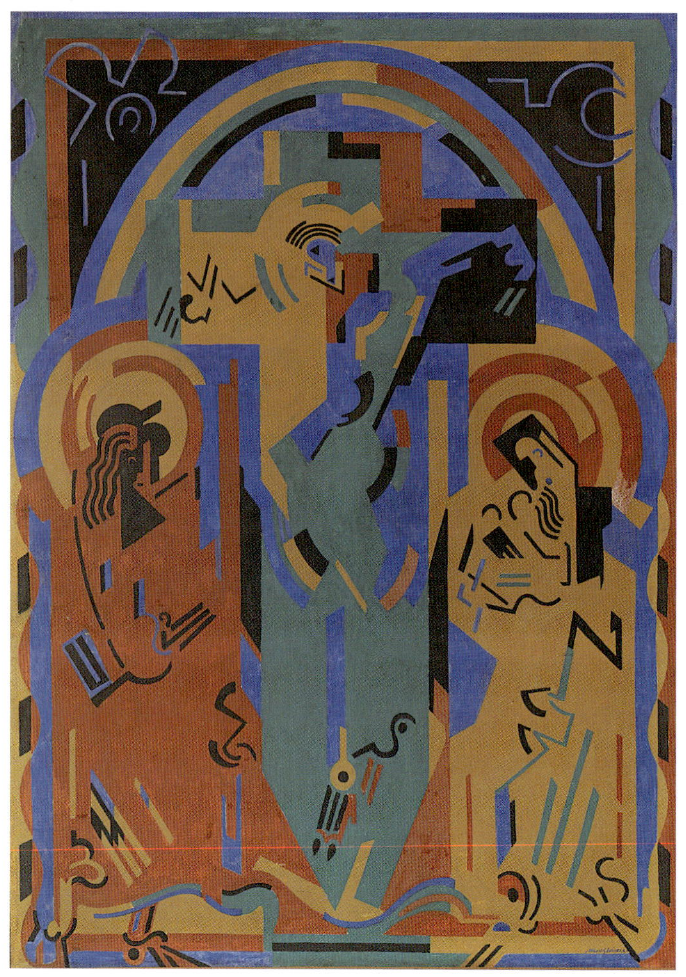

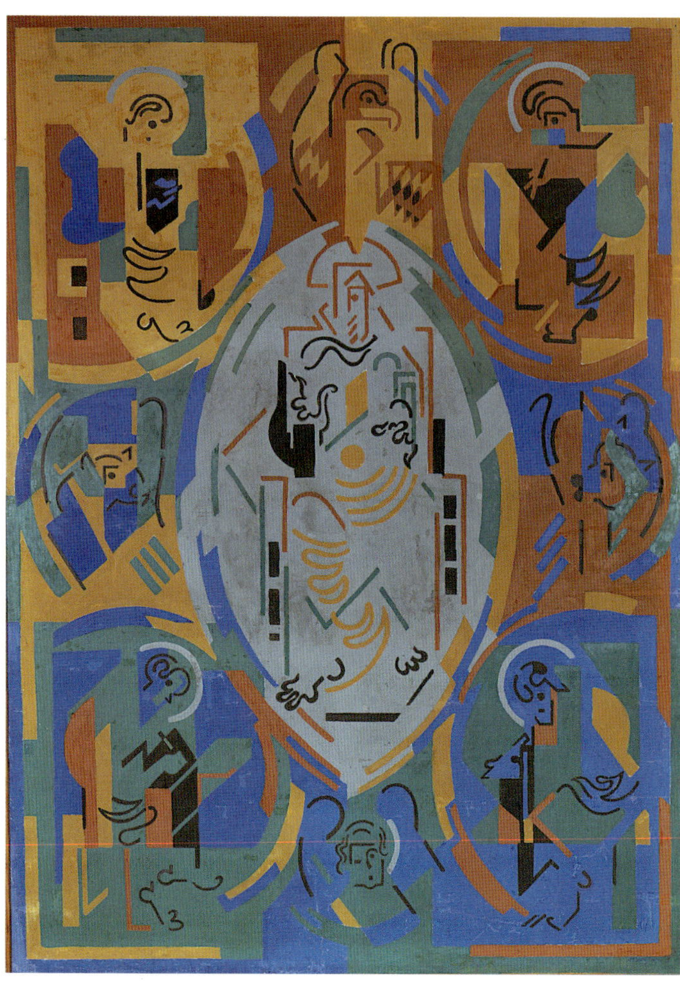

128. *Triptyque – la Crucifixion*, 1943. Oil on canvas, 288 × 200 cm. Musée des Beaux Arts, Lyon

129. *Triptyque – le Christ en gloire*, 1943. Oil on canvas, 288 × 200 cm. Musée des Beaux Arts, Lyon

'constants' that are of the stuff of human nature and therefore always accessible to us, even if the state of mind of the epoch comes closer to them or drifts away from them according to the play of the cycles.

These paintings are all in spiralling movement with a multitude of centres, and it is instructive to compare them with Delaunay's earlier *Rythme sans fin* series (Plate 33). The comparison is cruel. Gleizes's means are much greater than those of Delaunay. Delaunay's sinusoidal curves go beyond the limits of the painting; it is thus that he understands 'endlessness' – an advance along an infinite straight line. But the practical effect is to stop the rhythm. The eye stops at the edge of the canvas and cannot follow it any further and cannot return. We understand what Gleizes means when he says that the curve must be total – it must eventually join up with itself again. It must be circular in its principle, but it was not necessary that it should be a simple stated circle as in the paintings of 1935–8. It could be varied and irregular. In *La Forme et l'histoire II* and in the *L'Homme devenu peintre* of 1948, Gleizes evokes the principle of the rubber band to indicate all the fantastic variations the circle could undergo still without losing the principle of circularity.[17]

Delaunay shows a sinusoïdal movement which is quite unrelated to the whole surface of the painting; it is surrounded by dead space. In Gleizes's work,

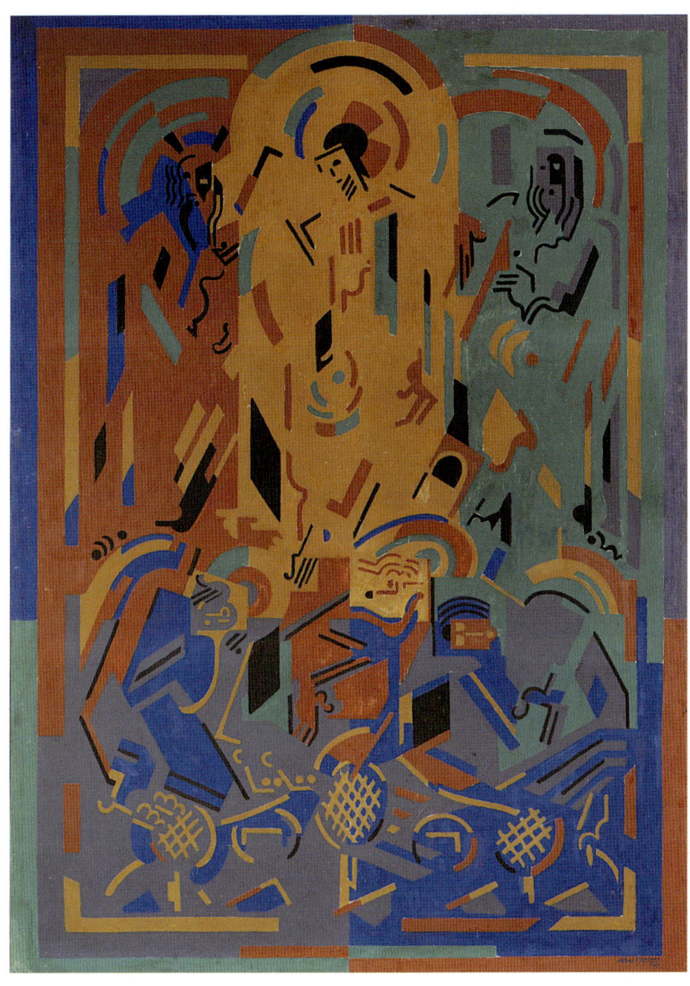

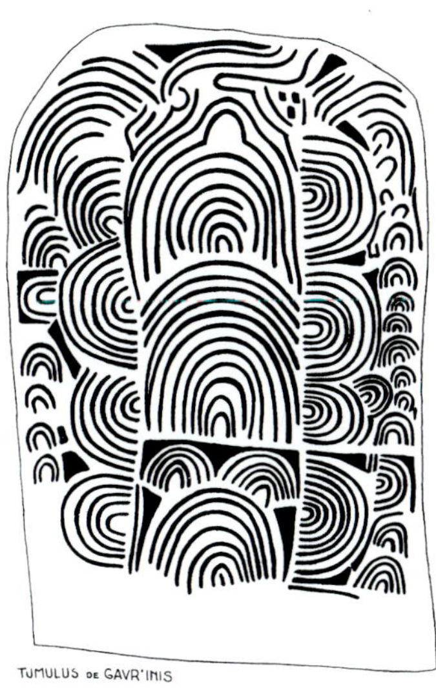

130. *Triptyque – la Transfiguration*, 1943. Oil on canvas, 200 × 288 cm. Musée des Beaux Arts, Lyon

131. Robert Pouyaud, *Tumulus de Gavr'inis, Morbihan.* Illustration from Gleizes, *Vers une conscience plastique: La Forme et l'histoire*, p. 9

every centimetre of the canvas has an essential part to play, despite the apparent irreconcileability of the rectangle and the sinusoide. All of Gleizes's Cubist 'analytical' research into the properties of the plane is brought to bear to slow the movement down, to providing many delightful distractions along the way, without ever stopping it entirely. We are back to the small figure walking through the wonderful, infinitely varied landscape of Meudon in 1911, or to a memorable passage in *La Forme et l'histoire* which reflects on the relation between the path leading up to the cemetery at Serrières, the line, moving in time, and the landscape through which it moves, space, always different every time the traveller stops to take a look at it (pp.186–7).

It is thus that these paintings, unlike Delaunay's *Rythmes sans fin*, can be called *Supports de contemplation*. They can be looked at, literally, for hours without ever finally yielding up their secrets and, during the time of looking at them, the mind is in silence. They may evoke all sorts of ideas, but those ideas are of no interest to the act of looking at them. It is a silent act, that evokes the consciousness of the soul as something other than a voice chattering in the head. It is a sacred painting, not because it uses any sacred imagery or allegory or any literary idea, but because it evokes the movement which, having nothing to do with an external mechanical displacement, is an internal property of the soul,

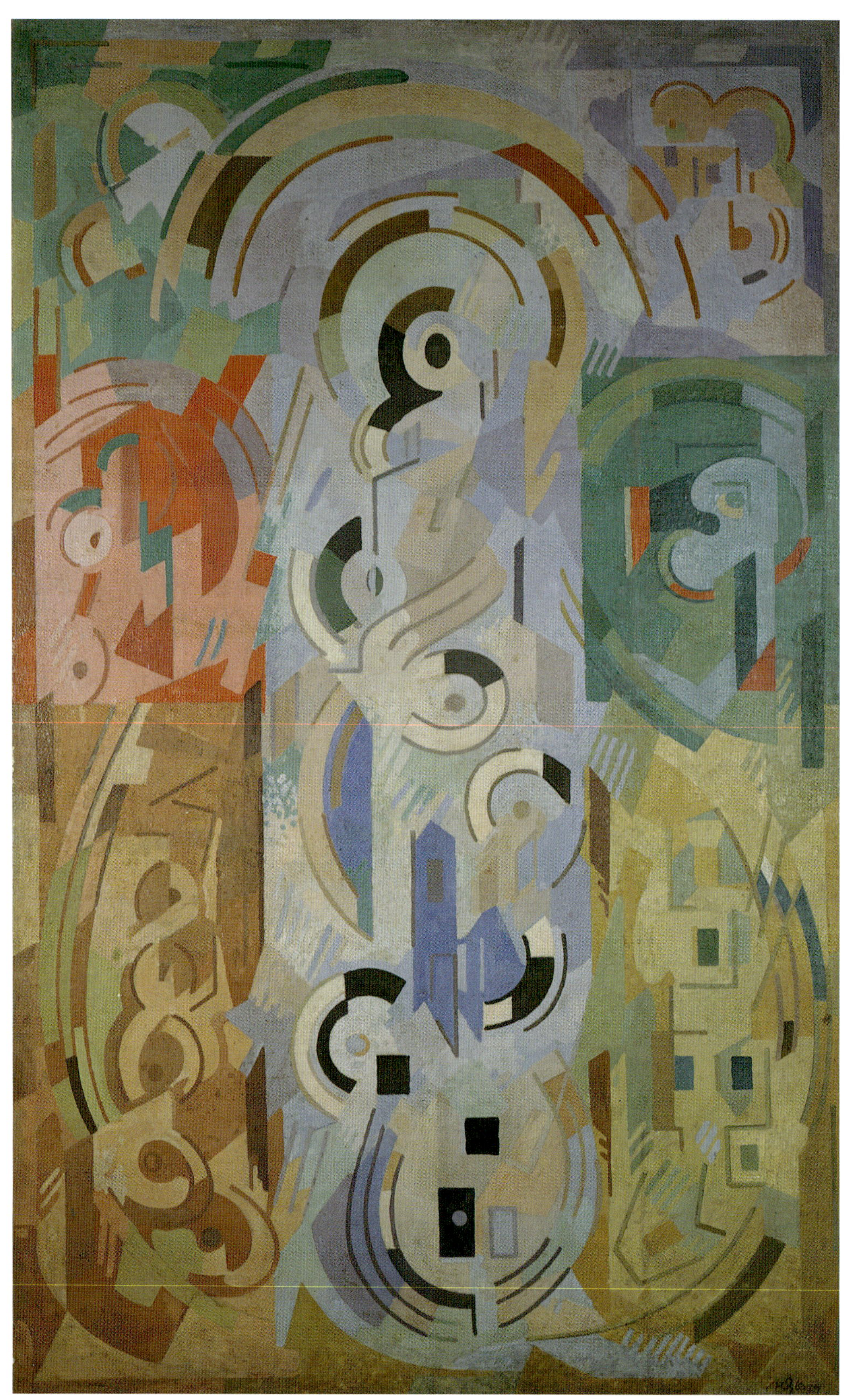

132. *Sept éléments*, 1943. Oil on canvas, 300 × 178 cm. Present whereabouts unknown

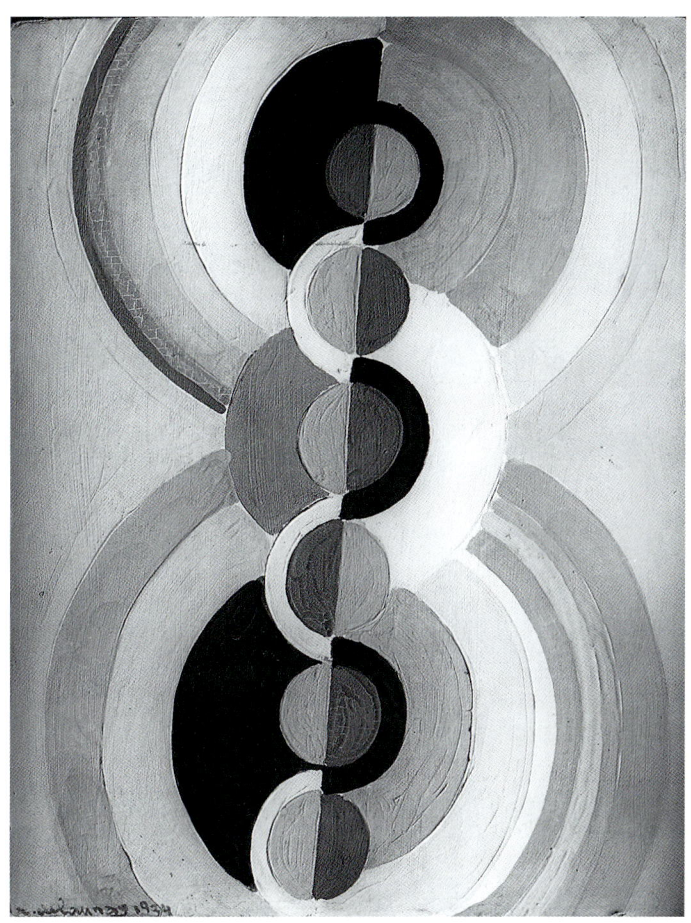

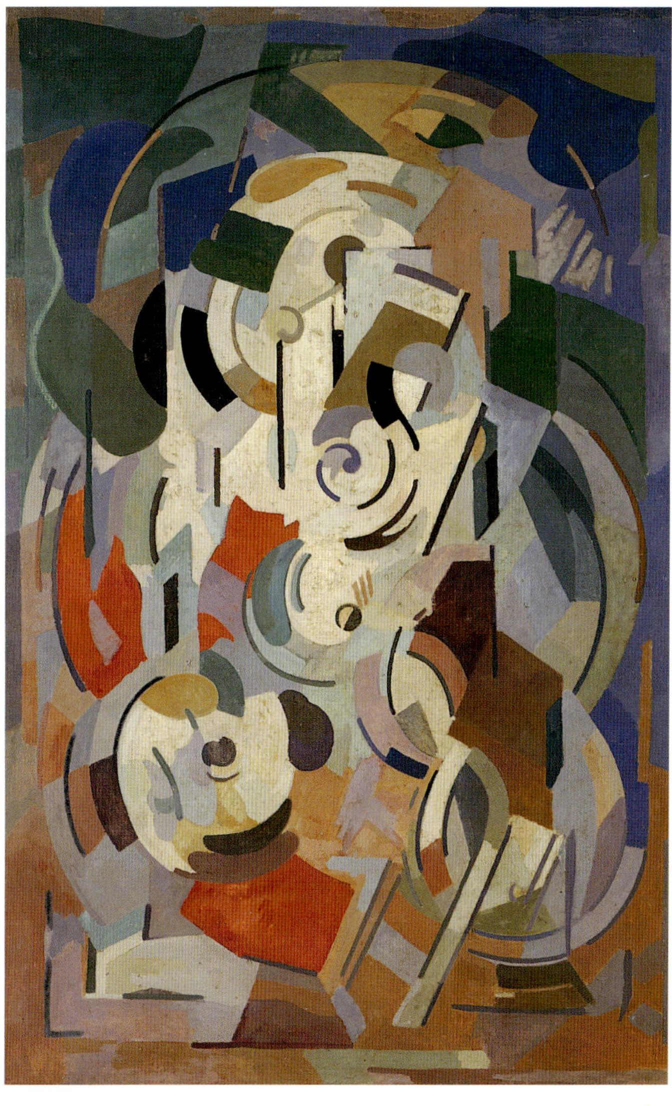

133. Robert Delaunay, *Rythme*, 1934. Oil on paper, 62.5 × 47.5 cm. Musée des Beaux Arts, Lyon

134. *Composition abstraite*, *c.* 1944. Oil on canvas, 212 × 132 cm. Musée National d'Art Moderne, Paris

ultimately linked to prayer. The painting helps the soul to rise from the material to the temporal, and prayer goes from the temporal to the spiritual. The three levels – measure, cadence, and unity/rhythm/ form – are still present but no longer stated symbolically. The unity is not given in the grey circle but in the eventual joining up of all the elements in the painting, a resolution which could never be precisely measured or situated but which is experienced in the 'endlessness' of the act of looking at it. We are reminded of what Gleizes had said nearly thirty years previously, in the letter he wrote to the composer Florent Schmitt in 1915:

> I have in vision the image that is made in the water by a stone which one has just thrown into it. A centre and, all around, vibrations which are translated into concentric waves that widen to arrive at a supreme development, finally dying in the whole that has, once again, become calm. I followed clearly the pattern of this drawing interlaced with arabesques, in which all the fantasy of your art was woven together in capricious dissonances. I saw circles

> spread out and stretch into ovals, these ovals turn, serpentlike, multiply in infinite folds, brutally, suddenly brought back to pure form, from which they fled again, playfully . . . Perhaps that is not what you wanted to convey, this game, this round of circles, developing, interpenetrating, escaping, breaking up, going in waves, incidentally assuming the characteristics of straight lines. It is doubtless not this explanation I have given that can translate the secret aims of your mind. But even if I am very far off the mark, my dear Florent, I don't mind. Once it has left you, your work is no longer yours, and it is I that listen to it.[18]

Robert Delaunay died at the end of 1941. André Lhote wrote to Gleizes, expressing his surprise: 'Our poor Delaunay is dead. The news, which came to me from Delteil without any details, has left me astounded. I thought him capable of living to be a hundred.'[19] Gleizes himself took up the thought in a new preface he wrote for his book on Delaunay in 1945: 'Robert Delaunay, who seemed as though he should have lived for a hundred years, died in December 1941.'

Delaunay, we have seen, was by this time the closest to Gleizes of all the original Cubist group. Gleizes was no longer in contact with his old friends of the Abbaye de Créteil, and was positively hostile in his attitude to the best-known of them, Georges Duhamel.[20] He seems to have had no contact with Léger, since their momentary coming together in 1926. He had very little contact with Metzinger, who wrote in 1942 expressing a typically worldly attitude to one of Gleizes's great passions: 'As for the "return to the soil", I sacrifice nothing more to it than is necessary for the feeding of a few rabbits.' [21] An interesting correspondence was to begin again after the end of the war, when Metzinger wrote to suggest republishing *Du 'Cubisme'*.

Gleizes continued after Robert's death to write to Sonia, treating her as a sympathetic colleague. He also continued in contact with Jacques Villon and – perhaps most importantly during the war – with André Lhote.[22]

Pouyaud wrote in April 1944, happy that Gleizes was still working and noting 'that literature has occupied the dominant place this winter'. He also expressed his regret at the 'suppression of any exchange, for example with Mainie and Evie, René Guénon and others who are not in this blessed Fortress Europe . . .'.[23] A fortnight later he had learned of Mainie Jellett's death in February, at the age of 47, from cancer:

> I remember as if it was yesterday our first meeting in your studio at Neuilly around 1923 [1924 – PB] and at once I am overwhelmed by the uprightness of her spirit and the depth of her faith in the picture as a means of expression. We were actually very close to each other, just as precise, as meticulous in our formal expression, just as rigorous in the manifestation of space and rhythm, expressions of the plane. . . [24]

When Pouyaud refers to Gleizes's 'literature' he probably has in mind the two essays *Spiritualité, rythme, forme* and *L'Arc en ciel, clé de l'art chrétien médiéval*, both written in December 1943 and both in their different ways destined to play an important role in Gleizes's life after the end of the German occupation. But this is also an important period in Gleizes's painting. I have described such works as the *Support de contemplation* of 1942 and the *Sept éléments* (Plate 132) of 1943 as the realisation of an ambition Gleizes had had since his letter to Florent Schmitt of 1915, and indeed as the closest Gleizes came to the perfect expression of his pictorial means. But this does not seem to have been Gleizes's own estimation. When he developed the 'traditional painting' of 1934, he continued to use it for four years during which he seemed to regard it as definitive. But he does not linger over the means he has developed for the *Support de contemplation* or the *Sept éléments*. In 1943, he seems to be changing course in a way that is difficult to describe or to explain.

The difficulty derives from the apparent lack of method. Gleizes's painting has, since the 1920s, been based on a very precise distinction drawn between the straight line (vertical or horizontal), the oblique straight line, and the curve. Now Gleizes is interested in much more fluid, more apparently arbitrary shapes whose precise role in maintaining the stability or contributing to the mobility is not always easy to identify. And yet the paintings retain the virtues of the earlier, more apparently systematic, works: there is a stability, there is a mobility, which is freer, but still controlled and not allowed to go too fast; and there is a unity, an overall form which, however, may be characterised as wholly transcendant and immeasurable – it is certainly not expressed in the simple form of the grey circle (Plate 135). It is, however, instructive to compare the construction of this period of largely non-representational painting with the construction of the non-representational paintings which led to the adoption of the grey circles in 1934.

The latter were characterised by their obvious construction – still built on a basis of the manipulation of identifiable plane surfaces. Or they show signs of the 'cadences' – repetitions of identifiably similar strokes of colour organised in a series that can be followed. Now the construction is barely identifiable, there is little sense of the existence of superposed plane surfaces, and little resemblance between the shapes that enclose the different colours. And yet there is unity and a coherent direction.

It is as if Gleizes who, in his writing, is drawing a clear distinction between the 'Absolute' and the 'relative', insisting on the absolute, transcendant unity of the object – is anxious to show that if measure, cadence and rhythm (space, time, eternity) are of the nature of the Absolute, the laws of translation-rotation-rhythm, by which he believes they can be expressed, are relative. The 'formula' by which we attempt to approach the Absolute must not be confused with the Absolute itself. This relativisation of the formula is not a rejection of it. Translation and rotation are still present in these paintings and will be to the end of Gleizes's life.

The continued presence of the stable, the mobile and the form-rhythm may be appreciated if we compare these paintings with those of Gleizes's younger contemporaries – Manessier, Bazaine, Le Moal (Plate 136), Estève, Bissière – who may be described as the

135. *L'étrange Musicien*, 1944. Oil on canvas, 182 × 111 cm. Present whereabouts unknown

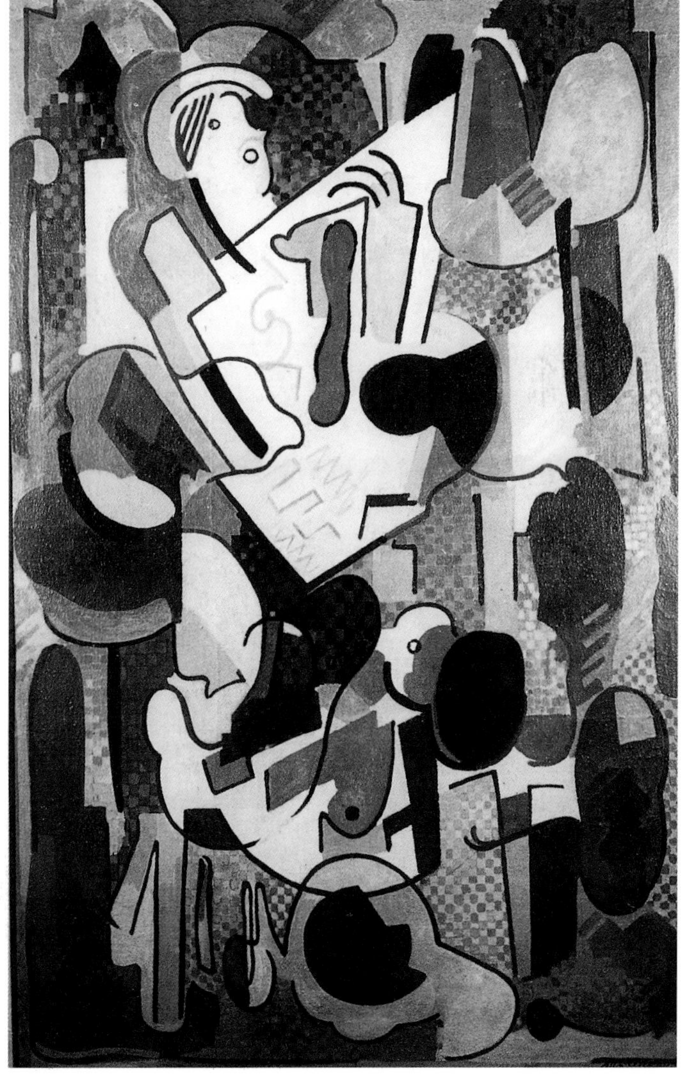

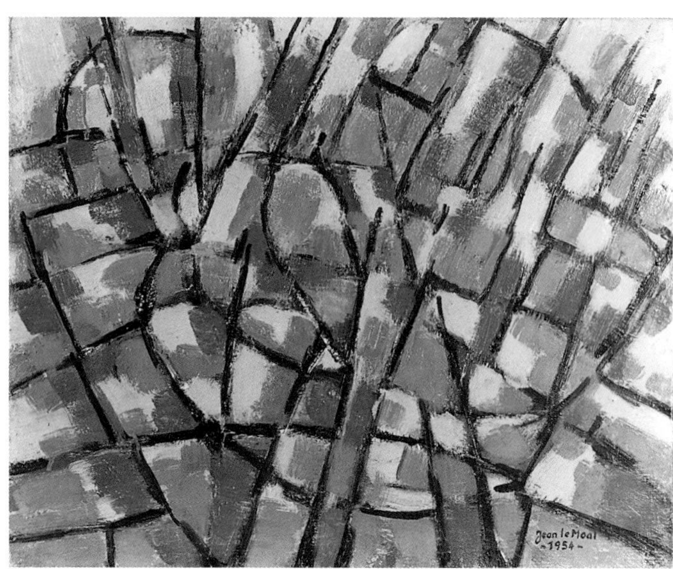

136. Jean Le Moal, *Sans titre*, 1954. Oil on canvas, 46.5 × 55.5 cm. Musée des Beaux Arts, Lyon

mainstream tendency of French non-representational art in the period immediately following the war, and who also claimed an affinity with Romanesque painting. Their works have in common a tendency to use warm, glowing colours in more or less uniform shapes, often structured by a dark 'grid' that has been interpreted as a reminiscence of Cubism. Sometimes, particularly in the case of Manessier and Estève, the juxtaposition of the colours is very beautiful; but it is an essentially static, atmospheric beauty. There is no resemblance to Gleizes's cadences; the eye is not guided from one colour to the other. This property of the eye (and the properties of the colours that evoke it) is unknown to them. The static, separated nature of the colours is all the more reinforced by the grid which, if it evokes the idea of structure, of construction, of scaffolding, does not derive from the overall plane surface on which it is placed. It therefore plays a role that is very different from the structures of Gleizes, or indeed from those of Braque, Gris and Metzinger when they are working with planes rather than with lines. It actually comes closer to the lines of construction used in Lhote's paintings and it may not be an accident that Bissière – the elder statesman of the group – had worked with Lhote. But a source that is more obvious than any source in Cubism is Rouault and, behind him, the lead-lines of stained-glass windows.

If we turn to Gleizes's new paintings and if, very improperly, we treat them like a jigsaw puzzle, an assemblage of the various shapes that appear in them, we find that each of those shapes, taken individually, is varied and irregular. Indeed, we may well be reminded of the paintings of Mirò or Kandinsky, but in the works of these latter the shapes retain their autonomy. They have no autonomy in Gleizes. The eye cannot settle on them and, in and of themselves, they have no interest. The eye is obliged to engage in the same activity it has enjoyed in Gleizes's other, more obviously methodical work. The change is more apparent than real, and we can see that, if the different elements cannot be assigned precise roles, the roles – vertical and horizontal line, oblique, curve – are still being played. The vertical and the oblique have less relation to the contours of distinct superposed planes than they used to do, the curve

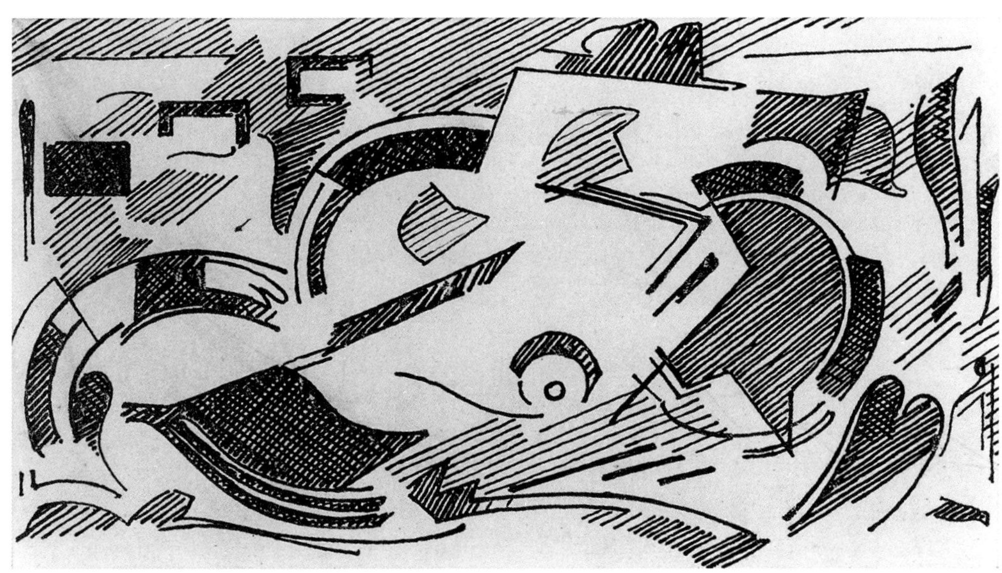

137. *Sans titre*, 1949 (?). Ink on tracing paper, 8 × 14 cm. Private collection

is moving from the circle to the arabesque (Plate 137). Indeed, this is the development Gleizes discussed in his *La Forme et l'histoire II*, when he used the example of a rubber band which retains the principle of circularity, returning on itself, but allows the eye to wander, hither and thither, in a freedom that is all the fuller and greater because it never loses sight of its limits.

So, this may now be asserted. The 'Absolute' – transcendant unity – that Gleizes evokes may well seem like the abolition of all distinction and variety, the death of all 'originality and personality' as Gleizes puts it, the imposition of a uniform totalitarianism, but this is to mistake its absolute and transcendant nature, its reality in Eternity. Religious totalitarianism becomes a dull uniformity, or an obstacle to human self-realisation precisely when the absolute, transcendant nature is forgotten and a relative concept, an opinion or, to use Gleizes's term, a 'subject' is given an absolute value. It may be premature to quote *L'Homme devenu peintre* which was written in 1947–8, but it was the theoretical statement of this period of Gleizes's work. This is what he has to say about the relationship between the relative and the Absolute in painting:

> However it might appear, or however well it may serve for our practical needs, a circumference closed on itself, in which the Alpha and the Omega come together, is impossible for us. The coming together of the Alpha and the Omega as we might imagine it in absolute terms never occurs, so that we can only pretend to spirals, to gyres, more or less close to each other, relative in relation to the Absolute of movement, which is no longer based on the differentiation of space and time.
>
> We can only pretend to spirals! What a stroke of luck for painters! For if we could effectively realise the circumference, we would no longer have any reason to leave the blessedness of its 'Nirvana'. And we advance towards this perfection, towards which every painter deeply committed to his work must tend, by continual and repeated experiments which are only possible through the countless varieties of paths available to the spiral. The circum-

ference and spirals dominated by the rotation of the eye are thus the primary lines of this movement. It is up to us to make them 'vibrate' according to our feelings and our knowledge of the rule which naturally conditions them – that is to say, optically. The movement of the eye has, as a direct consequence, the eye in movement, strolling along the line, where it will follow the course marked out by the periods we have proposed to it, cadences which trace the melodies of colour, and weave into counterpoint the places where they meet. Arabesque of line and colour, whose sinuosities are already enough to mark the cadences; periods broken at regular intervals, leaving the cadences open, as in the warp and woof of an invisible chain; the rotation of the eye allows every possible combination that can delight the painter's imagination; it gives free rein to his personal feelings, constantly subject to correction by the rule, which is the constraint that is common to all men, and permits communication between them.[25]

19

LA PIERRE-QUI-VIRE

Just after the war, as just before the war, Gleizes was very depressed. Robert Pouyaud quotes from a letter Gleizes sent to him in November 1945:

> I'm really disgusted with everything that's going on around us. What malice [*bêtise*] and what idiocy! So I'm continuing to work by force of habit but with a terrible feeling of uselessness. I look to my death as a liberation. I don't say any more, above all because I don't want to spread misery all around, I've already said too much.[1]

For once, the relationship between a normally pessimistic Pouyaud and a normally optimistic Gleizes was reversed. Pouyaud, like Anne Dangar, was enthusiastic for the Liberation.[2] Anne Dangar's loyalty had, we have seen, been sorely tried throughout the war by the Gleizes's political views and also by what she felt had been their lack of support in what was for her, as an Australian citizen, a very difficult time. In March 1945 she received a visit from her nephew, Geoffrey Dangar, with an American friend, both in full uniform. She describes the excitement of the children in the village who accompanied her as she rushed to meet them, her pride and happiness (and shame at what she thought was the squalid state of Moly Sabata). The next month she was with the Gleizes' on what she thought would be her last visit since she was determined – not for the first time – to return to Australia. After saying 'It is a privilege to work with Mr Gleizes, and he is very good and kind to me', she continued:

> Mme Gleizes is more painful than ever. Because the good God hasn't allowed her to run the world as she would like, she battles against him from morning to evening and mealtimes are very disagreeable because of her bitter and malicious comments.

The situation had not greatly improved when she went back in October 1946 (after she had definitely decided to stay in France):

> Imagine every evening with the wireless talking nonsense and Mme Gleizes talking politics ceaselessly, and me looking at the magnificent illustrations Mr Gleizes has made in Form and History or trying to read in his tiny, difficult handwriting some astonishing and so precious things St Augustine says in his On Free Will about the artist's eye . . .
>
> Once I dared to say to Mme Gleizes that I got no pleasure from always having to hear her hard reflections against my people and her excuses for everything the Germans do or have done – both of them accused me of being 'partisan', of having no religion, of hate etc . . .

> Oh, when the Gleizes' speak to me against the English, I feel I must go back to Australia, that I am a traitor staying here.[3]

Though one of her reasons for deciding not to return to Australia was that it would be painful to hear her Australian friends speaking ill of the French for their – to Australian eyes – inglorious role during the war.[4]

Gleizes does indeed appear to have been more sensitive to the horrors that accompanied the allied victory than he was to those that had accompanied the German occupation. As we have seen, he was persuaded that the rise of Hitler had been a result of the vindictive treatment of Germany at the end of the First World War, and that the need for war was itself a consequence of an uncontrolled commitment to industrial expansion which had found its highest expression in the now again victorious United States of America. Consequently, in his vision of things, an American victory could only be the prelude to yet more terrible wars. At the end of the Second World War (before the need was felt to cultivate Germany as a bulwark against the Soviet Union) the hatred directed against Germany was if anything greater than the hatred that had so horrified him at the end of the First World War. France in particular had a psychological need to identify itself with the Resistance rather than with Vichy or with the collaboration. It is difficult to situate Gleizes in any mainstream French political tendency but the one that comes closest is that strand of French pacifism which was seriously compromised in the collaboration. The case of the Provençal novelist Jean Giono, a miltant pacifist and advocate of the return to the soil, comes to mind. Giono had been much honoured by the Vichy government and was forbidden from publishing for some years after the war. Gleizes was not much honoured by the Vichy government but he was under suspicion of collaboration. Metzinger wrote in June 1945 with a proposal to republish *Du 'Cubisme'*:

> It wouldn't be a bad thing if you emerged from your hole to come and defend yourself. Profiting from the war, the second and third-class types have taken the first place . . . I had to withdraw my canvasses on the opening day [of the Salon des Tuileries – PB]. If it hadn't been too late, I would have sent you a telegram so that you could do the same. Your two pictures were placed outside the rooms, in a sort of box, without any possibility of stepping back from them . . . the desire to snuff you out was obvious. Your painting annoys those who have taken advantage of it. And do you know what I heard in a gallery in which non-figurative painting is all the rage, when I expressed my amazement that you weren't represented? 'Gleizes . . . but he has disappeared . . . it seems that he was a collaborator.'
>
> You are going to reply that all that has no importance, that you couldn't care less. You're wrong. Its immoral to let one's place be taken by people to whom one has shown the way. My old friendship is annoyed to see that you let yourself be robbed of the success that you deserve.

Thanking Gleizes for the preface he wrote for the new edition of *Du 'Cubisme'*, Metzinger wrote again:

> Your text is perfect. Unfortunately it gives a favourable mention to A. Salmon. Don't you know, then, that A. Salmon is accursed? No-one is pre-

> pared to shake his hand any more and he has been rejected. Literature! This quotation by itself is enough to give us problems.
>
> And speaking of this, I heard malicious remarks being passed about you yet again, not longer ago than yesterday. I hope there's nothing behind it and that it won't prevent our republication. It doesn't take much! There's nothing more terrible than these collective hysterics.[5]

Du 'Cubisme' did not appear until 1947, and Gleizes's preface does refer favourably to Salmon, even though Salmon's influence on the historiography of Cubism was, generally, unfavourable to Gleizes.[6]

What might have been behind these rumours of collaboration? In 1942, Gleizes joined a National Committee for Folklore supported by the Vichy government, though it had actually been created on a private initiative before the war. Gleizes was president of a commission established by this Committee for encouraging craftsmanship. In this context he spoke at a conference at Nice, and in his speech, published in the Committee's journal *L'Echo des Provinces*, he said:

> The Marshall has called us to an intellectual and moral revolution. If we obey him it will not be long before we discover the real meaning of Man, simply in the opposition that there is between craftsmanship and industrialisation.[7]

Little seems to have come of this initiative, which was really a continuation of activities the Gleizes' were already engaged in at the time of the Popular Front government in the wake of the Universal Exhibition. There are some letters in which Gleizes complains about tedious and fruitless committee meetings that were keeping him from his work at Les Méjades.[8] He told Walter Firpo: 'They made me an inspector, but they never allowed me to inspect anything.'[9]

The Gleizes' had a friend, Régis de Vibraye, who worked at Vichy and can be said to have belonged to the pacifist-collaborationist tendency (he had written books in the 1920s and 1930s advocating greater Franco-German understanding). In 1943 when Anne Dangar was summoned to Grenoble and, very briefly, imprisoned, the Gleizes' wrote to him to ask him to use his influence.[10] Also in 1943, Gleizes's Spanish workers were told that they had to go to work in Germany. Mme Gleizes set off for Vichy (missing a chance to meet Villon who had arrived at Les Méjades at just that moment). Failing to make contact with de Vibraye, she went straight to the German ambassador, whom she found very helpful. She says that she was much criticised for this but that through it she had saved all the Spanish workers of the region.[11]

That, so far as I can see, is the extent of Gleizes's actual collaboration but it is possible that he would have collaborated more had he been invited to. There can be no doubt where his sympathies lay. Whatever he may have felt about the Nazis (he alternated between sympathetic interest and revulsion) he had long been an advocate of Franco-German collaboration and he saw the British as being chiefly responsibe for prolonging the war and therefore for the train of horrors it produced. I have not found any material that tells how he felt about the war in the East, where most of the atrocities were concentrated. Nor do I have a clear idea of his attitude towards the German, or French, persecution of the Jews. With regard to his own personal opinions, there is a lengthy discussion in *L'Art dans l'evolution générale*, pp.234–41, in which the Jews are praised (together with the Freemasons) for their radicalising effect on French history and for their internationalism. In particular he says that it is perhaps thanks to the Jews that France was the first European country in which the state was freed from the 'industrial control of the Church, making a commerce out of problems of conscience . . . It was a liberation despite all the protests, the chains were broken forever, thick clouds swept out of the way of the future' (p.237). However, his understanding of the Jews – as a revolutionary people, responsible first for the capitalist revolution and now destined to play a leading role in the anti-capitalist revolution – rather resembles that of certain of the anti-Semites, except that what they saw as an evil influence, he sees as positive. Even in arguing against the anti-Semites, he takes their arguments seriously. We have seen his interest in Houston Stewart Chamberlain and his friendship with Camille Mauclair, and we may imagine, but I have little in the way of definite evidence, that, since he had praised the Jews as a progressive people, his attitude may have changed when he ceased to believe in progress. I have, and I regret it deeply, seen no evidence that he spoke against the deportations that took place under the Nazi occupation and can only think he saw the worst accounts as atrocity propaganda of the type that had so disgusted him in the First World War.[12]

If Gleizes was depressed in 1945, it was not in his nature to remain so for very long and he was soon to have good reasons for feeling encouraged. Already in 1945 his book *Vie et mort de l'occident chrétien* was published in an English translation. This was a proposal that had originally been made in 1940; it came from an unexpected source.

Marco Pallis was a mountainclimber who, climbing in the Himalayas in 1933, came upon and was deeply impressed by the Tibetan Buddhist culture of Ladakh. Here, he felt, was a society that was what a society ought to be, a hierarchy in which every level was touched and ennobled by a religious ideal embodied in its highest level – a monastic spiritual authority living a life of renunciation. In 1939, he published an account of his journeys, *Peaks and Lamas*. Ananda Coomaraswamy recommended the book to Eric Gill, who wrote in February 1942 to express his admiration: 'I believe there is an ultimate reconciliation between the Christian belief in the sanctity and reality of individual personality and the ultimate impersonality of 'the void' . . . But on our level, here and now, and as confronted by our mechanical capitalism . . . What then?'[13]

Pallis wrote to Gleizes in October 1940 saying that he had read *Vie et Mort* shortly before the war after seeing a review in René Guénon's journal *Etudes Traditionnelles*.[14] Pallis was to translate Guénon's *Introduction générale à l'étude des doctrines hindoues* and *Crise du monde moderne* into English and he may have played a role in persuading Guénon to modify his insistence that Buddhism was merely a deviation from the Hindu tradition as – in Guénon's eyes – Protestantism was a deviation from the Christian tradition.[15] Pallis believed that Gleizes's book could be especially useful for certain Indian friends of his who, while wishing to remain loyal to the Hindu tradition, thought that it could be reconciled with elements of modern civilisation. It was in *Vie et mort de l'occident chrétien*, we remember, that Gleizes argued that all forms of industrial production, especially industrial methods of agriculture, were destructive of the essential value of human life.

The proposal was taken up again at the end of the war and the book published with a preface by H. J. Massingham, well-known as an advocate of what is now called organic farming. Gleizes wrote to Pallis in May 1945 expressing his enthusiasm for *Peaks and Lamas*: 'Your Peaks and Lamas gives us a thousand subjects for conversation and we so much agree with it. My wife takes a very great pleasure in translating it and she frequently reads me the most striking passages. We rejoice together. . . .'[16]

•

The publication of the English translation of *Vie et mort de l'occident chrétien* was an important event on what might be called the Guénonian side of Gleizes's activities. 1946 was to see an important development in what might be called the Catholic side – his friendship with two people who were to play important roles in the development of French Catholic culture – the historian Régine Pernoud, and the Benedictine monk, Dom Angelico Surchamp, founder of the publishing house, Zodiaque, known for its books on Romanesque art. Before introducing them, however, it will be necessary to say a word about Gleizes's own immediate circle.

Gleizes's circle – Evie Hone, who came to visit him after the war, Pouyaud and Dangar – had now been joined by a younger group of recruits, more distinctively French and perhaps more influenced by the religious and philosophical, though not necessarily Catholic, side of his thought, particularly as it was expressed in *Homocentrisme*. We have already met Henri Giriat, working as a labourer at Les Méjades. Gleizes also had what could be described as a lieutenant in the person of Jean Chevalier. Chevalier was a schoolteacher who, from 1939 until the end of the war, was living in Vienne, situated in the Rhone valley between Lyon, to its north, and Moly Sabata, to its south. In Lyon, Chevalier was associated with 'Témoignage', a group of painters founded in 1934 which included the Paris-based Jean Bertholle and Jean le Moal, and the Lyon-based Louis Thomas and René-Maria Burlet, grouped round the gallery owner, Marcel Michaud.[17] Témoignage specialised in a religious, symbolic painting which, by the war, was developing in two directions, towards Surrealism and, largely mediated by Chevalier and by Michaud, towards Cubism as Gleizes understood it. The struggle was personified in the painter René Maria Burlet, whose 'Minotaur' studio was to be an important centre for discussion and teaching in Lyon for many years. Burlet's own painting has been described by Henri Giriat, quite aptly, as a sort of 'Cubist Surrealism'.[18] Chevalier was also in touch with Moly Sabata, where he took lessons with Anne Dangar.

Chevalier's correspondence is a mine of information as to Gleizes's interests and concerns, especially during the war. He was a voracious reader, devouring anything Gleizes recommended him to read and keeping Gleizes informed of everything he thought might interest him. He entered into correspondence with a number of Gleizes's own contacts, including Coomaraswamy and Lhote. After receiving a letter from Coomaraswamy, he wrote to Gleizes in August 1938 to ask if he knew anything about Eric Gill. Coomaraswamy had told him that 'he is the most important representative of that point of view which, in company with Mr Gleizes, interests you'.[19]

Chevalier argued for Gleizes in talks, in articles and in exhibitions. He gave a talk on Gleizes's *Le Pape et l'empereur* (which, we remember, was Gleizes's manifesto for the period of the French defeat) at an exhibition of the Témoignage group held at Michaud's gallery in December 1940. *Le Pape et l'empereur* was again the centre of an exhibition Chevalier organised in Vienne in May 1941.

Chevalier and his wife – both schoolteachers – stayed at Moly Sabata during the Summer holidays in 1942. Anne Dangar was initially happy to receive them but their relations quickly cooled. It is not clear why, but something of the reason may be guessed from a letter of Anne Dangar's to the Grimauds written in August, referring to an exhibition they were planning in Annonay the following month: 'Chevalier wants to make it a very snob exhibition (he's such an intellectual), but with the children's works, Lucie's pretty little napkins and tablecloths and lots of pottery, I think we're going to have a real Moly style exhibition.' [20]

Where Anne Dangar saw the exhibition as an opportunity to give the people of Annonay a treat, Chevalier saw it as an opportunity to fight for Gleizes's ideas. This disagreement among two people who considered themselves to be among his most devoted disciples was to be a foretaste of things to come.

Around 1942–3, Gleizes entered into relations with the musician, Joseph Olivier. The story has it that Olivier arrived at Les Méjades as an insurance salesman. It was Gleizes who opened the door to him and the two retired to Gleizes's study and spent the morning together. Mme Gleizes was furious that her husband should have wasted an entire morning with an insurance salesman but Gleizes replied that he had spent the morning, not with an insurance salesman, but with a representative of the ancient tradition of the 'tambourinaires' of Provence. This is the equivalent of the English tradition of the 'whittle and dub'. The musician plays a drum with one hand and a flute with the other. The flute has three holes, combinations of which enable the musician to find all the notes he needs with one hand.

The tradition died out in England in the nineteenth century, giving way to the concertina, and it was on the verge of dying out in Provence. Largely as a result of his meeting with Gleizes, Olivier gave up his job and returned to farming, devoting himself at the same time to the revival of traditional music. His experience was described by the Dominican, Thomas de Romefort, whom we shall be meeting shortly:

> Joseph Olivier practised one of the most modern of professions but, tired of the vanities of economic 'progress', wearied by its useless agitation, and strongly influenced by Albert Gleizes, he again picked up the implements he had known from his peasant upbringing. And it was in wielding his scythe that he realised that the movements of work followed rhythms that were physiological in their nature. This was the starting point for his research into the rhythm of traditional music, which is not indicated in the neumic notation of the Middle Ages. This discovery enables him now to play certain pieces of the eleventh and twelfth centuries which have been rather neglected by the musicologists. Joseph Olivier's group of *tambourinaires* is made up exclusively of young farmers who are not musicians and who learn the airs by ear and not by reading the notes.[21]

Mention of the musician Joseph Olivier provides an opportunity to mention the musician César Geoffray, though he does not fall into the category of Gleizes's new acquaintance. The Geoffrays had continued in Moly Sabata throughout the 1930s, living in a state of some tension with Anne Dangar, who felt that they were pursuing their own careers in Lyon and contributing very little to the local community. It was a charge which, in retrospect, as we have seen, Geoffray thought was just. He was briefly mobilised at the beginning of

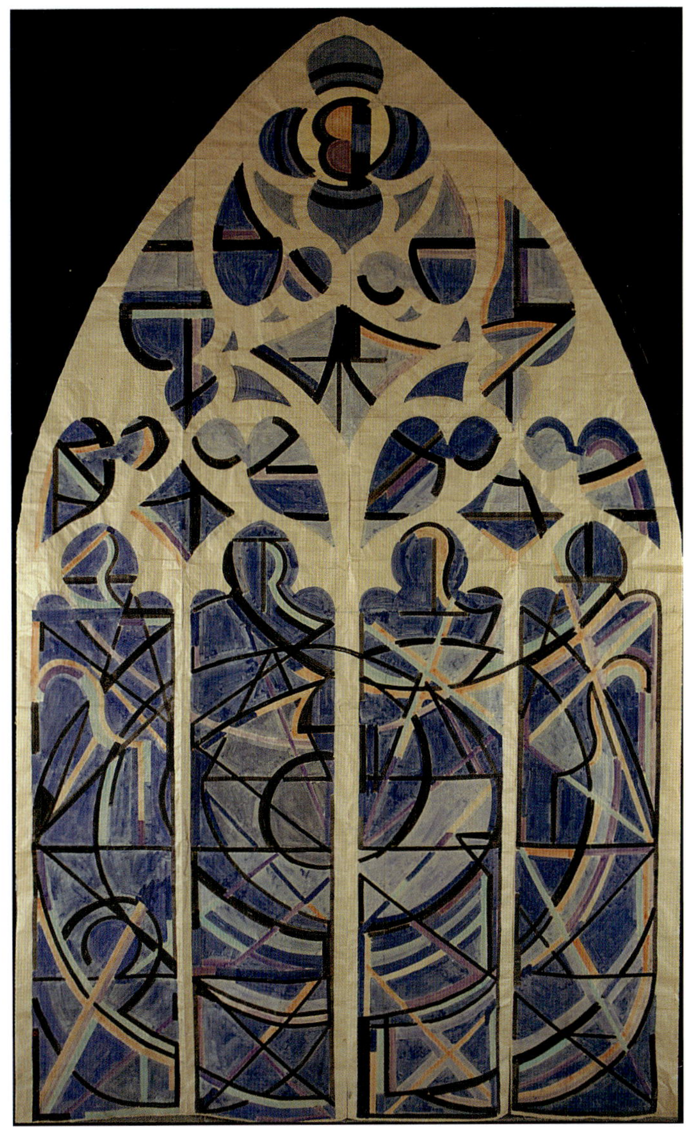

138. René Dürrbach, Cartoon for the third lower-level window on the north side of the Cathedral of Nevers, nd. Watercolour on brown paper, 651 × 396 cm. Private Collection. Photo communicated to me by Dr Max Célérier, President of the Association des Cahiers de Bourgogne

the war but returned to Moly in 1940 though he was now spending even less time there, so that even Gleizes was becoming annoyed. In 1940, after the French defeat, he received a visit from the 'Commissaire Nationale adjoint à la Route des Scouts de France' inviting him to conduct an improvised scout choir for a forthcoming radio broadcast. By that time, he says: 'I had learnt from Gleizes the sense of responsibility and the manner of conducting oneself that are proper for the artist in general who finds himself charged with a social role. I knew how authority should be exercised, competently and with goodwill and friendliness.[22]

The fifty boys and girls wanted him to stay with them to form a choir and the result was the Chorale du Scoutisme Français. In three months, the fifty had become over a hundred and Geoffray was invited to become singing master for all the scouts of France. For the music, Geoffray wrote his own arrangements of popular songs often using complicated modern harmonies. These were published in four collections during the war under the title *A Coeur Joie*. By the end of the war, twenty choirs had been formed using this material. A great reunion of French scouts at Strasbourg in 1946 brought together 400 singers and this proved to be the beginning of a national movement – A Coeur Joie – that went far beyond the limits of the scout movement and which is still going strong, with its headquarters in Provence at Vaison-la-Romaine. Geoffray himself died in 1972. In all his writings he insists that his two masters had been Florent Schmitt, who was his music teacher in Lyon in the early 1920s, and Albert Gleizes.

Gleizes's immediate circle in St Rémy included, in addition to Giriat and Olivier, the painters, Josep Franch-Clapers and Albert Coste. Clapers was Spanish and his paintings at the time he met Gleizes were sombre and representational, evoking the horrors of the Spanish Civil War.[23] He was later to work in mosaic in a style very obviously marked by Gleizes. Coste was a popular teacher of painting in the Art College at Aix-en-Provence, who had already worked with Maurice Denis.[24] Shortly after the war, the group was to be joined by the fresco painter Elizabeth Meyer, by René and Jacqueline Dürrbach and, once again, by Walter Firpo. René Dürrbach (Plate 138) was a painter and sculptor who was to realise the extraordinary stained-glass win-dows of the basilica at Charleville-Mézières, a work that lies outside the scope of this book but which, little known as it is, is one of the most impressive of twentieth-century works in the medium. His wife Jacqueline de la Baume Dürrbach was a weaver perhaps best known for her tapestries, done in conjunction with her husband and with Pablo Picasso, of the latter's *Guernica* and *Les Demoiselles d'Avignon*.

Firpo, whom we have already met at the end of the 1920s, re-established contact with Gleizes in 1946. His own development had occurred quite independently. In the 1920s he had been friends with Matisse and De Chirico. Both,

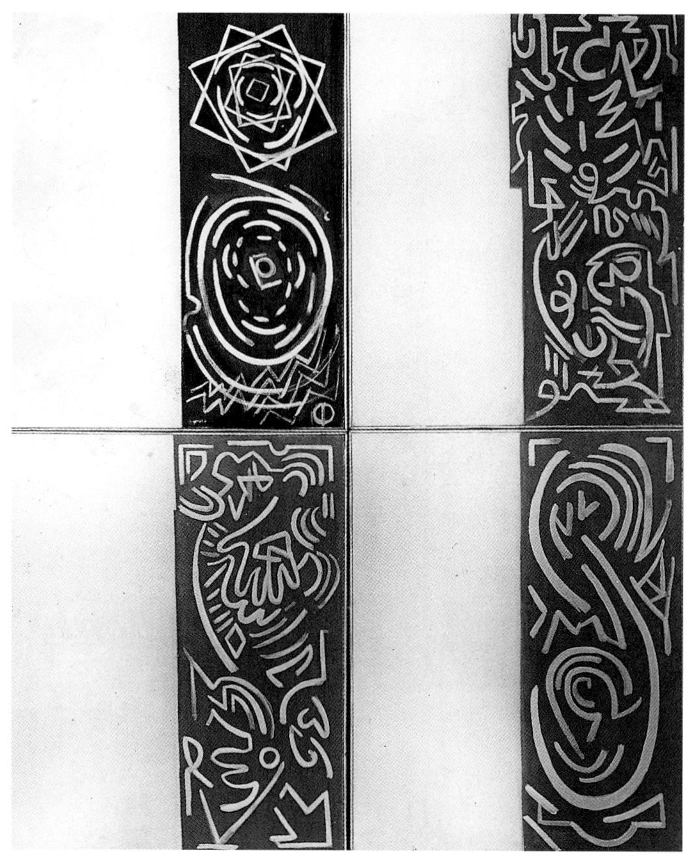

139. Walter Firpo, Four canvases from the series '*Domination du blanc*', nd. Exhibited at the Galerie Tony Spinazzola, Aix en Provence, 1961–2

he said, had impressed him deeply but it was only Gleizes who had really changed him. Gleizes describes the change that was taking place in the preface he wrote for Firpo's exhibition in 1947:

> If one looks at them [Firpo's paintings (Plate 139)] attentively, one will enter into their meaning which is so eminently human, and will discern that drama of the age in which two apparently contradictory attitudes are confronting each other – the subjective, inherited from the Renaissance, and the objective, forgotten, lost, which was that of the Christian Middle Ages. In fact, these two alternatives are specific to every living manifestation whether individual or collective. Firpo shows us the struggle he has conducted as a man to arrive at the witness that must be made by a painter. Unlike the intellectual who starts from the theory to arrive at the works, he starts from the work and struggles to draw lessons and certainties out of his experience . . . The conflict which began by opposing subject and object, the saying and the doing, is soon resolved and it is the first fruits of the reign of the object that we see with joy in his latest works . . .
>
> To live or to die? To be on the side of the seed or on the side of the atom?
>
> In his latest works, Firpo says eloquently that he has chosen the seed. He wants to live. He will live.[25]

Both Régine Pernoud and, at the time, Dom Angelico, could be described as intellectuals, starting with the 'saying' rather than the doing, but it was still the encounters with them which seemed at the time to offer the most possibility of an opening to the outside world.

Both came to Gleizes on the strength of his essay, *Spiritualité, rythme, forme*, written, we have seen, in December 1943 and published at the end of the war by the journal *Confluences*. We know something of the history of *Confluences* through the correspondence of Jean Chevalier; it started off in Lyon in 1940 as a proposal for a magazine to be called *Carrefour*. Chevalier had been invited to contribute, as had Burlet, and he had proposed an article on Gleizes's *Vie et mort de l'occident chrétien*. In March, the project had been changed to a monthly – *Disciplines* – owing to a shortage of paper. Chevalier was still invited, but since it was all on the themes of fatherland, Péguy, Claudel etc., he was doubtful if he should contribute to a review 'whose director, though full of enthusiasm and goodwill, is very far from our spirit'. By July, *Disciplines* had become *Confluences* – 'The title was imposed at Vichy' – which was to appear at very irregular intervals. Chevalier refers in December 1943 to the project of publishing a special issue wholly devoted to the plastic arts, and to the fact that Gleizes had been invited to contribute. In the event, this edition was not published until 1945, when it attracted a great deal of interest at a national level as a first glimpse of what French art after the war might be.[26]

Régine Pernoud had already published her book *Lumière du moyen âge* and had also taken a keen interest in modern art. She had visited a number of painters, including Hans Hartung, Manessier and Rouault, had taught history of art in the University of Aix-Marseilles and she envisaged giving a course in the history of modern art. She explained her project in her first letter to Gleizes in January 1946 and continued:

> So you can understand that the confirmation your article gives to views which I had built up intuitively was quite wonderful. Never before have I seen the relations between the two ages explained so clearly and your distinction between 'spatial periods' and 'rhythmic periods' seems to me to be essential to characterise what separates us at the present time from the Renaissance and from the centuries which followed it.[27]

Régine Pernoud was well connected in both academic and ecclesiastical circles and it seemed as though, through her, Gleizes's views could achieve a wide circulation. She told him in June 1946 that she had had to renounce the idea of writing an article on him because his ideas required a book: 'They enable us to uncover a whole collection of facts which, joined with what erudition has to offer, certainly constitute, as you yourself have said, a revolution in the history of art.' [28] It was through her that Gleizes entered into contact with the influential Dominican, Father Thomas de Romefort. She had written in April, copying an extract from a letter of de Romefort's, saying:

> I thank you for having brought Gleizes's article to my attention. It is very enlightening. I immediately plunged into the wallpaintings at St Savin. But what he says about painting is also true in other domains; I am currently trying to apply myself to 'rhythmic preaching'.[29]

When Gleizes went to speak at de Romefort's priory of St Maximin, she wrote that she was happy 'for these young brothers who are going to benefit (and will pass the benefit on to the Church) from so many ideas of which it is essential that the Church should become conscious'. In February, she herself was invited to speak in the Vatican and said that she hoped to speak about Gleizes.[30]

All this was very exciting, but we are tempted to ask what happened? The proposed book that was to explain the history of art in the light of Gleizes's teaching never appeared, and the correspondence peters out in 1948. Régine Pernoud wrote a great many books that have been widely read, but she rarely mentions Gleizes. A clue to the problem may be found in the piece she wrote on Gleizes for a special *Hommage* published in his honour in 1954, after his death. She praised him as one of the first to have pointed to the virtues of mediaeval art; his *Forme et Histoire* had been in advance of the work of the historians. The link between modern art and the sacred of which Gleizes was the prophet had now been realised in Matisse's chapel at Vence but Gleizes's own thought needed to be separated out from 'certain applications that were too narrow, too literal'.[31]

We may assume that the 'too narrow, too literal' application of Gleizes's thought refers to the precise idea that Gleizes wished to evoke with the word 'rhythm' which is what, apparently, initially attracted Régine Pernoud, but which she did not really understand, or which she rejected. Matisse's chapel at Vence is magnificent, but it is not 'rhythmic'; it remains, in Gleizes's termi-

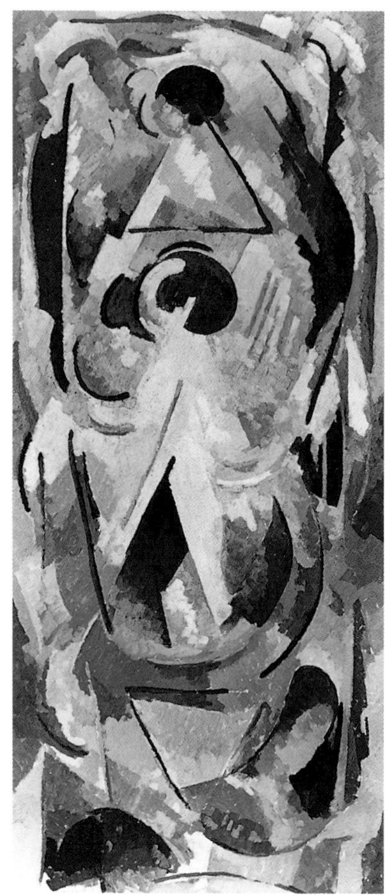

140. Jean Chevalier, *Etude à deux triangles*, 1955. Oil on canvas, 179 × 75 cm. Musée des Beaux Arts, Lyon

nology, 'spatial' – the eye is not put into movement. She admires Gleizes because he taught that there was a similarity between modern art in general and mediaeval art, but this was already becoming a cliché. She did not in the end accept what was specific to Gleizes's thinking.

More lasting was the connection with Dom Angelico Surchamp. The Benedictine Abbey of Ste Marie de la Pierre-qui-Vire is a nineteenth-century foundation situated in a wood in the Yonne region, not far from the great Romanesque basilica at Vézélay, and not far also from Clamecy, where Robert Pouyaud was living. Pouyaud had in fact visited it in the 1930s, when he went hoping to convert one of the monks, Dom Luc Lavergne 'whom I knew as a pupil of Maurice Denis. He was interested but still too much occupied to take up this new perspective'.[32] He described this visit in a letter to Gleizes written in 1934:

> Some time ago I went to rest myself for a few days in a Benedictine monastery situated in my region – Notre Dame de la Pierre-qui-Vire – a recent foundation, 1860. Godfather and godmother: Mr de Montalembert and Mme de Chatellier – an ideal situation in the gorges of the Morvan. I spoke of the things that are dear to us with the fathers and with the abbot, who is an extremely intelligent man. Even though I was disappointed to find that the monks had adopted modernism in the form of certain mechanical devices, I found that there was still something of true spirituality – really 'intelligence' seems to have found a refuge in these houses despite appearances to the contrary. The monks – even those of a modern tendency – are they not the only ones who are capable of preserving this sacred heritage? [As for the Gregorian chant, especially at night,] 'I couldn't even imagine such an exalted art . . .'[33]

Angelico Surchamp had entered the monastery in 1942, at the age of eighteen. His brother, Claude Jean-Nesmy, had been there since 1938. The difference in their names is explained by the fact that their father wrote popular novels under the nom-de-plume Jean Nesmy, which was then adapted by Claude. The abbot, Father Fulbert Gloriès, the same abbot Pouyaud had met, was a man of enterprise, living at a time when monasteries were being forced to justify themselves before the world, to raise funds to survive. During the war he encouraged Nesmy and some friends to launch a review, *Témoignages* (not at all connected with the Lyon group, Témoignage). In a letter to de Romefort, Nesmy explained this as a 'commitment to a rupture with the ivory tower'. [34] Chevalier had written to Gleizes in February 1944 on the subject of *Témoignages*: 'Even in the monasteries these days people turn out reviews; like the Pierre-qui-Vire. They talk about art and philosophy; they indulge in criticism and compile a review of the reviews. It is very profane and very regrettable.' [35] But Chevalier was soon to be writing for *Témoignages* himself.

Shortly before entering the monastery, the younger brother had spent some time with a sculptor, Henri Charlier, and, just before he took his final vows, the abbot wanted him to return to Charlier, presumably with a view to further diversifying the activities of the abbey. In the meantime, however, Surchamp had had an article published in *Témoignages* on Picasso. Despite the lack of enthusiasm the article displayed for Picasso, Charlier was annoyed by his failure to denounce modern art in all its forms and refused to take him unless he recanted. But Surchamp's interest in modern art had been further heightened by reading Gleizes's *Spiritualité, rythme, forme*. Obliged to choose, he decided that he wanted to go and work with Gleizes. His superiors raised no objections (it is possible that Pouyaud had prepared the way). As for Gleizes, as Surchamp put it without any exaggeration: 'in my desire to work with him, he saw a sign of Providence – a recognition of his painting by the Church since, in his eyes, in my person, it was the whole of the Benedictine Order that was coming to him!'

Surchamp spent a month with Gleizes in August 1946 and says that he found the experience very disorientating. He himself came from a conservative Catholic patriotic family. The Gleizes', for all their enthusiasm for the return to the soil and, in the case of Albert Gleizes, for the Church, were old anti-clericalist, anti-militarist, free-thinking Parisians. He describes Mme Gleizes in particular as 'inclining to Hinduism . . . or, rather, nihilist'. Nonetheless, his visit was a success and provided Surchamp with a whole programme of activities for his return to the monastery.[36]

By coincidence, Pouyaud, unaware of any of this, had gone back to La Pierre-qui-Vire and was there when Surchamp returned from Les Méjades. He wrote to Gleizes in September a letter that shows something of the almost excessive excitement of the moment:

> This year, after two months of exhausting work devoted to sculpting monuments to the glory of the Resistance in this region, I decided to go and rest for a few days in this same monastery and, still thinking about Dom Luc, I brought all my gouaches.
>
> You know what happened then – the meeting with Dom Angelico, who had just come back from St Rémy. Projects, talks, the establishment of a school etc . . . I thought I was dreaming!
>
> Since the day I met you, twenty-five years ago, I never doubted. I was sure that you had had a glimpse of the truth, and that it was necessary to work in this way despite all the opposition of the world about us. The contact, through R. Guénon, with the traditional sacred sciences, only confirmed the certainty . . .
>
> But a consecration was missing, a formal recognition, in a word, an initiation that has the force of authority. The great Benedictine family is offering us the possibility on a theological level. It is a first step, and we couldn't ask for anything better in the West.
>
> But we can hope, in the future, for a possible connection with the East, for the Pierre-qui-Vire has a foundation in Tonkin . . .[37]

Everything now seemed to suggest that a school of art based on Gleizes's principles was about to be formed under the auspices of one of the most influential Benedictine monasteries. Dom Angelico (he took his final vows in October 1946) opened a workshop – the Atelier de la Coeur Meurtry. *Témoignages* published a special study on Gleizes. And at Easter 1947, Pouyaud and Chevalier were invited to help Surchamp in painting a wall in the monastery chapel. Both had already had experience in wall-painting, using lime. Chevalier, indeed, had resigned his job as a teacher in April 1946 with a view to becoming a professional housepainter in accordance with Gleizes's insistence on the practice of a manual craft. Pouyaud had fallen so much out of touch with Gleizes's circle that it was only in January 1947 that he learned, through Surchamp, of Gleizes's reception into the Church.[38]

It would not be long, however, before this Benedictine idyll began to be disturbed. It very quickly became clear that Pouyaud's vision of 'an initiation that has the force of authority' into a 'Tradition' that went beyond the bounds of the Roman Catholic Church was not the idea of the Benedictines. And the very enthusiasm of the brothers, Dom Angelico and Dom Claude, was soon to arouse an old quarrel of which Gleizes had long been conscious and to which he had long attached a great importance – the quarrel between the Benedictine tradition and that of the Preaching Friars, the Dominicans, representatives of the thirteenth century and the opening of the 'spatial' age which, Gleizes hoped and believed, was coming to its end.

20

A CONTROVERSY OVER SACRED ART

In the immediate aftermath of the Second World War there was a widespread desire within the Roman Catholic Church for a change in the way in which the Church was presented to the world – a desire for greater openness and 'relevance' to the conditions of modern life. Its most radical expression in France was the 'worker-priest' movement – the movement of priests who, acutely aware of the divorce of working-class life from the Church, became workers, as indistinguishable as possible from their fellow workers, often actively engaged in the political struggles of the class led by the Communist Party.[1]

In art, the post-war period was characterised by a willingness to use well-known, sometimes controversial, artists, giving them considerable freedom, regardless of their own religious beliefs. The two names most prominently associated with this tendency were Fathers Marie-Alain Couturier and Pie Raymond Régamey, both Dominicans. They were to be behind the church at Assy, in the Haute Savoie, built between 1948 and 1950, with work by Léger, Lurçat, Matisse, Chagall, Bazaine and (especially controversial) a crucifix by Germaine Richier. They were also responsible for Matisse's chapel – realised for the Dominicans – at Vence (1948–51), and for Le Corbusier's church at Ronchamp (1955) and his Dominican priory at La Tourette (1960).[2]

A theory of modern art based on the teachings of Thomas Aquinas had already been worked out by Jacques Maritain in his *Art et scolastique*, published in 1920. In the Middle Ages, Maritain argues, the artist and the theologian – the two distinct disciplines of Beauty and Truth – worked together. The artist was set free from the theologian by the Renaissance which thereby rendered him at once the greatest and most miserable of men, delivered up to the search after Beauty in its own right, independent of theological truth. Though Maritain insists on a sharp distinction (which Gleizes would deny) between Truth and Beauty, Beauty is still a 'transcendental', it belongs to the divine order; but with the rise of the utilitarian order, the artist, longing for Beauty as an absolute end in itself, has become as superfluous and ridiculous a figure as the theologian or the saint. The nineteenth century saw the artist – or at least, in Maritain's conception, the poet, Baudelaire – attempting to reassert the transcendental nature of his art:

> When in an art gallery we leave the rooms of the Primitives for those which display the glories of oil-painting and a much more considerable material science, the foot advances over the floor but the soul sinks to the depths. It had been taking the air on the everlasting hills; it is now on the boards of a theatre – a magnificent theatre. In the sixteenth century, deceit installed itself in painting, which began to like science for its own sake and to give the illu-

> sion of nature, to make us believe that in front of a picture we were in front of a landscape or the subject painted, not in front of a picture.[3]

This states a position that was common ground to a wide range of artists, particularly those interested in religious art. It was a basic idea of the Benedictine school of Beuron in Germany, and of the French 'Nabis', the admirers of Gauguin, among them Maurice Denis whom Maritain quotes to the effect that a painted figure should look like a painted figure and not like a real figure. In England, it could have been written by Eric Gill, who was involved in the publication of the first English edition of *Art et scolastique* and whose own thought was strongly influenced by it. It could have been written by Gino Severini, who was to become a friend of Maritain's and whose *Du Cubisme au classicisme* is referred to favourably in a footnote in the later editions. It could have been written by Gleizes, especially prior to the 1920s and his discovery of the crucial difference between the rhythmic art prior to the twelfth century and the spatial art which followed it. But the passage continues with what is most probably a reference, very unfavourable, to Gleizes's and Metzinger's *Du 'Cubisme'*:

> Does Cubism in our day, despite its tremendous deficiencies, represent the still stumbling, screaming childhood of an art once more pure? The barbarous dogmatism of its theorists compels the strongest doubts and an apprehension that the new school may be endeavouring to set itself absolutely free from naturalist imitation only to become immoveably fixed in *stultae quaestiones*. . . .

A footnote explains that *stultae quaestiones* (the formula is taken by Thomas from Paul's Epistle to Titus, 3:9) 'are such as, if raised in any science or discipline, would run contrary to the first conditions implied by that very same discipline.' Maritain does not say what particular *stultae quaestiones* he has in mind but it is interesting to see here exactly the objection that the Dominicans would raise against Gleizes in the late 1940s: he was bothering his head with questions that did not concern him and were best left in the hands of professional philosophers and theologians.

Any mistrust that the Thomist theoricians may have felt for Gleizes was returned abundantly. In a letter written in 1929 to a Benedictine monk whom I have not been able to identify, Gleizes gave his own opinion of the movement associated with the name of Maritain. Nowadays, he said, many intellectuals were feeling a need to return to religion:

> But by what door do they think of entering in? By the easiest, that which demands the least by way of renunciation, the least humility, that in which, on the very threshold, all the intellectual values of the urban university are to be found, where Aristotle's philosophy rules supreme, where they are taught, as a priest told me one day, seeming to think it the most natural thing in the world, that in Heaven St Augustine barely touches St Thomas' ankle. In a word, the Dominican door . . .
>
> The real door . . . that will open on the order of St Benedict, exclusively theological and for that very reason guardian of a way of doing things that is living, in accordance with the scale of magnitudes of the individual – work with the hands as the necessary complement to intellectual work, authority given to the agricultural countryside and restoration of monastic schools in

which culture and technique are defined so well in the two categories of the *trivium* and *quadrivium*.

He cited the work done by the Benedictines in the nineteenth century on music – the development of plainsong – at the abbeys of Solesmes and Farnborough, and in painting (he presumably has in mind the School of Beuron):

> These efforts interest those who are nowadays called Thomists up to a certain point, but beyond that point these latter are no longer capable of grasping anything; and this can be understood, it seems to me, by those who are aware of the conditions imposed by their doctrine of non-renunciation. The future, insofar as it is in the hands of men, belongs to the Augustinians, of that there can be no doubt. Thomism is a step backwards, a timorous intellectual gesture; to go towards St Augustine is to go forward, an act of confidence and intelligence. . . .[4]

Gleizes's attitude towards Thomas was a little moderated in the 1930s, perhaps through his contact with Coomaraswamy who had a sharp eye for good quotations from him. But his basic idea remains constant. Thomas is of the thirteenth century, which is the period when the essentially theological view of the world associated with the Benedictines was giving way to a more intellectual and philosophical view of the world, associated with the Dominicans. The theological view attached more importance to the experience of form, to movement and rhythm; while the philosophical view attached more importance to the observation of external appearances (whose internal movement had necessarily to be slowed down to allow the observation to be made). The difference was easily discernible in the plastic arts and it is in the thirteenth century, not in the Renaissance – not even between the early Renaissance (the 'primitives') and later Renaissance – that it occurs.

•

In the post-war period, Gleizes was involved in a controversy with the Dominican and, consequently, Thomist Père Régamey. Régamey and Couturier ran a journal, *Art sacré* (founded in 1935 as *Cahiers de l'art sacré*. It changed its name at the beginning of 1947). In June 1945, Gleizes submitted his article *L'Arc en ciel, clé de l'art chrétien médiéval* – written in December 1943, at the same time as *Spiritualité, rythme, forme*. Régamey replied in March 1946, apologising for his lateness, saying that the article did not fit into the journal's programme and raising some objections to Gleizes's line of thought. He thought that Gleizes exaggerated:

> I very much liked your considerations on experience and, in particular, the distinction you make: 'Experience is an intimate participation with the living object; observation a distant, subjective appreciation. Everything that is produced by the fruit of experience is blessed: it is life.' But I do not think one can add: 'Everything that is produced with the combinations that are proposed by observation is damned: it is death.'[5]

The letter is still courteous and respectful. Régamey gave a lecture in Brussels in 1947 on *Les Principes d'un véritable renouveau de l'art sacré* in which he defended the use of non-figurative art:

> Some of the best among contemporary artists – for example Gleizes, Bazaine, Manessier – have made for themselves, in virtue of a real necessity of their nature, plastic languages whose eminent spiritual qualities will be recognised by our nephews. Unfortunately, such forces remain unused by the Church because we have thought about art only in the most narrowly didactic manner.[6]

Gleizes had a short article – a reply to a questionnaire – published in *Art sacré* which, discreet and polite as it is, could be read as a challenge to Régamey's programme. It states a doctrine of 'two kingdoms' – the kingdom of this world and the kingdom that is not of this world. This is a new element in Gleizes's terminology and we may see in it that he has abandoned all hope for the foreseeable future in the establishment of a 'spiritual authority' on earth. The kingdom of this world is the kingdom of space and time; the kingdom that is not of this world is the kingdom of eternity. The ambition of the Christian is to bring the two into harmony. At present, in Gleizes's eyes, the dis-harmony between them is total:

> It is, then, in the re-establishment of a religious state of mind – *religare*, to bring together – that the harmony between the two kingdoms can be achieved. First of all, incarnate man has to find himself again, to recognise [*reconnaître*] himself and to be reborn [*renaître*] through water and the spirit.[7] That is the urgent problem that faces us today. Its not a question of adapting oneself for good or ill to an existing political or economic state of affairs, but of posing questions as to the worth, human and divine, of this state of affairs, and of asking clearly: this state of affairs – is it a progress or a frightful deviation?

Under these circumstances:

> I can see no trace of anything sacred in what is called 'contemporary art'. Subjective opinions on spectacles or appearances, timid or daring, all products of individualism. Consequently subject to no traditional principle and standing in no relation to what is the necessary determinant of any religious manifestation and the more to what is its crowning glory – the sacred. . . .[8]

This is implicitly an attack on Régamey's desire to incorporate 'contemporary art' into church building which Gleizes would also see as a matter of 'adapting oneself for good or ill to an existing political or economic state of affairs'. The disapproval of Régamey's venture in Gleizes's circle can be seen in a letter from Chevalier to Gleizes in April 1947, after a visit to the Pierre-qui-Vire: 'Père Régamey . . . shows in numbers of his review architectures which, he says, show what must be done to help bring about a spiritual renewal but which, in reality – this is what Pére Claude [Nesmy] thinks and I think – would be just as suitable for secular schools or administrative offices.'[9]

Gleizes's piece in *Art sacré* also implies that the Church itself is implicated in the general 'deviation'. The article begins by insisting that insofar as it is part of the kingdom that is not of this world, insofar as it participates in the nature of eternity, 'on the supernatural plane', the Church is 'as pure as it was on the first day.' But, though Gleizes does not spell it out, this does not imply any infallibility on the part of the Church as a human institution, and there is an implicit assumption that the Church's own idea of itself is wrong. In his *Souvenirs* he says that the Church must die to be reborn.[10] We may remember Père Jérôme's annoyance at Gleizes's telling him: 'the whole of theology has to be taken up again'.

In 1947, Régamey had intervened with an article in the journal *Arts*, replying to two previous articles, one by Michaud, the other by Nesmy, which had presented Gleizes's painting as 'the traditional religious way' (Michaud), a way which 'can be taught' (Nesmy), and which the Church had to take on board if it was to be seriously interested in a renewal of sacred art. Régamey said he admired Gleizes's work 'very sincerely, but moderately' but complained that 'in singing the praises of Gleizes's system as the sacred art par excellence, because it is something that can be taught, we are being led back into a new academic painting, all the more disturbing because it is abstruse'.[11]

Jean Chevalier had two encounters with Régamey towards the end of 1947, both at exhibitions held in Lyon under the auspices of Marcel Michaud's group, Nouvel Art, in the Chapel of the Lycée Ampère, a former Jesuit seminary. The first was an exhibition of sacred art, one of a series organised throughout France by Régamey which included Gleizes's 1935 *Crucifixion*. The second was an exhibition devoted to Gleizes himself. Chevalier thought at the end of the first encounter that, on the whole, Régamey was well-disposed to Gleizes even if he didn't understand the 'living "mechanism" of the traditional language' and was suspicious of what he understood, wrongly in Chevalier's eyes, as Gleizes's symbolism and esotericism.

Gleizes's exhibition, held at the end of the year, was perhaps the biggest single exhibition ever held of his work during his own lifetime (the catalogue lists eighty paintings and fifty-nine gouaches and drawings, but Chevalier made an inventory which showed 115 paintings and 109 gouaches and drawings[12]). Chevalier gave talks at it every Sunday and on one of those Sundays, Régamey came down from Dijon, where his own Art Sacré exhibition was showing, and there was a major row – a 'bagarre' as Chevalier puts it. Régamey called Gleizes's painting 'dessicated academicism' and said that:

> the craft you talk about isn't 'the craft', with a universal value – but your own conception of the craft, that there is also Braque's craft, Picasso's craft, Manessier's craft etc etc . . . and finally that you betray the Romanesque painters, putting things into their works which are not there at all or only just sketched (for example in the Saint Savin wall-painting reproduced in the catalogue, the curve which becomes the fold of the garment . . .).[13]

Perhaps Régamey had been provoked by the fact that Michaud's programme for the Chapelle du Lycée Ampère – Régamey's exhibition followed by Gleizes's exhibition – looked like a problem (the incoherence of contemporary religious art) followed by a solution. This was certainly Michaud's own opinion. Also the catalogue, under the title *Le Cubisme et son dénouement dans la tradition*, included two articles by Surchamp, originally published in *Témoignages*, on this theme of Gleizes's painting as the traditional craft. The confrontation was to continue at the beginning of 1948 when *Arts* devoted a page to articles by Michaud, Nesmy and Gleizes, followed by a long article by Régamey in *Art Sacré* on the meaning of the word 'tradition'.

This turns into a polemical attack on Gleizes's *Homocentrisme*, in particular on all that Gleizes has to say about the 'temporal' nature of painting. The concept has no meaning for Régamey, for whom painting is uniquely spatial. He is therefore annoyed by Gleizes's insistence on the movement of the eye as necessary to painting as a support for contemplation:

> Gleizes does not want the contemplative, placing himself at the necessary distance, to embrace the whole of the painting with a single glance. That is a passive and profane attitude. As for us, we find every day that it can be eminently contemplative. But no! this eye must wander and turn about the surface, following the directions of the cadence to finish up at rest in the 'rhythm' of Eternity.[14]

Régamey's failure to be impressed by what must have been a wonderful exhibition can indeed be explained by Gleizes's argument on the two modes of activity of the eye – the static eye and the eye in movement. The static eye is simply unable to follow the cadences and directions – it can only experience them as Régamey experienced Gleizes's work – a too great, too intellectual, profusion of confusing details.

Introducing an article on Romanesque art in 1945, Régamey had criticised the author (a Benedictine, as it happens) for his view that Romanesque painting went beyond the image to arrive at the 'idea'. Régamey evoked by way of contrast 'our present day taste for a painting that would be like a cry . . .'.[15] What impressed him in Romanesque art was the apparent liberty with which the figurative subject was treated and this is what he missed in Gleizes – a subject deformed under the pressure of great emotion. We may note in passing that Régamey's idea does not correspond with that of Maritain. Maritain maintained the idea of Beauty as an existing objective reality and where, as we have seen, Maritain looks to the early Renaissance, before the development of oil painting, Régamey endorses everything in painting except the 'academic' style which he confuses with all attempts to formulate clear-cut principles. He is as opposed to the School of Beuron, to Sérusier and to an interesting little group formed round the Greek painter Praxitele Zographos as he is to Gleizes (we may, perhaps, wonder at his support for the extremely dogmatic Le Corbusier). His thinking corresponds to that of the champions of 'independent' art against the academy at the end of the nineteenth century.

•

Also in 1948, and after a long conversation with Régamey, Thomas de Romefort wrote to Gleizes offering to preserve his thought from 'an exaggeration which could seriously compromise its effectiveness'. We have seen Régine Pernoud telling Gleizes of the enthusiasm of the Dominican Père de Romefort for *Spiritualité, rythme, forme*, and for the distinction it draws between 'spatial' and 'rhythmic' – knowledge through spectacle and knowledge through act. De Romefort visited Les Méjades in the Summer of 1946, and Gleizes gave a talk in his priory at St Maximin the following winter.[16] Thereafter, their relations had begun to deteriorate – a deterioration that, on a much more 'intellectual' level, resembles the deterioration of Gleizes's relations with Père Jérôme.

De Romefort wrote defending Thomas Aquinas and, in so doing, he was defending the appearances of the external world:

> You confuse 'accessible to the senses' [*sensible*] and 'sensual'. So, you're right to react against the art of the Renaissance which is sensual, but you are wrong not to admit, in between the sensual and the spiritual, that which is accessible to the senses [*le sensible*] or, if you like, the spiritual incarnate [to which Gleizes added a question mark and an exclamation mark – PB] . . .
>
> [Thomas] was the first to show the existence of the spiritual in what is accessible to the senses. What is created is not for him just a reflection of the Spirit, no, there is also the spiritual in what is created itself . . . This vision of the Universe will be expressed plastically in Christian sacred art by figurative works, and even by works that are fully realist, such as the Christ on the cross . . .
>
> No, Père Régamey is not an aesthete. He is – a Dominican. He belongs to the thirteenth century. You jump right over the thirteenth century and want to start again at the ninth. He says to you: 'No. Take account of the *progress* which the tradition which you love realised in the thirteenth century. He is right. As a Dominican I stand by him . . .
>
> Without knowing it, you are opening up an old dispute – that of the Augustinians against the Thomists. But, don't forget, I tell it to you politely, that the Popes and, consequently, Catholicity, have opted for St Thomas.[17]

In his biography of Augustine of Hippo, Henry Chadwick remarks that he sees the world uniquely in terms of a confrontation between Man and God. The only phenomenon that interests him is consciousness, human or divine – he nowhere represents 'nature' as a subject worthy of study in its own right, independent of consciousness.[18] Where we think of consciousness as an epiphenomenon of matter, Augustine thought of matter as an epiphenomenon of consciousness (created by God). The enthusiasts for Thomas Aquinas (G. K. Chesterton, for one) argue that he, in a sense, 'discovered' nature as a subject of study, or at least rediscovered it through Aristotle and Averroës. He still understands Nature as having been created by God and therefore as embodying divine laws which can be studied within it. The long-term tendency of Oxford Nominalism, personified by Roger Bacon, was to study it in its own right as a mechanism which contains within itself its own sufficient explanation. For Gleizes, Thomas, by the mere fact of offering nature as a subject of study, external to Man, was preparing the way for the Nominalists. Thus, Gleizes had offended de Romefort earlier by saying that Thomas was 'the prototype of the modern age'.[19] Or, alternatively, Thomas was making concessions to a new order whose advance was inevitable in order to maintain something of the old. De Romefort had protested: 'No. St Thomas is not the defender of a tradition that is vanishing . . .'.

Gleizes, then, was very well aware that he was renewing the old case made by the Augustinians against Aquinas. He believed that we were living the thirteenth century in reverse. In the thirteenth century, the Augustinians had been obliged to give way to the Thomists and the Thomists eventually had to give way to the Nominalists. But now the Nominalists had to give way to the Thomists and the Thomists to the Augustinians. This was not a matter of winning intellectual arguments, and still less of papal directives. It was a matter of recovering the internal life which is common to all things and which is known not through observation or through a commentary on what is accessible to the senses but through an active participation. De Romefort, like Régamey, was unable to see that there was a rhythmic principle in Christian art until the twelfth century, which stops in the thirteenth century. De Romefort's own eye was stopped and he was himself, therefore – for all his goodwill and admiration for Gleizes's 'central intuition', as he calls it, of Actor against Spectator – the proof of the inadequacy of the purely intellectual, Dominican, Thomist formation that he was trying to defend: the 'rhetorician with white hands'. Gleizes must have felt that this was proved definitively when, at the end of his letter, de Romefort raised a series of objections to Gleizes's way of understanding the 'glories', the 'haloes', the great circles that surround the heads of the saints in Romanesque painting.

Gleizes had said in *Spiritualité, rythme, forme* that the halo:

> is the transformation of the figure predetermined by the shape of the head. Through its circularity, it immediately takes control of the to-ing and fro-ing of the cadences which are generated by the different directions established by the extensions in space. It adds an ever so slightly troubling element to the supreme purity of the rhythm. The halo confirms the gloriole and, unhesitatingly, it blends into it.[20]

De Romefort says:

> Above all, can it not be explained purely and simply by the habit the painters have of placing a 'centre of delight' in their works or, even more simply, by the desire to isolate the person represented and draw attention to him, in the way that a teacher does on a blackboard, putting a circle round an important word. . . .

21
THE QUARREL OVER GUÉNON

One of the reasons for Régamey's hostility to Gleizes had been a suspicion that perhaps he was not a Christian at all – that the 'tradition' which Gleizes wished to renew, if it was not a figment of his own imagination, was the 'tradition' evoked by René Guénon, a metaphysical system thought to be the real foundation underpinning all the major religions and transmitted from one generation to the next through a secret process of initiation. The question of the relations between Gleizes's thought and that of Guénon was soon to produce a serious rupture among Gleizes's small group of followers, and particularly between Dom Angelico Surchamp and Robert Pouyaud.

We have already seen how, partly on Pouyaud's initiative, Gleizes had become very interested in Guénon in the 1930s, how he promoted Guénon in his own circle and warmly recommended him, together with Coomaraswamy, in *Homocentrisme*. We know also that Gleizes did indeed see the fundamental distinguishing characteristics of 'sacred art' – the static measure of the straight lines; the mobile cadence of the spiral and of the succession of colours; and the eventual unifying form/rhythm – as common to all the great religious traditions, even if it was specifically the Christian Celtic and Romanesque tradition that he usually evoked. We know that Gleizes greatly appreciated Guénon's critique of modern civilisation given in his *Crise du monde moderne* and *Orient et occident*. He shared Guénon's view that societies, like everything else that is alive, develop in cycles – and that a long period in which the society is structured by a religious idea is followed by a shorter period of increasing religious chaos; that our society is in the last phase of such a period of religious chaos, necessarily heading for destruction; and that the task of those aware of the situation was to rediscover and reaffirm the principles on which a new religious culture could evolve.

Gleizes had re-established contact with Guénon as soon as possible after the Liberation and had offered to collaborate with Guénon's publisher, Chacornac, an offer Guénon accepted, though nothing seems to have come of it.[1] As we have seen, it was through Guénon's circle, through Coomaraswamy and Marco Pallis, respectively a Hindu and a Buddhist, that Gleizes's *Vie et mort de l'occident chrétien* was published in England. Guénon's *La Règne de la quantité* was published in October 1945. It was full of ideas that could be expected to appeal to Gleizes, not least the idea expressed in the title itself – that our age is obsessed with quantity, with whatever is measurable or quantifiable, to the exclusion of quality. The distinction between what can be measured and what cannot be measured had been fundamental to Gleizes since *Du 'Cubisme'* and had evolved into his way of understanding the distinction between space and time, the static and the mobile. His essay of 1931, *Art et production*, had been based on a distinction between quality and quantity, a terminology he had attributed to Guiglielmo Ferrero.

La Règne de la quantité was published by the highly influential publisher Gallimard. In the 1920s and 1930s, Guénon's work had been known only to a very small circle, but in the aftermath of the war he became fashionable, to the extent that in 1952, even André Breton was to express his admiration, though *La Règne de la quantité* subjects the confusion between the psychological and the spiritual – which is certainly how Guénon would have understood Surrealism – to withering criticism.[2] Gleizes wrote to Guénon to congratulate him on his book and Guénon replied:

> We are certainly fully agreed on the essential. I thought we could date the start of the modern deviation from the beginning of the fourteenth century, or at least that we could see its manifestation already appearing in certain fields; but you trace it back a century earlier. What would interest me would be to know rather more precisely what are the signs of naturalism you find in the cathedrals from the thirteenth century onwards; and also, in your opinion, how that can be reconciled with the fact that the builders of these cathedrals still unquestionably possessed a knowledge of certain things both of the distinct nature of initiation and of that of the traditional sciences. . . .[3]

This disagreement over the fourteenth or the thirteenth century indicates a very profound difference in approach which Gleizes was to discuss at some length with Pouyaud. Between the twelfth and thirteenth centuries a play of lines and colours that put the eye in movement had given way to a play of lines and colours that evoke the appearances of the natural world. The folds of the garments in the paintings and sculptures which had been organised in such a way as to contribute to the unifying rhythm of the whole painted or sculpted area became an imitation of the folds of the garments agitated by the wind or evoking the shape of the body underneath. For Gleizes this change was much more fundamental than any change in intellectual ideas. For Guénon, the intellectual idea, the metaphysical structure, was the foundation stone of all the rest. Thus it is sufficient that a correct understanding of his traditional doctrine is conveyed in the symbols and numerical proportions used by the artists. For Gleizes by contrast it is the 'cast of mind' that counts, and this is expressed at a much more fundamental level in the act of the artist than in anything – symbolism, metaphysical argument or whatever – that can be expressed in words.

•

Dom Angelico spent another month with Gleizes at Les Méjades in Autumn 1947 and, on his return, he visited Moly Sabata where he began an extraordinary and rich friendship with Anne Dangar. She, after long hesitations, had finally decided to stay in France, at least for the moment, and therefore to build her own pottery and kiln, since she could no longer bear the emotional trials and long journeys involved in working in the pottery at the neighbouring town of Roussillon. She had just had the kiln completed when Dom Angelico arrived and he placed with her an important order for objects to be used for the worship at La Pierre-qui-Vire. Catastrophically for Anne Dangar, who had invested a small inheritance she had received from an aunt in Australia as well as money she had borrowed from friends (a thing she hated doing but was obliged to do for the whole length of her period in France), the first four firings at Moly Sabata were spoilt – especially the second, which included the work she had done for La Pierre-qui-Vire. According to her friends among the local potters, the holes in the roof were too small, with the result that smoke turned back into the kiln and darkened the pottery. The problem was eventually resolved but, as a result of the time and money she had lost, she was obliged to take on a large job decorating a cinema in Serrières. At the same time, Gleizes was driving her to undertake a large project of thirty plates based on her own and on his designs for an exhibition of his work in Paris. She complained to Dom Angelico that Gleizes was always talking about the importance of the crafts, but that he had no idea of what the potter's craft involved:

> He's asked for impossibilities in a letter I received this week. To make, fire, wrap up and send these thirty pieces of pottery before the First April! He hasn't commissioned them – I have to find the money to have them fired and to send them to Paris: if they sell we will share the profits between us! While waiting, my commissions have to wait, my debts aren't paid, and how am I to live? Don't tell him about all that, please, father – he'll never understand and he'll be cross with me for gossiping. I can't do two firings before April, and I can't put more than eight of his pieces in the first firing which is still going to be an experiment. Every day the water in my workshop is frozen. I can't begin to turn until it has stopped freezing. But Mr Gleizes refuses to listen to these problems, problems which are of the nature of the craft: 'You can do it. Perform miracles!'[4]

> You have to juggle with the heavy plate on the palm of the left hand and let the colour flow from the beak of the little pot held in the right hand. It is above all through the movements of the left hand that the design is made with the thick flowing colour. Imagine the tension on the nerves while this work is being done! The colour flows too fast, it flows everywhere, or the beak is blocked up – you have to blow on it or suck it (copper oxide is a poison, but I forget that in these crucial moments), tap it – and at night the left hand is so tired.[5]

At the end of all that she was insulted by the owner of the gallery where the exhibition was being held:

> Mlle des Garets does not like my work at all. She acknowledged the reception of some pieces that had been sent from 'Folklore' [Marcel Michaud's gallery at Lyon] and told me that she couldn't show the two pieces signed by me and that she was suspicious that one of the plates was not based on a design by Gleizes: 'You must understand, Mademoiselle, that I have a very elegant gallery in Paris and that I am determined to maintain a certain class and presentation of high quality.' Actually, all the four pieces were decorated following my designs not Gleizes's. It was Mr Gleizes who asked me to send fifteen pieces with his designs and fifteen with mine. It was because of Mr Gleizes that I neglected all my orders, put off all the work I had intended to do, and it was he who told me what was required. I decided over eighteen years ago to turn my back on the 'very elegant galleries' of the big cities and

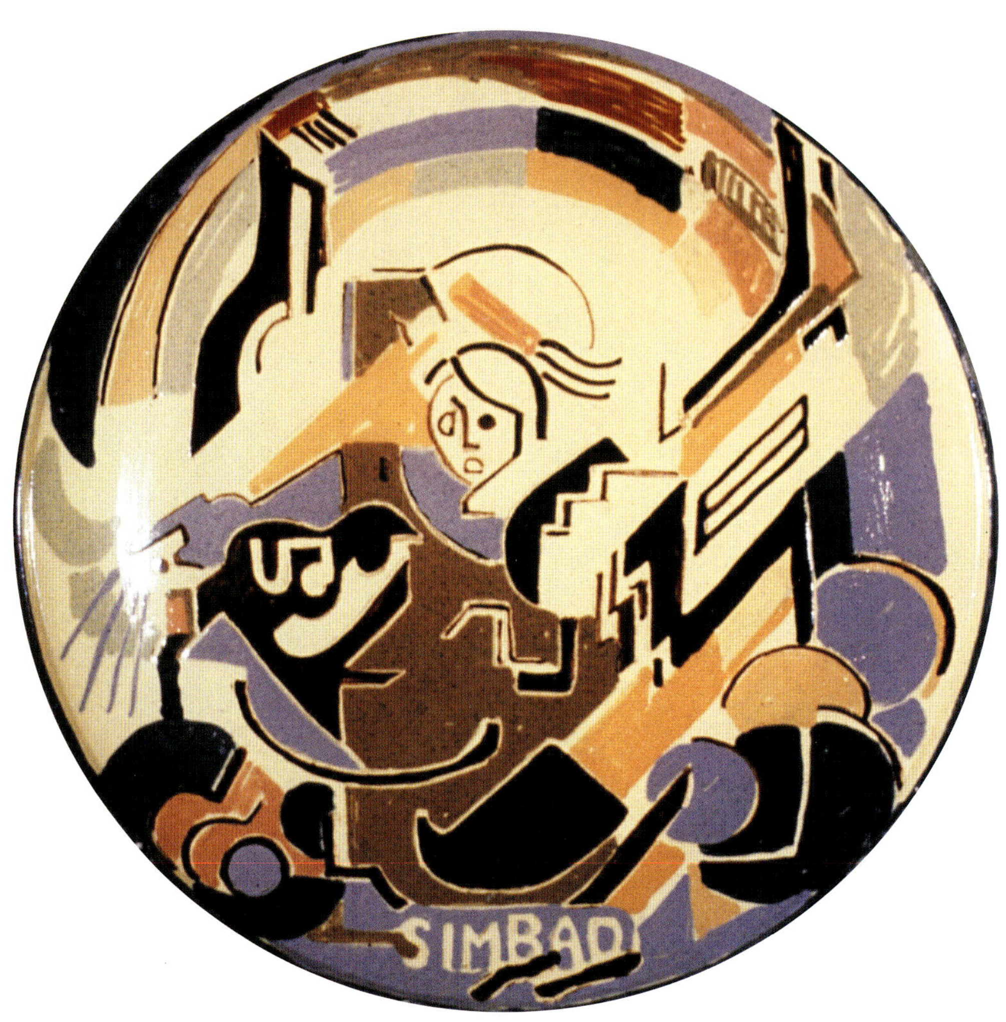

141. Anne Dangar, Plate - '*Simbad*', 1947–8 (?). Glazed earthenware with slip decoration, dia. 48.7 cm. Fondation Albert Gleizes

> there's nothing that annoys me more than being obliged to work for these exhibitions. I always do it only for Mr and Mme Gleizes, and I assure you that it is always a great loss for me. . . .[6]

Nonetheless, it should be said that these demands on Gleizes's part obliged Anne Dangar to work at a level that would not have been possible if all her time had been spent sensibly fulfilling the orders that enabled her to gain a livelihood. The plates in question, some of which are still in the possession of the Fondation Albert Gleizes – since they were not to the taste of Mlle des Garets' very elegant clientele – are among her masterpieces (Plate 141).

Perhaps Anne Dangar's frank way of speaking encouraged a similar frankness on the part of Dom Angelico. He was ordained priest in May 1948 and, as part of his training, he was studying theology. Increasingly he began to complain about what he felt was Gleizes's rather cavalier use of theological terms:

> If you continue to interpret the Bible as you do at present, on the basis of pure personal judgment, you will be acting as a Protestant without intending to do so – as, for a Catholic, it is always necessary to refer to tradition and to the teaching authority which – and its not really your fault – you sometimes fail

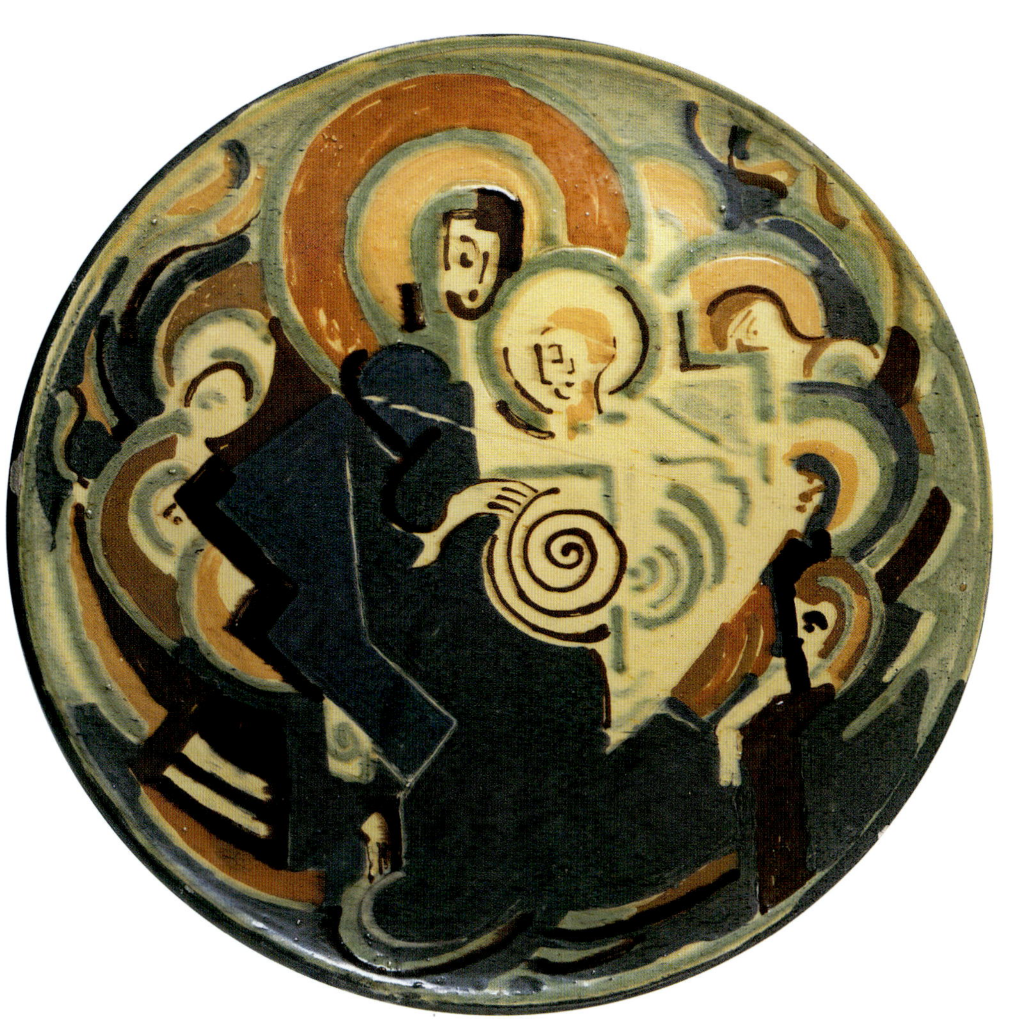

142. Anne Dangar, Plate – *Virgin and Child Surrounded by Angels*, 1942 (?), dia. 44.5 cm. Musée des Beaux Arts, Lyon. Gift of Jean Chevalier

to recognise . . . This is the enormous reproach that has to be made against Guénon. He wants to find tradition again but, right from the start, he refuses to consult it. Hence the interpretations of the Bible in an anti-Catholic sense on the pretext that the Bible must be in accord with the Vedas, the Vedantas etc. For us this is inadmissible. For us, the Catholic tradition is to be found with the Fathers of the Church as tradition in the plastic arts is to be found in Romanesque art, and we don't judge Romanesque art in relation to Hindu art but in relation to the Fathers of the Church. It is this difference in fact that divides us. It is immense because it is the whole passage from the natural to the supernatural. The Hindu religion is natural, the Catholic religion supernatural. It is a matter of faith – the incarnation of the Word in human nature cannot be proved. The Catholic theologian . . . can do no more than admire a fact that only faith enables him to perceive . . . A Romanesque painter wasn't a theologian. He gave himself into the care of those whose craft was theology . . . I tremble a bit to see you undermining our position before we have yet had time to consolidate it. That the craft of the painter can produce repercussions in theology, a theological formation, is – as a Catholic – impossible to maintain, as art is always part of the natural domain . . . while theology belongs to the supernatural, that is to say the revealed, domain. . . .[7]

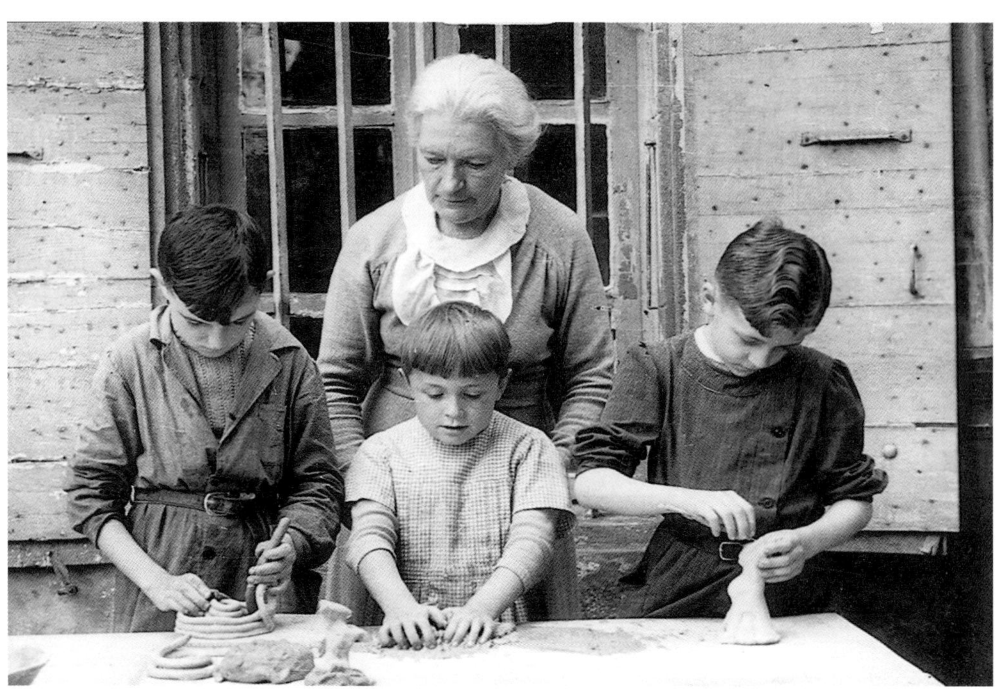

143. Anne Dangar with members of her class at Moly Sabata

Gleizes's theological speculations had been all very well, Dom Angelico thought, while he was alone in the world, but now there was a team about him, each of whom had their own speciality. Gleizes should leave theology to the theologians. It was, in fact, much the same argument as de Romefort's and even, though Dom Angelico was very hostile to him, Régamey's. Indeed the insistence that 'art is always part of the natural domain', quite separate from the domain of theology, is reminiscent of Maritain. It is a Thomist argument and indicates that, for all the apparent opposition between the Benedictines and the Dominicans, the theological formation Dom Angelico was receiving was Thomist. It belonged to the thirteenth century. For Gleizes it was axiomatic that the real meaning of theology had progressively been lost by the theologians, and that the thirteenth century had been the starting point of the process.

The theologians had long been engaged in a purely intellectual speculation divorced from real, everyday experience. It was thus that the most fundamental doctrines – the Trinity, the Incarnation, the Resurrection of the Body – had become matters of pure faith, to be marvelled at from a distance. Gleizes believed that, through his experience as a painter, he had rediscovered them as living realities (and if they were expressed as living realities in other religions in other terms so much the better).

•

Over the next few years, in his 'Atelier de la Coeur Meurtry', begun in early 1948 before his ordination, Dom Angelico laid the foundations of what was to become the remarkable adventure of the publishing house, Zodiaque. It was, of course, not to learn Gleizes's theology that the Abbot of the Pierre-qui-

Vire had sent him to Les Méjades, but to pick up enough of the rudiments of artistic practice to launch a venture that would have some possibility of commercial success. The Pierre-qui-Vire was also establishing a model farm, pioneering, among other things, the use of artificial insemination in animal husbandry. 'Poor Benedictines!', as Pouyaud would later remark. Against the probabilities it was, eventually, Zodiaque that was to prove the more successful venture,[8] but that was still in the future. During this early period, after his second visit to Les Méjades in 1947, Dom Angelico had very little contact with Gleizes. He had much more with Pouyaud, who lived in the region, and their relations, as reflected in their letters to Gleizes, were stormy. Expressions of outrage alternated on both sides with expressions of mutual affection and respect. Both felt deeply hurt when Gleizes failed to write to them. Dom Angelico in particular complained that Gleizes had never expressed any interest in his workshop, even though he was, he protested, faithful to Gleizes's principles and was initiating new people, such as the painter and sculptor, Marc Heinard, into them.[9]

A particular crisis blew up in 1949 with Pouyaud's publication of a little study, *Du 'Cubisme' à la peinture traditionelle*. This combined an exposition of Gleizes's practical principles of painting with passages on the symbolism of forms, numbers and colours which were much closer to Guénon, the whole presented in the impersonal and precise manner of a technical handbook. Both Gleizes and Guénon wrote to congratulate him, and Guénon's appreciation is worth noting since, for all his liking for Gleizes, it is by no means obvious why the great opponent of 'the modern deviation' should accept the argument that elements of the lost tradition had been rediscovered through Cubism. Pouyaud indicated that he was quite relieved by Guénon's praise – 'he who, all the same, is always ready to engage in acid criticism'. But Dom Angelico was far from sharing the general enthusiasm:

> My pamphlet has caused quite a stir at the Pierre-qui-Vire. Angelico wrote to me and, virulently, he condemns the ideas, the book and even the technique, he finds it too uncompromising, he won't allow the symbol in its pure form, nor a painting that has no reminders of anthropomorphic forms such as they exist in the memory. He won't allow the existence of a Tradition that is unanimous outside of the Catholic tradition. . . .[10]

Pouyaud during this period was gathering around him a group of sympathisers, including a priest, the Abbé Nicolas Boon, who shared 'our ideas and practices painting following our technique'. Two camps were beginning to develop, with Pouyaud and the Lyon painter, René Maria Burlet, in the 'Guénonian' camp and Dom Angelico and, increasingly, Anne Dangar, in the 'Catholic' camp. From Gleizes's point of view both could be seen as far too hypnotised by the symbol, whether the symbol 'in its pure form' – the circle, the swastika, the spiral – as Pouyaud wanted, or the Catholic symbolism that Dom Angelico wanted. The symbol presents an idea and it was not ideas that were needed, but acts.

While Pouyaud was becoming ever more insistent on the inseparability of Gleizes's 'traditional painting' and the esoteric philosophy of René Guénon, Dom Angelico seemed, in Gleizes's eyes, to be becoming ever more worldly in his writings on art. In the April 1949 *Témoignages* he published a 'Note sur l'art abstrait' which did not mention Gleizes, and an article on 'Picasso and the future of Modern Art' which approved Picasso's neo-classicism, his pottery, and even his eroticism. 'The sumptuousness of a Miro or that of a Picasso is all the more true the more it is simple . . .'. 'Picasso launches us into the mobile . . .'.[11] Surchamp was reading an enormous amount of literature on modern art and reviewing it without any clear reference to the body of ideas he claimed to be defending. This tendency came to a head in Gleizes's eyes with an article in which he praised the book on Juan Gris by Gleizes's old enemy D-H. Kahnweiler.[12] For Gleizes this was almost proof that the Pierre-qui-Vire was selling out, and was accommodating itself to the tastes of the artistic establishment. Dom Angelico seemed, like Régine Pernoud, to have succumbed to the charms of 'modern art' in general, and no longer to be committed to what was specific in Gleizes's teaching. It was this feeling that lay behind a quarrel that blew up between Gleizes and Dom Angelico in 1950.

Dom Angelico had written at the beginning of the year to say that he proposed organising a reunion at the Pierre-qui-Vire of all the growing band of young artists who claimed to be working according to Gleizes's principles. Gleizes approved the project and Dom Angelico sent invitations in May for the end of July, a time, he later said, that had been chosen by Gleizes himself. At the beginning of July he received a letter from Gleizes refusing to come, saying he was tired, and citing the Kahnweiler article as proof that Dom Angelico had abandoned him.

Gleizes was indeed tired. He had just completed the huge work of etching illustrations for Pascal's *Pensées sur l'homme et Dieu*, a major project which we will be looking at shortly. During this work, he had lost the use of his right eye. But his reasons for refusing to attend the Pierre-qui-Vire 'congress' remain unclear. It was certainly not a simple matter of supporting Pouyaud since Pouyaud himself reproached Gleizes and said that he should have been there. Some twenty years later, Dom Angelico wrote:

> In spite of all the assurances I received from Gleizes, I suspected that he had been warned against an attempt on our part to want to take his movement over . . . That disgusted me deeply, for I never entertained any such plans. I insist on paying homage to the man who had given me everything . . . but from that time onwards I kept my distance from the group . . . keeping hardly any deep relations except with Anne Dangar, relations which continued to gain in intensity and fervour up to the moment of her death.[13]

Gleizes did try to patch up his relations with a deeply wounded Dom Angelico, describing the incident as a 'lovers' tiff'.[14] It is tempting to speculate that, while Gleizes may well have wondered if there was any longer any meaningful sense in which Dom Angelico could be described as his pupil, another reason for his reluctance to attend may have been that, faced with the two parties – the 'Catholics' and the 'Guénonians' – he would have been forced to clarify his position with regard to Guénon. Anne Dangar believed that Gleizes was using his influence against Guénon, but that he was doing so discreetly so as not to upset Pouyaud. For example, he had converted the extraordinary air force pilot, Captain Montantême though, according to Anne Dangar, he was by no means sure that he had done well, since Montantême had swung to the other extreme and was now surrounded by 'Spanish Jesuit priests – miraculous medallions mass-produced in aluminium, grottoes full of tinsel and glitter . . .'.[15]

Shortly before the 'congress' at the Pierre-qui-Vire, Pouyaud, Burlet, Chevalier and some friends had met and decided to launch a new journal, *L'Atelier de la rose*. Anne Dangar wrote to Dom Angelico that 'it will not be in the spirit of Guénon, I assure you'[16] and indeed the first article in the first issue was by Dom Angelico. But Pouyaud, who was chosen as editor, had told Gleizes in May 1950: 'it ought to be in the spirit of *Etudes traditionnelles* but based on craft and technical questions'.[17] The first issue appeared in October 1950. By the time the second issue appeared at the beginning of 1951, the rupture was complete. According to Anne Dangar, it was in reaction against *L'Atelier de la rose* that Dom Angelico launched his journal *Zodiaque*.[18]

•

By this time, as Dom Angelico has said, his relations with Anne Dangar had grown in intensity and fervour. And it was in the context of this relationship that she, who had resisted Gleizes's bullying at the time of his own confirmation, was received into the Roman Catholic Church.

On New Year's Day 1950, she had attended Holy Communion in the Anglican Church at Lyon. It was an exceptional occasion. There had been no regular provision for Anglican worship in Lyon since the outbreak of the war. She wrote to her friends the Grimauds saying that she missed Communion terribly and that she sometimes thought of joining the Catholic Church 'but I can't regard all other Christians as infidels because they don't belong to the Roman church, nor believe that my saintly mother is in Hell'.[19] She could not pronounce the required abjuration of the Church of England. In March she was visited at Moly Sabata by the Abbot of La Pierre-qui-Vire, Dom Placide de Roton (Dom Fulbert Gloriès had died early in 1949), and was enormously impressed by him. In August she was in hospital after damaging her shoulder in a fall and the nuns looking after her told her that the Catholic Church recognised the presence of Christ in the High Church of England. By October, she wrote to say: 'I am in France – to serve God here, I cannot stay Anglican. There has been no Anglican priest in Lyon for eleven years.'[20] She had therefore decided to obey Dom Angelico, whose letters had for some time been urging her to join the Catholic Church.

She was probably also encouraged in her decision by the arrival in Sablons of a very sympathetic priest, Abbé Joseph Meyer, 'converted to modern painting some years ago by the books of my old teacher André Lhote, he was delighted to find Moly Sabata. He has asked me to help make the church less ugly . . .'.[21]

In January 1951, she went to see an exhibition in Annonay. She wrote to Dom Angelico to say,

> after a morning passed in the cold – I even ate in the cold park – I went to the Town Hall. The entrance hall was very warm and I couldn't find the exhibition room. I went to look for the concierge and I saw her standing in front of her door. I woke in the hospital two hours later. My friend Mme Filhol was there; I recognised her, but I had a very bad headache and was unconscious for another two hours. . . .[22]

She was writing to tell him that, as a result of this experience she now wanted to join the Catholic Church, recognising her own weakness. She had

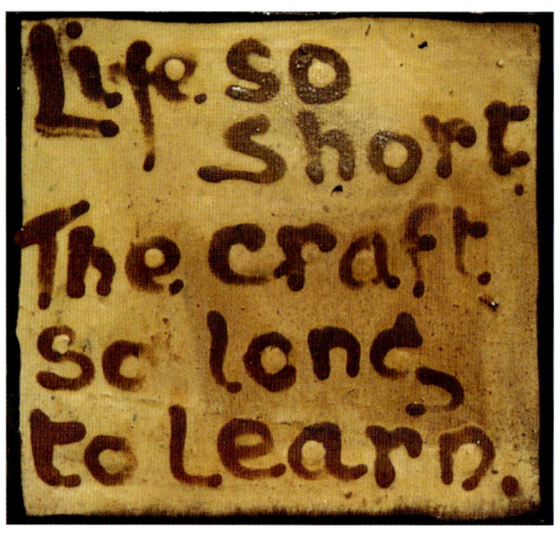

144. Anne Dangar, Wall plaque, nd. 17 × 17.5 cm. Private Collection

told the priest in the hospital that she regarded Dom Angelico as her spiritual director. In the same letter she mentioned that she had just heard of the death of René Guénon.

Anne Dangar was baptised in March by Abbé Meyer (the Roman Catholic Church recognises Anglican baptism but it appeared that she had not actually been baptised by an Anglican priest and she 'had always been worried about my baptism'[23]). Dom Angelico had come for the occasion and gave her her first communion. To her great relief he had brought with him a new formula for abjuration which did not require her to condemn the church in which she had been raised. Gleizes and Mme Grimaud had been chosen by her as her godfather and godmother: 'It was Mr Gleizes who opened my eyes, it was Cubism that made me think, search, meditate and understand. I would have liked my master, who had guided me right to the baptismal font, to have been there with me at my baptism . . .'.[24]

Anne Dangar's fall in Annonay in January had followed a series of health problems. She had spent three weeks with the Gleizes' in Les Méjades in April 1950 because her doctor had forbidden her to work, and she had, as we have mentioned, been in hospital in August after damaging her shoulder in a fall. At the time of her baptism she was still very weak and had even wondered if she would be able to go through with the ceremony on a day when Sablons was covered in snow. By May she seemed to have recovered and was preparing a new firing, but in July she fell ill again. In August her left side was entirely paralysed. She died on 23 September.

Lucie Deveyle, who had come to Moly Sabata as a maid with the Geoffrays and who had become a weaver at Anne Dangar's side, wrote to Dom Angelico that she thought Anne Dangar had been preparing her death since her fall at Annonay: 'Certainly, this last month she has made, I believe, the loveliest, the richest things of her life.' She had made almost enough to fill the kiln and Lucie herself, with Paquaud, the potter at Roussillon, would fire it. 'But I had the best part of everyone, that of having lived with her for nearly twenty years.'[25]

22

NEW REALITIES

In 1948, as the various religious quarrels were developing around him, Gleizes embarked on two projects which, in the light of his death in 1953, may be seen as testaments: the book *Peinture et de l'homme devenu peintre*, and the illustrations to Pascal's *Pensées sur l'homme et Dieu*.

L'Homme devenu peintre was written in response to the efflorescence of 'abstract' painting that was taking place all around him after the war. The book evokes the 'Salon des Réalités Nouvelles', re-opened in 1945 on the initiative of the art dealer Frédo Sidès. The Salon was reminiscent in its intentions and in its presentation of the Abstraction-Création of the early 1930s. Non-figuration was, at least at first, its only principle of selection; beginning in the Summer of 1946, it organised an annual exhibition and presented the catalogue of this exhibition as a review in which the artists were invited to give statements of their aims and objectives. There was a direct continuity of personnel from Abstraction-Création in Auguste Herbin (vice-president of the Réalités Nouvelles), Jean Arp, Sonia Delaunay and Gleizes who were all, from 1947 onwards, on its committee. As with Abstraction-Création one has the impression that Gleizes was not a very effective committee member since he was rarely in Paris, but also that he encouraged his own circle to participate. The 1947 exhibition included Jean Chevalier and Anne Dangar's pupil, Louis Raibaud.[1]

In a footnote to *L'Homme devenu peintre*, Gleizes says:

> 'People can say whatever they like, but that exists' was Bonnard's comment after visiting the Salon des Réalités Nouvelles in 1946. Frédo Sidès cannot be enough congratulated, nor those who helped him enough thanked for having brought this Salon into existence. But what will be its future? Is it not destined to open the door to all the heresies? (p.149)

The fact that so many painters young and old felt the need for a non-figurative painting was of itself significant. It was a phenomenon that was of the nature of the age we live in and, as such, it could help us to understand the age we live in. But it was still just a feeling. In itself, this feeling was entirely reactive. It had no intelligence or sense of direction and certainly could not act as a guarantee for the renewal of painting.

For Gleizes, the rejection of the 'subject' – in itself a very legitimate aspiration – amounted in many cases to no more than a continuation of the process by which the subject (so wonderfully affirmed at the time of the Renaissance) had been analysed, dissected and deformed in modern representational painting. The cast of mind was not so radically different as it might appear. What was required was that the obsession with the subject, and with the private and individual subjective tastes of the painter, should be replaced by a real understanding of the objective requirements of the painting itself – the objective nature of the act of painting corresponding to the objective nature of Man, living in the twin conditions of space and time and capable of rising to a third condition, that of eternity. Once this was understood, the question of whether or not the painting incorporated reminiscences of the external appearances of things became a very secondary question.

L'Homme devenu peintre is unusual among Gleizes's writings in that it deals almost entirely with painting; his broader historical concerns are mentioned only in passing. There is a history of the modern aspiration towards a painting without a subject, which he traces to Baudelaire and Delacroix. He quotes Baudelaire as saying:

> We find harmony, melody, counterpoint in colour . . . harmony is the basis of the theory of colour. Melody is unity in colour, or general colour. Melody needs a conclusion; it is a whole, in which all the particular effects are joined together in a single general effect. So melody leaves a profound memory in the mind. Most of our young colourists lack melody. The best way to see if a picture is melodious is to look at it long enough so as no longer to be able to understand either the subject or the lines. If it is melodious it already has a direction and it has already taken its place in the repertoire of the memory.

Delacroix says 'Painting does not always need a subject' and, writing to Baudelaire, evokes: 'These mysterious effects of line and colour which, alas, only a handful of adepts are able to feel . . . This aspect of music and arabesque . . . for many people it is nothing.' (pp.30–1)

These phrases recur like a leitmotif throughout Gleizes's book:

> Baudelaire and Delacroix make no mistake. Against the rules imposed by the classical subject, they, both of them, oppose a certain number of objective values that are of the nature of painting understood as such – values that are as definite and important as the human eye, from which they derive, and as the matter on which it works, which is not susceptible to change. These are the secrets of a traditional craft, always faithful to itself in its principles, which are part of its very substance. Secrets that can only be learnt through apprenticeship, work, application and talent. When we know how to use them automatically, then we are free, and the evidence of it can be seen in our work. (p.31)

Vie et mort de l'occident chrétien had been a study of society, arguing for rural society against the growth of the big towns. *La Forme et l'histoire* had been a study of the overall movement of history seen, beyond political and military events, in terms of the changes undergone by the 'cast of mind' of the epoch. *Homocentrisme* had dealt with the nature of Man seen as a three-tiered hierarchy – the senses, the intellect, the intelligence: that which can deal with the phenomena of the world rising, through the intermediary intellect, to that which is capable of entering into contemplation of the Divine. The unfinished second volume of *Forme et histoire* – *Mort et résurrection de l'occident chrétien* – applied this three-tiered hierarchy to politics. *L'Homme devenu peintre* is entirely to do with the painter's craft. Without recapitulating the argument of *Homocentrisme*, however, it insists that the craft is rooted in the physiological structure of Man, and especially, since it is to do with painting, of the eye.

For the first time since *La Peinture et ses lois*, Gleizes elaborates on the terms 'translation' and 'rotation'. He is deeply critical of the way in which he had understood these terms in 1922. He had seen them as properties of the plane – the canvas or the wall – and not as:

> the two natures of sight projected into the painter's work. It seems amazing that it should have taken so much time and effort to discover or, rather, rediscover things so simple and obvious. That is the consequence of the humanist state of mind which propelled Man out of himself and misled him to the point of imagining that what he observes exists quite independently of his own responsibility as an observer. . . . (p.53)

We have seen how in the 1930s, Gleizes had come to understand 'rotation' not in terms of an inclination of the initial proportions of the plane but as an actual circle, punctuated by a succession of different colours organised in a clear sequence which he called 'cadence'. The initial construction, dominated by straight lines, left the eye unmoving, at rest. It could be seen all at once. The cadence excited the eye into a movement which was ordered and circular. After four years of applying this as a more or less rigorous formula, Gleizes had begun to vary it, to play with it, to allow a variety of circular movements, eventually producing the great *Supports de contemplation* of 1942–3. Now he argued that the property of painting that corresponds to the eye's capacity for movement was 'line', that element that could almost be said to have been excluded from the Cubist experiment as it passed from a concern with volumes to a concern with planes. In evoking line in this way, Gleizes could be accused of entering into dangerous territory, of approaching the 'musicalism' of Henry Valensi, a painter we have mentioned in the context of the 1912 Section d'Or exhibition, one of the forgotten pioneers of non-representational art who also argued for an art of time, of movement, expressed in sinuous, interweaving lines.[2] The possible comparison with Valensi is all the more striking when, as we shall see shortly, Gleizes explains Rhythm, the unifying form of the painting, by evoking a very strong musical analogy. One of the elements that most clearly distinguishes Gleizes from Valensi is his insistence on the static element in painting – the 'translation'. But in *L'Homme devenu peintre*, Gleizes has little to say on translation, except to stress its immobile character. It is the mobility of the line, the 'aspect of music and arabesque' evoked by Delacroix that most interests him. It is the radical element on which he insists.

L'Homme devenu peintre also reflects the change that had taken place in Gleizes's understanding of 'rhythm', which, we remember, had been expressed in the 1930s in the clear, simple form of the grey circle. It has now become almost invisible, if still powerfully present:

> Let us take an example, not far from painting – the analogous case of a piece of music in which, also, there is no subject; a Bach fugue will suffice, without going any further back in history. I am only a listener who knows nothing about the technique. I let myself be enchanted by the interlacing sounds made by the ear and for the ear; they are there, they were there, and they will be there, right to the last moment. What will be left when the last note has gone away? Nothing that can be experienced; no past or future. So? But I don't even have to pose the question, I am so transfigured, so taken up with my whole being in a presence that is more real than the ebb and flow of the sounds I have just been

> listening to. Sensations, sentiments, perceptions, tensions, harmony in chords, melody in a rising and falling of waves, counterpoint – their place is taken by silence. But what a silence! The full, substantial silence of rhythm, which is not troubled by accident but which has a form, a form which touches my form and which, beyond the senses, beyond the heart, joins with the spirit. (pp.93–4)

L'Homme devenu peintre is very far removed from the dry, technical language of Pouyaud's *Du 'Cubisme' à la peinture traditionnelle*. If the emphasis is on the craft, the craft is poetic, not in the loose sense of something of the stuff of dreams, but of something that responds to the fullness of our own nature, something that cannot be evoked by any copy of the external appearances of things about us. *L'Homme devenu peintre* is the best expression we have of Gleizes's lifelong experience as a painter, a practical guide that, at every moment, refers us to the poetic end to be attained. Although it is a very great book, it may be doubted whether it can really be understood by anyone who has not engaged in the practice it describes. It is a book that is written for the workshop, to be used by master workmen rather than by art teachers. Pouyaud several times complained to Gleizes that they were not of the age they were living in and that the age would not be able to understand them. The circumstances in which *L'Homme devenu peintre* could realise its worth – the sort of workshop Gleizes envisages – as yet barely exist.

Certainly the age seemed to be against Gleizes's attempt to publish it. He clearly wanted to see it produced quickly since it was a response to the very immediate problem of the current fashion for abstract art. He had long been in the habit of publishing his books privately but for *L'Homme devenu peintre* he approached A. C. Gervais, a former associate of Jacques Povolozky who had been Gleizes's publisher in the 1920s and 1930s. Gervais was now working for the publisher Pierre Bordas. He wrote in December 1948 to say: 'he [Bordas] is naturally very attracted by the possibility of being able to count you among our authors,'[3] but he would not be able to publish the book for about six months. After six months, in May 1949, Gleizes wrote and was told that, owing to the exceptionally difficult circumstances of publishing, he would have to wait until the end of the year. In February 1950, Gleizes wrote again and Gervais replied, asking for another month. In April, one and a half years after he had virtually (but not quite) offered to publish, he sent Gleizes a letter that is a small masterpiece of its kind:

> I have just re-read your *Peinture et de l'homme devenu peintre*. I took the same pleasure and the same interest as at the first reading when you sent me your manuscript. Although the craftsman, the painter, is in the worst position to speak about his work and about his art, you have been able to bring to bear on it the necessary clarifications and explanations. Your book is a fascinating synthesis of the most excellent effort the history of Art has ever known. Doubtless to cast light on your subject you operate like de la Tour, disguising the luminous source as if it came from the interior of the objects. Perhaps our age needs a more crude lighting and if I was your publisher I think I would allow myself to propose certain changes. . .

Bordas was unable to publish it. Gervais would like to have proposed another publisher, Audin:

> The project interests me all the more because I envisage a collection on aes-

> thetics for which I already have, in particular, from Pierre Francastel, an extremely penetrating and original study on 'the evolution of plastic space from the quattrocento to our present time'. It is a most remarkable analysis, which has the same quality as your own.

But Audin was a more modest publisher than Bordas and had already undertaken an ambitious history of sculpture from pre-history to the Middle Ages. Gervais was therefore returning Gleizes his manuscript.[4]

•

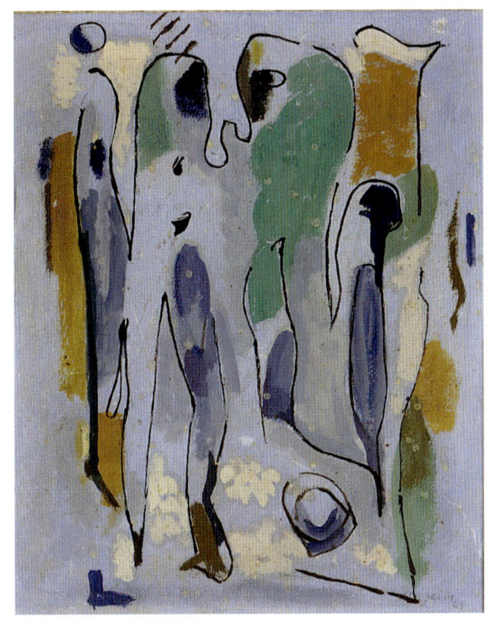

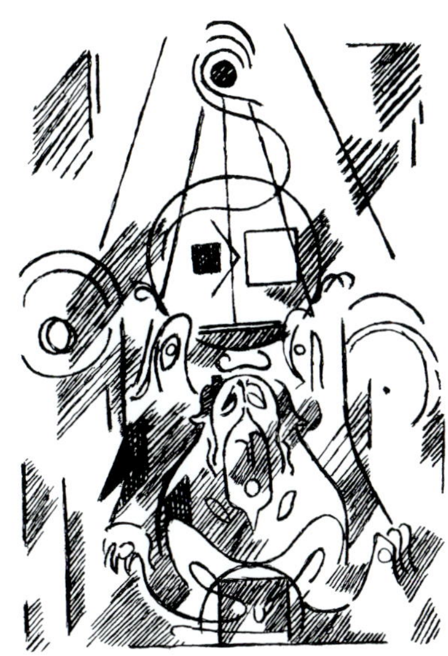

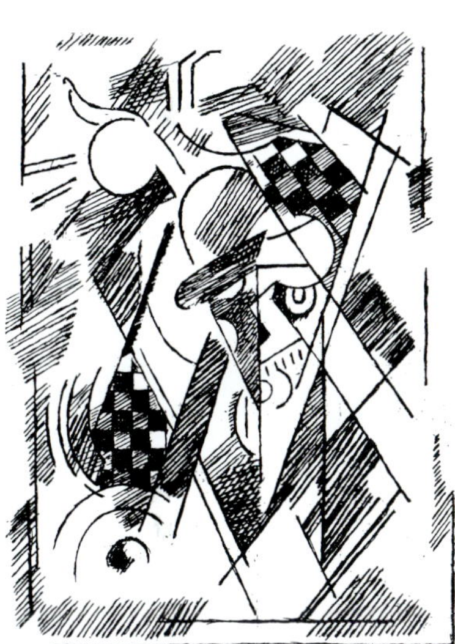

145. *Composition*, 1948. Gouache on cardboard, 33 × 27 cm. Fondation Albert Gleizes

146. *L'Injustice*, 1949–50. Etching, 15.5 × 10.8 cm. Pascal: *Pensées*, p. 49

147. *La Masque du divertissment*, 1949–50. Etching, 13 × 9.5 cm. Pascal: *Pensées*, p. 63

Gleizes's work immediately prior to *L'Homme devenu peintre* does not show much evidence of his new interest in line. It is one of the cases where Gleizes's thought seems to precede his practice. The paintings of the post-war period continue the tendency of his 1944–5 paintings in which the principles of construction used during the 1930s and early 1940s, while still present, become ever less obvious. The paintings become subtle to a degree that begins to risk a certain nebulosity. There are a number of paintings of the time in which Gleizes seems on the verge of entering into the 'informal' – the absence of form that is such a salient characteristic of post-war non-representational painting and which was, indeed, to tempt some of Gleizes's own associates after his death (Plate 145). We could see a possible justification for it in the passage just quoted on the silence that follows a performance of a piece of music. The form is present where it is not stated. It is a unity that transcends the manifestation that has led to it. However, it does not eliminate the need for structure in the manifestation itself, any more than the silence after a Bach fugue eliminates the need for the fugue.

If Gleizes was indeed heading in the direction of the informal, he could be said to have been pushed off course or, if we prefer, saved by the project of illustrating Pascal's *Pensées sur l'homme et Dieu*. The proposal had been made by Jacques Klein, a fine-art publisher based in Casablanca in Morocco. Gleizes started work on it in October 1948,[5] and it absorbed most of his energies through 1949. The book was printed in July 1950 in a limited edition of 200 copies. It includes fifty-seven etchings. A separate portfolio of fifteen supplementary etchings was also prepared. Gleizes had to master the art of engraving on copper plates and in the course of doing this very delicate, highly concentrated work he lost the sight of one eye.[6]

Pascal's seventeenth-century *Pensées* may seem an odd choice for a man who had been disputing with Guénon whether 'the modern deviation' had set in in the fourteenth century or the thirteenth century. But Gleizes liked to emphasise real human experience in opposition to abstract knowledge and it is probably the emphasis on experience rather than on pre-conceived religious ideas that he appreciated in Pascal. The publisher's introduction to the book says:

> We entrusted the illustration to Albert Gleizes because we saw in his own evolution as a painter and as a man an analogy with the evolution of Pascal – the use of reason in a direction other than that imposed by rationalism, finally able to situate the true, living reality in the transcendental, ineffable nature of the Divine Being. . . .

Pouyaud calls Gleizes's illustrations 'a *Summa* of his work'[7] and it is indeed almost as if Gleizes wishes to revisit his whole life as a painter. It is this that gives the book the appearance of a testament. There are etchings based on works from every period of his career from 1915 onwards. There is also a willingness to express a range of emotions, including negative ones such as horror, in an etching on the theme of a return from war, based on his wartime *Retour de Bois-le-Prêtre*; empty, pompous vanity, in his *Le 'Moi' haïssable* ; cruelty in *L'Injustice* (Plate 146). Gleizes obviously responded warmly to the moral and psychological drama Pascal evokes. But these dramatic etchings are interspersed with more serene, impersonal 'meditations', based on his more recent non-figurative paintings.

148. *Pour la Méditation*, 1949–50. Etching, 16.7 × 10 cm. Pascal: *Pensées*, p. 90

149. *L'Ange et la bête*, 1949–50. Etching, 24 × 17 cm. Pascal: *Pensées [hors texte]*, p. 106

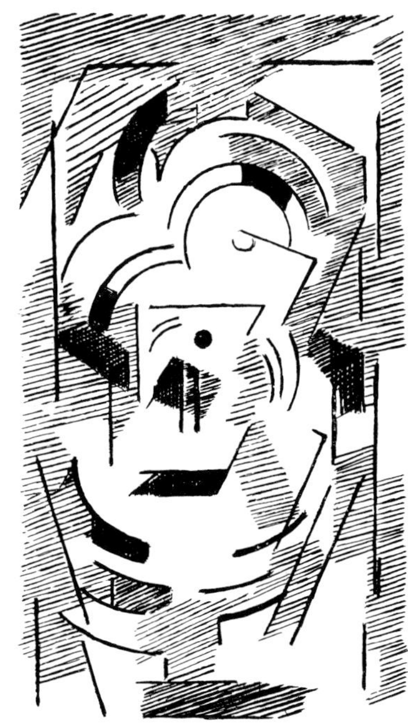

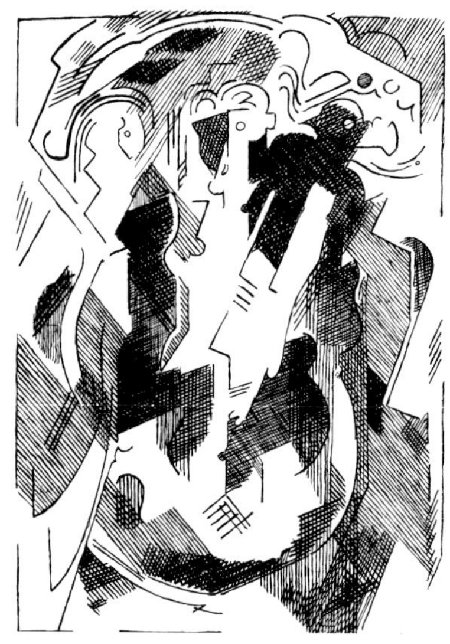

The book shows just how flexible Gleizes's technique has become. *L'Homme devenu peintre*, defending the use of figurative elements, had asked rhetorically: 'Have we finally decided to become forever the Jansenists of painting?' (p.70). The question is a little ironical in the present context given Pascal's sympathy for Jansenism, but the point is that Gleizes was disclaiming a puritanism that would admit only the highest religious emotions. The use of Gleizes's own earlier works is a reminder of the great variety of the feelings and ideas that had been expressed in the course of his single-minded search after principles for the organisation of the picture plane. There is a surprising sympathy established between Pascal's thought – varied, passionate and disturbed as it is – and the etchings of a painter who normally aimed at a certain serenity. Gleizes proves that his 'translation-rotation' is not just a formula for producing endless variations on the same painting but that in itself it is no more and no less than a language, not an expression in itself but a powerful means of expression.

The particular selection of Pascal's thoughts made for this book was divided into two parts: *Misère de l'homme sans Dieu* and *Félicité de l'homme avec Dieu*. Gleizes's illustrations for the second part include, strangely, a number of pieces that do not in any way embody his principles of construction, of translation-rotation. They present religious symbols in the most straightforward figurative manner, reminiscent of the expulsion from Eden sequence at the foot of *Le Pape et l'empereur*. It is difficult to account for these etchings, appearing as they do in what would normally be expected to be the 'higher' part of the book – that which deals with theological truth. It is almost as if Gleizes has agreed with Dom Angelico, who had claimed in opposition to the argument of *L'Homme devenu peintre* that the figurative representation of supernatural realities, rather than the non-representational support for contemplation, was necessary to achieving the highest possible level of Christian art.[8]

In notes written for a travelling exhibition that followed the book's publication, Gleizes described two of his etchings (*Le Baptême du Christ*, which is constructed according to the principles of translation-rotation, and *Annonciation*, which isn't) as having been based on the 'traditional requirements of the Guide de Mont Athos'.[9] Gleizes had been aware of the *Painters' Guide* prepared for the use of the monks at Mount Athos since at least 1935, when

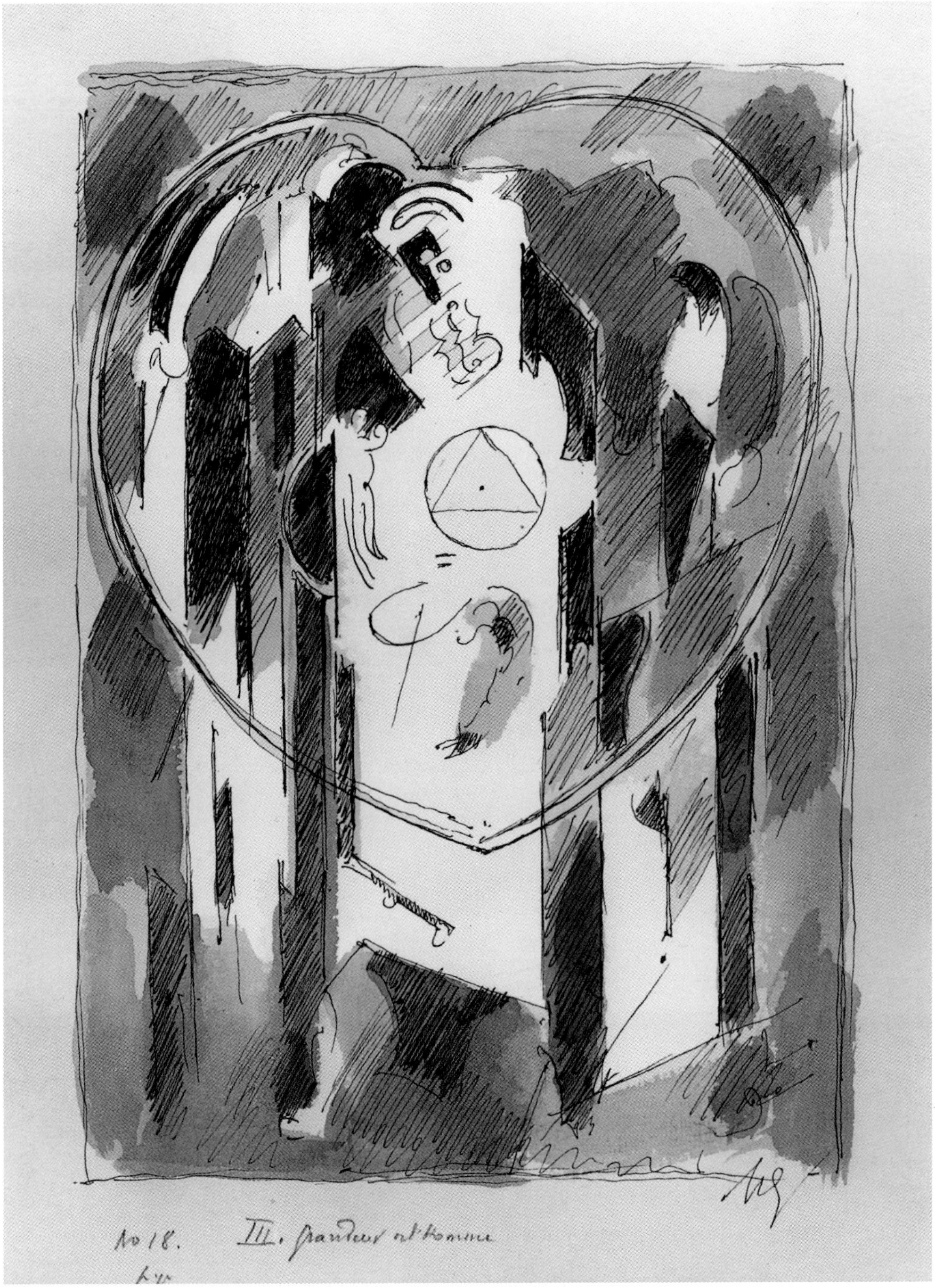

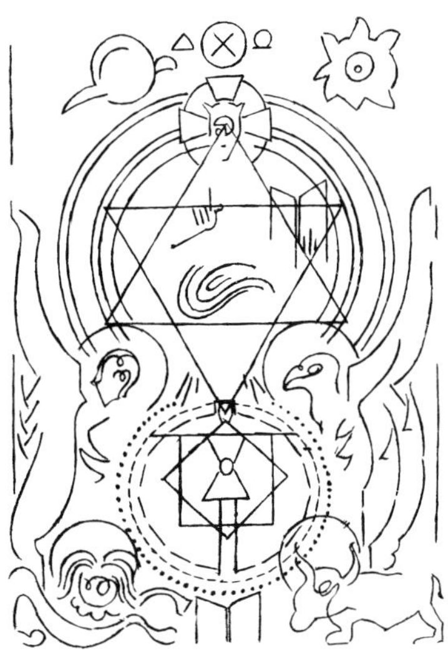

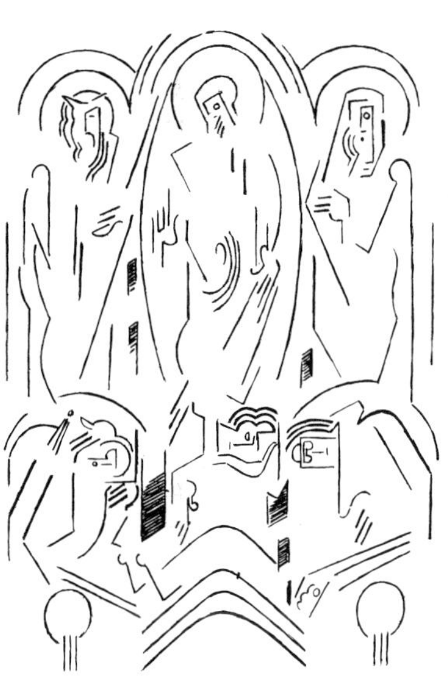

150. *Grandeur de l'Homme*, 1949 (?). Ink on paper, 32.4 × 24 cm. Solomon R. Guggenheim Museum, New York

151. *Les deux Royaumes*, 1949–50. Etching, 24 × 17 cm. Pascal: *Pensées*, p. 164

152. *Le Thabor*, 1949–50. Etching, 22.7 × 15.6 cm. Pascal: *Pensées*, p. 190

he mentioned it in a letter to Pouyaud as endorsing the use of the rainbow in sacred painting.[10] Pouyaud himself had a low opinion of it. He criticised it in an article in *L'Atelier de la rose* in which he complained that it had nothing to say about the structure of painting, giving only a host of rather dubious 'tricks of the trade' and meticulous details on the presentation of the figurative side of the painting: 'Nothing is left out, not even the colour and form of the beards and moustaches!'[11]

That, of course, is the main purpose of the book – to show painters in the

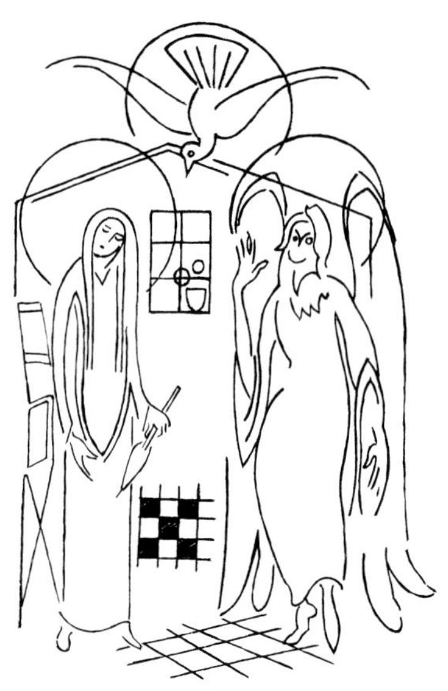

153. *Annonciation*, 1949–50. Etching, 19.5 × 12.9 cm. Pascal: *Pensées*, p. 201

Orthodox tradition how the saints and events celebrated by the church should be presented. Gleizes's interest in it seems to indicate a coming to terms with the fact that a church art would, necessarily, have to be figurative. What is rather disappointing is that the purely figurative etchings in the *Pensées* – those which show no signs of his own structural principles – have a sentimental character to them. They are, to use the term current in Catholic circles, rather 'Saint Sulpice' (resembling the artefacts sold in little religious shops grouped round the great church of Saint Sulpice in Paris). Given the strength of the purely figurative aspect of paintings such as *Le Pape et l'empereur* and the Lyon *Tryptique* done according to his principles, it is difficult to know why this should have been such a problem. He may have thought, as Evie Hone may have thought before him, that what was acceptable to the community of believers, must, by that very fact, have a certain authority. Henri Giriat remembers him, at the very end of his life, expressing the desire to find an iconographical figuration whose validity would be unquestionable.

23
THE ARABESQUE

It is in his paintings of the early 1950s, after he had finished the illustrations to Pascal's *Pensées*, that we begin to get some idea of what Gleizes meant in *L'Homme devenu peintre*, when he identified 'rotation' with 'line'. At first sight, there could appear to be a contradiction with the principle on which he insists right to the end of his life – that of 'measure', 'cadence', and 'rhythm'. 'Measure' implies that the work is to be based on small units which rise to continuity, to movement, through the 'cadence' – the order in which they are placed. That is what is illustrated most clearly in the 'traditional painting' of the 1930s, and Gleizes recommends this formula in *L'Homme devenu peintre* as an indispensable exercise for understanding the properties of colour. The affirmation of line as the principle of movement in painting runs the risk that the eye, following the line, will move too fast, like someone who runs through a landscape too fast to stop and look about.

Insofar as line seems to assume a more important role in the paintings of the mid-1940s, prior to *L'Homme devenu peintre*, it is a line that reinforces a movement that has already been established in the cadence of the colour. It is not continuous and it is not in itself the impulse behind the movement. As a simple consequence of the technique employed – etching – the illustrations to Pascal are linear. But, as we have seen, they largely take up constructions that had originally been developed in painting. It is in the supports for meditation that Gleizes comes closest to the ideal he evokes in *L'Homme devenu peintre* but the line is still – as it was in the paintings on which they were based – tied to the concentric circle. Like the eddies of a river it passes from one circular centre to another. The distinctive peculiarity of the *Pensées* – the use of purely figurative imagery – is certainly linear but has no pretensions to embodying the principle of rotation.

It is as if in the late forties Gleizes has an idea in mind that he does not yet dare to try; and as if, in the *Pensées*, he revisited his whole evolution as a painter to draw from it the strength that he would require. He stepped back, the better to be able to leap forward. It is in the fifties that he makes the leap, in his canvases – all non-figurative – some of which he called *Arabesques* (Plates 154 and 155); and also in the mural paintings he realised both for the Jesuit chapel at Gouvieux-Chantilly, and for a church to be built on an industrial estate at La Ciotat, near Marseilles.

What characterises all these works is, precisely, the apparent freedom of the line. The explicit circle that had been a distinguishing mark of Gleizes's painting for twenty years has almost wholly disappeared (with the striking exception of the centre of the fresco at Chantilly). The line dances and meanders apparently anywhere and everywhere. It would be impossible to attribute a

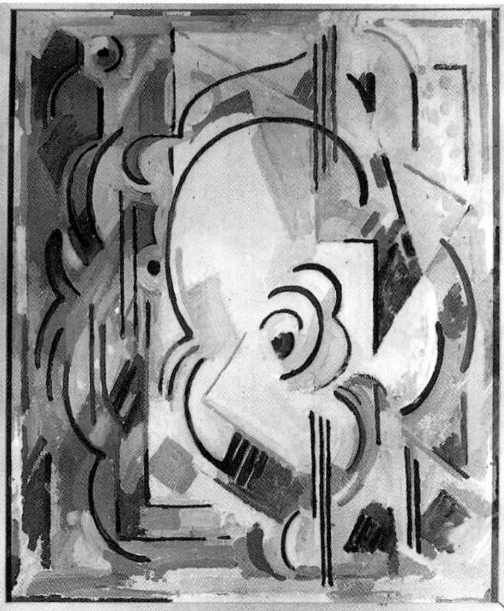

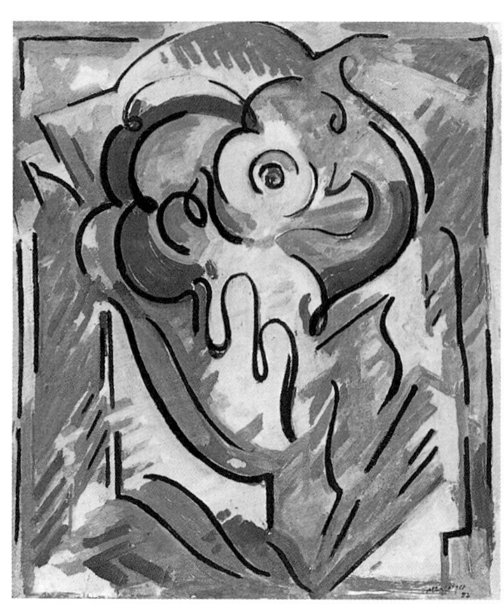

154. *Composition bleu-jaune*, 1952–3 (?). Oil on isorel, 73 × 60 cm. Present whereabouts unknown

155. *Arabesque, rose*, 1952. Oil on canvas, 53 × 46 cm. Fondation Albert Gleizes

principle to it except that ultimately it joins up with itself, even if it does so invisibly. The line never passes beyond the frame of the painting or of the wall.

It is also thoroughly rooted in the plane surface, itself still organised according to the principle of translation – but a principle of translation that had evolved enormously since the 1920s. Most obviously, of course, it incorporates the inclined planes that, in the 1920s, were called rotation. In the 1920s, the vertical and inclined planes combined to produce a distinct, unified 'figure'. This figure would still be present at the centre of the traditional painting of the 1930s. In the 1940s, it disappeared, and the translation became uniquely a principle of organisation applied across the whole picture surface. It was the new, spiralling, rotation, that gave the painting its distinct, unifying form. The figure, whether representational or not, had disappeared. Now it is the line that replaces the spiral and the circle at the forefront of the painting, but the sheer wealth of interest in the translation, in the landscape through which the line passes, invites us to slow down the trajectory imposed by the line, so as to taste it. In these paintings, one feels that Gleizes was at the beginning of a new adventure which might have taken him far, had it not been cut off by his death.

•

This was a period, like the late 1930s, when it appeared briefly as if Gleizes was about to receive something of the public respect to which he was entitled. In 1951 he was asked to sit on the jury for the Prix de Rome, he received the Légion d'Honneur, and he shared the Grand Prix at the Menton biennial.[1] He was also nominated for, but narrowly failed to be accepted by, the Institute of France (the body that incorporates the five great French academies).[2] At the same time he was invited to engage in what seems to have been a rather mournful exercise in nostalgia – a reunion of René Arcos, Charles Vildrac, Georges Duhamel and himself at Créteil, where the municipality had decided to install a memorial plaque on the old 'Abbaye' (which would eventually be pulled down as part of the transformation of Créteil into an ambitious city of the future, under the inspiration of André Malraux). Alexandre Mercereau, Lucien Linard and Albert Doyen were dead, and Henri-Martin Barzun was living in America. According to Mme Gleizes the house was in poor condition and Gleizes found his old companions very hostile to the religious direction he had taken.[3]

Gleizes was further to be reminded of his past by the organisation of a major exhibition in Paris in 1953 at the Musée National d'Art Moderne – Le Cubisme, 1907–14. At the end of 1952, he was engaged in a correspondence with one of the organisers, the art historian Bernard Dorival. He clearly hoped that as a result of his efforts the exhibition would at last present the existence of two major independent currents in the history of Cubism – that of the painters exhibiting in the salons, and that of the painters associated with the gallery of D-H. Kahnweiler. Gleizes had earlier been upset by Dorival's account of Cubism in his ambitious *Les Etapes de la peinture française contemporaine*, published in 1944. He had written, probably to Jacques Villon:

> The emptiness of Dorival's book troubles me. I can't bring myself to understand how a young man, standing at a distance from the events in question, can fall back into this fruitless, nameless, analytical confusion when he wants to establish the stages of contemporary French painting. He engages in accounts of the particular psychological formation of known painters and has no interest in what there might be that is human, beyond the particular case of the individual avatars.
>
> And yet it all seems to me to be so simple. The question Cubism posed, more vigorously and more visibly than the other movements of the nineteenth and the beginning of the twentieth century was, precisely: is it possible to realise a painting without the conventional support of a figurative reproduction – a painting which would be based on natural laws, not giving itself up to fantasy and anarchy?
>
> The proof can be seen in what has emerged from the logical consequences of Cubism, if, of course, you are willing to recognise them. The aspirations that appeared in the groups 'Abstraction-Création', 'Inobjective Painters' and others of like mind are the logical consequence of Cubism.
>
> What each painter has managed to do since, with great talent, outside this line, can only have a fragmentary, anecdotal interest, without any great profit for painting and its future, for the spirit that has to free itself from the individualist anarchy into which – a fact that is unique in our aesthetic history – the fine arts (like everything else) have fallen. . . .[4]

Villon wrote to Gleizes, probably in reply to this letter, to say that 'having come late into this domain he [Dorival] has mixed everything up and treated Cubism like the Kingdom of Heaven, where the last will be first. I believe him ready now to make an honourable amend and to correct his mistake should the occasion present itself.'[5]

The organisation of the Cubism exhibition seemed to present such an occasion. Gleizes obviously enjoyed his correspondence with Dorival which involved, among other things, uncovering the old debate on Cubism between Marcel Sembat and J. L. Breton in the Chambre des Députés in 1912.[6] But he was to be disappointed in the result. If the so-called 'minor Cubists' occupied a larger place than usual, the catalogue article still reaffirmed their dependence on Picasso and Braque thus, in Gleizes's opinion, reducing the history of Cubism to a matter of 'the particular psychological formation of known painters' – of no general usefulness for the future of painting. Dom Angelico mentions that about this same time, in the context of an exhibition of modern art he had organised at Vézélay, he came to know one of the organisers of the Cubism exhibition, Mme Gabrielle Vienne, who was to help him greatly with commissions and encouragement: 'She didn't like Gleizes, and warned me against him: "Don't trust Gleizes!" '[7] She may have been reacting to the fact that at the time Gleizes gave a public lecture contesting the catalogue's account of the history of Cubism.[8]

One of the reviewers, Georges Besson, wrote in *Le Soir*: 'It is undeniable that in this manifestation, among the stammerings of the supernumerary figures of whom Mr Gleizes is the most miserable specimen,' certain works of Picasso, Braque, Léger and Gris were 'clever, beautiful or interesting, but lost in so much mediocrity, muddy grey, sadness, renunciation of painting and of humanity that this exhibition is a place for the mortification of the soul . . .'.

Gleizes noted that it was as if he was once again hearing the voice of the old enemy of Cubism, Louis Vauxcelles, so many years ago, lamenting the 'return of an ignominious spirituality'.[9]

For Gleizes, unquestionably the most important development of the early 1950s was the commissions he received for the churches at Chantilly and La Ciotat.

Here again, Gleizes would have reason to look back over his life. His whole career could be presented as the story of a man who had championed mural painting against easel painting but who had never been given a wall. 'I paint on canvasses because I do not have any walls'[10] was the quotation Henri Giriat chose to preface the catalogue of an exhibition organised by the Fondation Albert Gleizes at St Rémy in 1990. His Cubist work prior to the First World War had already been on a monumental scale; he had argued for mural painting in his articles in *Clarté* in 1920. The *Décoration pour le gare de M* of the same year had been envisaged as a wall-painting. He had worked on mural projects in 1924 (for the Ecole de Pharmacie at Paris), in 1927 (for the church at Serrières) and in 1938 (for the Conservatoire des Arts et Métiers at Paris), all of which had been aborted after the preparatory work had been done. The commission at La Ciotat was to follow the familiar pattern. The church at Chantilly was (if we except the temporary decorations done for Rosenberg's apartment, for the Universal Exhibition and for the 1938 Salon des Tuileries) the only one of Gleizes's mural projects that was ever realised.

Gleizes's friend Walter Firpo, himself a Protestant, noted a moment at which the Dominicans in Gleizes's entourage gave way to Jesuits.[11] Among the Jesuits in question was the young seminarian Henri de Montrond, who wrote an article in the December 1951 issue of the Jesuit paper *Etudes* supporting the marriage of modern art and sacred art while criticising the initiatives of Régamey. Régamey had been running into difficulties with the church authorities, especially for Germaine Richier's violent crucifixion at Assy; Dom Angelico expressed some nervousness that a condemnation of Régamey could effect his own and Gleizes's initiatives as well. De Montrond presents Gleizes's painting as the reasonable alternative to Richier's tortured realism: 'the recovery of the value of the sign, the symbolic representation replacing naturalism, the reconquest of the sense of rhythm, stylisation, the hieratic nature of the painting and, finally, the spirit of craftsmanship again respected; these are the leading qualities with which Saint Savin [the great French Romanesque church] was built.'[12]

De Montrond published an account of the commissioning of the mural at Chantilly in a special edition of *L'Atelier de la rose*. He says that the Jesuit community of 'Les Fontaines' at Chantilly had returned to France after an exile of fifty years (following their expulsion during the church/state conflicts at the beginning of the century[13]). Gleizes had been invited to give a talk there in 1951 and, as a result, he was asked by the rector, Father Le Blond, to paint a tympanum above the altar of their new church. Gleizes himself was anxious to ensure recognition of the theological orthodoxy of his project and therefore submitted it for examination by teachers at the seminary of Fourvière, overlooking Lyon. The teachers were enthusiastic. According to de Montrond, they showed the work to the aged Father Victor Fontoynont who declared:

> Here is the appearance in all its simplicity of the true tradition of Christian iconography. It goes beyond the human figure without rejecting it; symbolism and history are united gracefully with harmony and rhythm.[14]

Fontoynont's support is highly significant. We have seen Gleizes in trouble with nearly all his acquaintances in the Church establishment, mainly because of his attitude towards Thomism, which had by that time almost become identified with Christianity itself. Fontoynont had been one of the pioneers of a movement within Roman Catholicism aiming to rediscover the wealth of the early, pre-Thomist, Fathers of the Church, both Greek and Latin. At the time Gleizes was working on his fresco, a group of Fontoynont's pupils were starting what was to become the huge publishing venture, Sources Chrétiennes, aiming to make this literature generally available in parallel texts, the original with a French translation. From a Christian point of view this is one of the most important publishing ventures of the century. It initially aroused considerable hostility among Thomist circles, though it was soon to be adopted by the Dominican publishing house, Cerf.[15] Gleizes had read some of the early volumes (including Origen's *Homilies on Genesis*, which he refers to in a marginal note on one of de Romefort's letters). It is highly significant that the man who was recognised as the primary inspiration of this venture saw Gleizes not just as an interesting painter but as, what Gleizes believed himself to be, a painter who had recovered the 'true tradition of Christian iconography.'

De Montrond also quotes Joseph Pichard, founder of Régamey's paper *L'Art sacré* and of the 'Salon d'Art Sacré', as saying 'not without a certain malice': 'Gleizes is really the ideal painter for young clerics all full of mysticism and gifted with a certain intellectualism'. Pichard, it should be said, was much less hostile towards Gleizes than Régamey. Régamey's *Art sacré au vingtième siècle?*, published in 1952, does not mention Gleizes. The Salon d'Art Sacré, by contrast, held a small exhibition in his memory after his death in 1953.

Gleizes worked on his design in 1952, but at the age of seventy, he did not feel able to execute it himself in what would have been, for him, the new and difficult technique of true fresco.[16] It was a technique that had been much studied in his circle, especially by the painter, René Maria Burlet, who had been

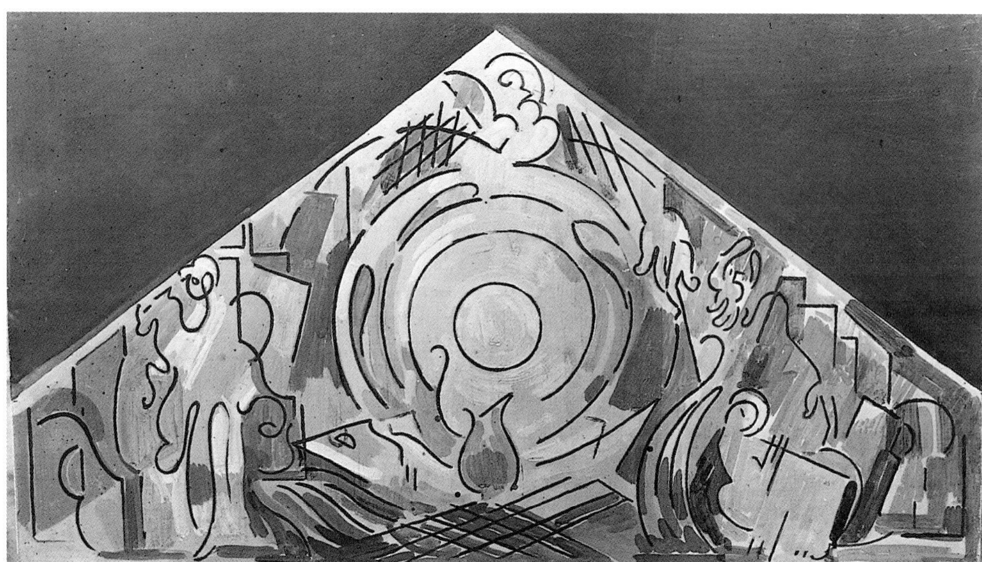

156. Study for *L'Eucharistie*, 1952 (?). Ink and wash (?). Dimensions and present whereabouts unknown

writing a series of articles on his own experience of fresco in *L'Atelier de la rose*. Gleizes entrusted the work to him, together with the master mason, Marcel Cluzel, another contributor to *L'Atelier de la rose*. They began work in August 1952 and took ten days to complete it. Gleizes himself was very impressed by the result.

The fresco is a dramatic illustration of the new-found liberty of line that Gleizes was proclaiming, a line in which the representational or symbolic elements appear almost as accidents along the way – an arabesque that is constantly surprising, seemingly arranged without any principle of order, like the apparently wandering melody of Gregorian chant. There is an interesting comparison between the principles of Gregorian chant and those of translation/rotation in the first issue of *L'Atelier de la rose*.[17]

The appearance of the figurative imagery in the line marks a considerable change in Gleizes's thinking. Previously the 'subject' – corresponding to the lowest level of the human hierarchy, that of the senses, was expressed in the 'translation' through the conjugation of straight lines and planes. The theme of the fresco at Chantilly is the Eucharist, shown as a circle flanked by the sacrifice of Isaac, as a type of the Old Testament, and the Good Shepherd, as a type of the New Testament (Plate 156). The sacrifice of Isaac and the Good Shepherd, both barely recognisable, are established entirely in the line. The linear, but static and conventional figures in the illustrations to Pascal's *Pensées* can perhaps be seen as a preparation for this new, mobile figure. The concentric circles in the centre suggest the colour circles of the 1930s paintings but where the latter derived from and turned round a central figure in translation, the figures – expressed in this highly mobile line which seems to destroy them almost as soon as it creates them – are now outside. The circle turns round a 'void', but a full, luminous void, the silence after the Bach fugue. It is as though the 'light' expressed in the grey circle that passed round the circumference of the coloured cadences of the 1930s has now replaced the static figure at the centre or heart of the painting.

A similar freedom of line, generating representational images only to go dancing beyond them, can be seen in the drawings Gleizes prepared for the

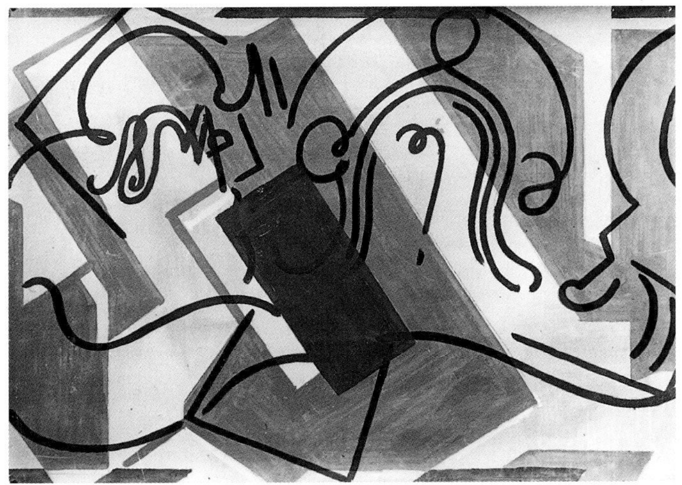

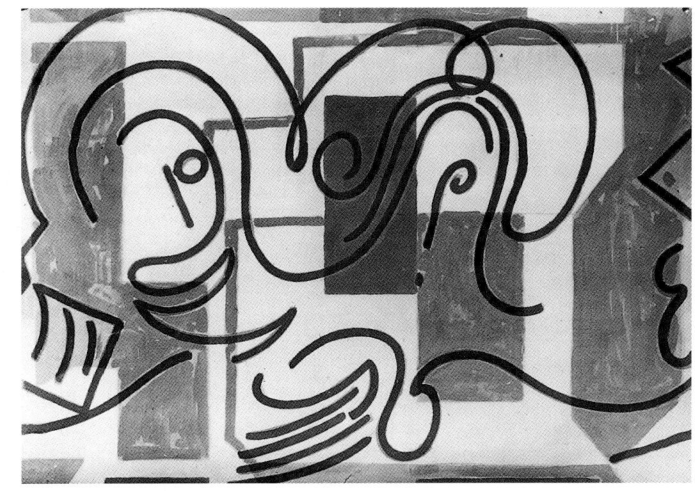

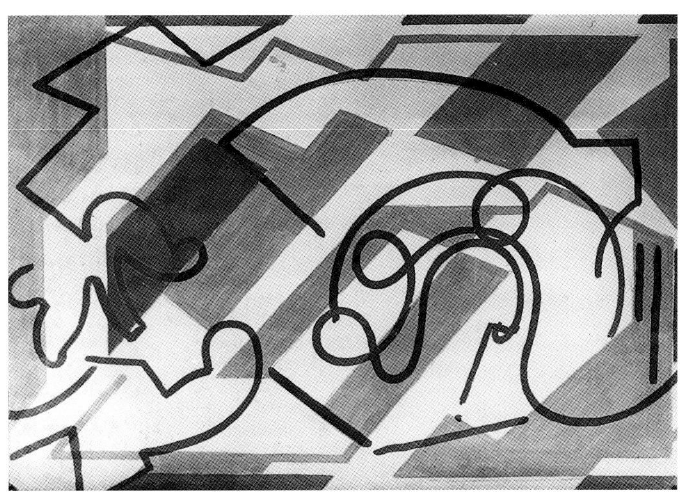

Chemin de la croix at La Ciotat – organised not in fourteen separate works but in a continuous frieze, each incident giving rise to the next, the whole punctuated by rectangles, vertical and inclined, slowing the movement down or projecting it on its way. In this case, Gleizes was to have been given control of the whole interior of the church. He envisaged the Stations of the Cross being realised in ceramic (probably, since the death of Anne Dangar, by Jean-Claude Libert who had spent some time at Moly Sabata just after the war) with vestments woven by Lucie Deveyle. Father Fontoynont, on being shown the maquette, commented:

> This is the first time to my knowledge that this subject of devotion has found a faithful interpreter. Up until now the artists dispersed the devotion to the Passion by their anecdotal representations, or even, in extreme cases, deprived it of its evangelical realism. Gleizes, while still respecting the scriptural character of each of the stations, draws them together, unites them in a gesture of sorrow about the single theme of the cross . . . Its a real discovery, this rhythmical interlacing.

157. *Chemin de Croix, no. 10*, 1951. Gouache on board, 7.5 × 10.7 cm. Musée des Beaux Arts, Lyon

158. *Chemin de Croix, no. 11*, 1951. Gouache on board, 7.5 × 10.7 cm. Musée des Beaux Arts, Lyon

159. *Chemin de Croix, no. 12*, 1951. Gouache on board, 7.5 × 10.7 cm. Musée des Beaux Arts, Lyon

The initiative for the project seems to have come from Walter Firpo. Firpo had been active on Gleizes's behalf in Marseilles, interesting collectors and gallery owners in his work. He was an ideal combination of committed enthusiast, poet, painter, theologian and salesman. Among the collectors he had succeeded in interesting in Gleizes was an important businessman, Auguste Terrin, who was to buy Gleizes's *L'Ecuyère* of 1919. In one of his letters, organising a meeting between Gleizes and Terrin, Firpo indicates something of the problems Gleizes posed for his more practically minded collaborators:

> Knowing our friend as I do, let me ask you not to insist too much on the over-inflated prices of pictures bought from the 'dealers', for our good friend has up till now been their most faithful client, and that could give him a

> certain feeling of unease. For him, it must be admitted, painting is little more than a sure investment – he is the enemy of everything that might provoke doubts as to the sureness and future of his previous purchases. We have to take people as they are and not as we would like them to be.[18]

It was Terrin who owned the land on which the church was to be built. In May 1952 the project was still going ahead, but Mme Gleizes says that, after some time, she began to be worried about hearing nothing. She pressed Gleizes to write and, as a result, he learned that there had been a series of violent strikes at the shipyard, followed by a lockout. The Trade Union representatives had, among much else, protested against the waste of money involved in constructing a church. The project had been abandoned. The ecclesiastical authorities too, alarmed by the storms provoked by Régamey's activities, had been lukewarm in their support.[19]

•

Albert Gleizes died in June 1953 from an unexpected complication that set in during a routine operation on the prostate gland. He was buried, together with Anne Dangar and, later, Lucie Deveyle, in the Roche family tomb in the graveyard at Serrières. A description of the path winding up from Serrières to the graveyard, meandering, disappearing, reappearing, but never losing its way, is among the most beautiful passages in *La Forme et l'histoire*.[20] The funeral cortège walked from the (long-abandoned) house at Serrières accompanied by the music of Joseph Olivier's group of Provençal fife and tambourine players.

At the time of his death, Gleizes was surrounded by a small but energetic group of admirers who believed that he had provided the means – practical and moral – by which the art of painting could be renewed. In their different ways, Pouyaud, Chevalier, Surchamp, Firpo, Lucie Deveyle, Coste and the Dürrbachs regarded him not just as an interesting painter among other interesting painters but as the man who, more than any other, had laid the foundations for the painting of the future. Two journals – *Zodiaque* and *L'Atelier de la rose* – were competing to be regarded as the vehicle of his teaching. *Zodiaque* was attached to the discipline of the church and increasingly open to other currents of modern art. It was soon to become part of Dom Angelico's great publishing initiative, the series of books which, with the support of influential figures such as André Malraux, was to do much to create and sustain a popular interest in Romanesque art throughout Europe. *L'Atelier de la rose*, with a very small circulation, was attached to the doctrines of René Guénon and developed a specialist interest in esoteric symbolism. An issue of *Zodiaque* devoted to Gleizes was published at the end of 1951, and another, the hundredth edition, in 1974. Gleizes wrote regularly for *L'Atelier de la rose* until his death.

In March 1953 an exhibition was held of Gleizes and his associates in the Ecole des Beaux-Arts in Paris, supported by its director, Raymond Untersteller, who had been behind Gleizes's appointment to the jury of the Prix de Rome, and the proposal that he be elected to the Institute. Gleizes had suggested the names of twenty-eight artists who could be invited to take part. The exhibition travelled to Aix-en-Provence, Saint-Rémy de Provence, Lyon and Vienne.[21] In Paris it was followed by another exhibition of 'Painters of the School of Albert Gleizes' (Jean Chevalier and Albert Coste).

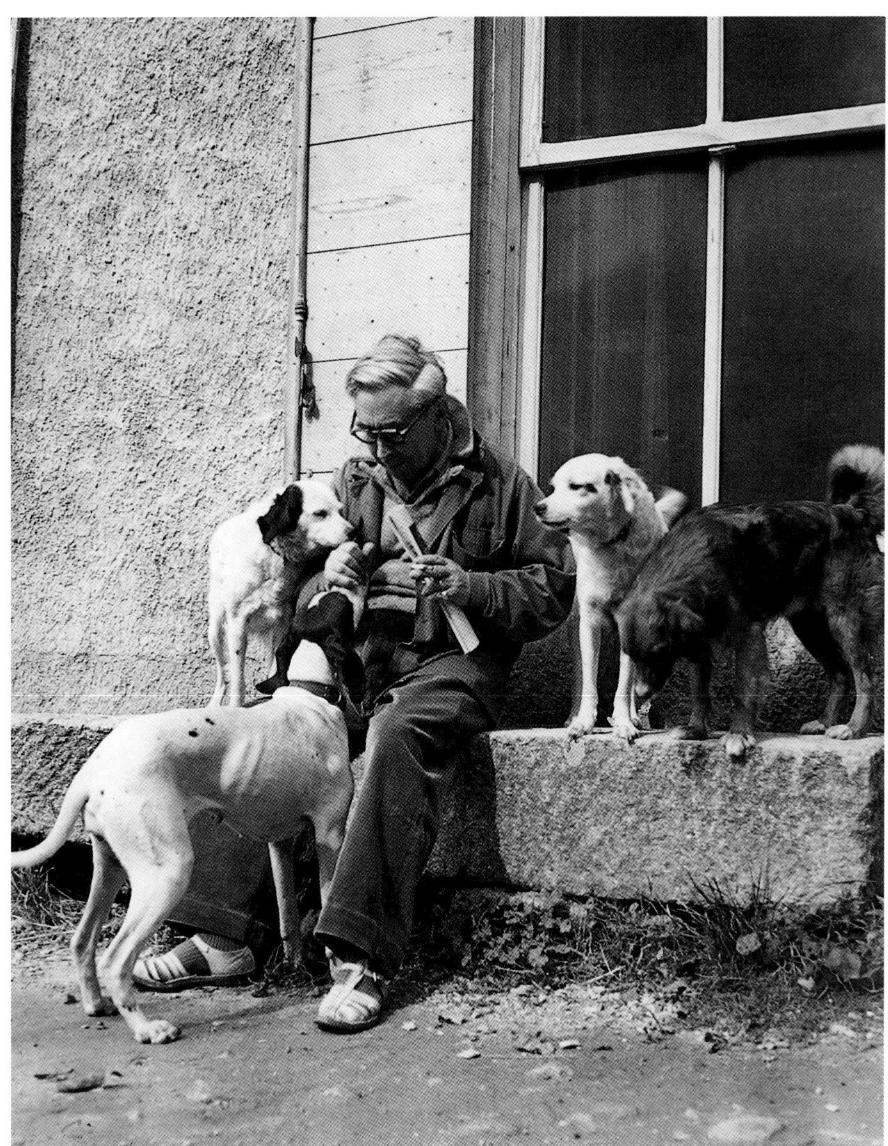

160. Albert Gleizes with dogs, *c.* 1950. Photo: Marcel Coen, Marseille. Communicated to me by Walter Firpo

At the moment of his death, then, Gleizes had every reason to believe that he had left, if not a 'school', at least a legacy – that he had prepared something which other painters could develop. He had written to Pouyaud in 1947:

> I've done what I could, as conscientiously as possible. Those who come after me will do better. You've already shown me the proof. Better and more decisive. I know where I come from and how hard I had to struggle against my regrets and feelings of remorse. But in the end I've still the feeling of having prepared the ground, and that's already something.[22]

However, very quickly, Gleizes's legacy began to run into difficulties. Mme Gleizes had a sharp, ironical intelligence. She understood her husband's ideas, sympathised with them, was able to explain them clearly, and had herself contributed, especially to the political side of his thinking. But she was still a Parisian in spirit. She had always been ill-at-ease with the rural, agricultural life on which Gleizes had insisted and, without him, she found it almost impossible to make anything of Les Méjades. Moly Sabata had been kept going with great difficulty by Anne Dangar and Lucie Deveyle, but was a heavy burden for Lucie Deveyle alone. She was to die, at a comparatively young age, in 1956, leaving the young potter, Genevieve de Cissey, in charge of the house. After a year, Genevieve de Cissey found it impossible to continue. A couple of subsequent attempts were made to revive it but without success. It is now being administered by the Fondation Albert Gleizes as an artists' residential centre, but with only a very limited reference to what is specific in Gleizes's teaching.

Anne Dangar had often reproached Gleizes for his naivety with regards to the practical problems of preserving and transmitting a craft. Gleizes himself had often written against the art school in favour of the workshop, with its ordered hierarchy of masters, companions, apprentices. But he had not himself been able – or even tried very hard – to establish such a workshop. Yet without it, there was no possibility of that 'tradition' whereby the experience of one generation can be passed practically, not just intellectually, to the next.

An 'Association des Amis d'Albert Gleizes' was formed in Lyon in 1954. It published a little booklet giving Gleizes's account from his *Souvenirs* of the early history of Cubism. The book had some effect in combatting the tendency among historians to see Cubism as uniquely the achievement of the painters associated with D-H. Kahnweiler – Picasso, Braque, Léger and Gris. The association also published a *Hommage – Albert Gleizes*, with tributes from a wide variety of people who had known him. But although a loose network of friendships was maintained, the painters in general went their separate ways, all acknowledging the profound mark that Gleizes had left upon them, but few prepared to argue for or to teach the general validity of the principles he had taught.

I was introduced to those principles through Walter Firpo, whom I met in 1963 when he was teaching a course in painting at a Summer school organised by the Collège Cévénol, a well-known Protestant school in the Cévennes mountains. I was greatly impressed by Firpo, as a teacher, as a painter and also as a poet, and we entered into a long correspondence. Firpo's letters were a mine of information and of insights on poetry and painting and I wanted nothing more than that he should himself be my teacher and guide in these matters. I was quite put out when I found him constantly referring me to Gleizes, especially since I had very little possibility of seeing Gleizes's paintings. Some years later, in 1969, I went to France specifically for this purpose and I remember standing in front of the great *Triptyque* in Lyon, wondering if I really liked it and if I had not come a long way only to be disappointed. And then my eye fell almost accidentally on a part of the painting and I found myself guided to another part and then to another and to another and soon I was caught up in the dance, the mobility of the eye, rotation – that quality on which Gleizes was to insist as the truly radical innovation of the twentieth century, the one thing that matters and justifies all the rest.

In the event, I was not yet able to understand how important this was. It seemed difficult to reconcile with the general direction of the intellectual life of my time, a direction which still had its attractions for me. My life took me off on a tangent. It was about thirteen years later that I went into the Tate Gallery in London and chanced upon the *Portrait de Jacques Nayral* of 1911, which they had only recently purchased. It is a painting in which Gleizes's knowledge of the rotative capacity of the eye is still undeveloped and yet, as he himself said, the Cubism of that period had reintroduced a taste for 'rambling', for taking one's time in passing in and out, around and about the painting. Thanks to Firpo all those years ago, I knew how to look at it. I was amazed, and bitterly reproached myself for having lost the fine thing I had once known.

I renewed the contact I had broken with Firpo and he insisted that I should go to a village south of Lyon in the Rhone valley, where I would be able to see a small collection of Gleizes's paintings. It was there that I made the acquaintance of the potter, Geneviève Dalban.

Geneviève Dalban had, as Geneviève de Cissey – a young girl just out of the art college of Dijon where she had specialised in ceramics – gone to Moly Sabata to meet Anne Dangar at the urging of the Lyon gallery-owner, Marcel Michaud. But Anne Dangar was weary of having to cope with people who had been sent to her from Michaud. She informed Geneviève that she had no time to lose with young girls who wanted to amuse themselves with clay: 'Pottery is a craft that is learnt from long experience, and the work is very hard.'[23]

As she had written in the first issue of *L'Atelier de la rose*:

> Over the last few years, 'pottery' has become the fashionable craft. Plenty of young people think it an easy craft that they can learn in a few months and

> then make plenty of money. All that they need to become potters is to buy an electric kiln, enamels and colours.
>
> At the same time the real traditional potteries are closing down; the enormous production of saucepans and kitchen utensils in aluminium has almost wiped out the good earthenware pots and plates and the true potters have abandoned the craft. So at Saint-Uze in the Drôme, how many potteries have disappeared.
>
> You, who love what is 'traditional', must not be indifferent to those masters of their craft who are still with us. For fifteen years, I worked with them, as one of them. Everything I know about the craft I learned from them. They possess the precious seed of tradition, they learnt the craft from their parents and their grandparents: 'We had', they told me 'to do seven years of apprenticeship before we could call ourselves potters!'[24]

Nonetheless, Geneviève de Cissey persisted and Anne Dangar soon recognised that her interest was serious. She took part in a course in painting organised by Anne Dangar at Moly Sabata in the Summer of 1949 and corresponded with her until her death. Geneviève took her at her word that pottery could only be learnt in a workshop and went to work with Paquaud, the potter at Roussillon, a hard-drinking and militant atheist environment that was disconcerting for a well-brought-up Catholic girl. After Anne Dangar's death, she lived for some time in Moly Sabata with Lucie Deveyle and she says that it was from Lucie, the modest, unpretentious former factory-worker and maid to the Geoffrays that she learnt most about Gleizes's principles.

Subsequently she married and settled in Ampuis, where she and her husband, Charles Dalban, rebuilt an old barn with a view to establishing a place suitable for teaching and for showing works of art – 'Art for life, not art for a spectacle', she insists. Many of those who had known Gleizes supported Ampuis and allowed works – their own or Gleizes's – to be exhibited there. In particular, Robert Pouyaud saw Ampuis as the continuation of Moly Sabata. The Association des Amis d'Albert Gleizes held annual meetings at Ampuis which were attended by, among many others, Pouyaud, Firpo, Dürrbach and Giriat. The venture was also supported by the historian, André Dubois, author of an important study, *Anne Dangar et Moly Sabata*, and by the publisher, Henri Viaud who, in the late sixties, published two collections of Gleizes's essays – *Art et religion* and *Puissances du cubisme* and who himself achieved the return to the country in his magnificent domain at Aubard in the Alpes de Haute Provence, where a large part of the present book was written.

Geneviève Dalban's own work as a potter, rigorously faithful to the principles of translation/rotation, almost always derived from the most elementary schema, is proof of the endless variety and interest of which those principles are capable. I have known her now for over fifteen years – a very difficult period during which she lost the use of her right arm and had to renounce turning and learn to decorate with her left hand. I have never ceased to be surprised and delighted by her work – the living proof that what we are dealing with is not a particular, individual, finished style, but that it truly deserves to be called a principle, an originating impulse that can give rise to many very different consequences.

I have chosen to finish this book not by dwelling on Gleizes's death but by evoking the continuity that I found at Ampuis. That continuity has been and

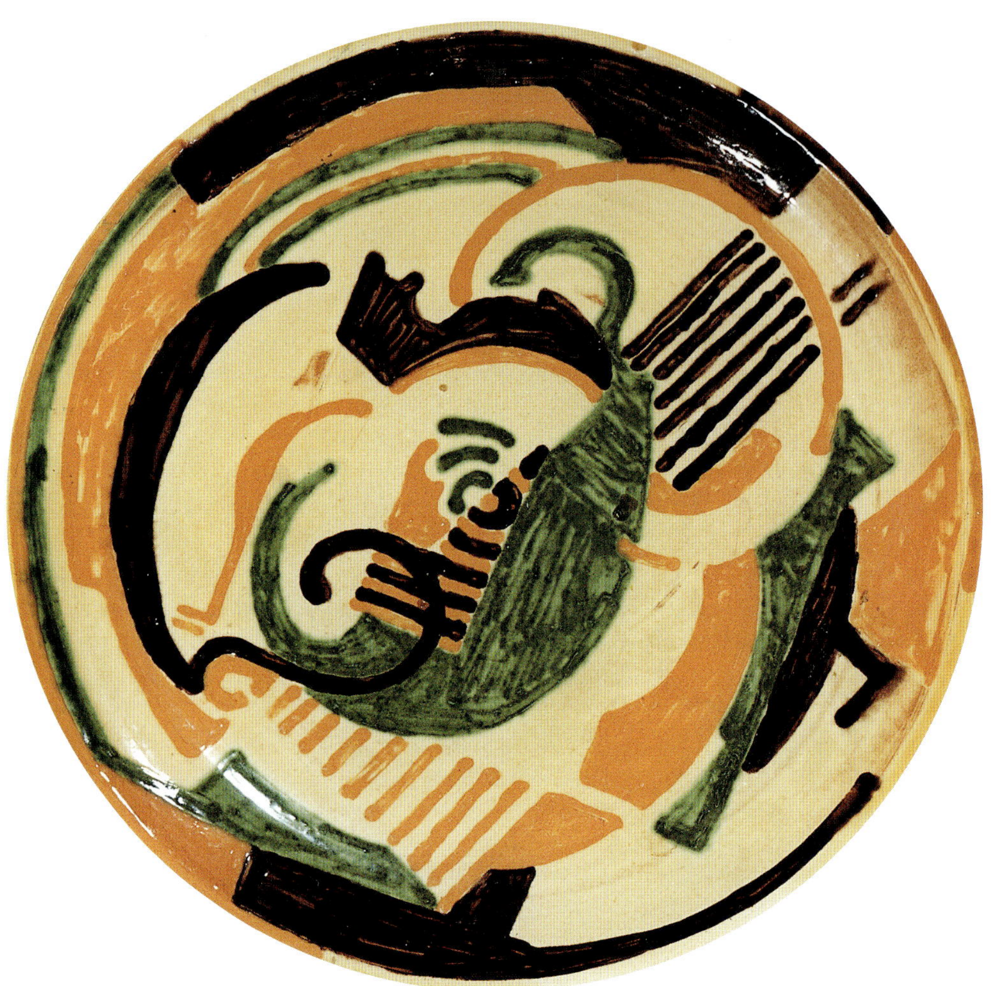

161. Geneviève Dalban, Plate with Cubist design, *c.* 1980. Glazed earthenware, dia. 39 cm. Private collection

still is very fragile, but it has lasted for forty years, which is already remarkable without any institutional support in an age that is obsessed with rapid change. During that time, a succession of young people have passed through Ampuis learning painting, pottery and weaving. But the problem of transmission, which is largely the problem of establishing a real 'traditional' workshop, is still far from being solved. It is no reproach to others who had the privilege of knowing and working with Gleizes that they have not solved it either. It is a problem of the age – a problem of the same order as that of the decline of the English arts and crafts movement. It is with a view to spreading a desire to address this problem – the feeling that such a transmission might be worthwhile – that this book has been written. To quote Anne Dangar, in a letter to Geneviève de Cissey, showing how removed we are from the sterile thing that the history of Cubism has become:

> Cubism is a state of mind – the rhythmic, traditional and religious spirit! It isn't a technique you can use or not, you feel it in you, it fills you. How can you not express it in everything that you do?[25]

NOTES

I
A Literary Prologue – The Abbaye de Créteil

1 My main source for this account of Gleizes' early life is the *Souvenirs*, written during the Second World War. Only a small part of the *Souvenirs* has been published (*Le Cubisme, 1910–14* and some parts relating to 1934, both published by the Association des Amis d'Albert Gleizes). There exists a typescript of the first section, *Enfance*. Page references are to the published fragments, or to the typescript *Enfance*; otherwise they are to the manuscript in the Musée National d'Art Moderne (MNAM), in Paris.
2 *Souvenirs – Enfance*, pp.16–18.
3 Ibid., p.33, cp *L'homme devenu peintre*, pp.99–103.
4 *Enfance*, p.26.
5 *Souvenirs – 1905–9, L'Abbaye de Créteil*, p.30
6 Ibid., p.31.
7 Ibid., p.34.
8 Ibid., p.40.
9 Ibid., p.31.
10 Ibid., p.49.
11 Christian Sénéchal: *L'Abbaye de Créteil*, p.138.
12 *Souvenirs – 1905–9*, p.44.
13 Ibid., p.45.
14 Mercereau against Duhamel in *L'Abbaye et le bolchévisme*; Duhamel on Mercereau in *Le Temps de la recherche*, pp. 61–7 Gleizes on Mercereau sending money, *Souvenirs – 1905–9*, p.51.
15 *Souvenirs – 1905–9*, p.37.
16 Sénéchal: *L'Abbaye*, pp.61–2. In a letter to Gleizes, sent while he was writing his book, Sénéchal says that he had visited Mme Ghil and discussed Gleizes with her: 'Your ears should have been blushing', Sénéchal to Gleizes, 16 November 1928.
17 Albert Gleizes: 'Vers une époque de bâtisseurs', in *Clarté* no.32, 11 September 1920. See below, ch.7.
18 Juliette Roche Gleizes: 'Mémoires – Le dadaïsme, 2e partie'. Mme Gleizes' memoirs consist of a large collection of very short typescript texts, each of which has its own title. It seems easier to give these titles rather than page references. There is an account of Ghil's relations with Mallarmé in Montal: *René Ghil*, esp pp. 29–30, though he does not give this story. In his *En méthode à l'œuvre* (1906), Ghil says, as we shall see in ch.7: 'nearly all the poets are but the degenerate leftovers of the rhapsodies of pleasure and sadness, who cannot do without Eden.'
19 Georges Duhamel: *Le temps de la recherche*, p.55.
20 *Souvenirs – 1905–9*, pp.35–6.
21 Sénéchal, *L'Abbaye*, pp.53, 55 and 66 (for Brancusi); p.66 for Marinetti. Marinetti was also involved, with Arcos, Duhamel, Mercereau and Vildrac, in a revival of Ghil's late nineteenth-century paper *Ecrits pour l'art* in 1905. See Montal, *René Ghil*, p.111.
22 *Souvenirs–1914–19, La guerre*, pp.10– 11.
23 Mercereau: *L'Abbaye*, p.16; Duhamel: *Temps de la recherche*, ch.5, p.57; Gleizes in Sénéchal, *L'Abbaye*, p.66.
24 *Mémoires – 1951 (2)*, pp.13–14. The Abbaye is also identified as Unanimist in ibid., *1934 – L'Angleterre et la guerre*, and in ibid., *1916*.
25 General account of Romains in Denis Boak: *Jules Romains, Twayne, New York, 1974*
26 Roger Fry: *Cubism*, pp.45–6.
27 There is a list of Abbaye publications in Sénéchal, *L'Abbaye*, pp.100–2
28 J.R.Gleizes: *Mémoires – 1916*.
29 Maxe, Jean (Pseudonym): '"L'Abbaye" et le Bolchévisme culturel', p.200.
30 Sénéchal, *L'Abbaye*, pp.110–11.
31 Gleizes: *The Abbey of Créteil, A Communistic Experiment*.
32 Sénéchal, *L'Abbaye*, p.89.

2
Towards Cubism. 1908–11

1 Albert Gleizes: *Souvenirs – Le cubisme, 1908–1914*, p.6.

2 It happens that at the end of his life, Gleizes made ink and wash drawings of a number of his earlier works, including works from this period, marking them with the original date. So that some of the works carrying this date are indeed by the same hand 'as that of the ink and wash drawings of the end of his life'. But I am referring here to the arabesques provided by such subjects as smoke or clouds and to the overall construction, which is still intuitive in the early works, becoming highly conscious in the later ones.

3 *Souvenirs – Le cubisme*, pp.7–8.

4 Ibid., p.9.

5 Accounts of Le Fauconnier in Robbins: 'Le Fauconnier and Cubism', and Cottington: *Cubism in the Shadow of War.*

6 Gleizes' tripartite division of the history of Cubism is developed in detail in his commentary to the illustrations in his book *Kubismus*, written for the Bauhaus. This will be discussed in more detail in ch. 9.

7 *Souvenirs – Le cubisme*, p.10. Though Gleizes had previously exhibited in the Salon d'Automne, in 1903 and 1904 (Barrer: *Quand l'art du vingtième siècle était conçu par les inconnus*, p.163).

8 *Souvenirs – Le cubisme*, p.11.

9 Loyer: *Gleizes et la majesté*, pp.19–20.

10 Apollinaire: *Chroniques d'art*, pp.158–9.

11 Ibid., pp.155–6. Of Metzinger he says: 'It is sad to see a cultured painter waste himself in this way in sterile efforts'.

12 Robbins: 'Formation and Maturity', pp.80–1. See also the account of the literature on the 1910 Salon in Robbins: *Jean Metzinger*, pp.14–15.

13 Account of the coup d'état in the Salon des Indépendants of 1911 in *Souvenirs – Le cubisme*, pp.15–20.

14 Gleizes on 'flânerie' in an unpublished notebook in the possession of Jean Chevalier, Lyon.

15 *Souvenirs – Le Cubisme*, p.21.

16 Ibid., p.24.

17 Ibid., pp. 25–6.

18 Albert Gleizes to Mme [Gabrielle Vienne?], nd [1953]. Further extracts from this important letter are given in Gleizes: *Gleizes sur Picasso et Braque.*

19 The story of Gleizes' involvement is told in Gleizes: 'Apollinaire, la justice et moi', pp.53–65. There is a good overall account of the affair in Richardson: *A Life of Picasso*, vol.2, *1907–1917 – The Painter of Modern Life.*

20 The view that 'Salon' Cubism is something more than a poor imitation of the 'essential Cubism' of Picasso and Braque is beginning at last to be generally accepted. See for example David Cottington: *Cubism in the Shadow of War.*

21 There is an account of Kahnweiler's policy and contracts in Gee: *Dealers, Critics and Collectors*. See also Assouline: *L'Homme de l'art*, and Richardson: *Picasso.*

22 In Metzinger: *Le Cubisme était né*, p.57.

23 Virginia Spate: *Orphism*, pp. 16–17. There is an account of Delaunay's relations with Uhde in Georges Bernier and Monique Schneider Maunoury: *Robert et Sonia Delaunay*, esp pp. 66–71. Sonia Delaunay had been married to Uhde, but it had been a marriage of convenience and they divorced without ill-feeling.

24 *Souvenirs – Le cubisme*, p.24.

25 Gleizes in *L'Art dans l'evolution générale*, p.148; Delaunay in a letter reproduced in *Du Cubisme à l'art abstrait*, p.123.

26 Robbins: 'Formation and Maturity', p.94. Apollinaire: *Chroniques d'art*, p.241. There is a curious confusion of dates in Richardson's account. He explains Apollinaire's support for the 'Salon Cubists' (p.207) by evoking his dissatisfaction with Picasso at the time of the statuettes affair in the autumn of 1911 (under interrogation Picasso denied that he knew him). We have seen, however, that Apollinaire had already been supporting the Salon Cubists, despite his attack on Metzinger at the 1910 Salon d'Automne, since the beginning of the year. If there is an inconsistency in Apollinaire's relations with the painters it lies in the attack on Metzinger. A portrait of Apollinaire by Metzinger featured in the 1910 Salon des Indépendants (it is reproduced in Cottington, *Cubism in the Shadow of War*, p.156).

27 Gleizes states that the order of the illustrations in *Du 'Cubisme'* reflects the chronological order of the adhesion of the painters in his Preface to the 1947 edition – Albert Gleizes and Jean Metzinger: *Du 'Cubisme'*, (1980 ed.) p.29.

28 Account of Apollinaire's relations with the Delaunays in e.g. the introduction by L.C.Breunig and J.Cl.Chevalier to Guillaume Apollinaire: *Les Peintres cubistes*, pp.22–7.

29 Robbins: 'Formation and Maturity', p.91 *et seq.*

30 Gleizes: 'Jean Metzinger', p.164.

3
Cubism. 1912–14

1 There is an account of the debate, giving substantial extracts, in Patrick F. Barrer, *Quand l'Art du XXe siècle*, pp.93–101.
2 Gleizes to [Dorival?], 2 January 1953.
3 Mme Gleizes tells the story in her *Mémoires – Le Dadaïsme, 1ère partie.*
4 Picasso, it is true, was able largely to dictate the terms of his relationship with Kahnweiler. He was in a very strong position owing to the success of his pre-Cubist work. Braque refused to exhibit in the Salon d'Automne after his early Cubist 'L'Estaque' paintings had been refused – by a jury which included Matisse – but this does not of itself explain his withdrawal from the non-jury Salon des Indépendants. It was only in 1912 that Gris began to appear as a serious Cubist painter. He signed up with Kahnweiler in February 1913. Léger only passed into Kahnweiler's camp (where he was received with suspicion by Picasso and Braque) in October 1913, at which time he signed a contract forbidding him from participating in the Salons. See Derouet et al: *Léger*, p.301. He justifies his departure from the Salons in his article 'Les réalisations picturales actuelles', p.52 *et seq.*). There is a general account in Assouline: *L'Homme de l'art.*
5 This is a central thesis of Robbins' doctoral thesis, 'Formation and Maturity of Albert Gleizes'.
6 William Innes Homer's *Seurat and the Science of Painting*, 1964, shows that, in his last paintings, Seurat was attempting a scientific approach to the problem of form, using methods proposed by Charles Henry, in much the same way as he had earlier used the methods proposed by Ogden Rood to develop his scientific approach to the problem of colour.
7 See William Rubin: *Picasso et Braque*, p.49. He argues that the first use of the terms 'analytical' and 'synthetic' Cubism to describe the change that took place in the work of Picasso and Braque around 1912 occurs in an article, probably written by the critic Carl Einstein, in the journal *Documents*, vol.2, no.3, 1930, published in close association with D-H Kahnweiler.
8 Quotations from Apollonio (ed): *Futurist Manifestos*, pp.28 and 92.
9 Cabanne: *Entretiens avec Marcel Duchamp*, p.31. See also Tomkins: *Duchamp*, pp.79–84. Although sharing the conventional view of Gleizes and his friends as a group of arid and unamusing dogmatists, Tomkins confirms that one of their main anxieties was the resemblance between Duchamp's painting and those of the Italians. He also points out that the *Nu descendant un escalier* was shown, without attracting any particular attention, in the Cubist exhibition organised by Gleizes' friend Jacques Nayral in Barcelona the following month, and at the Section d'Or exhibition in the autumn.
10 Severini in Jean Cassou et al: *Hommage à Albert Gleizes*, p.19. Without contradicting this view of Gleizes, Severini, in *The Life of a Painter*, gives a rather different impression of the general reaction of the Cubists. He says that the Parisian painters regarded the Italians with a certain condescension as rather backward country cousins, and that he himself shared their attitude and was rather embarrassed by the whole affair.
11 Cork: *Vorticism*, pp.248 and 279.
12 Daniel Robbins, in his preface to the 1980 edition, p.15. Unless otherwise stated, page references are to this edition. Extracts given are based on the English translation published in 1913.
13 *Du 'Cubisme'*, 5th ed, Paris (Figuière) nd [1912], p.44. The text differs from the 1980 edition.
14 e.g. p.45.
15 The possible influence of Nietzsche on *Du 'Cubisme'* is discussed in John Nash: 'The Nature of Cubism'. Gleizes quotes Nietzsche at the end of his article on Jean Metzinger in the Revue Indépendante. For the generosity of the Superman see e.g., in 'Of the Bestowing Virtues' in *Thus Spake Zarathustra*: 'Your soul aspires insatiably after treasures and jewels because your virtue is insatiable in wanting to give'. (p.100); and, in *The Will to Power*: 'Those who, from the fulness they represent and feel, involuntarily give to things and see them fuller, more powerful and pregnant with future - who at least are able to bestow something.' (p.30)
16 Louis Chassevent: *Quelques petits Salons*, p.32, quoted in Robbins: *Albert Gleizes*, p.20.
17 The question of Delaunay's attitude to Cubism is discussed in more detail in ch.13 below. Robbins in *Le Fauconnier and Cubism*. Léger in e.g. 'Les réalisations picturales actuelles' (*Fonctions de la Peinture*, p.52 *et seq.*, p.17 of the English translation in ibid.: *Functions of Painting*).
18 There is a lengthy discussion in Henderson: *The Fourth Dimension and Non-Euclidean Geometry in Modern Art.*
19 G.F.B.Riemann (the name is misspelt in

Du 'Cubisme') was one of the best-known nineteenth-century theorists of Non-Euclidean geometry.

20 Albert Gleizes: *La Peinture moderne*. The article was republished in Albert Gleizes: *Le Cubisme*, 1918, op. cit. Metzinger expresses his interest in the new geometries in letters addressed to Gleizes which I have reproduced in 'Jean Metzinger – Cubism as Realism', *Cubism*, no.8, Spring 1985.

21 The article is reproduced in Henderson: *Fourth Dimension*. I make a comparison between the thought of Gleizes and that of Malevich in Brooke: *Deux Peintres philosophes - Albert Gleizes et Kasimir Malévitch*.

22 Ozenfant and Jeanneret: *Après le Cubisme*, pp.16–17.

23 *Montjoie!*, 11–12 Nov–Dec 1913, which also included a brief essay by Gleizes on the Salon d'Automne. Valensi's presence in New York is mentioned in Borràs: *Picabia*. See also ch. 24 below.

24 In e.g. the afterword to the 1947 edition of *Du 'Cubisme'* and in *Le Cubisme était né*.

25 There is a magnificent full-scale reproduction of this work at Ampuis, executed in pencil by Geneviève Dalban.

26 Fry, *Cubism*, p.26.

27 Nicolas Berdyaev: *The Meaning of History*, Geoffrey Bles, 1936, pp.172–4; see also *The Meaning of the Creative Act*, pp.224–5.

28 Both quotations are in Signac, *D'Eugene Delacroix au néo-impressionisme*, pp. 50–1.

29 This provides the cover for Mark Antliff's book, *Inventing Bergson*.

30 Gleizes on Cézanne in *La Peinture et ses lois* and *Peinture et perspective descriptive*. Apollinaire, *Les Peintres cubistes*, p. 76.

31 In e.g. Firpo, *Albert Gleizes – Cubism with a future*.

4
In the Shadow of War

1 Account of Juliette Roche's first meeting with Gleizes in Pierre Alibert: *Gleizes - Biographie*, pp.62–3.

2 From a correspondence on Gleizes' painting between his father, Sylvain, and his uncle, Honoré. Alibert, *Gleizes*, pp.36–7, attributes this correspondence to 1909, but one of the letters, which Alibert had not seen, is dated February 1911.

3 Juliette Roche Gleizes: *Mémoires – 1914*.

4 e.g. in *L'Homme devenu peintre*, pp.32–8.

5 Juliette Roche Gleizes: *Mémoires – La tribu*.

6 Fry, *Cubism*, p.36.

7 Republished in Gleizes: *Tradition et cubisme, vers une conscience plastique*, p.22.

8 There is a warm tribute paid to Boccioni for having felt the possibility of pictorial dynamism in *L'Homme devenu peintre*, p.79.

9 Anna Paolo Massetto Campro: *Montjoie! ou la ronde des formes et des rythmes*. The book does not appear in Antliff's bibliography but it developes quite a thoroughgoing case for the 'Celtic' orientation of *Montjoie!*.

10 Severini, *Life of a Painter*, p.114. He complains that *Montjoie!* was 'too accessible to just anybody'.

11 Gleizes takes up the theme of a Gaulish/Frankish alliance against the Romans in 'Réhabilitation des Arts Plastiques', *Tradition et cubisme*, pp.82–3. Antliff expands on the populist anti-Frank character of the Celtic nationalist strand in French literature, pp.118– 19.

12 Quoted in Alibert, *Gleizes*, pp.63–4. A similar passage is given in Steegmuller: *Cocteau*, pp.115–16 and in Cottington, *Cubism in the Shadow of War*, p.193. Misia Godebska, or Misia Sert, or Misia Edwards, helped to finance Diaghilev's Ballets Russes. She organised the ambulance corps in which Cocteau served during the First World War. There are accounts of her in Steegmuller and in Frederick Brown: *An Impersonation of Angels*.

13 *Souvenirs*, op. cit., p.8. Steegmuller says that the music was to have been by Satie, conducted by Varèse (*Cocteau*, pp.132-6). Satie wrote *Five Grimaces for a Midsummer Night's Dream*. It was, according to Steegmuller, Varèse who introduced Cocteau to Picasso, in December. There is a fuller account, which also explains the role of the fourteen-year-old Georges Auric, in Olivia Matis: *Theater as Circus: 'A Midsummer Night's Dream'*.

14 Rudenstine: *The Guggenheim Museum Collection*, p.160.

15 They are in the Musée des Beaux-Arts in Lyon.

16 The account of this period of Gleizes' life is largely based on the *Souvenirs – 1914–19, La guerre*.

17 If we assume that he is the 'Dr Morinaud' whom Robbins identifies as the model in New York retrospective exhib. cat., 1964. See Varichon et al: *Catalogue raisonné*, p. 143.

18 *Souvenirs - La guerre*, p.6.

19 Ibid., p.7. A gouache of Valmier's portrait is reproduced in the catalogue raisonné by

Denise Bazetoux: *Georges Valmier*, p.45.

20 *Souvenirs – La guerre*, p.15.

21 Quoted in André Dubois: *Anne Dangar et Moly Sabata*, pp.69– 70.

22 *Souvenirs – La guerre*, pp.7–8. Gleizes' article – 'C'est en allant se jeter à la mer que le fleuve reste fidèle à sa source' – is discussed in Silver: *Esprit de Corps*, but Silver, like the French censorship, sees only the patriotic main text, not the subversive subtext. He also complains to the effect that Gleizes, stressing the French character of the avant-garde and that nearly all its leading representatives are at war, is trying to write Picasso out of the historical account. Given that the main point of the article was to reply to accusations, widespread at the time, that the new art was unFrench and Germanic, the criticism seems rather specious. Silver, op. cit., pp. 39–42 of the French edition.

23 He develops the argument in *L'Art dans l'evolution générale*, mainly written in 1916. See e.g. pp.18–19, and 61–6.

24 Perhaps because there was in fact a rumour of his death, which was formally announced in the Salon des Indépendants. See Signac to Gleizes, 31 January 1915.

25 Alibert, *Gleizes*, pp.95–6.

26 *Souvenirs – La guerre*, p.18.

27 'Gleizes – l'artiste – soldat patriote ...' Silver, *Vers le Retour à l'ordre*, p.40.

28 'Conférence faite au Twillight [sic] Club de New York', Novembre 1915, unpubld ms.

29 Alibert, *Gleizes*, pp.96–7.

30 Robbins, who knew her very well and liked her, calls her a 'peculiarly eccentric kind of snob', *Formation and Maturity*, pp.213– 14.

31 Ibid., pp.192–3.

5
New York and Barcelona

1 *La Vie des lettres et des arts*, Oct 1920, p.178 *et seq.*

2 e.g. Robert Rosenblum: *Cubism and Twentieth-Century Art*, p.182.

3 There is an interesting account of the source of these phrases in Rudenstine, *Guggenheim Museum*, pp.153–5.

4 Gleizes mentions Stella approvingly in 'Quand je suis arrivé à New York en fin septembre 1915 ...'. (unpublished ms).

5 'Les voyages que je viens de faire en Canada, Açores, Portugal, Espagne ...'. (unpublished ms).

6 *Mémoires – 1916 (1).*

7 *Souvenirs – voyages en Amérique*, pp. 6–7.

8 These are the texts, never published, which Gleizes collected under the general title *Le Cavalier du Dimanche. Le Minéralisation de Dudley Craving McAdam* was published privately in 1924. Account of Stieglitz' circle in e.g. Homer: *Alfred Stieglitz and the American Avant-Garde.*

9 *Souvenirs – voyages en Amérique*, p.9.

10 *Mémoires – 1916 (2).*

11 Robbins questions Gleizes' account in his *Expectations and Disillusion.* I think he exaggerates the extent of the Gleizes' expectations, but it is certain that their attitude at the time was ambivalent.

12 In *Le Cavalier du Dimanche.*

13 General account of Picabia, particularly interesting on the relation with the Gleizes, in Borràs, *Picabia*. Sonia Delaunay on Picabia and the possibility that Picabia may have helped pay for the book in Robbins, *Formation and Maturity*, p.153. Picabia helping to pay for the publication of Apollinaire's *Les Peintres cubistes* in Sanouillet: *Picabia*, p.25.

14 Anecdotes of the period are given in Alice Halicka: *Hier, souvenirs.*

15 Delaunay: *Du Cubisme à l'art abstrait*, p.194. The date attributions are very dubious. There is a correspondence between Delaunay and Gleizes during the war in the Delaunay MSS, both in the Bibliothèque Nationale and in the MNAM. See Bernard Dorival: 'Robert Delaunay et Albert Gleizes'. One of Delaunay's letters, apparently written in 1917, after Gleizes had written *L'Art dans l'evolution générale*, refers to the possibility of working together to organise a Rousseau exhibition in New York (Fonds Delaunay, MNAM). Others indicate intriguingly that Delaunay saw himself and Gleizes as allies in a state of virtual war with the tendency represented by Picasso.

16 '[C]onséquence d'émotions et de raison qui touche à sa limite' – Surchamp, quoting Gleizes, in *L'Itinéraire pictural et spirituel d'Albert Gleizes*, p.6.

17 The year 1917 is sometimes given for the 'the revelation of Pelham' but Mme Gleizes (*Mémoires – En Attendant la Victoire*) says it took place eighteen months after January 1917, when Gleizes finished *L'Art dans l'evolution générale* (subtitled *En attendant la Victoire*). Firpo in *Albert Gleizes – Cubism with a Future.*

6
Paris After the War – I

1 *Souvenirs– retour à la France, 1919-26*, p.2.

2 Alibert, *Gleizes*, p.106 (fn).

3 Green discusses this development under the

title 'Crystal Cubism' in *Cubism and Its Enemies*, e.g. pp.25–37. Green's book provides an indispensable background to the whole period of the 1920s and therefore to the next seven chapters of the present book.

4 e.g. in 'L'Epopée' and in 'Spiritualité, rythme, forme', both in *Puissances du Cubisme*, pp. 122–3 and 338 respectively.

5 Green, *Cubism and its Enemies*, pp. 7–10.

6 André Lhote: 'Le Cubisme au Grand Palais' in *Nouvelle Revue Française*, no. 78, 1 March 1920, pp. 467 *et seq.*

7 For Allendy see Frémont: *La Vie du Dr René Allendy*, and for Henry's relations with the Neo-Impressionists, Homer: *Seurat and the Science of Painting* and Herbert: '"Parade de Cirque" de Seurat . . .'. For Sérusier see Boyle-Turner, *Paul Sérusier*, which includes an interesting discussion of his practical teaching and for the school of Beuron see Krins: *Die Kunst der Beuroner Schule*. At the time of writing, English translations of both Sérusier and Lenz are being prepared for publication by Francis Boutle publishers.

8 Picasso never signed a contract with Léonce Rosenberg, but Rosenberg bought his work and had contracts with Gris, Metzinger, Rivera, Laurens, Lipchitz, Lhote, Zarroga, Hayden, Severini, Braque and Léger. See the very interesting account in Gee, *Dealers, Critics and Collectors*, esp. pp.225–42. The Galerie de l'Effort Moderne opened in 1918 with what must have been a wonderful series of one-man shows given, in order, to Herbin, Laurens, Metzinger, Léger, Braque, Gris, Severini and Picasso (Gee, op. cit., p.232).

9 *Souvenirs, 1919–26*, p.8.

10 Ibid. Elements of Rosenberg's correspondence with painters, especially with Gris and Léger, are being published by Christian Derouet, e.g. correspondence with Gris in Green: *Juan Gris*, p.286, and in Derouet (ed): 'Juan Gris: Correspond-ances avec Léonce Rosenberg, *1915-1927*'; Léger in Derouet (ed): *Fernand Léger: une correspondance d'affaires*. See also discussion in Green: *Léger and the Avant-Garde*.

11 Reyner Banham: *Theory and Design in the First Machine Age*, pp.205–6.

12 Albert Gleizes: 'Vers une Époque de bâtisseurs, pt iv' in *Clarté*, no.22, 26 June 1920.

13 Gleizes: 'Hommage à Mainie Jellett' in Mainie Jellett: *The Artist's Vision*, pp.29–30.

14 Gleizes in *L'Art dans l'évolution générale*, p.148. I quote the passage in Brooke: 'Albert Gleizes: Another Way of Cubism'. Delaunay in his letter to Nicholas Minsky, 1912, *Du Cubisme à l'art abstrait*, p.123.

15 Metzinger to Gleizes, 4 July 1916 and 26 July 1916, translated in *Cubism*, no.8, Spring 1985.

16 Villon quoted in Colette de Ginestet: *Géometrie poétique et sécrète de Jacques Villon*.

17 Gleizes' preoccupation with 'depth' in this period will be looked at in more detail in ch.8.

7
Paris After the War – 2

1 The involvement of former members of the Abbaye and their associates in post war politics is discussed in 'Jean Maxe' (pseud): *L'Abbaye' et le bolchévisme culturel*. See ch. 1 above. Gleizes' involvement with the Fêtes du Peuple in Lyon is mentioned in Alibert, *Gleizes*, p. 201.

2 *Souvenirs – retour à France*, pp.3–4. Specifically, Gleizes says that he left when the syndicate expressed its support for Paul Léon, Director-General of the Beaux-Arts. Green: *Cubism and its Enemies*, refers to the constant opposition put up by the 'arch-reactionary' Paul Léon to all the manifestations of 'l'art vivant'.

3 J.R.Gleizes: *Mémoires, 1920–5 – Clarté*.

4 My general remarks, here and in what follows, on the left-wing politics of the period are largely drawn from Daspre and Décaudin (ed): *Histoire littéraire de la France*, and Edward Mortimer: *The Rise of the French Communist Party*.

5 Mme Gleizes on Vaillant-Couturier's early ambition to be a Benedictine monk in *Mémoires – 1920–5*.

6 Gleizes on Vaillant-Couturier and Lefebvre in *Souvenirs – retour à la France*, pp.4–6.

7 Alibert, *Gleizes*, p. 114, suggests that Gleizes may have been disillusioned by Lenin's New Economic Policy in 1921; J.R. Gleizes: *Mémoires – 1920–5* refers to disputes with Vaillant-Couturier when, in 1925–6, the latter lost patience with the pacifist approach. Gleizes argued that the working class could only advance if it managed to develop the early Christians' capacity for 'martyrdom' – without fighting back. In a letter to Ilya Ehrenburg (25 July 1930), Gleizes criticises the Russian Revolution for failing to recognise that humanity had to be saved from machinism, and, as we shall see in ch.12, he remarks that it was when he turned definitely against the machine, in 1925–6, that Vaillant-Couturier stopped visiting him.

8 Gleizes: *Souvenirs – retour à France*, p.6.

He says that *Clarté* lost subscribers because of his articles, but refers to the letter of support from Lyon, which appears in *Clarté*, 17 April 1920.

9 Gybal's articles are in *Clarté* (new series) no.2, 1 December 1921 and no.3, 21 December 1921.

10 For Lunacharsky, see e.g. the preface by J.Cl.Marcadé to Malévitch: *Écrits*, tome 1, esp. pp.23–4.

11 Mercereau: *L'Abbaye et le bolchévisme*, p.4.

12 Subsequent history of *Clarté* and Rolland's dispute with Barbusse in Daspre and Décaudin, *Histoire litteraire*, pp.251–75.

13 'Vers une époque de bâtisseurs', pt i, in *Clarté*, no.13, 20 March 1920.

14 Green, *Cubism and its Enemies*, pp. 144–5.

15 J.R.Gleizes: *Mémoires – Jean Cocteau*.

16 Alibert, *Gleizes*, p. 134.

17 Cocteau to 'Juliette et Albert' [Gleizes] 5 August 1920. I should add that Gleizes' nephew, Claude Gleizes, has insisted in conversation with me that Mme Gleizes told him it was she, in opposition to Gleizes, who wanted to end the relationship with Cocteau.

18 Green's account in *Cubism and its Enemies*, p.50; Hans Richter: *Dada*, p.179; J.R.Gleizes: op. cit., and *Mémoires – Le Dadaïsme*, 3 partie – 'l'Affaire Dada'. The presence of Braque, normally reluctant to associate with groups of other painters, is worth noting. For a contemporary account from the Dada point of view see Dermée: *Excommuniés*.

19 *391*, xiv, Nov. 1920. Under the circumstances, it is tempting to question its authenticity, on which Tzara insists, loudly. Or, alternatively, to think that the two had been drinking rather heavily.

20 In *Dada*, nos 4–5. See Borràs, *Picabia*, p.200.

21 Gleizes: 'L'Affaire Dada' in *Action* no.3, April 1920. I have used the translation by Ralph Manhelm which is given in Robert Motherwell (ed): *Dada Painters and Poets*, pp.298–303. In what is probably a response to Gleizes' remarks on the Dadaists' sexual obsessions, Picabia accused Gleizes of impotency, on the grounds that the Gleizes were childless (*Cannibale*, no.2, May 1920).

22 Green on Fels and *L'Art Vivant* in *Cubism and its Enemies*, pp. 172–4 and 203–7, though I should specify that this refers to Fels' support for naturalist painters such as Vlaminck in 1925–6, not the 1920 period.

23 Mercereau, *L'Abbaye et le bolchévisme*, p. 17. His correspondence with the Gleizes at this time indicates that he viewed them as exceptions. Alibert, *Gleizes*, p. 125, says, following Mme Gleizes, that Gleizes met Beauduin, editor of *La Vie des lettres et des arts*, in the Summer of 1919.

24 Virginia Spate, *Orphism*, p.37 quotes an account by Beauduin of Apollinaire's lecture at the Section d'Or exhibition of October 1912. He says that Apollinaire defined 'Orphism' in front of paintings by Kupka, which arrived too late to be included in the catalogue. Kupka fits very well into the general atmosphere of *La Vie des lettres et des arts*.

25 I have seen a copy of Milosz's *La Confession de Lemuel* with the ms dedication: 'A Monsieur Albert Gleizes, dans le monde du mouvement, en attendant une communion plus parfaite dans le Seul Situé. O.V. de L. Milosz'.

26 e.g. M.A.Chaix: 'L'Instrumentation Verbale' on Ghil's ideas on poetry in *La Vie des lettres et des arts*, new series, vol. i, July 1920; a review by Ghil of Marcello Fabri: *L'Inconnu sur les villes* (published by Povolozky), vol.vii, Dec 1921; and a review of Ghil's *La Tradition de la Poésie Scientifique*, in vol.viii, Feb 1922.

27 *Clarté* no.32, 11 September 1920. See above, ch.1.

28 René Ghil: *Oeuvres Complètes, tome 3*, p.304. It is worth noting that Ghil had previously been published by Figuière.

29 Mondrian calls for a separation of words and meaning in *Le Néo-Plasticisme*, pp.8–9, though he admits that it is not yet possible (and Ghil is not advocating it. He is simply advocating a greater consciousness of the characteristics of words other than their prose meaning). Articles by Mondrian on Futurist experiments in music and drama appear in *La Vie des lettres et des arts*, ix, April 1922 and xi, nd.

30 In the ms of *'Cubisme' – Vers une conscience plastique. Essai de généralisation*, pp.40–1: 'The word, restored to its proper place, revealed its value as word, sonorous and resounding [*résonante*]; it contributed to the birth of a cadenced whole, in which it played the role of measure. It began to free itself from discussion, to count, and, consequently, to vibrate.' Poetry was the first of the arts to fall into intellectual subjectivism and the first to free itself from intellectual subjectivism, followed by painting. Part of this essay was published in *La Vie des lettres et des arts*, xxi, nd, dated 'Serrières Sept 1925', but it does not include the passage quoted here.

31 One of my reasons for wanting to mention

Ghil here is that I think that much of what Mark Antliff attributes to the influence of Bergson could equally be attributed to the influence of Ghil. Ghil and Bergson have much in common, most notably the attempt to, so to speak, spiritualise Darwin's theory of evolution. They participate in a common intellectual atmosphere, but Gleizes would have known Ghil before he knew Bergson. It should perhaps be said that 'influence' is a misleading concept. It implies that the person is an empty vessel filled with something from the outside world. Gleizes presents his most important intellectual encounters as a matter of meeting in someone else, perhaps more fully realised, something which he has already felt within himself.

8
Painting and its Laws

1 Metzinger, *Le Cubisme était né*, pp. 59–60.
2 Alibert, *Gleizes*, pp.130–3. Poznansky in J.R.Gleizes: *Mémoires – l'état de la peinture en 1925*. Account of Colette Allendy in Frémont: *La Vie du Dr René Allendy.*
3 Arnold: *Mainie Jellett*, p.59.
4 *La Peinture et ses lois* was published privately in Paris in 1924 after being refused by Povolozky (Povolozky to Gleizes 19 January 1924). The frontispiece describes it as an 'essay published in *La Vie des lettres et des arts*, March 1923'. It appears in *La Vie des lettres et des arts*, vol. xii, no.5, which, like many copies of the journal, does not carry a date. It is included in the catalogue of the Bibliothèque Nationale for the year 1922 and, on the assumption that *La Vie des lettres et des arts* was, as it claimed to be, bimensual, vol. xii should have been published in October 1922 (the last dated issue was vol. ix, published in April). It seems unlikely that Gleizes could have made such an error in dating so soon after the original publication, but there are several clear errors in the dates given for articles in *La Vie des lettres et des arts* in his *Tradition et cubisme*, published in 1927.
5 The printed text reads 'eastern'. This is corrected by Gleizes in one of his own copies of the book.
6 Reproduced in Gleizes: *Tradition et cubisme*, p.107. *Choses simples* was published in *La Vie des lettres et des arts* vol. vi, Oct 1921, not 1920 as stated in *Tradition et cubisme.*
7 *Tradition et cubisme*, p.128.
8 Ibid., pp.168–70. *Tradition et cubisme* gives 1921 as the year when 'Des "Ismes"' was published in *La Vie des lettres et des arts*. In fact it appears in vol. ix, April 1922.
9 Kasimir Malévitch: *Écrits*, tome 1. The term 'economy' used by both Malevich and Gleizes is discussed in Brooke: *Deux Peintres philosophes*, pp.11–15.
10 There are collections of these drawings in the National Gallery in Dublin and in the Ulster Museum in Belfast.
11 *Souvenirs – 1934–9*, pp.1–2. The passage is given in *Albert Gleizes en 1934*.
12 Arnold, *Mainie Jellett*, p.67.
13 Cavalaire in Alibert, *Gleizes*, pp. 136–9 and in J.R.Gleizes: 'Albert Gleizes'.
14 Gleizes: *La Forme et l'histoire*, pp. 197–206.
15 Charles Henry: 'Les Travaux français sur les problèmes de la Théorie de la Relativité'.
16 It is based on the formula devised by the German mathematician Johann Gauss to express what was common to all the polygons that could be inscribed in a circle. The relation between the polygon and the circle was to be important to Gleizes' thinking, especially in the 1930s.
17 'La peinture d'avant garde, le machinisme et l'art – reconstruction de l'Univers' in Severini, *Ecrits sur l'art*, p.80.

9
Back to the Beginning

1 Dangar to Crowley, 23 June 1931. Anne Dangar: 'Notes for classes at Moly Sabata', 1949 in Gleizes archive, Ampuis.
2 Green, *Cubism and its Enemies*, p.85.
3 Ibid., e.g. pp.78–84.
4 *Eclair*, 26 June 1924.
5 Green, op.cit., p.89.
6 Gleizes to Lhote, 23 September 1943.
7 *Tradition et cubisme*, pp.149–50. English translation, Gleizes: *Modern Art and the New Society*, p.9.
8 *Souvenirs – 1926–33*, p.4.
9 Arnold, *Mainie Jellett*, p.69.
10 Mainie Jellett, *The Artist's Vision*, p.48.
11 *Souvenirs – 1934–9*, pp.1–2; *Albert Gleizes en 1934*, p.4.
12 Arnold, *Mainie Jellett*, p.69.
13 Gleizes to Pouyaud, 7 August 1934.
14 *Souvenirs – 1934-9*, p.2; *Albert Gleizes en 1934*, p.5.
15 See pp.24–5.
16 Dangar to Crowley, 7 March 1931.
17 *Souvenirs*, *1926–33*, p.4.
18 *Souvenirs – 1919–26*, p.2.
19 e.g. in 'Spiritualité, rythme, forme', *Puissances du Cubisme*, pp.321–2.
20 *Mémoires – 1925*.

21 Pouyaud to Gleizes, 19 August 1924.
22 Gleizes on Pouyaud in *Souvenirs – 1926-33*, p.3.
23 Though, writing to Evie Hone in 1922, he insists that there can be no question of their paying him for advice sent by letter.
24 Gleizes to Pouyaud, 1 September 1924.
25 Anne Dangar: 'Notes for classes at Moly Sabata', 1949, Gleizes archive, Ampuis.
26 Pouyaud to Gleizes, 19 June 1925 and 29 July 1925.
27 'L'Epopée', in *Puissances du Cubisme*, pp.127–8, though Gleizes says that the exhibition was held in 1920. 1921 is given as the date in the list of exhibitions in Robbins, *Albert Gleizes*.
28 Though he was to complain that he was never paid for it, Gleizes to [-], 25 November [-].
29 'Cubisme et Culture Générale', written in 1925 and published in *Vers l'unité*, no. 41, May–June 1926, where, however, the references to the exhibition, which had already finished, were removed.
30 Green, Cubism and its Enemies, p.92.
31 Ibid., p.113.
32 Ibid., p.97, quoting *L'Intransigeant*, 7 January 1926.
33 Fernand Léger to Albert Gleizes, n.d. [1926].
34 In *Documents*, vol.2, no.3, 1930. See ch.3, fn 6 above. Einstein probably got the terms, via Kahnweiler, from Juan Gris, who had been close to Metzinger during the war. In the way in which they appear among modern historians they are, therefore, a deformed version of a notion current among the 'Salon Cubists', who used them to refer not to two successive phases of Cubism, but to two different parts of the painter's act – the 'deconstruction', to coin a phrase, of the visible appearance of the object in the external world, and its reconstruction as a 'total image' in the new conditions imposed by the painting itself.
35 I am grateful to John Minihane for his help in translating the German text of this commentary.
36 William Wauer, Prospectus for *Ars* in Wauer to Gleizes, 17 June 1926. Account of Mainie Jellett's search for an English critic in Arnold, *Mainie Jellett*, p.95. Gleizes to de Noailles, 6 September 1926. Noailles buying from *L'Art d'aujourd'hui* in Green, *Cubism and its Enemies*, p.138.

10
The End of an Illusion

1 *L'Art d'aujourd'hui. Exposition de 85 artistes de 24 nations.*
2 *Mémoires – 1916.*
3 *Vie des lettres et des arts*, no.xxi, nd. The ms is dated 1925. The passage is quoted in Gleizes: *Life and Death of the Christian West*, p.95.
4 *Souvenirs – 1926–33*, pp.1–2. The idea of investing the machine with a soul is taken from Bergson.
5 e.g. in a very interesting letter to an unnamed Benedictine, 28 October 1929.
6 Pouyaud to Gleizes, 19 June 1925.
7 e.g. Dangar to Crowley, 17 March 1932. The talks, sent in the winter 1934–5, are also in the Crowley MSS, Sydney.
8 The terms 'intelligence' and 'intellect' as used here correspond to the Greek 'nous' (also translated 'spirit') and 'psyche' (also translated 'soul') but the reader should note that these terms are often, as in the authoritative English translation of the Philokalia, translated as, respectively, 'intellect' and 'intelligence'. Philip Sherrard, one of the translators of the Philokalia, has pointed out that Augustine sometimes calls the supra-rational faculty 'intelligence' and sometimes 'intellect' but that either way his concept should not be confused with the Greek 'nous'. Augustine is talking about a higher faculty of the created soul while the Greek concept invoked by Sherrard is of a nature distinct from the soul and is itself divine and uncreated. Gleizes as I see it derived his terms from Augustine but often gives them a 'Greek' meaning. There is a masterly summary of the question in Sherrard: *The Greek East and the Latin West*, pp.139 *et seq.*
9 A similar view of monasticism as a longing for simplicity and the return to the soil in reaction against an over-intellectualised culture is given in J.H.Newman: *The Mission of the Benedictine Order.*
10 Stella Frost: *Evie Hone*. Account of Evie Hone's period at Truro in Arnold, *Mainie Jellett,* pp. 103–7.
11 In ch. 6. It should perhaps be mentioned that Verkade's book is rather reticent with regard to the distinctive principles of Peter Lenz, the main theorist of the school of Beuron, and, generally, to the idea of a scientifically based painting. This was a source of some friction between himself and Sérusier.
12 e.g. Jellett to Gleizes, 8 September 1926.
13 Letter of August 1926, quoted in White and Hone: 'Evie Hone', unpublished ms, nd., ch.9.
14 Account of Louis de Broglie in Gamow: *Thirty Years that Shook Physics*, pp. 80–1.
15 Gleizes uses the term 'metaphysics' similar-

ly as a term of reprobation e.g. in *L'Epopée*, (begun in 1925) referring to the representational idea of painting. See Gleizes: *The Epic, From Immobile Form to Mobile Form*, p.30 and fn.

16 'Biologie: Vie et survie', typescript in Gleizes archive, priv.coll., p.8.

17 *Essai de généralisation de la théorie du rayonnement*, p.137.

18 Juliette Roche: 'Charles Henry'; Albert Gleizes: 'Charles Henry Universitaire', in *Cahiers de l'Étoile*, no.13, Jan–Feb 1930, pp.31 and 122 respectively. See also J.R. Gleizes: *Souvenirs – 1926–33*, pp.3–4. Henry's argument for life after death is discussed in Mirabaud: *Charles Henry et l'idéalisme scientifique*.

19 'Charles Henry Universitaire', p.122.

20 'L'Inquiétude, crise plastique', ms version, p.2. *La Vie des lettres et des arts*, no.xx, May 1925.

21 Coleridge's word 'esemplastic' – formed into a unity – is a pleasing equivalent.

22 Later, as we shall see, Gleizes would talk rather about the transformation of geometry (tied to space) into arithmetic (which, unlocated, was able to enter into time).

23 The passage appears in both *L'Inquiétude* and *Cubisme: essai de généralisation*, both on p.5 of the ms versions.

24 *L'Inquiétude*, p.6.

25 *Essai de généralisation*, p.19.

26 *L'Inquiétude*, p.6.

27 *Souvenirs – 1926–33*, pp.5–6.

28 There are several references in the correspondence, e.g. Jean Baltus to Gleizes, 9 April 1930.

29 *Souvenirs – 1926–33*, pp.5–6; Mme Gleizes' version in Alibert, *Gleizes*, pp.189–90.

30 Dangar to Crowley 17 May 1936.

31 Pouyaud: *Moly Sabata*. J.R. Gleizes: *Souvenirs – 1926–33*, p.3.

11
Moly Sabata

1 Dangar to Crowley, 26 July 1932.

2 Dangar to Crowley, 23 November 1932.

3 Gleizes does not specify where but Severini in *Life of a Painter* says of this period: 'many foreigners soon flocked to Paris and at a certain point there were approximately forty thousand artists' (p.207).

4 Gleizes: 'Moly Sabata' (ms), pp.1–5.

5 General account of the story of Moly Sabata in Pouyaud: *Moly Sabata*, and in Dubois: *Anne Dangar and Moly Sabata*

6 Pouyaud to Gleizes, 11 June 1928.

7 *New York Herald*, 25 March 1923.

8 There is a letter from him to Gleizes, written after his stay in Moly, in which he says that he has been invited by Jean Paulhan to work for the *Nouvelle Revue Française*. Georges Dobo to Gleizes, 16 November 1928.

9 *Clarté*, no.15, 17 April 1920.

10 Manevy to Gleizes, nd.

11 This introduction is reprinted in Firpo: *Lettres adressées à l'Association des Amis d'Albert Gleizes*. Firpo's family moved to France from America before the First World War, but he never relinquished his American citizenship.

12 Quoted in Stella Frost, *Evie Hone*.

13 Pouyaud to Gleizes, 22 September 1929.

14 *Mémoires, 1927–9*.

15 Pouyaud to Gleizes, 2 October 1929.

16 *Mémoires – Congrès de Barcelone*, 1929.

17 e.g. Dangar to Jean Chevalier, 29 August 1938, quoted in Dubois : *Anne Dangar et Moly Sabata*, pp.41–2. There is an account of Ashton's circle and of Anne Dangar's career in Australia in Topliss: *Modernism and Feminism*.

18 Dangar to Crowley, nd [1931].

19 Dangar to Geneviève de Cissey, 28 August 1950, Gleizes MSS, Ampuis.

20 *Undergrowth*, Oct–Nov 1927, quoted in Humphrey McQueen: *The Black Swan of Trespass*, p.6. I am grateful to Bruce Adams for pointing out that the author of this letter was Crowley not Dangar, as stated in *Black Swan*.

21 Dangar to Gleizes 13 January 1941.

22 Dangar: 'Notes for classes given in Moly Sabata', August 1949, Gleizes MSS, Ampuis.

23 Dangar to Crowley, 23 June 1931.

24 Dubois: *Anne Dangar et Moly Sabata*, p.57.

25 Pouyaud to Jellett, 19 June 1930. Letter communicated to me by Bruce Arnold.

26 Pouyaud to Gleizes, June 1930; Dangar to Crowley, 17 September 1930.

27 Pouyaud to Jellett, 19 June 1930.

28 Dangar to Crowley, nd [1931].

29 Dubois: *Anne Dangar et Moly Sabata*, p.36. There is a good account of Charchoune in Waldberg et al.: *Charchoune,* Centre National d'Art Contemporain,Paris, 1971.

30 Dangar to 'Mr & Mme Gleizes', 29 May 1930.

31 *Mémoires – Arrivée d'Anne Dangar*.

32 Pouyaud to Gleizes, 5 September 1929.

33 Dangar to Crowley, 11 March 1934. The Crowley MSS are also the main source for other details in this paragraph.

34 Gleizes: 'Moly Sabata', *Sud Magazine*, no. 1021, 1 June 32.

35 Dangar to Crowley, 29 November 1934.

36 Dangar to Crowley, 23 June 1931. So much for Romy Golan's notion that Moly Sabata was partly supported by

'the financial contributions of an ex-student of Gleizes' (the Australian Anne Dangar)', *Modernity and Nostalgia*, p.86.

37 Dangar to Crowley, 2 March 1932.

38 Gleizes: 'Moly Sabata', *Sud Magazine*, no. 1021, 1 June 32.

39 Marcel Corneloup and Michel Burgard (ed): *César Geoffray par ses textes*, esp. pp.17–19.

40 César Geoffray: *Dix Ans de présence à Moly Sabata.*

41 His dismissive attitude is referred to in Arnold, *Mainie Jellett*, p.105.

42 Pouyaud, Anne Dangar and Dobo. Gleizes, showing a rather disgraceful flair for propaganda, divides Anne Dangar into two persons, a painter giving lessons to the village, and a potter.

43 *Mémoires – 1932.*

12
The Mystery of the Bread and Wine

1 J.R.Gleizes in *Zodiaque*, no.25, April 1955, p.35. Rohan's sympathy for German National Socialism in a review by Thomas Greenwood (a Roman Catholic mathematician who had been the English representative of the Unions Intellectuelles) of his book *Schikalsstunde Europas*, Graz, 1937, in *Sud Magazine*, no.148, May 1937.

2 An ms account of his contribution has survived: 'Le Professeur Carl Schmidt nous a souligné la necessité ...'.

3 An English translation is also available. See the bibliography. Gleizes: *Art et Religion* etc also includes a brief account of the tour by Mme Gleizes.

4 *Mémoires – 1930, Vie et mort de l'occident chrétien.*

5 So it is not, as Romy Golan calls it (*Modernity and Nostalgia*, p.86), an 'unpublished manuscript'. *Les Cahiers de l'Etoile* was the French journal of the international movement associated with J.Krishnamurti, the 'Order of the Star', developed for him within the Theosohical movement under the guidance of Annie Besant. The English equivalent was called *The Star Review*. Krishnamurti at this time was disbanding the Order of the Star and preaching a mystical unity that went 'beyond Good and Evil', encouraging the development of strong passions. This aspect was celebrated in articles by the editor, the poet Carlos Suarès, but the journal, aiming at an ambitious synthesis of modern thought, scientific and cultural, was very diverse. Gleizes' articles, calling for a return to Christian renunciation, square oddly with the anarchic and modernist tendency of the editorials. The journal stopped in 1930, with the publication of a major survey of the opinions of leading intellectuals, including Gleizes, on the 'anxiety' (inquiétude) of the age.

6 Gleizes to 'the editor of the *Tablet*', 15 September 1947.

7 *La Forme et l'histoire*, pp.365–7.

8 The historian Georges Duby, in his *Guerriers et paysans*, an account of the Dark Ages written from a rather different viewpoint than that of Gleizes, confirms that wheat and the grape – typically Mediterranean crops – were introduced throughout Northern Europe by the monks with their sacramental role in mind (pp.26–8).

9 Not to be confused with the Nudist movement, though the two overlapped given the Naturists' enthusiasm for the – at the time – radical practice of sunbathing.

10 Guénon was soon to become formally a Muslim but his terminology, epecially in the 1920s, is usually drawn from Hinduism.

11 It laid particular emphasis on developments in the new science of psychoanalysis, and regularly published the proceedings of Allendy's Groupe d'Etude Philosophique et Scientifique pour l'examen des tendances nouvelles.

12 Frémont: *Vie du Dr René Allendy*, Climats, e.g. pp.45–6 and p.55.

13 *Vie et mort*, p.28.

14 Ibid., p.35.

15 *Souvenirs – 1926–33*, p.2.

16 'Les manifestations du cubisme furent surprenantes ... ', extract from a French ms version of *Kubismus*, p.15. The passage does not appear in the published German *Kubismus*.

17 *Life and Death*, p.11.

18 Jacques Povolozky to Gleizes, 31 October 1930.

19 *Mémoires – 1930, Vie et mort de l'occident chrétien.*

20 Henry: 'Le Contraste, le rythme, la mesure', p.376.

21 Ibid., p.372.

22 *La Forme et l'histoire*, p.425. See also Gleizes to a Benedictine Abbot, 28 October 1929. Henry's 'aesthetic protractor' is reproduced in Homer: *Seurat and the Science of Painting*.

23 The argument of this paragraph is developed at length in *Art et science*.

24 *La Forme et l'histoire*, pp.217 and 246–8.

25 Plotinus: *Enneads,* vi.vii.32. See ch.8 above.

13
Robert Delaunay

1 'L'épopée', in *Puissances du cubisme*, p.122.
2 This essay, originally written in 1933, was re-worked in 1937 and again in 1945. It was never published. The most complete version, that of 1945, is in the Fonds Delaunay in the Bibliothèque Nationale.
3 Gleizes to Hone, 1922.
4 Gleizes to Pouyaud, 22 November 1926.
5 Pouyaud to Gleizes, 28 March 1927.
6 Dangar to Crowley, 29 March 1930 and 24 June 1930.
7 A summary appears in the papers of her pupil, Hélène de St Pierre. Photocopy communicated to me by Bruce Arnold.
8 Pouyaud to Gleizes, 3 December 1945 and 21 January 1946.
9 Dangar to Crowley, 29 March 1930.
10 Dangar to Crowley, 24 June 1930.
11 The Serrières story is given in Alain Tapié: *L'Art sacré d'Albert Gleizes*. The Ecole de Pharmacie in Mme Gleizes: *Mémoires – 1925*. Preparatory gouaches for the Ecole de Pharmacie are in the Musée de Beaux Arts at Lyon and in the Skissernas Museum in Lund, Sweden.
12 For Rood see Homer, *Seurat and the Science of Painting*, and for his influence on Delaunay, Roque: 'Les vibrations colorées de Delaunay', in Rousseau et al.: *Robert Delaunay*, p.63.
13 'La Lumière, la couleur et la forme', pp.7–8.
14 Le Contraste, le rythme, la mesure', p.364.
15 'L'épopée', in *Puissances du cubisme*, p.120.
16 See the preface by L.C. Breunig and J.Chevalier to the 1965 edition of Apollinaire's *Méditations esthétiques*, pp.22–4.
17 *Der Stürm*, no.144–5, 1913. *Du Cubisme à l'art abstrait*, p.146.
18 *Du Cubisme à l'art abstrait,* p.157.
19 Ibid., p.123.
20 Ibid., p.159.
21 Ibid., p.186.
22 Only the first sentence is given in quotation marks in the printed version but it seems to me to be evident that the whole passage goes together.
23 Ibid., p.182.
24 Ibid., p.179.
25 Gleizes to Delaunay, 12 December 1929.
26 Exchange of letters in *L'Intransigeant*, 4 November 1929 and 8 November 1929.
27 Delaunay to Gleizes, nd [*c.*1931].
28 Delaunay to Gleizes, 11 October [1930–31?].
29 The passages on Picasso are reproduced in *Gleizes sur Picasso et Braque*, pp. 10–13. See also 'L'épopée', in *Puissances du cubisme* and the English translation, *The Epic*.
30 Gleizes to Delaunay, Feb 1930.
31 Gleizes to Delaunay. I have seen two typescript copies of this letter in the Gleizes archives, one dated 9 April 1930, the other 9 August 1930. The earlier date seems more probable. Given Gleizes' handwriting, it is easy to see how a typist could have mistaken 'avril' for 'aoüt'.
32 Seuphor: *A Dictionary of Abstract Painting*, entry on Gleizes, p.179. Seuphor spent some time in Moly Sabata in 1932 and wrote a malicious fictional account of it, particularly hostile to Gleizes, in his *Les Evasions d'Oliver Trickmansdorff*.

14
1934

1 *Du Cubisme à l'art abstrait,* p.72.
2 Ibid., p.75.
3 'How could it not throw the immobility of classical space into confusion, colour, that is time itself?' – Gleizes: 'Robert Delaunay'.
4 Louis Hoyack: *Où va le machinisme?*, pp.106–8.
5 e.g. Dangar to Crowley, 19 June 1935. Pouyaud: *Du 'Cubisme' à la peinture traditionelle*, pp.41–2.
6 Gleizes says 'he', but the person in question could well be Mme Gleizes, who studied under Redon.
7 Dangar to Crowley, nd (1931 – the letter mentions the presence of J. Grelin, a young 'naturalist' who was at Moly Sabata in 1931).
8 Superimposed the drawing on the panel probably by means of a carbon copy.
9 Dangar to Crowley, 10 February 1931.
10 Gleizes to Pouyaud, 5 January 1931.
11 Pouyaud passed a gouache by himself with a correction by Gleizes to Genevieve Dalban at Ampuis. Both are dated by Pouyaud and Gleizes respectively '1926', but they seem to correspond closely to the description in this letter and to the work of both painters in 1931. They do not at all correspond to their work of 1926. I assume that the dates were added later, perhaps when Pouyaud visited Les Méjades around 1940, and in error.
12 Dangar to Crowley, 17 March 1932.
13 Jellett to Gleizes, 9 December 1932.
14 Herbin to Gleizes, 24 February 1933.
15 Gleizes to Delaunay, 12 January 1927.
16 Gleizes discusses his attitude to the word 'abstract' in Gleizes to Pouyaud, 22 November 1926. and in Gleizes to Graf, 9 September 1932. The whole question of

his attitude to the representational image is discussed more fully in my next chapter.
17 They appear in an 'Agenda' with the printed date 1929. The original is in the possession of Jean Chevalier, Lyon.
18 Gleizes to Delaunay, nd (Spring 1934).
19 *Albert Gleizes en 1934*, p.1.
20 Dangar to Crowley, 11 March 1934.
21 Gleizes' copy of *Les Aubes* is dedicated 'For Albert Gleizes, in unity of thought'.
22 These issues are discussed in his correspondence with Gleizes.
23 Largely reproduced in *Le Pouvoir des mots-clef*, (English translation: *Key Words*).
24 *Albert Gleizes en 1934*, pp.6–9.
25 In *Art et science, Art et religion, etc.* pp.77–9 (pp.73– 4 in the English translation).
26 Dangar to Crowley, 11 March 1934.
27 Arnold, *Mainie Jellett*, p.144. In the *Souvenirs – 1934–9*, pp.20–1, he says that it was when he saw these paintings at a one-man-show held 'in the unfamiliar surroundings of Abstraction-Création' (June 1934) that he was forced to admit the external nature of the grey circles.
28 Reproduced in *Albert Gleizes en 1934*.

15
From Figure to Light

1 Robbins in his review of Christopher Green: *Cubism and Its Enemies*, *Times Literary Supplement*, April 8–14, 1988; Dorival: 'Robert Delaunay et Albert Gleizes'.
2 Gleizes to Pouyaud, 22 November 1926.
3 *La Forme et l'histoire*, e.g. pp.98–103, 274–82, 372–80. Preference for wood over stone as a matter of principle not of technical incompetence, pp.387–8, and reluctance to 'modify the creator's work through the combinations put together by his own imagination', pp.276–7.
4 Gleizes to Graf, 9 September 1932.
5 See ch.13 above.
6 Herbin to Gleizes, 24 February 33, quoted above, ch.14. Gladys Fabre: *Herbin*, says that in 1934 there was a row over Herbin's taking decisions without consulting the committee and that among these was the decision to authorise a talk by Gleizes. The row resulted in the resignation of Hélion, Arp, Sophie Tauber-Arp, and Fernandez. This is presumably what is referred to in a letter from Gleizes to Hélion, 8 June 1934: 'I can't enter into these quarrels which, so far as I'm concerned, can only have one result – to please our enemies. That is why I deplore everything that's going on at present in A[bstraction] C[réation], and remain perfectly aloof from this dispute which I don't understand.' Hélion appears to have written to assure him that there was nothing personal against him in the dispute.
7 Pouyaud to Gleizes, 4 July 1933.
8 Gleizes to Pouyaud, 7 August 1934.
9 Pouyaud to Gleizes, 9 September 1934.
10 Gleizes to Pouyaud, 12 February 1935; Pouyaud to Gleizes, 17 February 1935.
11 Gleizes to Delaunay 26 February 1935.
12 Dangar to Gleizes, 18 January 1935.
13 Dangar to Crowley, 24 July 1933.
14 Dangar to Crowley, 24 March 1935.
15 Dangar to Crowley, 2 June 1935. The first reference to Michaud I have noted (though it is as if Crowley already knows who he is) is 17 May 1935.
16 Rosenberg to Gleizes, 15 [November?] 1934.
17 Rosenberg to Gleizes, 7 January 1929.
18 Gleizes to Rosenberg, 20 May 1934.
19 'Le retour à la terre' in *Beaux Arts*, Paris, 14 December 1934.
20 Arrival of Plasses in Dangar to Crowley, 30 March 1933.
21 *Mémoires – 1935, La 12eme gerbe.*
22 *Régénération*, no.64, Oct 1935, pp.28–9.
23 *Mémoires – 1936.*
24 Povolozky to Gleizes, 29 August 1935.
25 Rosenberg first mentions the project in Rosenberg to Gleizes, 8 February 1935.
26 Delaunay to Gleizes, nd [1935].
27 Rosenberg to Gleizes, 9 March 1935.
28 Rosenberg on Paul's survival in Rosenberg to Gleizes, 25 October 1934. On privations of his family see same to same, nd, [apparently following 29 November 1935].
29 Gleizes' objection to Valmier in an account of the dispute by Anne Dangar to Grace Crowley, 24 March 1935. She says – and we may assume that the idea derived from Gleizes – that the whole exhibition had been got up by Rosenberg to stimulate interest in Valmier, since he had invested heavily but unsuccessfully in him. Only five paintings by Gleizes, three of them small, were shown. Rosenberg attributed this under-representation to Cogniat and Wildenstein; Dangar, perhaps following Gleizes, attributes it to Rosenberg himself.
30 Rosenberg to Gleizes, 12 March 1935.
31 Gleizes: 'Les Créateurs du Cubisme' in *Sud Magazine* no.126, 15 April 1935. Gleizes even has a kind word to say for Valmier, who features in the illustrations (all of which, apart from those showing work by Gleizes and Delaunay, come from Rosenberg's collection).

32 Arnold, *Mainie Jellett*, p.119.
33 Huyghe to Gleizes, nd [early 1934]; Gleizes to Huyghe, 14 February 1934; Huyghe to Gleizes, 17 February 1934.
34 Rosenberg to Gleizes, 22 August 1935.
35 Rosenberg to Gleizes, 15 [Nov?] 1934.

16
The Universal Exhibition

1 Sympathy for Nazi agrarian reform in *Régénération*, no.49, March 1934, p.16; no.52, June–July, 1935, p.8; for Soviet agrarian reform in ibid., no.65, Nov. 1935, p.16 *et seq*.
2 E.B. Havell: *Ideals of Indian Art*, p.xvii. The piece was written by Sir George Birdwood, curator of the Indian section of the South Kensington Museum, who had in fact been an early defender of Indian craft against the competition of the English industrial system. Considering the usual western definition of the term 'fine arts' the statement is in itself, quite defensible. For the controversy surrounding Birdwood's views on Indian art, see Lipsey: *Coomaraswamy*, pp.30, 36 and 53.
3 Guénon to Gleizes, 4 December 1939.
4 Guénon, writing to Gleizes from Cairo in November 1931, says 'I would be happy to see you again.' Alibert, *Gleizes*, pp.207–8, citing Mme Gleizes as his source, says that they met in 1927 but, despite an immediate mutual liking, they did not meet again until 1930, when Gleizes re-established contact at the suggestion of Pouyaud. Pouyaud says in 'Les sept étapes d'Albert Gleizes sur la voie métaphysique', that it was 'around 1929 that we introduced Albert Gleizes to the work of René Guénon, through *Autorité spirituel et pouvoir temporel*, which had just appeared.'
5 Dangar to Crowley, 17 September 1930.
6 Coomaraswamy to Gleizes, 20 December 1936 and 26 January 1938. In a note published in the *Art Bulletin*, no. xx, New York, 1938, Coomaraswamy refers to 'such as [Eric] Gill, Gleizes, [A. Graham] Carey and me' (*Christian and Oriental Philosophy of Art*, p.86). Alibert, *Gleizes*, p.209 complains that Guénon never refers to Gleizes, but Gleizes' books were regularly and favourably reviewed in *Etudes traditionnelles*.
7 Rosenberg to Gleizes, 4 January 1936.
8 J.R.Gleizes: *Mémoires – L'état de la peinture en 1925*. The story is told as a development of an incident in 1926 when Gleizes indignantly refused Rosenberg's offer to artificially inflate the price of his pre-war canvas *La Chasse* (see also Rosen-berg to Gleizes, 27 April 1926). It is not clear when the contact with Guggenheim began but it was most probably 1929–30.
9 Rebay to Gleizes, 18 [December?] 1938.
10 Rosenberg to Gleizes, 2 October 1936.
11 Rosenberg to Gleizes, 10 February 1936, 12 February 1936, 19 February 1936.
12 *Mémoires – Albert Gleizes et l'exposition de '37*.
13 Gleizes to Delaunay, 25 February 1936.
14 Rosenberg to Gleizes, 17 September 1936.
15 Rosenberg to Gleizes, 16 February 1937.
16 Dangar to Crowley, 8 November 1937.
17 G.H.Pingusson to Albert Gleizes, 17 October 1934. A letter from Léger to Gleizes inviting him to participate is reproduced in Derouet et al.: *Léger*, p.331. Photographs of the works in question and of Gleizes working on them in Varichon: *Gleizes*, pp.505–8.
18 *Mémoires – Albert Gleizes et l'exposition de '37*.
19 Delaunay to Gleizes, nd (beginning of 1935); Gleizes to Delaunay, 26 February 1935.
20 *Edition catalogue critique du Salon de l'Art Mural*, 4–30 juin [1935]. General account of Salon d'Art Mural in e.g. Bowness: 'The Presence of the Past'. See also Muter: 'Une visite d'Eugenio Ors', *Sud Magazine*, no.120, 15 October 1934.
21 Pierre du Colombier in *Candide*, 27 June 1935. Gleizes' comment on Michelangelo is in the essay he contributed to the *Edition catalogue critique*.
22 *Mémoires – L'exposition de '37*.
23 *Mémoires – 1938*.
24 A list of the artists included is given in Barrer: *Quand l'Art du XXe siècle était conçu par les inconnus*.
25 Rosenberg to Gleizes, 2 March 1935.
26 Lhote to 'Mr Directeur des Beaux Arts', 4 January 1937 [sic. It should presumably be 1938]; Lhote to Gleizes, 30 November 1937; Mme Gleizes' account in *Mémoires – 1938, Albert Gleizes et Jacques Villon*.
27 Dangar to Crowley, 5 March 1938.
28 Two tapestries based on these paintings can be seen at the Ecole Technique de l'Armée de l'Air, Rochefort, France; and at the headquarters of the Organisation de l'Aviation Civile Internationale in Montreal, Canada. See Vanber: *A propos de la tapisserie 'Histoire du Vol'*.
29 Account in J.R.Gleizes: *Mémoires – 1938*.
30 Dangar to Crowley, 5 March 1938 (where the sum in question is described as '£40').
31 Rebay to Gleizes, 9 August 1938.

17
Under the Occupation

1 *Souvenirs – 1939*, p.1.
2 Some, but by no means all, of the transcripts of these sessions are included in Delaunay: *Du Cubisme à l'art abstrait*.
3 Jellett to Gleizes, 6 February 1939.
4 *Mémoires – 1938*. Some of the works in question appear in Varichon et al: *Albert Gleizes*, p.638.
5 'Hitler', unpublished typescript. It is in fact a letter, dated 8 January 1934, probably what Gleizes refers to as 'a reply, quite long . . . which I had to send a few weeks ago to some students of 18 to 20 years old who were preparing [the civil grade?] and who had asked me for my views on "what had to be done with regard to the government in Berlin. Should we or shouldn't we talk to Hitler?"' (Gleizes to Graf 4 January 1934).
6 Graf to Gleizes 3 August 1933, 6 November 1933, 27 December 1933. The correspondence thereafter seems to peter out but Graf does keep Gleizes informed of the régime's hostility to his own and Gleizes' forms of painting.
7 The problems with Mme Noguès in Anne Dangar's Moroccan correspondence with the Grimauds, with the Gleizes and with Lucie Deveyle.
8 Dangar to Gleizes, 23 June 1939.
9 Dangar to Raibaud, 23 July 1939.
10 Dangar to the Grimauds, 1 December 1939. Letters from the Fez potters in ibid., 14 April 1940.
11 Correspondence with the Gleizes, Grimauds and Louis Raibaud. Contrast between French attitudes and those of Australians in the First World War in Dangar to Gleizes, 13 January 1941.
12 See especially Dangar to Gleizes, 26 July 1940.
13 Gleizes gives an account of his movements at this time in Gleizes to Rosenberg, 23 December 1945. See also J.R.Gleizes: *Mémoires – 1939*, and Giriat: *Chronique des Méjades*.
14 Dangar to the Grimauds, 16 November 1940.
15 In 'Sur la lettre d'Anne Dangar'. But it should be noted that some of Gleizes' sketches for the painting carry the title *Le Pape et l'empereur*.
16 As we shall see later when discussing the illustrations to Pascal's *Pensées*, these are related to his interest in the *Guide de la peinture de Mont Athos*. He refers to the guide in a letter to Pouyaud, 12 February 1935.
17 Dangar to Raibaud, 29 December 1939.
18 Dangar to Gaston Grimaud, 15 June 1941.
19 Told to me in conversation by Geneviève Dalban.

18
First Communion

1 Giriat: *Chronique des Méjades*.
2 'She went on to talk of Gleizes. She knew him very intimately before his marriage. She says he was always deadly in earnest, but was then always arguing against religion, and she found it so very interesting that it was his work which had made him change and led him to understand Christianity in such a deep, logical way,' Dangar to Crowley, 11 June 1936.
3 Told to me in coversation by Dom Angelico.
4 Thomas Greenwood: 'L'esthétique religieuse du peintre Gleizes'.
5 *Mémoires – 1940, Le Père Jérôme*.
6 Ibid.
7 Giriat: *Chronique des Méjades*.
8 Dangar to Grimauds, 13 January 1942.
9 Dangar to Grimauds, 3 January 1950 and 19 October 1950. In this last, she says: 'though I do not despise the Protestant ministers, I would be frightened if I was sure I was going to be buried by one of them'.
10 Dangar to Gleizes, 13 January 1941.
11 Dom Angelico Surchamp, writing in 1947, criticises this notion as it appears in *La Peinture et ses lois*: 'The mistake is on the religious level which consists in representing religion as having disappeared with the Renaissance' – 'L'Itinéraire pictural et spirituel d'Albert Gleizes'.
12 Père Jérôme to Gleizes, 18 April 1942.
13 Gleizes would probably have agreed with Berdyaev, who says: 'The naturalistic element is very strong in the teaching of St Thomas Aquinas who tends to regard man as a non-spiritual being' – *The Destiny of Man*, p.61. See also Sherrard: *Greek East and Latin West*, e.g. p.150, and *The Rape of Man and Nature*, especially p.52 *et seq*. The question of Gleizes' attitude toward Thomism will recur, especially when we come to discuss the question of 'art sacré'.
14 Giriat: *Chronique des Méjades*, pp. 14–15.
15 Père Jérôme to Gleizes, 11 August 1943, 26 November 1943 and 6 January 1946.
16 Surchamp: *Itinéraire pictural*, p.15.
17 *La Forme et l'histoire II*, ch.2, p.31a; *L'Homme devenu peintre*, p.94.
18 See ch.4 above.
19 Lhote to Gleizes, 11 November [1941], Gleizes MSS, MNAM. Joseph Delteil was a

novelist, author of *Sur le fleuve amour*, published in 1923. Later, like Gleizes, he became an advocate of the return to nature, retiring to live in Languedoc in 1937.

20 This can be seen in his account of the Abbaye in the wartime *Souvenirs*. The disapproval was mutual. In an article in *Candide*, 28 June 1944, Duhamel says, speaking of the Abbaye: 'Albert Gleizes also took part in the discussions. Since he has devoted most of his life, with a most surprising self abnegation, to the defence and illustration of Cubism, it must be said that at this time Gleizes painted as a good pupil of Monet and Pissarro, that he had charming gifts, above all for landscape, that he practised an art of sensibility, and that he showed no signs of being grievously vulnerable to the attractions of ideology. *Et nunc intelligite . . .*'

21 Metzinger to Gleizes, 8 October 1942.

22 An important correspondence between them in 1943 has been published by the Association des Amis d'Albert Gleizes under the title *Sujet et objet*.

23 Pouyaud to Gleizes, 13 April 1944.

24 Pouyaud to Gleizes, 26 April 1944.

25 *L'Homme devenu peintre*, pp.85–6.

19
La Pierre-Qui-Vire

1 Pouyaud: 'Les sept Étapes d'Albert Gleizes sur la voie métaphysique', p.10.

2 e.g. in Pouyaud to Gleizes, 3 December 1945, in which he expresses great optimism about De Gaulle. He told André Dubois that, while he was working on restoring the church tower in Clamecy during the war, he had an excellent view of the militia headquarters and was able to report on its comings and goings to the Resistance.

3 Dangar to Grimauds, 4 March 1945, 22 April 1945 and 16 October 1946.

4 Dangar to Grimauds, 1 January 1947.

5 Metzinger to Gleizes, 21 June 1945 and 18 August 1945.

6 See e.g. his article on Picasso in *L'Esprit Nouveau*, no.1.

7 *L'Echo des Provinces*, May–June, 1942. General account of the 'Fédération des Associations Régionales et du Comité Nationale du Folklore' in special number, Sept–Oct, 1941.

8 e.g. Gleizes to Mme [-], 4 May 1943: 'Yes, you are right. France, defeated on the military plane, must and will triumph on the level of the spirit ' but 'I fear that we are for the most part just trying to amend our ways instead of making our mea culpa and taking many things up again from scratch ... I've had the occasion, over the last period, to attend many conferences at which a great deal of talent was lost in sheer waste over details, seemingly quite unaware of both the starting point and the end to be attained, earth and heaven ...'

9 Told to me in conversation.

10 De Vibraye to Gleizes, 5 March [1943]. Anne Dangar's account of the incident in Dangar to Raibaud, 8 May 1943. De Vibraye assured Gleizes that there was nothing to be done but in fact she was released in five days.

11 *Mémoires – 1943*.

12 It is a pity that Anne Dangar does not give us more detail about the conversations she had with the Gleizes after the war which she found so disagreeable. She herself is, somewhat bizarrely, the only member of the Gleizes group whom I have seen expressing antisemitic sentiments in her private correspondence. After the war, however, she visited Suzanne Alexandre, her oldest friend in France, who had studied pottery with her in Paris before she went to Gleizes. Suzanne Alexandre was Jewish and from her she learnt to her horror something of what the Jews had suffered. After that, she says she could not understand how Gleizes could continue to defend the Germans (Dangar to Grimauds, 9 February 1946).

13 Gill: *Letters of Eric Gill*, p.441.

14 Pallis to Gleizes, 7 October 1940.

15 This is suggested in Waterfield: *René Guénon*, pp.58–9 and in Sherrard: *Christianity – Lineaments of a Sacred Tradition*, p.77, which gives a number of bibliographical references for the relations between Pallis and Guénon.

16 Gleizes to Pallis, 26 May 1945.

17 Chevalier's circumstances emerge clearly from his correspondence with Gleizes. Michaud and Témoignage in Déroudille et al: *Marcel Michaud*. See also Giriat: 'René-Maria Burlet, une oeuvre, une vie' and Marcel Michaud: 'L'Eglise contre l'art sacré' in *Arts* 20 September 1946.

18 In a letter to the author.

19 Chevalier to Gleizes.

20 Dangar to Grimauds, 2 September 1942.

21 Romefort, talking to the Centre Interprofessionnel de Théologie Appliquée, Marseille. The quotation is given as the preface to Joseph Olivier: 'Jeunesse du rythme dans la musique traditionnelle'.

22 Account of Geoffray's career in *César Geoffray par ses textes*. Quotation on p.16.

23 Some of this work can be seen in: Franch-Clapers, Josep: *L'Exode. L'exile*,

exhib. cat., Barcelona, Palau Laja, June–July 1989.

24 See Bernard Muntaner: *Albert Coste*.

25 Reproduced in the preface to Firpo: *Lettres adressées à l'Association des Amis d'Albert Gleizes*.

26 Chevalier to Gleizes, 21 December 1940, 19 March 1941, 31 July 1941, 28 December 1943.

27 Pernoud to Gleizes, 22 January 1946.

28 Ibid., 16 June 1946.

29 Ibid., 11 April 1946.

30 Ibid., 1 November 1946 and 25 February 1947. Pierre Alibert, who has written a biography of Gleizes, had been a seminarian at St Maximin and it was there that he first heard and was impressed by him.

31 Jean Cassou et al: *Hommage – Albert Gleizes*, p.24.

32 Pouyaud to Gleizes, 30 September 1946.

33 Pouyaud to Gleizes. The practice of *a capella* Gregorian chant has since, unfortunately, been abandoned.

34 Nesmy to de Romefort, 26 May 1947.

35 Chevalier to Gleizes, 29 February 1944.

36 Surchamp's account of his relations with Gleizes runs through the early chapters of *L'Art roman, rencontre entre Dieu et les hommes*. Quotation, pp.56–7.

37 Pouyaud to Gleizes, 30 September 1946.

38 Accounts in Surchamp, Pouyaud and Chevalier correspondence.

20
A Controversy over Sacred Art

1 There is a good account of the worker priest movement and of the general problems facing the Roman Catholic Church in France at this time in Dansette: *Destin du catholicisme français*.

2 See e.g. Debuyst: *Le Renouveau de l'art sacré*.

3 Maritain: *Art and Scholasticism*, p.54

4 Gleizes to [–], 28 October 1929. It is surprising to see Gleizes in contact with Benedictines in 1929 though he visited Farnborough Abbey in 1934. It is also surprising to see at this date such a full statement of his reservations with regard to Thomas Aquinas.

5 Régamey to Gleizes, 15 March 1946.

6 Quoted in *Témoignages*, xxxvi, 1953.

7 The reference is to John 3.5.

8 *Art Sacré*, no.4–5, April–May 1947.

9 Chevalier to Gleizes, 22 April 1947.

10 *Souvenirs – 1934–9*, p.9; *Key Words*, p.15.

11 Michaud in *Arts*, no.85, 20 September 1945; Nesmy in ibid., 15 November 1946; Régamey in ibid., no.124, 18 July 1947.

12 Chevalier to Gleizes, 27 January 1948.

13 Ibid, 8 December 1947.

14 Régamey: 'A la recherche de la tradition', *Art Sacré*, May–June 1948.

15 *Cahiers de l'Art Sacré*, no.2, 1945.

16 Pernoud to Gleizes, 1 November 1946.

17 De Romefort to Gleizes, 2 February 1948.

18 Chadwick: *Augustin*, p.51.

19 De Romefort to Gleizes, 30 January [1947].

20 *Puissances du cubisme*, pp.328–9.

21
The Quarrel over Guénon

1 Guénon to Gleizes, 14 July 1945.

2 Breton's enthusiasm for Guénon is referred to, dismissively, in Pouyaud to Gleizes, 11 May 1952. Georges Ribemont-Dessaignes, the poet who had led the Dada attack on Gleizes back in 1920, refers to it, equally dismissively but for different reasons, in *Déjà-Jadis*, p.184. Bruce Adams has shown me evidence that suggests Breton had been interested in Guénon from a much earlier period.

3 Guénon to Gleizes, 23 February 1947.

4 Dangar to Surchamp, 29 February 1948. These letters have been published as Anne Dangar: *Lettres à la Pierre-qui-Vire*. This letter, p.40.

5 Ibid, 28 March 1948, *Lettres*, p.42.

6 Ibid, 18 April 1948, *Lettres*, p.44.

7 Surchamp to Gleizes, 31 December 1947.

8 Pouyaud to Gleizes, 11 May 1952. Surchamp: *L'Art roman, rencontre entre Dieu et les hommes*, p.88, refers to 'the farming exploitation, which had turned out to be a disaster'.

9 Surchamp to Gleizes, 6 September 1950. Heinard was responsible for an important work of stone and wood carving at the monastery.

10 Pouyaud to Gleizes, 19 May 1949.

11 *Témoignages*, xxi, April 1949, pp.223 and 230.

12 Surchamp to Gleizes, 24 November 1950.

13 Dangar: *Lettres*, introduction by Surchamp, pp.14–15.

14 Surchamp to Gleizes, 24 November 1950.

15 Dangar to Surchamp, 28 August 1950, *Lettres*, pp.117–8.

16 Ibid., p.118.

17 Pouyaud to Gleizes, 30 May 1950.

18 Dangar to Grimauds, 5 February 1951. It should in fact be 5 March 1951.

19 Ibid., 3 January 1950.

20 Ibid., 19 October 1950.

21 Ibid., 31 December 1950.

22 Dangar to Surchamp, 27 January 1951, *Lettres*, p.137.

23 Ibid., 7 February 1951, p.145 ('because of a stupid quarrel between the village

priest and my father over politics').

24 Ibid., 20 February 1951, *Lettres*, p.146.

25 Deveyle to Surchamp, 23 September 1951, *Lettres*, pp.175–8.

22
New Realities

1 *Réalités Nouvelles*, no.1, 1947. There is a general acount of its history in Lhotelier, André (ed): *Réalités Nouvelles.*

2 See note in ch.3 above. The talk by Valensi which is referred to there, published in *Montjoie!* in 1913, is worth quoting in the light of the present discussion: 'Rhythm will be translated in "pure painting" by line. The line, which will no longer be the conventional means of expressing the limit between a body and space, will have a personal expression which will derive its strength from within itself.'

3 Gervais to Gleizes, 12 November 1948. There is a letter from Gervais to Gleizes on Povolozky's behalf, 14 August 1935, in the Gleizes/Povolozky correspondence.

4 Gervais to Gleizes, 17 April 1950.

5 It is referred to in Firpo to Gleizes, 8 October 1948.

6 There are accounts in Jacqueline Loyer: 'Catalogue des Estampes et des Illustrations d'Albert Gleizes' in *Nouvelles de l'estampe*, 1976, and in Chevalier et al: *La Lumière et le trait*, exhib. cat., 1990. There is also a very interesting correspondence with Villon who gives Gleizes technical advice on etching. Villon finishes by expressing his admiration for what Gleizes had achieved (6 February 1950).

7 Pouyaud: 'Les sept Étapes', p.11

8 Surchamp to Gleizes 17 February 1949.

9 The Mount Athos Guide has been published in English as *The Painter's Manual of Dionysius of Fourna*. The text of these notes is given in Chevalier et al: *La Lumière et le trait*, pp.56–63.

10 Gleizes to Pouyaud, 12 February 1935.

11 Pouyaud: 'Le Guide de la Peinture du Mont Athos' in *Atelier de la Rose*, no.10, June 1953

23
The Arabesque

1 J.R.Gleizes: *Mémoires – 1951 (I)*; *Le Provençal*, 8 August 1951.

2 Ibid., *(II)*; Surchamp, *L'Art roman*, pp.59–60, reproaches Gleizes for his willingness to accept the Légion d'Honneur. Mme Gleizes says she initially revolted against the invitation from the Institute.

3 Ibid.

4 Gleizes to [Villon], 23 July 1944.

5 Villon to Gleizes, 7 January 1945.

6 The debate is mentioned in ch.3 above.

7 Surchamp (1993) op. cit., p.105. The letter on Gleizes' encounter with Picasso in 1911 quoted in ch.2 above was almost certainly addressed to Gabrielle Vienne.

8 Severini refers to this in his essay in Cassou et al., *Hommage – Albert Gleizes.*

9 *Le Soir*, 6 February 1953. Gleizes also refers to this remark of Vauxcelles at the end of *Spiritualité, rythme, forme.*

10 The same thought is expressed by Gleizes in different words in Surchamp: 'L'enseignement d'Albert Gleizes', p.23.

11 In conversation with the author.

12 De Montrond: 'Art sacré et théologie'.

13 There is a certain irony in the fact that this occurred in the context of the drive against religious involvement in education which Gleizes was supporting at the time through his involvement in the Association Ernest Renan.

14 De Montrond: 'Le Cadre'.

15 Early history in Etienne Fouilloux: *La Collection 'sources chrétiennes'.*

16 Another explanation, which has been given to me in private conversation, is that Gleizes was terrified of heights.

17 Marie-A. Devereux: 'De la mélodie rythmique de Solesmes et du "Cubisme"'.

18 Firpo to Gleizes, nd. In another letter, 17 October 1950, he says with regard to a prospective buyer for *La Chute de Babylon*: 'I think that, in the event of a dinner at Les Méjades to complete the sale, it would not be useful to enlarge too much on the differences, whether now or in the past, Gleizes and the art dealers – given that we find ourselves confronted with one of their leading representatives . . .'

19 *Mémoires – 1951 (II).*

20 *La Forme et l'histoire*, pp.186–8.

21 A series of letters on this exhibition from Henri Giriat to Gleizes, March 1953, shows what a difficult crowd Gleizes' followers could be.

22 Quoted in Pouyaud: 'Les sept Étapes'.

23 Dangar to Geneviève de Cissey, 28 February 1949.

24 Anne Dangar's article in *L'Atelier de la Rose*, no.1, nd [end 1950].

25 Dangar to de Cissey, 28 August 1950.

BIBLIOGRAPHY

Alibert, Pierre: *Gleizes – Biographie*, Galerie Michèle Heyraud, Paris, 1990.

— Albert Gleizes: *Naissance et avenir du cubisme*, Aubin-Visconti, St Etienne, 1982.

Allendy, Dr. René: *Le Symbolisme des nombres: essai d'arithmosophie*, Chacornac Frères, Paris, *1948* (*1st ed 1921*).

Antliff, Mark: *Inventing Bergson*, Princeton University Press, Princeton 1993.

Apollinaire, Guillaume: *Chroniques d'art, 1902–1918*, Gallimard, Paris, 1981.

— *Méditations esthétiques – les peintres cubistes*, Hermann, Paris, 1965. 1st ed, Figuière, Paris, 1913.

Apollonio, Umbro: *Futurist Manifestos*, Thames & Hudson, London, 1973.

Arcos, René: *Ce qui naît*, Figuière, Paris, 1911.

— *La Tragédie des espaces*, Edition de 'L'Abbaye', Paris, 1906.

Aristotle: *De Anima* (On the Soul), Penguin Books, Harmondsworth, 1986.

Arnold, Bruce: *Mainie Jellett and the Modern Movement in Ireland*, Yale University Press, New Haven and London, 1991.

— et al.: *Mainie Jellett, 1897–1944*, exhib. cat., Irish Museum of Modern Art, Dublin, 1991.

Assouline, Pierre: *L'Homme de l'art – D-H. Kahnweiler, 1884–1979*, Balland (Folio), Paris, 1988.

Augustine of Hippo: *Confessions*, Penguin Books, Harmondsworth, 1961.

— 'On True Religion' in *Augustine: Earlier Writings*, SCM Press, London & Philadelphia, 1953.

— 'The Teacher' in *Augustine: Earlier Writings*, SCM Press, London & Philadelphia, 1953.

— *Dialogues Philosophiques iv: La Musique*, Institut d'Etudes Augustiniennes, 1947. English version: *'On Music' in The Fathers of the Church*, vol.iv, Catholic University of America Press Washington D.C., 1969.

Banham, Reyner: *Theory and Design in the First Machine Age*, The Architectural Press, London, 1960.

Barr, Jr., Alfred H.: *Cubism and Abstract Art*, Museum of Modern Art, New York, 1974 (reproduction of 1936 ed).

Barrer, Patrick F.: *Quand l'Art du XXe siècle était conçu par les inconnus*, Arts et Images du Monde, Paris, 1992.

Barzun, Henri: *L'Ère du drame: fondation d'Europe, 1916–1920*, Atlas University, Paris, 1921.

Bazetoux, Denise: *George Valmier, catalogue raisonné*, Noème, Paris, 1993.

Berdyaev, Nicolas: *The Meaning of the Creative Act*, Collier Books, New York, 1962.

— *The Destiny of Man*, Geoffrey Bles, London, 1937.

— *The Meaning of History*, Geoffrey Bles, 1936.

Bergson, Henri: *Matter and Memory*, Zone Books, New York, 1991.

— *Essai sur les données immédiates de la conscience*, PUF, Paris, 1985.

Bernier, Georges, and Monique Schneider Manoury: *Robert et Sonia Delaunay – Naissance de l'art abstrait*, J.C. Lattès, Paris, *1995*.

Boak, Denis: Jules Romains, Twayne, New York, 1974.

Boethius, Anicius Manlius Severinus: *Fundamentals of Music*, Yale University Press, New Haven, 1989.

Borràs, Maria Lluïsa: *Picabia*, Thames & Hudson, London, 1985.

Bowness, Sophie: 'The Presence of the Past – Art in France in the 1930s, with special reference to Le Corbuisier, Léger, and Braque', unpublished Ph.D thesis, Courtauld Institute, London, 1995.

Boyle-Turner, Caroline: *Paul Sérusier, peintre de la Bretagne*, Edita S.A., Lausanne, 1988.

Brooke, Peter: 'Albert Gleizes – another way of Cubism', in Arnold et al.: *Mainie Jellett, 1897–1944*.

— *Deux Peintres philosophes – Albert*

Gleizes et Kasimir Malévitch, Association des Amis d'Albert Gleizes, Ampuis, 1995. English translation, ibid. 1996.

— 'Jean Metzinger – Cubism as Realism', *Cubism*, no.8, Spring 1985.

— see Gleizes: *Art et religion* and *La Peinture et ses lois*.

Brown, Frederick: *An Impersonation of Angels – a Biography of Jean Cocteau*, Longmans, London, 1968.

Burlet, René Maria, *see* Déroudille et al.

Cabanne, Pierre: *Entretiens avec Marcel Duchamp*, Eds Pierre Belford, Paris, 1967. Reprinted Somogy, Paris, 1995. Eng Trans: *Dialogues with Marcel Duchamp*, Thames & Hudson, London, 1971.

Campro, Anna Paolo Masetto: *Montjoie! ou la ronde des formes et des rhythmes*, Grabischena, Fasano, 1979.

Cassou, Jean et al.: *Hommage – Albert Gleizes*, Atelier de la Rose, Lyon, 1954.

Chadwick, Henry: *Saint Augustin*, Cerf, Paris, 1987.

Chevalier, Jean, et al.: *Albert Gleizes, l'oeuvre graphique – "La lumière et le trait"*, exhib. cat., Association des Amis du Musée de l'Imprimerie et de la Banque, Lyon, 1990.

Chevreul, Michel Eugene:*Des Couleurs et de leurs applications aux arts industriels à l'aide des cercles chromatiques*, J.B.Baillière et fils, Paris, 1864.

— *De la Loi du contraste simultané des couleurs*, Pitois-Levrault, Paris, 1839.

Coomaraswamy, Ananda K.: *The Christian and Oriental Philosophy of Art*, Dover publications, New York, 1956. First published as Why Exhibit Works of Art, Luzac & Co, London, 1943.

— *The Transformation of Nature in Art*, Dover publications, New York, 1956. Replication of second edition published by Harvard University Press in 1934.

— *see* Lipsey, Roger

Cooper and Gary Tinterow, Douglas: *The Essential Cubism, 1907–20*, exhib. cat., Tate Gallery, London, 1983.

Cork, Richard: *Vorticism and Abstract Art in the First Machine Age*, Gordon Fraser Gallery, London, 1976.

Cottington, David: *Cubism in the Shadow of War – the Avant-garde and Politics in Paris, 1905–1914*, Yale University Press, New Haven & London, 1998.

Dangar, Anne: *Lettres à la Pierre-qui-Vire*, Zodiaque, L'Abbaye de Ste Marie de la Pierre-qui-Vire, 1972.

Dansette, Adrien: *Destin du catholicisme Français, 1926–1956*, Flammarion, Paris, 1957.

Daspre, André and Décaudin, Michel (eds): *Histoire litteraire de la France*, tome 11, 1913–39, Editions Sociales, Paris, 1979.

Daumal, René: 'Le mouvement dans l'éducation intégrale de l'homme', *Régénération*, no.55, Nov 1934.

Debuyst, Frédéric: *Le Renouveau de l'art sacré, 1920–1962*, Nouvelles Editions Mane, Paris, 1991.

Delaunay, Robert: *Du Cubisme à l'art abstrait – documents inédits publiés par Pierre Francastel*, S.E.V.P.E.N, Paris 1957.

Delaunay, Sonia: *Nous irons jusqu'au soleil*, Robert Laffont, Paris 1978.

Dermée, Paul: 'Excommuniés', *391*, no.xii, March 1920.

Déroudille, René et al.: *Marcel Michaud*, exhib. cat., ELAC, Lyon, 1989.

— *Variations sur le nombre d'or – hommage à René-Maria Burlet*, exhib. cat., Musée des Beaux-Arts, Chambéry, June–Sept, 1993.

Derouet, Christian (ed): 'Fernand Léger: une correspondance d'affaires', *Les Cahiers du Musée National d'Art Moderne*, Musée National d'Art Moderne, Paris, 1996.

— 'Juan Gris, Correspondances avec Léonce Rosenberg', *Les Cahiers du Musée National d'Art Moderne*, Musée National d'Art Moderne, Paris, 1999.

— et al.: *Fernand Léger 1881–1955*, Centre Georges Pompidou, Paris, 1997.

Devereux, Marie-A.: 'De la mélodie rythmique de Solesmes et du "Cubisme"', *Atelier de la Rose*, no.1, nd [end 1950].

Dionysius of Fourna: *The 'Painter's Manual' of Dionysius of Fourna*, The Sagittarius Press, London, 1974.

Dorival, Bernard: 'Robert Delaunay et Albert Gleizes', *L'Oeil*, no.445, Oct 1992.

— *Les Etapes de la peinture Française contemporaine*, t. 2 – *Le fauvisme et le cubisme, 1905–1911*, Gallimard, Paris, 1944.

Dubois, André: *Anne Dangar et Moly Sabata, dissertation prepared for the University of Lyon*, 1971, published by the Association des Amis d'Albert Gleizes, Ampuis, 1998.

— 'Sur la lettre d'Anne Dangar', *Bulletin de l'Association des Amis d'Albert Gleizes*, no.1, Ampuis, 1986.

— 'Cubisme et Cubismes', *Travaux iv – Le Cubisme*, Université de Saint-Etienne, St Etienne, 1973.

Duchamp, Marcel, *see* Cabanne, Pierre.

Duhamel, Georges: *Le temps de la recherche*, Hartmann, Paris, 1947 (part 3 of *Lumières sur ma vie*).

— *Des Légendes, des batailles*, Edition de l'Abbaye, Paris, 1907.

— and Vildrac, Charles: *Notes sur la tech-*

nique poétique, Champion, Paris, 1925. First published 1910.
Dujardin, Edouard: *Le Retour éternel*, Moly Sabata, Sablons, 1934.
Einstein, Albert: *Relativity, the Special and General Theory, a Popular Exposition*, Methuen & co, London, 1920.
Fabre, Gladys C. et al.: *Abstraction-Création*, exhib. cat., Westfälisches Landesmuseum, Munster, April–June 1978; Musée d'Art Moderne de la Ville de Paris, Paris, June–Sept 1978.
— *Herbin*, exhib. cat., Musée d'Art Moderne, Céret, 1994; ADAGP, Paris, 1994.
Ferrero, Guglielmo: *Entre le Passé et l'avenir*, Simon Kra, Paris, 1926.
— *Entre les deux Mondes*, Plon-Nourrit, Paris 1913.
— *Grandeur et décadences de Rome*, 6 vols, Plon-Nourrit, Paris 1904–8.
Firpo, Walter: *Albert Gleizes – un cubisme d'avenir*, Association des Amis d'Albert Gleizes, Ampuis, 1996. English translation, *Cubism with a Future*, ibid., also 1996.
— *Lettres adressées à l'Association des Amis d'Albert Gleizes*, Association des Amis d'Albert Gleizes, Ampuis, 1995.
Forichon, F.: *La Couleur. Ses manifestations, son rôle dans les arts, ses harmonies*, Henri Laurens, Paris, 1916.
Fouilloux, Etienne: *La Collection 'sources chrétiennes'*, Cerf, Paris, 1995.
Francastel, Pierre, *see* Delaunay, Robert,
Franch-Clapers, Josep: *L'Exode. L'exile*, exhib. cat., Barcelona, Palau Laja, June–July *1989*.
Frémont, Marguerite: *La Vie du Dr René Allendy, 1889–1942*, Climats, Castelnau-le-Lez, 1994.
Frost, Stella: *Evie Hone*, Browne & Nolan, Dublin, 1958.
Fry, Edward: *Cubism*, Thames & Hudson, London, 1966.
Gamow, George: *Thirty Years that Shook Physics – the story of Quantum Theory*, Dover Publications, New York, 1985.
Gee, Malcolm: Dealers, *Critics & Collectors of Modern Painting, aspects of the Parisian Art Market, 1910–30*, Garland Publishing, New York & London, 1981.
Geoffray, César: *César Geoffray par ses textes. Textes rassemblés par Marcel Corneloup et Michel Burgard; 'A Coeur Joie'*, Lyon, n.d..
— 'Dix ans de présence à Moly Sabata', *Mémoires de l'Académie des Sciences, Belles-lettres et Arts de Lyon* – Séance de 13 June 1972.
Ghil, Réné: 'En méthode à l'Oeuvre' in *Oeuvres Complètes*, t. 3, Albert Messein, Paris, 1938. Developed from the *Traité du verbe*, first published with a preface by Mallarmé in 1886.
— *Oeuvre. II Dire de sangs. III Les Images du monde,* Eugène Figuière et cie, Paris, 1912.
— *Légende d'âmes et de sangs*, L.Frinzine et cie, Paris, 1907.
— *see* Montal, Robert.
Gill, Eric: *Letters of Eric Gill*, Jonathan Cape, London, 1947.
Ginestet, Colette de: 'Géométrie poétique et sécrète de Jacques Villon', *Revue de Tarn*, no.121, Spring 1986.
Giriat, Henri: 'Chronique des Méjades' in *Albert Gleizes à Saint-Rémy*, exhib. cat., Musée des Alpilles, Saint-Rémy de Provence, 1990.
— 'René-Maria Burlet, une oeuvre, une vie' in Déroudille et al.: *Variations sur le nombre d'or.*

Gleizes, Albert: 'Albert Coste', *Arts*, no.156, 5 March 1948.
— 'The Abbaye of Créteil, A Communistic Experiment', in Carl Zigrosser, *The Modern School,* Stelton, New Jersey, 1918.
— 'L'Affaire Dada', *Action*, 3, Paris, April *1920*, pp.26–32. Translated into English in Robert Motherwell ed: *Dada Painters and Poets*, New York, 1951, pp. 298–302.
— *Albert Gleizes en 1934,* Association des Amis d'Albert Gleizes, Ampuis, 1997. Extracts from Gleizes' Souvenirs. English translation: Albert Gleizes in 1934, ibid., 1996.
— 'Apollinaire, la justice et moi' in Marcel Adema (ed): *Guillaume Apollinaire, souvenirs et témoignages*, Eds de la Tête Noir, Paris, 1946, pp.53–65.
— 'Arabesques', *Cahiers du Sud*, vol.22, no.175, Aug–Sept 1935, pp.101–6. Special issue on 'L'Islam et l'Occident'. Article dated Serrières, November 1934. Also in *Puissances du cubisme.*
— 'L'Arc en ciel, clé de l'art chrétien médiéval', *Les Etudes Philosophiques*, nouvelle série, no.2, April–June. Reprinted in *Puissances du cubisme.*
— 'L'Art dans l'évolution générale', unpubl. ms, 1917. Photocopy in Gleizes archive, Ampuis.
— 'L'Art moderne et la société nouvelle', *Moniteur de l'Académie Socialiste*, Moscow, 1923. Reprinted in *Tradition et cubisme*, Paris, 1927.
— *Art et réligion, art et science, art et production*, Editions Présence, Chambéry, 1970. In English, translation with introduction and notes by Peter Brooke, as *Art and Religion, Art and Science, Art and Production*, Francis Boutle

publishers, London, 1999.
— 'L'Art sacré est théologique et symbolique', *Arts*, Paris, no.148, 9 January 1948.
— *Art et science*, Moly Sabata, Sablons 1933; La Presse Universitaire, Aix-en-Provence 1961. See also Gleizes: *Art et religion*.
— 'L'Art et ses représentents', *see* Jean Metzinger
— 'Bals Mornes III – Génie', dated 'New York, 1917', from 'Le Cavalaire du Dimanche', unpubl MS. Photocopy in Gleizes archive, Ampuis.
— 'C'est en allant se jeter à la mer que le fleuve reste fidèle à sa source', *Le Mot*, no.17, 1 May 1915.
— 'Charles Henry, Universitaire', *Cahiers de l'Etoile*, no.13, Jan–Feb 1930.
— 'Choses Simples', *La Vie des lettres et des arts*, vol.vi, Oct 1921 and in *Tradition et cubisme*.
— 'Les Créateurs du Cubisme', *Sud Magazine*, no.126, 15 April 1935. Reprinted in *Puissances du cubisme*.
— *Le Cubisme*, [no publisher given], Geneva, 1918.
— 'Cubisme: essai de généralisation', *La Vie des lettres et des arts*, no.xxi, nd., and 'Cubisme – vers une conscience plastique' in *Bulletin de l'Effort Moderne*, Nos 22–32, Feb 1926–Feb 1927. The ms is dated 1925. Photocopy in Gleizes archive, Ampuis. It was written as the theoretical section of *Kubismus* (qv), but only an extract appears in the published book.
— 'Cubisme et culture générale', *Vers L'Unité*, no. 35–6, Aug–Sept 1925.
— 'Cubisme et surréalisme, deux tentatives pour rédécouvrir l'homme, *Centres*, no. 5, 1 August 1946. Communication faite au 2ème Congrès International d'Esthétique et de Science de l'Art, Paris, 1937. Reprinted in *Puissances du Cubisme*.
— 'Le Cubisme et la tradition', *Montjoie!*, 10 February, 1913. Reprinted in *Tradition et cubisme*.
— 'Des "Ismes" – vers une renaissance plastique', *La Vie des lettre et des arts,* vol.ix, April 1922, and in *Tradition et cubisme*.
— 'Dieu nouveau', *La Vie des Lettres,* vol. ii (7th year), October 1920.
— with Jean Metzinger: *Du 'Cubisme'*, Eugene Figuière, Paris 1912. Reprinted with preface by Gleizes, *Compagnie Française des arts graphiques,* 1947, and Editions Présence, Aubard 1980. English translation, *Cubism*, T.Fisher Unwin, London 1913. A more literal but in my view less readable translation is given in Robert L. Herbert (ed): *Modern Artists on Modern Art*, Prentice Hall, New Jersey 1964.
— *Du Cubisme et des moyens de le comprendre*, La Cible (Povolozky), Paris, 1920.
— 'L'Épopée, de la forme immobile à la forme mobile', *Le Rouge et le noir*, 1929. French text of the historical section of *Kubismus*. Reprinted in *Puissances du cubisme*. English translation: *The Epic, From Immobile Form to Mobile Form*, Association des Amis d'Albert Gleizes, Ampuis, 1995.
— 'L'Exposition de la passion du Christ et le problème religieux', *Sud Magazine*, no.115, 15 *May* 1934.
— *Gleizes sur Picasso et Braque*, Association des Amis d'Albert Gleizes, Ampuis, 1997.
— 'Hommage à Mainie Jellett' in Jellett: *The Artist's Vision*.
— *Homocentrisme*, Moly Sabata, Sablons, 1937 and Association des Amis d'Albert Gleizes, Ampuis 1997.
— 'Individualisme', *Le Cahiers Idéalistes*, 1921. Reprinted in *Tradition et Cubisme*.
— 'L'Inquiétude' – reply to an enquiry, *Cahiers de l'Etoile*, no.18, Dec 1930.
— 'L'Inquiétude, crise plastique', *La Vie des lettres et des arts*, 2nd series, no.20, May 1925, pp.38–52.
— 'Jean Metzinger', *La Revue Indépendante*, no.4, Sept 1911.
— *Kubismus*, Bauhausbücher, 13, Albert Langen Verlag, Munich 1928. Reprinted, Florian Kupferberg Verlag, Mainz, 1980.
— 'La Forme et l'histoire', t.2, unpublished and uncompleted ms, Gleizes archive, Ampuis.
— *La Forme et l'histoire*, Jacques Povolozky, Paris, 1932.
— *L'Homme devenu peintre*, Fondation Albert Gleizes/SOMOGY éditions d'art, Paris, 1998. Written in 1948.
— *Life and Death of the Christian West*, English translation of *Vie et mort de l'occident chretien*, Dennis Dobson Ltd, London, 1947.
— *La Mission créatrice de l'homme dans le domaine plastique*, La Cible (Pobolozky), Paris,1921.
— 'Moly Sabata, ou le retour des artistes au village', *Sud Magazine*, no.1021, 1 June 32.
— 'Naturisme du Corps, Naturisme de l'Esprit. Vers la Régénération Intellectuelle, pt. 3', *Régénération*, no.46, July 1933; pt 4, ibid., no.47, Sept–Dec 1933.
— 'Originalité collectif', *Les Cahiers Idéalistes*, 1921. Reprinted in *Tradition et cubisme*.
— *Peinture et de l'homme devenu peintre*, see *L'Homme devenu peintre*.
— 'Peinture et Peinture', *Sud Magazine*,

no.125, 15 March 1935. In *Puissances du cubisme.*
— *La Peinture et ses lois, ce qui devait sortir du cubisme*, Paris 1924 and in *La Vie des lettres et des arts*, vol.xii, no.5, nd [1922 or 3]. English translation, *Painting and Its Laws*, Francis Boutle publishers, London, 2000.
— 'La Peinture Moderne' in *391*, no.5, 5 June, 1917.
— *Peinture et perspective descriptive*, Moly Sabata, Sablons, 1927. Reprinted in *Puissances du cubisme.*
— *Le Pouvoir des mots-clefs*, Association des Amis d'Albert Gleizes, Ampuis, 1993. Extract from Gleizes: *Souvenirs*. English translation, *Key Words*, ibid., 1995.
— 'Préliminaires à une étude sur les variations iconographiques de la Croix', *Témoignages*, no.xv, Octobre 1947.
— 'Le Problème de la lumière', *Les Cahiers du Sud*, March 1937. Reprinted in *Puissances du cubisme*. The essay is extracted from ibid.: *Homocentrisme*, pp. 71 et seq; Association des Amis d'Albert Gleizes ed, pp.21 et seq..
— *Puissances du cubisme*, Editions Présence, Chambéry, 1969.
— 'Le Retour de l'homme à sa vie', *Régénération*, no.49, March 1934.
— 'Retour à l'homme, mais à quel homme?', *Sud Magazine*, December 1935. In *Puissances du cubisme.*
— 'Le Retour à la terre', *Beaux Arts*, 14 December 1939.
— 'Le Retour à la terre et à l'artisanat', *Régénération*, no.48, Jan–Feb 1934.
— 'Robert Delaunay', unpublished ms, 1947, Bibliothèque de France , Fonds Delaunay.
— 'Souvenirs: le Cubisme, 1908–1914', *Cahiers Albert Gleizes*, Association des Amis d'Albert Gleizes, Lyon, 1957. Reprinted, Association des Amis d'Albert Gleizes, Ampuis, 1997.
— 'Souvenirs', unpublished ms, *c.*1942–3, Gleizes archive, Musée National d'Art Moderne, Paris.
— 'Spiritualité, Rythme, Forme', *Confluences – les problèmes de la peinture*, Lyon, 1945. Reprinted in *Puissances du cubisme*. English translation in *Association des Amis d'Albert Gleizes*, Ampuis 1996.
— *Sujet et objet – deux lettres adressées à André Lhote*, Association des Amis d'Albert Gleizes, Ampuis, 1996.
— 'La Terre et les Métiers Manuels', *Cahiers de l'Etoile* no.4, July–Aug 1928, no.5, Sept–Oct 1928. Reprinted in *Vie et mort de l'occident chrétien.*
— *Tradition et cubisme – vers une conscience plastique*, Jacques Povolozky, Paris, 1927.
— 'La Tradition et le cubisme' *see* 'Le Cubisme et la tradition'.
— 'Vers une époque de bâtisseurs', *Clarté*, Paris, no. 13, 20 March 1920, p. 3; no.14, 3 April 1920, p. 4; no. 15, 17 April 1920; 26 June 1920, p. 4; no. 32, 11 September 1920.
— *Vie et mort de l'occident chrétien*, Moly Sabata, Sablons, 1930. Extracts were first published in *Cahiers de l'Etoile*, 1928–9.
— 'Voyage Circulaire', *391*, no.x, December 1919.

Gleizes, J.R., *see* Roche-Gleizes, Juliette.
Golan, Romy: *Modernity and Nostalgia – Art and Politics in France between the Wars*, Yale University Press, New Haven and London, 1995.
Golding, John: *Cubism, a History and Analysis, 1907–14*, Faber & Faber, London, 1959.
— et al.: *Léger and Purist Paris*, exhib. cat., Tate Gallery, London, 1970.
Green, Christopher: *Juan Gris*, Whitechapel Art Gallery/Yale University Press, New Haven & London,1992.
— *Cubism and its Enemies*, Yale University Press, New Haven & London, 1987.
— *Léger and the Avant-Garde*, Yale University Press, New Haven & London, 1976.
Greenwood, Thomas: 'L'esthétique religieuse du peintre Gleizes', *Les Carnets viatoriens*, Jan 1955 and Zodiaque, no.25, April 1955.
Gris, Juan, *see* Derouet, Christian (ed).
Guénon, René: *La Crise du monde moderne*, Bassard, Paris, 1926.
— *Le Roi du monde*, Les Etudes Traditionnelles, Paris, 1939 (2nd ed).
— *La Métaphysique orientale*, Editions Traditionnelles, Paris, 1976 (first published in *Vers l'Unité*, no.41, May–June 1926).
— *Orient et occident*, Eds de la Maisnie, Paris, 1987 (first ed. 1924).
Halicka, Alice: *Hier, souvenirs*, Paris, éd du Parois, 1946.
Havell, E.B.: *Ideals of Indian Art*, John Murray, London, 1920.
Helmholtz, Hermann: *On the Sensations of Tone*, Dover Publications, New York, 1954.
Henderson, Linda Dalrymple: *The Fourth Dimension and Non-Euclidean Geometry in Modern Art*, Princeton University Press, Princeton, 1983.
Henry, Charles: *Essai de généralisation de la théorie du rayonnement*, J.Hermann, Paris, 1925.

— 'Les travaux francais sur les problèmes de la Théorie de la Relativité', *Courrier Médical*, nos 45 & 46, December, 1922.

— *La Lumière, la couleur et la forme*, Editions de l'Esprit Nouveau, Paris, 1922. First published in *L'Esprit Nouveau*, nos 6–9, 1921.

— *Sensation et energie*, A.Hermann et fils, Paris, 1911.

— *Application de nouveaux instruments de précision à l'archéologie*, Ernest Leroux, Paris, 1890.

— 'Le Contraste, le rythme, la mesure', *Revue Philosophique*, no.28, October 1889.

— 'Biologie, Vie et Survie', typescript in Gleizes archive, priv.coll..

Herbert, Robert L.: '"Parade de Cirque" de Seurat et l'esthétique scientifique de Charles Henry' in *Revue de l'Art*, no.50, 1980, pp.9–22.

Homer, William Innes: *Alfred Stieglitz and the American Avant-Garde*, Secker & Warburg, London, 1977.

— *Seurat and the Science of Painting*, M.I.T. Press, Cambridge, Massachussets, 1964.

Hone, Joseph, *see* White, James.

Hoyack, Louis: *Les Aubes de l'humanité*, Marcel Rivière, Paris, 1933.

— *Spritualisme historique, étude critique sur l'idée du progrès*, Marcel Rivière, Paris, 1932.

— *Où va le Machinisme?*, Marcel Rivière, Paris, 1931.

Janneau, Guillaume: *L'Art cubiste*, Editions d'Art Charles Moreau, Paris, 1929.

Jean-Nesmy, Dom Claude: 'De l'art abstrait à l'art sacré', *Arts*, no.148, 9 January 1948.

— 'L'Eglise et l'art sacré', *Arts*, no.15 November 1946.

Jellett, Mainie: *The Artist's Vision – Lectures and essays on art with an introduction by Albert Gleizes*, edited by Eileen MacCarvill, Dundalgan Press, Dundalk, 1958.

— *see also* Arnold, Bruce.

Kahnweiler, Daniel Henry: *Mes Galeries et mes peintres – entretiens avec Francis Crémieux*, Gallimard, Paris, 1961. English translation: *My Galleries and Painters*, Thames & Hudson, London, 1971.

— *Confessions esthétiques*, Gallimard, Paris, 1963.

— *Der Weg zum Kubismus*, Delphin-Verlag, Munich, 1920 (under pseudonym of Daniel Henry). French translation in *Confessions esthétiques*. English translation: *The Rise of Cubism*, Wittenborn-Schulz, New York, 1949.

Krins, Hubert: *Die Kunst der Beuroner Schule*, Beuron, Beuroner Kunstverlag, 1998.

Le Corbusier, *see* Ozenfant and Jeanneret.

Léger, Fernand: *Fonctions de la peinture*, Gallimard, Paris, 1997 (first published, éds Denoël-Gonthier, 1965). English trans: *Functions of Painting*, Thames & Hudson, London, 1973.

— 'Les réalisations picturales actuelles', *Soirées de Paris*, vol.iii, no.25, 15 June 1914. Reprinted in ibid.: *Fonctions de la peinture*.

— *see* Derouet, Christian (ed).

Lenz, Pierre: *L'Esthétique de Beuron* (translated by Paul Sérusier), Bibliothèque de l'Occident, Paris, 1905.

Lhote, André: 'Le Cubisme au Grand palais', *Nouvelle Revue Française*, 1 March 1920.

Lhotelier, André (ed): *Réalités Nouvelles, 1946–1956*, Musée de Calais, Calais, 1980.

Lipsey, Roger (ed): *Coomaraswamy*, Princeton University Press, Princeton, 1977.

Lombroso, Gina: *La Rançon du machinisme*, Payot, Paris 1931.

Loyer, Jacqueline: 'Catalogue des estampes et des illustrations d'Albert Gleizes', *Nouvelles de l'Estampe*, 1976.

— 'Gleizes et la majèste', *Nouvelles de l'Estampe*, 26, March–April, 1976.

Malevich, Kasimir: *Ecrits*, tome 1, *L'Age d'homme*, Lausanne, 1974. Preface by J.Cl. Marcadé.

Maritain, Jacques: *Art et scolastique*, Librairie de l'Art Catholique, Paris, 1920; new revised edition: Louis Rouart et fils, Paris, *1927*. English translation as *Art and Scholasticism with other essays*, Sheed & Ward, London, 1930.

Massenet, Michel: *Albert Gleizes*, SOMOGY Editions d'Art/Fondation Albert Gleizes, Paris, 1998.

Maxe, Jean (Pseudonym): '"L'Abbaye" et le Bolchévisme culturel', *Les Cahiers de l'Anti-France*, Paris, Eds Brossard, n.d. (after 1921).

McQueen, Humphrey: *The Black Swan of Trespass – The Emergence of Modernist Painting in Australia to 1944*, Alternative Publishing Co-operative Ltd, Sydney, 1979.

Mercereau, Alexandre: *Contes des ténèbres*, Figuière, Paris, 1911.

— *L'Abbaye et le bolchévisme,* Figuière, Paris, n.d. (after 1922).

— *La Conque miraculeuse,* Povolosky, Paris, 1922.

Metzinger, Jean: *Le Cubisme était né*, Présence, Chambéry, 1972.

— 'Note sur la peinture', *Pan,* no.10, Oct–Nov 1910.

Michaud, Marcel: 'Le Symbole – a-t-il été et peut-il être un véhicule de sacré?', *Arts,* no.148, 9 January 1948.

— 'L'Eglise contre l'art sacré', *Arts,* no.85, 20 September 1945.
— *see* Déroudille et al.
Milosz, O.V. de L: *La Confession de Lemuel*, La Connaissance, Paris, 1922.
Mirabaud, Robert: *Charles Henry et l'idéalisme scientifique*, Librairie Fishbacher, Paris, 1926.
Mondrian, Piet: *Le Néo-Plasticisme: principe général de l'equivalence plastique*, Galerie de l'Effort Moderne, Paris, 1920.
Montal, Robert: *René Ghil: du symbolisme à la poésie cosmique*, Editions Labor, Brussels, 1962.
Montrond, Henri de: 'Le cadre', *Atelier de la Rose*, no.9, March 1953. Reprinted in Gleizes et al.: *La Fresque "L'Eucharistie" d'Albert Gleizes*, Association de Amis d'Albert Gleizes, Ampuis, 1995.
— 'Art sacré et théologie', *Etudes*, dec 1951.
Mortimer, Edward: *The Rise of the French Communist Party, 1920–47*, Faber & Faber, London, 1984.
Motherwell, Robert (ed): *Dada Painters and Poets*, Wittenborn Schultz, New York, 1951.
Muntaner, Bernard: *Albert Coste (1895–1985)*, Marseille, 1990.
Muter, Mela: 'Une visite d'Eugenio Ors', *Sud Magazine*, no.120, 15 October 1934.
Nash, John: 'The Nature of Cubism', *Art History*, vol.3, no.4, December 1980.
Newman, John Henry: *The Mission of the Benedictine Order*, John Long Ltd, London, 1923.
Nietzsche, Friedrich: *The Will to Power*, Vintage Books, New York, 1968.
— *Thus Spake Zarathustra*, Penguin Books, Harmondsworth, 1966.
Nikodimos of the Holy Mountain and Makarios of Corinth (compilers): *Philokalia*, vol.1, Faber & Faber, 1979.
Olivier Joseph: 'Jeunesse du rythme dans la musique traditionnelle', *Atelier de la Rose*, no.12, Feb 1954.
Ozenfant, Amédée and Jeanneret, Edouard [Le Corbusier]: *Après le cubisme*, Editions des Commentaires, Paris, 1918.
Pascal, Blaise: *Pensées sur l'homme et dieu*, Editions de la Cigogne, Casablanca, 1950. Chosen and arranged by Geneviève Lewis. Illustrated by Gleizes.
Pernoud, Régine: *Lumière du moyen âge*, Bernard Grasset, Paris, 1944.
— 'Gleizes le prophète' in Cassou et al.: *Hommage*.
Philokalia *see* Nikodimos of the Holy Mountain.
Plotinus: *The Enneads*, translated by Stephen MacKenna, Faber & Faber, London 1956.
Pouyaud, Robert: *Du 'Cubisme' à la peinture traditionnelle*, Clamecy, 1948.
— 'Les sept Étapes d'Albert Gleizes sur la voie métaphysique', ms in Pouyaud archive, Ampuis. Talk given in 1970 in Chambéry.
— *Moly Sabata*, Atelier de la Rose/ Association des Amis d'Albert Gleizes, Lyon, 1955.
— '"Le Guide de la Peinture" de Mont Athos', *Atelier de la Rose*, no.10, June 1953.
Régamey, Fr Pie-Raymond: *Art sacré au vingtième siècle?*, Cerf, Paris, 1952.
— 'A la recherche de la tradition', *Art Sacré,* May–June 1948.
— L'Art sacré, sera-t-il chrétien?', *Arts*, no.124, 18 July 1947.
— 'Pour un renoveau de l'art sacré', *Arts*, no.4, 23 February 1945.
Ribemont-Dessaignes: *Déjà-Jadis, ou du mouvement Dada à l'espace abstrait*, René Julliard, 1973. Reprinted from 1958 ed.
Richardson, John: *A Life of Picasso*, vol.2, *1907–1917 – The Painter of Modern Life,* Jonathan Cape, London, 1996.
Richter, Hans: *Dada, Art and Anti-Art*, Thames & Hudson, London, 1978.
Robbins, Daniel: 'Le Fauconnier and Cubism' in *Henri Le Fauconnier (1881–1946): A Pioneer Cubist*, exhib. cat., Salander-O'Reilly Galleries, New York, 1990, n.p.
—'Jean Metzinger, at the Centre of Cubism' in Joan Moser: *Jean Metzinger in Retrospect*, Exhib. cat., University of Iowa, Iowa, 1985.
— *Albert Gleizes, 1881–1953*, a retrospective exhibition, Solomon R. Guggenheim Museum, New York, 1964 (French ed.: Musée National d'Art Moderne, Paris, 1964).
— 'The Formation and Maturity of Albert Gleizes, 1881 through 1920', unpublished Ph.D. thesis, New York University, 1975. Xerox University Microfilms, Ann Arbor, Michigan.
— 'Expectations and Disillusion' [typescript communicated to me by the author].
Roche Gleizes, Juliette: 'Albert Gleizes', *Zodiaque,* no.25, April 1955.
— 'Albert Gleizes et son temps', *Zodiaque,* no.100, April 1974.
— 'Charles Henry', *Cahiers de l'Etoile,* no.13, Jan–Feb 1930.
— 'Mémoires', unpublished ms, priv. coll. and in Gleizes archive, Musée National d'Art Moderne.
— *La Mineralisation de Dudley Craving MacAdam*, Paris, np, 1924.
Romains, Jules: *La Vie unanime*,

'L'Abbaye', Paris, 1908. Gallimard, Paris, 1983.
— *Les Hommes de bonne volonté*, Robert Laffont, Paris, 1988.
Romefort, O.P., R.P.Thomas de: 'L'art sacré à la Pierre-qui-Vire', *Témoignages,* xxxvi, Jan 1953.
Rosenblum, Robert: *Cubism & Twentieth-Century Art*, Abrams, New York, 1974.
Rousseau, Pascal et al.: *Robert Delaunay, 1906–1914, de l'impressionisme à l'abstraction*, Eds du Centre Pompidou, Paris, 1999.
Rubin, William: *Picasso et Braque – L'invention du cubisme*, Flammarion, Paris, 1990. French translation of *Picasso and Braque – Pioneering Cubism*, Museum of Modern Art, New York, 1990.
Rudenstine, Angelica Zander: *The Guggenheim Museum Collection: Paintings, 1880–1945*, vol.1, Solomon R. Guggenheim Museum, New York, 1976.
Salmon, André: 'Picasso', *L'Esprit Nouveau,* no.1 (n.d. Article dated May 1920).
Sanouillet, Michel: *Picabia,* Oeil du temps, Paris, 1964.
Sénéchal, Christian: *L'Abbaye de Créteil*, André Delpeuch, Paris, 1930.
Sérusier, Paul: *ABC de la peinture* (with study on Sérusier by Maurice Denis), Librairie Floury, Paris, 1942 (1st ed, Librairie Floury 1921).
— see Lenz, Pierre.
Seuphor, Michel: *A Dictionary of Abstract Painting*, Methuen & Co, London, 1958.
— *Les Évasions d'Olivier Trickmansholm*, Aubier, Paris, 1939 and Editions du Pavois, Paris, 1946.
Severini, Gino: *Du Cubisme au classicisme – esthétique du compas et du nombre*, Jacques Povolozky, Paris 1921. English translation, *From Cubism to Classicism*, Francis Boutle publishers, London, 2000.
— *The Life of a Painter*, Princeton University Press, Princeton, 1995.
— *Ecrits sur l'art*, Eds Cercle d'Art, Paris, 1987.
Sherrard, Philip: *Christianity, Lineaments of a Sacred Tradition*, T&T Clark, Edinburgh, 1998
— *The Greek East and the Latin West – a Study in the Christian Tradition,* Denise Harvey, Limni, Evia (Greece), 1995 (1st ed., Oxford University Press, 1959).
— *The Rape of Man and Nature*, Golgonooza Press, Ipswich, 1987.
Signac, Paul: *D'Eugene Delacroix au néo-impressionisme*, Hermann, Paris 1978. English translation in Rockefeller University Press, New York 1992.
Silver, Kenneth E: *Esprit de Corps*, Princeton University Press, Princeton 1989. French translation: *Vers le Retour à l'ordre*, Flammarion, Paris, 1991.
Spate, Virginia: *Orphism: The Evolution of Non-figurative Painting in Paris, 1910–1914*, Clarendon Press, Oxford, 1979.
Steegmuller, Francis: *Apollinaire, Poet among the Painters*, Penguin Books, Harmondsworth, 1986 (first published 1963).
— *Cocteau, a Biography*, Constable, London, 1986.
Surchamp, Dom Angelico: *L'Art Roman, rencontre entre Dieu et les hommes*, Desclée de Brouwer, Paris, 1993.
— 'Note sur l'art abstrait', *Témoignages*, no.xxi, April 1949.
— 'Picasso et l'avenir de l'art moderne', *Témoignages*, no.xxi, April 1949.
— 'L'enseignement d'Albert Gleizes', *Témoignages*, xiv, July 1947 (reprinted in Albert Gleizes, *Le Cubisme et son dénouément dans la tradition*, exhib. cat., Lyon 1947).
— 'L'itinéraire pictural et spirituel d'Albert Gleizes' in Albert Gleizes, *Le Cubisme et son dénouément dans la tradition*, exhib. cat., Lyon 1947.
Tapié, Alain et al.: *L'Art sacré d'Albert Gleizes*, exhib. cat., Musée des Beaux-Arts de Caen, 1985.
Tisdall, Caroline and Angelo Bozzola: *Futurism*, Thames & Hudson, London, 1977.
Tomkins, Calvin: *Duchamp, a Biography*, Pimlico, London, 1998.
Topliss, Helen: *Modernism and Feminism – Australian woman artists, 1900–1940*, Craftsman House, Roseville East, 1996.
Vanber, Albert: 'A propos de la tapisserie "Histoire du Vol"', *Pégase*, no.60, December, 1990.
Varichon, Anne et al.: *Albert Gleizes – Catalogue Raisonné*, SOMOGY éditions d'art/Fondation Albert Gleizes, Paris, 1998.
Verkade, Dom Willibrod: *Le Tourment de Dieu – étapes d'un moine peintre*, Paris, 1923.
Vildrac, Charles: *Livre d'amour*, Figuière, Paris, 1910.
— *Poèmes 1905*, L'Abbaye, Paris, 1907.
— *see* Duhamel, Georges.
Waldberg, Patrick et al.: *Charchoune*, Centre National d'Art Contemporain, Paris, 1971.
Waterfield, Robin: René Guénon and the Future of the West, Crucible, 1987.
White, James and Hone, Joseph: 'Evie Hone', unpublished ms, nd.

INDEX

PICTURE ACKNOWLEDGEMENTS

Studio Basset, 6, 23, 39, 124, 128, 129, 130, 133, 136, 140, 142, 157, 158, 159; Buttin, 46, 94, 95, 96; Marius Cochard (?), 38, 43, 71, 91, 98, 99, 100, 101, 102, 103, 105, 107, 108, 109, 116; Columbus Museum of Art, Ohio, 31; Fondation Albert Gleizes, 4, 132; Graydon Wood, 19; Peter Joyce, 51, 82, 97, 111, 137, 161; Laurent Lecat, 10, 59; Marcel Coen, Marseille, 1, 139, 160; Méziat-Burdin, Lyon, 24; Musée National d'Art Moderne, Paris, 7, 8, 12, 15, 30, 33, 45, 60, 90; National Gallery of Art, Washington, 16; Rajak Ohanian, Lyon, 155; Susan Paull, 85, 112, 141, 144; Perrodin, 138; Robert E. Mates © Solomon R. Guggenheim Foundation, NY, 20, 27, 28, 29, 34, 35, 37, 150; Zodiaque, 115, 127, 135, 143, 154.